Journeys through the Labyrinth

Latin American Fiction in the Twentieth Century

◆

GERALD MARTIN

VERSO

London · New York

First Published by Verso 1989
© Gerald Martin 1989
All rights reserved

Verso
UK: 6 Meard Street, London W1V 3HR
USA: 29 West 35th Street, New York, NY 10001–2291

Verso is the imprint of New Left Books

British Library Cataloguing in Publication Data

Martin, Gerald
  Journeys through the labyrinth : Latin American
  fiction in the twentieth century. – (Critical studies
  in Latin American culture).
  1. Fiction in Spanish. Spanish American writers,
  1910– – Critical studies
  I. Title II. Series
  863

  ISBN 0–86091–238–8
  ISBN 0–86091–952–8 pbk

US Library of Congress Cataloging-in-Publication Data

Martin, Gerald
    Journeys through the labyrinth : Latin American fiction in the
  twentieth century / Gerald Martin.
      p. cm. – (Critical studies in Latin American culture).
  Includes bibliographical references.
  ISBN 0–86091–238–8 ISBN 0–86091–952–8 (pbk.)
      1. Latin American literature — 20th century — History and criticism.
  2. Literature and society—Latin America.   I. Title. II. Series.
  PQ7082.N7M34   1989
    860.9'98—dc20

Typeset by Ransom Electronic Publishing, Woburn Sands, Bucks, UK
Printed in Great Britain by Bookcraft (Bath) Ltd

To my students

CRITICAL STUDIES IN
LATIN AMERICAN CULTURE

SERIES EDITORS:

James Dunkerley
Jean Franco
John King

This major series – the first of its kind to appear in English – is designed to map the field of contemporary Latin American culture, which has enjoyed increasing popularity in Britain and the United States in recent years.

Six titles will offer a critical introduction to twentieth-century developments in painting, poetry, music, fiction, cinema and 'popular culture'. Further volumes will explore more specialized areas of interest within the field.

The series aims to broaden the scope of criticism of Latin American culture, which tends still to extol the virtues of a few established 'master' works and to examine cultural production within the context of twentieth-century history. These clear, accessible studies are aimed at those who wish to know more about some of the most important and influential cultural works and movements of our time.

Other Titles in the Series

DRAWING THE LINE: ART AND CULTURAL IDENTITY IN CONTEMPORARY LATIN AMERICA by Oriana Baddeley and Valerie Fraser

PLOTTING WOMEN: GENDER AND REPRESENTATION IN MEXICO by Jean Franco

MAGICAL REELS: CINEMA IN LATIN AMERICA by John King

Contents

Acknowledgements

I should like to thank James Dunkerley for his patient encouragement from the very start of this project and invaluable assistance in its completion; John Kraniauskas for his generous help with information and bibliographical material; Colin Robinson of Verso for his forbearance and support at times when it looked as if his author would never deliver on any of his promises; and above all John King for his constant flow of advice, solidarity and bright ideas both now and in the past: without him this book would not have been completed. Neither he nor the aforementioned are responsible for any continuing errors or shortcomings. Last but never least, I thank Gail, Camilla and Leonie, who saw me through, yet again.

Thanks are also due to the following publishers for permission to use material from previous publications:

Forum for Modern Language Studies, '*Yo el Supremo*: the Dictator and his Script', vol. 15, no. 2, 1979; reprinted in S. Bacarisse (ed.), *Contemporary Latin American Fiction*, Edinburgh, Scottish Academic Press, 1980.

Pergamon Press, 'Boom, Yes; "New" Novel, No: Further Reflections on the Optical Illusions of the 1960s in Latin America', *Bulletin of Latin American Research*, vol. 3, no. 2, 1984.

Cambridge University Press, 'On "Magical" and Social Realism in García Márquez', in B. McGuirk and R. Cardwell (eds), *Gabriel García Márquez: New Readings*, Cambridge 1987.

Note on Translations

I normally give the title of works in English, followed by the original Spanish or Portuguese title and date of original publication in parentheses. Where no Spanish or Portuguese title is given (usually in the case of titles based on proper names), the original may be assumed to be identical.

Information given on translations usually refers to first editions, and has not been brought up to date. There are currently more paperback editions available of Latin American narratives than at any time in the past.

Where the work has not to my knowledge appeared in translation and the English title is my own, I have departed from conventional practice by continuing to italicize *and* using quote marks. The great majority of extracts quoted in the text are my own versions, but a bibliography of translated works is provided under 'Primary Texts'.

Preface

Latin American fiction, which first came to international attention some twenty-five years ago, is currently more widely read and appreciated than ever before in the English-speaking world, as the five hundredth anniversary of 'discovery' and 'conquest' approaches. Throughout the period of its enforced participation in Western history this underdeveloped region of the New World has proved an exceptionally open and fertile field for the implantation and cultivation of stereotypes and ideologies. It has seemed to me that the caricatures which appear to spring so naturally from our encounters with the subcontinent have been nurtured in more subtle ways by the image that most readers manage to decipher from its writing, especially from the anti-rationalist tradition of its 'fantastic literature' or the chaotic world of 'magical realism', both linked in strange and unpredictable ways – dialogically, perhaps? – with the resurgence of romance since the 1940s. It must be admitted that since the 'boom' of the 1960s some Latin American writers have contributed to the confusion by giving their customers from the First World the kind of exotic and melodramatic literary experiences which many of them appeared to want.

The present work is an interpretive history of the Latin American novel in the twentieth century, and is focused particularly on the period from the 1920s to the 1980s. There are several more or less reliable academic histories and handbooks of long standing (indicated in the bibliography), though none of them are up to date, and a number of more recent thematic readings which look at six or seven books from one or two points of view. This work attempts something different and perhaps more ambitious: to combine these two traditional approaches and in so doing to modify the perception that the majority of readers and critics seem to have of the historical development of Latin American narrative; and to achieve this not by recuperating unknown

works or marginalized writers or by inventing a social history of Latin
American fiction which – given the current state of research – would be
premature at this time, but by proposing new readings of the best known
writers and works (or confirming old ones) and, more especially, a new
interpretation of the relation between them. The book is therefore intended
both for those already fully familiar with the subject and for non-specialists,
and is conceived as a developing story, with a chronology and even a plot of
sorts. Its objective is unashamedly demystificatory, and although the
arguments are sometimes complex I have opted to risk oversimplification
through old-fashioned reduction rather than add one more dazzling
deconstruction to the critical debris surrounding us in the so-called
'Post-modern' era: the theoretical debates which have taken place over the
past twenty-five years – a period which coincides precisely with the rise of
the New Latin American Novel launched by the 1960s 'boom' – are here
very largely taken for granted. In that sense this is a book which takes a
number of liberties, for which as author I acknowledge that I may have to
pay, but that is an inescapable part of my project. If Latin American history
and fiction really are labyrinthine, as so many writers have assured us, the
objective of this critical journey is, in an intellectual sense, to assist in the
Bolivarian enterprise of liberating the labyrinth.

Thus at a moment when we appear to be 'post-everything' and the very
notion of any 'history' at all is open to doubt, this book seeks unity rather
than dispersal, fearful that Latin American culture is in danger of becoming
atomized in the name of yet another European redefinition before it has even
been provisionally fixed. In the face of an era of post-Modern writing, it
looks back not only to the 'boom' of the 1960s but also to the first great
wave of Latin American fiction in the 1920s: at a time when pluralism is the
great rallying cry, we look again at Latin America's historic quest for cultural
identity; and in an era when the great master narratives of the West are
supposedly in disrepute, this work sets out to recover the persistent unities in
Latin America's historical experience and to show how they have been
reflected in its literary expression. (This is the main reason why the emphasis
here is overwhelmingly on the novel rather than the short story.)

Paradoxically, perhaps, this is a book written with English-speaking and
European readers largely in mind, but one which, with modest intent, seeks
also to represent a Latin American perspective. To entangle the paradox still
further, I follow particularly the paths and frontiers between Latin American
and European culture. García Márquez expressed the problem well in his
Nobel Prize speech in 1982 when he noted that Europeans 'insist on
measuring us with the same yardstick with which they measure themselves,
without recalling that the ravages of life are not the same for all, and that the
search for one's own identity is as arduous and bloody for us as it was for

them. To interpret our reality through schemas which are alien to us only has
the effect of making us even more unknown, even less free, even more
solitary'.* 'Literature' can, if the reader chooses, be understood in rather an
abstract way, but for me the concept 'Latin American literature' can only be
understood in the context of Latin American history. If we are to confront
myths, ideologies and stereotypes in order to dissolve at least a few of them,
it is surely essential to turn to the clichés and commonplaces which Latin
Americans themselves have manipulated rather than to copy yet again the
image of our own face as we see it reflected in another, different culture. It
goes without saying that I recognize the inevitable irony of such a statement
as soon as these words come under the critical gaze of another.

One book can only attempt so much. This rather long work attempts to
reduce a complex history to accessible proportions; to show continuities over
time and space, however contradictory, and to identify major conjunctures; to
study, however transiently, most of the key narrative texts of the present
century and to give some sense of their texture by quoting briefly from them
and explaining their interrelation. My hope is that on finishing the reader will
feel that she or he has completed a long journey through the labyrinth of
cultural time and space and will be better positioned to understand the
specific nature of Latin America's always problematical relationship with the
so-called mainstream of Western culture, whose fictive reconquest by Latin
American writers is currently under way.

---

*Reprinted in B. McGuirk and R. Cardwell (eds), *Gabriel García Márquez: New Readings*,
Cambridge, 1987. Translation by R. Cardwell.

Introduction

We Americans rose up of a sudden and without prior knowledge... and, uncertain of our future destiny and threatened by anarchy in the absence of a legitimate, just and liberal government, launched ourselves into the chaos of revolution.... But shall we now be able to maintain the true equilibrium necessary for taking charge of a republic? Can one conceive of a people so recently unchained taking flight into the sphere of liberty, without their wings melting away like those of Icarus, and plunging back into the abyss? Such a prodigy is inconceivable, never yet seen. Thus no reasonable hope can encourage us in this venture.

Simón Bolívar, 'The Jamaica Letter', 1815

New worlds have to be lived, rather than explained.

Alejo Carpentier, *The Lost Steps*, 1953

1

Myths of the Mestizo Continent

I imagined a labyrinth of labyrinths, one sinuous spreading labyrinth that would encompass the past and the future and in some way involve the stars.

Jorge Luis Borges, 'The Garden of Forking Paths', 1941

Why struggle to define the character of Spanish American literature? Literatures have no character. Or rather, contradiction, ambiguity, exception and hesitancy are traits which appear in all literatures. At the heart of every literature there is a continuous dialogue of oppositions, separations, bifurcations.

Octavio Paz, 'Spanish American Literature', 1977

This first chapter outlines some of the key concepts which have marked the discussion of Latin American literature in the past century and which underpin the treatment of individual narratives in the rest of this book. These relate to literature itself, to history, and to ideology or myth. As regards the latter, I trust that the reader will not imagine that I am somehow 'advocating' ideas which, being part of the currency of Latin American cultural discourse, I seek merely to identify or describe.

Literature: American Content, European Form

The present work is a history of Latin American narrative fiction in the twentieth century. It will endeavour to map a path through the literary labyrinth (the metaphor is unavoidable), not only to facilitate the understanding of the region's key literary texts but also to shine a light on its cultural identity. Structurally, it concentrates on the parallels, relationships and developments between two great conjunctures: that of the 1920s, which initiated the first great moment of Latin American fiction; and the 1960s, when the Latin American 'New Novel' imposed itself, irresistibly, on world attention. Very broadly speaking, these are the moments of what we may call Social Realism, founded on the 'Novel of the Land', and Magical Realism, the most publicized version of the New Novel. What I seek to show is that this New Novel is not merely a belated, if exuberant, reworking of the post-Joycean Modernist new wave, but a part of that new wave. Its origins lie, precisely, in the 1920s, the period of the earlier Novel of the Land, and thus the celebrated 'boom' of the 1960s is actually a climax and consummation, not a sudden emergence from 'nowhere', that is to say, from underdevelopment.[1] It is not coincidental that the first moment follows the Mexican Revolution of 1910–17, whilst the second follows the Cuban Revolution of 1954–59. Both historical experiences brought about changes in consciousness which transformed the shape of narrative fiction in succeeding decades. Indeed, the term 'Latin American literature' (as against 'Spanish American and Brazilian', 'Ibero-American', 'South American', and so on) itself only began to achieve generalized currency in the later 1960s.

The periodization and systematization of what we should perhaps be calling the Latin American literatures from 1492 to about 1918 has been surprisingly stable for more than half a century. Indeed, it would be no exaggeration to state that a critical consensus began to emerge almost as soon as those literatures began to be seriously studied outside the region itself – mainly in France and the United States – from the 1930s on. This is partly because the traditional periodization of Latin American history itself is so straightforward, which in turn springs largely from the fact that the development of Latin America has been circumscribed by external forces and essentially colonial relationships throughout its development (making Latin American literature, inescapably, a branch of Western literature). Thus the discovery and conquest at the end of the fifteenth century coincide with the Renaissance and Reformation, giving a 'colonial' period and a predominantly 'baroque' style in art and literature, which for many historians continues to characterize Latin American culture to the present day through such phenomena as Magical Realism. Rebellion against Spain and Portugal at the beginning of the nineteenth century coincided with the end of the Enlightenment and the era of the French Revolution, giving a period variously classified as post-Independence, the Early National or the Neocolonial, and a literature which evolved from the Neoclassical, eventually identified with colonialist repression, to the Romantic, identified with American liberation, as imposed Iberian authority gave way to freely elected French influence. This oscillation between a nationalist, continentalist or Americanist impulse and a Europeanist, cosmopolitan or universalist impulse is the single most important phenomenon in Latin American cultural history, and is reflected in the works of the most representative writers of the twentieth century, as we shall see.

Towards the end of the nineteenth century 'Modernismo' – roughly an amalgam of such European literary phenomena as late Romanticism, Parnassianism and Symbolism – emerged in Spanish America. The movement is usually dated from the moment in 1888 when the great Nicaraguan poet Rubén Darío wrote the prose poems of his anthology *Azul* (*'Blue'*) until 1916 when he died. Principally a poetic movement, Modernismo coincided almost exactly in chronological terms with the Naturalist movement in fiction, to which, at first sight, it is diametrically opposed. Both schools were modelled on French originals, but whereas in France the gulf between Naturalism and Symbolism only served to accentuate a divorce – born of class struggle – which had been growing in Europe since the early industrial revolution and the rise of the Romantic movement, in Latin America writers almost unconsciously identified Naturalism with American contents and Modernism with European forms, and thus added a consciousness of imperialism to their perception of the contradiction.

On most of this critics broadly agree, doubtless because Latin American literature during that long 400-year period is interpreted as being overwhelmingly 'colonial' and hence mimetic and secondhand. This is an oversimplification which ignores countless examples of literary rebellion, resistance and recuperation, but as a generalization it retains its historical validity. Quite the opposite is the case with Latin American literature, and specifically fiction, in the period since the 1920s. Whilst such critical disarray is a worldwide phenomenon relating to 'Modernity', Modernism and Post-modernism, in which politics and aesthetics are inextricably entangled and – for the moment, at least – hopelessly confused – the Latin American case is all the more striking given the unanimity on the characterization of earlier periods. The lack of definition raises elementary questions about the relation of Latin American to European and North American literatures, and about the contradiction between these external 'influences', the specific character and traditions of Latin American literature(s), and the impact of Latin America's own social dynamic.

At present there is less agreement among practitioners as to what literary history is than at any time in the last hundred years. It was always a complicated task seen in the round: there are genres (poetry, drama, narrative, and so on); 'texts' (genres, forms, themes, relationships); authors (biographies, works, influences, relationships); movements (forms, themes, genres); and periods (historical, cultural, literary); all of which must be woven into a coherent narrative. The complete task is rarely done and even more rarely well done, even for single national literatures; but with regard to Latin America the problems are compounded by the need to compare its countries (including Brazil and Haiti), both amongst themsleves on a national and a regional basis (Caribbean, Central America, Andes, Southern Cone), as well and taken as a whole with Europe, North America and other 'Third World' areas.[2] It is part of the purpose of our present journey through the critical labyrinth to suggest that this complex literary–historical context poses particular problems to the Latin American artist, that the solutions encountered give that art a specific and definable character, and that this character has found its own expression and become internationally recognized in the period from the early twentieth century to the present. This does not imply any acceptance or approval of the labels conventionally used to classify Latin American literature, but their existence – like that of the more obviously social and cultural 'myths' which we shall be handling – is something that all readers have to recognize: indeed, the relation between labels of all kinds and realities has been one of the central themes of Latin American cultural discourse as a whole, as well as of Latin American literature itself. This was true from the moment Columbus's eyes first fell on the 'New World' (which, to compound the problem, he had wrongly identified in the first place as the 'Indies'), long before the twentieth century debate on the relation between signified and signifier began in Europe.

The most obvious reason for difficulties in classifying any literature since 1918 is that the period is too close to us. The second is that it has been unprecedentedly fast-moving. A third is that many critics have argued – even before the concept of Post-modernism was invented, though much more frequently since – that ours is the era which has seen the end of ideology, the end of criticism and possibly the end of the novel: totally new ways of conceiving and describing writing ('literature' itself being a mythical or ideological term) are now required. This is not unconnected to the mutual inextricability of literature and criticism since 1900, which the Mexican poet and essayist Octavio Paz was one of the first to point out, which the Argentine writer Jorge Luis Borges was one of the first to exploit with his 'fictions', and which has recently reached crescendo proportions with Derridean critical theory.

Fourthly, in Latin America itself this is the period in which the continent's literature began to assert its own creativity, independence and individual identity – largely unnoticed at the time by its critics, who were looking elsewhere. The fifth reason is a consequence of the fourth: it is the moment where the interaction between Latin American and external influences becomes increasingly complex, fertile and difficult to unravel, superimposing an additional screen of complexity over the long ideological labyrinth of ethnic, national, social and cultural identity which we shall be examining in this chapter. This last may be the decisive factor.

The literary period 1915 to 1945 in Latin America is most frequently thought of as the period which saw the emergence of the so-called 'Novel of the Land', 'Telluric Novel', 'Regionalist Novel' – and other similar depictions which may conveniently be summarized as Social Realist. Indeed until the 1960s this, too, was a near universal perception and critics disagreed only as to whether such fiction was or was not a good thing in aesthetic terms. It is more obvious now, and certainly more convenient conceptually, to think that Social Realism was the prolongation and culmination of Naturalism (and thus of Realism, which, given the absence of a fully hegemonic national bourgeoisie, has never flowered in Latin America). Social Realism was itself prolonged and transformed into documentary fiction from the 1960s to the present, as the specular illusion of 'realist' fiction, usually presented in the third person by an implied narrator with an objective and reliable point of view, became more and more difficult to sustain. The new fiction of the 1960s 'boom' era, for which Latin America is best known, made it more obvious that the 1920s had seen the development of a relatively unstudied avant-garde, itself an extension of Modernismo and precursor to the New Novel of the 1960s. This development of Modernismo in the Spanish American sense into Modernism in the European, North American and Brazilian sense (meaning Joyce, Kafka, Proust and Faulkner in the developed world; and Mário de Andrade, Miguel Angel Asturias, Jorge Luis Borges and Alejo Carpentier in Latin America) is thus the key literary phenomenon of the century, running from the 1920s to the late 1960s. The 1970s and 1980s see the emergence of Post-modernism, which sometimes seems to be best described as the as yet undefinable.

None of the above is intended to suggest that Latin American artists have ever merely imitated, or even mainly imitated, European or North American models: influences exist everywhere, and the question is only raised as a problem with regard to ex-colonial regions. Indeed, whereas most important Latin American fiction between the 1940s and the 1960s is recognizably 'Joycean' or 'Faulknerian', it is equally arguable that since the 1960s many of the most important new writers – Italo Calvino, Milan Kundera, Salman Rushdie, Umberto Eco – have had to become 'Latin American' novelists (see chapter 9). Nevertheless, it seems clear that not until the emergence of César Vallejo and Pablo Neruda in the 1920s did Latin American poetry become truly self-generating (thanks to the continental thrust of Darío's Modernismo in the previous thirty years), and not until Andrade, Asturias, Borges and Carpentier did Latin American fiction truly reach that stage (thanks to the continental thrust of the regionalist–Americanist fiction of the 1920s). What seems particularly striking in retrospect, however, is that in the 1920s Latin American fiction was already entering, however marginally, its Joycean, or more specifically 'Ulyssean' moment; it then entered its Faulknerian moment (again, these are merely shorthand depictions); it completed both of these in the 1960s; and has since then, along with the whole of Western literature, entered the 'Finneganian', or possibly 'Borgesian' moment, beyond which perhaps – for the time being – there may be nowhere to go. This may be defined as the moment where myth and history become totally confused, appearing at different moments diametrically opposed, as they were at the dawn of modernity, totally interpenetrative, as they have been during Modernism, or absolutely identical, as under Post-modernism, according to the point of view of the observer. That is why Gabriel García Márquez's *One Hundred Years of Solitude* (*Cien años de soledad*, 1967) may be the quintessential Latin American novel of the century, and the true heir to Cervantes's *Don Quixote* which inaugurated the modern novel, since it can be, and has been, read in each of these ways.

Myth: Father Europe and Mother America Weave their Labyrinth

> Generous spirits will always be concerned with the fate of a people striving to recover the rights which their Creator and Nature once bestowed on them.
> Simón Bolívar, 'The Jamaica Letter', 1815

Those who journey often over time through Latin American cultural history and its artistic expressions may come gradually to glimpse the outlines of a 'grand historical narrative' which is effectively the continent's own dominant self-interpretation and which, in its persistence and coherence through the trajectory of such phenomena as the New Novel, can safely be said to have the dimensions and the relative stability of a great cultural myth. What follows is an attempt to outline this complex ideological construction to prepare the ground for the literary readings in ensuing pages. The myth draws on the whole history of Latin America, but only began to become thinkable by Latin American artists from the 1920s for a number of reasons which will become more apparent in later chapters, although some of the factors have already been mentioned. Not the least of these is that Latin America's own decisive cultural transformation took place at the conjunctural moment of modernity itself, when Western culture as a whole was subjecting itself to a quite new gaze – what I will call the 'Joycean', or 'Ulyssean' moment. This itself was intimately connected with the rise of workers' movements worldwide, the increased mobility of the easily alienated intellectual strata, the beginnings of decolonization and the emergence of what we now call the Third World, of which Latin America has formed an important, though usually reluctant part.

The myth, Romantic in origin, Surrealist in focus, rebellious in orientation, is in essence about the relation of the New World to the Old. It tells of discovery and conquest, endlessly reproduced and repeated, and of desperate struggles, usually fruitless, to resist, rebel and liberate, to overcome solitude and attain some kind of collective unity and identity. And it shows how the people's dreams, utopias and occasional triumphs become internalized through folk memory and through art which, sometimes at least, can make itself the written record of that memory, and thus unite past, present and future at the level of representation.

In reality the Latin American myth is merely one version of the great master narrative of Western history: the road to freedom, progress and development through self-realization. Jorge Luis Borges notes in one of his fictions that 'the generations of men, throughout recorded time, have always told and retold two stories – that of a lost ship which searches the Mediterranean seas for a dearly loved island, and that of a god who is crucified on Golgotha'.[3] The word 'men' has rarely been used more ambiguously than here. It includes, fallaciously, 'non-Western men', and (as is usual) excludes, through invisibility, 'Western women': it is, in short, an innocently imperialist and patriarchal discourse. Still, Borges's reference to the Odyssey and to the Bible, the two great historic transformers of the oral and the experiential into the scriptural and the discursive, is an exact enough encapsulation of a cultural tradition. These two narratives have indeed been essential sources for the metanarratives of Western development (as well as the usual Greek meaning, 'meta' also signifies goal or objective in Spanish), currents flowing into the watershed of modernity, one of whose great expressions is Joyce's *Ulysses* (1922), which draws on both of them. When, after the illusions of the 1960s, the watershed was perceived to be a dam – manmade? – the era of Post-modernism was declared.

The United States, in the north of the New World, was able to carve out its own independent territory within the space of European – now Western – development, and could thus cultivate a self-satisfying foundational myth. Minorities fleeing from oppression had sailed the dangerous seas to freedom, set up small, democratic, God-fearing communities, and followed the sun and their own manifest destiny across a receding frontier from east to west, reluctantly defending themselves against wild animals and savage Indians to whom they had first offered the hand of friendship. Immigrants and their cultures could be simply aggregated to this scheme. One could say, then, changing our metaphors, that the capitalist prow cuts through the surface of reality, simplifying as it goes, but leaving the wash and spray of turmoil and confusion in its wake. Such an experience permits the repeated unfurling of the great myth of progress, the endless frontier, the one identity, the permanent march of capitalism, knowledge and freedom: 'man's search to know his world and himself', to quote Daniel J. Boorstin.[4] The fact that this 'triumph of the west', to cite another similarly enterprising history,[5] has involved racism, genocide, imperialism, the destruction of nature and the menace of the nuclear shadow, is easy to ignore (except in Faulkner's South), especially since the space age allows the myth another dimension through its literally endless frontier. These are just bad dreams, to be exiled from the garden of a nation that likes to 'feel good about itself'.

Latin American experience allows no such happy simplicities. In Latin America at the time of the conquest there were not just nomadic Indians, but a complex tapestry of great civilizations (defined, of course, by their conquerors as great organized barbarisms) and smaller cultural groupings, which could not all be moved on or ignored, nor even easily liquidated; besides, the colonization was not a family or community activity but a great state enterprise carried out on behalf of the Crown through the Army and the Church, without ordinary labourers and very largely without women, other than voluntary or involuntary Indian collaborators like Cortés's mistress and interpreter, Malinche. It was said to be a liberation from ignorance, but this was difficult to believe even at the time: there were too many enslaved survivors of the defeated for ideology to turn completely into myth. Moreover, since Independence in Latin America there has been a plurality of countries which have failed to become a United States of Middle and South America. Progress has been made, but usually for brief periods, erratically, sporadically, spasmodically; and hardly ever as a successful collective enterprise but through the efforts of individuals, often tyrants. There was not just one frontier; there were many different ones, sometimes within the fragmented nation states, sometimes across them. Nothing has ever been simple, unified and consistent, except through the ruthless will of some charismatic or authoritarian figure. Otherwise: improvization, intuition, inspiration, spontaneity; or lethargy, original sin, bad blood, sad tropics, sick people, a failure to assimilate and advance, sudden outbursts of violence, devastating continental, national and individual solitude. They had been marooned, isolated, banished, exiled, forgotten, negated, cursed; they were in hell, purgatory, limbo, nowhere; in a state of inferiority, second-class, comic-opera figures, caricatures, mimic men. Could they not escape and progress? No, because they were in chaos, darkness, obscurity, unpredictability – unknown and unpredictable even to themselves. When the great liberator Simón Bolívar saw the collapse of his continental vision, he declared: 'Those who serve a revolution plough the sea.'[6]

One could write an entire book on this thesis alone, but our subject is Latin American fiction and the concept must be summarized in a few pages. The architecture of the Latin American version of the myth is such that it can be read in different ways, and from different points of view. Certainly there are progressive and conservative readings, as well as male and female ones (the most radical version, needless to say, is anti-capitalist, anti-imperialist and anti-patriarchal). I am in no doubt, however, that the myth as a whole is neither a personal mirage nor an individual ideological construction, but a material collective phenomenon subject to external verification – which is not to deny, of course, that the vision through and from within the myth may be a grand historical illusion. The complete myth rarely if ever appears – Miguel Angel Asturias's *Men of Maize* (*Hombres de maíz*, 1949) would be one exception[7] – but usually partially, sometimes fragmentarily, and even momentarily, like a forest or a mountain glimpsed through the mist. The basic story is as follows:

Mother America, aboriginal, virgin, fertile, creative and productive – nature's muse[8] – was violated by the Spaniard, the European outsider, cold, rationalistic and covetous, motivated by theories, not experience, by lust and power, not love and understanding. The product of this assault was the illegitimate Mestizo (of mixed blood), the Latin American culture hero. Its effect is felt to this day whenever Latin Americans gaze at the spectacle of their history and ponder their identity: for theirs is not an identity but a duality: Indian/Spaniard, female/male, America/Europe, country/city, matter/ spirit, barbarism/civilization, nature/culture, and, perhaps most ironic in the context of Latin American fiction, speech/writing. What is the Latin American's origin? Native America in its multiple forms? Renaissance Spain (itself heir to Greece, Rome and Jesus)? Or the moment of violation in 1492? What is her/his future? A 'return' to Native America? A 'return' to European civilization? Or an acceptance of being for ever a member of a hybrid culture in a non-European continent?

Of course 'Europe', including North America, the vanguard of scientific, technological and cultural progress, is still there, although any relation with it has always thus far required the perpetuation of a dependent, neocolonial status for a Latin America still considered new, young and underdeveloped after almost five hundred years. Native America is gone, though Bolívar's '*La Patria Grande*', now Guevara's socialist America, may still beckon. But Mestizo America, oscillating, crucified between the two poles, remains the constitutive reality. This is not a complementarity but a conflict, an opposition, the variable sign for a real contradiction which determines many others.

Some dualisms are universal and are manipulated – in different ways – by all human societies, usually to range them in interlinking hierarchies which justify the dominant epistemology and prevailing social status quo. The existence of males and females and of day and night, for example, underpins the way in which human beings think about reality and organize their culture. These two oppositions alone account for much of the basic content of mythical thought, as numerous contemporary anthropologists have shown.[9] The key dualism in Latin American culture, however, is unmistakable and has a specific historic point of departure which happens to be a moment of cultural confrontation: between an already existing, known world of 'Europe', and a new, recently 'discovered' world named 'America'. Like the Romans before them, the Spanish imperialists defined that which was other as barbarous, and themselves as civilized, through a strategy which has certainly not outlived its usefulness even at this 'Post-modern' finale to the twentieth century.

That triumphant European world, suffused with Platonism and Christian philosophy, had long since proclaimed the dualism of soul and body, spirit and matter, which continues to dominate Western bourgeois commonsense to the present day and broadly corresponds, of course, to the distinction between use value and exchange value in the process of commodity exchange. In Spanish literature it was given classical expression by Cervantes in *Don Quixote*, initiating a tradition in which the main reflection of this dualism in literature – especially in Spain itself and Latin America – is the persistent theme of the gulf between the real and the ideal, or between truth and illusion, in the period between the Renaissance and modernity.

Moving to the twentieth century and contemplating this history of conquest through Freudian eyes (and through Greek mythology), we can see that in the Latin American version of Freud's 'family romance' the initial violation of the Indian mother by the European father, and its endless and still continuing repetitions, prefigures in metaphorical form the structure and Oedipal processes of the patriarchal bourgeois family, with its violent confrontation between male and female, word and flesh, law and fantasy, and their inevitable and self-perpetuating result: violence, rebellion, and a consciousness both raised and traumatized.

Viewing the same history through Marxist eyes, we can further see that the oppositions between use value and exchange value, country and city, manual and mental labour, can all provide metaphors for the antagonism between America and Europe which is reproduced within each Mestizo and within the culture as a whole. Like the Freudian perspective, these can serve to liberate Latin Americans from any sort of inferiority complex by inverting the terms of the civilization–barbarism polarity and attributing barbarism to the imperialist (and capitalist) camp.

Adding in the anthropological perspective of a Lévi-Strauss (who claims his lineage in the Enlightenment thought of Rousseau), we can see the distinction between nature and culture as another potential reversal of the hegemonic interpretation of the barbarism versus civilization opposition. The female–male polarity is identified with the nature–culture distinction in many cultures, and with renewed force in Western culture since Romanticism: in Latin American culture, indeed, such identification is almost universal. Again, Lévi-Strauss and others have insisted that 'savage thought' is more inherently civilized (because 'authentic') than Western rationalism, and thinkers both inside and outside Latin America have used this assertion to provide the most vigorous apologies for Shakespeare's Caliban and his underdeveloped but also less alienated world.

All these dualisms have journeyed inexorably throughout Latin American history and culture, along the forking paths of race, nation, class and gender, taking up ever new forms and combinations, slipping, superimposing, eliding, metamorphosing, yet somehow – as long as certain kinds of antagonism continue to exist – always reemerging over time in some new and unexpected guise. The myth we are tracing can exist wherever a 'civilization' vanquishes a 'barbarism' (it could have been written in England soon after the triumph of the Romans, or of William the Conqueror, or in Ireland at any time since the sixteenth century).[10] But only in Latin America, because of the emergence of the Mestizo culture and the enduring nature of the historical contradictions involved in its creation, have these essentialist human, Western and continental dualisms been given the force to create such an enduring historical and literary myth, whose time is not yet past.

Since 1492 the Latin American Mestizo has been forced to abandon the sedentary communities of his native forebears and, dialectically negating the historical mission of crusaders, explorers and conquistadors, has taken to the road in search of his own cultural identity, national expression and continental liberation (heir to Ulysses, Theseus, Prometheus, Dante, Quetzalcoatl). This unended and perhaps endless journey through the labyrinth has woven the myth of Latin America behind it, and, finally, contradictorily, integrated it into the Western culture from which it continues to feel itself alienated. A succession of mainly masculine writers, seeking to impose themselves on the colonized territory of Latin American culture, have found themselves, rather like the Irishman James Joyce, having to retreat to higher ground and to enlist unexpected allies, including natives and women. This is why in Latin American fiction the story is so often inverted and heroic biographies are so frequently underpinned by a mythical origin in virgin, Indian America, and a utopian objective in '*La Madre Revolución*' and '*La Patria Grande*'.

History: The Quest for Identity and the Field of Forking Paths

Given the imposed dualism of Latin America's Mestizo culture, the concept of choices, crossroads, forking paths or alternative destinies is inscribed in the very origin of the new continent. Their persistence explains why it is that the greatest Latin American novels are not just the vehicles of speculation, experimentation or playfulness, but determined explorations of Latin American reality.

Race: Iberians, others and illegitimacy

> We are but a small human kind, a world apart…, neither Indians nor Europeans,
> but a species half-way between the legitimate owners of the land and the
> Spanish usurpers.
>
> Simón Bolívar, 'The Jamaica Letter', 1815

In 1992 the world will be acknowledging the 500th anniversary of
Columbus's discovery of a region which has never acquired a settled denomination, although a majority currently call it 'Latin America'. The native
Americans, mistakenly labelled Indians, naturally refute the concept of the
'discovery' and have not taken any more kindly to the idea of 'celebrating'
the European invasion and occupation than the Australian Aborigines did in
1988. What they would certainly not refute is the concept of the 'conquest'.
A conquest there certainly was, an appropriation, a violation – many violations – and genocide. Followed by enslavement and the imposition of a new
alien religion.

Most histories of Latin America now begin not with 1492 but with the
story of the aboriginal cultures, the native Americans who were there before
the European invasion and colonization. Yet this is invariably a prelude, or
background, a preparation of the ground for the real history of Latin
America. In that sense it is usually treated as a prehistory, with all that this
still implies for us in the 'civilized West'. This is even more the case with
histories of literature: it is rare indeed for them to consider the literatures,
oral or written, of the ancient American civilizations and cultures, and again,
if they are considered it is merely as a gathering of the ingredients for the real
history to be narrated later.[11] It is only in the past half-century that such
assumptions have even been challenged, and in that sense the Latin American
situation is no different from that of other ex-colonies. Except in one crucial
respect: Latin America has been in existence as an extension of Europe for
500 years. Its republics have been formally independent for well over 150
years, and the attitudes and conflicts which the question of identity gives rise
to are long-standing internal problems, existing within national frontiers as
part of the national question; as well as also existing externally, between
Latin America as a whole and her old colonial masters (Spain, Portugal,
France, Britain) and new imperialist master (the United States).

Furthermore, the cultural problem caused by this dualism, this bi-
culturalism, has a unique pendular force, persistence and intensity in Latin
America. It originated at the moment of discovery and conquest, and specifically when the first rape of an Indian woman by a European took place and
the first Mestizo was born, a matter of months after Columbus's first landfall.
That child carried the conflict – conquest or resistance – within itself, and as

it grew was confronted with the same system of tensions outside itself, and therefore the choice (notionally, at least) as to which side to join and which way to go. This was the first great forking path in the Latin American historical labyrinth and its dilemmas remain unresolved today. Its most paradoxical aspect is that this disunity is perhaps the factor which most helps to integrate the separate republics into the overarching concept of Latin America: twenty-odd different nationalities united by geography and history, by the imposition of the two dominant Iberian languages, their culture and the Catholic religion on every other ethnic and social group existing in the continent before or since.

The conquest involved the penetration of alien territories and societies, the invasion of that cultural space and the creation of a new race of people, not by consent but by violation. To be made up of two separate and even antagonistic entities is difficult enough (our own culture has always denied the female in every male, the male in every female), but to be made up of two things because of a rape, in a symbolic context where the rapist is from the allegedly superior race, the victim from the inferior race, and where the child knows this, sympathises with but despises its mother, hates yet fears and even admires its father, and has to live in a society which perpetuates the same values, distinctions and hierarchies, is a painful experience indeed. One example among thousands is given in a recent Brazilian novel set in the colonial period, where the Mestizo Januário is lamenting his fate even to his black slave Isidoro:

> That's the best you can do, said Januário. You've got a race waiting for you, a night to shelter you. I don't have a race, I'm like a mule, stained at birth. They call me redskin sometimes, you know that. I'm not even that. I'm more of a whitened half-breed on account of my father. Neither white nor Indian. I'm not anything. I'm going to meet up with this nothing that is me.[12]

Eventually after three hundred years of that colonialist creed, an emancipation takes place, another system becomes official, and a future-oriented social philosophy is implanted. All men, and in due course women, are now in theory equal, not just because God's Church says so, but because the Enlightenment says so and the new Constitutions say so, though Biology and Ideology do not yet say so. The project of the quest for identity is declared, and has not yet run its course. Liberation becomes a permanent theme, revolution the accepted means of bringing about change, and eventually socialism becomes a standing item on the historical agenda.

However, objectives and ideals are one thing, ideologies and social realities another. Illegitimacy, one of the supreme forms of social injustice, lived on in the symbolic and psychological spheres into the nineteenth and twentieth centuries, and all Latin Americans, including artists and intellectuals, are constituted in the imaginative space marked out by these dilemmas. The Spanish family involved a patriarchal head, married to a perfidious female who was originally sinful and liable to be led further astray by serpents; her subjugation implied the rejection of nature and its gardens and the erection of an institution with bars and an inner courtyard called home, a chastity belt of stone and iron. A Spaniard's house was his castle and her prison. If this was a somewhat ruthless version of the Christian family unit, the classic Latin American structure referred to above is not a family at all. In that story an Indian mother was violated by a Spanish father, who never acknowledged his offspring: the child was therefore the product both of fornication outside of wedlock and of a violation on his mother's legitimate territory, which had become his father's by force of arms. As a half-breed he could look nowhere to his origin except to that act of violence and illegitimacy. His identity was that: unless he, looking forwards rather than back, decided to forge his own identity, in some different future. (Naturally, the Church, which in practice sanctioned the social status quo, always offered him the alternative vision of the Holy Family, to which of course that status quo paid hypocritical lip-service: a non-violent father, a virgin mother impregnated by the Holy Ghost, and a sacred child destined to die in crucifixion and rise again to join his parents in the other world.)

Illegitimacy, then, product of an unending dialectic of violation and vengeance, has remained a central theme of Latin American culture: the social and racial illegitimacy of the governed – and hence of the whole half-breed culture – has for most of its history been matched by the political and moral illegitimacy of their governors. The violence was there at the beginning and no myths can disguise it. The normal response has been the redemptionist, messianic countermyth of the charismatic, 'necessary' man, whether rebel or dictator. The colonial period, when a few Spaniards and Portuguese imposed their own legitimacy and everyone else's illegitimacy, was followed by a neocolonial period in which the cultural framework, ideas and definitions continued to come from outside. In these circumstances, the sense of illegitimacy and inferiority, now metaphorical rather than concrete, was difficult to fight and took a long time to dissolve – indeed, it took 'one hundred years of solitude', to quote the title of the novel which best encapsulates the period and its dilemmas.

Nevertheless the other story, against conquest, triumphalism and oppression, is the liberationist impulse, the courage to resist and survive against overwhelming or even hopeless odds, seen in the history of Haiti, Cuba, Paraguay, Bolivia, Central America and so many other small and defenceless countries, regions or social groups. Many Latin American writers – not necessarily the best known or the most successful – have borne witness to these struggles, which lie at the heart of Latin American history, as we shall see.

Nation: civilization or barbarism

We were, as I have said, abstracted and, so to speak, absent from the universe in all things relating to the science of government and the administration of the state.

Simón Bolívar, 'The Jamaica Letter', 1815

During the colonial period there was only Spain or Portugal. No outside alternatives existed, and those two powers exerted every conceivable form of monopoly – political, economic, cultural, religious and educational – until well into the eighteenth century. For all practical purposes there was also a racial monopoly, as we have seen, which perpetuated the relationships instituted by the conquest itself. Eventually independence became a possibility, and the leading settlers, the Creoles – or Spaniards and Portuguese born in America – opted for emancipation and set out to universalize their own self-interest.

Thus the nineteenth century saw the institution of some twenty national projects against a neocolonial background. It became clear that Latin America was not a *tabula rasa* or blank sheet of paper on which the Enlightenment could be inscribed, as so many had thought. On the one hand its freedom to manoeuvre was strictly limited by external forces; whilst on the other emancipation from Spain and Portugal did not allow it to forget, erase or escape from the Spanish and Portuguese past which lived on in its own political, social and cultural heritage. Nevertheless real alternatives now existed and real choices could and indeed had to be made about national cultural identity and about the paths to be taken into the future. Moreover, despite Creole dominance and European intervention, the social, racial and cultural project was now, finally, an American one, in which, logically, the Mestizo, the man who was no one, would gradually come into his own as the true American –although it was not until the 1920s that he began to do so, largely as a result of the cultural upheaval catalysed by the Mexican Revolution. Thus in the mid nineteenth century, as the national question began to monopolize the debate about choices for the future, two great themes began to dominate men's thoughts and cultural discussions.

The first was the conflict between 'civilization' and 'barbarism', a polarity which takes us back to the Romans, and which at heart is certainly not racial, as men then assumed, nor even anthropological, as some (Morgan, Engels) were beginning to think, but ideological. 'Civilization' implied the ultimately 'European' values of enlightenment, reason and sobriety, whereas 'barbarism' involved the violence, spontaneity and improvization of nature, identified with America herself, and served to explain the disillusioning

period of 'anarchy' which followed Independence in the first half of the nineteenth century. The dichotomy is as old as so-called civilization itself, and it
came as no surprise when in 1973 Chile's General Pinochet announced that
his barbaric coup had been carried out, like Spain's original conquest of
America and Franco's rebellion against the Spanish Republic in 1936, in the
name of Christian Civilization. On the whole, however, Latin America's
quest for political progress has been in the direction of Western-style democracy, however 'normal' dictatorial regimes may appear to be in the region.

The second theme, like the first, has appeared in numerous guises and has
undergone numerous metamorphoses over the centuries, but has been equally
tenacious, although more specifically Latin American: that of 'solitude'. This
is the principal metaphor arising out of Latin America's origin through conquest and destiny as a colonial, half-breed offshoot of Europe. Extensions of
it are themes associated with distance, and with divisions, separateness,
incommunicability. (There are parallels with the more recent Australian case,
and the dominance there also of themes of dishonour, solitude and distance,
although the differences are equally striking.) It is curious how little its historical meaning has been understood, however: even Octavio Paz, in his
famous psycho-historical essay *The Labyrinth of Solitude* (*El laberinto de la
soledad*, 1950) chooses to give it a metaphysical explanation not far removed
from an existentialist philosophy. Yet it is unmistakably the sense of isolation and abandonment of Europeanized minds in Mestizo bodies, the sense of
living nowhere and of living outside of history, a sense of total non-
transcendence and futility which took concrete root in Latin America long
before romantic spleen, the *fin-de-siècle* malaise, and the twentieth-century
absurd. Almost all the many weird and wonderful metaphysical theories
which Latin American *pensadores* ('thinkers') have developed over the past
150 years about the nature of the Latin American mind can be traced back to
these historical dilemmas and translated into the nucleus of themes relating to
colonialism, bi-culturalism, civilization and barbarism, solitude and illegitimacy. The reception of all external ideas and influences has been conditioned
by this perspective. To all of which the Latin American responded with the
quest for identity and the struggle for liberation; only to find that even the
horizon was a mirage and that his journey, inescapably, was destined to take
him through an apparently endless labyrinth.

The project had been independence followed by a process of civilization in
replacement of the dastardly Iberian feudal–Catholic heritage and the barbarous indigenous one. But if the project was liberation, the reality, everywhere,
was closure, tyranny, imprisonment, exile or death. The reason was in the
blood. Indian and Spanish, Black and Portuguese culture were even more ret-
rogressive when mixed, and this sick America could only be cured by mass
injections of European blood and European – especially French and British –

culture, including political culture. The nineteenth century saw the separation of Church and State in most of the new republics – this was the focal point of conflict between liberals and conservatives – but it was not until well into the second half of the twentieth century that Protestant religious movements made any significant headway in Latin America. Prior to that the effective choice was simply to believe or not to believe; and more than 90 per cent of the population have always claimed to believe.

Nineteenth-century thinkers and writers were debating these questions even when they were unaware of it, but there were two remarkable and pre-scient works whose influence is still with us: '*Facundo: Civilization and Barbarism*' (*Facundo: civilización y barbarie*, 1845) by the Argentine Domingo Faustino Sarmiento (1811–88), eventually President of the Republic in 1868, and *Revolt in the Backlands* (*Os sertões*, 1902) by the Brazilian Euclides da Cunha (1866–1909).[13] Both are passionate, hybrid works, written as if they were novels but intended as testimonial and ulti-mately political documents, in a tradition which is as vigorous as ever today. Sarmiento's work belongs to the early post-Independence period in which Enlightenment and Romantic currents were confused and imperfectly assimi-lated, whilst Da Cunha's work is a product of the Positivist era at the end of the century. (A quarter of a century later, in the new proletarian era, a third seminal work on the national question appeared, namely the Peruvian José Carlos Mariátegui's more overtly theoretical '*Seven Essays towards an Interpretation of Peruvian Reality*' (*Siete ensayos de interpretación de la realidad peruana*, 1928).

Facundo is surely one of the most remarkable works ever written after the birth of a new nation, in a panorama dominated by the gulf between dreams and realities, between the extraordinary deeds of great liberators (Bolívar, San Martín) and the ensuing chaos, violence and… barbarism of tyrants like Sarmiento's adversary, the dictator Juan Manuel de Rosas, in power between 1829 and 1851. Sarmiento, a self-educated man from the Andean foothills, exiled in Chile, gazes out in his imagination over the vast expanse of the recently liberated and newly enslaved Argentine Republic, and within a first part of less than a hundred pages outlines, in a vigorous, pioneering romantic prose the themes which will dominate more than a century of intellectual debate about the political, social and cultural condition of this newly consti-tuted nation: Europe versus America, civilization and barbarism, solitude and distance, frontiers, horizons and the unknown, individualism, violence and improvization. These ideas will recur again and again in Argentine literature and in the works of thinkers like Echeverría, Alberdi, Gutiérrez, Rojas, Gálvez, Martínez Estrada, Mallea, Murena, Hernández Arregui and Viñas, and the political questions will appear anew, eerily familiar, the first time as farce and the second as tragedy, during the two comings of Perón (see chapter 10).

However, the key to Sarmiento's work – the first of the great literary labyrinths of Latin America – is his robust grasp of alternatives, contradictions and antagonisms. These provide the momentum and architecture of his book and the outlines of the national debate in Argentina for 150 years. But at the same time Sarmiento falls victim to his own contradictions, which are those of Argentine nationalism itself, such as the need both to reject and to emulate what is foreign, the need to negate the Spanish heritage with an absolutism that seems inherently Spanish whilst ignoring the Indian legacy, and the unmistakable admiration, despite himself, for the self-reliance, individualism and, when necessary, savage violence of the gaucho pampa dwellers in the face of an untamed natural world. His portrayal of Facundo Quiroga, a provincial caudillo eventually murdered by Rosas, is almost startling in its modernity.

The problem which Sarmiento had perceived, but for which despite his originality he had no theoretical framework, was one which was already being explored by two German thinkers in a work which appeared soon after *Facundo*, namely *The Communist Manifesto*. Sarmiento was struggling to theorize the contradiction between the city and the country, between mental and manual labour – indeed, with uneven development – as he wrestled with the relation between Europe and America in terms of civilization and barbarism. He sees only too clearly that virtues fit for the city may be vices when they are transferred to the country, and vice versa, and that what is appropriate for European culture may not assist in the development of Latin America. But he also sees – what Paraguay's dictator Doctor Francia had tried heroically to ignore (see chapter 8 on *I the Supreme*) – that the development of the planet is unfortunately in one direction only and that the odds are stacked overwhelmingly against new nations trying to compete on equal terms.

Half a century later, in Brazil, a decade after the end of slavery and the dissolution of the monarchy, federal troops sent by the new republican government to the small community of Canudos in the Northeastern outback carried out the suppression and liquidation of messianic rebels led by the self-styled prophet Antônio Conselheiro. The event has since become a landmark in the process of imposition of civilization over barbarism, technology over religion, Europe over America, the city over the country, and the nation over the regions.[14] The army engineer Euclides da Cunha recorded his horrified response in *Revolt in the Backlands* (1902), a work whose tone is at once didactic and declamatory. The problems he perceived and analysed were almost exactly the same as those reviewed by Sarmiento sixty years before. But Sarmiento had Rosas's ruthless dictatorship to justify his crusade for civilization; his plans were all still aimed at an open future, and he was as much as anything arguing for the spiritual campaigns of universal education, a lifelong ideal. Da Cunha, however, had begun to see the limits of the civilization which his expedition represented – even before the watershed of the First World War – and had witnessed a horrific massacre which still haunts Brazil's historic memory (even if it is still periodically repeated in the Amazon, through the slaughter of forest Indians). Despite Da Cunha's own ambivalence, his sense of outrage is passionately and unforgettably conveyed. Up to that moment Latin America had almost always opted, as it has mainly since, for 'Europe' against its own native cultures and traditions. This remained overwhelmingly the case until the 1920s, in the aftermath of the Mexican Revolution, when a new consciousness began to develop, and another great thinker, José Vasconcelos, emulated Sarmiento's missionary zeal, only this time with a universalist education system and a 'cosmic culture' in mind.

Sarmiento had rejected both the Hispanic and the Indian heritage, and mistrusted the imperialist directions he perceived in British and French culture. Unlike almost all later thinkers, he held the United States to be the best available model for Latin America, and considered Argentina the country best suited to emulate it. By the end of the nineteenth century, when the great Cuban poet José Martí lived in exile in the United States, that nation was no longer the young creature which had cast off a colonial oppressor, but a robust and dangerous carnivore seeking an empire of its own. Martí saw these contradictions with great clarity, coming as he did from a Cuba then in the final throes of the struggle against Spain. He died a martyr in that struggle and did not live to see the United States replace Spain as effective master of Cuba after the decisive events of 1898.

Thus when in 1900 the Uruguayan thinker José Enrique Rodó (1871–1917) published his famous essay *Ariel*, neither he nor most of his contemporaries shared Sarmiento's admiration for the United States. Rodó, on the contrary, compared it to Shakespeare's Caliban, in possibly the first Third World use of a symbol which has been repeatedly employed in the decolonizing debate ever since.[15] Rodó declared that Latin America should not follow the United States model, but instead should take the Latin path which flowed through Iberian culture from the Greeks and Romans through the Italian Renaissance and the French Enlightenment. It hardly needs saying that this left little space for the Indians or Mestizos or Blacks of countries which, unlike Argentina and Uruguay, could hardly pretend they were 'white'. Still, the idea of Latin America's spiritual superiority over the Northern Anglo-Saxons was a useful and an influential one which gave comfort to many artists and intellectuals well into the 1930s (it was in a sense the ideology of Victoria Ocampo's magazine *Sur* in Argentina, for example).[16] Despite his temporary celebrity, however, Rodó's work was really the culminating essay in a nineteenth-century tradition of building philosophical castles in the air, and the continent was now ready for something different. The Parnassians and Symbolists of Brazil and the Modernist poets of Spanish America, for whom Rodó was essentially writing, were fast coming to the end of their era, and a new tough-minded age was about to dawn.

Class: capitalism or socialism

The Emperor Charles V made a pact with the discoverers, conquerers and colonizers of America which, as Guerra says, is our Social Contract.
                                                    Simón Bolívar, 'The Jamaica Letter', 1815

In the twentieth century the international context once again had a decisive hand in the transformation of Latin America. Just as the discovery and conquest were stimulated by the Renaissance, and the independence movements were a sequel to a process involving the Enlightenment, the United States battle for independence and the French Revolution, so developments in the twentieth century were launched by an even more extraordinary conjunction of world-shattering events. But this time momentous events in Latin America coincided with, rather than followed, events elsewhere. The First World War of 1914–18 and the Russian Revolution of 1917 coincided with the Mexican Revolution of 1910–17 and the continent-wide student movement which began in Córdoba, Argentina in 1918, whose influence has continued to be felt down to the present day, but particularly down to the Tlatelolco massacre of 1968 which effectively put a final full stop to the era of the Mexican Revolution and a symbolic end to an entire historical period.

The questions of class struggle, capitalism and imperialism made their first significant appearance on the Latin American scene in the 1920s, creating a dichotomy between nationalist and socialist perceptions which – like the contradictions between liberalism and nationalism in Sarmiento's mind – have been confusing but fertile in their effects down to the present time. Setting aside the old liberal and conservative parties, the major competition from this moment – sometimes comradely, usually not – was between the newly established Communist Parties and the Populist – usually also nationalist and Americanist – Parties born out of the combined ideologies of the Mexican Revolution's 1917 Constitution and the 1918 Córdoba rebellion. Such parties, inspired by dead literary heroes like José Martí (1853–95) and the Peruvian Manuel González Prada (1848–1918), actively sought student–worker alliances. The first and much the most influential was the Popular American Revolutionary Alliance Party (APRA), founded by the Peruvian student leader Raúl Haya de la Torre in 1924, which the Peruvian oligarchy successfully kept out of power until 1985.

For each Latin American intellectual from this moment the historical labyrinth became much more complex. The past remained largely a mystery, whilst the paths into the future, although more clearly marked than before, often proved to be mirages, so that increased options and combinations meant increased confusion. Before each writer in the 1920s, when the story of this book really begins, lay the vision of New York, home of capitalist modernity; Moscow, home of socialist revolution; and above all Paris, home of Latinity, high culture and the avant-garde, and unofficial capital in exile of a disunited American continent; and his own national capital, free from but also tied to all those other capitals. But then, within his own continent, and increasingly well-connected from then onwards, there were the many plural but similar Latin American nationalities and a few fast-growing, especially influential and fertile cities: Mexico, Havana, Lima, Rio and São Paulo, and Buenos Aires.

For a few heady years the panorama was alluring for all but the most conservative intellectuals. There seemed to be endless choices on offer, politically, culturally and artistically (most of them overlooked economics and sociology). There were Marx and Freud; the American way of life and the new mass culture; an avant-garde mesmerically concealing its elitism beneath an apparently juvenile and democratic image. And above all, one huge mirage: the populist Americanist belief that anti-imperialism (in the 1920s almost all Latin American intellectuals were anti-imperialists) was somehow the same as anti-capitalism. This was sometimes a sincere illusion and sometimes a convenient illusion, but it was certainly an influential and far-reaching one between about 1924 and 1964, after which the mirage again faded as the Cuban Revolution forced a division of the waters, a parting of the ways and a taking of sides. It was the new political consciousness, then, without a doubt, which in the 1920s provided the thread for Latin American intellectuals and artists to look back through the labyrinth of the past and forward into the labyrinth of the future, initiating a process which began in the populist era of the Mexican Revolution and reached its climax in the decade following the triumph of the first socialist revolution in America.

Gender: culture and nature

Can anyone calculate the transcendence of the liberation of Columbus's hemisphere?

Simón Bolívar, 'The Jamaica Letter', 1815

Women have not been allowed to play a very visible part in the development of Latin American culture, although men have used them as the inspiration and even the measure of their own imagination and creativity. Their treatment has not been essentially different from that which has characterized Western society as a whole, but given the especially stark contradictions of

Latin America's social processes their experience has been a particularly restricted and often intense version of the general pattern of exploitation and discrimination. Latin America is usually thought to be the natural home of machismo, the most exaggerated version of patriarchal sexism, though in truth the Latin American case is merely a more rugged, frontier expression of that code of honour and passion which has characterized Mediterranean society for at least 500 years.

In Latin America as elsewhere the rebellion of the workers, peasants and Indians has always overshadowed the concerns of women as such, but equally the emancipation of women was implicit in that other struggle and its time has now decisively arrived. In this book, due to its timescale (principally from the 1920s to the present) women will appear mainly as the objects of literature and of masculine meditation and imagination generally. However, the extent to which, paradoxically, they dominate that imagination invariably comes as a surprise to European and North American readers, even those familiar with such myths as that of 'Mother Russia'.[17] The particular architecture of what has been denominated above as the 'myth of Latin America' can help to explain this obsession, in a world where the trauma of the original violation of native America persists, and where the mythical fertility and creativity of natural America continues to inspire writers – self-appointed representatives of culture (and, implicitly, of civilization) – in the face of modernity and imperialism.

As in Europe, Latin American women have been able to express themselves through literature, and particularly through fiction, more effectively than in other ways, and there are many successful women novelists. The Mexican nun Sister Juana Inés de la Cruz (1648–95) was probably the greatest writer of the whole colonial period in Latin America, and in the nineteenth century the Cuban Gertrudis Gómez de Avellaneda (1814–73) and the Peruvian Clorinda Matto de Turner (1854–1909) are undoubtedly among the most significant novelists. Nevertheless, few of the best-known writers have been women, and none have been household names until recently, though the situation is now changing very rapidly, as the case of Isabel Allende shows. Whatever recuperations and vindications critics may undertake in the coming years – and we can be certain there will be many – there can be little doubt that the great era of women's writing in Latin America is still to come. Once Her-story begins to effect radical changes in His-story, and we at last cast light on the dark side of the moon, nothing will ever be the same again.

Culture: The Magic Labyrinth

I find myself in a conflict, between the desire to return the confidence you have placed in me and the difficulty of satisfying it, given both the lack of documents and books and my limited knowledge of a country as immense, varied and unknown as this New World.

Simón Bolívar, 'The Jamaica Letter', 1815

It is unusual these days to pick one's way through a literary supplement without coming across some fictional or critical work based implicitly or explicitly upon the concept of the labyrinth. Umberto Eco's *Il pendolo di Foucault* (1988) is only the best known recent example of a novel structured around a paradigm which may, retrospectively, dominate our vision of twentieth-century narrative.[18] In no literature, however, are images of labyrinths as persistent and pervasive as they have been in Latin American literature, not just recently but since the 1920s, and an astonishing number of works which do not even mention the concept nevertheless embody it in their structure or view of the world or both. Is it merely a fashion which has turned into a tradition? Or simply the influence of Jorge Luis Borges (1899–1986), author of the celebrated *Fictions* (*Ficciones*, 1944), who almost patented these concepts in elaborating his own conception of what reading, writing, thinking and culture are? Or that of Octavio Paz (1914–), who has applied the concept archetypally to the question of Latin America's historical identity in his influential *Labyrinth of Solitude* (1950)?

As we have seen, the colonial origin of 'Latin' America left its people with a traumatic self-conception whose inherent dualism inevitably heightened the 'natural' human tendency to think and advance by means of contrasts, differences and opposites. Latin America's history can thus be interpreted in retrospect as a field of forking paths, to refashion Borges's influential metaphor ('The Garden of Forking Paths' is one of his best-known stories), with the choice between 'Europe' and 'America' inaugurating and preordaining a whole series of later choices as the determinants of race, nation, class and gender construct, reconstruct and deconstruct individual and collective identities.

Labyrinths and mirrors

A labyrinth may be natural or man-made, above or below ground – the Ulyssean or Thesean variants – designed as a puzzle, entertainment, trap or prison.[19] It may be real or imaginary, metaphor, symbol or myth. It may be essentially symmetrical, or spiral, or have no discernible structure; its outer boundaries may likewise be of any shape. It may have a central focus, or several, which may or may not be at its topographical heart, which may give meaning to the whole, or rather to the journey or journeys which it implies, offers or demands. Most often, perhaps, one associates it with an underground quest, in the darkness, through spiralling corridors, in which one may easily get lost, downwards towards some intimidating centre; nocturnal, the space of our worst dreams but also the arena of our greatest triumphs and discoveries, including – perhaps above all – our identity and the meaning of our life. But then we find ourselves asking: is this an origin and purpose rediscovered or a name conquered for oneself? For Freud, and above all Jung, the labyrinth is, archetypally, uterine, symbolizing a simultaneous longing to return to the maternal origin and fear of regression to the preconscious world of chaos; or, more historically, the site of a journey from a dark, enveloping matriarchal consciousness into the light of knowledge and patriarchal civilization. Needless to say, the problem with this for either a colonized or feminine imagination is that all the signs may have to be reversed if liberation is to be achieved.

In the realm of cultural space as the twentieth century has conceived it, there are fields (language, culture, memory, texts) and paths (utterances, discourses, images, themes); and there are labyrinths or networks fusing and confusing the two (worlds, lives, books), embracing past, present and future, the collective 'we' and 'they' and the individual 'I', 'you' and 's/he'. A hall of mirrors is a kind of labyrinth in which there are not only unpredictable routes and corridors, but misleading and illusory ones, where what you see is not what you get: what appears to be a mirror may be a mirage. Perhaps one can step through the mirror to a non-reflecting world, an alternative reality through different doors of perception? These are questions which have been asked repeatedly in literature since the Renaissance, when the Realist perspective was born – the seminal text remains Cervantes's *Don Quixote* – although the nineteenth century had seemed for a time to liquidate the debate with the classic Realist moment of writers like Balzac and Dickens, emblematized by Stendhal's famous mirror image early in that century and reaffirmed, albeit temporarily, by Lenin's studies of Tolstoy early in the twentieth. But Symbolism was already undermining this mode of vision and such questions were taken up again with renewed urgency at the moment of Modernism with its labyrinthine passages from Flaubert through Proust, Kafka and Joyce, at one of the decisive conjunctures of world history (1870–1930).

To put things more crudely into focus, one can say that Realism began to move into crisis at the moment, in the second half of the nineteenth century, when writers perceived that modern history itself, the very basis of literary Realism, concealed prehistory, biology and psychology, chose to be informed by geography, economics, sociology, politics and even culture, not to mention science and technology, and struggled tenaciously and increasingly unsuccessfully with theology, philosophy, myth and ideology. This crisis of knowledge – confusion out of surfeit – preceded and indeed provoked the Modernist moment where history and myth, world and book, universe and self glided silently together under cover of the great political and cultural commotions of the era. At this moment the 'inner other' became partially visible, on the one hand (Freud, Joyce, Surrealism), and art began to reflect obsessively on its own process of production on the other (Joyce, Unamuno, Pirandello, Proust, Gide): self-referentiality both of text and author. The modern labyrinth was in place. Its most obvious characteristic was that each observer experienced it differently: most could not see that it was a labyrinth, and some could not see it at all.

Europe's last labyrinthine moment had been the era of the romance at the end of the Middle Ages. Then, like Latin America after Independence, Europe had been unknown unto itself, and the novels of chivalry charted the quest of European consciousness towards its own reconciliation of individual and collective identity. That discovery coincided with the vanquishing of the East and the discovery of the New World of the West. In the period after the First World War, when Europe again entered a labyrinth – recorded in literature by Joyce and Kafka – from which it has not yet re-emerged, Latin America's historical experience had been inherently labyrinthine for a century, but without the mental tools to think around its contours and without, as yet, the consolation that Europe was in a similar predicament. On the contrary, Europe provided, albeit temporarily, such models of reason as were still available. Thus famous twentieth-century novels like Miguel Angel Asturias's *The President* (1946) or García Márquez's *One Hundred Years of Solitude* (1967) portray the development of Latin America as a kind of tragicomic caricature of European history, or as a vicious circle, a repetitive nightmare in which the same sins and curses come to haunt the continent and its children through century after century – conquest, murder, violation, illegitimacy, and dictatorship – countered by the redemptive quest for legitimacy and identity and the struggle for liberation, inevitably involving a raising of consciousness, further repression from without and within, and a new round of disillusionment and despair. Little wonder, then, that the labyrinth has become a symbol of Latin American literature which may well stand ultimately for Latin American history itself. García Márquez has chosen to entitle his new novel on the great Liberator Simón Bolívar '*The General in his Labyrinth*' (*El general en su laberinto*, 1989).

Plots thicken

Yet somehow there must be a way out. When that way out has been found, Latin Americans will know where they are, who they are, where they have come from and where they are going. They will have escaped from the labyrinth of solitude, have completed the quest for identity: they will be able to look at themselves in the mirror and see what is truly there.[20] What does this involve? Above all, it involves exploration of their own Mestizo culture. As we have seen, the problem for a Latin American, more than for the members of any other major world culture, is that identity is not given: it has to be searched for, discovered or even invented. And it is always twice dual. The most cursory glance at Latin America's typical cultural expressions in the twentieth century would suggest that within each Latin American two mythical beings are always at war, an original Spaniard (or Portuguese, or Frenchman) and an original Indian (or Negro, especially in Brazil, Cuba and Haiti); and beyond this inner conflict, he and she are permanently crucified between their own, already dual America and the external world of Europe (and later North America). A Latin American must face the fact that s/he is both part of and the product of many cultures, but *at least two*: hence the proliferation of concepts like bi-culturalism, transculturation, the neobaroque, or Magical Realism, as codes for the social reality and cultural expression of the colonized Mestizo continent – whose project, nonetheless, in the modern era, must surely be that of the truly multicultural and polylingual space.

This only very recently desired outcome – first visible in Asturias's *Men of Maize* (1949) – means choosing a future which is different from the past, maybe even a negation of the past. It means not seeking to impose oneself by violence, not conquering as a means of establishing identity, not repressing the other, weaker part of oneself; possibly even encouraging all the traditions of resistance and rebellion, seeking out the suppressed democratic, cooperative and ecological currents of the culture, seeking to fuse rather than split, to unite rather than separate, because America took the wrong road at the start and must take a different road in the future if the way is to be found. If this is done, the Latin American republics may be better placed to confront the world that is to come than other nations with a willed – rather than inherited – lust for progress through violence.

As we have seen, Latin American reality itself, by the 1920s, was already extraordinarily complicated – twenty separate nation states unified and divided by history and geography and by inextricably interwoven concepts of race, nation, class, gender and culture. But the problems of decipherment were getting more formidable as they went along. As the Western world itself, in the age of modernity, entered its own twentieth-century maze, Latin Americans were obliged, more than ever before, to understand what we now call the 'First' and 'Second' Worlds of Europe and North America in order to understand themselves, which implied travelling simultaneously through two superimposed labyrinths without any guide to tell them how to read the signs. For the irresponsible this created an endless playground, a gigantic hall of mirrors in which all paths led to the truth – or none. For the committed avant-garde writer, however, who sought to combine political and aesthetic revolution in the age of cultural Modernism – Joyce and/or Kafka – the challenge was momentous.

As a matter of fact, things were even more complicated than this suggests. What critics complacently call 'the labyrinth' (dissolving differences) or 'labyrinths' (multiplying differences indefinitely) is really three – among many – different phenomena. First and last, it is an image of 'life' (the Borgesian version), that is, the human condition, the eternal perplexity of what some American film-makers like to call 'man', condemned to journey perpetually through a time and space odyssey towards death, without ever knowing why. But equally, as we have already seen – and in this case perhaps more decisively – it is also 'history' (Paz's variant), however abstractly conceived, and in this instance the history of Latin America, of each of its individual republics and each of their individual inhabitants, and of the relation of each of these to each other and to the rest of the world. The literary debate about the relation of these two categories is interminable. My simple contention is that the greatest novels, in Latin America or elsewhere, attend simultaneously to both dimensions. The quest, then, is for identity, for the meaning of life, oneself, one's culture, nation, continent, in relation to others. The triumph is finding it, defining it, taking possession of it: liberating the labyrinth. The tensions between the verbs I have chosen are self-evident, derive from the dialectic of Latin American history, and help to explain the contradictory dynamism of recent Latin American writing.

Finally, however, to complete the elements of an explanation, one should not fail to add that the art form which has charted the rise of bourgeois consciousness and the development of the nation state, namely the novel[21] (which, ironically enough, neither Borges nor Paz have ever attempted), is also the genre which has most closely reproduced 'man's' labyrinthine experience – his quest for meaning and identity. Moreover, it has also, in the twentieth century, most closely approximated in form as well as content to the concept of the labyrinth itself: book as world, world as book. Joyce's exploration of language and culture, Proust's odyssey around the mind, Kafka's journey through the corridors of the absurd – in short, the birth of the metafiction – are phenomena which belong to the period 1913–22, when the novel attained heights and depths of complexity which have never been surpassed. Since that time fiction has also been about the nature of fiction (as it has been at so many of its definitive moments: Boccaccio, Rabelais,

Cervantes, Sterne). The Mexican writer Carlos Fuentes has often talked about this:

> The novel is the privileged arena where languages in conflict can meet, bringing together, in tension and dialogue, not only opposing characters but also different historical ages, social levels, civilizations and other dawning realities of human life. In the novel, realities that are normally separated can meet, establishing a dialogic encounter, a meeting with the other. [22]

Little wonder that the Latin American New Novel is the artistic phenomenon which has heralded the region's reappropriation of the West's attention in the late twentieth century, and little wonder that it has assumed what one might call the 'Joycean', or 'Ulyssean' (or even Bakhtinian) form.

Journeys through the labyrinth

> It is indeed a grandiose idea to form out of our New World one single nation with one single link connecting all its parts to one another and to the whole. Since it has one language, one origin, one set of customs and one religion, it ought, in consequence, to have one federal government to unite the different states to be formed; but this is not possible because remote climates, different situations, opposing interests and dissimilar characters divide America.
>
> Simón Bolívar, 'The Jamaica Letter', 1815

Race, nation, class and gender may be taken as ciphers for the great forking cultural paths which Latin Americans have been forced to travel since the conquest. These exist in each nation and bifurcate further and differently according to the specific origins, conditions, composition and history of each one, forming a vast, multiple Latin American labyrinth, always static in the past (we can move back through it), but always mobile in the present and the imagined future, and of course in the human mind and memory themselves. Historic individuals, fictional characters, authors and readers are all confronted by these paths and alternatives, either in reality or in their imaginations. [23] In general, Latin American novelists, being more socially and politically committed than most, show us that their characters may see the choices before them correctly or incorrectly; if incorrectly, it may be either because they they make technical – that is, philosophical – errors, or because they lie to themselves out of cowardice or self-interest; if correctly, they may then make moral or immoral choices, either because they lie to themselves about the possibilities of action or, again, out of cowardice or self-interest.

The myth outlined earlier is, so to speak, Latin America's master narrative about itself. It is the writers' collective interpretation of what Latin American history has been about. Each writer, each national literature, can see the myth as their own individual journey through the labyrinth of life (consciousness, knowledge, memory, morality), history or fiction itself. Thus the life of a nation or a continent can be identified with the life of a writer or a fictional character, especially as in this case the continent itself has a date of birth and a prehistory, as do each of the republics some three hundred years later. However, assimilation of the full complexity and coherence of the myth was impossible before Independence, and, despite the prophetic vision of Sarmiento, who gave the first – patriarchal – version, it took a century of solitude before writers, who did not even know what they were waiting for, could see enough of the outline to begin to explore the contours of this newly discovered imaginative geography. The period of exploration and conquest, or of revolution and liberation – needless to say, there are always at least two versions – occupied the period from the 1920s to the 1960s, and forms the main focus of the chapters to follow. Each novel, each fictional construct, is itself a journey through the labyrinth.

The quest for identity, then, has been the central problematic of Latin American culture and the central theme of Latin American literature, the material framework for its cultural horizon and historical perspective. The Social Realists of the 1920s perceived this, opened up a cultural space for literary exploration, thought they saw the horizon (development, nationality, identity), pointed to it like Adam, and prophesied paths, directions, destinies. They saw mirages, thought the road was straight and clear, however arduous, and failed to understand the labyrinthine complexity of language, of myth, of urban consciousness, or, in a word, modernity. It is as if Latin Americans have struggled desperately to assume their imposed destiny – sharers in the European trajectory of progress and development – but repeatedly been frustrated in the attempt by the prior existence of 'Europe' itself. The novelists of the 1960s completed this process of self-discovery at another moment of radically enhanced expectations. Borges had proclaimed that all reality, all experience was labyrinthine, and his leading contemporaries agreed; but most were not at all convinced that the puzzle was insoluble or that the problem of identity could not be resolved. They established it, or thought they did, and their discovery and conquest of that historical knowledge, the way into the future, is the subject of our own journey through the labyrinth.

PART I

Social Realism

2

Openings:
Rediscovering America

What impression must be left in the mind of any inhabitant of the Argentine
Republic by the simple act of fixing his gaze on the horizon and seeing... seeing
nothing? Because the more he sinks his eyes into that uncertain, hazy, indefinite
horizon, the further it recedes, the more it fascinates and confuses him, sinking
him ever deeper into contemplation and doubt. Where does it end, this world he
vainly seeks to penetrate? He knows not! What lies beyond his gaze? Solitude,
danger, savagery, death. And hence poetry.

D.F. Sarmiento, *Facundo*, 1845

The history of Latin America is the history of a frustration, of newness,
youthfulness or freshness repeatedly denied and repressed, of a past that has
never been assimilated and a future that never seems to come, or, if it does,
arrives too late. Its continuity of frustration and disappointment reminds us
only too clearly why men so often prefer myths and dreams to realities and
truths, and why fantasy reigns so powerfully so often in history. At the close
of the nineteenth century the poet and martyr José Martí, in the face of a new
imperialist threat from the North, had insisted that the Latin American
republics should unite around the intimate and emotive family surname of
'Our America'. In the 1920s, as intellectuals and artists began the quest for
identity in earnest, its most important literary explorer, Pedro Henríquez
Ureña, in his aptly named 'essays in search of our expression', summed up
the experience of the nineteenth century:

'I will do great things; what they are yet I know not.' The words of the mad king
are the motto inscribed for a hundred years now on our banners of spiritual
revolution. Shall we overcome the disillusionment provoked by so many
successive revolutions? Shall we fulfil our ambitious promises? No sooner had we
emerged from the dense colonial cloud into the burning sun of independence, than

35

we shook off our spirit of timidity and declared our rights to the future. Virgin world, newly born liberty, republics in ferment, ardently devoted to the immortal utopia: here would be created new arts, new poetry. Our lands, our free lives, demanded their expression.[1]

This seminal essay, now largely forgotten, is also one of the first in Latin America to use the concept of the labyrinth as its central image:

> We have come to the end of our journey through the confused palace, the weary labyrinth of our literary aspirations, in search of our own original and authentic expression. And here at the exit I feel I have returned with the hidden thread which has been my guide....
> The search for perfection is the only norm. If we content ourselves with the discoveries of others, foreigners or compatriots, we shall never communicate our own intimate revelation; if we make do with a lukewarm and confused enunciation of our intuitions, we shall distort them for our listeners and they will appear vulgar. But when we achieve the firm expression of an artistic intuition, it will contain not only universal meaning but the essence of the spirit that possessed it and the savour of the land in which it was nourished.[2]

Henríquez Ureña's goal was only fully achieved in the 1960s, although, as we shall see, some writers were able to unite the local and the universal as early as the 1920s, when his statement was made. Broadly speaking, the nineteenth-century search saw a pendular movement in Latin American literature. The Neoclassical style and ideology which had characterized the late colonial and early independence periods had given way to a more appropriate Romantic mode: vigorous, rebellious, optimistic, popularly oriented and explicitly Americanist in the early decades, though increasingly disenchanted later, on the European model, as chaos and dictatorship supplanted early illusions. Towards the end of the century the widely perceived failure of the ideals of the independence era prompted a swing back to explicitly European forms of art. The phenomenon was profoundly contradictory and took on paradoxical forms. On the one hand fiction, which seemed directly concerned with the realities of Latin America from an objective standpoint, was produced mainly by apostles of Zola's Naturalism. They subjected Latin America's 'backward' or underdeveloped societies to the gaze of European ideology, under the mask of scientific neutrality, with all its implications in terms of social Darwinism and racial inferiority. In poetry, on the other hand, the new 'Modernist' movement in Spanish America, which in most respects appeared to be almost slavishly deferential in its imitation of European aesthetic fashions, was nevertheless, with its flair, confidence and unifying impulse, the first genuinely continental artistic movement and the first to influence developments in Spain.

The Modernist movement's point of departure was French Parnassianism and Symbolism, but it also gathered up the strands of earlier, only partially assimilated movements such as Romanticism and even Neoclassicism, to form an exquisite, elegant concoction which was the prototype of the alert, flexible cosmopolitanism which has characterized Latin American bourgeois art and thought to this day. For the first time Latin American artists were both united among themselves and integrated with European artists. Rubén Darío's smooth, musical medium was a great historical achievement, but its limitations were manifest. He declared that his creed was beauty and renounced the false mirrors of Naturalist art; yet beauty, too, was skin deep, and Darío had no way in to the labyrinths of consciousness, language and meaning. His art had no cutting edge.

By contrast the Cuban José Martí was less concerned with the possible reactions of some potential European audience. His simultaneous commitment both to poetry and to politics placed him at the very margins of bourgeois expression at the time, announcing that the 'hour of the furnaces' was at hand and forging a mode of revolutionary Romanticism which remains one of the pillars of radical artistic expression in Latin America to this day.

The Land and the People

Another such pillar comes from Argentina, as do most of Latin America's nineteenth-century prototypes and archetypes. It is the gauchesque poem *Martín Fierro* (1872) by José Hernández, as close to a national epic as one can find in Latin America and the true precursor of the 'telluric' novels which were to dominate the 1920s and 1930s.[3] In most respects a history of Latin America seen through Argentina is inevitably a distortion because this is the country which has least accepted and assimilated its Mestizo status,[4] which is why, paradoxically, Sarmiento's *Facundo* remains representative not merely of the Europeanist perspective on the national and continental questions in general, but also, intensely, of its own country of origin. *Martín Fierro* is its dialectical opposite: rural, popular and egalitarian, refusing to reject what exists in the name of idealist projects for the future, opting for tradition because the modernization on offer promises no freedom, no justice, only incorporation and marginalization on the terms of others. For Sarmiento liberal capitalism and civilization are synonymous, or rather, if they are not, will have to be deemed so for practical purposes. Hernández and his gaucho hero want other terms. None are available. The gaucho can die out or become a hired hand. He becomes a hired hand and dies out, though in the process he becomes a national myth – a continental one too, whose spirit rides on through the Cuban *Barbudos*, the Tupamaros, the Peronist Montoneros and the cantering throb of every Latin American protest song of the last twenty-five years. Like Fierro, each of those singers sits himself, as it were, with the great Latin American landscape open before him, to create songs in which, characteristically, politics and the meaning of the cosmos become somehow united.

On foot Martín Fíerro sits and strums his guitar as he laments his fate or announces his rebellion. When he rides the horse's hooves echo the beat and mark out his revolutionary journey. The man on horseback, good and bad, dominated the history of Latin America from the sixteenth century to the time of the Mexican Revolution and Sandino, and his images, traditions and myths live on in the present. By the 1920s the horse had begun to be superseded in most parts of Latin America. The first century after Independence had belonged increasingly to the steamships which brought the foreigners, entrepreneurs and immigrant workers, but also and most especially to the railways, although their function on the whole was to undertake the economic purposes of others, the foreigners, rather than to unite Latin Americans within or between national boundaries. The twentieth century has belonged to the combustion engine – above all the long-distance bus – and to the airplane (above all in Brazil), and there is little doubt that the novels of the 1920s, which so often represented travellers on foot or on horseback, were, like the movies then being made, narrated as it were by observers who themselves were riding on trains, cars or planes, observers who were, precisely, not local, but who now knew how these dwellers of the interior fitted into the regional structure of their still disunited nations. The story of the 1920s, then, is the story of a mapping, a story of fields, paths and horizons, in which knowledge, progress and development were seemingly no longer problematical, the only frontier the line between present and future, the known and the knowable, the developed and the as yet undeveloped. If, as frequently occurred, novels were records of failures, these tended to be confirmed only on the last page as if to emphasize their imminent resolution.

The Novel of the Mexican Revolution

The twentieth-century apotheosis of the man on horseback came with the Mexican Revolution, almost a war between cowboys viewed through its Hollywood image. For some it is this century's first great social revolution. Certainly it changed the face of Latin America as no event had done for a century and no other would until the Cuban Revolution of 1959. For thirty years the regime of the dictator Porfirio Díaz had been a nineteenth-century archetype, the dreams of Positivism made flesh: ports, telegraph lines and railways carrying European civilization to cities with French-style boulevards, political opposition all but invisible, workers and peasants suppressed. After 1900 he found things more difficult: liberals and anarchists began to stir up revolt and the opposition gradually united under the bourgeois industrialist Madero ('effective suffrage, no re-election') and the peasant leader Zapata ('land and bread'), in an anti-feudal and anti-imperialist insurrection. Madero˙was unable to restructure the authoritarian institutions of the Díaz state apparatus and was assassinated. The struggle only intensified, and a whole country took to the roads and railways. The new dictator, the assassin Huerta, was defeated by the combined forces of the modernizing North – the landowner Carranza, self-educated soldier Obregón and rural bandit Villa – and of the underdeveloped South – the peasant leader Zapata. At the crucial convention of Aguascalientes in 1914 mass impulses and individual passions meshed with national and foreign ideologies to produce a chaotic, desperate confrontation. The revolutionaries divided, Villa and Zapata against Carranza and Obregón. What was a petty-bourgeois intellectual to do?

Why, ride with Pancho Villa if he wished to lose the political battle but win the literary war. A whole succession of writers, already well-known or soon to become so, including the American John Reed, the Peruvian José Santos Chocano and innumerable Mexicans – most notably Mariano Azuela and Martín Luis Guzmán – did precisely that and wrote reports, poems, novels and film scripts about their experiences, which other writers and film-makers have continued to use or refashion to this day.

Mariano Azuela, *The Underdogs*

> The riders go on down the steep mountain trail exhilarated by the glorious morning. No man thinks of the bullet that may await him round the next bend. The joy of the trail is in the unexpected. And so the horsemen sing and talk and laugh for all they're worth. The old nomadic longings fill their hearts. It matters not from where they come or where they're going; only to ride and keep on riding, never stop; take possession of the valleys and the plains and high sierras, just as far as the eye can see.
>
> Mariano Azuela, *The Underdogs*, 1915

Mariano Azuela (1873–1952) was the first and in important respects the greatest of the so-called 'novelists of the Mexican Revolution'. By general consent this also makes him the first of Latin America's great Social Realist writers and arguably, with *The Underdogs* (*Los de abajo*), the author of Latin America's first genuinely modern novel, whose formula – political liberation opens the road to modernity – although frustrated, inaugurates the 'regionalist' current of the 1920s and 1930s. All accounts of modern Latin American narrative must really start from here. As a matter of fact Azuela had also written the first 'novel of the Revolution' in 1911, with '*Andrés*

Pérez, Follower of Madero' (*Andrés Pérez, maderista*), an embittered fictional account of his own early experiences in the conflict. Like many middle-class intellectuals, Azuela always really felt that the 'ideals' of the Revolution had died with the murder of President Madero in 1913. Socialists, on the other hand, tend to believe that the real revolution only began after that event.

In 1914, confronted with incomprehensible alternatives, Azuela opted for Pancho Villa's Northern Division and enlisted as an army surgeon, writing much of his novel in between battles. In *Facundo* and *Revolt in the Backlands*, as we saw, an implicit acceptance of a heterogeneous form of expression for a heterogeneous reality had been the key to success: the Latin American artist, more than most, has had to make a virtue of imperfection, improvization and contradiction. *The Underdogs*, a short and in some respects rudimentary novel, is epic, comic, lyrical and tragic by turns. Summarized, it begins as an epic and ends as a tragedy; a tragedy it is, then, and one which has been repeated many times in Latin American history and literature, that of the illiterate peasant – in this case Demetrio Macías – who has neither the consciousness nor the technology to defend his own interests and carry out a successful revolution or even to participate actively in the process of modernization. He is outmanoeuvred by opportunistic petty-bourgeois intellectuals.

Although perhaps misguided – he never fully understood the real political issues at stake in the Revolution – Azuela was scrupulously honest. The novel is not narrated from the peasant's point of view, and Azuela is careful only to enter the consciousness of middle-class characters like himself, but the title emphasizes that the peasant is the principal protagonist of the novel as he was of a revolution which was taken away from him by the rising agrarian and industrial bourgeoisie. Sarmiento's whole concern had been to prevent the gauchos from behaving in a wild and spontaneous way, outside the law, and since then the people – these 'underdogs' – had never been seen acting in Latin American fiction. Now here they were:

> A whirlwind of dust, swirling along the highway, suddenly broke into violent hazy masses, swelling chests, tangled manes, dilated nostrils, wild eyes, flying legs and pounding hoofs. Bronze-faced men, with ivory teeth and flashing eyes, brandished rifles or held them across their saddles.[5]

The peasants are coming, along the road of history, which will dissolve them like ghosts, and the intellectuals are watching and focusing their image. What will they do: watch, criticize, condemn, support, commit themselves, act? What they will do less than almost anywhere else in the Western world is lie to themselves about the prospects and the choices. Naturally the same cannot be said for the characters. Here is the opportunist Luis Cervantes trying to decipher an unfamiliar reality – across the frontier between two different worlds – shortly after capture by the brutal and illiterate rebels whom he claims he has come to join:

> Lost in the shadows of the starry night, Luis Cervantes had not yet managed to establish the exact shape of the objects about him. Seeking the most suitable resting-place, he laid his aching bones on a pile of fresh manure beneath the blurry mass of a huizache tree. More exhausted than resigned, he closed his eyes, determined to sleep until such time as his fierce keepers, or the morning sun, burning his ears, should chance to waken him. Something vaguely warm at his side, then a hoarse and weary breath, caused him to shudder. He opened his eyes and, feeling about him with his hands, sensed the coarse bristles of a large hog which, resenting the arrival of a companion, began to grunt.[6]

Once accepted by the revolutionaries, Cervantes, a journalist and former medical student, persuades himself temporarily of their cause, and is shocked to hear the conclusions of Solís, a friend who has focused his own perceptions somewhat differently:

> Cervantes... invited Solís to explain the circumstances which had so destroyed his illusions.
> 'Circumstances?... Insignificant, trivial matters, things most other people never see; instantaneous, a line that contracts, eyes that shine, lips that flare; the fleeting meaning of a phrase that fades. But all circumstances, gestures and looks which, rearranged in their logical and natural expression, make up a frightful image, the grotesque and frightful image of a race.... An unredeemed race!'[7]

Azuela, leaving the nineteenth century behind, is already in the realm of the metafiction, with this self-referential passage which effectively explains how his novel is to be organized and interpreted, transforming a labyrinth of unfocused glimpses into a clear and legible composite image. The seeds of the new fiction are perfectly visible here. Nevertheless, he is ultimately more concerned with conception than perception:

> 'Facts are bitter, my dear fellow; so are men.... Enthusiasm, hopes, ideals, happiness – all empty! After which there's only one alternative: either you turn bandit, like the rest of them, or you leave the stage and hide yourself away behind the walls of a fierce and impenetrable egotism.'[8]

These intellectuals will be there, writing the books or appearing in them, sometimes as heroes and martyrs, failed leaders of abortive struggles (not infrequently mere struggles of conscience), more often as cynical opportunists, but most often of all as feckless ditherers, speculating about the meaning of life and the purpose of literature as their illiterate countrymen starve and immolate themselves in futile rebellions, or agonizing as to whether they can and should sacrifice their own class interests by identifying themselves with the *pueblo* and committing themselves to its cause.

The persistence of these themes is not surprising. The absence of the so-called middle sectors is a long-standing factor in Latin American society, as in other ex-colonial regions. After the overthrow of the colonial monarchy there had been no constituted authority in that continent of illegitimates. What authority, following the overthrow of Díaz and his 'generals and doctors',[9] could they respect, follow or identify themselves with? So if, like Darío, they effectively supported dictators, they would – the occasional dedication apart – write about something else, something 'universal', and evade the issue. Nevertheless, the main line of Latin American literature is undoubtedly progressive, liberationist and frequently revolutionary, sometimes obviously so, sometimes implicitly, and sometimes – as in Azuela's case – without the artist himself being fully aware of it.

What did the Revolution achieve? It began to unify and modernize the country (see my discussion of Fuentes's *The Death of Artemio Cruz* in chapter 7, below), gave it an international identity, prepared it for full capitalist development, and made possible the next stage of the debate about the national question in Latin America. What did *The Underdogs* achieve? It provided Latin America with its first important Social Realist novel – however 'primitive' – and preserved the essence of the Mexican Revolution in literature for posterity. Azuela, who so deplores almost everything he narrates, and is even disillusioned by Demetrio Macías, his crude but good-hearted hero, has given numerous expressions of the quest for land and liberation which was so much a part of the true meaning of the conflict:

> Back astride his chestnut horse, Demetrio felt a new man; his eyes had recovered their peculiar metallic gleam and the hot red blood flowed once more through his coppery Indian cheeks.
>
> The men threw out their chests as if to breathe in the distant horizon, the vastness of the sky, the blue of the mountains and the sweet fresh air perfumed with all the aromas of the sierra. They spurred their horses to a gallop as if in that wild chase they sought to take possession of the land itself. Who among them now remembered the ruthless chief of police, the surly gendarme or rascally politician? Who gave a thought to the pitiful hut where he had lived as a slave, under the eye of the boss or the cruel and heartless foreman, forced to rise every day by dawn...?
>
> They laughed, they sang, they whooped, drunk with the sunlight, with the air of the wide open spaces, with life.[10]

In general, Azuela's eye for telling detail and ear for popular speech are essential aspects of his art. His simple and illiterate peasant hero becomes a historical archetype – oppression, darkness, rancho, land, wife and child – who rides out of the maize fields and on to the highway of history, to die without achieving his objective:

> His famous marksmanship fills him with joy. Where he plants his gaze, he plants a bullet. He loads the gun once more… takes aim.…
>
> And at the foot of the carved rock-face, huge and sumptuous as the portico of an old cathedral, Demetrio Macías, his eyes fixed in an eternal gaze, keeps on pointing with the barrel of his gun. [11]

In its dynamic, almost cinematographic urgency, its frank recognition of the gap between city and country, mental and manual labour, intellectuals and peasants, Azuela's novel was in many respects more 'modern' than any of the works which followed it, and in retrospect seems the only novel of the Revolution produced in colour.

Martín Luis Guzmán, *The Eagle and the Serpent*

Azuela's Indian is simple but not stereotyped, rustic but also contradictory. No other novel of the Revolution focuses on him in the same way, leaders or intellectuals elsewhere taking centre stage. Azuela's only major literary rival is Martín Luis Guzmán (1887–1976), a general's son who joined the Revolution and opted, like Azuela, for Villa. *The Eagle and the Serpent* (*El águila y la serpiente*, 1926) is a gripping documentary novel based on Guzmán's own experiences, and for some critics Mexico's most important chronicle or 'true history' since the work of Bernal Diaz at the time of the conquest. Guzmán personally encountered most of the leading protagonists of the Revolution, and each of them appears in an acting and speaking role in this remarkable gallery of Mexican historical personalities. So vivid indeed is Guzmán's portrayal of character and scene that some of his portraits have made permanent contributions to our image of key figures in the conflict, and historians have leaned perhaps too confidently on the pictures and interpretations it constructs. Chapters such as 'A Night in Culiacán', 'Fiesta of Bullets', 'The Hangman's Knot' or 'Zapatistas in the Palace', are classics of twentieth-century Mexican prose and provide images and anecdotes which were to become the stock-in-trade of the Mexican nationalist cinema of the 1930s and 1940s.

Azuela, although disillusioned, had waited until after Villa's first defeats before fleeing, but Guzmán, having decided that both houses were plagued, invented a pretext and fled for the border after bidding farewell to the fearsome guerrilla leader:

> 'Right, Doc', said Villa, 'now go take a rest. And listen: from tonight you stay here with me. I'm gonna order them right now to get Luisito's office ready for you,

because you're gonna be my secretary. Or do you have any objections? Speak up like a man.'

Once again my life was hanging by a thread; still I had no choice but to go on to the end.

'I'd like to ask you one favour, General.'

'Speak up, then, straight out now.'

'My family left Mexico City on the last train. They could be in Chihuahua, I don't know. Or maybe in El Paso... I'd like... if it were possible... with your permission... to go and look...'

Villa leaned his face towards me. He fixed me with a look, and held me by my lapels again. He was quiet for a few seconds, then he said:

'You, too, going to abandon me?'

I thought I saw death pass across his eyes.

'Me, General...?'

'Don't run out on me, Doc; don't do that, will you, because I'm your friend, believe me. You wouldn't run out on me, would you?'

'General...'

'And go look for your family, you have my permission. Do you need anything, would you like a train all to yourself?'

Then I breathed again...

Now the train ran, swiftly through the shadows of the night. How big Mexico is! Fourteen hundred kilometres to the frontier.[12]

The image of the intellectual as opportunist or deserter, already memorably recorded by Azuela, is one that will recur repeatedly in works of twentieth-century fiction in Latin America. Guzmán fled into exile in the United States, returned after the fall of Carranza, plotted against Obregón, and fled again, this time to Madrid, where he wrote a brilliant novel about Mexican politics, 'The Shadow of the Caudillo' (La sombra del caudillo, 1929), which earned him the enmity of yet another president, General Calles. In Spain he became the secretary of a different kind of leader, Manuel Azaña, President of the Spanish Republic, and took Spanish nationality, but was then forced to flee Spain itself at the outbreak of the Civil War. Curiously, after his definitive return to Mexico, Pancho Villa, the jaguar-like barbarian, became a lifelong obsession, and from the time of Lázaro Cárdenas's presidency, Guzmán devoted many years and more than a thousand pages to his unfinished novelized chronicle, The Memoirs of Pancho Villa.[13] The work not only confirmed Villa's image as a beloved popular legend, but made him in due course a member of the approved pantheon of national revolutionary heroes.

Even Villa was a great leader, however. Guzmán was never interested in the secondary characters of history, still less the masses. His sinister, unforgettable evocation of the Revolution is convincing but severely limited in focus, viewed from the standpoint of the liberal intellectual and drawn with the power (though not the heart) of a Rembrandt, through scenes based on small dots and threads of illumination against a prevailing obscurity as the serpent of darkness gradually overwhelms the eagle of light. The chiaroscuro of heroism and villainy, cynicism and idealism, recreates a vivid sense of the impossibility of knowing which was the right side to be on, morally or opportunistically, for more than a day or two at a time. A former member of the intellectual Atheneum of Youth (1909), Guzmán has little sympathy for the popular cause, as is made amply clear by his classic account of the occupation of the National Palace by the Zapatistas and his contempt for their intellectual adviser Antonio Díaz Soto y Gama.

Gregorio López y Fuentes, '*The Land*'

Pancho Villa had become immortal even before his assassination, for showing the gringos how, and his legend dominates the fiction of the Revolution. Zapata's more genuinely mythical, Indian presence was slower to take hold, and the only major novel to feature his story was '*The Land*' (*Tierra*, 1932) by Gregorio López y Fuentes (1897–1966), which helped to fashion the image of another national hero:

> The news, like a hungry dog, goes diligently from door to door. It is passed on in whispers, in huddles, by men at the plough and women at the well. He has been seen. So it's true he's not dead...
>
> 'Do you know who saw him? Old Albina. She's telling the whole thing to anyone who'll listen. And mind, old Albina's not one to lie. She'd rather swing. This is what she told me:
>
> "I saw him with these same eyes the worms will eat. Such a beautiful moon when he rode up to the verandah... Like midday. Just one look told me who it was. I recognized him straight off. Hat pushed back, like always, them same trousers with the buttons, and that moustache you could tell a mile away. Just as I was about to invite him in for a cup of coffee, he turned his horse away and set off at a canter, in that direction; look, as if he was heading for Anenecuilco..." '
>
> ... Along the old road, opaque in the dusk, two yokes trudge side by side. Thin as they are, the oxen walk and chew with statuesque dignity. As if they were made of pumice stone. Behind the oxen, using their goads as staffs, walk two men, as hazy as the animals they are driving, murmuring about what is said around the fires, in porches and along the furrows.
>
> 'That's what they say. And that old Albina saw him.'
>
> The two pairs of oxen nod in time. The two men immersed in their thoughts. Fireflies light up the hedges by the wayside. There is a light on the mountainside. A fallen star?
>
> Both men turn their heads. They are certain they heard the trot of a horse. They see, perhaps silhouetted against the clear horizon, a man on horseback. They rub their eyes with their hands, like people who have emerged from darkness into light. There is nothing. Only the perfect silence of the fields.[14]

Zapata and the other peasant revolutionaries live on in the paintings of Rivera, Orozco and Siqueiros, and in popular poetry and song. Around this time a different Indian peasant was invented for the new 'revolutionary' party, for speeches, slogans and murals. A dark Indian dressed in white, who wants to learn to read and write in Spanish and is grateful to the party; his children are healthy and can choose whether to stay in the rancho or migrate to the new life in the cities. Meanwhile Azuela's real Indian reappears from time to time in literature, most notably in the works of Juan Rulfo (see chapter 6), prostrated in a long unrelenting agony which goes on today.

The peasant has appeared, then, and with him the intellectual. They have a long road to travel together over the next half century, in the era of Social Realism. Sometimes the one is in focus, sometimes the other, though there is no need to say who is doing the watching and the writing, not to mention the reading. In the nineteenth century the peasants had been no more than a part of the scenery, whilst the founding fathers of Romantic fiction made arrangements for them and, above all, for the emblematic earth-rooted females who connected the ruling classes to the land – over the heads of the peasants and peons, so to speak – and were thus awarded the titles of so many novels: *Soledad*, *Amalia*, *Inocência*, *María*.

On the whole the novels of the 1920s were written by men who originated in the provinces and moved to their national capital (or, though less frequently, vice versa). They themselves were part of the flow from the inferior, interior regions of the national body to the head, the capital, where knowledge and experience are stored. From that new standpoint they then looked back at the country from the city and its perspectives. The expansion of those big cities had resulted from the growth in international trade, increases in population combined with the decline of the old landowning classes, incipient industrialization and the rise of workers' movements, all of which combined to bring a belated end to a colonial period which should have died in the early nineteenth century. The prospect of such economic, social and political transformation gave most writers a renewed feeling of liberation, as if only now was Latin America really gaining its independence and the chance to discover itself instead of being discovered and defined by others. Themes relating to the road, the frontier and the horizon – Azuela's revolutionaries galloping along the highways of history – gave a sense of possibility and a perspective on the future which transformed the Latin American intellectual's ability to think about his country and his continent. Novels by the Venezuelan Rómulo Gallegos (1884–1969), such as *Canaima* (1935), abound with images of open doors and open books, deeds waiting to be done and histories waiting to be written:

Mouth of the Orinoco. Doors, barely ajar, to a region still dominated by the age of violence and adventure.... Every so often one would see the odd solitary heron, motionless, as though waiting for that retarded world to finally emerge; then, for long stretches, like the sleeping channels of some silent labyrinth, the solitude of the plants was absolute in the midst of the cosmic waters. But the boat moves on and its journey is time, ages of the landscape.... Channels and more channels! A wondrous labyrinth of soundless waterways with the landscape lying as if shipwrecked along the dead surface. Deep perspectives towards other solitary waterpaths, mysterious turnings prepare for the sudden striking appearance, expected at any moment, of some strange dweller of that uncompleted world.... Venezuela, her discovery and colonization as yet uncompleted.[15]

In the nineteenth century Latin Americans had not been ready for their independence. They lacked the technology, the education and the sheer manpower to explore and develop their own countries. The moment of optimism after the First World War suggested that this time, for sure, the *tabula rasa* was not an illusion, the horizon was open for economic and cultural development, the continent was an open book waiting to be written in. Thus peasants and workers become the principal narrative focus during the half century which the Mexican Revolution inaugurates in Latin America; but although they are the apparent subject of fiction, they are little more than the objects of the petty-bourgeois artist's friendly but profoundly ambivalent gaze; for intellectuals often change their mind and point of view, and their favourite subject is almost always themselves. The people's quest for economic justice and social liberation offers a way out to the frustrated and disenchanted middle sectors trapped in the prisons of their Creole cities after what would later be perceived as a hundred years of solitude. The French Revolution had been so long ago, and was for Europeans, not for inferior unenlightened ex-colonials; whereas anyone could join the proletarian struggle, which, since Marx and Bakhunin, had convincingly universalist ideologies and an internationalist framework. The Mexican Revolution, the events in Europe, the Latin American and student movements opened paths into the future, to the frontier – the cultural horizon: development, modernity, national integration – and on to the as yet undefined but now, at last, definable. That was how it seemed to Latin American writers in the 1920s.

The best known of the Social Realist novels have the archetypal quality of primitive epics, which is what they were: national myths carved out of the rawest of materials by men who had barely emerged from the nineteenth century, suddenly ready to embark on their cultural mission of defining national identity within the process of national integration and thus to embrace the people, whose folk traditions offered some authenticity in a disillusioning past and whose struggle for liberation seemed to point the way to the future. It had not been possible to write such novels before and it is no longer possible to write them today. Thus these novels are profoundly historical even though for the most part they present themselves – given their epic intentions – as timeless and archetypal, featuring characters who are at once symbolic, typical and – despite what some later sophisticates would say – individual.

The mighty jungle: José Eustasio Rivera, *The Vortex*

> Ah, jungle, mistress of silence, mother of solitude and mist! What evil spirit left me a prisoner in your green dungeons?.... How often my soul wanders sighing through your labyrinths in search of the star that colours the purple horizons of my homeland, above its unforgettable plains and the snowy peaks that crown the cordillera!
>
> José Eustasio Rivera, *The Vortex* , 1924

One of the earliest of the great regional novels and one of the most remarkable for its self-awareness and its author's implicit self-criticism was *The Vortex* (*La vorágine*, 1924) by the Colombian José Eustasio Rivera (1889–1928). Until quite recently critics generally failed to acknowledge the extraordinary fertility of a novel in which some of the seeds of Alejo Carpentier's *The Lost Steps* (1953) and even of García Márquez's *One Hundred Years of Solitude* (1967) lie planted. Rivera, born and raised in the Colombian interior, began his literary odyssey as a Modernist bard in an era in which that form of expression was outmoded, and ended up as a boundary commissioner, exploring the Amazon jungle much as the great Guyanese novelist Wilson Harris would later do. This experience, at a time of ruthless capital accumulation, rapidly transformed Rivera's view of the world, and of his country; through his narcissistic protagonist, the failed poet Arturo Cova, he looked back on the previous century in dismay and saw his own frustrated career ambitions as a symbol of Colombia's national futility:

> Who established the imbalance between reality and our insatiable souls? Why give us wings in the void? Poverty was our stepmother, ambition our tyrant! Through gazing only at the heights we stumbled on the ground, through attending to our wretched stomachs we failed in affairs of the spirit. Mediocrity passed on its anguish. We were heroes of the second rate!....
>
> As I tried to get away with my illusions, unknown forces launched me far above reality! I passed beyond fortune, like an arrow missing its target, unable to correct the fatal flight and with no other destiny than to fall! And this was my much vaunted future![16]

Rivera's novel anticipated by two years Henríquez Ureña's lamentations on Latin America's Lear-like empty boasts, quoted above. The absurd and truculent romantic rhetoric, like a Latin popular song of anguish and betrayal, dominates this entire first-person narrative, as in the opening lines, which deserve to be anthologized as a pastiche of Latin American romantic attitudes even today:

> Before I fell in love with any woman, I gambled my heart with Destiny and it was won by Violence. I knew nothing of intoxicating swoons, nor sentimental confidences, nor the tremor of cowardly glances. Rather than a lover, I was always the dominator whose lips knew no entreaty. And yet I longed for the divine gift of an ideal love to set my spirit alight, so that my soul would sparkle in my body like the flame within the branch that feeds it.
>
> When Alicia's eyes brought me misfortune I had long since abandoned hope of a pure emotion.... She was an easy conquest; she gave herself without hesitation, on the promise of the love she sought in me. She had not even thought of marrying me when her relatives conspired to arrange a wedding, urged on by the priest and resolved to subject me by force. She alerted me to this contemptible scheme. I'll die alone, said she: my misfortune stands in the way of your future.
>
> Then, when they threw her out of the family bosom and the judge told my lawyer that he would see me rot in jail, I said to her one night, resolutely, in her hiding place: How could I abandon you? Let's flee! Take my fate, but give me love.
>
> And we fled![17]

Most readers have assumed that we were meant to take this seriously, and there is little doubt that Rivera is having his Romantic cake and eating it. But on the contrary, this is the novel that puts an end to a century of Romanticism, using firstly the antidote of parody and secondly, and increasingly as the novel progresses, of documentary realism, so that what begins as a case study of almost psychopathic individualism ends as a defence of communal values and a denunciation of capitalist development, undertaken by the rubber barons of the Amazon, and involving imperialist infiltration and ecological devastation.

Rivera follows the distant example of Sarmiento and the more recent example of the classic Uruguayan short-story writer Horacio Quiroga (1878–1937) in recapturing the sense of awe and primordial terror evoked by Latin America's natural scenarios. In particular Rivera is the first novelist to begin to organize his fiction in mythological zones of the kind later analysed by semiologists, based in turn on the dramatic contradictions of Latin America's national geographies. Thus here, as in Gallegos's *Doña Bárbara* (see below, p. 54), the great plains or Llanos are conceived as everyday reality, the sunlit present stretching straight into future progress, an epic land where achievements mirror intentions and the human mind mirrors external reality. Like Azuela, Rivera perceives the potential national symbolism of popular independence and liberty in such a setting:

> 'Mulata', I said to her, 'which is your country?'
> 'Here where I am.'

'Are you Colombian by birth?'

'I'm just from the Llanos, round Manare way. They say I'm from Cravo, but that ain't so; or from Pauto, but I ain't from there neither. I'm from all these here plains! What more country would I be wanting with them so wide and beautiful? As the saying goes, Where is your God? There, where the sun comes up!'

'And who is your father' I asked Antonio.

'Child, the important thing is you was born!'

With a pained smile I enquired:

'Mulato, will you travel to Vichada with me?'...

'That's just jungle and more jungle, where you can't take a horse, what for? I'm like the cattle: I just want the grassland and my freedom.'[18]

Similarly when Cova challenges a cowboy of the plains the man gives a reply that will be heard often in the fiction of these days:

'Listen', the man rejoined, 'up above me there's my hat. However big the earth is it fits beneath my feet. I ain't messin' in your business, but if you're looking for trouble, I got plenty you can have!'[19]

When Cova and his companions flee the plains to take refuge in the Amazon, the same theme of freedom reappears, and again we sense the disenchantment of a new generation with a whole era of frustrated ideals in the independent but unhappy continent:

The moment had come to free our horses, which had given us such comfort in our adversity. They recovered the virgin pampa and we lost what they so joyfully regained, that zone where we had suffered and fought so uselessly, committing our hopes and our youth. As my sorrel, sweating, shook itself free of the harness and galloped off with tremorous whinnies in search of the faraway waterhole, I felt alone and abandoned, and I fixed the vision of my surroundings on my sad gaze, with the bitterness of the condemned man resigned to the final sacrifice as he sees the last sun turn red above the landscapes of his childhood.

Descending into the ravine that separated us from the canoe, I turned my head to the limit of the plains, lost in a soft haze, where the palm trees now bade me farewell. Those vast solitudes had wounded me, and yet I somehow wanted to embrace them. They had been decisive in my existence and had become a part of me. I know that at the moment of my death the most lasting images will fade from my glassy eyes; but as my spirit wings upwards through the everlasting atmosphere I shall see again the half-tones of those enchanting twilights which, with strokes of opal and pink, showed my soul the way into the beckoning sky towards the supreme constellation.[20]

The whirlpool of the title is of course the vast Amazon jungle, and indeed savage nature itself, the feminine, dark, magical, mysterious, the pool of corruption and death as romantic minds conceive it. Arturo Cova has a momentary intuition that the wide open spaces of the plains were a nineteenth-century illusion, as they had been for Azuela's peasants, and that life, the world, culture is a pre-existing labyrinth as complex as the human mind itself. Far from Latin Americans having put the 'sadistic virgin jungle' behind them, thinks Rivera's protagonist, that same forest still awaits them with its prehistoric network of flora and fauna engaged in a frenetic danse macabre. This is reflected in turn in the ruthless behaviour of capitalist exploiters in the most primitive phase of commodity fetishism, as they compete in a battle for survival whose monstrously epic quality Rivera reluctantly admires:

> Yet it is civilized men who are the knights of destruction. There is something magnificent in the epic of these pirates who enslave their peons, exploit the Indian and battle against the jungle. Trampled by misfortune, they hurled themselves from the anonymity of the cities into desert zones, looking for any way out of their sterile existence.... The rubber traders in Colombia destroy millions of trees every year. In Venezuela the *balatá* has disappeared. In this way they are busy defrauding future generations.[21]

Thus the whirlpool of fate, of nature, embodied in the jungle, becomes modern capitalism, cruel, insatiable, insanely competitive, and mere men, like every other form of commodity, end up sluiced away down the jungle plughole. Arturo Cova has a premonition of all this in the first pages of the novel, where, surprisingly enough in such an early work, the ruthless development of the natural world, then only just beginning, is identified with Cova's own sexual exploitation of the hapless Alicia. Both impulses are reduced to a lust for power and possession which he, comically, is unable to bring to a climax. The novel's last line is possibly the most quoted in Latin American literature: 'The jungle devoured them.'[22] Rivera died in 1928 during a visit to New York to publicize the novel and attend to its English translation. Legend has it that illness brought about by his sufferings in the Amazon were the direct cause of his early death.

The great plains: Ricardo Güiraldes, *Don Segundo Sombra*

> The countryside had returned to its former desolation. Almost nothing remained of the roundup, either out on the plain or in my memory. It might all have been just imagination, now denied by the solitude of the grasslands. Solitude that somehow seemed to me eternal....
>
> We set off at a gallop, headed for the pampa, which swallowed us bit by bit in its indifference.
>
> Ricardo Güiraldes, *Don Segundo Sombra*, 1926

This era in Latin American fiction is the moment of the Latin American equivalent of the 'Western' – the 'Southern', perhaps? Mexican vaqueros, Venezuelan llaneros, Chilean huasos, Argentinian, Uruguayan and Brazilian gauchos. Strong, wild men had been riding through Latin American literature since independence, in gauchesque poetry and in works like *Facundo* and *Martín Fierro*. The Spanish word for a gentleman is *caballero*, a horseman, and the conquest of America was undertaken by great equestrian heroes. During the colonial period the *peones de hacienda*, invariably Indians, were also – literally – travellers by foot, as well as workers by hand, the usual situation being that only gentlemen could ride horses and Mestizos mules, whilst Indians were forbidden to ride in most countries until after Independence. The independence struggles themselves were won by guerrilla armies heavily reliant on horsemen, and equestrian statues of the great liberators are to be seen everywhere in Latin American cities and on the continent's prints and stamps. This has made the man on horseback a peculiarly potent and contradictory figure, given the prior tradition of knight errantry and aristocracy, crusades and conquests, hunting and cattle herding, not to mention more elemental associations between taming and mounting horses and the physical domination of the environment and of women.[23] The horse, in other words, is a complex symbol of power over nature, social status and privileged mobility.

The greatest of Latin American cowboy novels, greater perhaps than any North American version, is the Argentine elegy *Don Segundo Sombra* (1926) by Ricardo Güiraldes (1886–1927), which anticipates many of the twentieth-century Western's conventions before Hollywood had fully explored them. This profoundly conservative work, exquisite in style and technique yet popular in tone and ambition, artfully conciliates the aristocratic and *machista* tensions in the figure of the plainsman. Güiraldes provides a landowner's vision of the gaucho to attenuate the epic, popular thrust of *Martín Fierro*. His novel evokes the horseman's ride into the sunset whilst silently expressing the fears of a whole feudal class in the face of modernity, capitalist development, wage labour, immigration, industrialization, urbanization and workers organizations, none of which are even hinted at in a novel confined to the mythical image of the pampa in bygone days.

Güiraldes was born into a wealthy landowning family and his early life involved frequent alternations between the family estancia, Buenos Aires and Paris, where his family resided for long periods at a time. During the prewar period of the Belle Epoque most Latin Americans in Paris wrote about Paris itself and about their excitement at being there. After the war America looked different – new, healthy, open – and attitudes radically changed. Güiraldes's novel is accordingly the first in that decisive interwar period to apply the aesthetics of the Parisian avant-garde (in his case little more than an assimilation of Impressionism and Symbolism) to the realities of Latin America. The result is a pampa seen through a lens made in Paris, an unforgettable emphasis on the positive and suppression of the negative which has made this Argentina's best loved novel and a permanent influence on the mentality of its young men.

If *The Vortex* explored the labyrinths of motive, *Don Segundo Sombra* travels back along the winding trails of memory. It tells the story of Fabio, an illegitimate orphan in a small settlement on the edge of the pampa, brought up by two sterile aunts and imprisoned in the small town, the house and petty-bourgeois culture. For this reason it has often been compared to *Tom Sawyer* and *Huckleberry Finn*, though *Le Grand Meaulnes* is perhaps a closer analogy. It looks back on freedom from reluctant immobility, innocence from knowledge, morning from nightfall. One day, long ago in the past, as dusk began to fall, Fabio had seen a man on horseback ride by and had felt strangely drawn to him by some magnetic attraction:

> Motionless, I watched it move away, a silhouette of man and horse, mysteriously magnified against the luminous horizon. I felt I had seen a ghost, a shadow, something passing more as an idea than a being; something that attracted me with the force of a pool sucking in the current of a river with its depth.
>
> With my vision inside me, I reached the first paths and was able to quicken my pace. More strongly than ever I felt the desire to leave the mean little township for ever. I foresaw a new life made up of movement and space.[24]

This is Don Segundo Sombra, the gaucho hero, strong and mainly silent, sober and self-contained, who becomes knight to Fabio's squire (one recalls the title of a Zane Grey novel, *Knights of the Range*, 1939), and teaches him how to become a gaucho and a man:

> 'I can't fall further than the ground', the horse breaker will say, responding to the taunts of those who predict his downfall, giving to understand that there's a limit to everything and power lies in not being afraid. 'I can't go further than death', seemed to be my godfather's motto, 'and when it comes I won't be afraid and I'll be ready'.
>
> When everyone else was on the way to death, he was on his way back. Pain, I saw it more than once, was like his daily bread, and only the impossibility of moving an injured limb could bring him to complain. The 'skeleton', as he called his body, oughtn't kick up at any job it was asked to do.[25]

Don Segundo's stoicism is born of a peasant philosophy that says that the world is not susceptible to positive historical action, since nothing can change our fate:

Poor Dolores had not foreseen the woes he'd have to suffer to meet his fate. Such is the destiny of man. No one would begin the road if they were shown what they were in for.

   In the clear mornings, when the gaucho changes ranches, he sees a dot up ahead, like the end of his journey, but hell, when he makes it the pampa stretches out ahead just the same! So goes man, pursuing what he sees with his eye, with never a thought to the misery awaiting him over every hill. Step by step his hope helps him on, like the extra oxen on the slopes, as he travels towards his skeleton. But why talk of things that can't be changed?[26]

Thus all historical action is pointless, Argentina is going nowhere, for there is nowhere, in a world of mirages, to go: 'On the pampa all impressions are rapid, spasmodic, soon erased in the vastness of the landscape, leaving no trace.'[27] The entire novel, constantly interweaving images of the river as time and the trail as man's life, reasserts the sentiment of one of Spain's best known poems, Manrique's *Lines on the Death of my Father*, from the fifteenth century, which reads 'Our lives are the rivers which flow into the sea of death.' But perhaps the best parallel is with another influential American novel written that same year, Scott Fitzgerald's *The Great Gatsby*, which also asserts that life is lost in the living of it, and that the American Dream was a particular kind of historical mirage: 'So we beat on, boats against the current, borne back ceaselessly into the past.'

   Many years later, with *Shane* (1954), the United States writer Jack Shaeffer gave another version of the theme, with a child's hero-worship of a mysterious outsider whose epic era is past, and many of the same literary conventions, but the principal difference is a striking one: in the North American version the child is from a solid, indeed archetypal settler family. In the Latin American version Fabio is both a bastard and an orphan, though by the end of the novel he comes into a huge inheritance and becomes a reluctant landowner:

Three years had passed since I had changed, from being a simple cowboy, into a boss through my inheritance. My inheritance! I could look all around me and say all this is mine. The words meant nothing. Yet when, as a gaucho, had I ever felt I was riding through other men's fields? Who owns the pampa more than a gaucho does? It made me smile even to think of all those estancia owners stuck in their houses, always suffering from the cold or the heat, frightened of every danger from a frisky colt to a stampeding bull or a wild rainstorm. Owners of what? A few patches of land might appear as theirs on the map, but God's pampa had been truly mine, for I'd mastered its secrets through my own strength and skill.[28]

Again, the conclusion of the novel is remarkably similar to the film version of *Shane* – and in other respects to Ford's *The Searchers* – except that in the

North American version it was the gunfighting hero who was bleeding at the conclusion (in the tradition of such legendary heroes as the Cid, Robin Hood or Ivanhoe), whereas in the last pages of the Argentine version it is the narrator and reluctant landowner whose life seems to have come to an early end rather than that of the mythical protagonist:

> 'Shadow', I repeated. Then I thought almost violently about my adoptive father. Pray? Let my sadness simply flow? I don't know how many things piled up in my solitude. But they were things a man would never admit even to himself.
>
> Concentrating my will on carrying out the smallest acts, I turned my horse and, slowly, went back to the houses.
>
> I went as one whose life-blood was ebbing away.[29]

These concluding sentiments follow Don Segundo's definitive ride into the sunset, glistening through Fabio's tearful gaze as he recedes into the distant horizon, misted by memory, creating the most powerful literary myth in Argentine culture to this moment. The trail is an illusion, there are no roads into the future, epic deeds exist only in the past (Borges is also prey to this ideological conceit, as a review of his poetry will show), yet boys may still grow straight and tall by absorbing these spiritual qualities. Ironically enough, Güiraldes, like Rivera, was a sick man by the time the publication of his novel brought him definitive recognition, and he died in Paris, in 1927, in an apartment in which James Joyce would later reside.

The epitome of the enlightened aristocrat, Güiraldes carefully sublimated his own class perspective and true historical standpoint, provided a philosophical justification for violence, machismo and the necessity of the charismatic, authoritarian leader, and suffused his novel with an underground charge of eroticism linked to power and death; he portrayed women as inherently contemptible, unreliable and irrelevant, implicitly justifying their exploitation and violation; and he painted a picture of the gaucho far more potent than reality, one which, if it ever had any true historical content, belonged to a bygone age, basing his portrait of 'Don Segundo', almost unbelievably, on a man who was a hired hand on the family estancia during his childhood. The freedom Güiraldes advocates is the freedom to ride in circles, and to dream. This strategy of implicitly announcing closure when apparently exalting a libertarian way of life (albeit confined to the past) allowed his work to become the most influential conservative novel in Latin American history and a notable exception among the best-known of the so-called Novelists of the Land, thereby providing a first clue to the direction and character of the Argentine literary mainstream since that time.

A thousand and one paths: Rómulo Gallegos, *Doña Bárbara*

From beyond the Cunaviche, beyond the Cinaruco, beyond the far-off Meta! From further off than never, said the plainsmen of the Arauca – for whom, none the less, everything is always – from way beyond those forests. That was where that tragic half-breed girl had come from. Engendered by the violence of the white adventurer and the sombre sensuality of the Indian, her origins were lost in the dramatic mystery of the virgin lands.

Rómulo Gallegos, *Doña Bárbara*, 1929

A few years before *Canaima* (1935), Rómulo Gallegos (1884–1969) wrote what for most critics at the time appeared to be the novel which Latin America had been waiting for in that new era of progress and opportunity after the First World War. *Doña Bárbara* (1929) is without doubt the most optimistic novel of the era; not suprisingly, it is also one of the most ingenuous. It is almost, if not entirely, the dialectical opposite to *Don Segundo Sombra*: both, in a sense, are bosses' books, but Güiraldes speaks for the landowning classes who wish to keep the future at bay, whilst Gallegos represents the new rising bourgeoisie hungry for power. Gallegos is, without question, the novelist of the Latin American frontier. Strategically enough, the central character of *Doña Bárbara* is a landowner who wants to become businesslike. Santos Luzardo, whose fratricidal family history sums up that of his country, has lived in the city and longs to bring its essentially European values to Venezuela as a whole; whereas he has inherited a ranch on the Llano, the soul of Venezuelan nationhood and field of conflict between barbarism (the jungle) and civilization (the city). In no other novel is the essential dualism of Latin America's historical experience so overtly, indeed naively expressed, from the very first scene in which we see Luzardo travelling back upriver to rediscover his wild former abode.

Despite a somewhat wooden and occasionally rudimentary nineteenth-century technique – really more of a belated romance than a novel – *Doña Bárbara* structures most of the themes of the century since Independence into a single narrative and is thus, inescapably, the key text of a formative era, the 1920s. Its subject, the problematic of development, is a fictional continuation of Sarmiento's polemic on civilization and barbarism, as the name of its eponymous female villain, Doña Bárbara, openly proclaims. (Like Sarmiento, in 1948 Gallegos became president of his country, although he was ousted by the military 'barbarians' after a few months.) Fifty years ago it was the most admired novel in Latin American history. Then, twenty-five years ago, as the flood-tide of the 1960s 'boom' washed all else away, it fell into disrepute and Gallegos was deemed to be less the novelist of underdevelopment than an embarrassingly underdeveloped novelist, whose work was as devoid of real people as the vast empty savannahs he depicted.

The more sympathetic critics, like Alejo Carpentier, conceded that his limitations were due to the frontier nature of Latin American reality itself, still largely unexplored in fiction, and the lack of an established literary tradition. Both factors in turn were connected to the absence of a broadly based middle class or national bourgeoisie, without which there could be no complex psychological introspection or exploration.

Gallegos's novels, in short, viewed from a Lukácsian perspective, conceive Latin America as something essentially problematical, yet the central characters of his best known works, *Doña Bárbara* and the jungle novel *Canaima*, are essentially epic figures, like those of the Mexican novels of the Revolution, always actually at home in the world of the novel, if not, supposedly, in the world depicted therein. The same applies to the form: language is transparent, plot moves like clockwork, characters dance like marionettes. As those characters explore the Venezuelan interior Gallegos purports to be exploring their inner being; yet although he appears to be asking questions he is really, for the most part, only giving answers (always 'reporting', never 'rendering', to echo Henry James), and he could have done so equally well or better outside the novel, as the preacher, lawyer and teacher he had successively aspired to be, or like a nineteenth-century *pensador*, always pointing not the magic finger of Adam but the deadening finger of positivist didacticism and turning living reality unerringly into stone.

But those who look for European virtues of character, psychology and plot in a Latin American novel are apt to overlook the solutions which its writer may well have improvised (and which would eventually bring about the literary revolutions of Magical Realism and the New Novel), in this case a complex but undoubtedly coherent weave of themes and motifs whose meaning is ultimately historical – in the long sense – and the product of profound meditation. Gallegos worked the seam of Hispanic romance, with its labyrinths of fate and chance ('I only sing my song to those that ride with me'), and anticipated the theme of one of Latin America's most popular revolutionary songs of recent years, 'Traveller, there is no road: you make the road as you go.' In *Cantaclaro* (1934) a rider is said to have been 'carried away by the road as it opened up before him'; whilst a chapter of the first part of *Doña Bárbara* is entitled 'One path and a thousand different paths', and ends 'The sun began to set, on the pathfinders' route across the savannah which is, all of it, one path and a thousand different paths.'[30] The concept foreshadows the conception and original Portuguese title of one of Latin America's greatest novels, João Guimarães Rosa's 'Great Sertão: Passages' (*Grande sertão: veredas*, 1956), translated into English as *The Devil to Pay in the Backlands* (see chapter 6). Both works are in one sense Saussurean (ironically enough, given Gallegos's positivistic conception of language and representation), seeing the great plains – and Latin American history as a whole – as one vast 'field' (*campo*) of significance to be explored, with an infinite number of 'paths' (*caminos*) through it, like human life itself, which is always apparently the same, at the level of myth, but always different at the level of the specific experience of history; or, extrapolating, like a novel, which always has the same words in the same order, but through which the reader can take a thousand different paths – and believe any one of them to be the true one. Gallegos thus anticipated Borges's well-known view that 'every event, however humble, implies the universe' ('El Zahir').

Again, a merely reductive historical reading would view *Doña Bárbara*, with its landowner hero applauded for turning his feudal estate into a vehicle for capitalist agriculture, as a grotesquely inadequate impression of the Venezuela of its time. But a review of the previous one hundred years of history in Bolívar's homeland, a succession of caudillos culminating in the monstrous Gómez dictatorship of 1908–35, can help us to understand how much an ambitious novelist needed to pack into such a historical metaphor and thus to appreciate the scale of his achievement and his importance as a precursor of the 'Ulyssean' novelists to come. Chapter 8 of the first part gives another image of the Llanos: 'Great land lying open and outstretched, made for work and grand deeds: all horizons, like hope, all paths, like will.'[31]

This feat of literary condensation seems to summarize Gallegos's shaping conception of Venezuela as the land of the future, virgin nature, providing a positivist happy ending to a century of endless failure marked by anarchy, violence and dictatorship. This vision is conjured anew at the novel's end: 'Great plains of Venezuela! Land fit for labour as once for grand deeds, land of open horizons where a fine race loves, suffers and waits!'

This messianic land was still in truth a jungle-dominated world – where the savage Doña Bárbara came from in the novel: the 'Venezuela of the incomplete discovery and colonization', as *Canaima* would put it, a realm of darkness and chaos like that of Genesis before God's light came to give it form; a world of 'ancestral slime', to quote *Doña Bárbara* – the world, indeed, of Doña Bárbara herself, swamplike (now we quote the German philosopher Keyserling), fount of original sin (to quote the Argentine thinker Murena), labyrinth of solitude (to cite Paz once more). Gallegos's problems with female sexuality and his identification of the feminine with barbarism are evident from his metaphors and from his – at first sight incredible – choice of a woman as the malevolent representative of Venezuelan *caciquismo*.

Sarmiento had set out to lead the Latin American people, through the vanguard of Argentina, out of this slough and into the promised land of orderly development, but as in North America the cost proved heavy in the blood of the barbarians, the true Americans, to whom Gallegos would belatedly turn in *Canaima* (1935) and '*On the Same Earth*' (*Sobre la misma tierra*, 1943). However, as if a curse had been sown, other forms of barbarism had risen to replace these disappeared Indians. Now, eighty years later, in quite different political and economic circumstances, Gallegos renews Sarmiento's call for orderly progress through education and enlightenment towards the horizon of economic development and urban civilization, towards what Santos Luzardo conceives as a kind of illuminated labyrinth of the mind, 'an ideal city as perfect in its complexity as a brain, where every stimulus becomes an idea, and every resulting action carries the stamp of conscious efficiency'.[32] The Llano, like Mexico in the first part of *The Underdogs*, like *Don Segundo Sombra*'s pampa, like the Colombian Llano in *The Vortex*, is a vast open space, with few distinguishing features – the same panorama, metaphorically, as the face of Latin America, or indeed its literature, as Gallegos and his contemporaries gazed upon them early in the century. It was an open book, waiting to be written in.[33] Thus once again the river, carved out by nature, is the flow of time itself, sleeping, unconscious, the agent of myth (Doña Bárbara herself is the 'daughter of the rivers'); and the road, constructed by man, is the vehicle of history deliberately and consciously willed (Santos, as pathbreaker, eventually brings not only roads and fences but the railway); whilst the *canto*, the poem or song, sung to a guitar which strums purposefully like the drumming of horses hooves driving into the future, stitches myth and history together, as man's reflection upon his journey into that future, towards the frontier and on to the horizon, which for Gallegos – if not perhaps for Rivera, and certainly not for Güiraldes – can only mean urban civilization, development and modernity.

These ideas are not so popular these days, although they still dominate our lives and shape the destiny of the planet: in 1929 they were perceived as the key to Latin American progress, however contradictory. Few people today would celebrate the coming of 'the barbed wire, the straight lines of man within the curved line of nature', see the railway as 'progress penetrating the plains and barbarism retreating defeated', nor indeed overlook the phallocentric implications of the imagery. Gallegos had no conscious misgivings, however. The two forms of property out on the range were land and livestock, and much of the novel involves a struggle over property and its boundaries, conceived as the location of the frontier between civilization and barbarism. Thus the Llano is divided into two *hatos* (haciendas), two zones, black and white, like a chessboard, with a few central characters as signposts to the outcome of the battle between the old Venezuela and the new. The novel is naturalistic about its villains and idealistic about its heroes: the former are those who fail to overcome the inheritance of bad blood and a savage environment, whilst the heroes of course triumph absolutely against nature, not least their own.

The patriarchal complacency of such images should not blind us to the complexity of their integration. That Gallegos was viewed almost universally at the time as a progressive novelist merely underlines the fact that it is important to understand the historical heritage which his work was seen as contesting. Judged as politics rather than as a nationalist myth, the novel was ideologically reactionary and conceptually simplistic even in its day (we have learned to call this successful communicative formula 'Reaganite' in the re-enchanted 1980s). Although Santos is viewed briefly as a 'centaur', just as Doña Bárbara is likened to the 'sphinx', spirit triumphs over matter and the animal within him is eliminated completely, whilst the beast in Doña Bárbara prevails until the very last moment. Santos solves both Venezuela's major national 'problems' – impediments to progress – namely racial and technological inferiority, by the time-honoured methods of eliminating his enemies or marrying them and by enclosing and improving his land. He represents the replacement of a barbaric, semifeudal elite which did not bother to validate its activities through a supposedly neutral legal system by a new educated elite which is just as absolute in its belief in private property and its faith in the values of liberal individualism. Finally, the ideological axes along which the text travels – spirit/matter, word/flesh, good/evil, male/female, Europe/America, city/country, development/underdevelopment, culture/nature and civilization/barbarism – are marshalled together for the first time in a Latin American novel and brought into lucid coherence, giving the concept of the 'frontier' its fullest, its most Latin American meaning and opening up a whole literary continent for exploration. This sets the pattern for the next forty years, until the culmination of the 'boom', whose high-point coincided with Gallegos's own death in 1969, as writers struggled to reverse the direction of the signs he had mobilized.

To understand the breadth of Gallegos's achievement we might go to the comments of another 'South American' writer (he would not thank us for calling him thus), V.S. Naipaul, who was born in Trinidad, very close to Gallegos's native Caracas in 1932, shortly after Gallegos wrote Doña Bárbara and shortly before he wrote Canaima. Naipaul, by his own account, came to understand his dilemmas as a potential Third World, colonial or underdeveloped novelist through his reading of another only slightly less marginal writer, Joseph Conrad. Conrad himself had said that in attempting to evoke the far-flung outposts of empire through fiction, 'the problem was to make unfamiliar things credible. To do that I had to create for them, to reproduce for them, to envelop them in their proper atmosphere of actuality'.[34] Naipaul, reflecting on Conrad's work on the tropics, says the following:

> It came to me that the great novelists wrote about highly organized societies. I had no such society; I couldn't share the assumptions of the writers; I didn't see my

world reflected in theirs. My colonial world was more mixed and second-hand, and more restricted. The time came when I began to ponder the mystery – Conradian word – of my own background: that island in the mouth of a great South American river, the Orinoco, one of the Conradian dark places of the earth, where my father had conceived literary ambitions for himself and then for me, but from which, in my mind, I had stripped all romance and perhaps even reality: preferring to set *The Lagoon*, when it was read to me, not on the island I knew, with its muddy rivers, mangrove and swamps, but somewhere far away.

It seemed to me that those of us who were born there were curiously naked, that we lived purely physically. It wasn't an easy thing to explain, even to oneself. But in Conrad, in that very story of *Karain*, I was later to find my feelings about the land exactly caught: 'And really, looking at that place, landlocked from the sea and shut off from the land by the precipitous slopes of mountains, it was difficult to believe in the existence of any neighbourhood. It was still complete, unknown, and full of a life that went on stealthily with a troubling effect of solitude; of a life that seemed unaccountably empty of anything that would stir the thought, touch the heart, give a hint of the ominous sequence of the days. It appeared to us a land without memories, regrets and hopes; a land where nothing could survive the coming of the night, and where each sunrise, like a dazzling act of special creation, was disconnected from the eve and the morrow.'[35]

Naipaul concludes:

I found that Conrad – sixty years before, in the time of a great peace – had been everywhere before me. Not as a man with a cause, but a man offering, as in Nostromo, a vision of the world's half-made societies as places which continuously made and unmade themselves, where there was no goal, and where always 'Something inherent in the necessities of successful action... carried with it the moral degradation of the idea'. Dismal, but deeply felt: a kind of truth and half a consolation.[36]

Similarly, to return to *The Lagoon*, Naipaul notes that 'there is a lot of Conrad in it – passion and the abyss, solitude and futility and the world of illusions'. To understand Conrad, then, 'it was necessary to begin to match his experience. It was also necessary to lose one's preconceptions of what the novel should do and, above all, to rid oneself of the subtle corruptions of the novel as comedy of errors.'[37]

These concepts and emotions convey exactly the problems and ultimately the typical fate of Gallegos's protagonists. Although his own impulse, and that of his novels, is towards order and progress, most of his characters, like the nineteenth century as a whole in his perception, relapse back into chaos and darkness, men and women who leave no mark, no name. In chapter 10 of his first novel, *Reinaldo Solar* (1920), for example, the protagonist laments:

Now, after so many years uselessly wasted in seeking my own path, I find myself once again at the crossroads, the perennial crossroad of my own lack of self-confidence! This is dreadful, atrocious! To look for oneself all one's life, along every road, and never find oneself! To be a shadow and not know who is projecting it! A voice and not know who is speaking![38]

And he asks himself: 'Must we always be a people marching across a sandy desert followed by a fatal wind rubbing out its footsteps?' The answer comes at the end, when we contemplate 'the ruin of a man, which is all that was left of the vigorous and generous youth of Reinaldo Solar'. For readers of Rivera's *The Vortex*, both the answer and the question are strikingly familiar, and indeed summarize the Latin American novel's verdict on the nineteenth century as a whole.

Clearly, Gallegos' perspective is both nationalist and capitalist: hence the search for a populist solution. We could say of both him and Naipaul what Edward Said has said of *Nostromo*, one of the earliest novels about 'neocolonialism' and a work he much admires:

Conrad writes as a man in whom a Western view of the non-Western world is so deeply ingrained that it blinds him to other histories, other cultures, other aspirations. All Conrad can see is a world dominated by the West, and – of equal importance – a world in which every opposition to the West only confirms its wicked power. What Conrad could not see is life lived outside this cruel tautology. He could not understand – or so we would have to conclude from reading him – that places like Latin America (and India and Africa for that matter) also contain people and cultures with histories and ways not controlled by the gringo imperialists and liberal reformers of this world.[39]

Said's own article, however, concedes that Conrad's novel was as lucid as any subsequent work of fiction about imperialism and therefore implicitly confirms how little has changed in the eighty years in between.

Returning, however, to Naipaul's reflections on Conrad's achievement, we can review some of our own earlier discussion. Conrad was able to place European colonies within the context of European history itself, whereas like most of his generation of novelists Gallegos had never travelled to Europe and remained marooned in his Latin American 'solitude'. Although we can acknowledge that Alejo Carpentier intended his famous remark about so-called regionalist fiction to be generous, if patronizing – in the absence of known cultures and contexts, he said, the role of the novelist was to point his finger and name things, like Adam – it was also profoundly misleading.[40] Gallegos, for all his own simplicities, actually had to cut his way into new territories to see what he then pointed out to his contemporaries. His striking symbols – which are, admittedly, only clumsily connected to psychological realities – were not already given but had to be hacked out of living reality to create the founding myths of a nationalist and Americanist literature foreshadowed by Sarmiento but only fully achieved by the writers who stretch from the Mexican Revolution to the time of the Cuban Revolution. From this perspective, that of national development, perceived through an essentially populist consciousness, there is no body of fiction more important than that of Rómulo Gallegos and no single novel more important than *Doña Bárbara*. This was augured by the first lines of his first novel: 'The dawn was scarcely beginning to break, when Reinaldo was up and about, anxious to start with the day the new life he had planned. Through the open window, the country sunrise was spreading its generous warmth and hazy light. From all around came echoes of morning labours'.[41] Although this, like so many of his works, is ultimately about failure, almost every word of its first paragraph denotes the dawn of new beginnings, the openness of beckoning possibility, the thrust of the human will, the light of intellect, and the infinite material potential of the Venezuelan land. No wonder such a man eventually stood for president!

Few of the other novelists shared so confidently in his belief in capitalist development and incorporatist politics, but it is this, precisely, which makes him the most significant representative in literature of the dominant economic and political ideologies of the coming era: developmentalism and populism. At the same time his perception was irremediably idealist and voluntarist: the past, entrapped in a barbaric, nocturnal, maternal–material web, was certainly like a labyrinth, but a new era had dawned and the path into the future was now clear. His is a world of middle-class leaders, all imbued with the rhetoric of honesty, decency and democracy, who wish to get rid of a corrupt and reactionary ruling class (identified with the Spanish colonial heritage), and anxious to convert servile peons into docile wage-earners. He rejects caudillismo, messianism and violence, but these qualities are firmly imprinted on even his consciousness: all his main characters are judged, in the end, by the extent to which they fulfil their 'promise' by becoming leaders, and there is little suggestion that they might transform themselves through political action as such. The subsidiary characters invariably involve one or more truly decent, loyal peasant or proletarian characters, who know and appreciate an innate and worthy leader when they see one, that is to say, a working class which knows how to recognize a reliable fraction – intellectuals and schoolmasters, presumably – of the bourgeoisie, and will follow them to the ultimate consequences. These no doubt would be transformed into the collaborationist trade union leaders within an institutionalized, mass-participatory capitalist state on the model advocated by APRA (see the section on Ciro Alegría p. 80 below) and fully achieved only in Mexico after the 1920s, although Vargas in Brazil and

Perón in Argentina found temporary success in the 1930s and 1940s.

Nevertheless Gallegos also learned and changed. In *Doña Bárbara*, Mr Danger, the North American who longs to violate young Venezuela, simply pushes off when he sees Santos's resolute determination. Later novels, especially '*On the Same Earth*', would take imperialism more seriously. Also in *Doña Bárbara* Santos puts a disgusted stop to the erotic antics of Venezuelan folklore when the peons dance around the camp fire, whereas the affectionate *Cantaclaro* (1934) is one long hymn to Llano traditions conceived in consciously Homeric terms. Finally, whereas Doña Bárbara's whole problem was her Mestizo background, in *Canaima* the protagonist, Marcos Vargas, a young man of great promise, returns to immerse himself in the jungle with an Indian community in order to begin a new mixed culture and start afresh. In so doing he helps to end the regionalist novel and points the way to the more labyrinthine fiction which was to come.

It is crucial, however, to remind ourselves once more of the true context and true scale of Gallegos's achievement. There is a sense in which his oeuvre gathers together and assimilates Latin American literary experience from the time of Sarmiento to the time of the Mexican Revolution. In his '*Allocution to Poetry*' (*Alocución a la poesía*, 1823), the great Venezuelan thinker Andrés Bello had urged literature to 'direct its flight/ to the grandiose scenarios of Columbus' realm/ where the earth is clothed still in her most primitive garb'. In *Facundo* Sarmiento had given this entreaty a more historical orientation: 'If a glimmer of national literature is to shine momentarily in these new American societies, it will result from the description of our grandiose natural settings and above all of the clash between European civilization and Indian barbarism, between intelligence and matter' (I, 2). In taking an Argentine work of the 1840s as his point of departure in *Doña Bárbara*, Gallegos was not only settling accounts with Sarmiento himself but also adopting an Americanist perspective for the first time in a major work of fiction and thereby already turning a national literature into a continental one. It is as if the *Leatherstocking* tales of the James Fenimore Cooper which Spanish America never really had (Brazil can boast a rough equivalent in José de Alencar, 1829–77) were in need of a larger literary panorama than any single Spanish American country could offer and only became finally writable at the dawn of the proletarian era.[42] Thus Gallegos ends romance and inaugurates Social Realism in one difficult but decisive literary undertaking.

3

Closures:
Conflicts and Commitments

The traversing of the backland trails is more exhausting than that that of a barren steppe. In the latter case, the traveller at least has the relief of a broad horizon and free-sweeping plains. The *caatinga*, on the other hand, stifles him; it cuts short his view, strikes him in the face, so to speak, and stuns him, enmeshes him in its spiny woof, and holds out no compensating attractions. It repulses him with its thorns and prickly leaves, its twigs sharp as lances; and it stretches out in front of him, for mile on mile, unchanging in its desolate aspect of leafless trees, of dried and twisted boughs, a turbulent maze of vegetation standing rigidly in space or spreading out sinuously along the ground.

Euclides da Cunha, *Revolt in the Backlands*, 1902

Gallegos was the last major novelist able or even willing both to celebrate Latin America's natural landscapes and to underwrite their historical promise in one and the same narrative construct. In that sense he was 100 years, or even 400 years, out of date. By the early 1930s a new wave of disillusionment was sweeping the subcontinent, against an international background as sombre as the world had ever known. Writers now gave less attention to grand historical symbols and focused more closely on their characters, albeit from a sociological and economic rather than a psychological standpoint.

Brazilian Fiction in the 1930s: From Peasant to Worker

Brazil is almost a continent in itself, and separated from Spanish America by the Portuguese language, a distinct historical experience, and the special influence of African culture. Brazilian literature, perhaps because of this relative isolation within the continent, tends to follow European patterns rather more closely and is much less influenced by the Spanish-speaking literatures than they are by each other. Moreover, although the pattern of Brazilian literary development is broadly similar century by century to that of the Spanish-speaking countries, the rhythms tend to differ over any given period.

In the 1920s the Brazilian modernist movement, centred on São Paulo, allowed Brazil to leap into the vanguard of contemporary Latin American developments, with a revolution in painting, sculpture, architecture, music and poetry. Even in fiction, which had been through an arid period since the days of Machado de Assis, the new wave produced Marío de Andrade's remarkable *Macunaíma* (1928), arguably the first Magical Realist novel of Latin America (see chapter 5). Equally as important, Brazilians, including Mário himself, began to theorize the relation between Brazilian and external influences in new and radical ways, most notably through the *Pau–Brasil Manifesto* of 1924, which raised the question of the one-way historical relationship in terms of literary borrowings, and the *Anthropophagous Manifesto* of 1928, which took the idea further by arguing that Brazilian artists should unashamedly cannibalize and Brazilianize foreign cultures, but be fully aware of what they were doing so that the final result was more than an unconscious imitation of outside models. A different response was that of the *Verde–Amarelo* movement of 1926 which, named after the colours of the Brazilian flag, argued for a straightforward literary nationalism, rejecting all external ingredients and working for an entirely Brazilian culture through a sort of *bandeirismo mental* or literary pioneering spirit. Nevertheless Brazilian narrators were still having difficulty in finding their identity and voice, and in 1928 Paulo Prado published a bitter essay, '*Portrait of Brazil*', which saw the country as an unfortunate amalgam of 'three sad races'.

At the same time, as the avant-garde began to negotiate the symbolic terms on which the country might be better integrated into international culture, regionalism was also gaining new impulse, notably in the declining Northeast where Gilberto Freyre (1900–), Brazil's most influential cultural propagandist of the century, launched his Regionalist Movement in Recife in 1926. Alarmed by the political, economic and cultural shift away from the Northeast to Rio, São Paulo and Rio Grande do Sul, Freyre argued, above all in his classic *The Masters and the Slaves* (*Casa-grande e senzala*, 1933), that the soul of Brazil still lay not in the cosmopolitan South but in the old sugar plantation zones along the northern coast and the interior wastelands of the Sertão. The result, a little later in Brazil than in Spanish America, but even more cohesively, was a vigorous Social Realist movement known as the 1930 Movement, coinciding with the end of the Old Republic and the dawn of Getúlio Vargas's *Estado Novo*.

In Brazil, then, 1930 makes a more convenient dividing line than else-where in Latin America. But everywhere the naive faith in development and modernization which had characterized the 1918–29 period – quintessentially expressed in *Doña Bárbara* – evaporated, and political ideologies now began to separate intellectuals and artists with a decisive force that had not been evident in the 1920s. The world now had to be planned, and literature, like politics and economics, became more programmatic. The supposedly 'scientific', objective realism of late nineteenth-century Naturalism became transmuted into a more sociologically critical form of realism, as writers incorporated the perspectives of socialism and, much more gradually, psychoanalysis. The rather diffuse humanist commitment of the 1920s, characteristic of the archetypal romances discussed hitherto, evolved into more ideologically explicit forms of commitment in the 1930s, and determined once more a historically decisive parting of the ways, in which non-socialist writers retreated into metaphysics, fantasy or the new Catholic existentialism. The 1929 crash and the collapse of international trade made the 1930s years of relative isolation in Latin America, where the story was essentially one of radical assaults on a status quo whose response was authoritarian retaliation. The outward-looking Americanist works of the 1920s were succeeded – paradoxically, given the growing internationalist influence of world Communism – by another period of national introspection. The committed, ideologically explicit works which now appeared in most countries were contested by a growing tendency towards essays written by *pensadores* obsessed, in the wake of Spengler and visits by foreign thinkers like Count Keyserling, Waldo Frank and José Ortega y Gasset, with national character and the metaphysics of the Mexican, Argentinian or Brazilian 'being'. It was at the start of such a process that the influential Argentine magazine *Sur* (1931–76) was inaugurated. These metaphysical tendencies, significantly enough, continued until the mid 1950s, when the new middle classes had satisfactorily established their historical identity, with new university sytems and the development of the social sciences; and the vogue is long since past.

It is of course essential to remind ourselves that regionalism is nothing more than the other face of literary nationalism. Indeed, regionalism at this moment in history was a sign of the impulse for national integration, at a time when the incorporation of Latin America into the world economic system, which had been accelerating ever since the 1870s, was still not complete. Americanism for the nationalist was a means of integrating an artist's own national identity and that of the entire continent within an anti-imperialist perspective. For a socialist, of course, the various forms of nativism, nationalism and Americanism afforded a vehicle for his own internationalist and anti-capitalist project. It is this multitextured literary–ideological complex which Latin American Social Realism represents between 1915 and 1945, despite the efforts of liberal critics since the 'boom' of the new novel of the 1960s to discredit the movement through contemp-

tuous slogans and dangerous oversimplifications.

Regionalism was particularly important in Brazil precisely because national synthesis was still so far from being achieved. Rio's elegant nineteenth-century classicisms had given way in the 1910s and 1920s to São Paulo's various modernisms, but it came as something of a surprise when, in the 1930s, the focus of literary attention again shifted to the decaying Northeast. The polarization which had been intensifying throughout the Republic ever since Prestes's long march (1924–26), encouraged a marked radicalization of fiction, as the coffee slump in São Paulo coincided with a further convulsive lurch in the Northeast's decline and an associated political crisis, culminating in the Revolution of 1930. Whilst the same phenomenon of radicalization was visible in other artists such as the painter Cándido Portinari and the musician Villa-Lobos, as a new mass-oriented populist culture began to assert itself, it was in the Social Realist regionalist novels of the Northeast that all these tendencies were most directly reflected, making the 1930s and 1940s one of the golden ages of Brazilian fiction.

Its immediate point of departure was *Cane Trash* (*A bagaceira*, 1928) by José Américo de Almeida (1887–1980), pioneer of twentieth-century regionalism in the Brazilian novel. Like *Doña Bárbara*, Almeida's novel, which was published two years after Freyre's regionalist congress, portrays the modernization of the hacienda or *fazenda* system, in this case that of the Brazilian sugar plantation or *ingénio*. A lawyer by training, Almeida had other things in common with the Venezuelan novelist, not least his lifelong commitment to struggle on behalf of the people. Closely involved with the *tenentes*, he was one of the leaders of the 1930 Revolution and Vargas made him minister of transport and public works from 1930–34. In 1935 he became a senator and launched an unsuccessful bid for the presidency in 1937, after which he became governor of Paraíba, returned to his former ministerial post in Vargas's second government, and later held diplomatic office.

Cane Trash was set in the Northeastern sugar belt between the great drought of 1898 and that of 1915, tracing not only the permanent hostility of nature but also, like *Doña Bárbara*, the transition from labour-intensive to machine-based cultivation. It is a curiously contradictory work, unmistakably sincere in its sympathy for the plantation workers and landless peasants of the region, but little different in style, aesthetics and ideology from the kinds of sub-Zolaesque, Naturalist novels tinged with Romanticism which were so prevalent in Brazil in the last two decades of the nineteenth century. In a sense it was typical of an entire sociological line in Brazilian fiction – heavily influenced by Comtian Positivism and Zola's laboratory techniques – with famous titles from the past like *Memoirs of a Militia Sergeant* (*Memórias de um sargento de milícias*, 1853) by Manuel Antônio de Almeida, 'The Guarani' (*O guarani*, 1857) and 'Man of the Sertão' (*O serta-*

nejo, 1875) by José de Alencar, '*The Mulatto*' (*O mulato*, 1881), *The 'Boarding-House*' (*Casa de pensão*, 1884) and '*The Tenement*' (*O cortiço*, 1890) by Aluísio Azevedo, or '*Flesh*' (*A carne*, 1888) by Julio César Ribeiro, to name just a few. The principal plot concerns the relation between a beautiful *retirante* (refugee from the drought), Soledade, and an idealistic young student, Lúcio, and between Lúcio and his father, the sugar baron, who eventually takes away both his woman and, for the time being, his hopes for social progress. Despite *Cane Trash*'s undoubted anachronism in a number of decisive respects, it undeniably inaugurated a new complex of such subjects as the sugar mill, the drought, the migrant refugee and the bandit which other more talented novelists would develop after 1930.

The first narrator to extend Almeida's contribution was, remarkably, a woman, Raquel de Queirós (1910–), a judge's daughter and, at the age of fifteen, a qualified teacher. Her first novel, '*Back in '15*' (*O quinze*, 1930), picks up precisely where *Cane Trash* had finished, with the terrible *sêca* or drought of 1915 which ravaged the entire Northeastern territory and sent tens of thousands of desperate *retirantes* wandering in search of food, water and work. All her work was notable, like so much writing by Latin American women, for a sober, neorealist kind of style, making effective use of everyday dialogue and showing sensitive insight into the personal aspects of social situations, above all the inequality of women. '*Back in '15*' was followed by three further novels before she was twenty-eight, after which she renounced fiction and turned to the theatre and documentary writing. During this period Raquel de Queirós was involved in the politics of Communism, and in 1937, when her third novel, '*Path of Stones*' (*Caminho de pedras*), appeared, was in a Trotskyist phase which resulted in a three-month prison sentence. Later in life, like her mentor Freyre, she became a more conservative figure and became more preoccupied with folklore and popular tradition.

Two years younger than Raquel de Queirós, but influenced by her both in his equally precocious literary career and in his political militancy was Jorge Amado (1912–), the son of a merchant turned coffee planter. Amado, undoubtedly Brazil's best known twentieth-century novelist, was educated in Salvador and Rio, lived in the former as a somewhat bohemian journalist in the late 1920s and then returned to Rio at the end of the decade to study law. It was there that he produced his first novel, '*Land of Carnival*' (*O país do carnaval*, 1931), the expression of a lost generation looking for some nationalist ideal in the midst of corruption and decay. He then embarked upon a series of militant novels, shrewdly combining socialist and populist ingredients, the first of which, '*Cacao*' (*Cacau*, 1933), portrayed the life of workers on the cocoa plantations of Ilhéus, and was followed by a sequence of urban novels set in Salvador, including '*Sweat*' (*Suor*, 1934) and *Jubiabá* (1935). Amado's political trajectory in this period was a complex and difficult one. For a brief period in 1935 he was involved in Vargas's Aliança Nacional Libertadora, and also worked as head of publications for the José Olympio editorial. His relationship with the second Vargas regime was more troubled, however, and he was imprisoned on several occasions between 1937 and 1942. In the 1930s Amado had travelled throughout Brazil and most of Latin America, and his works began to be widely translated. In 1942 he wrote the '*Life of Luís Carlos Prestes, Cavalier of Hope*', and also what for many critics remains his greatest novel, *The Violent Land* (*Terras do sem-fim*), a work of great power and sobriety which picks up themes and characters from '*Cacao*' and portrays the decline of the old rural *coronéis*. Of all the Brazilian novels of this period, this is the most profoundly historical and in that sense closes an era. In 1946 Amado became a member of the Brazilian Communist Party and went into exile when the party was proscribed, travelling widely in Eastern Europe and elsewhere and producing works which openly followed the party line such as '*Peace in the world*' (*O mundo da paz*, 1950) and '*Tunnels of Freedom*' (*Os subterrâneos da liberdade*, 1954). After the 1956 thaw he began to compose a succession of works calculated to appeal to a much wider popular audience in the capitalist West, the first of which was *Gabriela, Clove and Cinnamon* (*Gabriela, cravo e canela*, 1958), a worldwide bestseller. These new novels, which for most critics show the real Amado – sentimental rather than ideological, voluptuous rather than passionate, and inherently colourful and picturesque – have made him as successful in the capitalist world since the 1960s as he was in the Communist world in the 1950s, and without doubt the most marketable Brazilian novelist of all time. His sexy, larger-than-life female leads have undoubtedly offered a more independent image of Latin American woman than most traditional versions, although many readers feel that they merely substitute one form of exploitation for another.

Older than Amado but a slower starter, José Lins do Rego (1901–57) was just as prolific once he found his literary vein in the early 1930s. He had spent his childhood in the big house of one of his maternal grandfather's sugar plantations in the state of Paraíba, and this experience became the essence of his literary oeuvre. He moved in the same literary circles as Freyre and Almeida in Recife, where he was studying law. He is still best remembered for his unforgettable *Sugar-Cane Cycle* of 1932–36, a literary complement to Freyre's influential historical essay *The Masters and the Slaves*. *Plantation Boy* (*Menino de engenho*, 1932), *Doidinho* (1933), *Bangüê* (1934), *Ricardo, Black Boy* (*O moleque Ricardo*, 1935) and *The Mill* (*Usina*, 1936), based on the plantation of his legendary grandfather *coronel* Zé Paulino, are stages in a personal search for lost time as the young protagonist, Carlos, is educated and socialized against a background in which slavery and plantation life is giving way to the mechanized practices of the sugar mill. Lins do Rego achieves a remarkable fusion of emotional memoir and analytical document, which is, in the last instance, and despite his undeniably tragic vision, remarkably impartial given his own class experience. He claimed that his narratives were unplanned and largely spontaneous, comparing himself somewhat improbably with the blind singers at Northeastern regional fairs. Years later, in 1943, he wrote 'Dead Fire' (Fogo morto), a more historically distanced assessment of the decline of the old order, and most critics would consider this not only the belated culmination of the literary sugar cycle but also his greatest work. He also wrote two further novels on the Northeast, Pedra Bonita (1938) and 'Bandits' (Cangaceiros, 1953), both depicting the messianic movements for which the region is known. No writer of the period developed a more forceful yet modulated literary language than Lins do Rego, and his insight into one of Brazil's most formative historical experiences was unrivalled. His treatment of slavery and black culture gives him a unique position in Latin American fiction, but since his work was largely retrospective in orientation we have no space to treat him in detail here.

Graciliano Ramos, *Barren Lives*

He looked all around him. Beyond the roofs hemming in the horizon stretched the hard dry countryside. He remembered his family's painful trek across that land, their hunger and exhaustion. That they'd escaped with their lives seemed a miracle, he didn't know how they'd done it.

If there were anywhere else to go, he'd shout out loud that he was being robbed. Apparently resigned, he felt an immense hatred for everything that at one and the same time was the dry land, the boss, the soldiers and the prefect's agents.

Graciliano Ramos, *Barren Lives*, 1938

For all Lins do Rego's undeniable importance, a still older writer from the Northeast, who began publishing at about the same time, was to become acknowledged, in due course, as Brazil's greatest literary stylist since Machado de Assis. Graciliano Ramos (1892–1953) was the eldest of the fifteen children born to a rather brutal middle-class couple. His father was a storekeeper who took the family to live in Palmeira dos Indios in 1910 and eventually became its prefect from 1928–30. Graciliano began writing his first novel, 'Caetés', in 1925, but did not complete it for publication until 1933, by which time he was living in Macéio and knew Queirós, Amado and Lins do Rego. Caetés's provincial realism was compared with that of the great Portuguese novelist Eça de Queirós, but Ramos was on his way to something quite original. In 1934 São Bernardo appeared, one of the first

Latin American novels to communicate through a first-person narrative the worldview of an uneducated anti-heroic protagonist, in this case the self-made landowner Paulo Honório, who narrates with intense economy the shocking and sordid story of his failed marriage to a schoolteacher. In a sense the novel is reminiscent of the Uruguayan Juan Carlos Onetti's later novel '*The Pit*' (*El pozo*, 1939; see below, p. 112), in which another nondescript anti-hero takes it upon himself to become a writer. Similarly his next novel, *Anguish* (*Angústia*, 1936), set in an urban background like Onetti's novel, tells the story of the existential torment of an insignificant functionary with frustrated literary ambitions. In March 1936 Ramos was imprisoned for alleged subversive activities, suffered brutal maltreatment, and was not released until March of the following year, instilling in him, as in the case of the great Peruvian poet César Vallejo a decade earlier, a sense of bitterness and resentment which had always been with him but was now confirmed for life. In 1938 his masterpiece *Barren Lives* (*Vidas sêcas*) appeared, the story of a family of illiterate refugees struggling to survive against almost impossible odds, in the face of hostile natural and social forces. Despite its unrivalled economy of expression and objectification, this novel, turned into a famous film in 1964, is one of the most moving works of fiction to have emerged from Latin America, comparable with the Mexican Juan Rulfo's *Pedro Páramo* in its insight into rural desperation or with the Paraguayan Augusto Roa Bastos's *Son of Man* in its epic bleakness of vision, although Ramos's painfully spare prose makes even those two writers appear 'literary':

> No doubt, everyone was against him. He was used to that, his hide was tough, but sometimes it would quiver. There was no patience in the world could endure it all.
> 'One day a man'll do something bad and get himself in trouble.'
> Couldn't they see he was flesh and blood? His duty was to work for others, he knew his place. Sure. That was the destiny he'd been born with and no one was to blame for him being born with that hard luck. What could he do? Could he change his fate? It would have astounded him to think it possible to change his situation. He'd come into the world to break in strays, cure wounds with prayers and fix fences summer and winter. That was his destiny. His father'd done the same, his grandfather too. Cut thorns and slap leather, that was in his blood. He accepted his fate, he wasn't after more. If they gave him what was his, all well and good. But they didn't. He had a dog's luck, 'cause they only gave him bones. And then rich folk even took away a part of them bones. [1]

This simply told tale of suffering and humiliation, pathetically limited ambitions and ingenuous dreams, is beautifully paced and structured and provides a classic picture of the desperate *sertanejos*. For the protagonists of the novel existence is a series of endlessly repeated yet disconnected scenes, unified only by their persistent anguish. It is one of a handful of works to find a solution to the problem of communicating illiteracy and inarticulate-ness with sensitivity, tact and precision. Even the family dog is treated with respect and affection by the author in a world where no respect of any kind is available to the desperate trekkers. Moreover Fabiano, the illiterate labourer and cowhand, is shown to be in awe of his more enlightened wife, Vitória, whose idea it is that they should abandon the hopeless conditions of the coun-tryside and migrate to a new life in the city:

> Little by little a new life, however confused, began to be conjured up. They would settle in some small town, which was difficult for Fabiano to imagine, having been raised to run loose in the endless bush. They'd work a bit of land, then move to the city, where the kids would go to school and be different from them... He was enraptured by Missy Vitória's words. They would press on to an unknown land. Fabiano was happy and believed in that land, because he didn't know where it was or what it was like. Meekly he repeated Missy Vitória's words, the words she murmured because she had faith in him. And they headed south, inside their dream. A big city, full of strong people. The kids at school, learning difficult and necessary things. They, Vitória and Fabiano, would grow old and end up like dogs, useless, like poor Baleia. What would they do? They hesitated, fearful. They would come to an unknown and civilized land, and there they'd be imprisoned. And the Sertão would keep on sending people there. The Sertão would keep on sending strong, ignorant people, like Fabiano, Missy Vitória and the two boys.[2]

Barren Lives is a novel carved out of drought, sand, brush and cultural poverty: clear, stark, arid, brutal and compelling, an early Third World mas-terpiece. In 1945 Ramos joined the Communist Party and in 1953 published '*Journey*' (*Viagem*), a work on his impressions of a visit to the Eastern bloc. In the same year *Prison Memoirs* (*Memórias do cárcere*) appeared, as a grim record of his time behind bars. Like Vallejo, Rulfo and Roa Bastos, Ramos was a writer who had suffered like his characters, and continued to suffer on their and his own behalf. His sombre and unyielding austerity of vision makes his work the classic expression of the Northeast during this period.

The High Sierras

> The field of wheat rippled gently, ripe in the evening sun. One stalk is like another, and all together they are pleasant to behold. One man is like another, and all together they, too, are pleasant to behold. Likewise the story of Rosendo Maqui and his children was as the history of each and every one of the other villagers in Rumi. But men have heads and hearts, while the wheat lives only through its roots, and that makes the difference between them.
>
> Down below there was a village, and he was its mayor and perhaps a doubtful future awaited them. Yesterday, today... The words teemed with years, with centuries.
>
> Ciro Alegría, *Broad and Alien is the World*, 1941

Some critics have suggested that with *Canaima*, his literary journey into Indian country and exploration of his continent's Mestizo culture, Rómulo Gallegos had effectively put an end to the Spanish American regionalist current which he best represents, and had opened the way to a more complex, problematical and indeed labyrinthine form of writing. While this may be true of Gallegos's own trajectory, it effectively brought his development to a full stop since his later works showed no further ability to explore the worlds of myth, language and consciousness which such a new conception would seem to imply. Moreover Rivera's *The Vortex*, more than a decade earlier, had marked out much of the ground to be covered in this journey through the jungle of signs, and other younger writers – like Mário de Andrade, Miguel Angel Asturias and Alejo Carpentier (see chapter 5) – had embarked on that odyssey long before Gallegos himself. Nevertheless Gallegos's belated recognition of the centrality of what many Latin Americans insist on calling 'the Indian problem' in Latin American history was highly significant.

During the postwar period, Social Realist literature on Indian themes had been through the same range of options as regionalist literature as a whole. If the jungle provides the most dramatic and intense version of the natural world which is the context of American social and economic reality, the Indian is America's original autochthonous inhabitant. Nineteenth-century literature had seen numerous magnificent savages residing nobly in the past, from José Alencar's '*The Guarani*' (*O guarani*, Brazil, 1857) to Juan León de Mera's *Cumandá* (Ecuador, 1879) and Juan Zorrilla's *Tabaré* (Uruguay, 1879). The relation of the masculine denominations of these long-dead Indians to the foundational females of nationalist myth-making of the same period (*Soledad*, *Amalia*, *Inocência*, *María*, etc.) is a fascinating topic which unfortunately cannot be treated here. At any rate, these were clearly exoticist works, called 'Indianist' in Latin American critical terminology. The best known novel on the Indians of the Andean sierras and the forerunner of twentieth-century 'Indigenism' (like the Novel of the Mexican Revolution, a branch of Social Realism) was Clorinda Matto de Turner's *Birds without a Nest* (*Aves sin nido*, Peru 1889), not dissimilar to Beecher Stowe's *Uncle Tom's Cabin*. Its sentimental title conveys the fact that the novel remained essentially romantic despite its admirable militant intentions.

The first great work of twentieth-century *indigenismo* is '*Race of Bronze*' (*Raza de bronce*, 1919), a powerful novel by the Bolivian Alcides Arguedas (1879–1946). His pathbreaking though permanently controversial achievement is even more remarkable when one considers that a primitive version, *Wata Wara*, appeared in 1904, five years before his bitterly pessimistic sociological study '*Sick People*' (*Pueblo enfermo*, 1909), which attributed Bolivia's problems to its individually unfortunate and collectively catastrophic racial ingredients. Arguedas, later an influential historian, was another writer who, like Horacio Quiroga and José Eustasio Rivera, had participated in the Modernista movement and was now exorcising the errors of his own escapist past. Son of a landowning family from the Bolivian Altiplano and a regular visitor to Paris, Arguedas captures in his novel the almost incredible level of brutality between landowners and peons on Bolivian haciendas, which was to continue up to the Revolution of 1952 (and later still in Peru). Long before the Mexican Revolution managed to produce a similar ode to its own indigenous population, Arguedas's work displays, despite his own inherent conservatism, a keen insight into the social, legal and political framework of the inhuman feudal systems prevailing in all Latin American nations where there was a substantial Indian population. It also satirizes the fatuous attempts of Modernist writers to convey Latin American realities, whilst managing itself to give a number of memorable evocations of the grandiose scenarios of the Bolivian Andes from Illimani along the Cordillera Real.

Jorge Icaza, *Huasipungo*

Other indigenist works appeared in each of the 'Indian' republics in the 1920s, following Arguedas's example and the new indigenist policies of the Mexican Revolution, but most writers, like the rural judge López Albújar (1872–1966) in Peru, for example, still saw the Indians as inherently inferior, irrational and superstitious. Their integration seemed unlikely, if not impossible, to such people, then as now. Politics eventually modified the perceptions of other observers, and it was in the 1930s when the movement reached its climax, or rather two different kinds of climax. The first was through a literary bombshell entitled *Huasipungo* (1934) by the Ecuadorean Jorge Icaza (1906–1978), which may just be the most controversial novel in the history of Latin American narrative. Born not in the tropical coastlands of Guayaquil, where most of Ecuador's great Social Realists of the era were located, but in the highlands of Quito, Icaza spent time on the hacienda of relatives as a child, and gained some early acquaintance with the lives and problems of the Indian peons. He lost both parents at an early age, and this may have freed him for the controversial path he was to take through contemporary Ecuadorean culture (despite the fact that he was for most of his life a minor bureaucrat and bookseller). He worked as an actor and playwright in a theatre company in the 1920s and published his first work of fiction, 'Mountain Clay' (*Barro de la sierra*), only in 1933. His lasting claim to fame, however, was established in the following year, coinciding, appropriately enough, with Zdhanov's notorious intervention in the writers' congress in the USSR and the institution of Socialist Realism.

Huasipungo – the title refers to the plots of land the Indians were allowed to farm on feudal estates until the Liberal reforms of 1918 – is perhaps the most brutally laconic and unyielding novel ever published about the condition of the Indians and the shameful realities of the hacienda system which dominated Latin America from the colonial period to the present century. Most Latin American fiction about the Indians portrays them as beggars on golden stools, the degraded inhabitants of some of the most imposing natural landscapes on the planet. Icaza has different intentions:

> Night was falling when the cavalcade entered the village of Tomachi. The winter, the winds coming down the hillsides from the wilderness, the misery and indolence of the people, the shadow of the high peaks which corral them, have made of that place a nest of mud, filth, wretchedness, where everything and everyone crouches and cowers. The huts crouch along the single mud road; children crouch in the doorways as they play in the dirt or chatter on the fever of an old malaria; women crouch by the fire, morning and evening, to boil up the barley mush or potato soup; the men crouch from six until six, in the fields, mountains or plateaux, or disappear along the roads after the mules carrying loads to neighbouring villages; the water crouches and murmurs in the ditches tattooed along the road, filthy water where the animals from the huasipungos slake their thirst, where the pigs make beds of mud to cool their ardour, where the drunks urinate and the children crouch on all fours to drink.[3]

No Latin American novel before or since has ever been so single-minded. Indeed few novels anywhere have provided such a clear example of the idea that 'the sum total of the relations of production constitutes the economic structure of society, the real foundation, on which rises a legal and political superstructure and to which correspond definite forms of social consciousness'. First Icaza shows us the mental life of the upper class:

> Landlord and priest held long, substantial and sometimes entertaining conversations: the fatherland, progress, democracy, morality, politics. Don Alfonso, using and abusing his liberal tolerance, showed the cassock a friendship and confidence without limits. The priest in turn – Christian gratitude and understanding – allied himself to the lord of the valleys and the mountains with all his material and spiritual powers.[4]

Such cynical idealism contrasts with the involuntary materialism of the Indian protagonists' thoughts:

> In the minds of the Indians... on the other hand, were woven and unwoven anxieties about immediate needs: for the roasted corn or the flour not to run out, for the mist to lift so the cold will end, for the time to pass so they can return to their huts, for the huasipungo to be without calamities – the kids, the wife, the parents, the guinea pigs, chickens, pigs, crops – for the bosses not to give painful orders impossible to carry out, and the water, the land, the poncho, the blouse...[5]

As can be readily seen, the novel is written in a kind of brutal shorthand. The contrast between a clichéd, hypocritical, degraded but guileful bourgeois–Creole mode of speech and the spontaneous, whining, primitive but above all collective utterance of the Indians is maintained throughout the novel. In the previous extract we saw that Don Alfonso the landowner is a liberal; so liberal, indeed, that he foregoes the usual anti-clerical posture for tactical ends. He is, so to speak, the body, the agent of economic control, at the level of institutions, whilst the priest is the soul, the agent of ideological control; in other words a replication of the base and superstructure relationship within the superstructure itself. We also see that their words are truly empty words: their use of language is essentially political and manipulative, and their hollow conceptualizations merely conceal the true motivation of their behaviour. The Indians, by contrast, have no such room for manoeuvre, either in reality or in their consciousness: so they cringe, whine and bleat like the beasts of burden they have become:

> Don Alfonso went on:
> 'Andrés is to go first with me, then Juan with Lolita. The others can carry the trunks.'
> After wiping their sweating and rain-soaked faces with the sleeve of their blouses, after rolling up their rough cotton breeches to the thigh, after taking off their ponchos and folding them like an apache headscarf, the Indians named by the master humbly presented their backs for the members of the Pereira family to move from the backs of the animals to theirs...
> Andrés, staggering under Don Alfonso, went first. It was not a walk. It was an instinctive groping with the feet to test the danger. It was a slow sinking and rising in and out of the mud.[6]

Here the Indians carry the white landowning family across a stretch of muddy land where even the horses cannot keep their footing. The image is unwaveringly concrete and shows that the Indians have been dehumanized to mere beasts of burden; that the beautiful world of nature, so important in most indigenist writing, has itself been degraded whenever necessary; that the Indians stand between the upper classes and the mud, thereby cushioning them against material reality at the same time as they 'carry' the economy through their labour; and that they also know the countryside, and can interpret its signs in the interests of the usually absent landlords, who depend upon them to do this.

Now it is well known, as mentioned before, that realism chronicles the fortunes of the European middle classes, and that whenever Latin American novelists have tried to write a realist novel they have lapsed into Romanticism, 'Costumbrismo' (the novel of customs) or Naturalism. There has been no rise of the Latin American middle class comparable to that of

Europe in the eighteenth and nineteenth centuries. When a close enough approximation finally emerged in the 1940s, its dependent status, whose psychological and other realities had to be disguised at all costs, produced – Icaza and those like him would argue – the carefully refracted mythologies of Magical Realism, the fantasies of Borges, and in due course the linguistic riddles of the New Novel. Icaza, in the first pages of *Huasipungo*, sneers at the landowner's penchant for self-dramatization by terming it 'the mystery and emotion of a romantic novel'. This he will avoid throughout his own novel, giving his readers no possible escape into the spiritual or psychological realms. Of course Icaza's extremist Naturalism translates a political stance not far removed from Ramos's *Barren Lives*. Since there are people who have nothing, and since a whole socio-economic system condemns them to having nothing, why should anyone feel entitled to anything? He therefore gives importance only to what people share in common, their primary needs and basic drives, and systematically demythologizes all those abstract religious and political principles which validate the social and economic status of elites. Thus religion, for example, is reduced to a sublimation of the sexual instincts for the upper classes and a means of socially and economically controlling the lower classes. Oligarchical codes of honour and Cholo (Mestizo) machismo are similarly put in their place.

Using your Marxism, then – the most modern theory for conceptualizing and controlling the world – you start from the bottom up, from those primary needs which determine the infrastructure. The Indians, who when they are not working spend their time in the novel writhing, defecating, vomiting, spitting, bleeding and dying, have nothing to offer but themselves – the labour of the men and the bodies (for sexual exploitation and wet nursing) of the women. They have nothing but their *huasipungos* and one another. The novel shows the attempts – usually quite incidental – to separate them from one another and from the *huasipungos* which they believe are legally theirs, though we are shown in the first pages of the novel that this is a mistaken supposition. The book therefore not only emphasizes the 'vulgar' base–superstructure duality, but also follows the implacable logic of the socio-economic system on the basis of one case study, the building of a road through the hacienda by a North American lumber company. It shows that all situations in real life flow from the logic of the infrastructure. Imperialists, their economic interests (the debt problem today?), their relations with the oligarchies in dependent societies (the drugs problem today?), eventually drive anonymous *huasipungueros* out of their hovels.

Innumerable critics have said that this crude and brutal novel betrays both literature and the Indians, whom it dehumanizes. They have sometimes further insinuated that things cannot really have been as bad as Icaza has painted them. This is true: the story of the Latin American hacienda is even worse than Icaza's portrait. He notes that it is difficult to be human when subjected to inhuman treatment. The higher one's social class, the more 'worlds' one has available. These Indians have only one available world, as the Ecuadorean novelist is at pains to show us:

> He searched for some mental support but found everything around him elusive and alien. For the others – Mestizos, gentlemen and bosses – an Indian's woes are a matter for scorn, contempt and disgust. What could his anguish over the illness of his wife possibly signify in the face of the complex and delicate tragedies of the Whites? Nothing![7]

Thus Icaza counterattacks by forcing literature on the defensive too. He wilfully eschews the normal virtues of literature because literature, being predominantly the vehicle of the ruling class of any given society, is an important means of validating the dominant culture through its superior virtues of style and tone, concepts which were giving way at the time to that of 'technique' under the influence of the New Criticism. Icaza is not concerned with imagination, fancy or romance, and he refuses to allow us to set our imaginations to work: the world he knows is not complex. He does not wish us to wonder what will happen in his narrative, since its whole point is to ensure that there can be no doubt. There is, in other words, an implicit criticism of writers who see the Indians as exotic, or who escape from the cruel world of documentary fact into the world of the imagination. For Icaza, like his Indians, there are not many worlds: there is only the world of matter, in the first and last analysis.

Thus of all Latin American novelists, Icaza is the most concerned to prevent his readers from bolting into the nearest imaginative or ideological labyrinth. He denies us the satisfactions of literariness, as commonly understood, and refrains from assuaging our sense of shock and guilt by showing, for example, that the Indians have their own, say, mythical culture, which may even be superior to ours despite or even because of their poverty. It is a novel which in its time raised vital questions about the relations of literature to society in underdeveloped countries. Whatever view one takes of this approach to writing, it seems reasonable to suppose that each literature can afford at least one *Huasipungo*. It can seem almost incredible that at the same time that Icaza and his contemporaries were writing such works in Ecuador and elsewhere, as others have continued to do until this day (not to mention their extension into straightforward documentary testimony), Borges and his circle in Argentina were writing their complex and labyrinthine inquisitions. There could hardly be a clearer example of what the concept of unequal development might mean as applied to cultural expression.

Ciro Alegría: dogs and Indians

Nowhere in Latin America, then, has the relation between literature and society been more direct, or more turbulent, than in the Andean republics of Peru, Bolivia and Ecuador, due in part no doubt to the starkness of the relation between three great inextricable problematics: the national question, the agrarian question and the ethnic question. In no Latin American republic have the contradictions determined by these problems been more acute than in Peru, and in no other republic is it more painful — to judge from literary expression — to be excluded from the fragile and always unjust national social consensus. This gives Peruvian cultural expression a characteristically bitter quality which is unlike that of any other country. Even those novelists influenced by European and North American Modernism have tended to adopt a bitter and satirical stance towards national society, and with good reason: the ruthless dictator Leguía, thought of as the ultimate in repressive government styles whilst in power in the 1920s, was only the beginning. The Apra movement, to which many important writers adhered, would never be allowed to govern despite being the single most popular party, and ruthless repression would be the normal government response to any form of social movement originating in either city or country.

Haya de la Torre and Mariátegui between them developed the two main alternatives to conservative or liberal rule in the continent, and must indeed be counted the two most important ideologues this century before the emergence of Castro and Guevara. Mariátegui's *Amauta* (1926–30), unique among the leading avant-garde magazines of the day, provided a vehicle for the great social, political and cultural debates of the era, and can be read with profit still, like his own seminal *'Seven Essays towards an Interpretation of Peruvian Reality'*. From the 1920s onwards, through López Albújar (1872–1966), César Falcon (1892–1970) and others, nativist writing became a major current within Peruvian fiction, with a brand of muscular, visceral writing not unlike that of Icaza and his generation in Ecuador. Even the great avant-garde poet César Vallejo (1892–1938), a Communist, turned to Social Realism with *Tungsten* (*El tungsteno*, 1931), a work which gives a deliberately stereotyped presentation of sierra reality with a crude, though hardly exaggerated insight into class and racial exploitation and the impact of United States economic exploitation in the shape of 'Mister Take'.[8] This style was to dominate Peruvian fiction for the next half century, as Haya de la Torre's Aprismo, Mariátegui-inspired Marxisms, and traditional oligarchic reaction fought for control of the country.

Haya's wilfully eclectic Apra ideology was forced to fight on two fronts, both against traditional conservatism and against the various Marxisms. He believed that the Mexican Revolution showed the way for other Latin American countries and characterized it as follows:

First, a great citizens' upheaval against a feudal dictatorship, that despotic suppressor of democratic rights; then, a peasant uprising against the class which that government represented; and finally, a joint action of the masses of city and country – peasant, worker and middle class – which crystallized juridically in the Constitution of Querétaro of 1917. The socio-economic content of that fundamental law of the Mexican Revolution is anti-feudal and anti-imperialist, in Article 27, and pro-worker and semi-classist, in Article 123, and semi-bourgeois or liberal in its total inspiration.... We need our French Revolution, or to speak in our own idiom, our Mexican Revolution, combining the struggle against feudalism with the struggle against imperialism and establishing a precursor era to later transformations. This is not pure socialism? This profanes the sacred doctrines inspired in the revolutionary books? This may be, but it is reality. Let the hairs rise on the necks of the theorizers of criollo Communism, bad interpreters of true Marxism![9]

It would be difficult to exaggerate the impact of Aprismo throughout the continent over the next half century. It was in fact the credo of Ciro Alegría (1909–67), undoubtedly the most important Peruvian indigenist novelist of the entire regionalist era. He spent much of his childhood on his grandfather's hacienda close to the River Marañón in Huanachuco. Later, in Lima, he joined Apra and was imprisoned during the events of 1932, escaped and was rearrested, before becoming an exile in Chile in 1934. There he fell seriously ill with tuberculosis, and later became paralysed and lost the faculty of speech, but produced two episodic novels, *The Golden Serpent* (*La serpiente de oro*, 1935), about the boatmen of the Marañón, and '*The Hungry Dogs*' (*Los perros hambrientos*, 1938), about the Indian and Cholo peasants of the high cordilleras and their struggle against an indifferent nature and a hostile society. '*The Hungry Dogs*' is not his best-known novel (though many critics think it his best), but warrants a brief stop as perhaps the classic expression of populist reformism in the literature of the period. Alegría was to become the last of the great regionalist novelists, as well as the best known outside Latin America. Moreover, this was his first work about the sierra Indians, written not long after *Huasipungo* by his Ecuadorean contemporary Jorge Icaza, on similar subject matter and at similar length. There, however, all similarities end: we are still in the Andes, but in a quite different world. Here the narrator is not only omniscient, as in Icaza's novel, but clearly audible:

It was a large flock, for it was composed of a hundred pairs, without counting the lambs. Because it must be understood that both Antuca, the shepherdess, like her parents and brothers, counted in twos. Their arithmetic went up to five, and then had to start again. And so they would have said 'five hundreds' or 'seven hundreds' or 'nine hundreds'; though, in truth, they never needed to talk of such fabulous quantities. Moreover, to simplify matters still further, these pairs were firmly rooted in Indian accountancy by custom. After all, why mess about?

Counting is a job for treasurers, and a people who never knew money and kept to simple bartering aren't likely in all logic to engender descendants with much insight into numbers. But those are other matters. We were talking about a flock.[10]

We know this man. He is an old friend of ours, though we may not have expected to find him amidst the conflicts of the Peruvian highlands in 1938. This is the benevolent tone, the knowing chuckle of the conventional nineteenth-century narrator at home in his world (only this is not the nineteenth century nor is it his world), who understands all and forgives all, confident that he is speaking, on behalf of the Cholos and Indians (who at this time could only vote if they could read and write in Spanish and were male), direct to other members of his own class, namely Western literate bourgeois society in its Peruvian version. Confident, indeed, that even the things he leaves unsaid – almost everything – will also be understood.

In addition to the continual explanation of local detail and the naive psychology of the natives, the constant interposition of the author between the reader and the signified, several salient points emerge. Firstly, although Peru's difference from other places is almost the novel's condition for existence, it is in one important respect the same as anywhere else, because it has a middle class whose novelists know how to turn Peru's extremely raw materials into a story: it is largely a matter of adopting the right tone and knowing how to translate the simple into the slightly more complex. Secondly, this is, after all, 'only a story'. Rather like Gallegos's novels, it is something static and one-dimensional – like a piece of paper – which exists in Alegría's head, which can be read off, picked up and put down at will. Thirdly, the story belongs to Alegría, he has the rights to it. Peru belongs to the middle-class intellectual (his time is coming), because only he can 'translate' it for strangers and foreigners, unlike the fascist-inclined landowners who think that they own it all. Alegría's posture, however unconvincing, has actually been the position of most Latin American intellectuals since Independence, and in the twentieth century it has been populist parties like Apra which have most effectively assumed its perspective politically. They speak for the masses, although without fully mobilizing them, naturally, either in reality or in literature, and often enough without the masses even hearing them. Such a position will be familiar enough to followers of the British scene ('our people', etc.).

The narrator himself is in history, clearly enough, but the Indians are not:

And so they passed the day, watching the turbulent Andean peaks, the bleating flock and the sky, now blue, now cloudy and threatening. Antuca span and chatted, shouting and spinning at times, at others in silence, as if one with the vast and profound silence of the mountain ranges, made out of stone and immeasurable solitary distances.... Such are the idylls of the cordillera. Her companion was more or less the same age as she. Their young ripe flesh would win out in the end. Doubtless they would come together and have children who, in their turn, watching over the animals up in the highlands, would meet other shepherds. [11]

The emphasis is on the indissoluble link between the Indian and nature, which nothing can sever. (In Icaza's work the Indians were already alienated from the land.) This is a world of eternity, infinity, silence and solitude, all symbols of the 'immeasurable', transcendental world beyond the material plane, a life which alternates between winter and summer, rain and drought, health and sickness, fertility and sterility, and other eternal peasant values, a pendular motion summarized as 'that stream of lights and shadows called time'. This time is not historical but cyclical, and for Alegría the silence between an Indian mother and her baby is 'the same as it would have been four hundred years ago', just as when the domestic dogs of the title began to starve due to the drought, 'time ceased to exist: they were now three nomadic dogs from the stone age fighting over that prey caught out in the wild open spaces'. This ideology was that of Haya himself, who, although from a 'pure' Creole family of the upper classes, prided himself on his 'Indian' profile, and believed in the enduring nature of Indian blood and culture:

> In the writings of Keyserling we, who feel beneath the lack of pigment the beating of an Indian heart, see many truths. They are painful sometimes, because they cruelly strip off the veneer of the Europeanizers to show them the profound depth of their Indo-Americanism.... We are not ashamed, then, to call ourselves Indo-Americans. We recognize that in the heart of our continent, as in each of our hearts, is the Indian, and it must influence us even though it no longer shows on the surface and sons refuse to admit it. [12]

This is the familiar indigenist vision of the world (Alegría says in his novel that 'the heart is a fertile soil'), familiar in the responses of many anthropologists and utopian travellers, essentially ahistorical and idealist. Alegría's emphasis is almost exclusively on man's relation with nature, not on social relations, which are treated obliquely except at moments of crisis. Icaza, in contrast, was concerned primarily with social and economic relations, and pushed nature to the background. There is some social criticism in Alegría's work: we see military press-ganging, the corruption of regional officials and, crucially, the reaction of the landowner, Don Cipriano, to the drought, when he continues to feed his own animals but ignores the plight of the human beings. This is where Simón Robles makes his famous speech on behalf of Indians and Cholos:

'Don't boot us out as if we was no more than hungry dogs, patrón...'
Simón Robles fell silent, and the peons felt that he had spoken through the mouth, the heart and the ravaged stomach of each one of them. [13]

Don Cipriano effectively tells the Indians to go eat cake and shoots a few of them for good measure. Then, however, typically in this classic reformist text, the oligarchy feels sorry ('everyone regretted those deaths') – we are all human beings – though it is still not forthcoming with material aid. But then again, we are shown that the natural world is pretty much like the social world, merciless and indifferent, so what else can one expect – except from exceptional characters like Simón Robles. Finally, in the next chapter, without any change in the social and economic system, the rain returns and all is well. So what are we to think? That, though no doubt deplorable, the outrages we have witnessed are on one level aberrations (extreme cases), and on another level (the eternal plane) supremely irrelevant. Thus at harvest time we find Don Cipriano the landowner united with his men:

Evening is falling as they sow the last plot. Don Cipriano Ramírez himself has scattered the wheat on the fragrant earth, evenly, with a sure and skilled hand as befits a veteran in these jousts. They've been happy days these when, having lost almost the whole harvest last year, they have seen the rain come down again, they have ploughed again, and sown again. Bosses and peons have merged in a joyous embrace with the earth. [14]

Clearly for Alegría this is the basic human reality, man's love for the earth, beyond any concept of ownership or class relationship. Only actual hunger separates men definitively. If only Cipriano would be a little more flexible during periods of starvation, within a concept of national multi-class unity, all would be well. Following this episode come several pages attacking a number of Apra targets: centralism, government corruption and inefficiency, and mediocre or wicked presidents. But again, in classic liberal–reformist style, Alegría attacks only the symptoms, not the causes. He believes that if left alone the Indians would be all right: it's just awkward old society and culture getting in the way. He appears to have no awareness of the fact that the Indians and Cholos are already the product of a complex historical development, that they may eventually have to migrate to shanty towns (like Fabiano's family in *Barren Lives*), or – the lucky ones who are not enslaved by landowners – divide up their small plots until faced with starvation or social conflict. For Alegría they will always be there, throughout eternity, immune from change. His apparently mature acceptance of 'life' is actually an acceptance of the inevitability of the status quo and of injustice, even though he sincerely fought for social change.

Because of this idealist conception, in which truth, man, nature and human nature exist, Alegría purports to demonstrate what all reformists seek to show, namely that others (women, children, blacks, the working class and, in this case, the Andean Indian peasants) are 'just like us', yet the very tensions involved in his efforts at persuasion reveal transparently an uneasy consciousness that this is not the case. (His unease would have been cured had he understood that their difference arose precisely from 'our' discrimination and oppression). In order to make the Indians accessible and, more important, acceptable (he suspects that it is the same thing) to us, he unconsciously evaluates them as people are evaluated in our own society; he classifies them. These are actually outstanding Indians and outstanding dogs:

> Antuca was helped by four dogs, Zambo, Wanka, Güeso and Pellejo. Excellent sheepdogs, famous throughout the region, where they had scattered many relatives whose skill in no way contradicted the genius of the race. Their owner, the Cholo Simón Robles, was as famous as his dogs, due in part to them and in part to his talent with the flute and drum, not to mention other graces.... Race? Best not talk about it. They were as mixed as Peruvian man himself... Hispanic and native ancestors were mixed in Wanka and Zambo, just as in Simón Robles and all the other cross-bred people in those parts.[15]

Moreover the dogs are as robust yet well-intentioned towards the sheep as the good old English bobby used to be towards the workers:

> They had never incapacitated an animal and imposed their authority by barks close to the ears. Some other ignoble animals lose their temper when faced by a stubborn sheep and end up killing it. Zambo and the others were patient and secured obedience with a knock or by pulling gently on the wool, measures which they applied only as a last resort.... Finally they had a puppy, called Chuto, which means mongrel, because his small size and lack of breeding contrasted with the abundant heraldic background of the dogs from the big house... Chutín always got his way, even from cattle, through his determined bark, his careful nips, his tireless agility and good humour.[16]

Thus the Indians become a kind of responsible, socially conscientious caricature of the middle class; and the dogs become the equivalent of the labouring classes: willing, servile, loyal, and they only cause trouble if you actually starve them. The landowner, like Lima, is completely out of the picture for most of the novel: he is not built into the structure. In any case, if the reader is disturbed by the murder of the protesting Indians, even the protagonist Simón Robles is shown having to do unpleasant things. For example, half-way through the novel he is forced to drown some new-born puppies because of the drought, just as Don Cipriano has to shoot a few Indians for the same reason. Finally, if Güiraldes's *Don Segundo Sombra*, as so many critics have said, was a piece of ventriloquism, with Güiraldes's smoking jacket clearly visible under the narrator's gaucho blanket, Simón Robles here appears to be something close to Ciro Alegría with a poncho on:

> He was a born story-teller. But this does not mean, of course, that he was a charlatan. On the contrary: he was capable of profound and meditative silences. But when his speech sprang from his breast, his voice flowed with the spontaneity of water and each word occupied its proper place and had the required accent.[17]

Robles has the same narrative qualities that Alegría himself is seeking, behaves throughout with great dignity, unquestionably deserves to survive, and does. Can one possibly overlook the link between his personality, his particular qualities and his survival when others starve? He has precisely the virtues of the bourgeoisie as perceived by its own myths. Haya had thought them crucial to any Latin American revolution:

> It is necessary to establish the fundamental difference existing between the historical role of the middle classes – petty bourgeoisie of city and countryside – of Europe and the middle classes of Indoamerica. In Europe the dominant class is the high bourgeoisie. In Indoamerica it is the large landowners.... The belligerent capacity of the middle classes, therefore, must be used to the benefit of national liberation. They must join in the defence of the anti-imperialist state.[18]

By contrast with Robles's survival the Indian Mashe starves and, very poetically, only possesses the earth in death. Robles, behind his folksy socialist rhetoric, looks suspiciously like the middle classes asking the land-owning elite for its political and economic rights, like Apra riding to power – as it believed – on the backs of the workers and Indians. And the drought then begins to look suspiciously like that other fatal phenomenon about which nothing can be done, an economic slump, just as nature as a whole looks disconcertingly like the economic infrastructure, far beyond the power of men to control.

As he was completing 'The Hungry Dogs' Alegría came up with a possible title for a chapter to be called 'Broad and Alien is the World'. Deciding that it had a certain ring about it, he omitted it and made it the title of his next novel, which he wrote in four months in 1940 for a Pan-American competition organized by Farrar and Rinehart. Like the earlier work it has a certain willed authority and simple grandeur which could be said, albeit somewhat ironically, to make them Latin America's most accomplished nineteenth-century novels. Painted on a vast historical, geographical and social canvas, the narrative centres on the free community of Indians of Rumi in Northern Peru between 1912 and the 1930s, led by their mayor, Rosendo Maqui, at one time considered one of the great characters of Latin American fiction:

> The Indian Rosendo Maqui squatted there like an ancient idol. His body was brown and gnarled as the *lloque* – of knotted, iron-hard trunk – because he was part plant, part man, and part rock. His thick lips were set in an expression of serenity and firmness under his flat nose. Behind his hard, jutting cheekbones shone his eyes, dark quiet lakes. The eyebrows were like beetling crags. It was almost as though Rosendo Maqui were cast in the image of his geography; as though the turbulent forces of the earth had fashioned him and his people in the likeness of the mountains. His temples were white like those of Urpillau. Like the mountain, he was a venerable patriarch. [19]

As in most indigenist novels, the Indians are cheated of their land by a ruthless and unscrupulous landowner and forced to wander the earth, only to discover that Peru is broad and alien, and that neither pacificism nor banditry nor socialist insurrection can solve their problems. The novel duly won the competition, and was praised by John Dos Passos, a member of the jury, making Alegría one of the two or three best known Latin American novelists of the era. His book is ambitious, panoramic and the only one of the great regionalist works to have a genuine historical framework. The Indian search for land and justice takes us to the jungles and the rivers, the mines and the cities, among the bandits and the trade unionists. Unlike the much briefer 'The Hungry Dogs', this novel is unwieldy, poorly organized and erratic in style, as well as having all the technical and ideological limitations already mentioned. Nevertheless, it is majestic despite its unevenness and moving despite its sentimentality, and does provide the reader with a means by which to imagine the experience of the Andean Indians. It seems destined to endure as a great, if somewhat clumsy, monument to the indigenist doctrine of an entire era.

Of course fifty years later the Indians remain hungry, though Apra's hunger for power has at last been answered. However Alegría himself left the party in 1948 and joined Belaúnde's Acción Popular. This was after spending the Second World War in New York translating United States propaganda into Spanish. In the 1950s he went to Cuba and was forced by poverty to write an endless history of the Bacardi Rum company: contradictions dogged him to the end. Icaza managed things, including fate, much better. He spent the 1930s organizing theatre companies and was eventually appointed Director of the National Library. Despite his Marxist ideology he never devoted himself to direct political activism as the less radical Alegría had done, and was therefore never exiled and hungry, as Alegría was.

Needless to say, there is nothing unusual in the vision of Alegría which has been outlined here. His sincerity is not at issue. Writers have for several centuries, but particularly in the past two, been writing of people from different classes and cultures as if they had real insight into them – the same goes for the stories told by anthropologists[20] – and critics have been assuring us that they, especially the truly great writers, really did have such insight. This is problematical even between writers of the same class, nationality and gender – none of us has ever had even a second's true insight into another's mind, and this illusion is perhaps the greatest of all of fiction's many fictions – but in Latin America the social and cultural gaps are so wide as to make the problems starkly obvious. Many Latin Americans are barely aware, if at all, of their nationality, still less of what 'Latin America' is. Most of them are functionally illiterate, and only a minute proportion have ever read a 'serious' novel. In these circumstances the role of the writer in constituting the myths of nationhood remains extraordinarily important, and yet the fictionality involved in such an endeavour is extraordinarily transparent. To that extent one has to demur from Benedict Anderson's assumption in *Imagined Communities* that, for example, the Philippine novelist Jose Rizal's *Noli me tangere* (1887) has, in its point of view and structure, certain unmistakable signs of a specifically colonial nationalist spirit.[21] On the contrary, the strategies employed seem little different to those of, say, Dickens. The point is that Dickens, in all probability, really did persuade himself that there was an already existing national community to which he could address himself, either one that was contradictory but existent for all that, or one of men of goodwill like himself into which the evil members of his own class and the poor ignorant masses could be integrated. Rizal knows equally well that no such sense of nationhood exists in his Philippine world, but imagines and indeed 'invents' such a community in order to delude or encourage others into accepting and thus magically creating it: this is literally an act of propaganda and even of enchantment ('Our revels are only just commencing…'?). The difference lies not in the literary devices employed but in the actually existing relationships between writer and audience.

José María Arguedas, *'Everyone's Blood'*

The solitary lark flew out of the pisonay tree; the light from the snowy peak smiled on his black and yellow feathers as they winged on the air. He covered the courtyard, the whole sky, with his song, in which everything was weeping, from the smallest flowers to the river torrents, and the great precipice that rose up on the other side, taking in all the sounds and voices of the earth. But its slow flight before the uneasy eyes of the lord and master, as he tried to answer the Indian's question, lit up the multitude.

José María Arguedas, *'Everyone's Blood'*, 1964

While Alegría was producing his two major novels a younger writer, José María Arguedas (1911–69), was preparing his own early works, *'Water'*

(*Agua*, 1935) and *Yawar Fiesta* (1941). He is now considered perhaps the greatest indigenist novelist of the continent,[22] mainly due to *Deep Rivers* (*Los ríos profundos*, 1958: see chapter 6) and '*Everyone's Blood*' (*Todas las sangres*, 1964). Although the interest of his works is in some respects circumscribed by their strictly Americanist orientation and, it must be said, by some limitations of technique, Arguedas is today counted among the most important Latin American novelists this century. He is also unique. He lost his mother early and suffered rejection from his own family, living for much of his childhood among Quechua Indians. Quechua, indeed, was his first language and one of the fascinations of his writing is the relationship between the Spanish in which it is mainly written and the Quechua thought patterns and structures which lie beneath. The divorce between the two worlds, reminiscent of that which had mentally crucified the Inca Garcilaso de la Vega (1539–1616) more than three hundred years before, was an unremitting agony of Arguedas's life, which his anthropological training did little to relieve, and which he was never finally able to resolve.

It is really for this reason that the heavy reliance on Arguedas by Angel Rama and others as the leading exponent of 'bi-culturalism', 'transculturation' or 'pluralism' in Latin American narrative is somewhat problematical,[23] since the impossibility of reconciling the two worlds which had existed in mutual hostility for four hundred years is precisely what brought him into conflict with the 'boom' writers, notably Julio Cortázar (see chapter 8), and finally drove him to suicide in 1969. Nevertheless Rama has effectively described Arguedas's dilemma, torn as he was between the universalist and provincialist impulses:

> Arguedas lived within a game of mirrors which sent him from one hemisphere to another: as an Indian, he sought to insert himself within the dominant culture, to appropriate a foreign language (Spanish) by forcing it to express another syntax (Quechua), to find the 'subtle disorderings which would make Castilian a fit vehicle, an adequate instrument', in short, to impose his cosmovision and his protest on a foreign territory; but simultaneously he is transculturating the literary tradition of the Spanish language by appropriating an Indian cultural message with both a specific thematic and an expressive system. As if that were not enough, he has also to cope with the universalist demand which the incipient avant-garde had posed to the regionalist generation, to which he must give an answer.[24]

The classic answer Arguedas gave was to summarize his projects as follows: 'I tried to convert into written language what I was as an individual: a link, strong and capable of universalizing itself, between the great imprisoned nation and the generous, human section of the oppressors.'[25] Rama concludes that Arguedas's paradoxical solution was to make himself 'a White acculturated by the Indians'.

Arguedas's longest work, '*Everyone's Blood*', is possibly the last of the great indigenist novels, an appropriate sequel to *Broad and Alien is the World* (though published, ironically enough, in the midst of the 'boom'). Indeed one might say that it repeats in a sense the subject matter of Alegría's novel, but treats it from the kind of perspective which Icaza employed in *Huasipungo*, albeit with much greater complexity. Simply as a source of information it must be ranked as one of the most important literary documents in Latin American history; for, with the magic of literature, this is a text which moves: if *Huasipungo* is the classic of vulgar Marxism, '*Everyone's Blood*' is the classic of dialectical materialism.[26] It would appear to be set in the 1950s, in the period shortly before the Cuban Revolution, the foundation in Peru of the Apra Rebelde led by Luis de la Puente Uceda, in 1959, and the peasant upheavals in the Valley of La Convención and Lares led by Hugo Blanco. It presents a kind of microcosm of Peruvian history by detailing the social transformations taking place around the small town of San Pedro when the old patriarchal landowner Don Andrés dies and curses his two sons, Bruno, a reactionary religious fanatic who wishes to maintain the feudal system yet eventually assists the Indians in their uprising, and Fermín, a ruthless modernizing capitalist, a member of the new nationalist bourgeoisie, who owns the local wolfram mine and is involved in a desperate struggle with a foreign multinational company. Bruno's hacienda and Fermín's mine dominate the otherwise decaying local economy, where the gentry are in decline and the Cholos scrape to make a living. Nearby are two free Indian communities, the prosperous Lahuaymarca and the poor Paraybamba. Within these social sectors the widest possible range of ethnic groups, classes and fractions of Peru is represented.

This is a story which has been told many times in Latin American Social Realist literature, but never with such a sense of contradiction, mastery of detail and dynamic movement. The principal protagonist is Rendón Willka, an Indian who was exiled from the community as an adolescent for standing up for his rights at school. On his return eight years later Willka is an indigenist militant, a kind of Christ figure, one of the most complex and attractive character creations in Latin American fiction, a man who knows both of Peru's component social parts and thus has understanding beyond that of the other characters. Perhaps the most significant of his many insights is that his destiny and that of the capitalist entrepreneur are intimately linked, for both are 'modernizers', Don Fermín as an industrialist and Rendón as an Indian who needs to proletarianize his fellows in order to save them:

> 'Don Fermín suffer more. I'll make him. That's why I'm here. You not know? Don
> Bruno is full of filth, no eyes, the God inside him won't let him see; just molten
> lead. Don Fermín's much worse. He's deaf, body like dry leather... but that's all

right... Him I'll follow, go with him. I'll control him; he'll control the town.... But I say too much! Talk like fool! Not good talk when blood boils. Head look, heart push.'[27]

Willka also sets about tutoring the next generation of Indian revolutionaries, ensuring that Indian affairs will pass into their own hands and out of the power of the white politicians:

'Remember', said Rendón. 'In prison you learn plenty. Schools there. Listen to the politicians. The world is big. But don't follow what politicians say; by our own thoughts we must learn what they teach. They are different from us. No one knows us. You see! You're a man, Davicho; you'll be more than me. We've talked. They're coming to take you.... Wait for them in your house, quiet, no anger. Already you can sign, in prison you'll learn writing. Let them take you to Lima.'[28]

The same inevitability applies when the troops return to suppress what the authorities consider a 'Communist' uprising. Willka knows – and it is as if Arguedas were prophesying all that has happened in Peru, Brazil and Central America these last twenty-five years – that the Indians will have to be prepared to die if they are ever to live in the way they choose and according to their own ancestral cultural traditions:

'Can you see the sun's light? The gendarmes will come, tomorrow maybe, maybe three days, and they will try to put out the sun. Can they put it out? They cannot. Let every man die in the place the hacienda has set him to work. The hacienda belongs to Father Pukasira. He made this land before the white men came to our land.... Soldiers come, maybe they kill me. No matter. There will still be leaders, one hundred k'ollanas. Can they kill us all? When you hear the rifles thunder don't be afraid; think of it like the sound of roasted maize popping in the fire. When you see the blood run, much blood, don't be afraid; think of it like the coloured water of the ayrampu. And don't run. If you run you'll lose your life and land. If you stand firm they'll kill a few, then go away. How can they kill us all?[29]

This involves the recognition that his own self-sacrifice through death is inevitable if he is to maintain the Indian communal tradition of selflessness and solidarity whilst converting mere endurance into conscious resistance. His job throughout the novel is to do whatever is necessary to encourage Indian culture and social organization to survive. As the government troops converge on the Indians in the final sequences of the novel – as they do at the end of all the classic works of indigenism: 'Race of Bronze', Huasipungo, and Broad and Alien is the World – Willka has evidence that his task is completed:

'You are all communists', said the captain.

The woman did not reply at first. Then she said:

'You must be the communist, sir.'

'I've come here to kill communists. Martial law has been declared throughout the province.'

'Kill communists? Go somewhere else, sir; you won't find what you're looking for here.'

'Indian she-fox, trained by a fox. I'll shoot you too if you don't tell me where Willka and his people are.'

'Rendón Willka? His people? He doesn't have people. We are the community, all over the hacienda, everywhere.'

Willka heard the woman's answers with quiet rejoicing. 'Now they can shoot me. It doesn't matter now!' he thought. [30]

Resistance has, precisely, reached the moment where it is ready to be turned into revolution. The woman's son is shot and she after him, before Willka himself joins the endless chain of Latin American revolutionary martyrs:

'Against the wall, Indian!'

'I won't. Kill me here next to my son.'

'Fire!' shouted the captain.

The woman fell on the boy's body. She stretched out her arms, as if to move towards the firing squad and collapsed face up. Her blood shone beneath the still strong sun; poured shining from a hole in her neck. The flowers of the pisonay tree were shaken off by the wind. And everyone saw that they were opaque and silky beside the colour of the blood of that woman with children. The tree shook in the wind; and it alone wept long and hard in the immense courtyard. Everyone saw it shake its warm flowers on the cobbles and send them, rolling, towards the two dead ones.

'Captain! Captain, sir!', said Rendón Willka in Quechua. 'Here, now, in these towns and haciendas, only the great trees weep. Your rifles cannot put out the sun, nor dry the rivers, still less take the lives of all the Indians. Keep firing. We don't have manufactured weapons, they're no use. Our hearts are fire. Here, everywhere! We've found our country at last. And you can't kill our country, sir. There it is; it looks dead. No! The pisonay weeps; will spill its flowers throughout all eternity, still growing. Now out of grief, tomorrow out of joy. Your rifles are deaf, like wood; they don't hear. We are men who will live for ever. If you want it, if you need to, give me death, my little death, captain.'

The captain had him shot. But he was left alone. And, like the other soldiers, he heard the sound of great torrents which shook the earth below, as if the mountains had begun to walk. [31]

When Willka cries that the Indians have 'found their country at last', he is not talking about the neocolonial, capitalist state which has been developed – or, rather, underdeveloped – since Peru gained its formal independence in the early nineteenth century. Rather he looks forward to a new, genuinely plural society when 'the Peruvian' has finally managed to emerge from the ethnic labyrinth of blood and cultural conflict. The 1980s have seen a new era of debate about the 'national question' in Latin America, and nowhere more intensively than in Peru, where the rise of Sendero Luminoso has given the discussions a still more desperate quality.[32] Arguedas's heart-rending novel will remain one of the indispensable documents of the entire era.

Ciro Alegría's works already showed just how closely regionalism, nationalism and Americanism have been related in this era. Indeed, *Broad and Alien is the World* is precisely about the problematical unity and hoped for unification of the nation. Rosendo Maqui was the last of literature's innocent, traditional Indians, and his successor Benito Castro was the first of a new generation – forerunner to Rendón Willka – which would have to take part not merely in regional but in national politics, becoming proletarians without ceasing to be Indians. Since that work Peru has become one at last for all its people (it has been one for centuries for the ruling oligarchy, though even their territory would be dwarfed by a revived Inca Tahuantinsuyu), but only in the sense that it is now one great social, political and economic battlefield. Thus, rather like his Indian character, Alegría is the last of the great 'innocent' novelists, and *Broad and Alien* is the last of the great innocent novels, nineteenth century in conception, construction and above all ideology, and liberal in perspective without appreciating or even seeing the contradictions of liberalism for a continent in which neocolonialism means that self-determination and national integration are idealist objectives, Quixotic goals to be set but never achieved.[33]

The difference between Alegría's vision, which ends in a hopeless massacre, and those of Arguedas and Roa Bastos (see p. 94), which also end in defeat, is that the latter have a more militant vision – in part the benefit of hindsight – and have come to believe that death and sacrifice are not only happening but are inevitable and that liberation can only be achieved by struggle. The title of Alegría's work itself acknowledges the historical cul-de-sac. The Indian peoples may once have occupied the whole of America, but not even Tahuantinsuyu will ever again be theirs: there are too few of them, their communities are too insignificant, their technology will never overcome that of the Whites and Mestizos, and there is a vast world outside of Peru which for the forseeable future can be relied upon to back the interests of these groups. Apra's early Third World ideology was integrationist, accepting the inevitability of capitalist development, the market economy, commodity exchange, wage labour and even large-scale international trade. The rather desperate hope was that this could be achieved on favourably negotiated terms, so that if exploitation of the national workforce was essential it would be exerted by national politicians according to national policies: if any bourgeoisie is to get rich, let it be a national one. Alegría perceived this dilemma and structured it into his novels, but metaphorically and through unconscious displacement. Arguedas saw it much more clearly, and unforgettably dramatized, though of course he could not resolve, the contradictions involved.

The difference of course was ideology and militancy. Arguedas, despite the powerful surge of religiosity in his work – quite absent from Alegría's mechanical pantheism – and its accompanying sentimentality, is more angry and indignant than supplicatory. Indignation could only take the form it does in his work when there is some possible solution, and the solution of course was some form of Peruvianized Marxist doctrine. This development had been fermenting ever since Icaza's *Huasipungo*, and was soon to open up an ideological fault line right the way across Latin American fiction. Eventually, as we shall see, it would lead to the effective end of Social Realism as a major current, partly because its epistemological limitations gradually became untenable but also because the increasing urgency of political commitment forced writers both to total austerity and to immediacy of response, whereas a great historical novel usually requires at least thirty years' distance from its subject matter. Great realist works will always exist, but there will equally be only one or two to commemorate each era, and they will not appear during the era to which they refer. This partly explains the relative paucity of good fiction about the Cuban Revolution. We can expect it to emerge before the end of the century.

Augusto Roa Bastos, *Son of Man*: the limits of regionalism

One of the most interesting novels at the end of the 1950s, almost a premonition of the literary and political future, was *Son of Man* (*Hijo de hombre* 1960), by the Paraguayan Augusto Roa Bastos (1917–). Indeed all the more interesting in retrospect since this was one of the last of the recognizably 'regionalist' or 'pre-boom' novels by an author who was in due course to write one of the most remarkable 'post-boom' works, *I the Supreme* (1974). His first novel, like that of Arguedas, deals with a bi-cultural and indeed bi-lingual society; and also, like Arguedas's, it paints a truly moving picture of appalling oppression and suffering, matched by heroic powers of resistance on the part of the usually anonymous poor, and raises the question of commitment in a form which presents the reader himself with inescapable dilemmas. It has to be said that on the whole the great novels of the 'boom' rarely achieved such emotional force of identification with the suffering of the Latin American people as the tradition which extends from the Social Realists of the 1920s through Graciliano Ramos, Miguel Angel Asturias, José María Arguedas and Roa Bastos himself, and on to the documentary fiction of the 1970s and 1980s. Whilst never committing himself absolutely to any specific ideology, Roa's concerns are uniquely those of the Latin

American Left as a whole during the period from the 1950s to the 1980s. A long-time supporter of the Cuban Revolution, an advocate of Latin America considering itself part of the Third World, Roa has taken his novels closer than those of any other major writer to the debates of Fanon, Mao, Castro, Guevara, Liberation Theology and so on in recent decades. Yet he is the least dogmatic of novelists. His first work put an appropriate end, at the very moment of the Cuban Revolution, to the Social Realist or regionalist movement which had begun with *The Underdogs*, that other novel about the relation between the intellectuals and the people written at the height of the Mexican Revolution.

Son of Man tells the dramatic story of two Paraguayan communities, lost in the outback, over a period of three decades from the early 1900s to the time of the Chaco War with Bolivia and its aftermath in the 1930s. The novel juxtaposes two views of Christianity, that of the official Church and that of the Indian peasants who interpret Christ's torment as a reflection of their own agony:

> It was a harsh, primitive, rebellious ritual, fermented in some resentful upsurge of collective insurrection which, as though roused by the smell of sacrificial blood, broke out at the ninth hour on Passion Friday in this demonstration of fear and hope and anger.
>
> This was the ceremony which gave us villagers of Itapé the name of fanatics and heretics. The people of those times came year after year to unnail Christ and carry him through the town like a victim they wished to avenge rather than a God who had wanted to die for men's sakes.[34]

Roa has often said that the people have a capacity for heroism and self-sacrifice which is in itself utopian and carries the seeds of the future:

> The complacent supporters of submission and oppression may consider utopia as the expression of irreality, of hopeless projects and endless frustration, but the temper of our oppressed but undefeated peoples sees precisely in utopia the model for and the path to their liberation made reality in the essence of their being, with the impulse of their acts.[35]

Moreover Roa perceived early on and with unusual clarity the problems of intepreting a 'Third World' culture and history through the distorting mirror of ideology and colonialism:

> The understanding of Paraguayan reality is particularly difficult even within that collection of 'anomalous' societies which make up Latin America and which, since their origins, have been subjected to uninterrupted colonialism and dependency. The formation of the Paraguayan nation has followed a very particular path in the historical context of a continent which has been distorted, pillaged and alienated in

the interests of the colonial domination which has weighed on it for centuries and which has only changed hands and methods....

The difficulty of a correct 'reading' of Paraguayan reality is increased by the enormous confusion produced by the fanciful interpretations of sociologists and historians both from home and abroad who have made of Paraguayan 'culturology' an activity that seems infected with somnambulism or delirium.

From such a standpoint, there is no view of that country which does not present this strange sensation of irreality. Nowhere offers, to the same extent as Paraguay in its endless vicissitudes, the features of a bitter fable whose most incredible images are, precisely, the events of its own history.[36]

This is an implicit critique, *avant la lettre*, of the excesses of Magical Realist or 'carnivalesque' exuberance, which were about to be redoubled as Roa's first novel was published. *Son of Man* is an attempt to resolve the contradictions in these perceptions of his underdeveloped country, from which he has been exiled since 1948, and specifically, somehow, to maintain a measure of optimism in its future whilst documenting the horrors of the past and the injustices of the present. This requires reconciling the contradiction of writing about the oppressed and illiterate masses in the very construction of his text. The protagonist is a petty-bourgeois intellectual, Miguel Vera, who leaves Itapé as a boy to become a soldier and is thus alienated from his own environment and country people as a whole. Of all the important novelists of the past half century, Roa is the one who has most insistently built the experience of exile into his fiction:

I am nothing more than a writer of fiction in exile; and as we all know, expatriation, uprooting, are not the best school for observing with 'objectivity' the environment from which one is physically absent....

I began to write impelled irresistibly by that 'incessant clamour' which resounded deep inside me like an imposition of my bad conscience or false consciousness: that of the deserter, the fugitive.[37]

By the end of the novel Vera has reneged on the army and allied himself with the peasant rebels, but his moral weakness and hesitation bring them only disaster. In an epilogue to the novel after Vera has committed suicide a woman doctor comments on his life:

I believe that he was... an exalted being, full of lucidity but completely incapable of action. Despite having been born in the country, he had neither the level head of the peasant, nor his blood, nor his sensibility, nor his capacity to resist physical and mental pain. He was unable to orientate himself in anything, not even within the 'permitted aspirations'. He could lose himself even when he was on the road.... He was horrified by suffering, but was unable to free himself from it. He escaped therefore into desperation, into symbols.[38]

The main line of socialist criticism since the Russian Revolution, passing through Zdhanov and Lukács, has viewed the labyrinthine excursions of Modernist writing as, at best, petty-bourgeois escapism, and at worst sheer irresponsibility, cowardice or reaction. Roa's essential posture in *Son of Man* brings to mind the Third Worldist ideology of a Fanon, and indeed recalls the comments made by Fidel Castro in 1971 when the relation between writers and society in post-revolutionary Cuba came to its definitive crisis, with implications for the whole of Latin America. At the National Congress on Education and Culture in April, Castro rounded furiously on those 'boom' writers – his erstwhile supporters – who had dared to criticize the regime's arrest of the dissident poet Heberto Padilla:

> Why should I even refer to that garbage? Why should we elevate to the category of problems of this country problems which are not the problems of this country? Why, my dear bourgeois liberal gentlemen? Can you not feel and touch the opinions expressed by millions of students, millions of families, millions of professors and teachers, who know only too well what are their true and fundamental problems?[39]

Roa has confessed that Latin American reality is so stark, and his separation from it so painful, that in *Son of Man* he was forced to see events in simple terms (the almost impenetrable *I the Supreme* is, in this sense at least, the polar opposite):

> I sensed that in *Son of Man* the splitting of the narrative consciousness between Miguel Vera – as the guiding thread of the narrative more than as an excluded witness – and the mass character, or the characters who represent the mass of the oppressed, 'crucified as they wait for a time without destiny', represented the opposition between two worlds: the world of men, animals and things connected to nature, and the artificial, degraded, debased world corresponding to that false culture which engenders violence and ridicule against the anonymous mass of the martyred and the oppressed.[40]

Vera thus represents the classic middle-class intellectual, whose own personal crisis, brought on precisely by his alienation from his society, is projected outwards and identified with the human condition as a whole. Castro's comments to the National Congress on Education and Culture were re-echoed in the final declaration, which represented a brutal condemnation of the 'boom' writers and the moral direction of the New Novel as a whole, and again the similarity to Roa's views is almost complete (which is not of course to say that, faced with the need to act, Roa would take the same line as the Cubans):

We condemn those false Latin American writers who after initial successes gained with works which still expressed the drama of our peoples, broke their links with their countries of origin and took refuge in the capitals of the corrupt and decadent societies of Western Europe and the United States to become agents of imperialist metropolitan culture.

In Paris, London, Rome, West Berlin and New York, these pharisees find the best field for their ambiguities, vacillations and miseries generated by the cultural colonialism which they have accepted and profess. Among the revolutionary peoples they will find nothing but the contempt which traitors and turncoats deserve....

We reject the pretensions of this mafia of pseudo-leftist bourgeois intellectuals to turn themselves into the critical conscience of society. The critical conscience of society resides in the people themselves.[41]

By dramatizing these problems in the novel, Roa, as he is only too well aware, can have his own moral crisis and assuage it through the narrative's inbuilt criticism of the separation between intellectuals and people. The lives of the people in the story are literally ravaged by the effects of oppression, state violence, revolution and war, and Roa's writing returns obsessively to classic Latin American motifs of trauma, illegitimacy and violation. In the third of the novel's nine parts, the adolescent Vera is about to leave his small hometown and his erstwhile friends to become a cadet:

All morning I was struggling to get the boots on to my feet, roughened by knocks and chases, torn by the thorns in the bush, the roots on the river bed, in all that time of wanderings and liberty which was now coming to an end, as all things come to an end, without me knowing as yet whether to be glad or sorry.[42]

Once donned, the military boots separate Vera from his fellows: 'Our two shadows grew smaller in the midday sun, until they disappeared beneath our feet, his bare, mine wrapped in field boots.'[43]

Roa shows us that the petty-bourgeois mentality deliberately, if only half-consciously, confuses epistemological difficulties with ethical ones. Since reality itself and human memory are already labyrinthine, this confusion makes concepts of truth and sincerity more than problematical. The novel begins with a representative of the folk memory, Macario, who was the best part of a century old when Vera was a child: 'He was lonely, blind, his memory gone, and he was treated with indifference, which is the worst form of neglect. I remember him well at that time. A handful of dust thrown by a child was enough to blot him out.'[44] Macario's stories fascinated the children in earlier days: '[Macario told the story] changing it slightly each time. He superimposed facts, changed the names, dates and places, as perhaps I am doing today without realizing it, because my own uncertainty is even greater than that of the silly old fool, who was at least pure.'[45] Vera therefore doubts not only his perceptual ability to know or remember anything, but his moral capacity to do so:

> I was just a boy then. My testimony can only be half useful. Even now, as I write down these memories, I feel that the innocence, the wonder of my childhood is mixed in with my betrayals and omissions as a man, the repeated deaths of my life. I am not reliving these memories; perhaps I am expiating them.[46]

Later in the story Vera expresses Roa's more general unease about the very basis of narrative fiction: 'I knew the story; well, the poor bare part that can be known of a story one has not lived through oneself.'[47]

Everything in life then is in doubt except that fundamental resistance of the human will exemplified in peasant characters such as old Macario the story-teller, the carver Gaspar Mora who contracts leprosy, exiles himself and becomes identified with Christ by the people, Casiano and Natividad Jara, whose tragic story of suffering and oppression is actually an everyday experience in Latin America, Crisanto Villalba, the Chaco veteran who blows himself and his abandoned shack to pieces, and the heroic peasant leader Cristóbal Jara, the novel's closest equivalent to Rendón Willka. Their stories, which of course evoke the horrors of Paraguayan history itself, above all the War of the Triple Alliance against Brazil, Argentina and Uruguay (1865–70), in which three-quarters of the male population was lost, recall nothing else in fiction as much as the documentary narrative of Euclides da Cunha relating the appalling massacre at Canudos. Unlike the intellectuals, contemplating the 'ecstasy of the privileged navel', the peasants

> care only for the future. They feel themselves live in events. They feel themselves united in the passion of the moment that projects them outside of themselves, linking them to a true or illusory cause, but to something... There is no other life for them. Death does not exist. Thinking about it is what corrodes and kills. They simply live.[48]

It is in the character of Cristóbal Jara, the peasant revolutionary who becomes a war hero, that these characteristics reach an almost Maoist coincidence of theory and practice, as he drives a water truck through enemy lines to reach the desperate Paraguayan troops at the front:

> What could destiny be for a man like Cristóbal Jara, but to drive his obsession like a slave through a narrow trail in the jungle or across the infinite plains, filled with the savage smell of liberty. To force a path open through the inexorable undergrowth of facts, leaving his flesh in it perhaps, but transforming them also with the element of that will whose strength grew precisely as it integrated with them. What men cannot do, no one else can do.[49]

Jara's death (he is killed in error by a deranged and delirious Vera, subject to another literary hallucination) reveals to us the meaning of the kind of sacrifice which Rendón Willka made in '*Everyone's Blood*' and which, inexplicable though it may have been to some European intellectuals, Che Guevara made in Bolivia, with the same Christ-like associations which recur so frequently in Latin American history. It was for this reason that Roa advocated a form of literature which he himself might not be able to write, a literature which could be made as the guerrillas then in action in Latin America were making the revolution:

> Literary activity once again means the necessity of embodying a destiny, the will to inscribe oneself in the vital reality of a collectivity in its true moral environment and social structure, in the complex system of relationships of contemporary reality, that is to say, projecting itself towards the universal world of man.... We feel the need to make a literature that is not just literature, to speak against language, to write against writing: a literature, in short, which, through a wide range of nuances and possibilities expresses the world of the personal identity of its authors in consonance with the identity of the real context to which they belong.[50]

Clearly this was a call for an epic narrative rather than the alienated fiction so familiar in the West since Romanticism. Roa's posture is suspicious of the petty-bourgeois consciousness, of literature as an institution, and of language itself. Irremediably, words separate the intellectual from the worker and the peasant. Words, indeed, on this view – effectively an extension of what Oscar Lewis called the 'culture of poverty' and Glauber Rocha called the 'art of hunger' – can create false worlds, or empty worlds, which comes to the same thing. Possibly the best expression of the possible falseness of words is Vera's reaction when he hears the story of Casiano Jara's epic struggle to push the abandoned railway carriage which is his only home across the Paraguayan desert:

> Suddenly I felt hollow. Was my breast not also an empty wagon which I was carrying, full only with the sound of the dream of a battle? Irritated with myself, I rejected this sentimental thought, worthy of a spinster. Always the same duality of cynicism and immaturity alternating in the most insignificant acts of my life! And that love of big words! Reality was always much more eloquent![51]

In short – is this demagoguery or plain speaking? – the empty heart of a more or less privileged individual is of little consequence in comparison with the empty stomach of another person, or millions of other persons. The reader is lured into involuntary identification with Miguel Vera throughout the novel. He too feels cheated by the conduct of the lieutenant, all the more so when he realizes he has fallen into a trap carefully prepared by Roa, who as the novel ends is pointing an accusing finger. If Vera and Roa are 'traitors' and 'hypocrites', what of us, his readers?

What Roa asserts is that the concrete experience and beliefs of the people should be the first, if not the last concern of the Latin American novelist. Thus although Roa himself does not share the messianic Christianity of his desperate peasant characters, he presents it with respect and indeed underlines its socio-economic content. In this regard, as Roa himself modestly pointed out, he anticipated the development of Liberation Theology and the Church militant which was to be such a force in Latin America in the coming years:

> The collective rebellion [in *Son of Man*], mythical and real at one and the same time, existent and imaginary, not only questioned the meaning of a crushing and inhuman social situation, but also confronted the reactionary power of the official church, as one of the pillars of this regime of oppression and violence. It thus turned out, on this plane, to be a premonitory presentation of the transformation that was to take place ten years later, in the insurgence of the progressive post-conciliary currents which are taking part today – especially through the movement of the Third World clergy – in the struggle for social justice and the political and economic liberation of our peoples.[52]

Both Arguedas and Roa Bastos were classed as 'regionalist' writers at this time, but their work takes us to the very limits of such a denomination. Both emerged from that tradition, but Arguedas's earlier *Deep Rivers* was in many respects a 'proto-Ulyssean' novel (a portrait of the anthropologist as a young man), as we shall see, and Roa's *Son of Man* was already experimenting with alternating narrators (first and third person), and showing an understanding of the nature of myth as shaped by and shaper of consciousness, memory and legend which was quite different from that of a Güiraldes or a Gallegos. Together with his conviction of the inadequacies of language for communication, this understanding took him to the very edge of the labyrinthine consciousness which we shall be exploring in chapters 5 to 7. As the 'boom' of the 1960s washed over his moving fictional testimony and made even its relatively dialectical approach seem unsophisticated by raising the question of language, myth and consciousness on the Joycean model, Roa was himself developing a new narrative mode. Nevertheless he was to choose a very different route: his suspicion of language and memory was of a qualitatively different kind from that of a writer like Borges (see chapter 5), and places them light years apart in different ideological universes.

Roa's insistence in *Son of Man* on his own kind of degree-zero writing – the writing of hunger – makes his work the logical culmination of a Marxist, and hence internationalist focus, which had been developing from Icaza's vulgar and Arguedas's dialectical 'Old Left' perspectives to the kind of Third

Worldist 'New Left' vision we glimpse in *Son of Man* itself. How Roa, in the age of both the Cuban Revolution and the New Novel, resolved the contradictions involved will be seen below, when we come to *I the Supreme* (chapter 8). Suffice to say for the present that he responded in the most unexpected fashion by dialectically negating the 'boom' – with *I the Supreme* – just as he had negated Social Realism and 1930s alienation with *Son of Man*.

4

Dead Ends: Cities and Prisons

The next day in the morning we came to the broad causeway that leads to Ixtapalapa. And seeing so many peopled cities and villages standing in the water, and other great towns on dry land, and that mighty road leading straight and flat to Mexico, we wondered greatly, and said that it was like the magic tales they tell in the book about Amadis, on account of the towers and pyramids and other buildings in the water, all of brick and mortar, and some of our soldiers even asked whether they were really seeing it, or whether it was all a dream, and no one should be surprised that I write it here thus because there is much to think on't and I know not how to tell it: to see things never heard of, nor seen, nor even dreamed of, as we did.... I say again that I looked at it, and I thought that nowhere else in the world could other lands like these be discovered, because at that time there was no Peru nor news of it. Now all is cast to the ground, lost, none of it is still standing.

Bernal Díaz, *True History of the Conquest of New Spain*, 1568

Between 1850 and 1930 the population of Latin America as a whole grew from 30 to 104 million, proportionally more than that of any other region save the United States.[1] From about the 1870s on, the frontier began to advance again for the first time in a century, and internal migration began from the sierras to the coastlands and in particular to the regions which were being newly developed through international trade. The global increases were due not only to internal demographic growth but to heavy immigration into some countries: 4 million into Argentina between 1870 and1930 (equal to an astonishing one-third of the 1930 population), 2 million into Brazil, and 600,000 into both Cuba and Uruguay, in the latter case out of a population in 1930 of only 1.6 million. Needless to say, the cities had to absorb most of the population growth, expanding with astonishing rapidity over the course of the present century and transforming themselves from 'bourgeois' into 'mass' conurbations.[2] As the population of the subcontinent doubled during the second half of the nineteenth century a number of large cities had developed: more than a million in Buenos Aires, three-quarters of a million in Rio and half a million in Mexico City, although there were still only six other cities in the whole of Latin America with more than 100,000 inhabitants in 1900. Since then expansion has been vertiginous. To take just two examples at random: Lima, which had 130,000 inhabitants in 1900, had 330,000 by 1930, 1.8 million in 1960 and has nearly 6 million today; whilst Mexico City's half million had expanded to 1.5 million by 1945, 4 million by 1970 and may be as high as 17 million today.

The dialectic between country and city in Western history can be reduced to no easy patterns or formulae. No society has ever been free to choose between these two political and economic alternative realities nor between the different lifestyles which they have determined – although artists and intellectuals have often liked to imagine that they could – because only in the historical relation between the two milieux can social meaning exist.[3] That relation of course is one of power, which is why ruling classes have always had both country estates and urban mansions. Needless to say, in the colonial or neocolonial setting the relation between city and country, like all other economic relations, looks much more simple, even brutally simple, but is actually much more complex – it is, indeed, labyrinthine. The process which a city like London underwent in the nineteenth century in a society far better able to control the conditions of its own expansion was a relatively comfortable affair compared with the experience of, say, São Paulo in the last one hundred years. If one imagines Fabiano's family in *Barren Lives* turning up in São Paulo around 1938, the characters of Arguedas's novels flooding into Lima in the 1960s, or the children of Roa Bastos's peasant characters forced to emigrate from Paraguay to Buenos Aires in search of work in the 1970s, one can see that the Latin American city in this era replicates within itself the tension between city and country which characterizes each nation as a whole, and this in turn reflects, in the most variable ways, the relation between 'Europe' (including the United States) and Latin America as a whole within the international division of labour. Conceived in this way, and bearing in mind the history of 'forking paths' outlined in the first chapter, it is understandable that the labyrinth – the curtailment of vision, the closing down of horizon – should have come to seem an invaluable structural metaphor for Latin America's temporal, spatial and cultural experience, and it is not surprising that Borges and his Americanist adversaries have been implicitly struggling over its meaning since the 1920s.

Writers from Latin American urban backgrounds were from the start aware of the provincial and possibly caricatural status of their own neocolonial and dependent cities compared to the world's great metropoli past and present: parasitic enclaves, comprador corridors between city and country, the nontranscendence of life in them seemed somehow even more stark than in European cities, whose existence was justified both functionally and literally by the whole weight and authority of European history, however alienating urban life as such might seem to be to any given observer. Moreover, in a certain sense those Latin American cities hardly existed: they were unknown to the rest of the world and they had not been given an identity or historical physiognomy by Latin American literature.

In the early 1960s Alejo Carpentier, in a celebrated article, declared that Latin American artists had a duty to do for their cities what Balzac had done for Paris, Dickens for London, and Joyce for Dublin, but noted that his fellow Americans had an especially difficult problem, since not only were their readers unaware of the context of any literary re-creation but these were in any case cities 'without style' or, perhaps, with 'a third style, the style of things that have no style'.[4] At the very time that he was writing, around 1960, the novel of urban settings was indeed finally beginning to predominate, as it may be expected increasingly to do. Novelists like Cortázar, Fuentes, Vargas Llosa and Puig are unmistakably 'urban' in background and orientation, but even Cortázar's *Hopscotch* (1963) actually 'barbarizes' Buenos Aires in comparison with Paris, as we shall see, and both Fuentes's *The Death of Artemio Cruz* (1962) and Vargas Llosa's *The Green House* (1966) are novels in which the rural setting is at least as important as the urban one. In short, it is the contrast, the relationship between them which continues to be perceived as important, partly because the cities themselves are so often viewed as ugly or alienating, and partly because the relationship, as mentioned above, is an inverse metaphor for the wider relation between Latin America and the developed world. (In chapter 8 I examine some of the novels which have been devoted, not always successfully, to celebrating Latin American cities on the lines proposed by Carpentier.) Given what has been said about the subcontinent's involuntary role in the Western myth, it is clear that Latin America may be destined always to be 'country' to Europe's 'city', and that, given its landscapes and state of development, the novels of the land may continue to be important for a very long time.

It is also true that although Hispanic culture has for many centuries been urban and highly centralized in orientation, the idea of city life has generally assumed very negative characteristics. The city is not so much the site in which knowledge and experience are concentrated or the arena in which interests compete, as the garrison from which the country and the natural world in general are dominated, constrained and defined. One of the more positive things to be said about the British and Anglo-American cultural tradition at home (colonies are another matter) is the absence of what one might call prison literature. Nor, come to that, is the image of the monk or nun writing from his or her cell one which comes to mind when thinking of our literary history. Quite the opposite is the case with Hispanic culture, due to the twin traditions of absolutism and Catholicism. Oppression, inquisition, imprisonment, torture, execution or exile have been historical constants and a feature of most of the literatures written in Spanish or Portuguese. This applies on many symbolic levels as well, down to the chastity belt imposed upon the wife and the bars on the window of what Spaniards have rarely called home. Moreover, to the traditional Hispanic mentality, the body itself is a prison in which the soul (or heart, or mind) is imprisoned, while life itself, as Calderón told us, and as fictional characters in books from *Don Quixote* to *One Hundred Years of Solitude* have lived it, is a dream – or, for all too many of them, a nightmare.

> I merely dream that I lie here
> locked in this prison cell,
> but have also dreamed of another time
> when fate treated me right well.
> What then is life, but a fiction,
> a shadow, an illusion, naught else,
> and the greatest good is as nothing,
> for all of life is but a dream,
> and likewise dreams themselves.[5]

When the lugubrious Philip II built his great castle in Spain it took on the sombre shape and appearance of a vast prison. The military, civil guards, rural militia and secret police have played a role in Hispanic countries whose prominence would have seemed horrific in British society at most periods. It may be that this is why 'dictator', 'liberator' and 'liberal' seem to have peculiarly Spanish associations, and why guerrilla, pronunciamiento, caudillo, cacique and macho have entered the international lexicon.

Latin America's first writers were from among the European explorers, soldiers, priests and merchants who 'discovered' and conquered the continent in the late fourteenth and early fifteenth centuries. During the colonial period in Spanish America, urban life was concentrated above all in the two great viceregal cities of Mexico and Lima, with their main square (plaza de armas), garrison, government palace, cathedral and provision stores. Most of what literature was produced during that 'Baroque' period was produced by priests or nuns under the most constrained circumstances. Narrative fiction was prohibited, as were all works of the imagination about the native Indians. Not surprisingly, the writers best remembered are precisely those whose work appears to rebel against these conditions and to point the way to some different future. In Peru the Mestizo writer, the Inca Garcilaso de la Vega (1539–1616) recalled the execution of the last Inca emperor by the Spaniards in Cuzco:

> They brought the poor prince out on a mule with a rope around his neck and his hands tied, and a town crier in front proclaiming his death and the reason for it, that he was a tyrant and a traitor to the crown of his Catholic Majesty.... The Indians, seeing their Inca so close to death, felt such grief and pain that they began to murmur, cry out and wail, so that nothing else could be heard. The priests who were speaking to the Inca asked him to bid the Indians fall silent.... Then they cut off his head; a sentence and torment which he endured with the valour and greatness which the Incas and noble Indians have always shown when treated with any form of cruelty and inhumanity; as have occurred in our history of Florida, and in this one, and other wars the Spaniards have fought in Chile with the Araucanians, as many of the authors of those acts have recorded in verse, without mentioning many others done in Mexico and Peru by very distinguished Spaniards, some of whom I have known; but let us say no more lest we make our history odious.... Thus was the end of the Inca, legitimate heir to that empire by direct male line from the first Inca Manco Capac, as Father Blas Valera says, through more than five hundred, almost six hundred years. This was the general feeling in that land and the story told out of the compassion and pity of Indians and Spaniards. It may be that the viceroy had other reasons to justify his action. Once the sentence had been carried out on the good prince, his children and other relatives were exiled to the city of the Kings, and the Mestizos to various parts of the New World and the Old... God be praised for all.[6]

The Mexican Creole nun Sister Juana Inés de la Cruz (1648–95), recently studied in Octavio Paz's remarkable biography,[7] wrote numerous poems which provide excellent examples of the power of the prison metaphor over even the most abstract ideas:

> Stop, shadow of my elusive good,
> image of the enchantment I most adore,
> fond illusion for which I would happily die,
> sweet fiction I live so painfully for.
>
> If my heart serves as obedient steel
> to the magnetic attraction of your charms,
> why do you make me love you through flattery,
> if then you deceive me and flee my arms?
>
> But you cannot boast in satisfaction
> that your tyranny has triumphed over me;
> for even if you slip free from those tight bonds
>
> that entrapped your fantastic form,
> there is little good in eluding arms and breast
> if my fantasy builds you a prison around.[8]

Mexico City and Lima continued to be centres of literary activity in the nineteenth century, but in the South Buenos Aires and Rio de Janeiro began their rise to preeminence. In Mexico City *The Itching Parrot* (*El periquillo sarniento*, 1815), a belated picaresque work by Fernández de Lizardi (1776–1827), was the first true novel to be produced and published in the continent, set in an urban context, with a satirical view of what was still a colonial society. In Brazil the first important fictional narrative was the surprisingly realistic *Memoirs of a Militia Sergeant* (1853) by Manuel Antônio de Almeida (1831–61). In Lima later in the century Ricardo Palma (1833–1919) produced a stream of humorous satirical stories, the *tradiciones*, about life in the city during the colonial period, with the usual Hispanic emphasis on soldiers and lawyers, monks and nuns, capes and swords, adultery and duels.

Novels about the city on the lines of Balzac and Dickens did not emerge until very late in the century, by which time Zola held sway, though few of his imitators at that time had his mastery of detail or understanding of social motivation. Latin American capitals were very small and largely provincial in character until well into the twentieth century. A notable exception to the general picture was Brazil, where in the period preceding and following the abolition of slavery and the declaration of the Republic in 1888 and 1889, the mulatto writer Joaquim Maria Machado de Assis (1839–1908) became Latin America's only truly great novelist in the century after Independence and one of the masters of the genre in the Western world. The secret of his achievement lay in finding a humorous, parodic, iconoclastic form with which to negotiate the difficulties of living in a semicolonial city, long before the similar responses of a Borges or a Naipaul. The conclusion of The *Epitaph of a Small Winner* (*Memórias póstumas de Brás Cubas*, 1880), supposedly written from beyond the grave by a narrator long since dead, gives the flavour well enough:

> This last chapter consists wholly of negatives. I did not achieve celebrity, I did not become a minister of state, I did not really become a caliph, I did not marry. At the same time, however, I had the good fortune of not having to earn my bread by the sweat of my brow. Moreover, I did not suffer a death like Dona Plácida's nor did I lose my mind like Quincas Borba. Adding up and balancing all these items, a person will conclude that my accounts showed neither a surplus nor a deficit and consequently that I died quits with life. And he will conclude falsely; for, upon arriving on this other side of the mystery, I found that I had a small surplus, which provides the final negative of this chapter of negatives: I had no progeny, I transmitted to no one the legacy of our misery.[9]

No Spanish American novelist of the nineteenth century comes close to Machado's mastery of the subtleties of the genre, which has done so much to mould fiction in Brazil since that time. In Argentina the novel *Amalia* (1851) by José Mármol (1817–71) had been the first to evoke post-colonial Buenos Aires, but unfortunately it was a Buenos Aires suffused with the terrifying atmosphere of the dictator Rosas's police state. A much more benign view appeared later in *'The Great Village'* (*La gran aldea*, 1884) by Lucio Vicente López (1848–94), an ironic and wistful title in retrospect and a last literary look at a city which by the time of the First World War was one of the world's largest metropoli, the 'Goliath's Head' of Argentina, and one of the great poles of Latin American culture. That title itself suggested the dynamic movement between city and country, a relation already dramatically emphasized in Sarmiento's *Facundo* and later in Da Cunha's *Revolt in the Backlands* and re-examined in a whole series of Latin America's most representative novels down to the present day.

In 1885, not long after *'The Great Village'*, another Argentine, Eugenio Cambaceres (1843–88), produced *'Going Nowhere'* (or *'Aimless'* – *Sin rumbo*), a heady mix of decadent Romanticism and Schopenhauerian Naturalism which, in its raw brutality, became a prototype for narratives both about the predicament of the anguished neocolonial intellectual and the imposition of urban consciousness upon rural life. Andrés, the protagonist, is a wealthy landowner who lives part of the year on his large estancia and part in Buenos Aires. He also travels to Paris as often as he can. He is a nihilist, who uses sex and violence to fill his existential void. The description of the view from his French-style house, standing on an estate in the midst of the wilderness, is particularly revealing:

> From above, you had a clear view all around: in front the living vault of a street of holy-trees opening out into a broad semicircle of conifers around the house; behind, towards the other buildings of the estancia, a patio shaded by vines, and, on either side, beyond fields of peaches and willows crossed by long lines of poplars, you could see the infinite tableland of the pampa, green reflection of the blue sky, unprotected, alone, naked, splendid, taking its beauty, like a woman, from its very nakedness.[10]

In a century of nation-builders Cambaceres's sense of futility, solitude and isolation was the truer guide to the literary future viewed from the big cities. Andrés's obsession is to strip away the false clothing of bourgeois culture, ornament and rhetoric to reveal the emptiness beneath, dramatized in his repeated seductions of the women – a local Indian girl whom he effectively rapes, and an Italian opera singer who becomes his mistress – who provide the keys to his psychological and philosophical development, as in so much other Latin American fiction. His only fleeting hope in life comes when an illegitimate daughter is born to the wretched Indian girl, but she dies in childhood, whereupon he disembowels himself with a cross-shaped gash as his estancia blazes in Wagnerian climax.

Needless to say, there is nothing democratic in Andrés's perspective on his fellow man (still less his fellow woman), but his insistence on criticizing his own society from a lofty and indeed unreal vantage point which implicitly identifies him with European 'civilization' and its imperialist ambitions, is representative of many intellectuals and artists over the following century, not least in Argentina itself. '*Going Nowhere*' may be the continent's first important work on a theme which sooner or later, over the next half century, would become important in most Latin American countries, as in the southern United States, namely the decline of the old plantations and haciendas, the relative liberation of the slaves and peons, and the historical redundancy of the old landowning oligarchies, with their pseudo-aristocratic airs and paternalistic but ruthless ways of relating to their fellows. Rulfo's *Pedro Páramo* (1955) is perhaps the best known expression of the theme, but there are vestiges of it even in the works of García Márquez. Cambaceres's novel is typical of the era which it opens in ascribing psychological and philosophical anguish to idealist causes rather than to historical motivations, but again the labyrinthine realities of being no one (a non-European) and living nowhere (in Latin America), adds a particularly acute slant to such familiar *fin-de-siècle* pessimism. Güiraldes's *Don Segundo Sombra* would later give a classic, if mystificatory version of this syndrome.

In Brazil one of the first protest novels about city life and its injustices was '*The Sad End of Policarpo Quaresma*' (*Triste fim de Policarpo Quaresma*, 1915) by Afonso Henriques de Lima Barreto (1881–1922), another mulatto who was in some sense the successor to Machado de Assis, though he never attained Machado's social respectability. In 1917 the Chilean Eduardo Barrios (1884–1963) followed their example with another novel of urban alienation and despair, '*A Loser*' (*Un perdido*), in which the hopeless protagonist fails to find any meaning or satisfaction in life. In the 1920s the Argentinian novelist Roberto Arlt (1900–42), now belatedly considered one of the most important writers of the continent, gave an early indication of the extent to which Latin American fiction, particularly in Buenos Aires and Montevideo, would be able to pick up on European currents of nihilism and absurdism. As we have seen, this was precisely because for writers or protagonists with a European mentality and European nostalgias – which was almost impossible to avoid, especially as few nation-builders write novels (there are exceptions, like Mitre, Gallegos, Ramírez and Sarney) – Latin America was either nothing, nowhere, a caricature, or all three. Transcendence was difficult to find in these post-colonial, neocolonial cities. It is not surprising that Camus's philosophy came from colonial Oran: *The Outsider* is not a world away from '*The Metaphysical Disease*' (*El mal metafísico*, 1916) by Manuel Gálvez (Argentina, 1882–1962), '*The Pit*'

(1939, see below p.112) by Onetti, or Arlt's remarkable sequence of urban nightmares, 'The Rabid Toy' (El juguete rabioso, 1926), Seven Madmen (Los siete locos, 1929) or 'The Flamethrowers' (Los lanzallamas, 1931). At any rate, Arlt's city-based fiction, like that of the rural Quiroga before him, situated reality somewhere between alienation, madness, depravity and criminality, with neither the author nor the characters able to distinguish satisfactorily between these elements of the existential analysis. In a world without fulfilment, in which the bourgeoisie's official ideology of honour, hard work and decency is contradicted everywhere by reality, the only way of asserting or elevating oneself is through crime or madness. This Dostoyevskian tradition hails from Cambaceres in the River Plate region, and goes on through Onetti, Marechal, Sábato and many others. Ironically enough, Arlt was for a time Ricardo Güiraldes's secretary, a fitting conjunction in a sense, for it was Güiraldes whose Don Segundo Sombra bade a reluctant farewell to the gaucho era, and indeed to literary interest in the rural sector as a whole, whilst Arlt's novels signalled that in Argentina at least the age of urban fiction had definitively arrived.

In Peru Duque (1934) by José Diez-Canseco (1905–49) gave an equally sordid picture of social dissipation and existential despair amongst the upper classes. As we saw in the last chapter, the Brazilian Graciliano Ramos saw constraints and prisons everywhere, including his own provincial origins, recalled in Childhood (1945), and small-town life, as portrayed in Caetés (1933). In São Bernardo (1934) even an ignorant landowner is seen as imprisoned within his own cultural poverty, and Barren Lives applied the same perception to the retirantes of the backlands. It is in Anguish (Angústia, 1936), however, that Ramos applies the vision to the urban setting, continuing the tradition of the novels already mentioned, with a peculiarly hopeless slant:

> I got up about thirty days ago, but I don't think I've fully recovered yet. Some of the visions which haunted me through those long nights still remain, shadows which merge with reality and make me tremble.
>
> There are people I can't abide. Beggars, for example. They seem to have all grown bigger. Each time they approach I'm afraid that instead of whining and pleading they'll shout, make demands, take things off me...
>
> If I could, I'd give it all up and go back to my travels. This monotonous existence, tied to a bench from nine to twelve and two to five is just stupid. A snail's life... I go back to thinking about my corpse, withered, teeth bared, eyes like two skinless cherries, cigarette-blackened fingers folded across my sunken chest. [11]

Looking back at the 1930s, most literary historians agree that if Ciro Alegría was the last of the old-style 'regionalist' authors, or Novelists of the Land, the Uruguayan Juan Carlos Onetti (1909–) was the first and perhaps the most important of a new generation of urban novelists. His first book, 'The Pit' (El pozo), was published in 1939, and demonstrates that novelists living in Montevideo or Buenos Aires had no need to wait for Céline, Sartre or Camus to discover that they were alienated, anguished or both. Onetti's fiction picks up where Arlt left off, although Onetti always achieves the necessary distance from his materials to be able to impose the coherence of art on even the most contradictory reality. His novel tells the story of an anomic university-educated journalist, Eladio Linacero, who is frustrated but also mediocre, lives in a room like a prison cell with an ignorant Communist militant ironically called Lazarus, and vainly longs to become a writer. Like Cambaceres's Andrés and so many others, Linacero also has a series of self-revealing relationships with different women. These include an adolescent acquaintance, Ana María, whom he sexually assaulted, only to make her a life-long fantasy when she died (she comes in from the snow, naked, to visit him in his imaginary log cabin, whenever he calls), his wife Cecilia (less compliant and therefore less satisfying), the prostitute Ester and his latest mistress Hanka.

In a brief novel we note Linacero's inability to relate either to women or to the 'feminine' world in general through any agency other than hostility and violence, and his fixation on images of masculine domination despite an essential weakness and underlying insecurity in his personality. As in 'Going Nowhere', the theme of violation is fundamental, and is linked with the subject of virginity and the adolescent female. The Lolita syndrome undoubtedly takes on extra force through a curious combination of the Spanish social preoccupation with female honour and shame, the Latin American motifs of newness, natural spontaneity and primordiality, and the universal commodification of the raw and untouched through the process of exchange. This familiar complex of ideas and values leaves the male protagonists of numerous Latin American novels from The Vortex to Puig's The Kiss of the Spider Woman (1976) constantly cutting, penetrating and thus destroying everything they most desire, from their women to the natural landscape.[12] Typical of the contradiction is Eladio's weakness for the male-dominant images he sees in movies from North America, a culture he impotently affects to despise but which evidently castrates him psychologically. And beyond the appalling city which Montevideo has become, lies a Uruguay without history: 'Behind us, there is nothing: one gaucho, two gauchos, thirty-three gauchos.' The image is striking, and the more so if we reflect that these 'thirty-three gauchos' were the symbolic heroes of Uruguay's liberation struggle. We are very far from Gallegos and the other Americanists here. This is a continent with nothing worth writing about, beyond the writer's own anguish. The novel ends in existentialist despair:

This is the night. I am a solitary man smoking somewhere in the city; the night surrounds me, as in a ritual, gradually, and I have no part in it.... The extraordinary confessions of Eladio Linacero. I smile in peace, open my mouth, clash my teeth and gently bite the night. Everything is pointless and you should have the guts at least to avoid excuses. I would have liked to pin the night to my paper like a great moth. Instead, it has raised me in its waters like the livid body of a dead man and drags me, inexorably, through the cold foamy mist, downtime.

This is the night. I shall fall into bed, chilled, dead tired, trying to sleep before dawn comes, with no more strength to wait for the damp body of that girl in the old log cabin.[13]

Onetti gives perhaps the most persistently lucid expression to urban alienation in Latin American fiction, possibly because he is always more concerned to communicate a vision than to make a point. His later fiction elaborates a picture not only of city life (Montevideo, Buenos Aires and his invented 'Santa María') but also of reality and consciousness themselves as labyrinthine, a world of perceptions and motives impossible to disentangle and clarify, but always tending to weariness, boredom, frustration and defeat. Onetti's Faulknerian vision, which proclaims its Uruguayan specificity in the early works, gradually becomes more and more undifferentiated and indecipherable – in 'The Pit' the protagonist is in a labyrinth, but the reader and author are not – until it becomes a generalized and universal view of the world. This is a line of fiction particularly prevalent in the River Plate, where the Argentinian Eduardo Mallea (1903–82) gave it a rather portentous and burdensome philosophical slant from the 1930s to the 1950s, whilst the Uruguayan Mario Benedetti (1920–) concentrated more closely on the social and historical origins of that same grey, heavy despair during the 1960s and 1970s.

If the jungle had previously been a trap for urban dwellers, now the city, it seemed, had become a trap for all those who live in it, and particularly for those who migrate to it or are aware that their parents have only recently done so. As in other regions during the 1930s, Latin American novelists appeared to have the worst of both worlds: the country was primitive and barbarous, but the cities were meaningless and alienating: they blotted out the landscape and abolished optimism and hope. They were galleries without exits, dead ends. Even their most important inhabitants could find themselves caught in a maze of illusion, deceit and disenchantment. In the nineteenth century the country or interior had been a savage nowhere in which one could become lost or swallowed up (Sarmiento, Cambaceres, Da Cunha), whilst the tiny cities had represented nuclei of progress, the objective, the ideal or, in a word, the future; but cities soon concealed the horizon they once represented, and became the labyrinth they were once an escape from, and thus the city–country dialectic moved on. The Latin American dream died in the cities from the 1920s onwards, and as soon as this began to be assimilated the country became again what it had briefly been after the discovery and after Independence: natural, authentic, and above all productive, creative and fertile, the fount of true wealth and the connection to the cosmos, past, present and future. This required a new, more consciously mythological conception, that of what has come to be called Magical Realism (see chapter 5). By contrast, almost all novels about the cities written since that time, viewed from disenchantment, turned out to be 'memoirs of under-development', to translate the Spanish title of the Cuban Edmundo Desnoes's post-revolutionary novel from 1967.[14]

There can be little doubt of the novel which, in the period following the Second World War, confirmed the rise of urban fiction that had already been signalled in Argentina and Uruguay. Ironically enough, the work in question, *The President* (*El señor Presidente*, 1946) by Miguel Angel Asturias (1899–1974), was about a very small capital city, that of Guatemala, and it was set in the period of the First World War, before the process of Latin American modernization had become generally visible. The novel is studied in more detail in the next chapter, but we may pause to look at Asturias's presentation of the dictator's spy network as a labyrinth of horror,

> a monstrous forest that separated his Excellency the President from his enemies, a forest of trees with ears which at the slightest sound began to turn as though whipped up by a hurricane wind... A web of invisible threads, more invisible than the telegraph wires, linked each leaf to the President, alert to all that went on in the most secret fibres of his citizens.[15]

In this terrorist state, a distant Central American echo of Rosas's regime in Buenos Aires almost a century before, no one can escape the asphyxiating presence of the 'Father of the Fatherland'. Even the beggar Pelele, mute, deformed and deranged, finds himself trapped in a Buñuelian hallucination which is ultimately a projection of the collective nightmare:

> Half in reality, half in a dream, Pelele ran, pursued by dogs and the needles of a light fall of rain. He ran with no fixed aim, beside himself with terror, mouth open, tongue hanging, foaming, panting, arms outstretched. Doors and doors and doors and windows and doors and windows went by on either side of him... Suddenly he stopped, covering his face with his hands, defending himself against the telegraph poles, but when he saw they were harmless he cackled and went on, like someone escaping from a prison whose walls of mist stretch ever further the more he runs.[16]

At the other extreme from Guatemala City, back in Buenos Aires, Ernesto Sábato (1911–) produced in 1961 a novel, *On Heroes and Tombs* (*Sobre héroes y tumbas*) which, curiously enough, has been more admired outside than inside Latin America. Onetti's nauseated, exasperated mode had by then been widely influential in Argentina and Uruguay. Even Onetti, however, lacks the hysterical, hallucinatory edge to be found in Ernesto Sábato's fiction, notably *The Tunnel* (*El túnel*, 1948), *On Heroes and Tombs* and '*Abaddon the Exterminator*' (*Abaddón el exterminador*, 1974). If the first named puts us into Arltian territory, continuing the line of '*Going Nowhere*', '*A Loser*' and '*The Pit*', *On Heroes and Tombs* attempts a vision of Argentine history which is Dostoyevskyan in ambition, if not in realization, giving one of the most terrifying interpretations of the way in which the Argentine personality conceptualizes national reality and viewing the horrors and disappointments of the early national period as indissolubly connected to the neurotic, and sometimes insane social phenomena of Sábato's own lifetime as he perceives it. One does not have to share his interpretation in order to acknowledge how often such views have been dramatized in Argentine fiction. The work is at once a meditation on the condition of mankind in the twentieth century and on the development of Argentina from the time of Rosas to the time of Perón. A poor boy, Martín, neglected by his mother (who becomes a mythical 'mother–sewer' in his tormented mind), falls in love with Alejandra, a descendant of the nineteenth-century ruling aristocracy, whom he idealizes, little knowing that she has an incestuous relationship with her father, whom she eventually kills before burning herself to death in the family home. A harrowing story of criminal depravity, Sábato's novel views Buenos Aires through an intertext which links Homer, Dante, Freud and Sartre, on the one hand, with Arlt, Marechal, Borges and Cortázar on the other. Like Asturias's Guatemala, Sábato's Buenos Aires is home to nightmares:

As I went down I heard the sound of running water and knew I was approaching one of those underground channels forming a vast and labyrinthine network of sewers beneath the city... I thought of the people above, in gleaming salons, beautiful delicate women, with unctuously mannered bank managers and school teachers saying that no dirty words should be written on walls... whilst down below, in obscene and pestilent torrents, flowed the menstrual discharges of those romantic lovers, the excrements of those dreamy young ladies, the contraceptives used by those sober managers, the dead foetuses from thousands of abortions, the leftovers from millions of houses and restaurants, the immense, endless garbage of Buenos Aires.
And everything floated towards the Nothingness of the ocean through secret underground tunnels, as if Those Above were trying to forget, affecting to know nothing of this part of their truth. As if heroes in reverse, like me, were destined to the infernal and accursed task of bearing witness to that reality.[17]

Sábato attempts to end the novel on a somewhat anti-climactic note of optimism. History has justified its lack of conviction.[18]

Arlt, then, was perhaps the decisive moment in the turn from rural to urban fiction, and from his time fiction was gradually moving to the metropolitan realm away from the rural, though the latter continued to dominate until the late 1950s. As can be seen, however, given the contemporaneity of Arlt's major works, written in Latin America, and Asturias's *The President*, written in Paris, the process overlaps with the growth of the Modernist or 'Ulyssean' novel. Arlt's narrative, one might say, anticipating the terminology of our next chapter, is 'pre-Ulyssean', since it is written by the son of immigrants who does not himself have experience of the lost homeland. Asturias, by contrast, had travelled from Latin America to Europe and thus was able to metaphorize his own experience and function as a bridge between the modern world of Europe and the backward, traditional or rural world of Latin America. Needless to say, it was the 'boom' novelists who turned Latin American fiction decisively, indeed definitively, towards the urban realm at a time – the 1960s – when the great capitals of the continent were huge, contradictory and multiple metropoli of millions of people. And these great sprawling cities were much more heterogeneous, much more contradictory than had ever been the case in Europe, even with the 'guest workers' of the 1950s, 1960s and 1970s, and now contained a quite large and well-educated middle-class population ready at last to read fiction by their own writers.

Sábato's *On Heroes and Tombs*, although published in 1961, was really the last of the pre-'boom' urban narratives. For all his intensity of vision, Sábato's failing was in his rather wooden approach to language and technique. A new era was dawning, in which writers like Carlos Fuentes, who had already published *Where the Air is Clear* (*La región más transparente*, 1958), and Cortázar, with his dazzling surreal short stories and his novel *The Winners* (*Los premios*, 1960), would give urban fiction a sophisticated sheen which it had previously lacked. The new message, really, was the one Asturias had implicitly posited with the contrast between content and expression in *The President*: if the cities are physical and ideological prisons, perhaps they may at least be partly redeemed by language, imagination and new techniques. Thus conceptions elaborated to encompass the transformation of New York and other great cities in the 1920s and 1930s, at the onset of modernity, were reinvented for Mexico City, Lima and Buenos Aires in the 1960s and 1970s.

Carlos Fuentes adopted the literary conception of John Dos Passos to capture Mexico City in *Where the Air is Clear*, complete with panoramic montage and 'seeing eye'. The conclusion, involving yet another unspoken communion between Latin American intellectual and working-class personage, is characteristic of the new mode:

and on the Nonoalco bridge Gladys Garcia pauses, swift also within the dust, lights the night's last cigarette, tosses the match down towards the corrugated iron roofs and breathes in the great city's early morning, the somnolence of flesh, the smell of gasoline and alcohol and the voice of Ixca Cienfuegos, running, through the tumultuous silence of all those memories and the dust of the city, wanting to touch her fingers and tell her, just tell her: This is our place. What can we do. Here where the air is clear.[19]

However it was Mario Vargas Llosa, with *The Time of the Hero* (*La ciudad y los perros*, 1962) and, climactically, with *Conversation in the Cathedral* (*Conversación en la Catedral*, 1969), who most comprehensively painted the real face of the Latin American cities of the 1960s, with their penthouses and shanty towns, beggars and plutocrats, and the injustices, squalor and almost incredible contradictions which linked them together. The *Time of the Hero*, like *Where the Air is Clear*, sets out on the mission of the classic works of realism, both to criticize and to redeem, to expose the injustice of life in these great modern cities but somehow also to recuperate the hopes and dreams of their often desperate inhabitants. But as so often, realism lurched, disillusioned, into Naturalism, and in the hypnotic *Conversation in the Cathedral*, Lima is presented as a decaying labyrinth of vice and corruption, like the consciousness of the bourgeois intellectual protagonist, Santiago Zavala, and indeed like the novel itself, with a structure which makes the act of reading like journeying to the middle of a vast urban web hung with rotting corpses. The first page gives the flavour:

From the doorway of the *Crónica* Santiago looks down the Avenida Tacna, without love: cars, uneven and faded buildings, the skeletons of neon signs floating in the mist of a grey noon. At what precise moment had Peru fucked up? Newsboys prowl in and out among the vehicles stopped by the red light on Wilson shouting out the afternoon headlines and he sets off walking slowly towards the Colmena. Hands in pockets, head down, escorted by other people also making for Plaza San Martin. He was like Peru, Zavalita, he'd got fucked up at some moment. He thinks: when? Opposite the Hotel Crillón a dog comes up and licks his feet: might have rabies, get away. Peru fucked up, Carlitos fucked up, everyone fucked up. He thinks: there is no solution.[20]

A few pages later Santiago, drunk in a sordid bar, looks back over his privileged but futile life, and thinks of his dead father:

A whirlpool inside him, an effervescence in the heart of his heart, a sensation of suspended time and that smell. Are they talking? The juke-box stops pounding, pounds again. The thick river of smells seems to ramify into streams of tobacco, beer, human sweat and the remains of meals circulating warmly through the heavy air of 'The Cathedral', to be suddenly absorbed by an invincible higher pestilence: neither you nor I was right, Dad, it's the smell of defeat, Dad.[21]

Six hundred pages later, as the novel ends after an unceasing catalogue of sordid and violent events, passing frequently through brothels and prisons, the reader realizes that the author agrees with his character about 'Lima the horrible': there is no solution.[22]

As a matter of fact the major writers of the 'boom' era have been freer to speak their minds than any generation before or since them. In the 1920s and 1930s, and again in the 1970s and 1980s, innumerable Latin American writers have ended up behind bars, or disappeared completely. The Peruvian case was particularly persistent during that earlier period. Some of César Vallejo's revolutionary poems in *Trilce* were written in prison. Ciro Alegría was imprisoned under Sánchez Cerro in the 1930s, and ended up composing '*The Hungry Dogs*' in a Chilean sanatorium. Juan Seoane (1899–) was imprisoned between 1933 and 1935, falsely accused of trying to murder the same dictator, and recorded his experience in '*Men Behind Bars*' (*Hombres y rejas*, 1936). Serafín del Mar (Reynaldo Bolaños, 1901–), incarcerated at about the same time, responded with '*Sun, They are Destroying your Children*' (*Sol, están destruyendo a tus hijos*, 1943) and '*The Land is Man*' (*La tierra es el hombre*, 1943). Similar works included '*Prisons by the Sea*' (*Prisiones junto al mar*, 1943) by Armando Bazán (1902–62) and '*The Prison*' (*La prisión*, 1951) by Gustavo Valcárcel (1921–), set later, in the Odría period. José María Arguedas, in '*Prison Number Six*' (*El Sexto*, 1961), provided an unforgettable account of his time in the notorious Lima jail under the Benavides government. Mario Vargas Llosa was never imprisoned, but has taken a close interest in the theme, and prisons appear in several of his novels: indeed, in *Conversation in the Cathedral* Santiago Zavala has an overnight stay in gaol after a brief flirtation with Marxist politics at university.

The Peruvian experience was, however, echoed throughout the continent. Numerous writers ended up in prison during the Gómez dictatorship in Venezuela. Miguel Angel Asturias and others were briefly locked away following student unrest in the time of the dictator Estrada Cabrera (1898–1920), and the Guatemala in which he was born and the one to which he returned in 1933 are variably metaphorized in his works as totalitarian prisons, cemeteries or enveloping nightmares. Alejo Carpentier spent time in prison under the dictator Machado in the 1920s. Even Borges was threatened with prison by Perón, but was designated Inspector of Chickens and Rabbits instead. Pablo Neruda narrowly avoided capture and imprisonment in Chile in 1948 by fleeing into hiding and eventual exile. In Ecuador Alfredo Pareja Diezcanseco (1908–) wrote '*Men without Time*' (*Hombres sin tiempo*, 1941) to recreate life in the García Moreno Penitentiary where he had been imprisoned. In Brazil Graciliano Ramos, like Jorge Amado, was imprisoned by Getúlio Vargas and produced his two-volume autobiographical account,

Prison Memoirs (1953). José Revueltas (1914–76), Mexico's equivalent to Arlt, began and ended his narrative trajectory with prison novels, '*Walls of Water*' (*Los muros de agua*, 1941), written when he was a member of the Communist Party, and '*Lockup*' (*El apando*, 1969), during his incarceration following the Tlatelolco massacre which put an end to the 1968 student movement, of which Revueltas had been a spiritual leader. That even Mexico, where relations between writers and the state have generally been well managed – or manipulated – should go in for imprisoning novelists seemed to presage the horrors to come. After that things took a turn for the worse all over the subcontinent. We have not by any means yet seen the last literary results of the atrocious repression of the past twenty-five years, but already there is a long list of documentary, semi-fictional and fictionalized accounts from Brazil, Chile, Argentina, Uruguay and Central America, as will be seen in chapter 10.

In short, there have been a great many novels deploring city life and its repressive aspects, and very few indeed celebrating it as a liberation. The raw materials of virgin America, home of the fertile and the immanent, end not in Gallegos's city, perfect as a brain, but on a garbage dump, an ash heap, a world of exchange values where everything is bought and sold, where everything wears down, grey and illusory; or, worse still, where everything ends black and nightmarish: police van, cell, torture chamber, morgue, cemetery. It is a world of alienation, reification, consumption and exhaustion, compared to the cosmic fertilization and global significance of the indigenous world which preceded it, as celebrated in the works of numerous writers during the present century. Waiting at the end of this trail, we see, is the cosmic catastrophe which now confronts us all, most dramatically exemplified in the apparently suicidal trajectory of Brazil.[23]

Magical Realism

Material Realism

5

Into the Labyrinth:
Ulysses in America

Intimate friend of visions, Ulysses
journeyed back t'ward his destiny of mist,
as if returning to his own from other
countries. Yet his heart, salt kissed,

Ploughed through the diminutive seas
and the vast sea of oblivion through his desire,
caulking other loves within the great dry dock
of the thirst he bore. Thirst, magnet, fiery

Needle falling seasick midst Sirens
and chimeras, that route, long anticipated
by his flesh and soul now made foreign;

His wife was waiting, they are happy we learn
in legend, though not life for, belated,
he went back but he never returned.

Miguel Angel Asturias, 'Ulysses', 1928

Looking outside the cities at the novels in chapters 2 and 3, we can briefly reconsider the question of denomination. Certainly they all considered the land problem in this great empty continent, and go well beyond the Romantic obsession with mere landscape or mere spirituality, but the concepts – once so popular – of 'Novel of the Land' or 'telluric novel' seem ever more inadequate, especially when the key point in every one of them is to define the relation between the inhabitants of the different countries and the natural and social world which they inhabit. Equally, 'regionalist novel' is imprecise and perhaps even misleading. These are not novels which advance little local nationalisms, merely works set in scenarios in the interior, hinterland or backlands as against the cities or abroad. Most of the writers, indeed, if not born in their capital cities, had long since resided in them, though of the major 1920s writers only Güiraldes had lived outside Latin America.

In a sense, then, one might advance the hypothesis that such works were 'regional' not in the sense that they were 'sub-national' but precisely because, from this moment, 'America' (meaning Latin America) was conceived as one large though not yet integrated nation made up of numerous 'regions' (the twenty republics). There is much textual evidence that this was so.[1] In other words, it is not so much a regionalist spirit as a nationalist and Americanist impulse which informs the novels of Latin America's first important narrative moment, integrating the country and the city within one nationhood and linking each of these, sometimes explicitly but more usually implicitly, within an Americanist supra-nationhood or continental vision. Clearly this is not the same as identifying Latin America's place within world culture, a process which the Modernists tentatively initiated, albeit on unequal and semi-colonial terms. This latter, definitive literary–historical achievement – one which ends an entire literary epoch – began at the same time as the novels studied thus far were being written, but was undertaken by a different kind of writer and only completed in the 1960s and early 1970s.

If one accepts, then, that regionalism and Americanism are two sides of exactly the same impulse, one also sees that the concept 'Novel of the Land' was actually a symbolic designation: 'the land' is not so much the telluric earth as the American continent itself as a field of endeavour and object of reflection. Perceiving this, and seeing individual works oscillating within the semantic field marked out by these two poles – region and continent – as part of a shared vision, we can then also appreciate that the capital cities depicted in the novels studied in chapter 4 are not usually conceived as capitals of that regional, American interior. On the contrary, they are enclaves of European civilization, Trojan horses, either treacherously conspiring or weakly collaborating in the exploitation of natural raw (including human) materials, or with their backs turned on the regions – like Lima, Rio and Buenos Aires – and gazing out longingly over that ocean that leads back to Europe, a Europe ironically and unbearably infinitely more alluring than the one their forebears left behind to travel to America in the first place. Of course the more positive statement of this position is that cosmopolitanism is an inevitable reaching out to the world, a natural wish to integrate Latin America into the universal (read Western) order of things, to take its place among the cultures, recognizing and being recognized. However the same cosmopolitanism that is counted a virtue if America is seen as constricting or provincial, becomes neocolonialism, betrayal, collaborationism, the ideological assertion of an alien civilization against a barbarism actually willed, preserved, maintained, as a justification for whatever policies are required for the imposition of capitalism on these plantation and mining economies.

What is posed in each of the regionalist works, completing the debate initiated by Sarmiento and Da Cunha, is the national question. Are these strangely shaped territorial entities really nations? And if so, what sort of community is a nation? How do regions smaller and larger than the nations relate to them? If they are not nations, but nationhood is the project, how should they become so? What is a national culture and what are the 'cultures' currently so called? How do the existing nations relate to one another, and in what sense is this a unified continent (identity) and in what sense diverse (plurality). Or, synthesizing dialectically and returning to the point made above, to what extent might Latin America be conceived as a unified plurality which might perhaps only make sense at the level of the continent and therefore only makes unified writing possible at a continental level? If this is indeed the case, the reason for it is obvious as soon as one considers the matter closely. In Europe problems of frustration or non-transcendence have to be explained either by the hopeless futility of existence or by theories of class struggle, both of which crystallize as literary motifs in the 1920s and 1930s. In Latin America both explanations are also available, and their exploration in that period universalizes them for the first time (the decline of the West and the absurd on the one hand; imperialism and class struggle on the other; plus psychoanalysis as a second universalizing force explaining the fantasies and evasions of the bourgeois mind; and anthropology and myth adding one further dimension of universalization which incorporated the colonial peoples on an equal footing for the first time in history).

At that moment in the 1920s, the specific reality of Latin America's own history came to bear on the perception of some writers in a quite new way. After all, Latin Americans were united by a common origin. Their history had begun, as we have seen, with many tribal peoples and civilizations, all united under the denomination 'Indians', being colonized by two – both Iberian – Western peoples, who defeated those Indians, unified their respective empires, brought slaves in ships, and so on. Given the largely meaningless nature of individual nationalities in Latin America, writers decided that individual identity – whether national or personal – could only be established at the continental level, and that the national and continental questions could only be satisfactorily handled within the international or 'universal' context, though by keeping the image steady and the focus precise, without going over either to cosmopolitanism ('all nations are equal') or 'universalism' (no nations exist at all).

Numerous Latin American novels either take or signal this trajectory from small town to provincial capital to national capital to international metropolis (usually Paris). Sometimes, as in Rivera's *The Vortex* or Carpentier's *The*

Lost Steps (and Fuentes's *The Death of Artemio Cruz*), they take it in reverse. Other times, as in Arguedas's *Deep Rivers*, the symbolic zoning is internal to an institution or even a house. All of them – and *Doña Bárbara* and *Men of Maize* are further examples – deal with spaces ('fields'), paths and frontiers, the demarcation of temporal, historical, cultural, economic, political and psychological borders or barriers, according to the particular definition which each particular work adopts. So with each novel we read we should be alive to the geographical and historical frame of reference and the possible inversion of conventional divisions and definitions according to symbolic, metaphorical or allegorical design.

Nineteenth-century novels had founded nations and established who the ruling class was. Naturalist novels had examined the pathology of the lower classes and found them wanting. The 1920s 'regionalist' fiction looks again and takes a more positive view, not only of the lower classes, but of the possibilities of relationship between the rulers and the ruled. The interior is not now just declared, not just a field for imagination and romance, but for epic and social exploration, for knowledge and definition. So the journey from capital to interior is begun, and then, ironically, comes the realization that the future is not after all clear: firstly, because everything is more complicated than was thought, not least because alliances with the workers involve commitments which may not always suit the interests of the volatile petty bourgeoisie; and secondly because the road into the future still appears to lie through Europe, whether capitalist or socialist. Thus to the chain from capital to village is added the journey from there back again to the capital and across the seas to Europe – and then back again to the village, with all that newly acquired knowledge inside the consciousness of the writer. This indeed is the fundamental explanation of what I would call the 'Ulyssean' writer and the growth of the 'Ulyssean' novel, inaugurated and given definitive form by perhaps the greatest of all Modernist writers, James Joyce.

Indeed, taking a wide-angled focus, the only truly persuasive description for Latin America's most distinctive brand of fiction since the 1920s is Modernism in the European and North American sense, and it is an interesting question why that brand, given a new and distinctively Latin American character, has been more persistent in the new continent than in either Europe or the United States. One answer may be quickly advanced. European Modernism, despite the fertility of Joyce, Proust, Woolf or Faulkner, has no programme, no system, no theory, beyond the 'spirit of the age' (which most of its adherents secretly deplored and used their works to capture): at most, some general concepts of temporal fracture, structural complication, interior monologue and stream of consciousness, all connected in quite diffuse and usually undefinable ways to the new metropolitan experience;[2] and then the arrival of Kafka, Céline and Sartre takes us off into alienation and the absurd, which communicate the philosophical response to modernity rather than the experience of it. By contrast a Latin American writer, regardless of his or her politics, is always pulled in two directions and thereby learns to balance different realities and different orders of experience and thus to find their way into history as well as myth. Thus the real heart of what has been called Magical Realism (itself a form of Modernist discourse), as was anticipated in chapter 1, is the juxtaposition and fusion, on equal terms, of the literate and preliterate worlds, future and past, modern and traditional, the city and the country, corresponding to chapters 2, 3 and 4 above.[3] It requires the application of indirect discourse and the treatment of folk beliefs, superstitions and myths with absolute literalness. Joyce and Faulkner had shown the way, and both were from marginal regions with something of the bi-culturalism required, but neither of them needed to formulate this as an explicit part of their system or project, whereas in Latin America all writers are from the 'periphery' and all narratives, inevitably, bear the imprint of this origin in their structure.

The 1920s and Modernism in Latin America

Between 1918 and 1929 Latin America truly entered the twentieth century, a period identified at the time as the decade of the 'new' and of 'modernity', or, retrospectively, as one marked by the economics of integration and the politics of incorporation. In that decade many young Latin American students still yearned to be poets, usually at first on the model of a Darío whom they knew only too well to be outmoded (even though, with visionary foresight, he had called his own movement 'modernist'); like him they wanted to travel to the 'City of Light', there to undergo aesthetic, erotic and political adventures; like him, most of them turned to journalism as a means of earning a living, travelling the world ('from our correspondent in Paris...'), and engaging in writing as a profession; although unlike him, in that decade in which the aesthetic and ideological attractions of France intermingled inextricably with the speed, dash and sheer athleticism of the American Way of Life, they embraced the role of reporter 'enthusiastically', if not wholeheartedly, for their inner soul still yearned for Art. The period of Spanish American literary Modernismo was over, and the period of Vanguardismo or 'avant-gardism' (that is – confusingly – what in Britain, North America and Brazil is known as Modernism) had begun – and may even still continue.

One of the striking features of Latin American literature at the time, we can now perceive, was the contrast between the image of poetry and that of fiction. In poetry at least, the continent was already fully modern, in the sense that numbers of poets – Vicente Huidobro, Jorge Luis Borges, Mário de Andrade, Manuel Bandeira, César Vallejo and Pablo Neruda – were writing poetry fully as 'up to date', innovative and recognizably twentieth-century as anything being produced in Europe, the Soviet Union or the United States. Moreover, poets like Luis Carlos López, Baldomero Fernández Moreno and, above all and again, Vallejo, were initiating a line of deliberately prosaic, conversational poetry which remains fertile and relevant today. The novel, however, is always slower to mature and in the 1920s, the age of both Mexican muralism and the cosmopolitan avant-garde, there emerged in literature, broadly speaking, a contrast between a poetic expression whose dominant mode was cosmopolitan, produced by international experience and orientated in the same direction, and the various forms of 'nativist' fiction – regionalist, Creolist, telluric, indigenist, etc. – which we examined in chapters 2 to 4, and which, because they lay somewhere between realism and Naturalism, we are calling Social Realism. Its impetus had been both shaped and accelerated by the Mexican Revolution, and at that time was thought, not entirely paradoxically, to be the most innovative as well as the most typical current in Latin American literature, at a moment when no one dreamed that Latin Americans could simply participate in cultural discoveries and developments on equal terms.

Superficially this looks like a divorce between the genres in terms of the approach to form and content. Yet the novelists who were closest to the poets (and were usually also poets themselves) were young avant-garde writers like the Brazilian Mário de Andrade with his pathbreaking novel about the Brazilian culture hero *Macunaíma* (1928), the Guatemalan Asturias, author of the quasi-ethnological '*Legends of Guatemala*' (*Leyendas de Guatemala*, 1930), the Argentinian Borges, who was already intermingling literature with criticism in quite new ways, and the Cuban Carpentier, with his Afro-American *Ecue-Yamba-O* (1933). It was to these writers that the future truly belonged. Joyce had shown the way into the great labyrinth of modernity and had effectively ordained the literary systematization of Modernism. Once seen, the labyrinth could not be ignored and had to be traversed. In the case of the Spanish American trio just cited, the full dimensions of their talents would not become apparent until the 1930s and – due to the nature of the 1930s and the intervention of the Second World War – would only become visible after 1945; and even then, only relatively so, because not until the 1960s did the complex interaction between Latin American and international conditions of education, readership and publishing combine to produce a situation in which the achievements of Latin American art could be relatively quickly and generally recognized, both in Latin America and further afield.

Joyce and Latin America

> Dispersed in dispersed capitals,
> solitary yet many, we played
> at being the first Adam
> who gave things their names.
> Down the vast slopes of night
> that merge into the dawn,
> we searched (I recall) for the words
> of the moon, death, morning
> and other habits of man....
>   You, meanwhile,
> in the cities of exile,
> that exile that was
> your hated and chosen instrument,
> the weapon of your art,
> erected your arduous labyrinths,
> infinitesimal and infinite,
> wonderfully matter of fact,
> more populous than history itself...
>
>   Borges, 'Invocation to Joyce'

More than one hundred years after his birth and nearly seventy years after the publication of *Ulysses*, James Joyce remains a surprisingly polemical figure. Anyone attempting to write on Joyce and 'English' – rather than, say, North American – literature since 1922 would, as is well known, be embarking on a critical odyssey full of dangers, not least that of returning to his point of departure considerably older but little wiser than when he set out. Few works ought to have transformed the world as much as *Ulysses* or *Finnegans Wake*; but rarely has the nature, extent and desirability of an influence been more keenly, even bitterly, disputed. The Latin American case is eloquent in this regard. Since my view is that this is the century of Joyce in Western literature, and that the 'Ulyssean' design is especially relevant to Latin American fiction, this critical journey is one which risks shipwreck at the hands of both the English literature traditionalists and Latin American nationalists. As to the former, I can do nothing. However the latter assault, I believe, would be based on a misunderstanding: not only do I believe that Latin America's development of a 'Ulyssean' fiction springs largely from its writers' own experience, but I also believe that the Latin American contribution to Modernism has been decisive in its later evolution and in the process of communication between First, Second and Third World cultures.

It is of course impossible to separate Joyce from his century. Indeed, in the discussion that follows, 'Joyce' is merely a cipher for a far-reaching cultural phenomenon involving countless intellectuals and artists; and the 'Ulyssean novel' an abbreviation for a certain kind of literary text existing before and after 1922, but for which *Ulysses* constituted the watershed, and, up until now, the archetype. The world has seemed 'Joycean' to many people ever since *Ulysses* appeared. Indeed, as Richard Ellmann has said, 'Joyce is now read all over the world and influences even those who have never heard of him',[4] raising complex questions of the distribution of direct and indirect 'influences' or mere parallelisms.[5] Moreover, among those other great 'Modernist' names in fiction, such as Kafka, Proust and Woolf, are two North American narrators whose direct influence on Latin American narrative is at first sight even more substantial than Joyce's own, namely and particularly William Faulkner, especially with regard to 'rural' fiction, and John Dos Passos, especially in the 'urban' sphere.[6] Although there is no Faulkner without Joyce, and always remembering that Faulkner learned from the Joyce who had written *Ulysses* and not from the one who went on to write the *Wake*, it seems clear that, paradoxically, Faulkner and his compatriot were the more accessible influences in the Latin America of the 1930s, 1940s and 1950s, whilst Joyce, whose 'magic wand of language' (Miguel Angel Asturias), 'complex beauty' (Alejo Carpentier), and 'total reality' (Jorge Luis Borges) had mesmerized not a few budding young writers in the twenties,[7] would finally exercise his full impact only in the 1960s and 1970s. This is not really so surprising: it is my view that what Faulkner, and to a lesser extent Dos Passos, actually permitted was the renovation and restructuring of the Latin American social novel which we looked at in previous chapters through the next thirty years,[8] whereas, despite the bedazzlement he inspired in a generation of young Americans in Paris, Joyce's impact on most authors – if not, crucially, on the most important of them – remained largely fragmentary or superficial except in poetry – this too is ironic in view of Joyce's own rather conventional approach to poetry – and was only generally assimilable in the 1960s, the age, indeed, of the final flowering of Latin American Modernism in the shape of the 'boom' novel.

The discussion that follows has three possibly ambitious objectives: to recapitulate briefly Joyce's contribution to Modernism, given the similarity of his achievement to that of subsequent Latin American writers; to examine the conditions for his assimilation by such Latin American writers; and to trace the main directions of the actual assimilation in the subcontinent in the early years. Joyce's legacy, from *Ulysses*, may be synthesized as follows:

First, is the structural incorporation of myth – public or private – into the novel, to an extent previously unimagined, this following a long century of classical and folkloric studies in Europe, and of anthropological studies both in Europe and the United States. Joyce's own point of departure was a synthesis of classical, Catholic and native Irish materials, and obvious parallels can be made with Latin American writers like Asturias, Carpentier and Guimarães Rosa.

Second, is the exploration of language through and in fiction, to a degree unparalleled in any previous novelist, although with the similarly structured and self-conscious antecedents of Rabelais, Sterne and Carroll, and the discoveries of poetic symbolism. The result has rarely been more succinctly conveyed than in the following synthesis by the Brazilian critic and Concrete Poet Haroldo de Campos:

> The 'verbi-visual' elements of Joyce's prose – the 'montage' or 'portmanteau' word considered as a unit built up of mosaics or as a basic textual node ('silvamoonlake', 'platealunalago', for example) – were emphasized from the very beginning of our Concrete Poetry movement. The Joycean 'micro-macrocosm', which reaches its peak in *Finnegans Wake*, is another fundamental feature. Joyce's implacable poem–novel is also, in its own way, a triumph of structure, one in which the counterpoint is *moto perpetuo*. It achieves the status of ideogram through its superimposition of words – genuine lexical montages – and its general infrastructure is 'a circular design, each of whose parts is beginning, middle and end' (Campbell and Robinson).[9]

A particular aspect of Joyce's approach is an orientation towards linguistic humour, parody and satire.[10] This had been largely absent from Latin American fiction, but Asturias was an early exponent of this vein in *The President* (completed 1933, published 1946), followed by the Argentinians Leopoldo Marechal and Julio Cortázar, the Cubans José Lezama Lima and Guillermo Cabrera Infante, and later by others like the Mexican new-wave novelists of the 1960s in the age of pop culture and the mass media.

Third, comes the exploration of the nature and experience of consciousness in narrative fiction,[11] following the examples of Flaubert, James and other exponents of the 'well-wrought' psychological novel, at a time when Freud's theories were affecting all artistic genres and in particular Surrealism, whose own impact on Latin American literature was particularly strong; and, concurrent with this, an exploration of the relation of consciousness to time (the theories of Bergson), and of history to myth (the discoveries of ethnology). For many Latin American novelists and critics in the 1930s and after, Joyce's supreme legacy was the stream of consciousness and the interior monologue. It is here that his example merges early with that of his principal mediator, Faulkner, to affect writers as different as Marechal, Asturias, Onetti, the Mexicans Yáñez and Rulfo, García Márquez, Fuentes and Vargas Llosa. In the 1960s the anti-psychologistic 'exterior monologue' of *Finnegans Wake* would be echoed by yet another vogue in Latin American fiction.

Fourth, uniting all the foregoing, is the search for totality – Borges perceived this aspect of Joyce's achievement as early as 1925, but decided to confine his own quest within a nutshell – for the vast all-embracing cosmogenic-scriptural creation, on the model of Dante's *Inferno*, Rabelais's *Gargantua and Pantagruel*, or Cervantes's *Don Quixote*, works for which there had been no equivalents in the profane post-Renaissance bourgeois period (merely 'big' books like *War and Peace* being a quite different case);[12] but also, tied in with this, we have the ancestral European mythology of the road, individual destiny, the quest for identity (not to mention the appropriation of the identities of others...), associated above all with the *Odyssey*, but also, in terms of the search for meaning through self-realization, with Christ's trajectory and Dante's reenactment of it, and, in the Hispano-European ambit, with the novels of chivalry, *Don Quixote* (again) and the conquest of Latin America itself.[13] In that continent, whose dependent status gives such quests for identity a peculiarly anguished edge, Marechal's '*Adam Buenosaires*' (*Adán Buenosayres*, 1948), Asturias's *Men of Maize* (1949), Guimarães Rosa's *The Devil to Pay in the Backlands* (1956), Cortázar's *Hopscotch* (1963), Lezama Lima's *Paradiso* (1966), García Márquez's *One Hundred Years of Solitude* (1967) and Fuentes's *Terra Nostra* (1975) would all be good examples of the genre. Their very titles suggest the symbolic nature of the exercise.

Fifth, journeys along a road almost always end in a town, as Walter Benjamin has shown, and *Ulysses*, secretly a tale of two or many cities – Dublin viewed from a composite of European capitals – exploits to the full the tension between the road ('freedom') and the city as 'home' or, as is more common in Hispanic literature, as 'prison' (see chapter 4). Whenever European man set off on his voyages of exploration into 'Otherness', he would depart from and return to his own capital city, like Ulysses himself (invariably to another, perhaps colonial, country – in the case of Latin America, to distant parts of his own country, or maybe even just outside the capital city; maybe even inside it, over the road); but by the end of the First World War he was only too aware that such adventures were all but over even for heroes, while for lesser mortals – the new 'anti-heroes' of fiction – the city's claustrophobic aspects as a grid or screen for consciousness were uppermost in the mind.[14] More yet than Dos Passos, Joyce's genius made his reproduction of everyday life in the big city – even diminutive Dublin – an existential and linguistic adventure of inexhaustible textu(r)al fertility, even if the underlying message, as in the case of the Spanish baroque before it, was one of grim sterility and decay: hence the need for a 'collideorscape'. *The President*, '*Adam Buenosaires*', *Where the Air is Clear*, *Hopscotch*, *Three Trapped Tigers* (Guillermo Cabrera Infante, 1963) and others have continued this line of writing in the American subcontinent.

Sixth, the search of the European petty-bourgeois consciousness for the Other involved the return of Art to the roots of popular culture and tradition by the 1920s. Joyce's obsessive quest for totality immersed him in an affectionate journey, despite himself, into his own cultural underworld,[15] one which would find its full fruition in *Finnegans Wake*, though *Ulysses* itself was already heavily imprinted by popular poetry and song, music hall and silent cinema, advertising and the tabloid press, those diverse Signs-of-the-Time.[16] The other 'Other' is the female: and here the Nora–Molly–Anna Livia chain is reiterated in innumerable mythical female figures in the works of Asturias (especially María Tecún in *Men of Maize*), Carpentier (Rosario in *The Lost Steps*), Rulfo (Susana San Juan in *Pedro Páramo*), Guimarães Rosa (especially Diadorim in *The Devil to Pay in the Backlands*), Roa Bastos (especially Salu'í in *Son of Man*), Cortázar (especially La Maga in *Hopscotch*), García Márquez (almost everyone in *One Hundred Years of Solitude*), Fuentes (especially Regina in *The Death of Artemio Cruz*), and Vargas Llosa (especially Lalita-Toñita-Bonifacia in *The Green House*). All are descendants of Cervantes's Dulcinea, needless to say, but Joyce's remarkable oscillation between a view of the female as Musa–Musica or as Mater–Materia, deriving from his Irish Catholic agrarian heritage (Ireland the helpless sufferer of English domination), is one that has been emulated repeatedly in Latin America up to the present, for historical and cultural reasons that are self-evident.

Seventh of Joyce's deadly virtues is the incomparable synthesis of craftsmanship and artistry, professionalism and dedication, which itself stems from the paradoxical interpenetration of his twin inspirations – Symbolism and realism – and his consequent determination to recreate the whole and all the parts of the real world through a perfectionist aesthetic technique.[17] The supreme antecedent here is Flaubert's example of the purist approach to impure material. In terms of a general attitude to literary creation, Borges learned from this devotion in his brief 'fictions', as he did from Valery;[18] in terms of full-scale results, Carpentier, Asturias, Rulfo, Cortázar, Vargas Llosa and Fuentes are all examples of writers who have gone to remarkable lengths to make the realist–Naturalist novel an art form.

If these seven overlapping and interweaving features are taken into account, it is not difficult to see why Joyce's monstrous novel effectively inaugurates the twentieth-century literary labyrinth. Yet if *Ulysses* demanded criticism in order to be read at all, *Finnegans Wake* defied it, indeed defied all criticism, so to speak. Here, surely, was the end of literature as we knew it, or, at least, the end of literature that was separable from critical discourse.[19] Borges said in 1939 that the *Wake* was 'like a sentence from *Urn Burial*, arduously achieved across a century or a dream'.[20] Haroldo de Campos, in an article entitled 'Latinized Sanscrit' (as if to anticipate the concept of *One Hundred Years of Solitude*), has claimed that Latin Americans were quick to appreciate and exploit the full potential of Joyce's pioneering endeavour:

It is important to underline here a most significant fact. Whilst numbers of erudite North American and European critics insisted on reading Joyce (and in particular *Finnegans Wake*) as a kind of blind alley or cul-de-sac, we Brazilians who founded the Concrete Poetry movement (members of the Noigandres group of 1952) were using the *Wake* to stimulate and focus our poetic experiments, considering it not as the apocalyptic end of Western literature, but rather as an open field full of diverse possibilities, seminal.[21]

Finnegans Wake has still not been translated into either Spanish or Portuguese.[22] It remains the point beyond which our lettered civilization cannot go. A number of Latin American writers have followed, on a smaller scale, the Joycean trajectory from *Dubliners* to *Finnegans Wake*, that is, crudely, from Social Realism to the cryptographic novel, with Asturias, Fuentes, Cabrera Infante and Roa Bastos perhaps the best examples, while Juan Goytisolo offers a Spanish illustration of the paradigm.

Translation, of course, is one of the principal factors militating against Joyce's assimilation. Borges, proudly proclaiming himself 'the first Hispanic explorer to have ventured into Joyce's novel', translated the famous last page in 1925,[23] and that same page remains the only extract read by many educated Latin Americans to the present day. *Ulysses* appeared in Spanish, albeit in a controversial translation, in 1945, at the moment when the New Novel was in its infancy, gestation having taken place between 1922 and 1945. At the same time we remember that Joyce himself was multilingual, and there is little doubt that the most effectively Joycean writers from Latin America have been those versed in different European languages, notably English and French. *Ulysses* was first published in France – Joyce's rejection and notoriety in Britain and the United States only increased his attraction for the Parisian avant-garde – and presented to the cosmopolitan milieu in the French capital by Valery Larbaud and a team of translator disciples. (Faulkner, too, was admired earlier and more widely in France than in his own country.) Although a Borges could read it in the original English, Carpentier, Asturias and others like the Venezuelan Uslar Pietri made their fragmentary readings of the novel through the medium of Larbaud's translation, which would have given them an insight into the scale and structure of the work, if not a full sense of its true texture.[24]

However, James Joyce had been a long time coming and it would be some years before a convincing Latin American equivalent could be elaborated. Nevertheless, the seven lessons outlined above were noted early and the seeds began to grow. This was much more the case when, from the 1940s onwards, English began to replace French as the educated Latin American's first foreign language, eventually producing writers like Carlos Fuentes and Guillermo Cabrera Infante, men with a superb command of the imperialist tongue. Four other conditioning factors in the assimilation of Joyce have been:

Cosmopolitanism: the Paris link in the 1920s is fundamental as the vantage point from which the European avant-garde chose to view the contradictory impact of, on the one hand, the revolutionary experience of Russia, and, on the other, the implantation of the American way of life. Europeans, North Americans, Africans, Asians and Latin Americans intermingled in the French capital in the postwar period, just as the mass media and communications generally began to proliferate. Intellectuals 'escaped' from their own stifling provincialisms into Parisian multiplicity, and then restored unity at the level of a 'Ulyssean' textual consciousness which was in reality the material product of travel: Everyman had become tourist.

Exile: the other side of cosmopolitanism, or nostalgia in place of excitement. Joyce would not have written *Ulysses* had he remained in Dublin, and his central character might not have been a Jew. He was already, as an Irishman, peripheral to a major culture zone, an experience which has been shared by innumerable Latin American writers.

Catholicism: the essential ambiguity of Joyce's relations with his native religion has been duplicated in a number of Latin American writers – Carpentier, Asturias, Mário de Andrade, Jorge Amado, Yáñez, Marechal, Rulfo, Guimarães Rosa – with the variant that many of them emphasize the play between native American tradition and classicism more than Joyce does between classicism and native Irish tradition.[25] Concomitant with this perspective is an attitude to sexual matters – desire and its repression – similar to that displayed in Joyce's own works, with a corresponding freedom, verging at any given moment on the 'scandalous' or the 'blasphemous', of sexual subject matter and language.[26]

Language, national and regional: not only was Joyce culturally dependent on the imperial British state, but he wrote in its tongue, to which there was in fact a nationalist alternative in the shape of Gaelic. A similar case applies to all novelists from Latin America, and with particular force to such truly bilingual writers as José María Arguedas and Augusto Roa Bastos, both of whom decided that they had no choice but to use the language of the oppressors.

None of the above factors apply in the same way to Faulkner, and a detailed examination would therefore allow one means of distinguishing the relative influence of the two writers. As has been seen, Joyce's material influence on the Latin American novel began early, because it was irresistible, both in the short term and, much more so, in the longer trajectory of the period which was just then beginning. But 'Joyce' was not at all what the Latin American novel was looking for in the 1920s. What he did give young writers immediately, however, was the most remarkable among many examples of linguistic exploration and the confidence to experiment with words in the era of what Latin Americans call *jitanjáfora*, or word play. This influence was accordingly more accessible in poetry or, indeed, in prose poems, than in full-scale novels, though of course the exercise would gradually lead to a long revolution in the language of Latin American prose works. The American critic John Brushwood has noted, for example, that young Mexican writers of the time like Novo, Owen, Torres Bodet and Villaurrutia

> were poets by nature, and it well may be that their poetic intuition allowed them to sense the possibilities of this new type of narrative without necessarily giving them the preparation required for writing longer works. Their novels did use the narrative techniques learned from Joyce and Proust, techniques which it is sometimes thought were introduced into Mexican narrative at a much later date.[27]

Another particularly influential poet who used Joyce as a springboard for his own experimentation was the Chilean 'creationist' Vicente Huidobro.[28]

Joyce was in Paris by 1920, and so were many young Latin American writers and intellectuals – more, indeed, than at any time before or since. At the moment when the prewar 'Modernista' movement, already fading in the last years of the Belle Epoque, was giving way to the avant-garde of the années folles, these young writers, who had made the pilgrimage to Paris aided by the plunge of the franc, began to found and participate in a succession of new and exciting magazines with futuristic titles (in Buenos Aires Proa, 'Prow': in his 1925 review in that same magazine Borges said that Joyce himself was 'audacious as a prow', in other words, an avant-garde explorer and adventurer; in Havana Revista de Avance; in Mexico Contemporáneos; in Paris itself Imán, 'Magnet'), in all of which the name of Joyce would appear, usually as a rather distant, almost legendary figure. One magazine, Ulises ('Ulysses', Mexico, 1926–8), was actually named in honour of his achievement.[29]

Pride of place in all this must go to Borges, who saw in Ulysses a 'wild and entangled land' into which only the most foolhardy would venture.[30] Joyce's work of course made almost everyone feel and look not only foolish and inadequate, as it has done ever since, but also anachronistic, and Latin Americans noted this humiliation of his fellow Europeans from more hegemonic cultures with some satisfaction. Borges's lifelong debate with the Joycean oeuvre is worth a study in its own right. At first sight two more different writers would be difficult to find, and Borges's initial enthusiasm was soon renounced, just as he would in due course also renounce his own avant-garde moment – ultraísmo, his localist Fervor de Buenos Aires, his 'too vulgar' story 'El hombre de la esquina rosada', any plot which involved social or psychological realism (mere 'specularity'), all wilful obscurity and baroqueries. He would come to describe Ulysses itself as 'a failure', a work of microscopic Naturalism with, paradoxically, 'no real characters'.[31] Yet whenever Borges wishes to explore the nature of literary language, he turns to Joyce's example, just as he does whenever he wishes to discuss translation, comparativism, literary purity, artistic devotion, or totality. Moreover Borges, one of the writers who made possible the concept of 'intertextuality', frequently names Joyce as a key innovator in this regard: 'For classical minds the literature is the essential thing, not the individuals. George Moore and James Joyce have incorporated in their works the pages and sentences of others.'[32] In later life Borges's own blindness seemed to reconcile him to Joyce, as to Homer and Milton, and the poem 'Invocation to Joyce' is an unqualified homage to the Irishman's achievements. It ends:

> What care I for my lost generation,
> poor dim mirror,
> if your books can make it good.
> I am the others. I am all those
> rescued by your stubborn rigour.
> I am those you know not whom you have saved.

In his review article in *Proa* in 1925, Borges had acknowledged the role of Valery Larbaud in publicizing Joyce's formidable new novel. Larbaud's relations with Latin American writers like Alfonso Reyes and Ricardo Güiraldes are well known, and he and his disciples, together with other figures of the day like Adrienne Monnier, acted as a medium between French, Latin American and Anglo-Saxon writers and culture at this crucial conjunctural time. Another member of the 'ABC of twentieth-century Spanish American fiction' (Asturias, Borges, Carpentier), Alejo Carpentier, always alive to the movement and contours of cultural history, was quick to perceive the true nature of the Irish exile, placing him in 1931 in a trio with Stravinsky and Picasso as one of the great artistic revolutionaries of the age, the man who had transformed not only the direction in which the novel would develop but the language in which it would be written. The post-Joycean era, declared the young Cuban, had arrived.[33] Later, Carpentier, whose first experimental work, *Ecue–Yamba–O*, was written between 1929 and 1933, and whose *The Lost Steps* (1953), has been dubbed 'Joycean' (perhaps unconvincingly, though it is certainly 'Ulyssean'), would demand, as we have seen, that Latin American writers emulate Joyce's achievement by defining the physiognomy of their own great cities. This the New Novelists of the 1960s did indeed begin to achieve.

Joyce in the 1920s provoked precisely the same feelings of admiration and intimidation in young North American writers, notably Hemingway and Scott Fitzgerald, as Julio Cortázar was to evince in Spanish Americans like

Fuentes and García Márquez in the 1960s. Not surprisingly, he appeared even more formidable to tongue-tied young Latin Americans. One who confessed that he never plucked up the courage to hail the frequently espied Irish genius in halting French was Miguel Angel Asturias, who nonetheless acknowledged the extraordinary effect which Joyce was to have increasingly on generations of Latin American writers. Asturias always insisted that Joyce's impact was at the time confusingly and indistinguishably bound up with that of Surrealism, another subject which would provide enough material for a book in itself: the case of Cortázar, Spanish America's Joycean Surrealist of the 1960s, would later provide a paradigmatic example. Both the Joycean and Surrealist aspects of Asturias's own *The President* and *Men of Maize* are plain to see. Enrique Anderson Imbert has underlined the stream of consciousness, particularly in the chapter 'Whirlwind' of the former work,[34] whilst *Men of Maize* is literally a cosmic odyssey of Amerindian man with innumerable Joycean parallels at both macro and micro levels.

In the 1920s, then, Joyce dazzled the Latin American eye, and young poets in particular rushed to catch the sparks before they dimmed. In the 1930s Faulkner and Dos Passos showed how to apply the new Modernist techniques to narrative fiction and provided the means for updating the social or regionalist novel. Joyce supplied a strong but by no means dominant complementary impact. The point, however, is that his influence began before either, was more widespread if not more powerful, and grew slowly but surely to a crescendo in the 1960s and 1970s. Moreover in a few literary milestones of the following era – Yáñez's *The Edge of the Storm* (*Al filo del agua*, 1947), Asturias's *The President* (1946) and Marechal's '*Adam Buenosaires*' (1948) – the particular combination of interior monologue and stream-of-consciousness techniques with other devices, especially wordplay and myth, made critics correctly conclude that their historically fundamental works were more Joycean than Faulknerian. It was in 1945, four years after Joyce's death, that Salvador Rueda published the Salas Subirat translation in Buenos Aires, opening *Ulysses* at last to those who had never been to Paris and were unable to read the book either in English or in French. Three years later saw the publication of perhaps the most comprehensively Joycean – though, again, not 'Ulyssean' – of all the Latin American novels published before the 1960s 'boom', Marechal's '*Adam Buenosaires*' (1948; see chapter 8), which makes similar use of Dante's *Inferno* to that made of the Odyssey by Joyce in *Ulysses* and which occupies a mere forty-eight hours of real time, so that one can say of it, as Borges said of *Ulysses*, that Marechal's unfolding of a few hours of his hero's life requires many days of hard work from his readers.[35]

Argentine fiction – indeed River Plate fiction as a whole – has throughout the twentieth century been characterized by a tendency of the fictional artefact to draw attention to the conditions and phases of its own elaboration. The line runs from Macedonio Fernández (1874–1952) through Borges and Marechal, on to Cortázar – quintessentially – and then to Nestor Sánchez and Manuel Puig. (In justice, one should say that the precursor of them all is the Brazilian Machado de Assis, himself a nineteenth-century descendant of Sterne.) A particularly notable point about '*Adam Buenosaires*', in this sense similar to Asturias's *Men of Maize*, is that the book was scarcely read until the 1960s, by which time the so-called New Novel had retrospectively rendered it legible, thereby underlining its extraordinary pathbreaking achievement. Nevertheless, despite such occasional Joycean gestures, Faulkner, given Latin America's overwhelming 'rural' orientation in the literature of the 1920s to the 1950s inclusive, continued to be more obviously influential into the early 1960s on writers like Rulfo, García Márquez or the Asturias of the *Banana Trilogy* (1950–60); and even such 'urban' novelists as Onetti, Mallea, Sábato and Revueltas wrote many of their desolate urban tragedies largely in the mode of Faulkner or Dos Passos. At the same time, as we have seen, such works coexisted with more traditional, albeit updated versions of the regionalist novel, notably those of Arguedas and Roa Bastos, as well as a whole range of second-rank but still worthy writers from the provinces or from the smaller republics.

Then, around 1960, came the famous 'boom' of the New Novel, with its pronounced shift of gravity to the urban realm and the emergence and consolidation of the 'big four' – Cortázar, Fuentes, García Márquez and Vargas Llosa – followed by others like Lezama Lima, Cabrera Infante and Donoso. In an article on these new Latin American novelists in 1977, Emir Rodríguez Monegal, their principal academic propagandist, made an unequivocal retrospective assessment of the major influences on all the works of the previous decade:

> Joyce's achievement was to be imitated in many languages. Slowly, and through many successful works (Borges achieved in his stories a scale reduction...) and through some literally monstrous attempts (Leopoldo Marechal's '*Adam Buenosaires*'), *Ulysses* became the invisible but central model of the new Latin American narrative. From this point of view, Cortázar's *Hopscotch*, Lezama Lima's *Paradiso*, Fuentes's *A Change of Skin* and Cabrera Infante's *Three Trapped Tigers*, are Joycean books. Whether or not they are obviously Joycean, they do share the same secret code. That is, they agree in conceiving of the novel as both a parody and a myth, a structure which in its topoi, as much as in its private symbols, reveals the unity of a complete system of signification.[36]

So large a claim for Joyce's universal significance and specific impact in Latin America would not be supported by all Latin American critics – although it is shared, ironically, by all the principal antagonists of the New

Novel, mainly traditional literary or continental nationalists, and by many socialist commentators, as we shall see in chapter 8. Rodríguez Monegal himself had tended in the 1960s to stress the influence of Faulkner, and otherwise to see Joyce as just one influence among many within a generally Modernist trend. This writer shares his later perception, however: critics always need to stand well back if they are to attain a focused perspective on the full panorama. What Rodríguez Monegal does not consider is what the astonishing phenomenon which he identifies really means. Is the new (post-Joycean) novel truly a sign of the independence and liberation of contemporary Latin American fiction, as he and others frequently claim; or is this final catching-up merely a deepening of its dependent neocolonial phase, as his detractors often suggest? Is 'Joyce' something that is bound to happen to each or to most cultures anyway at a given moment of technocratic–capitalist development, or did Latin America simply imitate an original model some forty years too late, when the conditions for such assimilation were finally favourable? No answers to such questions are forthcoming in the works of Rodríguez Monegal and other publicists of the 'boom', but the radically uneven quality of Latin American literary development to this day suggests that they should continue to be asked.

These questions will be more comprehensively examined in later chapters. Taking the long view of Joyce's contribution, however, it seems to me an unmistakable *summa* of European Culture-in-Progress, a monument to several centuries of literary development – we are all living in the Afterjoyce, or in his *Wake*, so to speak. One of the most decisive accolades paid to Joyce was that of the Mexican novelist Fernando del Paso:

> I consider that *Ulysses* is a sort of sun installed at the centre of the Gutenberg Galaxy, which illuminates not only all the works which followed it but all of universal literature that preceded it. Its influence is definitive and unique in modern Western literature.... *Finnegans Wake* is a comet of great magnitude moving away from us at the speed of light, in danger of becoming lost for ever. But there is also the possibility that it will return one day and be better understood. Joyce's most important aspect for me is what has been called his 'total' or 'totalizing' practice of fiction, because I am interested in books not only as macrocosms but also as microcosms. This attitude implies two further aspects: the mythical background and linguistic revolution. But it also implies an anticolonial posture, because it presupposes a very highly personal analysis by the writer of history, that of his country, the West as a whole, and the world – quoting from memory, 'History, that nightmare from which I am trying to awake'. But it also implies sexuality, of course, which only acquires human dignity when it is liberated.[37]

Such an encapsulation, by the author of the Ulyssean '*Palinurus of Mexico*' (*Palinuro de Mexico*, 1977), explains convincingly why the Joycean paradigm has been so attractive in Latin America. There seems little doubt that the epoch-making crystallization, in *Ulysses*, of the transition between the psychological and the linguistic novel formed part of a continuous process in Western fiction from the epic–historical–romance (Cervantes, the picaresque, Fielding) through the sociological–historical (Stendhal, Balzac, Zola, Dickens, Tolstoy, Mann) and psychological–historical (Proust, *Ulysses*, Woolf, Faulkner) and on to the linguistic limits, beyond 'legibility' (*Finnegans Wake* and aspects of the *nouveau roman*). Whether we are now on our way, in the age of space exploration, cybernetics, possible nuclear holocaust and ecological catastrophe, beyond 'Post-modernism' to the 'cosmic' fiction, as the end of the dialectical trajectory from tribal poetry to the global village, can only be speculated. Seen in this long but essential trajectory, however, it becomes obvious that Latin America as a whole, from a far lower baseline, took less time to assimilate Joycean writing than, say, a number of the English-speaking literatures for which such assimilation was easiest and, moreover, assimilated it more completely. This would seem to confirm, for those who doubted it, that Latin America really is a part of Western civilization and that its cultural identity was of such a nature as to provide both a replication of the Joycean trajectory and optimum conditions for its assimilation.

The ABC of Magical Realism

> This story is over and its glory has faded away. There is no longer anyone left. Sorcery and bad luck have finished off the scions of the Tapanhuma tribe, one by one. The places they knew – those spacious savannas, those clefts and gullies, those balata bleeders' trails, those abrupt ravines, those mysterious forests – they are all now as solitary as a desert. An immense silence slumbers over the river Uraricoera. No one on this earth knows how to speak the language of this vanished tribe, nor how to recount its flamboyant adventures.
>
> Mário de Andrade, *Macunaíma*, 1928

If 1920s and 1930s literature, and much of what has continued to be written since, may be called Social Realism, what was the literature of the 1950s, 1960s and 1970s? The answer comes quickly to the contemporary reader's lips: Magical Realism. When applied to Miguel Angel Asturias and Alejo Carpentier alone, as it used to be, together with like-minded writers like Venezuela's Arturo Uslar Pietri (1906–) and Ecuador's Demetrio Aguilera Malta (1909–), the term, albeit unsatisfactory, was attractive and acceptable. Now that, like the concept 'baroque', it has become an almost universal description of the 'Latin American style' – exotic and tropical, overblown and unrestrained, phantasmagorical and hallucinatory – it is so ideologically dangerous that it should really be rejected. However, we would be prudent to bear with it for the time being. It is now most current precisely in Britain and the United States, for reasons which would be interesting to explore, particularly as a result of that second boom in the fashion for reading Latin American literature which has occurred, against all expectations, in our own recent past, the 1980s. It is now routinely applied to many writers quite different from Asturias and Carpentier – who of course sat at the same Surrealist cafe tables in the 1920s – and their imitators. Interestingly, though, many of the best-known writers – Fuentes, García Márquez, Vargas Llosa – have increasingly written in this vein since the 'boom', in order to give the international public – which, to be fair, now includes their own Latin American readers – what they seem to want, and the market is not yet saturated. Moreover, the term may even be on its way to becoming decolonized now that writers like Salman Rushdie, Bruce Chatwin and even Anthony Burgess (despite his disparaging comments about 'South American novels') have tacitly acknowledged its influence and allure.

The one great avant-garde system which coincides with Modernism in the 1920s, but was never such a significant influence in either Britain or the United States – both far too empirical for such schemas at this time – was Surrealism. Its emphasis upon the unconscious, and therefore the primitive, its insistence that there was a world more real than the visible 'reality' of commonsense and positivism, the idea that art is a journey of discovery involving free association and the liberation of the repressed, were all tailor-made for Third World interpretations and applications, and therefore for cementing the growing cultural relationship between France and Latin America following Independence and the assertion that what the British persist in calling 'South' America was actually 'Latin'. Moreover, this relationship in which, instead of superordinate to subordinate, imperialist to colonial, France exchanged her rational civilization on equal terms (she had no colonial axe to grind in Latin America) with the New World's supposed instinctual barbarism, was ideally suited to the interests of both parties, and has been fertile, fruitful and productive ever since.[38]

Thus far the rather frothy, mystified external conception. A more respectable explanation for the term is that the 'magic' derives from the cultural sparks which fly from the juxtaposition and clash of different cultures at different levels of development, but this seems not to be the explanation for its attraction. In the era of Hollywood stars, Coca Cola and the intensifying fetishism of commodity exchange, it ought not to be too difficult to understand why a 'magic' realism would give us pleasure and conciliate a number of painful contradictions. Otherwise it would seem much more logical to go for the concept of 'mythical realism'. It is myth – the universal currency of communication through translation and transformation – which is the only unifying facet between, say, Andrade, Asturias, Borges,

Carpentier and García Márquez, who, in other terms, are quite different kinds of novelist.

Mário de Andrade, *Macunaíma*

It is a curious irony that although the Ulyssean novel depends heavily on an international consciousness, and is usually doubly involved in a journey – a journey by the author in both mind and body, and a journey by the characters both real and metaphorical – Mário de Andrade (1893–1945) had never been abroad when he wrote *Macunaíma* (1928), and most of what he knew about Brazil had come from books – unlike, say, the composer Villa-Lobos who saw much of Brazil during his youth. Like the composer, however, and like Alejo Carpentier, Andrade was interested in music and in a wide range of ethnographic subjects. He knew more than enough about mythology to understand the concept of the culture hero and invented Macunaíma, 'our national Pantagruel', as Haroldo de Campos called him, the hero without an identity and without a name, symbol paradoxically uniting the Brazil of the past with its contemporary plural society and uneven development. He found a literary form through which to narrate this avant-garde folk tale, and thus Magical Realism was born, except that name did not yet exist and *Macunaíma* became a key text of the famous 'anthropophagous' movement. Oswald de Andrade, counteracting the general incomprehension and even derision with which the book was greeted, said, with foresight astounding in the year of the work's publication: 'Mário has written our *Odyssey* and with one blow with his club has created the cyclical hero and the national poetic style for the next fifty years'.[39]

As a writer from a country with no great pre-Columbian civilization on which to found a national myth, and without even a national classical style and heritage, Andrade was forced to confront the themes of tribalism, totemism, sacrifice, cannibalism and magic. This was a world inaccessible to one born in sophisticated São Paulo other than by force of imagination:

> The vanished tribe, the family turned into ghosts, the tumbledown hut undermined by termites, Macunaíma's ascent to heaven, how the parrots and macaws formed a canopy in the far-off times when the hero was the Great Emperor, Macunaíma: in the silence of the Uraricoera only the parrot had rescued from oblivion those happenings and the language which had disappeared. Only the parrot had preserved in that vast silence the words and the deeds of the hero.
>
> All this he related to the man, then spread his wings and set his course for Lisbon. And that man, dear reader, was myself, and I stayed on in order to tell you this story. That is why I came here. I crouched in the shelter of the leaves, picked off my ticks, struck a few chords on my little fiddle, and with a sweeping touch started the mouth of the world singing in vulgar speech the deeds and words of Macunaíma, the hero of our people.
>
> There's no more.[40]

It is safe to say that the 'carnivalization' of Latin American literature and the development of the 'polyphonic novel' begin here. Andrade's first version was composed in 1926, the year in which Volosinov (Bakhtin) wrote 'Discourse in Life and Discourse in Art', and published in 1928, the year in which Propp's *Morphology of the Folk Tale* appeared. Mário explained his book in his usual humorous way: 'The Brazilian has no character because he has neither a civilization of his own nor a traditional consciousness... He is just like a twenty year old boy.' Towards the end of the novel there is an intriguing moment when the hero loses his consciousness in a battle with a giant, and the narrator announces:

> Macunaíma got into the canoe, took a trip to the mouth of the Rio Negro to look for his consciousness, left behind on the island of Marapatá. And do you think he found it? Not a hope! So then our hero grabbed the consciousness of a Spanish American, stuffed it in his head, and got on just as well.[41]

Mário de Andrade was one of the first writers in the Third World to dare to take not only myth but also magic seriously and unapologetically, as a system of ideas and practices for working on the natural world as an alternative to our cold and instrumental science and technology. Religion exists in both spheres – the primitive and the 'civilized' – and the civilized version, monotheistic and individualistic, is of course seen as superior to the inchoate, collectivist polytheistic variety. Magic has nothing to do with religion as such, but is another way of relating to nature. Appropriately and ironically enough, Andrade is said to have written his book in six days flat: only such cosmic energy could have achieved the momentum to create a synthesis of Brazilian culture – in other words, a Brazilian character – virtually out of nothing, with such enveloping flair.

Alejo Carpentier, *Ecue–Yamba–O*

The brief novel *Ecue–Yamba–O* (*Praise be to Ecue*) by the young Alejo Carpentier (1904–80) was published in 1933, though its first version was signed 'Havana Prison, 1–9 August 1927'. It is worth noting, then, that both Carpentier and Miguel Angel Asturias were partly inspired to write by brief experiences of imprisonment. The Cuban was later unwilling for the work to be republished. He felt that although it was based on people he had known as a child, he had failed to grasp either the essence of their psychology and way of life or the linguistic medium needed to convey it. He only relented at the very end of his life, when a clumsily produced pirate edition appeared. While it is undoubtedly true that Carpentier's novel on the culture of Cuba's Black population was more interesting for what it promised than for what it achieved, its project was similar to that of *Macunaíma* and to Asturias's

'*Legends of Guatemala*'. Both he and Asturias were from small countries with large ethnic populations which made the question of a unified national identity more than usually problematical. Both were closely associated with the Surrealists in Paris in the 1920s; both knew of Joyce, both believed in the power of myth, metaphor, language and symbol, both were Freudian in orientation, *Marxisant* and revolutionary by instinct. They would each, from that moment, through the dark hibernatory age of the 1930s and 1940s – a fertile, global unconscious for both of them – gestate these ideas and in due course, around 1948, each would start to talk of 'magical realism' (Asturias) or 'the marvellous real' (Carpentier), whenever given the opportunity to do so. It was fitting that *The Kingdom of this World* and *Men of Maize* should have appeared in the same year, 1949.

Carpentier was an active member of Cuba's rebellious 1923 Generation, which attempted both to revolutionize national culture and to oppose the dictatorship of Gerardo Machado. Perhaps the guiding thread of their quest for identity was Afro-Cubanism, the effort to integrate the Black experience into Cuba's national self-expression, underpinned by the pathbreaking folkloric and ethnological work of Fernando Ortiz (1881–1969). Two of Carpentier's stories inspired compositions by the Mulatto composer Amadeo Roldán, and Carpentier subsequently became a leading authority on Cuban music in his own right. *Ecue–Yamba–O* includes several attempts to recreate the intense experience of Afro-Cuban music:

All the voices broke in on the same rhythm. The keys clashed together, three long beats, two short. The sounds went straight to the head as smoothly as alcohol. Louder and louder. Now they were all shouting, shaking their shoulders in bodily longing for movement. Black Antonio began to dance alone, pulling at the corners of a multi-coloured kerchief. A circle formed around him.

> *Hear the maracas rattle!*
> *Hear the drum-drum-beat!*

Exclamations like those at the cockpit urged the dancer on, as his waist turned wasplike in its elasticity and his hips began to swivel with an erotic motion. He threw his kerchief to the ground and, without missing a step, turning in a spiral, picked it up with his teeth, to shouts of enthusiasm.

The music rose higher. Menegildo entered the circle. The two dancers eyed one another like wild beasts spoiling for a fight. They began to move in circles, swaying their shoulders and arms in uneven movements, pursuing and brushing past one another alternating sexes as they enacted a ritual flight of the female from the male in rut.

'Get him! Burn him!' shouted the musicians. And the circular chase took on yet more meaning. Each tried not to show his back to the other, avoiding being made 'female' by a sudden step which symbolized the most abnormal of violations. Menegildo, already drunk, was dancing with such deliberation that they let him gyrate alone. Four hands started a *ñáñigo* beat. The sudden desire to reaffirm loyalty to the Cult – threatened by the insolence of the Goats – had stirred the musicians to profane, for a few moments, the sacred rhythm.[42]

The reader – intended but unable to become a spectator – senses that the writer has not yet decided what his objectives are. Carpentier has not quite succeeded in finding the balance between dramatic evocation, which was never to be his strong point, and explanation, his forte. He is still hesitating, palpably, between the divergent temptations of facile exoticism and avant-garde iconoclasm. As he notes in his prologue to the 1979 re-edition, 'To be "nationalist", yet also "avant-garde": that was the question.... A difficult project, because every nationalism rests on some form of respect for tradition, whilst "avant-garde" meant, inevitably, a break with all that'.[43] Nevertheless, at a time when the African contribution to Latin American culture was commonly represented in poetry and music, *Ecue–Yamba–O* was one of the first attempts to characterize the Black presence in narrative, and one which would be effortlessly surpassed in *The Kingdom of this World* two decades later.[44]

Miguel Angel Asturias: dreams and nightmares

By the time *Macunaíma* appeared, the young Guatemalan Miguel Angel Asturias (1899–1974) had almost completed a Spanish American equivalent in Paris, where he was studying ethnology at the Sorbonne. The first public readings took place in 1928, the year that *Macunaíma* was published. Asturias's deceptively titled '*Legends of Guatemala*' (1930), still virtually unstudied to the present day, is the first major anthropological contribution to Spanish American literature. The title actually suggests Asturias's desire to integrate and incorporate, rather than to negate and alienate. Since the Romantic period the evils of magic and witchcraft had been reduced to harmless 'legends', 'folklore' and 'superstition', but Asturias shared Mário de Andrade's awareness of just how much these ideological attitudes continued to associate the continent with Caliban's brutish ignorance and inherent inferiority. Like Andrade, who responded with the call for an American 'cannibalization' of European culture, Asturias thought attack the best form of defence and communicated a radically different vision, revealing a Latin American world as yet unimagined:

Vague accounts of earlier cities. The vegetation had covered the ruins and sounded like ravines beneath the leaves, as if all were rotting trunks, ravines and pools, ravines inhabited by creatures as lively as creepers, who spoke in low murmurs and who, in coils of ancient lianas, enveloped the gods to reduce their magical powers, as the vegetation had enveloped the earth, as clothing had enveloped woman. And thus it was the peoples lost their intimate contact with the gods, the earth and woman, folks say.[45]

It was a world originally discovered in books, but not necessarily inauthentic for that. It was time that Latin America, especially its lost past, appeared in books, especially books written by its own people, rather than out there in lost reality or in the fevered imaginations of others. In this Asturias shared the vision of Gallegos, whose own endeavour was to begin to recuperate oral culture for written record, but Asturias's voyage to Paris revealed tools that were not available to the Venezuelan, and showed him that the return journey was not across the open plains but through the winding paths of the indigenous cultural 'jungle' and the 'labyrinths' of Parisian avant-garde culture itself.

Moreover, Asturias's small country had behind it what Andrade's huge one lacked: a great native civilization. Thus the second part of his cultural strategy was to relate the 'primitive' (we were all 'Indians' once upon a time, in the tribal era) to the classical maize-based civilizations of the pre-Columbian era: Mayas, Aztecs, Incas. All were earth, maize, sun and star worshippers, space men. In Asturias's work the prehuman forces and creatures of native myth are given new life, and the Indians themselves are inserted into that landscape: the Spaniards here are very late arrivals, and their late arrival is always treated much more seriously than in most other writers. Asturias was also the first major novelist to perceive in Quetzalcóatl the greatest of all American myths and a convincing alternative to Jesus as a searcher, a culture hero, all-embracing and integrative, without separations, borders and exclusions:

Inside the jungle the forest closes off all paths. The trees fall like flies into the web of the impenetrable undergrowth. And at each step the agile hares of echo leap, run, fly. In the amorous depths of the penumbra, the murmur of doves, howling of coyotes, gliding of tapirs, padding of jaguars, soaring of kites and my tread awoke the echoes of the wandering tribes that came from the sea. Here their song began. Here their life began. They began their life with their hearts in their hands. When the paths had disappeared in opposite directions – the four corners of the heavens are opposites – the darkness returned like a sponge, filtering them in the darkness until they were dust, nothing, shadow... Isolated in a thousand snake coils, concupiscent, clumsy, I had the sexual agony of feeling roots growing out of me... Delirious night! My roots grew and ramified, filled with geocentric desire. I drilled skulls and cities, thought and felt through my roots, longing for the mobility of when I was neither wind, nor blood, nor spirit, nor ether in the ether that fills the head of God.[46]

Clearly when we speak of Ulyssean (or Thesean or Dantean) novels, we must not forget the possibility of a Quetzalcoatlian novel.

Asturias's most famous work, *The President*, briefly discussed in chapter 4, had actually been started in 1922 and was completed by 1933, thirteen years before its publication in 1946.[47] It is, in many ways, an avant-garde novel born of the clash in Asturias's consciousness between the Guatemala he had lived in until 1923 and the Paris he inhabited between 1923 and 1933. In that sense it is, with the arguable exception of *Don Segundo Sombra*, the first fully-fledged version of what I call the 'Ulyssean' novels, works which are not necessarily about the interrelation of Europe and America (as *The Lost Steps* and *Hopscotch* would be), but bear the imprint of the writer's own European odyssey in their interweaving of one reality with another, or in the superimposition of their enlarged, partly Europeanized, consciousness on Latin American reality. *The President*'s audacity of vision, imagery and meaning make its composition and appearance one of the key events of Latin American literary history. Indeed, the famous opening sequence is effectively the 'first page of the boom', according to a recent writer:

> Boom, bloom, alum-bright, Lucifer of alunite! The sound of the prayer bells droned on, humming in the ears, uneasily tolling from light to gloom, gloom to light. Boom-bloom, alum-bright, Lucifer of alunite, over the sombre tomb! Boom-bloom, alum-bright, over the gloomy tomb, Lucifer of alunite! Boom, boom, alum-bright... bloom, alum-bright... bloom, alum-bright... boom, bloom...[48]

Asturias's entire life until the age of twenty-one had been overshadowed by the fearsome dictatorship of Manuel Estrada Cabrera, and his own father's legal career was ruined by the tyrant. Thus in a primary sense, *The President*, in which every action and every thought is in some way circumscribed by the real dictator and his mythological aura, reflects in the most concrete form the horizons of Asturias's own childhood and adolescence. From that darkness, that imprisonment (not only the dictatorship, but also Hispanic traditionalism, semi-colonial provincialism, Catholicism and the family), he travelled to Paris, 'City of Light', to undertake his cultural apprenticeship to the twentieth century, in a capital which offered perhaps the most extraordinary confluence of ideas, schools and personalities assembled in one Western city since the Renaissance. The contrast between that light and the earlier darkness, perceived retrospectively and at first unconsciously, is perhaps the most important shaping phenomenon of the novel, and explains why Hispanic artists like Dalí, Buñuel, Neruda and Asturias were perhaps better able to fashion Surrealism for practical literary purposes than the French writers to whom many of its tenets, however fervently believed in, were really just ideas.

The President exemplifies more clearly than any other novel the crucial link between European Surrealism and Latin American Magical Realism. It is, indeed, the first fully-fledged Surrealist novel in Latin America, if we insist that a 'novel' must retain some social signification and a coherent plot. Since Surrealism posits a surface, rational or conscious reality and a profound, irrational or unconscious surreality (or subreality), Magical Realism attributes the conscious – and artificial, inauthentic (and in that sense unreal) – dimension to the European aspect of its culture, and the unconscious – and magical, creative, fertile and spontaneous – dimension to the autochthonous American aspect, though of course in practice the Magical Realist formula is really the interpenetration – one might almost say a miscegenation and indifferentiation – of the two. This is also, in another sense, what 'bi-culturalism' and 'transculturation', concepts invented to avoid the negative and colonized concept of acculturation, are intended to convey.

The President is an original work, both of and ahead of its time, which inevitably leaves it with something of a period flavour today. Because its subject – dictatorship – is so obvious, its more universal dimensions are easily overlooked. It remains the single most famous dictator novel of Latin American history, projected on to the screen of the reader's consciousness like a slightly tinted, flickering black and white silent movie. It provides an implicit critique of the concepts of progress and development, perceiving the extent to which, under Porfirio Díaz, Estrada Cabrera and other 'positivist' dictators, modernization was merely an ideology used for the advantage of a small elite. It was, as noted, probably the first major novel in Latin America to attempt a revolution in literary language, to exploit the relation between myth and language, and between both of these and the unconscious; it was also the first to underscore the functionality of myth in social and political life, to show that myth could be operative at the level of the text itself, and indeed to perceive that a narrative could also unfold as a kind of myth. The way in which the novel begins in darkness, flickers and ends in darkness, suggests a number of additional dimensions (birth–life–death, night–day–night, sleeping–waking–sleeping and absence–knowledge–absence) to the experience of watching a movie in the cinema, which is one of the dominant reference systems Asturias uses to frame and screen his narrative:

Immensity in movement. Her moving. Everything immobile inside her, moving. Words of surprise played on her lips as she saw the sea for the first time, but when she was asked what she thought of the spectacle she said with a foolish blase air: 'I'd already seen it in pictures!'...

Everything moving. Nothing stable. Picture after picture merging, turning, leaping in pieces to form an ever fleeting vision, in a state which was neither solid, nor liquid, nor gaseous, in which life is in the sea. The luminous state. In the pictures and the sea.

    With her toes curled up in her shoes and her eyes everywhere, Camila went on watching what her eyes had not yet seen. If in the first moments she'd felt her pupils empty to take in the immenseness, now the immenseness was filling them. It was the return of the tide to her eyes.[49]

The President was also the first important novel to unite the call for a revolution in politics and society with the call for a revolution in language and literature, to challenge patriarchy and authoritarianism at the level of consciousness, and thus to question the very basis of Latin American social life and psychic existence. This in turn makes it one of the first works – following *The Vortex* – to reverse the ideological signs of the century after Independence, which had involved an almost unquestioning march towards Europe, technological progress and modernity, a process which attained its literary culmination in *Doña Bárbara*. Asturias implicitly warns that for Third World regions no such march is possible, the vision is a mirage and Latin America, like its deadly yet ridiculous dictators and sycophantic social elites, will end up either as a mere caricature of Europe or as its dependent in a world of grotesque inauthenticity signified by the marionettes which inhabit Asturias's fictional galleries. In an article written in 1931 about the new Latin American narrative then appearing, Asturias gave one of the first intimations of the dominant direction which literature would take during the next three decades:

> One can see in it the tremendous struggle which has been fought out in America for the past one hundred and fifty years: the search for its spirit. Men of flesh and blood, peasants of flesh and blood, city-dwellers of flesh and blood, are battling against all things Spanish, which in the independence period meant everything spiritual, traditional, imported from Europe: an alien God, alien concepts of society and law. America, flesh and blood, rebels and raises ragged banners, on which are traced, as on giant leaves, the veins of its sons and daughters, clamouring everywhere: Liberty![50]

The youthful enthusiasm in this early statement of a materialist ethic, which we have already seen echoed in Roa Bastos's *Son of Man*, was to reach perhaps its classic expression in Carpentier's elegant conclusion to *The Kingdom of this World*:

> It was then that the old man, resuming his human form, had a supremely lucid moment. He lived, for the space of a heartbeat, the finest moments of his life; he glimpsed once more the heroes who had revealed to him the power and the fullness of his remote African forebears, making him believe in the possible germinations the future held. He felt countless centuries old. A cosmic weariness, as of a planet weighted with stones, fell upon his shoulders shrunk by so many blows, sweats,

revolts. Ti Noël had squandered his birthright, and, despite the abject poverty to which he had sunk, he was leaving the same inheritance he had received: a body of flesh to which things had happened. Now he understood that a man never knows for whom he suffers and hopes. He suffers and hopes and toils for people he will never know, and who, in turn, will suffer and hope and toil for others who will not be happy either, for man always seeks a happiness far beyond that which is meted out to him. But man's greatness consists in the very fact of wanting to be better than he is. In laying duties upon himself. In the Kingdom of Heaven there is no grandeur to be won, inasmuch as there all is an established hierarchy, the unknown is revealed, existence is infinite, there is no possibility of sacrifice, all is rest and joy. For this reason, bowed down by suffering and duties, beautiful in the midst of his misery, capable of loving in the face of afflictions and trials, man finds his greatness, his fullest measure, only in the Kingdom of this World.[51]

The President, the first real dictator novel, was also the first to show Latin American political, social and psychological life as a labyrinth or web of corruption, and indeed the whole tissue of human experience as a web or network of perceptions, emotions and ideas which have to be deciphered by the reader in order to reconstitute them and make sense of the world. No previous novel had so vehemently demanded the existential, emotional, moral and political commitment of the reader through the raising of consciousness, nor incorporated the real world of beggars and the deformed, showing them sleeping on their rubbish dumps and undergoing torture, intimidation and murder, to an extent which readers in the 1940s thought exaggerated. Now it may strike us as underplayed or mundane, though Asturias's fervent search for ways of forcing reader empathy through imagined identification with the poor and oppressed was almost unique at the time and remains remarkable to this day. His love of popular culture and understanding of its motivation and psychology was also unusual in fiction, as was the innate sympathy shown for feminine emancipation from his earlier works, in contrast with the contempt shown for women by authors as different as Gallegos, Güiraldes, Arlt and Onetti.

Finally *The President* was the first book since *Amalia* in 1851 to show that whole countries, entire cities, could be prisons, or that under a dictatorship, with terror and repression internalized, the human consciousness itself becomes a prison, rendering still more invisible all the other biological and psychological determinisms which we cannot entirely know but cannot entirely escape. Asturias could see this clearly from Paris (not that his later works show any illusions about the ultimate meaning of European civilization), which is why his novel, in its oscillation from the light of that great city to the darkness of Guatemala, from enlightenment to barbarous obscurity, so dramatically exemplifies the concept of the Ulyssean text. Given his subject matter, the writer achieves our enlightenment through

characters who themselves never discover it, or if they do, too late. The effect
has been well summed up by Gabriel Venaissin:

> I doubt if any novel has managed to create a greater sense of asphyxia. But the
> remarkable thing about this book lies in having used this universe to attain
> something else. Asturias invents a language of almost total freedom. Despite his
> point of departure in a poisoned world, there is not a single instant in which we do
> not feel ourselves projected towards the sky and the stars, launched towards space,
> pushed towards liberty from a reality in which liberty is dying at every moment.[52]

Readers have found something characteristically Latin American in this
contrast between imprisonment and freedom, reality and utopia. It was in the
1920s and 1930s, then, in the transition between the Novels of the Land and
the new 'labyrinthine' fiction, between Social Realism and Magical Realism,
that the liberation of Latin American fiction began.

Jorge Luis Borges: universality circumscribes and erases

> Like all men of the Library, I travelled in myyouth; I journeyed in quest of a
> book, perhaps the catalogue of catalogues; now that my eyes can barely
> decipher what I write, I am preparing myself to die a few leagues from the
> hexagon in which I was born.
>
> Jorge Luis Borges 'The Library of Babel', 1941

> Was I now, despite everything, going to die? Then I reflected that everything
> that happens to one does indeed happen, precisely, now. Century upon century,
> and only in the present do events occur; innumerable men on the air, the land
> and the sea, and everything that really happens happens to me...
>
> Jorge Luis Borges, 'The Garden of Forking Paths'

Borges was different from the others. He had been a leading avant-garde poet
in the 1920s but he was never any kind of revolutionary in the usual meaning
of the word. He was never interested in magic, nor in the primitive – the
rural, maybe, but only in so far as it is the forerunner of or adjacent to the
urban present – nor in Freud, and certainly not in Marx. Joyce was an early
fascination, but mainly in the sense that he had produced new 'ideas' about
what a book, a writer, a person, life and words are. Yet if Andrade, Asturias
and Carpentier brought about the opening to myth, oral expression and
popular experience which was to allow the exploration of Latin American
culture from the 1920s and thus to provide the essential basis for the New
Novel, it is Borges, unmistakably, who supplied the sense of precision and
structure which permitted the intertextual systematization of that culture and
the creation of the Latin American literature in which, incidentally, he never
believed.[53]

Borges is a masterly player of the dualist game, the inventor of the labyrinth in which all options appear to be neutral but are actually dominated by class, race, nationality and gender – not for nothing did he have an English education. Indeed he was able to read and write English more effectively than Spanish during his childhood, and spent his entire life endlessly crossing and recrossing the frontier between the two cultures.[54] For Borges all men are equal in the realm of ideas, but some much more equal than others – and inherently so – in the realm of reality. This double game – all values are relative and thus things are bad everywhere, but worst of all here in the empty continent; or, all men and all cultures are equal, but in practice some (the Indians, the gauchos) must be suppressed in the name of others – is characteristic of Latin American bourgeois writers, but Borges has raised it, in the most literal sense, to a high art within high culture. Rather like his contemporary Güiraldes, Borges's works are riven with violence, as Dorfman has shown, and with villains and illegitimates, as Paul de Man has noted.[55] Ultimately, after a childhood spent reading English adventure stories, he admired men on horseback, especially conquerors, not least his own ancestors: he thus managed to convert Argentina's nineteenth-century independence movement exclusively into one more triumph of the West, rather than an emancipatory, anti-colonial gesture. But then, it would be hard to find evidence in his work of any enthusiasm for emancipation in any of its forms. Thus, whilst giving him his brilliant due, my remarks on him here are concerned more to modify the most normal readings and to indicate not only his literary but his ideological importance for Latin American literature. Those who wish to use him either as an abstract thinking machine or as a justification for their own evasions can find an almost infinite bibliography elsewhere.

In the 1920s Borges was one of the best-known members of the youthful Hispanic avant-garde, prominent in the 'Ultraist' movement and a tireless cultural animator and contributor to little magazines. At the same time his early poems entitled 'Fervour of Buenos Aires' (Fervor de Buenos Aires, 1923) demonstrate that he, too, was at that time torn between the cosmopolitan lure of Europe and travel on the one hand, and nostalgia for the local and the picturesque on the other. Needless to say, the pleasures and pains of both are heightened, for the Ulyssean writer, by the contrast between them, which can only be fully experienced in the labyrinth of time, space and memory. In the 1930s the still young writer renounced both nativism and the avant-garde as infantile disorders and began to effect a long, slow revolution, first in Latin American fiction and eventually in Western literature as a whole. For some critics the publication of A Universal History of Infamy (Historia universal de la infamia) in 1935 marks the birth of Magical Realism in Latin America. But although this honour, as we have seen, must go to Andrade, Asturias and Carpentier – all writers with more convincingly 'native' cultures than Borges's disappearing gauchos – there seems little doubt that the book, a distant relative of Kafka's work, does mark the birth of Latin America's distinctive tradition of 'fantastic literature', a tradition most firmly rooted precisely in Argentina and Uruguay: Macedonio Fernández's '*Museum of the Novel of the Eternal One*' (*Museo de la novela de la eterna*, Argentina, 1967), an influence on the artistically dehumanized writings of both Borges and Cortázar, was conceived in the 1920s and written in the 1930s. The two styles – Magical Realism and 'fantastic literature' – were by no means the same, but certainly overlapped and both took on characteristically Latin American features, not least in their obsessive dualism. The tropical Magical Realism, centred on the Caribbean and Brazil, specifically set out to fuse an elemental but 'fertile' native culture with the more – but also less – knowing gaze of European consciousness; whereas the labyrinthine metaphysic of fantasy emanating from the River Plate, in the absence of such an alternative culture, fused the local reality, perceived as drab and second-rate, with a fantastic dimension which was really, perhaps, a sign for the superior 'metaconsciousness' of the Europe by which Argentines and Uruguayans felt they were inevitably defined and to which they hopelessly aspired. Borges's whole endeavour would be to resolve this tension through a strategy of relativization and redefinition.

The 1940s saw the great breakthrough. In 1940, together with his friends Adolfo Bioy Casares and Silvina Ocampo, Borges published an *Anthology of Fantastic Literature* (*Antología de la literatura fantástica*), and then his two incomparable collections of stories (for want of a better word), *Fictions* (*Ficciones*, 1944) and *The Aleph* (*El Aleph*, 1949). After that, and once he had collected his articles (for want of a better word) in *Other Inquisitions* (*Otras inquisiciones*, 1952), rather like a Galileo or an Einstein, Borges's work was effectively at an end. He continued of course to write poems, stories and essays, despite increasing blindness, but never again with quite the revolutionary verve of his work in the 1940s. The stories of *Fictions* and *El Aleph* are not studied individually here, but may be found scattered through the rest of this book (in much the same way that they are scattered through the rest of Spanish American literature).

There can be no doubt that Borges's reputation in Latin America grew in proportion to its growth outside. (His influence, however, had been growing since the 1930s, almost clandestinely, through his writings in the magazine *Sur*.) In the early 1960s most writers and critics in the subcontinent regularly dubbed him a 'European' and a 'reactionary', but gradually they realized that this was a losing battle and since about 1969 have – some grudgingly, others generously – made the best of a bad job. Borges, after all, as it transpired, was the man who inspired Michel Foucault to read the signs in the teacups of Western history and has been quoted repeatedly by no less an authority than

Derrida. Thus later writers like Carlos Fuentes came to suggest that without Borges there would not even have been a 'modern' Latin American novel, which is clearly untrue but none the less remarkable given his years as a political outcast and the fact that he never felt remotely tempted to write anything as gross as a full-length narrative. Nevertheless, there is some truth in the fact that if you strip the flesh from many contemporary Latin American novels, you will soon be feeling Borges in the bones.

Of all major Latin American writers, then, Borges is the least obviously 'Latin American', in the commonly understood sense of the phrase, not because he is from the most 'Europeanized' country, nor because his sources are apparently eclectic (closely examined, they are not), but because in his case repulsion from Latin America always outweighed attraction. More than almost anyone, Borges has felt the horror of being nowhere (a cultural vacuum frequently disguised as geographical distance), as a poem about his generation, 'Nineteen Hundred and Twenty-odd', makes crystal clear:

> We, remote from chance or hazard,
> Believed we were exiled in a time outworn,
> Time when nothing can happen.
> The universe, the tragic universe, was not here
> And maybe should be looked for somewhere else.[56]

So indeed he turned towards the Argentine writer's true heritage, the universe. Mocking those who believe that Argentines find themselves 'in a situation like that of the first days of Creation, an existential condition of primeval solitude and loss', Borges opts for a rather special version of universality:

I believe our tradition is all of Western culture, and I also believe we have a right to this tradition, greater than that which the inhabitants of one or another Western nation might have.... We should feel that our patrimony is the universe; we should essay all themes, and we cannot limit ourselves to purely Argentine subjects in order to be Argentine; for either being Argentine is an inescapable act of fate – and in that case we shall be so in all events – or being Argentine is a mere affectation, a mask.[57]

It is difficult to gainsay this statement, but it is also difficult not to notice that it begs virtually all of the important questions about the moral relation of an author to reality and to his readers.

Thus the only possible or desirable definition of a Latin American writer for Borges was one who was born there, and he periodically reminded his readers of the compensations of the Latin American condition, particularly for Argentines: 'The chief advantage of belonging to a rather traditionless land (for of course we are neither Spaniards nor red men) is that one has to fall back on the Universe or, at least, on Western culture'.[58] Rarely has so complete an ideology been packed into so few words. Even with regard to Western culture, however, Borges is the only major writer who has largely dispensed with those twin sources of Latin American inspiration, the literatures of France and Spain. Furthermore, within his favourite field of English literature, he opted perversely for writers ranking from the popular to the frankly mediocre. Thus Eliot, Yeats and even Joyce he would sometimes openly scorn, but Chesterton, Stevenson and Wells, who were among the first writers he read in the course of that Victorian childhood in Argentina, are nearly always 'right' and a reading of them invariably reveals extraordinary truths, at least to Borges. That the tongue is in the cheek should not deceive us: it is there as a defensive reflex, a characteristic double-bluff.

A superficial reading of his stories might lead one to think that he admired Arabic and Chinese culture as much as European, but let no one believe it: Borges was a classicist and an imperialist. At a certain point a reader of his work comes to the excited conclusion that his momentous project may have been to do for the 'universe' what Mário de Andrade did for Brazilian culture in *Macunaíma*: find the code, the structure, and hence the form, for articulating a unified discourse and thus, by structuring the heterogeneous, searching for an integrated global culture within which Latin American culture may be situated. This may already seem a little disappointing, not to say problematical, given Latin America's dependent status, but the sleight of hand – feigning a desired but impossible equality at the level of culture – represents an extension of Darío's achievement with the Modernista movement, and hence a bridge to some real equality in the future. The achievement is undeniably real, although the irony is that Borges would never have seen it this way: it is an achievement despite him, against the grain of his own conscious intentions. Moreover Borges's eclecticism is actually a fairly rigorous selectivism. Chesterton and Stevenson were part of his typically English reading childhood, and Chinese and Arabic culture came to him through the same route. He quoted Spanish writers only from the period of Spain's imperial splendour, identified unmistakably with England in its great colonial era, and in his later years gave himself over unhesitatingly to United States culture in its own great imperialist moment. Are these coincidences? I think not. The contemporary world is a mix of many cultures, and all ideas are in principle equally valuable, but Borges was glad that he descended from the Greeks and Romans, and glad too of his association with imperial England and the imperialist United States.

Outside of English literature, the universe was essentially chaotic, and philosophy for Borges was 'that organization of the essential perplexities of man'.[59] In a continent where despair and disillusionment are only the other side of a ferocious need for faith, he believed only in his own scepticism: reality may or may not exist, but it is certainly unknowable. Thus it is that Borges only played with philosophical ideas. He imposed order on the universe by considering it a vast kaleidoscopic jigsaw puzzle – one of those healthy activities recommended for keeping Victorian boys out of trouble – and what life comes down to is a process of organizing the pieces, however temporarily. No one has ever made them fit together more neatly than Borges, which is why his anti-humanist stories were such favourites with the Structuralists and Deconstructionists. This lonely Argentinian, writing from his blindness and from the gloom of a 'house in a far-off port in South America',[60] took the vision of the alienated bourgeois writer to its very limits, and it is at once ironic and wholly appropriate that such a man should have set off on the kind of literary epic quest which is supposed these days to be no longer feasible.

Borges thus compiled his own eccentric catalogue of books, writers and ideas in order to chart his own course through Western literature, demonstrate that its central themes are really no different from those of the Orient, and thereby justify his fundamental belief that 'universal history is the history of a few metaphors'.[61] To this end he invoked the spirits of Poe, Croce, Shelley, Schopenhauer, Kafka and Hawthorne, among others, to support Carlyle's observation that 'history is an infinite sacred book that all men write and read and try to understand and in which they too are written'.[62] From this he deduced what may be the key to an understanding of his influence, namely the idea that all writers are many writers and that 'each writer creates his precursors' – that is, 'each writer's work modifies our conception of the past as it will modify the future.'[63] This approach in the scintillating essays of *Other Inquisitions* (1952) allowed him to make such outrageous statements as that Chesterton 'restrained himself from being Edgar Allan Poe or Franz Kafka', or that, with regard to the two versions of a certain tragic history, 'the original is unfaithful to the translation'.[64] Perhaps his most complete statement is in the essay 'The Flower of Coleridge':

Around 1938 Paul Valéry wrote that the history of literature should not be the history of the authors and the accidents of their careers or the career of their works, but rather the history of the Spirit as the producer or consumer of literature. He added that such a history could be written without the mention of a single writer. It was not the first time that the spirit had made such an observation. In 1844 one of its amanuenses in Concord had noted: 'I am very much struck in literature by the appearance that one person wrote all the books...' Twenty years earlier Shelley expressed the opinion that all the poems of the past, present and future were episodes or fragments of a single infinite poem, written by all the poets on earth.[65]

In this extraordinary statement we see a reconciliation of the Spanish ballad tradition (all songs, in all their variants across time and space, are the work of 'the Spanish people') and the first and last lines of *One Hundred Years of Solitude*. Such tricks might have provided no more than momentary diversion were it not for their systematization across Borges's entire oeuvre, revealed in his remarkable ability to find the pieces for his puzzles in the most unlikely places. His *Extraordinary Tales*, for example, compiled with Bioy Casares, form an anthology of stories taken from Cicero, O'Henry, Chesterton, the *Folk Tales of Bengal*, Cocteau, Kafka, Valéry, Ah'med el Qalyubi, Stevenson, Gibbon, Diderot, Ah'med el Ibelichi, *Chinese Ghosts and Goblins*, and *The Weekend Companion to Wales and Cornwall*.[66] All of them could easily have been written by one writer, and of course the most likely man for the job would be none other than Borges himself. There is more to all this than meets the eye. In an essay entitled 'The Modesty of History', Borges blames Cecil B. de Mille retroactively for the traditional historian's tendency to think in terms of 'great days which changed the world', and suggests that 'history, real history, is more modest, and its essential dates may be, for a long time, secret.'[67] Borges was as modest as history, too, one might think – certainly most critics have accepted him at face value – but it gradually dawns on the reader that Borges is confident that he at least can read the great Text of Texts, and identify the essential dates, and that since all writers create their precursors, it is in fact he who is able to give meaning to all the earlier writers whose works he favours and whom he weaves together into such an appealingly eccentric pattern. The humble archivist is suddenly revealed as great prophet (only joking, of course).

Borges has, it seems, taken to extremes that other very English sort of hobby – collecting – by accumulating certain kinds of ideas, arranging them into sets and sticking them into his own album. In doing so he has created a series of anthologies, or perhaps just one anthology, which illuminate the processes of reading, writing and criticism in the most remarkable and unexpected ways, and in particular has opened up the debate on self-referentiality, intertextuality, reader participation and other current preoccupations. This makes the anthologies of his own writings, especially *Dreamtigers* (*El hacedor*, 1960), particularly interesting, since there for him is 'the distilled quintessence' of his own work. (It is amusing to see that the man who finds novels to be mainly 'episodic, illustration, psychological analysis, fortunate or inopportune verbal adornment',[68] should have taken his own precept seriously by condensing even the already stark 'fictions'.) By this means he has been able to define his own place in literary history, see his own face in the pattern of his precursors. It is, despite the mask of indifference and the pretence that all is just a game, an effort to defeat a permanent sense of loss increasingly heightened by the passage of time, and within this, an attempt to pre-record the image of his own face for posterity.

Life, then, is on one view just a system of mirrors; the identities of men are interchangeable; all things are happening continuously or being endlessly repeated. (My own involuntary homage to Borges is repeated each time I write about him: I find it almost impossible to use any other tense than the present.) We do not understand whether there is fate, causality or free will; we do not understand time and space; and we do not comprehend reality (which may be a mirage) or identity (which may be an infinite plurality, or another mirage). The labyrinth is all. James Irby has said:

> Borges once claimed that the basic devices of all literature are only four in number: the work within the work, the contamination of reality by dream, the voyage in time and the double. These are both his essential themes – the problematical nature of the world, of knowledge, of time, of the self – and his essential techniques of construction.[69]

Thus Borges is able to find himself (or anyone else, he would no doubt have said, if challenged) reflected down the ages in the images of other writers in other world literatures. His *aficionados* swallow this whole and willingly join in the illusionist's game. Thus Anthony Kerrigan, in his introduction to the *Extraordinary Tales*, blandly assured the readers that Lucretius was 'more Borgesian than Borges'.[70] Borges himself had clearly chosen his own epitaph in an essay on Paul Valéry in *Other Inquisitions*: 'A man who, in a century that adores the chaotic idols of blood, earth and passion, always preferred the lucid pleasures of thought and the secret adventures of order.'[71] A man, one might add, who, like Hamlet, whom he quotes at the beginning of one of his most celebrated stories, though bounded in a nutshell ('few things have happened to me, and I have read a great many'), yet counts himself a king of infinite space.[72]

The other side of this perspective brings us close to a lonely little boy, grown old, who told himself endless stories about the horrors of the universe the better to keep those horrors – increasingly close to him – at bay:

> A man becomes confused, gradually, with the form of his destiny; a man is, in the long run, his circumstances. Rather than a decipherer or an avenger, more than a priest of the god, I was a man incarcerated. From the tireless labyrinth of dreams, I returned as if to my home to the cruel prison.[73]

The more upbeat perspective is provided in his most satirical story, 'The Aleph', where the awful poet Carlos Argentino describes his vision of modern man:

> 'I picture him... in his study, as if in the watch tower, armed with telephones, phonographs, radio telephones, cinematographs, magic lanterns, glossaries,

timetables, almanacs, bulletins....'

He observed that for a man thus equipped the act of travelling was futile; our twentieth century had transformed the fable of Mahommed and the mountain; the mountains, now, converged on the modern Mahommed.... 'The journey I narrate is... *autour de ma chambre*.'[74]

In 1970, in the flush of his belated recognition and international celebrity, after many years without producing a new collection of stories, Borges published *Doctor Brodie's Report* (*El informe de Brodie*). It was distressingly illuminating. He declared in the preface that he had taken the opposite course to Kipling, since he, Borges, had begun his fictional career by writing exotic, maze-like stories, but wished to end as Kipling began, with 'a series of brief tales written in a straightforward manner'.[75] This, regrettably, was an apt enough description of a collection whose most striking motif turned out to be the ironies of fate in the seedy slums and suburbs of Buenos Aires at the beginning of the century, when Borges was a child and the city appeared to him to be populated largely by petty criminals, bartenders, gauchos and eccentric old ladies, and the air was heavy with an obsessive yet inconsequential violence. All Borges's stories are concerned in some way with time, and most of them end in death, which of course rather helps to sharpen the problem. The *Brodie* stories, however, appeared to have been written not to speculate serenely about time but to defeat it by taking him back to his roots, as his poetry did increasingly in his later years. And the violence was very much more concrete than before, as though the infant Borges's first encounters with brutality and mortality were freshening in his mind with the passing years.

Curiously, *Brodie* suggested that despite Borges's protestations to the contrary, his celebrity beyond the frontiers of Argentina enabled him to overcome his feelings of cultural inferiority and recognize his origin by once again exploiting the country's store of local colour in a way openly spurned when his works were written purely for local consumption. Sadly, the stories themselves lack the striking economy of *Fictions* and *The Aleph*, perhaps precisely because the lucidity of those earlier collections was emphasized as much as anything by the invariable triumph of each individual story over its own frequently eclectic and labyrinthine subject matter. The whole trick was that their very form built a logical prison from which, like Houdini, the great illusionist would leap miraculously free in the closing lines. Now it seemed that the master felt it was simply enough to put in an appearance, since the crowds of admirers were themselves sufficient proof of his magic. But it is hard not to suspect that the magic lay more in the name than the performance. Indeed, the preface read like a heavy-handed parody of Borges's earlier statements on creative writing, literary influences and translation. Many examples of the familiar lovable prejudices, the same old literary jokes, the same lupine arrogance disguised as sheepish modesty, were here crammed into four short pages where previously they might have come one or two a page. They had presumably been recognized as trade marks and the result read as if some internal producer had monitored the noisiest laughter and applause from Borges's successful United States lecture tours and then pieced the best moments together into one super self-congratulatory spectacular. And although age and overexcitement might have seemed the most reasonable explanation, one would have to ask a different question. Did success spoil Jorge Luis Borges?

Certainly, many of the 'boom' writers were subsequently drawn into the academic and publishing showbiz industry, but it was particularly hard to reconcile this in Borges's case with his longstanding and jealously maintained posture of ironic detachment and lofty disinterest. He was in fact carried like a banner around the North American campus circuit. He claimed in the preface to *Brodie* that 'now, having passed seventy, I believe I have found my own voice.' This was not quite exact. The truth was that Borges was now actually speaking in his own voice – let us be fair: one of his own voices – in his stories. The quietly modulated, eminently civilized voice that spoke in the *Fictions* and *El Aleph*, in the belief that only an initiated few would ever hear, was now declaiming stridently in the knowledge that all the world was listening. The message may have appeared to be different, but was not entirely so. It is just that all that had been left discreetly unspoken in those inimitable achievements of twenty-five years before was now openly articulated in tales narrated in the unashamed voice of reaction (the voice that had already applauded the invasion of Santo Domingo and the death of Che Guevara, and which would in due course thank Pinochet for an honour bestowed in Chile). It is a familar story: when you turn up the volume the quality of tone is diminished. Thus, for example, the first of the *Brodie* stories, 'The Gospel According to St Matthew', though apparently merely a narrative with an intriguing twist, operates most effectively as a statement that it is best not to educate the illiterate masses, since although they will not be able to understand 'our' teachings, they will nevertheless turn them against 'us' (the parallel with Shakespeare's Caliban, who learned to curse and maybe worse, is evident). Many of the other stories have similar morals.

It is obviously disturbing that despite his undoubted old-world courtesy and charm the man who may turn out to be Latin America's most important, or influential, writer of the twentieth century should be – virtually alone among significant contemporary authors – almost ingenuously Eurocentric, ethnocentric, phallocentric, a vicarious militarist and imperialist contemptuous of tribal cultures and native peoples everywhere: in short, an anti-Latin Americanist ashamed, like a significant stratum of Argentinian and

Uruguayan society, to share the continent with Bolivians and Paraguayans, an idealist, an ideological perpetuator of the civilization–barbarism dichotomy (your barbarism confirms my civilization), and thus a brilliant player of the double game, duplicitous as well as dualist.

It is important to say this because Borges's achievements are undeniable, in three respects above all others. First, he has, almost single-handed, revolutionized our ability to think about reading and writing. In real respects he has demystified these processes and even more profoundly the concepts of authorship and originality by foregrounding the artifice of art. This is the more extraordinary when one considers that reading and writing is what writers and critics are supposed to be meditating on all the time, yet it took a sceptic like Borges to penetrate the myths which have prevailed since Romanticism. Second, almost equally as important, is his approach to influences and his demonstration – again, despite himself – of the materiality of thought, language, literature and culture. The implications for an ex-colonial literature are far-reaching. Third, since he was, despite everything, a Latin American his revolutionary effect on literature and criticism has enormously advanced the international image and reputation of Latin America and its participation in Western culture.

All these achievements are supremely ironic, and one has to say of Borges what Marx and Engels said of Balzac's remarkable ability to write himself out of his own conscious ideology. Borges's effect within the most superficial strata of political consciousness is unquestionably and intentionally conservative, but his impact upon the conception and practice of literature, despite some insignificant side-effects, is overwhelmingly progressive. Contrary to common belief, philosophical and cultural relativism can be just as easily used for cynically justifying repression as absolutist systems. Borges himself was typically casuistical about this, having been through a dialectic of four levels of consciousness. First, his early 'Fervour of Buenos Aires' phase of nationalism; second, his period of shame when he retreated into complete universalism, which was actually Europeanism (Argentina is nowhere, Europe is somewhere); third, a move to universalize instead of privileging Europe (if Latin America is nowhere, Europe can be too); fourth, following his international success, a return to an acknowledgment of his roots, anticipated perhaps by his 'Conjectural Poem' about the thoughts of Doctor Laprida as he died at the hands of the first Montoneros in 1829:

> I who longed to be another, a man
> of judgments, books, opinions,
> will lie in marshes beneath the sky;
> yet my inexplicable heart exults in
> secret joy. At last I have found

my South American destiny.
   To this sombre evening was I led
by a multiple labyrinth of steps
woven by my days since one day in
childhood....
   In the mirror of this night I see
my unsuspected eternal face. The
circle now will close. I will it so. [76]

Ironically enough, Borges himself died in Geneva, the European city where he had lived as an adolescent. His permanent motto, 'all is relative', is an abstract concept concealing a very concrete 'all is hierarchy' in the real world. His relativism might be taken to imply that the whole planet is 'Mestizo', that all cultures have a reciprocity of influences, and thus we are all citizens of the world and the universe. This carefully overlooks oppression through class, race, gender and imperialism, and hence the unequal nature of all 'influences' in societies such as we inhabit, and would thus exclude the possibility that there are relations of domination and subordination among discourses or that language and consciousness are the site where conflicts actually take place. (As we shall see in chapter 8, the further elaboration of this debate is one of the major means by which Roa Bastos, with *I the Supreme*, implicitly counteracts what we can fairly call the Borgesian heritage.) Nevertheless, whatever its motivations, the assertion of relativity does – in practice – attenuate the deference to European and Europeanized thought systems, and does neutralize them through irony, which makes it all the more ironical that Borges is so often accused of being a 'European' writer. He is of course one kind of archetypally Latin American writer (the Mexican Alfonso Reyes was similar), one who takes cosmopolitanism to a connoisseur's level, but in an absolutely Latin American way. One could say more convincingly of Borges what Harry Levin said of Proust: 'No one has gone further in magnifying connoisseurship into a world-view, in visualizing one's self as heir of all the ages, as the soul adventuring among masterpieces.'[77]

Moreover, as has been noted, behind his revolutionary approach to writing and authorship was a supremely ironic stratagem which has been generally overlooked, namely that although Borges sees all writers as part of the same process, all different fragments of the same one face, and that if pressed he will always cautiously include himself in this, it is also possible to infer that he is, as it were the last of those great writers and great voices, the summit and supreme seer, the end of literature, after which, even if the same process continues, it will be downhill from that focal point of vision. There is therefore a special edge to John Updike's statement that Borges is a man for whom literature has 'no future'.

More important still in the long run is the insistence on the materiality of language, literature and culture. You are what you eat, as *Men of Maize* will teach us in the next chapter, but you are also, as both Borges and Asturias himself show us, what you hear and read, and the lesson applies as much to our learning of the simplest words at the dawn of time as it does to our readings of different contemporary authors and the 'influence' that each of these has upon us at the moment of 'creating' or 'producing' a text. Clearly this contradicts the relativistic idea of all men and women thinking exactly the same thoughts and being exactly the same person. Such a perception, which one can trace retrospectively through that famous line of self-referential texts from Boccaccio through Cervantes, Sterne and Machado de Assis, has been systematized with such force and rigour by Borges that even if, as seems unlikely, our culture were now to want to forget it again, as it did following each of those other writers, it could not now be forgotten. Indeed, the perception strikes so woundingly at the mystiques and mythologies of all writing, especially creative writing, in history, that one wonders whether it is not in itself a sign that the video and computer worlds are about to undermine the whole basis of old-style literacy, as thinkers from McLuhan to Steiner have hoped or feared.

We are of course talking about high culture (for Borges no other kind really exists). This materiality is never applied to low or popular culture, to the experiences of economics, class, race, gender or the oral culture and material experience of everyday life. For Borges's analyses this entire realm – which most people permanently inhabit – simply does not signify. There is no level of absolute specificity to counterpose against the life of absolute ideality which reduces all experience to abstract archetypes and all philosophies to vague relativities. The extension of this sense, stronger in Borges than almost any other writer (it is a motivating force) is that just as all human beings are no one (Shakespeare being the paradigm), so Latin America is nowhere, a place cursed to be empty of history, culture and even people, mere shadows or echoes of other places and other times (this might seem to be the vision of a Juan Rulfo, except that he has an explanation in feudalism and medieval Catholicism); or if there is a Latin America, it is just a hybrid chaos of imperfect copies, incoherent fragments, second-rate gestures – the world, in fact, of Asturias and García Márquez, except that they too have a ready explanation in the deconstructive phenomenon of imperialism. Far from this being a straightforward, all-encompassing view of reality, then, this is the ideological construction of a middle-class member of a Third World community who is ashamed of his background, humiliated by his national – and still more his continental – culture, and who has reacted against this existential predicament by emphasizing the futility and emptiness of all human existence in a world without God or meaning. Such an attitude would be more easily admired if it were born of defiance – though still more comfortable than courageously asserting the viability of one's own Third World or national culture for its own sake – but there can be little doubt that it was born of embarrassment, shame and a sense of inferiority which is in itself a symptom of a colonial mentality.

None of this prevented Borges from being one of the most influential writers of the century, and possibly, along with Darío (of whom similar judgments may be made), the most influential writer in the history of Latin America. A whole swathe of twentieth-century literature from Kafka, Pirandello and Unamuno to Calvino, Kundera and Eco (not to mention Cortázar and García Márquez) only makes the kind of unified sense it currently does thanks to the meaning which Borges's way of seeing retrospectively confers on these writers whilst also linking them backwards to their great distant 'precursors', as mentioned above. In Latin America itself this gives confirmatory legitimacy to a certain form of cosmopolitanism, which has been necessary for cultural communication and even survival, a certain way of being in and out of, part of and separate from Western culture, and at the same time a global approach to culture, knowledge and other men and other nations which is somehow wholly appropriate to the continent which completed humanity's knowledge of the world. The hierarchies and power relations really exist, and a serious observer must take account of them, explain them and confront them if the world is to be understood and changed. So the elementary questions still must be: who is talking, where, when and with what purpose? But equally the Structuralists and their Post-modernist successors in contemporary thought will continue to see both the whole of the past and the whole of the present as their domain, within their purview, available either as mouldable raw materials or simply as resources for the free play of the intellect and the imagination, for reality to be unified and contradictions abolished. In a sense Borges's contribution to this process is one version of a possible revenge of the Latin American mind, its reconquest of global space through the intellect when force of arms, science or philosophy are not available for the task.

Now the role of a second, shadow world, or authoritative master reference system, the basis of comparativism, was formerly provided by classical culture for the European nations and their intellectual ruling classes, as part of their ideological weaponry against the barbarism within their own borders or outside them. Borges, who, significantly, has not the slightest interest in or knowledge of anthropology, that – in principle – most humanistic and unifying of all the sciences, has made the whole world, above all the past, available as a kind of huge classical culture, and has therefore made the Latin American perspective – the latest, and in that sense, culminating Western perspective – a surprisingly privileged tool at what many feel to be the twilight of European culture, the culmination of modernity. In this he has given an advance figuration of Carpentier's prophecy that Latin America is destined to play a very special role in the future of humanity, as a melting pot of widely dispersed cultures, one which finds itself at a morally advantageous historical disadvantage.

This, again, is what Andrade and above all Asturias contributed in their own ways, at the level of popular culture and American mythology. Borges Americanizes universal culture and Asturias and Andrade universalize American culture, whilst Carpentier constantly theorizes the relation between these two activities. Asturias is the anthropological, mythological novelist par excellence, whose archaeology of the senses and anthropology of gestures and the body make him perhaps the most humanistic novelist in the history of Latin America. It is not surprising that his achievements have been more unequivocally recognized by the Senegalese poet Léopold Sedar Senghor and the Martinican Aimé Césaire than by the indigenist or purely cosmopolitan writers of Latin America, who sometimes dislike his literary approach to indigenism on the one hand or his raising of specific culture traits to a universal level on the other. Carpentier's constantly elegant and illuminating comparativist activity in relating Latin American to other cultures gives some kind of insight into what Borges himself might have achieved had he turned his formidable skills to an exploration and classification of Latin American cultural manifestations: he might have been the Lévi-Strauss of Latin American historical culture.

If we look at things in this light we can see what a remarkable contribution this ABC of writers made to Latin American culture in this century, in the transition between a traditional and a modern world, and between Europe and Latin America. They were the great cultural bridge, effective intermediaries between two worlds, and thus the first Ulyssean narrators. None of the 'boom' writers can claim to have been an authority on anything – even Latin American, still less global – in comparison with the erudition of that quartet of great writers from an earlier generation (to whom, for the purposes of this discussion, one should undoubtedly add Octavio Paz), who came to first maturity in the 1920s when the 'primitive' Social Realists were achieving their fame and influence. Why should this be? It is a problem that needs careful thought, though the answer must surely lie in the different historical experience of the two generations. When Andrade, Asturias, Borges and Carpentier began to write, in the mid-1920s, Latin America had barely begun to experience modernity, whereas the writers who attained celebrity and wrote their greatest works in the mid-1960s had grown up with it all their lives and absorbed the new pace and variety of contemporary urban experience without even thinking about it. For them, indeed, the city and its inhabitants were the primary reality and it was the countryside which was abnormal. For the earlier generation the motor car, airplane, gramophone, cinema and radio were all new experiences to be absorbed after childhood, but modernity as a whole, and life in a great modern conurbation were recent enough in origin to be perceived as essentially non-American experiences.

In that sense, then, 1920 was really the last moment where the divorce between modernity and underdevelopment could ever be quite so visible and quite so shocking in the Latin American environment. And this is simply to refer to the impressionistic, perceptual level, without theorizing the impact of transformations in relations of production and class dynamics or transformations in the literary legacy – positivistic Naturalism and idealist Modernismo – which they had inherited; nor the impact of the world's first Communist revolution in 1917 as most of them were reaching adulthood. Other writers of that generation, like Uslar Pietri and Aguilera Malta, came close but did not quite achieve the same integrated vision that Borges achieved through philosophy, Carpentier through cultural history, and Asturias and Andrade through anthropology: all of them great comparativists, great integrators, great fixers and definers of what Latin America was in comparison with other places and cultures. The generation of Reyes and Henríquez Ureña were too early for this, and Cortázar and Lezama Lima were too late, veering off into post-Borgesian archetypes. Men who did achieve the same mix of European and Americanist currents over the same period were the poets Vallejo and Neruda.

This, surely, was Latin America's decisive artistic generation (for much the same phenomenon is visible in music and the plastic arts); and despite various retrospective attempts at parricide it was also, thanks to its privileged experience of historical change, probably the most talented one. Its writers were the first to achieve a decisively focused synthetic vision of world history and Latin America's place in it from a specifically Latin American cultural perspective. Their own continental experience was already that of a transition between nineteenth-century traditionalism and modernity, but was not so traumatic as to diminish the culture shock, the *éblouissance* of their confrontation with Paris in the 1920s, a unique moment in a world which had still not decentred, was still focused on the one cultural arena, where they could still rub shoulders as they grew up with the great names of the international cultural world. The Modernistas had arrived there in the 1890s from cities already aping anciens regimes in the early years of the Belle Epoque; but the American way of life and the democratic avant-garde were quite a different matter. The writers of that era were culture shocked, in two meanings of the word: eyes and minds opened, liberated, everything now possible and all one had to do – it was the new ethos – was to work on the raw material of experience. Marx and Freud spoke of other forms of liberation (or deconstruction), for which, again, one needed neither culture, class, race nor style. Divisions, including those between the developed and underdeveloped worlds, poetry and prose, and each of the arts, vanished, were exploded. This, ironically, gave them the confidence to acquire a world culture for the first time. It is difficult to see how such a phenomenon can ever occur again; but then for Latin America it will never be necessary again.

The 1960s generation by contrast grew up modern. No one was modern before 1914, and no one who was middle class was exempt from it thereafter. They therefore never had their eyes opened quite so radically as the previous generation. On the other hand, the developed–underdeveloped dichotomy now existed fully and completely within their own countries – you did not have to go to Paris or New York to see an ultra-modern city – and therefore the Mestizo culture and the possibility of Ulyssean travel was now achieved almost as easily in the imagination or by staying at home (perhaps not quite: all the 'boom' writers were in fact great travellers – you had to travel to make the images and contrasts really move).

First World intellectuals had been experiencing the shock of industrialization, urbanization, imperialism and modernity slowly and gradually, from the 1850s, yet even they were stunned by the shock of events between 1910 and 1918. But the period from 1918 onward was the crucial moment for Third World intellectuals. No shock was greater than that experienced by Miguel Angel Asturias, from darkest Guatemala, confronting the dazzling reality of Paris in 1923, but his reaction was nevertheless representative of an entire generation. Surrealism was ideally conceived to sustain and respond to the contradictions involved and to build the necessary bridges between First and Third World intellectuals, both of whom – moving in opposite directions – were now heavily involved in the Ulyssean journey.[78] The next generation grew up with modernity and with the contradiction between the modern and the traditional, the urban and the rural – what sociologists eventually would call dualism – as part of normality. Paris, when they got there, was no longer such a privileged 'centre' and was only slightly more stimulating than Mexico City, São Paulo or Buenos Aires. They were used to Freud and Marx part one, but they did have two additional impulses: first, that previous generation from Latin America itself, which was actually the vanguard of their own movement, and which was itself already modern; and second, the example of the great European and North American Modernists, who had not been fully incorporated by that previous generation (not to mention by Europe itself, where they have still not been superseded: in Britain, at least, we too still feel in the shadow of Joyce, Woolf, Eliot, Lawrence and Yeats).

Then came politics again, as it had in the 1920s, separating the younger from the older writers. After a period of economic growth and patchy political democratization came the New Left (a new Marx, after Stalin, and a new Freud, following Reich), Third World liberation, women's liberation and sexual liberation. And above all Cuba, which in the early 1960s at least seemed to conjugate all the above. These writers were upcoming anyway, but this conjuncture of forces moulded and shaped them with an irresistible momentum and centrifugal force which at first carried them close to the heart of Latin American reality, and then – the market, capitalist economics, a different politics in the 1970s – away again and, in many cases, back into the merely cosmopolitan realm. Let us simply note, at this point, that Ulysses goes to the dangerous isles of Europe and comes back, inevitably, another; just as Stephen also went to France, and wrote *Ulysses*. (Gide: 'in order to find oneself, one must lose oneself first'.)

We shall be looking at this story in more detail, though from other angles, in subsequent pages. Borges apart (his importance is as the polar opposite of Social Realist Americanism), the first great example of the new vision is Asturias's *Men of Maize* (written and published at about the same time as another Ulyssean–Thesean–Dantesque work, '*Adam Buenosaires*', and the first fragments of Lezama Lima's *Paradiso*). It was followed by *The Lost Steps*, *Pedro Páramo*, *The Devil to Pay in the Backlands*, *Hopscotch*, *The Death of Artemio Cruz*, *The Green House*, *One Hundred Years of Solitude* and *I the Supreme*. These are the works we shall be examining in detail in the chapters to come. They are all novels in which the symbolism of national (within international) history is fused with the symbolism of individual (within universal) myth. And they are books about countries rather than books about cities. Interestingly, and significantly, none of their authors managed to write two such works – though Carlos Fuentes has tried valiantly with *Terra Nostra* – because each of them is a novel which unites the history of a continent, a country and an individual, the writer himself. All are written roughly under the sign of both Marx and Freud, whilst all are provided with an approximately Faulknerian solution, given his prior experience in uniting a vast outback with a cosmopolitan city experience. This, overall, is the background to and framework for the production of Latin America's great Ulyssean works during this decisive period of post-emancipation history.

6

The Rise of the New Novel

Given the virginity of its landscapes, the formation, the ontology, the challenging presence of the Indian and the Negro, the Revelation caused by its recent discovery, the fertile Mestizo cultures it has produced, America is far from having exhausted its stream of mythologies.... Through the dramatic singularity of its events, the fantastic aplomb of the characters who met, at a given moment, at the magic crossroads of Cap Français, everything turns out marvellous in a story impossible to situate in Europe, and which is nevertheless as real as any exemplary event recorded, for the edification of schoolchildren, in textbooks. But what is the whole history of America if not the chronicle of a marvellous reality?

Alejo Carpentier, Prologue, *The Kingdom of this World*, 1949

For Borges, in the South of Latin America, Argentine reality was not fantastic unless refracted through the vision of an imagination which was, by definition, individual, and could thus commune with other heightened individualities transmitted down the ages. Asturias and Carpentier, by contrast (Mário de Andrade never pursued the line initiated in *Macunaíma*), stimulated by their contacts with the Surrealists, and further encouraged no doubt by Breton's bedazzlement when he visited Mexico in 1937, were inspired by the idea that Latin American reality was inherently magical, and was simply awaiting a new generation of novelists to communicate it. Like Pablo Neruda, who was undertaking the same task in poetry with his '*General Song*' (*Canto general*, 1950), they took up exactly the opposite point of view to Borges: writing, an individual act, was self-indulgent unless conceived as the representation of a collectivity. Private mythologies were the sign of an alienation. Asturias's *The President* had been devoted almost entirely to fantasy, but its purpose was precisely to reveal the collective origin of indi-

171

vidual experience and to assert that no fantasy could ultimately ward off the power of the terrorist state. The beggar Pelele, an idiot, sleeping on his rubbish tip, is one of the first creations of this vertebral current in Magical Realism:

> Covered in scraps of paper, leather, rags, skeleton umbrellas, brims of straw hats, saucepans with holes in, broken china, cardboard boxes, torn books, pieces of glass, shoes curled up by the sun, collars, egg-shells, bits of cotton and food – Pelele went on dreaming...
>
> He heard the rustle of starched petticoats – wind and leaves – and ran after her with tears in his eyes.
>
> He found relief at his mother's breast. The bosom of the one who had given birth to him absorbed like blotting paper the pain from his wounds. What deep, imperturbable refuge! What abundant love! My pretty baby! My big baby! Hugging him, cuddling him...
>
> Pelele lifted his head and without speaking said:
>
> 'I'm sorry, Mamma, I'm sorry.' And the shadow tenderly stroking his face, replied: 'I'm sorry, my son, I'm sorry.'[1]

The New Novel, then, which in retrospect began its trajectory at the end of the Second World War, followed the different paths marked out by the writers who had undergone the 'Ulyssean' experience in the 1920s, above all Asturias, Borges and Carpentier. It is perhaps surprising, at first sight, that the most important novels to emerge during this period, following another great war, should again have been 'regional' or 'telluric' in orientation. Not until the 'boom' itself in the 1960s were Latin American writers able regularly to produce great works of urban fiction in response to the growth of a well-educated middle-class audience and the increasing concentration of the population in large cities. One might say, oversimplifying inevitably, that this was the moment in which the Faulknerian impulse predominated in Latin American fiction and that the Joycean moment would only fully crystallize in the 1960s, after the publication of *Hopscotch*.

Faulkner himself was of course a 'Ulyssean' writer in both senses of the word. He had travelled the world and then returned, 'weary of wonders', as Borges would put it (in his poem 'Ars Poetica'), to perceive that 'Art is that Ithaca, of green eternity, not of wonders', and thus to make a world, Yoknapatawpha County, Mississipi, out of his original world. And he was also a Modernist, Joycean writer, who was inspired by the Irishman's unrivalled exercise of formal freedom and adapted the interior monologue and stream of consciousness to his own purposes. The rather grand story of Faulkner's relation to both the French *nouveau roman* and the Latin American *nueva novela* remains to be told.

Ironically enough it was Borges, never a lover of long fiction, who made the most significant contribution to Spanish American awareness of Faulkner by translating *The Wild Palms* in 1940, the year after its first publication, just as he had translated the last page of *Ulysses* in 1925. *The Wild Palms*, with its juxtaposition of distinct realities, is perhaps the closest predecessor of a narrative line which would culminate in Vargas Llosa's *The Green House* in 1966. For Faulkner's realm is the unfinished, traumatized rural environment of the American South, an accursed land like the lands of Juan Rulfo, João Guimarães Rosa and Gabriel García Márquez. Indeed, Faulkner's imagination, like that of García Márquez, was dominated by a legendary colonel, in his case his great-grandfather. And one of the old man's spare-time activities was writing pulp fiction, a favoured subject for Faulkner's satirical ambiguities which foreshadows one of Vargas Llosa's richest veins. Moreover Faulkner himself was for three years a postmaster, just as García Márquez's own father was a telegraphist. Faulkner's characters are Black, Red and White, rich and poor (though usually the former declining into the latter), portrayed over three hundred years but particularly since the early nineteenth century, all struggling to discover a destiny and assert an identity which can never be forged collectively against a tragic history of violation, extermination, slavery and civil war, and a legacy of guilt, despair and solitude.

In the third volume of *Memory of Fire*, Eduardo Galeano evokes Faulkner in 1942:

Sitting in a rocking chair on the colonnaded verandah of an old crumbling mansion, William Faulkner smokes his pipe and listens as the ghosts confide in him.

The plantation owners tell Faulkner of their glories and fears. Nothing fills them with more dread than the mixing of races. A drop of black blood, just one drop, is a destiny which curses a life and compels one to an eternity amongst the black flames of hell.[2]

Galeano has understood what others have so often overlooked, namely the precise nexus of themes and techniques which makes Faulkner such a formidable influence on the Latin American New Novel – miscegenation and its contrasts and juxtapositions foremost among them. Like Faulkner, then, the leading Latin American writers were by the 1940s citizens not only of their own lands but of the world and they looked on their continent and its culture with a radically transformed gaze, mapping the cultural landscape through their geographical, social and historical explorations. It was, in short, a process of internalization of Latin American history. Rivera's *The Vortex* had begun the effort to get beneath the surface of reality through the resonances of Romantic poetry, and Gallegos through the use of folklore in *Cantaclaro* (set on the plains) and *Canaima* (set in the forest). *Canaima* had concluded that in order for Latin Americans to become Mestizos, to assume and accept that status, they first had to become Indians, and this is one of the symbolic acts of assimilation which the next generation of writers attempted to undertake.

Miguel Angel Asturias, *Men of Maize*

Men of Maize (1949) by Miguel Angel Asturias was the first unmistakable Magical Realist – Joycean rather than Faulknerian – novel, remains by far the most ambitious to this day, and there are powerful reasons for arguing that it is the greatest. Ariel Dorfman perceived its importance as early as 1968:

> Although its origins fade into remote regions and its socio-cultural coordinates are still disputed, the contemporary Spanish American novel has a quite precise date of birth. It is the year 1949, when Alejo Carpentier's *The Kingdom of this World* and Miguel Angel Asturias's *Men of Maize* saw the light of day. The latter, both the fountainhead and the backbone of all that is being written in our continent today, has met with a strange destiny, like so many works that open an era and close off the past.[3]

One is tempted to think that if Asturias had somehow been able to wait to write it in the 1970s, after the rise of the new revolutionary Left, after Lévi-Strauss and Lacanian psychoanalysis, in the new green age of ecology, feminism and global consciousness – all of which it anticipates – it might have staked a convincing claim to being one of the world's great novels of the century. It is a profound meditation on the history of Guatemala, contained within a symbolic history of Latin America since the conquest, contained within the history of humanity's passage from so-called barbarism to so-called civilization since the Greeks, contained within the novelist's own reflections on the human condition based on his own experience of life in the half-century 1899–1949, which is the novel's own approximate timespan. Everything fits: the complexity and precision of the overall conception, which was unquestionably achieved through a process of literary bricolage, is breathtaking.

Surprisingly, this is the only one of Latin America's best-known novels which begins not with the conquest, but with the native Indians themselves. There are, to be sure, many novels centred on the Indians, but all the novels which juxtapose both worlds see the conquest as their uncontested point of departure – and therefore as the given or pre-existing – and inevitably view the Indians from that perspective as some form of problem. This is true even of José María Arguedas, whose direct experience and knowledge of the Indians is so much greater than that of Asturias.

Men of Maize is in six parts, the last as long as the first five taken together. In the first part a group of native Mayan tribesmen, primitive guerrillas, led by chief Gaspar Ilóm, struggle in vain to defend their ancestral homeland in the mountain forests of Guatemala against the encroachment of private property, market forces and the capitalist state. They are thus defending the loss of the earth's natural covering and the magical dreaming time which it protected. This would be at the end of the nineteenth century, following the suppression by the Liberal governments then in power of communal indigenous territories in favour of capitalist agriculture. Ilóm is abandoned by his woman, Piojosa Grande, and defeated by the outsiders, just as his forefathers were abandoned by their gods and defeated by the Spaniards, and he vanishes into the world of myth. In parts 2–4, seven years pass, during which the surviving Indians attempt to hold out against the government forces and achieve some temporary victories which allow them to recuperate and partially stabilize their maize-based communal culture. In part 5, however, after many more years have passed, the blind Indian beggar Goyo Yic is deserted by his ever-pregnant woman María Tecún. Yic has his sight restored, takes to the road in search of his lost wife, and becomes, successively, a pedlar, a liquor trader and a jailbird, but never finds her. The section is evidently transitional between tribal and class society, between oral and written culture ('I'm looking for a woman I know only by ear, I've never seen her'), and between native religion based on the natural forces of fertility and sterility and the Christian world of good and evil symbolized by the Cross.

Part 6 sees the events of the earlier parts forgotten as history but dimly preserved as myths, legends and folklore, about which a variety of characters speculate from their widely different standpoints. The two main characters, intermediaries between the country and the city, are an Indian postman, Nicho Aquino, bearer of messages to which he is indifferent, and a Mestizo muleteer, Hilario Sacayón, bearer of commodities which belong to others. The two central myths 'invented' by Asturias are both well-known phenomena which appear in a variety of forms within Middle American folklore, but the author gives each a radically historical and psychoanalytical treatment: that of the 'tecunas', or runaway wives, no doubt signifying a lost relationship to the earth and the community, and that of the 'nahuales', or animal counterparts, communicating the repression of natural impulses. The Indian postman loses his woman, just as Ilóm and Yic did before him, but he is so alienated from his own culture that he can find her only by means of a journey through the undergrowth labyrinths of geology, biology and psychology. The Mestizo muleteer, true son of Spain (Don Juan or Don Quixote, that is the question...), never really has his woman in the first place, because, through the ideology of romantic love, he constructs an idealized version of her, the legendary Miguelita, which then becomes the site of both personal and nationalist ideologies. The novel ends enigmatically. The tribal chief is long since dead, but his lost woman makes a mystical rain-clad reappearance as the mother goddess of a forgotten matriarchal and collectivist era which may be pre-Mayan as well as pre-Hispanic; postman and muleteer fade into alienated anonymity; but Yic, the Indian who can still recuperate the fertile blindness of his past, is reunited at last with his woman, his children, the communal heritage and the maize-bearing land which is both his past and his future.

In each of the three phases – tribal, feudal/colonial and capitalist/neo-colonial – an Indian protagonist is defeated, loses his woman and, cut off from the earth and the maizefield, turns to drink and despair. Each is more alienated and distanced than his predecessor. The three phases based on modes of production are aligned, in mythological fashion, to the tripartite Mayan cosmic design – underworld, earth, sky (past, present, future) – which is the trajectory of Quetzalcóatl, the plumed serpent and Meso-American culture hero for whom, as for Asturias, the irruption from darkness or 'pre-history' is the model for all cognitive processes. His inherently Freudian trajectory, of course, is itself based on the sun's daily journey around the sky and beneath the earth and reflects the annual cycle of maize cultivation, whose rhythms and symbolism dominate the entire narrative with its powerful submerged imagery.

In *Men of Maize*, then, the Indians are there first, the novel's past is their past, and it is the Spaniards and Ladinos (Mestizos) who are the problem:

> The matapalo is bad, but the maizegrower is worse. The matapalo takes years to dry a tree up. The maizegrower sets fire to the brush and does for the timber in a matter of hours. And what timber. The most priceless of woods. What guerrillas do to men in time of war the maizegrower does to the trees. Smoke, flames, ashes. Different if it was just to eat. It's to make money. Different, too, if it was on their own account, but they go halves with the boss, and sometimes not even halves. The maize impoverishes the earth and makes no one rich. Neither the boss nor the men. Sown to be eaten it is the sacred sustenance of the men who were made of maize. Sown to make money it means famine for the men who were made of maize. The red staff of the Place of Provisions, women with children and men with women, will never take root in the maize plantations, try as they will.[4]

Asturias invokes here the sonorous echoes of Mayan sacred texts such as the *Popol Vuh* or *Book of the Community*, the so-called 'Maya Bible', as he establishes the elementary contrast between the sacred and the profane, use and exchange values. But this is also a novel which has both the classic Ulyssean design – a journey round the world and back to home – in the shape of the character Goyo Yic, and the Thesean design – a journey into the under-world (the past, the unconscious, nature) – in the shape of Nicho Aquino, only for the reader to realize by the end that the two patterns together make up the trajectory of Quetzalcóatl, as mentioned above. (*Mulata*, 1963, fuses the experience of Quetzalcóatl with that of Dante.) It was the first Latin American novel to attempt a synthesis of the Marxian and Freudian concepts in one perspective, to build ecology into a world vision, and to invert the normal patriarchal symbols so that instead of the woman representing the land in some immobile sense she represents a relationship to it, and far from deserting the male she is actually fleeing from his oppression. And beyond this, Asturias was the first writer to appreciate that myths have their own history, and that in some respects culture is the shadow of a shadow of a shadow. The theme of the conservation of the natural landscape and vegetation goes hand in hand with the concept of the conservation of culture and language through memory and resistance:

> Gaspar is invincible, said the old folk of the town. The rabbits with maize-leaf ears protect Gaspar, and for the yellow rabbits with maize-leaf ears there are no secrets, no dangers, no distances. Gaspar's hide is mamey skin and gold his blood – 'great is his strength', 'great is his dance' – and his teeth, pumice stones when he laughs and flint stones when he bites or grinds them, are his heart in his mouth, as his heelbone is his heart in his feet when he walks. Only the yellow rabbits know the mark of his teeth in the fruits and the mark of his feet along the paths. Word for word, that is what the old folk of the town said. You can hear them walking when Gaspar walks. You can hear them talking when Gaspar talks. Gaspar walks for all who have walked, all who walk and all who will walk. Gaspar talks for all who have talked, all who talk and all who will talk. That is what the old folk in the town told the maizegrowers. The storm beat out its drums in the hall of the blue doves and beneath the sheets of cloud over the savannahs.[5]

No novel has gone deeper and wider in exploring the labyrinths of Latin American cultural history. Asturias even has an unmistakable affection for – and much more direct knowledge of – the peasant, Mestizo culture which partly created him but which, as part of the Western heritage, he questions and even deplores, so that folk culture from the European side is as well represented as the myths and legends of the contemporary Indians and their pre-Alvaradian ancestors. The narrative's point of departure, the resistance of Gaspar Ilóm at the beginning of the century, is based on a real historical incident. This was itself representative of a historical process which still continues both in Guatemala and Latin America generally – the destruction of the Amazon jungle and its native inhabitants is only the most dramatic example – and was in turn part of a global development identified by Lenin as the imperialist scramble through which capitalism climbed to its peak of world dominance. It is the most complete enactment of a process whose chain-like structure is also visible in 'Race of Bronze', Huasipungo, Broad and Alien is the World, 'Everyone's Blood', and The Green House, namely that of the native Indian uprooted from his culture and ejected from his homeland by the typical processes of Western capitalism, who either rebels or sets out defeated on the road to loneliness and alienation. Clearly, in that sense, this is a retrospective, assimilative work, a panoramic examination of a historical landscape, a meditation by a city man on the origins of a national and continental culture, an all-absorbing immersion in the labyrinths of the past and present.

The novel moves on from this, however, to explore the sense of loss experienced by all peoples and all individuals due to the passage of time and the growth of knowledge itself, as when the blind beggar Goyo Yic has his sight restored:

> The little bird – it looked more like a fallen leaf – came, stopped, gave three hops, and flew away. Minimal. Nervous. An electrified coffee bean. His eyes flew away, too, eyes which, now they had emerged from their shells, would always be running away from him.[6]

Many years later, after Yic and his lost wife, María Tecún, have become legends, another character rides past the great rock into which the runaway woman is said to have been turned. He hears the blind man calling her name:

> Who has never called, never shouted the name of that woman lost in his yesterdays? Who has not pursued like a blind man that being who went away from his being, when he came to himself, who kept on going and still keeps on going from his side, a runaway, a tecuna, impossible to hold because if she stops time turns her into stone?...
>
> The voice of that blind man who, so folks say, left the clouds of his eyes behind when he regained his sight up there in that place, only to lose it again with that soapy water which allows no image to stand still, fix itself in one spot, they all go sliding by, marching away, erasing one another like those great slate blackboards down in rocky hollows where the stones look like the bodies of petrified lizards, or like those abandoned trees, stripped of leaves, which look less like trees than the antlers of giant animals sunk in glaciers.[7]

Here in this sixth part, the detribalized and desacralized Indians have been set 'free' from tradition and thenceforth subjected to 'the constant revolutionizing of production, uninterrupted disturbance of all social conditions, everlasting uncertainty and agitation', to quote Marx and Engels. The contradiction between use and exchange values, Asturias's point of departure, was also Marx's in *Capital*; and production and reproduction, the foundation of Engels's *The Origin of the Family*, are his two pivotal themes; together with an interpretation of the primacy of matriarchy which Marx and Engels took from Morgan and which, however 'mythological', has been adopted more recently by a number of feminist thinkers. Derrida and Lacan are then anticipated, as castration, inscription, truth and law are invoked; the gaze, absence and the abyss are explored through the adventures – road, desire, discourse, memory – of Goyo Yic and those who seek to retrace his steps. For the Mestizo characters in the novel, the absences which dominate their lives prove irretrievable, but the Indian characters are shown to be capable of recuperating and assimilating the past through collective memory and myth, as the old witch Nana Moncha explains:

> We often think we've invented things that other people have forgotten. When you tell a story that no one tells anymore, you say: I invented this, it's mine. But what you're really doing is remembering – you, through your drunkenness, remembered what the memory of your forefathers left in your blood... and if it hadn't been you it would have been someone else; someone would have told it, so it wouldn't be forgotten, because its existence, true or false, is part of the life, part of the nature of these places, and life cannot be lost, it's eternally at risk but it cannot be lost eternally.... Tales are like rivers, they pick up what they can as they flow past, and if they can't pick up something and carry it along, they carry its reflection.[8]

Setting aside Borges' concentration on universality, such a quotation shows beyond doubt how closely the Guatemalan and the Argentinian were actually thinking at this time within their different spheres of concern.[9] However it was Asturias's emphasis on the material intertextuality of Latin America's own cultural collectivity which was to set the path for the next twenty years, culminating in Vargas Llosa's *The Green House* and, above all, García Márquez's *One Hundred Years of Solitude*. When individualism reasserted itself, in the midst of the 'boom', Borges's emphasis upon mythologies which were at once private and universal finally came to the fore.

Juan Rulfo, *Pedro Páramo*

There have been a number of variations on Asturias's model. The first was *Pedro Páramo* (1955) by Juan Rulfo (1918–86), perhaps the most precisely executed short novel in Latin American fiction by an author who with *The Burning Plain* (*El llano en llamas*, 1953) had already composed some of the continent's most compelling short stories. His writing is very reminiscent of the Brazilian Graciliano Ramos. *Pedro Páramo* is a work in which recognizable motifs like the Oedipal, Thesean and Dantean quests are perfectly subordinated to the requirements of a metaphorical presentation of the colonized, feudal heritage of a whole country, a whole continent, unified by the power of myth:

> I came to Comala because they told me my father lived here, one Pedro Páramo. My mother said so. And I promised her I'd come to see him as soon as she died. I squeezed her hands as a sign that I would do it; because she was about to die and I

was in a mood to promise anything...

   But I didn't mean to keep my promise. Until just now when I started having day dreams and turning over illusions in my mind. And gradually a world began to grow around my hopes in that man called Pedro Páramo, my mother's husband. That's why I came to Comala.[10]

As in *Men of Maize*, Rulfo's novel operates on both the national (Mexican/ Latin American) and individual (universal) planes, and once again a critical vision compatible with the new Marx and the new Freud underpins the entire narrative. Without such a framework it becomes unreadable and spins off into labyrinths of 'magic' and 'mystery':

   This town is full of echoes. You would think they were trapped in the hollow walls or beneath the stones. You feel them shadowing your steps as you walk. You hear creaking. Laughter. Old laughter, as if it was tired. And voices worn out by use. All that, you hear. I think a day will come when those sounds will fade away.[11]

As the design for his novel, Rulfo – who never managed to write another – dreamed up a brilliantly simple conception, worthy of Kafka. All the characters in the novel are dead when it begins and the town they inhabit, Comala, is a dead town. Do they exist in myth, in memory, in the historically constructed consciousness of every Mexican peasant or, indeed, every modern Mexican? We do not know. We do not need to.

The Underdogs was the first Mexican novel because of its post-Flaubertian immediacy of presentation and its ironical, implicit self-referentiality, its awareness that a book is a constructed reality. It is difficult not to think that Azuela's strong sense of this truth in his novel derives from his own role as a man who was a participant in the Revolution and yet at the same time mainly a passive observer. Behind, and as it were out of, the historical actions of the characters a mythical image – that of the 'Mexican' – was gradually con-structed, as history and myth fused in the same way that they later would in *Don Segundo Sombra* and *The President*. Rulfo's *Pedro Páramo* is one of the many direct descendants of *The Underdogs*, and shows the identity of history and myth in the Mexican countryside, since its characters are unable to escape the world of religious false consciousness, and are thus formally dead. In this case world and book, both full of 'echoes and murmurs', seem effectively to fuse, and the reader's task, as in *Men of Maize*, is that of the archaeologist and the detective: the assemblage of clues and evidence, the establishment of interpretations based on cryptography and imaginative reconstruction.

   Now this can obviously operate at the level of a good idea, or of metaphor – look what happens to uneducated people held in the grip of a semi-feudal social formation (the Catholic Church and the hacienda system) over the course of four hundred years – but it also has another more immediate, yet apparently invisible level (judging by the mostly hallucinatory critical glosses on the novel). What Rulfo has actually done – and this, as we have seen, is the only convincing justification for Magical Realism – is to structure his entire novel and its perspective according to the worldview of the characters. It is a technique which Joyce did not entirely invent but which he formally inaugurated in the first pages of *The Portrait of the Artist as a Young Man*, and which Asturias emulated to some extent in *The Bejeweled Boy* (*El Alhajadito*, 1961), first written in the 1920s. Rulfo's Mexican peasants truly inhabit a world – similar to that conjured by the great engraver Posada – in which the Church as an institution no longer believes, in which the air is full of tormented souls wandering around in search of a redemption which, to judge from their terrestrial experience, is unlikely ever to come. In other words, the problem of belief in the novel lies not between the reader and the novelist, nor between the peasants and God – his existence or otherwise is not Rulfo's concern – but between the peasants and the Church:

Illusions? They cost a lot. I paid dearly for living more than I should.... I went so long without raising my eyes, that I forget all about heaven. And even if I'd looked up, what would I have gained? Heaven is so high, and my eyes so hopeless, that I was content just to know where the earth was. Besides, I lost all interest in it after Father Rentería told me that I would never know glory. That I wouldn't even get near it.... It was on account of my sins; but he oughtn't to have told me. Life's hard enough as it is. [12]

It is in fact social relationships which govern this apparently most ethereal of novels. This is of great importance, since *Pedro Páramo*, perhaps even more than *One Hundred Years of Solitude*, has been used time and again to justify the belief that Latin America is magical, mysterious and irrational, and that its literature celebrates this strange 'reality'; whereas for half a century most important writers have been attempting to carry out a deconstruction of the myths elaborated over the previous 450 years.

One is reminded inevitably of the response to Kafka's work, which so many bourgeois critics have celebrated as an expression of man's anguish in the world, thereby prompting a knee-jerk reaction in socialist critics who have dubbed him an escapist. Ernst Fischer has given the definitive response to this:

The plunge into the 'world's sleep', into the archaic, the inchoate and the inarticulate, is mostly an escape into irresponsibility. At the same time, however, the reaction against naturalism and the search for new forms of expression gave rise to Kafka's method of apparently transforming social reality into myth. Kafka did not write of man's anguish 'in the cosmos' or 'in the origin of things', but in a

particular social situation. He invented a marvellous form of fantastic satire –
dream interwoven with reality – to present the revolt of the lonely individual
hopelessly struggling against obscure powers in an alien world, and longing for
some form of community.... These images of social conditions have been
interpreted as symbols for supposedly 'eternal' ones. [Critics have] constructed a
mystical whole out of a scattered handful of mystical elements in Kafka's work,
and presented the new means which Kafka employed to describe life under the
Habsburg monarchy – a life both real and ghostly – as a kind of mysteriously
coded record of religious experience and illumination. Kafka, thus misinterpreted,
has done a great deal of harm, and has encouraged many mystifications.[13]

Alienation, reification, false consciousness – the concepts come drifting
into the light as soon as the reader begins to reflect seriously upon this exqui-
sitely crafted novel. All is distorted and inverted. The main peasant character,
Juan Preciado, and the priest, Father Rentería, both have names suggesting
price and exchange. The principal character, Peter, is the rock on which the
superstructure of the church is erected, whilst the main female personage, his
childhood sweetheart and eventual reluctant wife, Susana San Juan, the only
truly 'down-to-earth' character in the novel, has a name ironically suggesting
the metaphysical overtones of the Catholic Church. Most interesting of all is
the fact that the landowner himself, who perceives the illusory nature of
religious belief, falls victim to just the same mirages through the unconscious
structure of his own pattern of desires:

> I was thinking of you, Susana. When we used to fly kites in the windy season. We
> heard down below us the living murmur of the town, from up above, on top of the
> ridge, as we let out the string pulled by the wind. 'Help me, Susana.' And gentle
> hands pressed on our hands. 'Let out more string.'[14]

> Hundreds of metres, high above the clouds, far, far beyond everything, you are
> hidden, Susana. Hidden in the immensity of God, behind his Divine Providence,
> where I can neither touch you nor see you and where my words cannot reach.[15]

Ironically, however, Susana herself, whom Pedro eventually marries after a
separation of thirty-five years, when he has become a powerful landowner, is
the only relatively normal, unrepressed character in the novel, which is why
all the others think her mad and eventually drive her into that state. She longs
for her dead first husband Florencio:

> It was early. The sea was flowing and falling in waves. It threw off its foam and
> went back, clean green water in the silent swell.
>   'In the sea I always bathe naked,' I told him. And he followed me the first day,
> naked also, phosphorescent as he emerged from the sea. There were no seagulls;
> only those birds they call 'ugly beaks', that grunt as if they were snoring and

disappear after the sun comes up. He followed me that first day and felt lonely, even with me there.

'It's as if you too were an "ugly beak", one of the crowd', he told me. 'I like you more at night, when we two share the same pillow, beneath the sheets, in the darkness.'

And he went.

I came back. I'd come back always. The sea wets my ankles and goes; wets my knees, my thighs; puts its gentle arm around my waist, rolls around my breasts; embraces my neck; hugs my shoulders. Then I sink deep into it, all of me. I give myself over to its fierce pounding, its gentle possession, leaving no part of me outside.

'I love to bathe in the sea', I told him.

But he doesn't understand.

And the next day there I was once again in the sea, purifying myself. Giving myself up to the waves.[16]

This passage – which provides the only brief moment in the novel when we escape the asphyxiating grip of Comala, religious and social repression, and the arid Mexican interior – reveals not the virginal, immaculate Susana whom Pedro has invented and whom he worships, even though or because she frustrates him; nor is it the mad woman whom the other characters both pity and despise. On the contrary, she is the only character in the entire novel who is not prey to idealist illusions, and, as the passage shows, she stands for a specifically female sexuality attuned to the rhythms of nature and its alternation of darkness and light, which is reminiscent of *Men of Maize* and the discoveries made by its central male characters about the feminine other.

Everyone else in the novel is bitterly frustrated – sexual frustration is only the sign for every other form of impoverishment and longing – and the reader shares in their experience, though he or she alone gains satisfaction by the end. It has been said that the novel is pessimistic. Certainly Rulfo himself was, and it is difficult to see any other conclusion for a book reflecting the experience of the Mexican peasants in the past century. Yet Pedro is murdered: the Revolution may be shown – as by Azuela – to be confused, cynical or opportunistic, but in however indirect a way (and how else would anything happen in this Mexican world, this labyrinth of solitude?), one of the landowner's illegitimate sons does take his revenge and the pile of barren rocks which is Pedro's regime does finally come crashing down:

Pedro Páramo replied:
  'I'm coming. I'm on my way.'
  He leaned on Damiana Cisneros' arms and tried to walk. After a few paces he fell, pleading inside. He hit the earth and began to crumble like a pile of stones.[17]

João Guimarães Rosa, *The Devil to Pay in the Backlands*

The year after *Pedro Páramo*, the Brazilian João Guimarães Rosa (1908–1967) produced arguably his country's most important single novel of all time, again set in the unyielding, mysterious, exasperating and apparently eternal barren wastes of the Sertão, in this case that of Minas Gerais. The work has been compared with *Gargantua and Pantagruel*, *Don Quixote*, *Ulysses* and *One Hundred Years of Solitude*. Rosa was the writer who turned Brazilian fiction away from Social Realism in 1946 (as Asturias and Carpentier were doing in Spanish America), with his first collection of stories, *Sagarana*. In 1956, the same year as *The Devil to Pay in the Backlands*, the even more challenging narratives of '*Body for Dancing*' (*Corpo de baile*) appeared. The title communicates the idea of the Sertão itself as a 'body' or store of themes for narrating or an instrument for playing. Later collections were *The Third Bank of the River and Other Stories* (Primeiras estórias, 1962), '*Trifle (Third Stories)*' (*Trifle (Terceiras estórias)*, 1967), and '*These Stories*' (*Estas estórias*, 1969).

The Portuguese title of his greatest novel may be approximately translated as 'Great Deserts: Oases' or 'Great Plain: Rivulets', suggesting the same concept of the field and the paths as in '*Body for Dancing*' – one which we earlier saw in *Doña Bárbara* – the great labyrinth in which the plain may represent both life itself (individual and universal) and the book which recreates it. Its conception, however, is much closer to another novel by Gallegos, *Cantaclaro*, though the difference in sheer erudition and literary panache is evident. Rosa takes almost as many chances as Asturias in the novel's hermeticism and reliance upon dense layerings of imagery, symbolism and regional vocabulary. The story is narrated by one Riobaldo ('dry river'), a former cowboy and bandit from the Sertão, now a landowner, who addresses some unknown interlocutor – the writer? the reader? the devil? – as he recalls his adventures and perplexities over a long and passionate life riding the great plains at the end of the last century:

> You, sir, knew nothing about me. Do you now know much or little? A person's life, all the paths into its past: is it a story that touches upon your own life at all, sir?[18]

We come to believe Riobaldo when he says that 'The sertão is as big as the world', and to understand him when he says that a story 'spread everywhere, traveled more, you may be sure, than you or I'. Stories, as Asturias's Nana Moncha told us in *Men of Maize*, are like paths or rivers, branching everywhere and through everything. Rosa, through Riobaldo, maps the Sertão, its history and mythology, the folk consciousness of the Brazilian backlands, where medieval epic and romance still live, and where the destiny of man is still played out in ways long since lost to Europe and the United States. Riobaldo has two major concerns: his preoccupation with good and evil and the obsessive desire to know whether the devil exists; and his nostalgic recollection of Diadorim, a fellow *jagunço* whom he loved but resisted, and who turns out, melodramatically but magically, to have been a woman, a discovery Riobaldo makes only after she has died. Little by little our vision of the Sertão becomes inseparable from Riobaldo's philosophical meditations:

> How can God not be? With God existing, there is always hope: a miracle is always possible, and the world will settle its problems. But, if there is no God, we are lost in the turmoil, and life is meaningless. There is constant danger, on great and small occasions, and we must not be negligent – accidents can always happen. Having God, it is not so serious to be a little careless, for it will all come out right in the end. But, if there is no God, then we have no leeway at all! Because suffering exists. And man exists in a labyrinth: take the wrong turn, and things happen, like the deformity of those children without arms and legs. Doesn't pain hurt even in babies and animals – even in lunatics – doesn't it hurt without our needing to know why or how? And aren't people always being born? Ah, the fear I have is not of death, but of birth. Fear or mystery. Don't you see, sir? What is not of God is of the devil's domain. God exists even when they say He doesn't. But the devil does not need to exist to be – when people know that he does not exist, then is when he takes over. Hell is a limitless thing which cannot even be seen. But if people want Heaven it is because they want an end, but an end where they can see everything. If I am talking nonsense, please stop me. That's how I am. I was born different in my ways from anybody else. What I envy, sir, is your education. [19]

Gradually this magnificent novel clarifies all the mysteries about Riobaldo's historical existence, but this only serves to heighten the greater mysteries that can never be clarified, as when Riobaldo compares the beautiful but conventional Otacília, whom he eventually married, and the ineffable Diadorim:

> Diadorim and Otacília. Otacília was a quiet force, like those wide expanses of backwater on the Urucúia, which is itself a riotous river. Diadorim is far away forever. Alone. On hearing the music of a guitar I remember him. Just a little tune that can't even be danced to. Isn't God in everything, as they say? But everything is stirring and moving too fast. God could really be glimpsed only if everything were to stop, just once. How can you keep your mind on the ultimate things – death, judgment, heaven, hell – if you are bogged down in all these other things? All that has been is the beginning of what is to be – we are forever at a crossroads. Living is a dangerous business; and yet, it is not. I don't even know how to explain these things. [20]

If the novel is about Brazil, then it underscores the impossibility, recognized by so many Brazilian writers, of ever going beyond the concept of the nation as an irreconcilable plurality. In that sense it anticipates Vargas Llosa's *The Green House* (see chapter 7). If it is about man's condition in the world, then it underlines, like Asturias's *Men of Maize*, that Western man's destiny is to arrive forever at a crossroads, torn always between impossible choices and dualities, good and evil, male and female, objective and subjective, history and myth, in a world which, like fictional stories, is ultimately impossible to interpret:

> Ancient sertão of the ages. One sierra calls for another and it is from these heights that you can discern how the sertão comes and goes. It is no use turning your back on it. Its border lies near and in far-distant places.... A journey through it is dangerous, as is the journey through life.... I could turn back from there, couldn't I? Or perhaps I could not? Do I know or do you know? Who knows: perhaps all that is written is subject to constant change, but we don't know the road we are on, whether good or bad, while the changes are taking place.[21]

Evidently *The Devil to Pay in the Backlands* shows more clearly than most just how much the Latin American novel of its era was forced to reconcile the requirements of the twentieth-century Modernist text with the impulse of romance, a medieval genre which is still fully relevant in a world of loose ends, a still unwoven social and historical reality where more things are unresolved than identified, and where messianic movements promising transcendent meaning, the triumph of good over evil and imminent or eventual salvation are still invested with a force which no socialism has yet managed to marshal in South America. Lévi-Strauss's 'sad tropics' remains dominated in its own consciousness by the three sad races – the Portuguese, with their *saudade*, still missing Europe; the Africans, liberated from slavery only a century ago, longing for their magical past; and the Indians, staring into space, pining for their long-lost world. The combination has failed to produce even the beginnings of a successful democracy, but capitalism has taken firm root through the efforts of outsiders, including optimistic immigrants from all over the world. Thus we see a ruthless process of primitive accumulation sweeping in from the Amazon, an all-pervading medieval mysticism wafting from the Sertão, and a residual tribal–slave black magic reverberating from the Bahian coastlands, all miscegenating with a dynamic and unusually barbaric commodity fetishism which has taken root in the big cities. Little wonder that the largest republic in the region offers the perplexing image of a country with a national identity that strikes outsiders as unusually distinctive, whilst Brazilian artists and intellectuals themselves continue to insist that the nation remains a mystery unto itself, as we shall see later when we come to Lispector's *The Hour of the Star* and Ribeiro's *An*

Invincible Memory. In the meantime Rosa's Riobaldo undoubtedly communicates this contradiction to us, his silent interlocutors, whilst Rosa himself shows just how much can be achieved by a novelist who is equally aware of the historical, literary and linguistic context of his endeavour.

José María Arguedas, *Deep Rivers*

Guimarães Rosa was a plantation owner's son – perhaps it is not therefore surprising that the illegitimate Riobaldo comes unexpectedly into his inheritance almost at the end of the novel, through his 'godfather', like Fabio in Güiraldes's *Don Segundo Sombra* – and later a rural doctor and eventually a diplomat. He knew the Sertão inside out both through personal experience and through lifelong study of natural history and geography, and he spoke several languages, had read the world's classics, and had studied not only Catholic doctrine but Buddhism and Taoism. The Peruvian José María Arguedas (1911–69) had been from a similarly privileged background which fell to pieces about him, so that he suffered from all the agonies of Peru's divided cultural inheritance at the most tender age and was never able to develop the sophisticated cosmopolitan culture which characterizes a writer like Rosa. Nevertheless he became an anthropologist and produced what is by common consent the most important body of indigenist writing to have come out of Latin America, with '*Water*', *Yawar Fiesta*, *Deep Rivers* (*Los ríos profundos*, 1958) and '*Everyone's Blood*' (see chapter 3).

Of all twentieth-century writers Arguedas came closest, both through childhood experience and apparently irremediable personal choice, to understanding and representing the searingly painful half-caste duality of the early colonial period – his experience in many ways shadows that of the great Inca Garcilaso de la Vega in the sixteenth century – and he underwent a lifelong struggle to reconcile those two worlds within himself. *Deep Rivers* is indeed semi-autobiographical:

I was fourteen years old; I had passed my childhood in an alien house, watched over constantly by cruel people. The master of the house, the father, had eyes with red lids and thick brows; he liked those who depended on him to suffer, servants and animals. After, when my father rescued me and I wandered the towns with him, I found that people suffered everywhere.[22]

In those days of confusion and dismay, I remembered the farewell song the women sang for me in the last *ayllu* where I lived, as a refuge, whilst my father was hiding from persecution. Fleeing from cruel relatives I threw myself upon the mercy of an *ayllu* where they grew maize in the smallest and most delightful valley I have known. Thorn bushes with blazing flowers and the song of doves lit up the maizefields. The family heads and the ladies, *mamakunas* of the community, looked after me and imbued me with the priceless tenderness which fills my life.[23]

Arguedas's own harsh life ended bitterly in alienation from many of his Latin American literary contemporaries, given the different orientation of most of the 'boom' writers from his own. This conflict climaxed during his polemic with Julio Cortázar (see chapter 8), and with his suicide in 1969. *Deep Rivers* strikes its reader as in many ways an old-fashioned regionalist novel, comparable with Roa Bastos's *Son of Man*, although even that novel had a wide panoramic sweep, a counterpointed plot and a range of different characters. The strength of *Deep Rivers*, however, lies in its juxtaposition of two worlds, its uniquely poetic approach to the realm of nature, and its innovative conception of language and myth in a narrative tradition previously dominated by the conventions of the European bourgeois novel.

Once again, the conquest is the effective point of departure, the traumatic rupture which initiates a world order. Ernesto accompanies his father on a visit to an old, unpleasant and conservative relative in the ancient capital of Cuzco. Everything in the episode bespeaks the imposition of Hispanic over Inca culture, from the dead stones of the Spanish churches restraining the dancing, singing stones of the earlier Inca temples to the old relative himself, dressed in black, bigoted, cruel and authoritarian, repressing all he controls and sterilizing all that he touches. Cuzco is no longer a home for people or for culture: it is a fortress, a garrison, a church, a market. Ernesto recalls his first encounter with the mobile stones of the Incas:

> The stones of the old Inca wall were bigger and stranger than anything I had imagined; they swirled beneath the whitewashed second floor which ran blindly along the narrow street. Then I remembered those Quechua songs that repeat one constant pathetic refrain: *yawar mayu*, river of blood; *yawar unu*, bloody water; *puk-tik*, *yawar k'ocha*, lake of foaming blood; *yawar wek'e*, tears of blood. Could one not say *yawar rumi*, stone of blood, or *puk'tik*, *yawar rumi*, stone of boiling blood? The wall was static, but it boiled along all its lines and the surface was ever changing, like rivers in summer, when they have a crest along the middle of the torrent, which is the fearsome zone, the most powerful. The Indians call those turbulent rivers *yawar mayu*, because in the sun they make a shining motion, like that of blood. They also use *yawar mayu* for the violent phases of warrior dances, the moment when the dancers fight.[24]

The whole novel is a kind of cantata on Benjamin's perception that all stories are either about homes or roads. Ernesto is born into a world that is both broad and alien, and his childhood is shown to be a search for the maternal warmth, security and love which has always eluded his tragic father, a travelling lawyer alienated from his own people but incapable of standing up to the hatred and hostility which meets him everywhere he goes in his journey around the sierra towns of Andean Peru:

Whenever my father confronted his enemies, and more so when he stood and gazed at the mountains, from some town square, and it seemed that rivers of tears were about to spring from his blue eyes, tears he always held back, as behind a mask, I always thought about Cuzco... But he would always move from one town to another when the mountains, the roads, the playing fields, the place where the birds slept, the details began to form part of his memory.[25]

When Ernesto reaches fourteen his father decides to leave him at a school run by the Church in the highland city of Abancay. The rest of the novel is taken up with the youth's gradual realization of the true character of Peruvian society and growing ability to fortify himself against its worst excesses. He had already learned from his father that Indian music and the world of nature could have a therapeutic effect in consoling victims of injustice:

My father liked to hear *huaynos*; he could not sing, and danced badly, but he remembered which song corresponded to which town, which community, which valley... The Indian harpists play with their eyes closed. The voice of the harp seemed to come out of the darkness inside it; and the *charango* created a whirlpool that engraved on the memory the words and music of the songs...

In each town, at a certain hour, the birds can be seen heading for the places they know. Orchards, river beds, bushes that grow along the banks. And their flight changes according to the time. The locals don't notice these things, but travellers, people who will have to leave, never forget them.[26]

One of Ernesto's most important experiences is his relationship with another boy, Antero, from a landowning family. Although Antero has some sympathy with the plight of the Peruvian Indians oppressed by his own class, Ernesto comes to perceive that this concern is purely intellectual and is not felt by the whole self. Initially they become close friends and swim in the great Andean rivers together. But gradually Ernesto realizes that whereas he is instinctively communing with the ebbs and flows of the cosmos, Antero is testing and measuring himself against that same natural world, and ultimately seeks to impose himself upon it. With a vision remarkably similar to that of Asturias in *Men of Maize*, Arguedas shows that the Westernized mind seeks always to separate itself from nature, on the one hand, and to differentiate by gender, class, race and nationality, on the other. (Another Peruvian novel, Vargas Llosa's *The Green House*, gives a similar version of national divisiveness.) Ernesto, by contrast, is constantly trying to narrow distances, blur edges, conciliate differences. He seeks always, as it were, to transform the magnetic fields of society and nature in such a way as to connect rather than to separate things and people. The *zumbayllu* or spinning top, which is the boys' favourite entertainment in the school yard, becomes for Ernesto a symbol of the harmony of the universe, and in chapter 6 of the novel

Arguedas gives a long poetic explanation of the meaning of the word based on its Quechua associations. As Ernesto finds his way through the labyrinth of Indian and Hispanic semantics we see a metaphor for his journey of discovery through Peruvian history.

Thus what at the beginning of the novel appears to be merely an Andean variant of romantic sensibility towards nature – exemplified typically in Ciro Alegría's '*The Hungry Dogs*' – develops, through gradually accumulating reverberations, into a mythical conception which is one of Arguedas's major contributions to Peruvian and indeed Latin American narrative. Through his sense of integration with nature, Ernesto is able to identify himself with the Indian and Mestizo communities, despite all the formidable social sanctions exercised by his own class, and when a local rebellion breaks out late in the novel he commits himself joyfully towards it. Unlike his father, who had always run from his problems, Ernesto has begun to find himself and establish his own identity. As the narrative nears its conclusion he leaves the school and sets off with confidence to engage as an adult with the intimidating social contradictions of Peru.

Alejo Carpentier, *The Lost Steps*

The role which belongs to Alejo Carpentier (1904–80) as an outstanding cultural historian of Latin America, particularly of the Spanish and French Caribbean, puts him at the forefront of the Latin American cultural debate, even before one considers his eminence as a musical historian and of course his towering stature as one of the greatest of all Latin American novelists. A number of these attributes came together in 1949 to produce his first internationally successful novel, *The Kingdom of This World*, about the Haitian independence struggle against French colonial rule. Carpentier must have taken an ironic satisfaction from that work, since his own roots were as much in France as Borges's were in England, and he spent the period 1928–39 in Paris, engaging in numerous cultural activities and writing a torrent of articles for newspapers and magazines with the same nationalist and Americanist fervour as his contemporary, Miguel Angel Asturias.

As we have seen, the introduction to *The Kingdom of this World* contains Carpentier's reflections on what he calls '*lo real maravilloso*', Latin America's marvellous reality, which was effectively the manifesto of what, many years later, would be known as Magical Realism. He recalls Rimbaud's 'Alchemy of the Word' (and, presumably, Breton's quotation of it), but implies that the Surrealists tried in vain, and through typically artificial devices, to escape from their own European rationalism by phoney juxtapositions. Ironically, however, Carpentier's justly celebrated document implicitly suscribes to the Surrealists' Eurocentric conception of Latin America as one of the great homes of irreality, where the surface of everyday existence is magical, in much the same way that Spain is supposed to be the home of the grotesque (which makes the great Spanish novelist Valle-Inclán's *Tirano Banderas*, of 1926, about a Latin American dictator, a particularly suggestive work).

I have already argued that Latin American Modernism originates in the 1920s, most obviously with Andrade's *Macunaíma*, coincides with and assimilates the Joycean paradigm, and continues today. In many respects Carpentier's Magical Realist manifesto of 1949 provides the rationale for the vital central phase of the 'New Latin American Novel', which was born in the late 1940s and reached its pinnacle with *One Hundred Years of Solitude* in 1967. A recent study of Carpentier has described his endeavour as the effort to 'rediscover the imperatives of romance within the context of the modern novel'[27] and quotes Northrop Frye's conception of romance in *The Secular Scripture*: 'Reality for romance is an order of existence most readily associated with the word identity.... Most romances end happily, with a return to a state of identity, and begin with a departure from it.'[28] As I have shown in chapter 1, identity is an 'always already' problematical question in Latin America, so that both the point of departure and the ultimate destination are perennially in doubt. This is why the methods of traditional romance have come to fuse with the 'Ulyssean' journey and the Borgesian labyrinth to produce such a distinctive family of narrative fictions since the Second World War. The four principal 'boom' writers, Cortázar, García Márquez, Fuentes and Vargas Llosa, in explaining why the Latin American novel has generally eschewed the realism that has mainly defined the genre in Europe, have frequently restated Carpentier's ideas as if they were their own.[29] In doing so, as exponents of a genre which only became possible in Latin America after Independence, they have ironically joined the Cuban in exalting such great Hispanic romances and novels of chivalry as *Amadis of Gaul* and *Tirant lo Blanc*. Criticism of these, needless to say, was the purported point of departure of *Don Quixote* which, together with its descendant *Ulysses*, is effectively the point of departure of the New Novel itself, as if Hispanic fiction had somehow been interrupted for more than 300 years.

The novel which remains Carpentier's most important, despite the attractions of the even more ambitious *Explosion in a Cathedral* (*El siglo de las luces*, 1962) and '*Rite of Spring*' (*Consagración de la primavera*, 1978), is *The Lost Steps* (*Los pasos perdidos*, 1953), which, like Asturias's *Men of Maize* and Rosa's *The Devil to Pay in the Backlands*, though with different results, brings to bear thirty years of reflection about the nature of Latin American culture and its relation to the Europe which Carpentier in particular knew and loved so well, despite his passionate Americanism. It is the most programmatic of all novels about the relationship between Latin America (above all the Caribbean and Venezuela) and 'Europe' (above all Spain and

France), and between Latin America and 'modernity' as represented by the United States. In that sense it is an indispensable cultural document of Latin America's twentieth century. The title echoes Breton's Surrealist project, although the search for lost time and primitive roots actually takes place against a later Gallic background, that of postwar existentialism, in which a sometime Latin American, living in self-inflicted exile in New York, is nonetheless imbued with the absurdist ideas of Camus, though with none of the rebellious voluntarism of Sartre. The anonymous protagonist is a musician, a scholar and artist living an existence of utter alienation from both true values and from his Latin American cultural origins, selling his art in the capitalist market place by writing the music for advertising films. The picture Carpentier paints in part 1 of the life of a great modern metropolis in 1953 anticipates, with remarkable prescience, the kind of world which Marcuse and the whole New Left would excoriate in such works as *One-Dimensional Man* more than a decade later:

> Overhead, into the thinning mist, rose the peaks of the city... the large hospitals where White Eminences officiated beneath classical entablatures designed by those architects who, early in the century, sought to lose their way in an increase of verticality. Solid and silent, the funeral parlour with its multiple corridors seemed a reply in grey – with a synagogue and concert hall between – to the huge maternity hospital whose bare façade displayed a row of identical windows that I used to count on Sunday mornings from my wife's bed when topics of conversation ran low.[30]

However, Carpentier's work moves to another dimension, when his narrator makes a belated return visit to the country in which he was born. Here he encounters a Latin America at once arbitrary, unpredictable and profound, in contrast with his Baudrillardian perceptions of a New York emptied of all human content. During his journey he comes across three young artists whose dream is to do as he did in his youth – escape to civilized Europe in search of the truth and beauty invisible to them in their own continent:

> Culture, observed the Negro painter emphatically, was not to be found in the jungle. In the musician's opinion, the artist today could live only where thought and creation were really alive, returning to that city whose intellectual topography was engraved on the mind of his comrades, given, they confessed, to dreaming with open eyes before a *Carte Taride*, whose Metro stations were marked by heavy blue circles: *Solferino, Oberkampf, Corvisard, Mouton-Duvernet*. Between these circles, above the tracery of the streets, intersected from time to time by the clear artery of the Seine, ran the routes themselves, criss-crossed like the web of a net.... Years later, having frittered away their youth, they would return, with vacant eyes, all initiative gone, without heart to set themselves the only task appropriate to the milieu that was slowly revealing to me the nature of its values: Adam's task of

giving things their names.

That night as I looked at them I could see the harm my uprooting from this environment, which had been mine until adolescence, had done me; the share the facile bedazzlement of the members of my generation, carried away by theories into the same intellectual labyrinths, devoured by the same Minotaurs, had had in disorienting me.[31]

This is the very heart of the cultural debate whose alternatives are dramatized in the progress of so many protagonists embarked upon so many Latin American journeys through the labyrinths of fiction.

Effectively travelling back through the ages as he travels across geographical space, the narrator eventually reaches what the Victorians used to call the dawn of time. Before that, during a brief revolutionary uprising, he reflects on the extraordinary juxtapositions constantly thrown up by Latin American culture, that is, by uneven and combined development:

> Because of an incredible chronological discrepancy of ideals, the conflict between the conservatives and those who seemed to represent extremist tendencies gave me the impression of a kind of battle between people living in different centuries.
>
> 'That's very acute', replied a lawyer wearing an outmoded frock-coat, who seemed to accept what was going on with surprising calm. 'You must remember that we are accustomed to living with Rousseau and the Inquisition, with the Immaculate Conception and *Das Kapital*...'[32]

Ironically enough, the work smoothes out all these inconsistencies by imposing Carpentier's own rational lucidity on Latin America's fractured cultural space. For all its erudition and expressive brilliance, the novel is entirely schematic and depends on a series of exceptionally unlikely coincidences. The narrative functions as a contemporary allegory, a journey through different zones of geographical, historical and cultural time and space, each of whose stages is signposted in advance by the epigraphs which inaugurate the six parts. Thus New York is glossed by Deuteronomy ('And thy heaven that is over thy head shall be brass, and the earth that is under thee shall be iron.... And thou shalt grope at noonday, as the blind gropeth in darkness'); the return to Latin America is preceded by Shelley's 'Ha! I scent life!'; and the arrival at the primeval jungle is announced by a quotation from the Mayan *Book of Chilam Balam*: 'it will be time for him to take to the road, untie his mask and speak, vomit up what he swallowed and throw off his heavy burden.' In this regard, however, Carpentier is able to make the best of his own literary vice – an incorrigible discursiveness – since the protagonist's whole problem is his need to distance himself from reality in order to apprehend it logically. This ultimately makes it impossible for him to achieve the immediacy and spontaneity which he strives to experience, still less to find the means of expressing it. This is one of the defining preoccupations of Latin American fiction from *Don Segundo Sombra* to Cortázar's *Hopscotch* (see chapter 7). Since the novel is related in the first person, the dilemma is reflected in the very texture of the narrative form itself. As so often in Latin American fiction, we perceive the extent to which irony is a product of hierarchies and distances (not least that between the reader and the sophisticated but nonetheless ingenuous narrator), producing the pastiches, parodies and self-conscious melodramas which so frequently characterize the continent's New Novel. Lukács's perception that the very structure of the novel as a narrative form is based upon irony takes on added force in a milieu where the gaps between social strata are so wide and so numerous.

Once the narrator arrives in the jungle he falls in love with a Latin American Mestizo woman, a mixture of the continent's three great ethnic groupings, and forgets his North American wife and French mistress, giving himself over to a spontaneous eroticism which is also a cosmic ritual. His return to the maternal realm of nature stimulates him to write a long-cherished symphony based on Shelley's *Prometheus Unbound*, only to find that in order to obtain the materials to complete it – not to mention seeing it performed – he must return to the alienating civilization from which he has so recently escaped ('Today Sisyphus' vacation came to an end'). When, after a frustrating time in New York, he tries to journey back once more to the little jungle community, he finds that the waters of the river have symbolically risen and he cannot find the way through the labyrinth of trees and water. The conclusion is that there is no turning back – artists and intellectuals are, after all and above all, the antennae of the race:

> Within two days the century would have rounded out another year, and this would be of no importance to those around me. There the year in which we live can be forgotten, and they lie who say man cannot escape his epoch. The Stone Age, like the Middle Ages, is still within our reach. The gloomy mansions of romanticism, with its doomed loves, are still open. But none of this was for me, because the only human race to which it is forbidden to sever the bonds of time is the race of those who create art, and who not only must move ahead of the immediate yesterday, represented by tangible witness, but must anticipate the song and the form of others who will follow them, creating new tangible witness with full awareness of what has been done up to the moment.[33]

Intellectuals, then, should – indeed, must – return to their origins, know and remember everything they can about their ancestors, in order to know themselves, but it is also their duty to live fully in the present and to aim their work determinedly at the future, with the objective, of course, of trying to bring about a better one. Carpentier's statement echoes Neruda's declaration in his '*General Song*' ('I come to speak through your dead mouths'),

Asturias's cosmic dialectic of enlightenment in *Men of Maize*, and Rulfo's vision of Susana San Juan's rejuvenating relationship with the waters of the ocean in *Pedro Páramo*. It effectively argues for the integration of past and present, America and Europe, experience and knowledge, and communicates Carpentier's own version of the recuperative, testimonial impulse which lies behind the New Novel as a whole. It explains why Borges's full influence was delayed until the 1960s, as individualism gradually fought a winning battle with collective sentiment during the course of the 'boom'. Carpentier sometimes had his tensions with the Cuban Revolution – he was in some respects the most authentically cosmopolitan, if that is not a contradiction in terms, of all Latin American writers – but his lifelong objectives were not, in truth, much different from those of the early Castro and Guevara. Carpentier became head of the national publishing house in Havana and eventually – appropriately enough – represented the Cuban Revolution in Paris (as Asturias, Neruda, Uslar Pietri, Fuentes and many other writers represented their respective countries). The very title of his last major novel, '*Rite of Spring*', underscores his consistent attempt to reconcile the artistic and the political avant-gardes.

However, what makes *The Lost Steps* so important at the present stage of our own journey through the labyrinth is its particular perspective. All Magical Realist works implicitly and inevitably view a Latin American autochthonous reality from an implicitly European – perhaps we should say 'universal' – standpoint, but certainly from an extra-Latin American one. But whereas *Men of Maize*, *Pedro Páramo*, *The Devil to Pay in the Backlands* and *Deep Rivers* are focused on the rural interior and the European viewpoint is, so to speak, largely out of the frame, or rather is the frame itself, there is another series of works, of which *The Lost Steps* was the first, and *Hopscotch* the most influential, which either have a European-style narrator or set out purposefully to contrast Europe and Latin America, or the capital and the interior, or the city and the country. This was always there to be done, and of course had already been done long before by writers in the early nineteenth century; but it was only now, in the mid twentieth century, when it began to be done systematically, by the mainstream of the literature as a whole, and it was only now that writers had the technical skills required to juxtapose or superimpose and hence explore both realities. This they did in a number of different ways, in a world where the confrontation of the two opposed but dialectically connected realities began to be – as we see in *The Lost Steps* itself – a mere airplane journey apart, something which has become a cliché in terms of the vacations which city-dwellers can now spend in primitive or merely exotic places.

7

The 'Boom' of the 1960s

The novel in Latin America, in countries ruled permanently by censorship and terror, has become the first free territory. For me the first free territory of America is not Cuba; Cuba has undertaken an important political experience, but the first truly free territory of America is the Latin American novel... which has created a new way of looking at reality. For me this is crucial, because in my opinion if Latin America is to carry out its great political project, it must first liberate its imagination.

Manuel Scorza[1]

The Lost Steps was a novel written by a man steeped in the experience of the 1920s and 1930s in Paris, who was symbolically and ironically distancing himself both from that experience and from the world-weary and war-weary existentialist philosophies of 1950s Paris. Between the Second World War and the 1960s, as we now see, the New Novel was beginning its remarkable rise to world attention, virtually unnoticed at first, with each new achievement in some part of Latin America remaining unrelated by either writers or critics to what was going on elsewhere. Latin American society was searching for its new direction, frustrated both by outside intervention, as with the United-States-backed coup in Guatemala in 1954, and internal reaction, as with the ousting of Perón in 1955. Yet economically and politically a different age seemed to be dawning and there was some optimism that the Latin American middle classes, with liberal democratic regimes to represent them, might be on the verge of some new era of political stability and real economic expansion. The novel which first reflected this changing and essentially urban reality was Carlos Fuentes's *Where the Air is Clear* (1958), which now, with the benefit of history, appears clearly as the first novel of the 'boom' and the signal of the developments in Latin American narrative that were shortly to occur. Paradoxically, of course, these developments became visible at the very moment that the Cuban Revolution was about to transform the whole perspective of Latin American history by proclaiming a Third World, anti-urban and anti-bourgeois ideology. We shall be examining this ironic and contradictory scenario in the next chapter. In this chapter we examine what I take to be the representative works of the 'boom', conceived as the culmination of the New Novel.

The birth of the 'boom': Julio Cortázar, *Hopscotch*

Naturally, there are various possible outcomes.... In the work of Ts'ui Pen, all those outcomes occur; each one is the point of departure for other possible ramifications.

Jorge Luis Borges, 'The Garden of Forking Paths', 1941

He thought that good literature is very common and that almost any street discussion achieves it. He also thought that the aesthetic act cannot dispense with some element of amazement and that to be amazed from memory is difficult.... For those countless 'imperfect writers', Quain composed the eight narratives of his book *Statements*. Each one prefigures or promises a good story, deliberately frustrated by the author. Some – not the best – insinuate two plots. The reader, misled by vanity, thinks he has invented them.

Jorge Luis Borges, 'Review of the Work of Herbert Quain', 1941

If Fuentes's novel was the first true harbinger of the 'boom', there is no doubt which work effectively inaugurated the new moment by continuing the interrogation of Latin American identity which Carpentier had pursued in *The Lost Steps*. In 1963 a sensational new novel specifically and unforgettably juxtaposed Paris itself (symbolizing 'Europe') with Buenos Aires (symbolizing 'Latin America') in a fashion which has been widely recognized as paradigmatic. That novel was *Hopscotch* (*Rayuela*) and the author was the Argentinian Julio Cortázar (1914–84), arguably Carpentier's true successor. His achievement lies, first, in having updated and synthesized the twin traditions of 'Joycism' and Surrealism which were the legacy bequeathed by Andrade, Asturias and Carpentier from the 1920s; and second, in having fused them through an intense reading of the ideas and forms explored before him by his compatriot Borges. No other novelist and no other novel so comprehensively embody this triple heritage.

Cortázar's first novel, *The Winners* (*Los premios*, 1960), about an allegorical journey on a European cruise liner – tickets won by lottery and going nowhere – was already a rather timid fusion of Joyce (in structure and linguistic texture), Kafka (in theme and symbolic design), Borges, and other Modernist currents. Its culminating moment, when the passengers capture the bridge, only to discover that no one is navigating the ship, is one of the great defining moments of Latin American literature, anticipating not only the vision of post-Modernism as a whole – of which the Argentine writer's own story 'Blow-up' ('Las babas del diablo') was an early path-finder – but also the 'boom' writers' overwhelming sense of cultural emancipation from 'Europe':

> It was true, now he came to think about it: the bridge was entirely empty. An ash-grey horizon, a leaden sea, the curve of the rail... a sharp, cutting sensation, an almost painful plenitude in that instantaneous realization that when all was said and done the bridge was completely empty but that it didn't matter, it hadn't the slightest importance because what mattered was something else, something that couldn't be grasped but was trying to show itself and define itself in the sensation that was exciting him more and more. [2]

The emphasis upon sensation, spontaneity, imminence and the primacy of experience over conceptualization is one which characterizes Latin American fiction from its origins in the early nineteenth century. It was appropriate that Azuela's images of the revolutionary upheaval in Mexico should have marked the beginning of the effort to express these themes through the form of the narrative, a process which reaches its culmination in Cortázar's novels and stories.

Although many readers believe that the short stories are his outstanding achievement, *Hopscotch* is the work with which Cortázar is identified. Many have argued that it was to Spanish American fiction what *Ulysses* had been for European and North American literature as a whole in 1922. Alfred MacAdam has explained it thus:

> *Rayuela* is a point of crystallization for so many subjects that one is tempted to set it at the head of a movement. This of course would be a falsification. Authors like Machado de Assis, Bioy Casares, Roberto Arlt, Juan Carlos Onetti and Felisberto Hernández, dead, forgotten or simply ignored for one reason or another, all did what Cortázar did. His importance lies in having done it all at the moment when he was able to make a huge impression on a new generation of readers and writers.... What *Rayuela* is, then, is not so much an innovation as a gathering place in which an entire catalog of innovations is put on display. [3]

MacAdam underrates Cortázar's power of innovation and overrates the achievements of his predecessors: amidst the inevitable damp squibs Cortázar achieves some of the most extraordinary moments in modern literature (Berthe Trépat's piano recital, the conversation against the background of Rocamadour's death, Talita's journey across the plank, to name just three). He has a unique ability to move from the discursive to the uncanny or hallu-

cinatory, based on his belief that 'the fantastic always springs from the everyday' and that 'apart from our individual destinies, we form part of designs
which are unknown to us'.

However, it is certainly true, as MacAdam says, that *Hopscotch* was a
major point of crystallization and that it was particularly significant for its
timing – published early in the 1960s. Moreover its very structure is a comparison of two cities, moving from an exploration of art and its media and
institutions in the first part, 'Over There', to an analysis of consciousness and
language themselves in the second, 'Over Here'. There are many quite tangi-
ble Joycean influences: for example, choosing one at random, the dialogue
about reality and our perception of it between Oliveira and Ronald in chapter
28 ('You and I see that lamp', etc.) is clearly inspired by the conversation
between Stephen and Lynch in chapter 5 of *Portrait of the Artist* ('"Look at
that basket", he said', etc.). Cortázar's use of the epiphany is again clearly
Joycean, as are aspects of his particular assault on bourgeois sensibilities. At
the same time Cortázar's work invokes Surrealist concepts not present in
Joyce and existentialist considerations which postdated him. And much of
Hopscotch explores, tragicomically, the obscure and often sinister motives
which lie behind the most frivolous or inconsequential behaviour, in a way
reminiscent of Borges's 'El Aleph'. Most of all, though, Cortázar's work
attempts an interrogation of the nature and implications of avant-garde postures which give his work its own unique place in contemporary narrative.

This, then, was the novel most admired by the other writers of the 'boom',
the one which made it visible and recognizable, the work situated at the other
pole from *One Hundred Years of Solitude*, with which the literary firework
show reached its grand crescendo in 1967. Yet curiously, despite first impressions to the contrary, *Hopscotch* is really a variant of the conceptual model
underpinning *Men of Maize*, *Pedro Páramo*, the later *The Green House* and,
indeed, *One Hundred Years of Solitude* itself, a work which rejects the
rationalistic logocentrism of European civilization and posits a return to the
natural, authentic world of America. Whether America – least of all
Argentina, least of all Buenos Aires – can convincingly be considered in any
sense spontaneous or natural is a questionable point, but the essential thrust
of this position is that it is by definition newer, younger and more spontaneous than Europe or North America (which has on the whole – jazz apart –
sacrificed spontaneity for mechanization), no matter how unspontaneous it
may actually be on its own terms. This posture turns Europe's constant use of
Latin America for catharsis to America's advantage, inverting the Surrealism
which so influenced Asturias, Carpentier, Neruda, Paz and Cortázar himself,
as if to suggest that Europeans irremediably approach Surrealism from the
wrong side, whereas the Latin Americans can always come from the fertile
maternal darkness of autochthonous America into the dazzling light of

rational knowledge, and then, with their new knowledge aboard, can plunge back into the night and the underworld once more, as the earth itself does, growing, changing, advancing dialectically to the rhythm of the whole universe. Thus jazz, sex and all other improvizations suggest hidden paths to a revolution in consciousness:

> Why would I not love and possess La Maga beneath dozens of hotel ceilings at six hundred francs a time, in beds with frayed musty covers, if in that dizzying hopscotch, that careering advancement, I recognized and named myself at last and escaped for a while from time and its cages with monkeys and labels, shop windows Omega Electron Girard Perregaud Vacheron & Constantin ticking off the hours and minutes of sacrosanct castrating obligations, in an atmosphere where the last ties began to fall away and pleasure was a mirror of reconciliation, a mirror for larks but a mirror, something like a sacrament between one and another, a dance around the altar, the approach of sleep mouth against mouth, sometimes without uncoupling ourselves, sexes warmly united, arms like creeping plants, hands still caressing a thigh, a neck.[4]

Of course, Argentina is not the Caribbean, but Cortázar, unlike most of the famous Argentine writers – who had a fully articulated literary and intellectual world available to themselves as sophisticated as most places in Europe – gradually made himself into a Latin American writer (Güiraldes had been the last important one) and identified successively with Cuba, Chile and Nicaragua (he was also a translator with the United Nations, with which Latin Americans have a special relationship), thereby demonstrating that his views on spontaneity, revolution and the 'new man' (Breton and Guevara) could be kept true to practice as well as to theory. Ironically enough, at the time of writing *Hopscotch* he had not yet undergone this conversion: the epigraph to part 1 is from a letter from Jacques Vaché to André Breton: 'Nothing kills a man off like having to represent a country.' Like García Márquez, but unlike Fuentes and Vargas Llosa (respectively left and right of the liberal democratic centre), he retained his revolutionary socialist credentials, once acquired, to the very – and tragically premature – end. He, more than any of the others, and despite his age and his decision to take French citizenship, was the key writer of the youthful 1960s. He was the one whose work was used by Antonioni for the seminal film of *Blow-up* – and probably *Zabriskie Point* – long before the fashion for Baudrillard, whose perceptions of modernity are almost identical; and he, ironically, was the one who sent so many others unwittingly in the wrong direction, celebrating what he deplored, as his own course – after aimless drifting up to *The Winners* – became progressively straighter, though no less experimental after he found the socialist morning star as a point by which to navigate and Third World liberation as the objective of his journey.

Hopscotch is one of the most intellectually dazzling of contemporary novels (though a significant minority have considered it a pretentious fake), a work which – rather like Roa Bastos's *I the Supreme* – considers the state of the world today, the condition of being a Latin American, and the relation between Latin America and Europe. (In Cortázar's case, for the time being, the analysis largely excluded politics.) It also examines, with equal rigour, the nature of reality, fiction, language, art and, of course – and in this its connection with *The Lost Steps* is evident (as also in the Paris link, the underlying Rousseauism, the influence of Surrealism and the alienated hero) – the nature of the avant-garde. Cortázar's analysis works at two levels. Firstly, its anti-hero, Oliveira, is consumed by a thirst for rational knowledge and an equally desperate contrary desire to penetrate beyond it to some realm of pure intuition, some 'kibbutz of desire', whilst his lover, ironically but also quite seriously called 'La Maga', the sorceress, is already in that other, magical, deeper realm (although, as we have seen, Cortázar does not believe in depth, but in 'something else', something quite beyond words):

> There are metaphysical rivers, she swims in them like that swallow swimming in the air, swimming dizzily around the bell tower, dropping only to rise all the higher on the up-current. I describe and define and desire those rivers, she swims in them. I seek them, find them, watch them from the bridge, she swims in them. And she doesn't know, just like the swallow. She doesn't need to know as I do, she can live in disorder without any awareness of order holding her back. That disorder which is her mysterious order, that bohemianism of body and soul which opens the real doors wide to her. Her life is disorder only to me, sunk in prejudices which I despise and respect at one and the same time, condemned to be absolved irremediably by La Maga who judges me without knowing it. Ah, let me enter, let me see some day through your eyes. [5]

No male writer would be quite so nonchalantly phallocentric these days, but such insouciance only goes to underline the extent to which Cortázar is writing from within the same myth of Latin America which we examined in chapter 1. Second, then, shadowing this relationship exactly, the male–female axis is paralleled by the Europe–America axis, because Oliveira returns to Buenos Aires in the second part and fails to find La Maga there, but finds her female double, Talita, married to his old friend and male double, Traveller, and thus a world of successively unfolding dualities rather like that of *Men of Maize*. Beyond these two absolutely fundamental polarities, which return us to the very beginnings of Latin America as historical entity, are others like culture–nature, civilization–barbarism and their familiar echoes. Cortázar, however, adds a third section, of 'dispensable chapters', dominated by a literary experimentalist called Morelli (Macedonio Fernández? Borges?), as if to offer the opportunity of some dialectical escape from the oppositions which leave the human prisoner pacing endlessly back and forwards between the walls of his prison-like condition:

> The Orient isn't as great as the Orientalists make out. As soon as you get into its texts you get the same old feeling, intellect's inexplicable attempt at suicide by means of intellect itself. Like the scorpion stinging himself, fed up with being a scorpion but needing his scorpionness in order to kill off the scorpion. [6]

By extension, there is another interesting aspect of the novel which has been insufficiently noted. Reflecting the flight from civilization and culture back into barbarism and nature there is a trajectory from Literature and the other arts to Language and other artistic tools, and thus to the supposed 'raw experience' which the Surrealists, Sartre, the hippies and so many other thinkers since Rousseau and the Romantics have sought to find. Of course language is not actually raw, as Oliveira and Cortázar, following Joyce, realize only too well, but the concept provides a metaphorical frame which takes us beyond the then fashionable post-Saussurean Structuralism:

> 'I don't need words to feel, to know that I'm here', Ronald insisted. 'I call that reality. Even if that's all it is.'
>
> 'Perfect', said Oliveira. 'Except that that reality is no guarantee either to you or anyone else, unless you transform it into a concept and from there into a convention, a useful scheme. The very fact that you're on my left and I'm on your right makes reality into at least two realities, and note that I don't want to go any deeper by pointing out that you and I are two beings totally incapable of communicating except through our senses and words, things one must mistrust if one is going to be serious....
>
> One has the impression of following dead trails, like fussy little schoolboys going over old dusty arguments no longer of any interest. And all, my dear Ronald, because we speak dialectically. We say: you, me, the lamp, reality. Take a step back, please. Go on, it won't hurt. Words disappear. That lamp is a sensorial stimulus, nothing more. Now take another step back. What you call your sight and that sensorial stimulus become an inexplicable relation, because to explain it you'd have to take a step forward and the whole thing would go to the devil. [7]

As in Carpentier's *The Lost Steps*, then, we move from a world of institutions and false myths – usually signalled in both novels with capital letters or hyphenated phrases – to a world of authentic experience and archetypes, where things will again take on their primary meaning or presence. Cortázar's short stories, where his intuitions do not need impossible completion, are among the most brilliant of the century.

The 'boom'

This, then – the publication of *Hopscotch* – marks the precise moment at which 'Joycism' appeared to assume the main thrust of Spanish American fiction. Indeed, the epigraph to part 2 is overtly 'Ulyssean', Apollinaire's 'Il faut voyager loin en aimant sa maison'. The majority of writers were now ready for 'Joyce' instead of a mere few who had, literally, caught sight of him in Paris forty years before. From this precise moment also, the Faulknerian influence would dissolve, as the incomparable Irishman became the principal influence and point of reference, implicit and explicit trademark of Modernism and cosmopolitanism for another generation. Nevertheless, in the climax to the 'boom', what actually happened was something quite complicated. Cortázar marks the moment where Joyce rules, but the other major novelists who seized that particular historic opportunity – Fuentes, Vargas Llosa and García Márquez – were all already Faulknerian writers, and their greatest works, written during the 'boom', are recognizably in Faulknerian vein. Nevertheless, each of them also has an unmistakable additional element, and this is the labyrinthine, historical–mythological national quest motif which Joyce initiated in the 1920s and which Asturias, Carpentier, Guimarães Rosa and Cortázar had been elaborating progressively since the 1920s. Nothing written since, in my opinion, has yet superseded those great works, the culmination – for the time being – of 400 years of Latin American cultural development and – possibly false – consciousness. Like Joyce in the First World, they seem for the moment to have put an end to the possibility of further developing the novel as we know it. The current moment is one of assimilation and aggregation.

Nevertheless, as has been shown, the Joycean apotheosis signalled above all by *Hopscotch* had been coming for several decades, since 1922 itself; and for this reason the overtly Modernist works of the era were swiftly perceived as a 'boom', which swelled rapidly towards a climax with *One Hundred Years of Solitude* and then shattered into the glittering but perhaps illusory fragments of the 'post-boom' – or perhaps post-Modernist – novels of the 1970s, which appear once more to have a somewhat French look about them. It was a confused and contradictory moment, marked deeply by the Cuban Revolution, which at first was itself so pluralist that writers like Cabrera Infante were able to publish extracts from Joyce – as well as Trotsky: both were later effectively proscribed – in revolutionary arts journals like *Lunes de Revolución*. The sense of diverse ideological alternatives offered by Cuba and the various social democratic experiments of the day, combined with the new cosmopolitanism bred by a consumption-oriented capitalist boom and an expansion of the Latin American middle classes (nouveau read?) – buyers and consumers of novels – created a period of intense artistic activity throughout the subcontinent.

In Europe Modernism and its overflowing streams of consciousness had corresponded to a suddenly heightened complexity of experience and perception at a particularly dramatic and longlasting juncture of European historical development. Admittedly, Cervantes, Rabelais and Sterne had all in turn seen the potential for literary and philosophical 'intertextuality', but had simply not encountered the twentieth-century networked consciousness at the level of everyday simultaneity of experience – crossing a huge city or flying above one, tuning a radio and switching between channels, watching faraway places on cinema or television. I am reminded of Perry Anderson's critique, 'Modernity and Revolution', of Marshall Berman's *All that is Solid Melts into Air*. Briefly, Anderson rejects Berman's thesis that artistic Modernism opened the way to a new, universal aesthetic and presents an interpretation of the period quite similar to my own.[8] Speaking of the 1960s, which he explicitly compares with the 1920s, Anderson sees the perspective for artists and intellectuals as one of

> ambiguity – an openness of horizon, where the shapes of the future could alternatively assume the shifting forms of either a new type of capitalism, or of the eruption of socialism – which was constitutive of so much of the original sensibility of what had come to be called modernism.[9]

After asserting that Modernism lost its creative thrust after 1930, Anderson continues:

> This is not true, manifestly, of the Third World. It is significant that so many of Berman's examples of what he reckons to be the great modernist achievements of our time should be taken from Latin American literature. For in the Third World generally, a kind of shadow configuration of what once prevailed in the first world does exist today.[10]

Anderson's article, and Berman's reply, 'The Signs in the Street', are essential reading for anyone interested in the debate on Modernism and the directions of contemporary art and criticism.

Although Joycean novels continued to be published occasionally in the West, no achievement ever matched his. *Ulysses* was the supreme literary product of a peculiarly fertile, highly charged conjuncture, at the moment where the old European regime really was – or so it seemed – finally about to be laid to rest, and where some new modern world – which might be either Communist or capitalist – was imposing itself with a speed and vigour which the mind could barely encompass, due to a confluence of forms which Anderson summarizes as follows:

European modernism in the first [thirty] years of this century thus flowered in the
space between a still usable classical past, a still indeterminate technical present,
and a still unpredictable political future. Or, put another way, it arose at the
intersection between a semi-aristocratic ruling order, a semi-industrialized
capitalist economy, and a semi-emergent or -insurgent, labour movement. [11]

Suddenly, writers of the period, above all in the 1920s, were able to take a
step back, gain perspective, and write words which were no longer, in their
one-dimensional 'realist' historicity, secret metaphors for their own terminal
lifespan, but metaphors for the whole of human experience since the earliest
times. It was of course the development of the social sciences, especially ethnology, which had made such a development possible, viewed from the
standpoint of a Western civilization whose own belief systems were in a state
of disarray, at once underlining the relativity of culture and making mythology and mystification ever more alluring to the – reluctantly – profane mind
of capitalist consciousness. Only in Latin America, however, due to its specific bi-cultural circumstance, was the magical balancing act regularly
performed.

For a Latin American, from that time, the transition represented by
Modernism was not so much from a univocal, monolinear, patriarchal nineteenth-century realism to a complex, multi-perspectived twentieth-century
'modernism', as from a 'realism' which had never corresponded to his or her
experience anyway to a sense of pluralism that provided the opportunity for
tailor-made works and a genuine rendition of the experience of historical bi-
culturalism and narrative transculturation. Asturias had met the challenge
audaciously in his early *The President*, whereas others influenced by
Surrealism, like Carpentier and Cortázar, preferred to leave their intellectual
protagonists, as so often in Latin American fiction, stranded on the 'other
side', half grasping a reality which they cannot express through words. Does
it, then, have to be spelt out that what they long for is not another world, but
true contact with the people – which, at the very start of our story, Azuela
decided he could not have (or did not want) – true insight into their thinking
and their preliterate magical consciousness? Beyond this lay the equally revolutionary step envisaged by these same male writers, either to enter the
world of women or to imagine some democratic modification of reality
which might bring about a changed and equal world in which they could
more regularly and more completely express themselves.

Carlos Fuentes, *The Death of Artemio Cruz*

Almost at once I understood; the garden of forking paths was the chaotic novel;
the phrase 'various futures' (not all) suggested the image of a bifurcation in
time, not space. A re-reading of the whole confirmed this theory. In every

fiction, each time a man confronts diverse alternatives, he opts for one and eliminates the others.

Jorge Luis Borges, 'The Garden of Forking Paths', 1941

Carlos Fuentes (1928–) will have forgotten it by now, but in the early 1960s he was one of the younger writers most dazzled and most intimidated by Cortázar (whom both he and Vargas Llosa gradually ceased to quote, after the political parting of the ways over Cuba in 1971). At that time, despite being the oldest member of the 'boom' group, Cortázar was and remained its *enfant terrible*, the most way-out and the most hip throughout the 1960s and 1970s, in some avant-garde bohemian hangout of his own. Fuentes, born in 1928, was already Mexico's outstanding younger writer, and, as we have seen, could fairly lay claim to having written the first genuine 'new' novel in the pre-'boom' era. *Where the Air is Clear* (1958) remains perhaps the single most evocative novel about twentieth-century Mexico City, in a style almost entirely modelled on Dos Passos, complete with seeing eye in the shape of the protagonist Ixca Cienfuegos, but also with some of the most memorable pages in Mexican fiction. After *'Adam Buenosaires'* (see chapter 8), it is the first great hymn to a Latin American city, as though to respond to Alejo Carpentier's lament that Latin American cities had no individual style, or if they did it had gone unnoticed and therefore had not been properly fixed and celebrated in literature.

Possibly more than any other Latin American novelist, Fuentes has pursued the theme of identity, which in Mexico since the Revolution has at times taken on the proportions, among intellectuals at least, of a national obsession. The bourgeois characters of *Where the Air is Clear* engage, as if in a novel by Huxley or Lawrence, in seemingly endless discussions:

> Rather than being born original, we become it: one's origin is one's self-creation. Mexico must find its originality by looking ahead, it won't find it in the past.... Mexicans never know who their father is; it's their mother they wish to know, defend and rescue. The father is lost in a misty past, an object of resentment, violator of our own mother. He achieved what we can never achieve: the conquest of the mother. He is the true macho, and we hate him for it. [12]

For many people, however, *The Death of Artemio Cruz* (*La muerte de Artemio Cruz*, 1962), written partly in Havana at the very beginning of the 'boom', is Fuentes's oustanding literary achievement. It is also, appropriately enough, seen as the work which effectively puts an end to the cycle of novels of the Revolution (for some critics they ended in 1917, when the Revolution ended, for others in 1940, when Cárdenas left office, for others after the Tlatelolco massacre of 1968; whilst for others they will only come to an end when the ruling PRI ceases to hold power). It is, intriguingly, a vision of the legacy of the Mexican Revolution seen from the standpoint of the then still youthful Cuban Revolution, at a moment when writers like Fuentes and Vargas Llosa supported it more or less unequivocally. Nevertheless, we find that Fuentes – like Vargas Llosa a bourgeois realist at heart – leaves the tell-tale prints (soul marks) of liberal idealism everywhere in his text, and it came as no surprise when such writers ultimately turned away from the Cuban Revolution and back to Western liberal democracy.

The Death of Artemio Cruz is, like most of the novels of this era, retrospective (the character, on his death bed, looks back over his own life and over the history of Mexico and its Revolution; these are the same and the book is their story), and of course labyrinthine. Men quest into the future and then into the past, and novels shadow those quests in ways which, in the twentieth century, are increasingly complex. Fuentes's novel is the most straightforwardly labyrinthine of all ('Chaos: it has no plural'). We see this most clearly when Fuentes confronts his character overtly half way through the novel:

desire: desire that your desire and the desired object be the same thing; dream of the immediate fulfilment, the identification without separations of desire and the desired:
    recognize yourself:
    recognize others and let them recognize you: and know that you will oppose each other individual, because each individual is one more obstacle to the fulfilment of your desire:
    you will choose, to survive you will choose among the infinite mirrors just one, just one which will reflect you irrevocably, will cast a black shadow over all the other mirrors, you will kill them before offering yourself, once more, those infinite paths from which to choose:
    you will decide, you will choose one of those paths, you will sacrifice the rest; you will sacrifice yourself as you choose, ceasing to be all the other men you might have been, you will want other men – another – to fulfil on your behalf the life you mutilated by choosing: choosing yes, choosing no, not allowing your desire, identical to your liberty, to point out a labyrinth, but your self-interest, your fear, your pride.[13]

The first Latin American novelist to vary his technique according to his subject matter within the same novel was Asturias, first in *The President* with the Surrealist and concrete poetry sections, and then, with a vengeance, in *Men of Maize*, where an initially indecipherable indigenist text gradually achieves almost complete Western legibility by the conclusion. Cortázar experiments with this to a remarkable degree – his is one of the most 'experimental' of all Latin American novels – in *Hopscotch*, whilst Vargas Llosa (who would claim that the procedure really started with Flaubert), wrote *The*

Time of the Hero in this fashion, but took it close to its limits in *The Green House*, in his own inimitably functional way. Practice corresponds of course to particular situations in particular texts, but it is not surprising, given Latin America's dualist history and the tension between plurality and identity as alternative solutions, that this inherently Joycean–Ulyssean approach should have proved so widely compelling a technical solution to the problem of communicating a given cultural reality.

In *The Death of Artemio Cruz* Fuentes uses the familiar pattern, already seen in *The Vortex*, 'The Pit', *The Lost Steps* and *Hopscotch*, in which the male protagonist's trajectory is signposted and measured by his relation with a series of different women. Here the first, Regina, is closest to the ideal of the natural female and the compulsive no-holds-barred relationship, symbolizing the passionate convulsion of the Revolution itself. Regina dies in this novel at the same historical moment where, in *The Underdogs*, the erstwhile revolutionary comrades divided against one another, and thus suggests to us – in an achingly familiar theme of revolutionary reflections before and since – that the earliest days were the best, that good times can never be repeated, and that something called the 'original ideals' of the Revolution have been betrayed and have died.

Despite its structural contradictions Fuentes's novel is a stirring exploration of Mexico's twentieth-century history, one which fully engages the reader. If one had to recommend just one novel as an introduction to the subject, this would undoubtedly be the one. It is divided into twelve sequences, based on different periods of Cruz's life. Each sequence is cut across by three strands – 'I', 'you' and 'he', narrated respectively in the first, second and third persons – conceived as different ways of perceiving and narrating reality. Like *Men of Maize* and the later *One Hundred Years of Solitude*, it narrates its history on the basis of concentric circles, superimposing on the life of Cruz the history of the Mexican Revolution since 1910, the history of Mexico and Latin America as a whole since 1492 and the story of 'Everyman' since the dawn of time. It is worth noting that most Latin American novels, for obvious reasons, go back further than *Ulysses*, which looks back to the Greeks and the 'dawn of civilization'. In that sense they have more in common with *Finnegans Wake*, given its excursions into tribalism and timeless folklore. Unlike most of these novelists, however, Fuentes does not breathe his own experience into Artemio Cruz, no doubt due to the writer's own difficult relationship with Mexico, though one might speculate that Cruz's almost aboriginal alienation is some expression of this problem. At any rate, Fuentes's distance from Cruz means that the tensions within him are somewhat abstract and unreal, and the lack of personal identification results in an enormous symbolic and allegorical weight being placed upon the character which he can scarcely bear.

Those who have followed the history of the Mexican Revolution through literature will perceive echoes of Mariano Azuela (in the prison dialogue with Bernal) and Juan Rulfo (in the discussions with the workers on Bernal's ranch), as well as a conception of the Mexican character closely based on Octavio Paz's *Labyrinth of Solitude*. Azuela and Rulfo, however, were separated by their implicit philosophies, and in practice Fuentes, for all his apparent sophistication, reverts ultimately to the liberal perspective exemplified by Azuela. This is seen most clearly of all during the prison conversation with Bernal and in the subsequent episode where the parvenu Cruz, once a peasant, decides that he will never be able to win the love and respect of his upper-class wife Catalina. He therefore turns instead for consolation to that traditional landowner's recourse, the Indian girl. As for love – or revolutionary ideals or even common 'Christian' decency – forget it:

> He looked up to the sky, carpeted that night with all its flickering lights.
> 'Do you see that big shining star? You'd think you could reach it with your fingers, wouldn't you? But even you know that you will never touch it. We have to say no to all we can't grasp with our hands.' [14]

This, which appears to be a critique of Cruz, turns out eventually to be his justification. For in reality Fuentes thinks the same. We have realized this long before the conclusion, where, in an unforgettable final sequence, the adolescent Cruz waits up in the mountains for his godfather, the mulatto Lunero, as they prepare to escape from oppression into a new world:

> You will be there, on the first slopes of the mountain which will grow in height and air at your back.... You will try to fix your sight on just one star and take in all its light, that cold light, as invisible as the broader colour of the sun... but that light cannot be felt on the skin... You will narrow your eyes and in the night as in the day you will be unable to see the true colour of the world, forbidden to the eyes of man.... Dead in its origin, yet alive in your senses.... Lost, burned out, that well-spring of light will keep on travelling, now without origin, towards the eyes of a boy in a night in another time..., incarnated in this curious being which is you, a child, now an old dying man, you who link, in a mysterious ceremony this night, the tiny insects crawling up and down the rocks of the mountainside and the immense stars wheeling in silence out in the infinite depths of space.... And you will wait for a mulatto and a horse to cross the mountains and start to live, fill time, execute the steps and gestures of a danse macabre in which life will advance at the same time as life dies; a mad dance in which time devours time and no one alive can stop the irreversible course of disappearance.... You exist.... You standing there on the mountain.... You answering Lunero with a whistle.... You are going to live.... You are going to be the focus and the reason for the ordering of the universe.... Your body has a reason.... Your life has a reason... You are, will be, were the universe incarnate... For you the galaxies will light up and the sun will

blaze.... For you to love, live and be.... For you to find the secret and die without passing it on, because you will only possess it when your eyes close for ever.... You, erect, Cruz, thirteen years, on the verge of life...[15]

But his beloved Lunero is killed before they can meet up, and Cruz, already an orphan, already illegitimate, is left alone to find his own destiny in life. The Borgesian motifs are more than obvious. And when, despite having raped her, he finds love with Regina in the Revolution, that too is cut short before it has time to grow, confirming that for Fuentes life is one long vale of tears – not for nothing is his hero called 'Cross' – in which history always dissolves into the essential truth which is myth.

We see here what the 'down-to-earth' quality of liberal thought actually amounts to – namely that 'ideals' are by definition unattainable, which is precisely the attitude implicitly criticized by Rulfo, for example, through Pedro Páramo's conception of Susana. It bears repeating, then, that 'magically' inclined writers like Asturias, Carpentier, Rulfo or Roa Bastos are actually translating or directly articulating the perception of the people, whereas Fuentes, in his very effort at a critical realism, falls straight into the trap of his own bourgeois idealism. This is slightly different, as we shall see, from the case of Vargas Llosa, who perceives with absolute clarity the nature of bourgeois idealism, and accepts it, just as Flaubert did.

However, for Fuentes as for the lonely Candelaria Reinosa in *Men of Maize*, stars are a beautiful illusion, symbol of absence and sign of all that we can aspire to but never possess: hence its attribution to Hollywood's successfully created superhuman images. Whereas for a revolutionary writer, like Asturias for example, the stars, like seeds, are the symbols of all we may one day harvest.

Artemio Cruz, to the extent that he can be imagined outside of the novel, is, like Pedro Páramo, a cynical and callous man, though in his heart of hearts he has the same sentimentality and even the same beautiful dreams as his predecessor. Fuentes subjects him to a trial under bourgeois law, in which all the mitigating circumstances of existence – fatality, original sin, biology and the like – including the social determinisms – poverty, illegitimacy, discrimination – are put on one side of the balance, and all Cruz's negative qualities and actions – sacrificing others instead of himself, in refusal of Christian and revolutionary doctrine – are placed on the other. Needless to say, in this frothy concoction of social democratic values masquerading as revolutionary criticism (Fuentes was a 'young Marxian' at this time, with concepts of alienation, reification, use and exchange values, free love), mixed in with a gentle-Jesus revolutionary Christianity, the trial is something of a sham and Cruz is condemned when we are shown that he is subject, 'in spite of everything', to the 'blade of liberty'.[16] Never was a character more explicitly judged, and yet rarely was the evidence more obviously 'fixed'. As Cruz is finally wheeled into the operating theatre for heart surgery, the novel begins its ending on the same fatalist note as *Where the Air is Clear*:

> You will hear the rifle shot following Lunero's call.... On your head will fall, as if returning from a long journey through time, without beginning or end, all the promises of love and solitude, of hatred and endeavour, violence and tenderness, love and disenchantment, time and oblivion, innocence and surprise.... You will hear the silence of the night, without Lunero's call, without the echo of hooves.... In your heart, open to life, tonight; in your heart, open... [17]

The Aztec overtones here are unmistakable. Perhaps the most troubling aspect of the novel, though, is Fuentes's unfavourable comparison of the Mexican Revolution with the Spanish Civil War, as exemplified through his treatment of Cruz's son Lorenzo, who, unlike his father before him, dies heroically in the Iberian conflict – as if Mexico is inherently incapable of the 'true' ideals which are put into practice elsewhere.

It is important nonetheless to do justice to the audacity and complexity of this novel, its often brilliant writing, its superb evocation – precisely in and because of its contradictions – of contemporary Mexico, and its ability, 'in spite of everything', to give the reader the opportunity to meditate on Mexico and its Revolution, the thread of power and the difficulty of making choices in the actually existing world. Like Azuela, Fuentes's negative judgment on Mexican history merges with a hymn to his turbulent and contradictory country, creating a curious bitter-sweet tension all its own:

> your land
>   you will think there is a second discovery of the land in that warrior quest, that first step upon mountains and gorges which are like a defiant fist raised against the painfully slow advance of road, dam, rail and telegraph pole...
>   you will inherit the earth...
>   you will inherit the faces, gentle, distracted, without tomorrow because they do everything today, say it today, in the present and are the present: they say 'tomorrow' because tomorrow doesn't matter to them: you will be the future without being it, you will consume yourself today thinking of tomorrow: they will be tomorrow because they live only for today:
>   your people
>   your death: animal which forsees its death, you sing your death, tell it, dance it, paint it, remember it before dying it:
>   your land:
>   you will not die before returning:
>   this little town at the foot of the mountains: inhabited by three hundred people and barely perceptible from a few patches of roof peeping up through the trees. [18]

Of all contemporary Latin American novels this is the one which highlights most clearly the problematic of identity and the thematic of life as a series of choices or crossroads, through which we make or reveal ourselves; and which, in its very structure, embodies the complexity of reality: what is the universe, what is perception, what is knowledge, what is myth, religion, morality, politics, what is nationality? – these are just a few of its concerns. In constructing it, as and when he did, Fuentes made more visible the structure of contemporary Latin American fiction as a whole, just as his own relation to Mexico, Latin America and the New Novel, as both practitioner and critic, makes visible the inner thread which ties all the literary and personal relationships together (see chapter 8).

Mario Vargas Llosa, *The Green House*

> Your ancestor did not believe in a uniform, absolute time. He believed in an infinite series of times, in an expanding and maze-like network of diverging, converging and parallel times. That interweaving of times that approach, ramify, cross or entirely ignore one another, comprehends all possibilities.
>
> Jorge Luis Borges, 'The Garden of Forking Paths', 1941

The Green House (*La Casa Verde*, 1966), by Mario Vargas Llosa (1936–), is for me one of the three or four greatest novels ever written in Latin America. Indeed, with the passage of time its representation of the lives, dreams and illusions of ordinary Latin Americans becomes ever more compelling, and the fact that its author wrote it at the age of thirty, and – following the success of *The Time of the Hero* (1962) – under pressure of immense audience expectation, makes the achievement all the more remarkable. Nevertheless, despite the acclaim with which it was greeted – it was very much a necessary work if the 'boom' was to be sustained – it has not been as popular with readers and critics as other novels by Vargas Llosa. One suspects that again it is a question of the breadth of ambition going unnoticed: in a sense this is another version of Asturias's *Men of Maize*, written in another version for another generation.

Like Carpentier, Vargas Llosa based his novel on personal experience of a brief visit into the jungle. Typically, for a writer often branded a Naturalist, and himself a devotee of Flaubert, he made a second journey into the Peruvian Amazon to check details and add to the authenticity. The result is a picture of a cruelly divided Peru, riven by every internal tension imaginable in a contemporary nation, and the novel reflects this in its structure in both obvious and more subtle ways. The book is effectively in two halves, the one corresponding to events which take place in the jungle, around the mission and garrison of Santa María de Nieva, and the other to the city of Piura on the edge of the northern desert, near the coast, which happens to be the first city founded by the Spaniards on their arrival in what is now Peru.

This counterpointed story is told in four narrative sequences plus an epilogue, and each of these sequences is broken up laterally, so to speak, by five strands which run through the entire novel and which adopt different narrative modes to reflect the different kinds of reality they convey or the different kind of narrative effect which Vargas Llosa seeks to produce. Like Flaubert, and all subsequent cine-montage specialists, Vargas Llosa is an expert – the great expert in Latin American fiction – in the knowing production of specific effects, which must be counted one of the great tests of narrative art in the contemporary era. The structural comparisons with Fuentes's *The Death of Artemio Cruz* are obvious, though in a sense the two books are opposite endeavours: in Fuentes's book the whole of the architectural complexity is designed to reflect the architecture of human consciousness, which is the remembered experience of a long past life, through which we see everything else, above all the experience of twentieth-century Mexico in particular and what it is to be a man in general. In Vargas Llosa's novel a similar architecture is erected for quite different purposes. Like Fuentes's work, *The Green House* had to resist the inevitable criticism that the structures and techniques integrated into its texture are merely mechanical and that its art is too obvious. Vargas Llosa is more than equal to the charge. On the one hand the apparently mechanical progression of the novel is part of its message about the determinism of contemporary life in Peru; at the same time its apparently mechanistic strategies become ever more complex until a quite unpredictable but almost breathtaking monumentality comes about – without the author himself changing pace, launching climaxes or in any other way modifying his imperturbable posture. Part of the explanation lies in the lucidity with which Vargas Llosa sets his objectives. His two basic devices – 'communicating vessels' (alternating stories) and 'Chinese boxes' (stories within stories) – operate as both theme and technique, at both macro and micro levels, creating a remarkable mirror effect. They are, moreover, if we conceive them as forms of juxtaposition or superimposition, the two fundamental devices for all comparisons or fusions of 'European' and Latin American realities.

Fuentes's novel took place almost entirely in Cruz's consciousness, as a kind of dialogue between author and protagonist. In *The Green House*, however, there is almost no interiority: as in a film, virtually everything is either visual, or purports to be – as in Vargas Llosa's curiously hypnotic use of the third person imperfect as reported dialogue – or is audible. The only moment at which there is any sustained interiorization is during what turns out to be the dying soliloquy of one of the major characters – in an important sense, *the* major character, Anselmo – and of course precisely because the device has not been used before its effect is immeasurably heightened. The emphasis on the external, the visible and the audible, a common enough device since Flaubert, and more so since the French *nouveau roman*, creates a notable impact of mysteriousness when applied to the Amazon forest and juxtaposed with contemporarary urban consciousness:

'Do you remember when we burned your maps,' said Aquilino. 'Sheer rubbish, people who make maps don't realize that the Amazon is like a hot woman, she don't stay still a moment. Here everything moves, the rivers, the animals, the trees. What a crazy place we ended up in, Fushía.'[19]

As it crosses the desert the wind from the Cordillera hots up and hardens: armed with sand, it follows the river and when it reaches the city it hangs between earth and sky like some dazzling breastplate. There it empties itself: every day of the year, at twilight, a dry fine rain like sawdust, which only stops at dawn, falls on squares, roofs, spires, belfries, balconies and trees, and paves Piura's streets white.[20]

This is a novel in which the effects created take place in the mind of the reader, as Vargas Llosa's theory of the 'communicating vessels' would suggest, and the effect of the whole seems somehow the opposite of what one would expect to emerge from a summing of the parts. The world of Peru seems to emerge from itself, to be self-generated, truly 'there' before us. Henry James achieved something similar in his *The Ambassadors* phase, but Vargas Llosa's true precursor, after Flaubert, is Faulkner, and not even he was more successful in rendering to us the evil and mysterious beauty of a contemporary, dual world bereft of moral meaning. The achievement is all the more remarkable since the Amazon, apart from its sensationalist possibilities – so difficult to realize in fiction – does not at first sight appear to be ideal material for such techniques. The result, though, is that by the time we are through with *The Green House* we can see the novel's inner logic – like a path through the jungle – we can see the effectiveness of its techniques and where they have been leading; whereas in *The Death of Artemio Cruz*, for all its ingenuity, we can see the artificiality of the design, structured that way because of the artificiality and ultimate incoherence of Fuentes's judgment on Cruz and the Revolution.

Thus we come to realize after hundreds of pages that *The Green House* is counterpointed between Santa María and Piura because two characters, Lituma, 'the Sergeant', and Bonifacia, 'Jungle Girl', meet and get married, linking through their relationship the two hopelessly incompatible realities of urban and rural Peru. Later we perceive that the moment of their marriage is not only the spatial – and cultural – but also the temporal dividing line of the novel, and that, structurally and symbolically, everything which takes place in the jungle is chronologically prior to everything which happens in Piura (other than Anselmo's early experiences there) – at which point we understand why each of the two is known by their own name in their birthplace but by a stereotyped nickname in other regions, and we thereby come to see that the novel is also very much about that 1920s theme, regionalism, and about innumerable attempts by the characters, usually vainly, to achieve some kind of unity and reconciliation across the regional, racial and even sexual divide; then we further see that this point of departure based on a man and a woman, Lituma and Bonifacia, allows the careful and precise integration of diverse strands threading through the entire novel, some of which last only thirty days and others sixty years of historical time whilst occupying the same number of pages of narrative time.

The sixty-year-long story, that of Anselmo the harpist, founder of the brothel called the Green House, and fountain of myth and local legend in the novel – though it turns out that he is not from Piura, still less its popular quarter the Mangachería, but from the jungle – is also used, in another *tour de force*, to replicate (and even parody: 'In the first month after his arrival in Piura, nothing happened') the narrative techniques of the nineteenth-century realists and, no doubt, the 'preliterature' of the 1920s Novelists of the Land in Latin America. Then, gradually, this mode is dissolved and fuses into the stream-of-consciousness techniques used in those same 1920s by Joyce and later Faulkner, ending with Anselmo's dying meditation:

> And one more time ask yourself if it was better or worse, if life has to be like that, and what would have happened if she hadn't, if you and she, if it was all a dream or if things are always different from dreams, and then one last effort and ask yourself if you ever really resigned yourself and if it's because she died or because you are old that you are so accepting of the idea of dying yourself. [21]

Like Asturias and – as we shall see – García Márquez, Vargas Llosa used a great deal of biographical material, and its associated emotion, to construct the novel, which in one sense is an attempt to link his youthful experiences in Piura with his visit to the jungle as a university student, all viewed from the standpoint of a man who had later lived both in the capital, Lima, and in Europe. Always controversial, and increasingly right-wing after the moment of this novel – his most progressive work by far – Vargas Llosa's literary elaboration of the brothel he spied on as an adolescent is unlikely to appeal to feminists, since, like García Márquez, he presents it as an exciting, liberated zone where not only the sexes can meet, but also different social classes and races in a situation of shocking intimacy which otherwise usually appears only in novels themselves. Vargas Llosa goes even further, however. The Green House of the novel exists in reality, but much more so in legend, and obviously its very name is a metaphor for the vast Amazon jungle from which Anselmo and Bonifacia come. Green symbolizes both fertility and sexual frankness in Latin American culture. Clearly a brothel is anything but a house, but Vargas Llosa appears to believe that it is in some way a site of relative compromise even in the midst of exploitation, and that despite appearances a woman in a brothel is more adventurously free than a woman enslaved behind the bars of her convent-like home under the ideology of the Catholic Church in a patriarchal society. That this is his perception and one of the shaping motivations of the novel is seen in the fact that the jungle characters on the whole triumph over the urban ones, that the jungle's fertility is constantly juxtaposed with the sterility of the dry and dusty city, that the two most macho characters – Fushía and Lituma – end up in abject humiliation, the one with a withered penis and the other living involuntarily off prostitution, whilst the magnificent Anselmo, the dreamer of the 'North Star' (Piura, a bar, a woman), is supplanted by his own daughter, the frightful but entrepreneurial Chunga, for whom he eventually works as part of a musical trio playing romantic songs about unrequited love.

Of course one should not exaggerate. The world depicted is a male one, and the most cherished fantasies are masculine. The world of nature is seen only too clearly as an ideological construction which provides both a justification of masculine domination and an ever available means of escape from the class hierarchies of an unjust social order. Bonifacia, the Indian girl, is known as 'Jungle Girl'; Lalita, Fushía's jungle sex slave is obviously related to Nabokov's Lolita; and the theme reaches its climactic moment with Anselmo's passion for Toñita, the Latin American dream girl, beautiful, adolescent, blind and mute, but capable of feeling and hearing, and therefore a receptive instrument – like a harp – in the hands of the male, who can use her for any kind of fantasy and therefore as an effective aid to his own masturbatory desires. Thus Anselmo in his tower – explorer, conquerer, exploiter, creator of of fantasies and fountainhead of myth (from epic hero to popular street singer) – is one of the most complete and radical visions of the patriarchal complex, presented by Vargas Llosa with an almost perfect blend of ambiguities which at once holds, recreates, exposes and subverts. It is an unusual achievement in Latin America where, on the whole, the partisan character of narrative psychology – based on a a largely unmediated and none too subtle real history of violence and repression – leads most novelists into presenting villains as villains even unto themselves. Like Rulfo, Vargas Llosa shows us a far more human and thus tenacious social and psychological reality, without in any way diminishing its lamentable and despicable aspects. The narrative appears to end, like *Time of the Hero*, on a note of reconciliation. A novel predicated on the impossibility of crossing the social dividing lines which Peru's geography itself embodies, seems to close in a mood of compromise, which is ultimately an acknowledgment of defeat by the underdogs and another triumph of the status quo.

After *The Green House* Vargas Llosa brought us, in *Conversation in the Cathedral* (1969), with an exasperated pessimism and loathing, Latin America's most complete and desolate picture of one of its great cities, dominated by the political corruption necessary to maintain an unjust and immoral society. By now, however, for all its mesmeric brilliance, it was becoming clear that Vargas Llosa was lamenting the human and social condition rather than specific societies, and that like Borges and so many others before them, he was saying that society was everywhere corrupt, but even worse – hopeless – in the place he had been cursed to be born in.

Vargas Llosa had been searching for the 'total novel', but his stubborn rootedness in concrete reality made it difficult for him to achieve it except through the Joycean device of underpinning everything with some mythological substratum. In *The Green House*, with its carefully integrated substructure of myth, fantasy and ideology, he came as near to the perfectly integrated book as he ever would again. We now turn to the most seamless achievement in Latin American fiction, García Márquez's incomparable *One Hundred Years of Solitude*.

Gabriel García Márquez, *One Hundred Years of Solitude*

'An ivory labyrinth!' I exclaimed. A minimal labyrinth.

'A labyrinth of symbols,' he corrected. 'It has fallen to me, English barbarian, to reveal the diaphanous mystery. After more than a hundred years, the details are irrecoverable, but it is easy enough to work out what happened. Ts'ui Pen once said: I'm going away to write a book. And later: I'm going away to build a labyrinth. Everyone imagined two works: no one thought that book and labyrinth were one and the same. The Pavilion of Limpid Solitude rose up in the centre of a possibly intricate garden'

Jorge Luis Borges, 'The Garden of Forking Paths', 1941

In 1967, the year in which Asturias would become the first Latin American novelist to win the Nobel Prize, and Che Guevara would die in the mountains of Bolivia, the 'boom' reached its climax with the publication of its most famous literary manifestation, *One Hundred Years of Solitude* by the Colombian novelist Gabriel García Márquez (1928–). If the opening to Asturias's *The President* is the first page of the New Novel, it is arguable that García Márquez belatedly provides the first page of Latin American narrative as a whole:

Many years later, as he faced the firing squad, Colonel Aureliano Buendía was to remember that distant afternoon when his father took him to discover ice. Macondo at that time was a village of twenty adobe houses, built on the banks of a river of transparent water that ran along a bed of polished stones, which were white and enormous like prehistoric eggs. The world was so recent that many things lacked names, and in order to mention them it was necessary to point one's finger.[22]

Could anything be clearer? This innocent, fairy-tale beginning has the transparency of the great works of childhood, like *Robinson Crusoe*, *Gulliver's Travels* or *Treasure Island*. Almost anyone can understand it. And yet this remarkable book, despite its limpidity, is also one of the most deceptive and impenetrable works of contemporary literature, a worthy successor to those other children's works for adults, *Don Quixote*, *Gargantua and Pantagruel*, *Tristram Shandy* and *Alice through the Looking Glass*.

What firing squad, when, where and why? Who is Colonel Buendía? We are well used by now to not having such questions answered on the first page of a novel, if indeed they are ever answered at all. If there are problems here they lie elsewhere. Do colonels have fathers? Doesn't everyone know what ice is, without having to discover it? And why is that first sentence a labyrinth of tenses, times, people and places, a rotating mirror of events, experiences and memories reflecting endlessly back and forth until we tire of circular imag(in)ing and move on to the next lines?

'The world was so recent....' Who is talking, anyway? The first sentence approached the reported speech so familiar in contemporary literature and we realized that we were meant to come close to seeing things through Colonel Buendía's childhood gaze and adult reminiscence, or perhaps through the adult memory of his childhood gaze. Now someone else is talking, in solitude, a narrator, or perhaps – if fiction were logical – another inhabitant of the village, or maybe the voice of the community (whether representative or self-appointed). 'The world was so recent....' Just like that, a matter of fact, in a matter-of-fact voice. Except that we, the readers, in our knowing way, are already outside this knowing voice, already calmly superior to this knowledgeable equanimity. After all (which is where readers are), if there are colonels the world cannot be recent. Therefore this is not 'the' world (our all-encompassing world), this is merely 'a' world which is nevertheless all the world for the narrative voice which, in turn, represents – we presume (too much) – that community of twenty houses. This narrator seems to know everything, thinks he (he?) knows everything, but 'we', from our truly universal position in the international community of readers, naturally know much more than he or she does. This is not the Andean world of Ciro Alegría.

Yet we play the game, we accept the voice, we admit the logic. We know that really the world cannot have been new and 'recent', as if the stones in the river really were 'prehistoric eggs' and not merely similar to them. We know that a narrator who can use the concept 'prehistoric' cannot really believe that the world was recent, and thus we cannot believe that it was necessary to point with one's finger to communicate because things lacked names (yes, this is beginning to be comic, but things are also becoming serious), as if the inhabitants, in an age of colonels, were actually primitive savages.... But hold, we know (some of us) today (what we did not know 25, 50 or 100 years ago) that primitive savages had language, had names for everything, did not need to point with their fingers (except when they were invaded by ignorant foreigners). Does the narrator know this? What joke, what trick is he playing? What is he doing to us? Is this sleight of hand or word, *trompe l'oeil*? Who points with their fingers anyway?

Children do? Is there a child here? Why, Colonel Buendía. Yes, on the level of the fable. And Gabriel García Márquez, the author of the story (a he, according to the cover), going with the author of his days to discover ice, evidently a magical experience in the upside down world of tropical underdevelopment. And also the reader, who has also been a child (though not all readers have been male children – except when they read novels). Again, the labyrinth thickens, or thins (bifurcates): not only time but identity, we are already the colonel, the author and ourselves, as we shall be any narrative voice he decides to introduce. How shall we tell? Difficult, indeed, because in this novel the tone of the narrative voice will never change, even for a moment: everything, normal and absurd, comic and tragic, possible and inconceivable, will be recounted in that same tone of calm and absolute certainty.

So this, then, is childhood, a recent world. A recent world is a new world, and García Márquez is from Colombia (according to the dust jacket), in South America, the continent we call the New World, even though it is now 500 (as well as millions) of years old. Novels, of course, carry the concept of newness in their very name, new readings of old histories. If we knew about the literary history of Latin America (see chapter 1), we would know that in the 1920s a generation of writers appeared in republics up and down this by now ageing 'new world' and produced a series of rudimentary but vigorous narratives, Social Realist in orientation, which critics decided to call 'novels of the land' (see chapter 2). Many years later, in trying to evaluate them, Alejo Carpentier, a great Cuban novelist, far more knowing (naturally) than any of that earlier generation, said that they had performed a valuable historic service to Latin American culture by depicting Latin American realities for the first time in literary form, defining things and 'naming them, like Adam'. Many years later still, a novelist from an even more knowingly sophisticated generation, Mario Vargas Llosa, said that those early novels were not really worthy of the name at all: they were merely 'preliterature' (suitable, presumably, for prehistory: definition – everything before myself).

Thus do history and myth interweave, overlap, accrete, obscure and occasionally illuminate one another. It is this relationship that I have been seeking to examine in this book, aware that definitive readings are not available in this world but believing that this is an appropriate moment for attempting to redefine the image of Latin American fiction and through it the image of Latin America itself: plural, multiple, constantly changing, but not just anything, not just any vision, any image, any magical reality that any given author may wish to invent. To that extent, in challenging the absolute freedom of the artistic imagination – on ethical grounds: this is not a book based on show trials, exiles or disappearances – our endeavour is to illuminate the labyrinth.

García Márquez is as good at closing a novel down as he is at discovering beginnings:

> Only then did he discover that Amaranta Ursula was not his sister but his aunt, and that Francis Drake had attacked Riohacha solely so that they could search for one another through the most intricate labyrinths of blood, until they engendered the mythological animal which would put an end to their family line. Macondo was already a fearful whirlwind of dust and rubble being spun about by the wrath of the biblical hurricane when Aureliano skipped eleven pages so as not to waste time on facts he knew only too well, and he began to decipher the moment he was living, deciphering it as he lived it, prophesying himself in the act of deciphering the last page of the parchments, as if he were looking into a speaking mirror. Then he jumped again to anticipate the predictions and discover the date and circumstances of his death. But before he reached the final line he had realized that he would never leave that room, for it was ordained that the city of mirrors (or mirages) would be swept away by the wind and exiled from the memory of men in the instant when Aureliano Buendía finished deciphering the parchments, and that everything that was written in them was unrepeatable for always and forever, because those races condemned to one hundred years of solitude would have no second chance on earth. [23]

How does a Latin American begin and end a story? How does the story of Latin America itself begin and end? Every schoolchild knows the answer. It begins with a discovery and conquest (1492, when Columbus sailed the ocean blue) and ends with a revolution (in this case 1959, when Castro said this land is thine). So it is with this novel, which is about a frustrating and frustrated history, beginning with revelations and ending with a revolution in consciousness – a dialectical transformation, a critical awareness of the self in history after a hundred years of self-absorption – even if what seems to be happening is a death and a disaster. Who is talking?

García Márquez reminds us that those who read stories read the story of their own lives, and the consciousness of author, character and reader slide into overlap again. Those of us who are not as simple as this extraordinary novel makes us feel may well have read the books of Jorge Luis Borges, a verbal magician if ever there was one, and the true master of the twentieth-century literary labyrinth – in his case, not just the Latin American one, not just the recent world, but 'universal' reality, travelling back down through the history in which he always declined to believe:

> A man sets himself the task of portraying the world. Through the years he peoples a space with images of provinces, kingdoms, mountains, bays, ships, islands, fishes, rooms, instruments, stars, horses and peoples. Shortly before his death, he discovers that that patient labyrinth of lines traces the image of his face. [24]

Goodness, said Alicia, this is truly amazing. Borges knows that man is narcissistic, solipsistic, unmoving, unchanging. You can't fool him with mere appearances. But he can fool you. Has he fooled García Márquez and the entire 'boom' generation and taken them away from the path marked out by his contemporaries Andrade, Asturias and Carpentier? It is an important question

This, after all, is the novel which, more than any other, was taken to confirm the historical demise, not only of Social Realism, but of the kinds of Modernist works which, despite their experimental aspects, nevertheless sought to produce 'cultural knowledge', and therefore to herald the arrival of the linguistically inclined, experimental or post-Modernist novel.[25] But this is surely a complete – and sometimes, one suspects, wilful – misreading of *One Hundred Years of Solitude*, which contains a greater variety of carefully encoded material relating to the positivistic orders of social psychology, political economy and the history of ideas than almost any other Latin American novel that come to mind. Angel Rama's verdict on García Márquez's early work is equally applicable to *One Hundred Years of Solitude*: 'I do not believe any other novelist has so acutely, so truthfully seen the intimate relationship between the socio-political structure of a given country and the behaviour of his characters.'[26]

The main reason why so many readers have missed these otherwise obvious facts is, as hinted above, the elementary one that García Márquez presents most aspects of reality from the standpoint of his characters, while he himself, as narrator, adopts a perspective based – largely but not entirely ironically – on the mainly metaphysical views of the *pensadores*, those 'thinkers' or ideologists who dominated Latin America's interpretation of its own history until after the Second World War. Sarmiento's struggle between civilization and barbarism, Rodó's exaltation of Ariel against Caliban, the sick continent diagnosed by Carlos Octavio Bunge and Alcides Arguedas, Count Keyserling's swamp-like dawn of creation and *tristeza criolla* (creole sadness), Ezequiel Martínez Estrada's view of Latin Americans as victims of a historical mirage, Eduardo Mallea's incommunicability, and – perhaps above all – Hector Murena's original-sin thesis: these and many other mad and marvellous theories of Latin American history jostle for supremacy throughout the novel, only to find themselves circumscribed, at the last, by a conception which coincides closely with the rather more lucid kinds of perspective which emerged in Mexico after 1945, namely Octavio Paz's assertion that Latin Americans were now the contemporaries of all men and Leopoldo Zea's thesis that it was time, at long last, to break out of the labyrinth of solitude and assimilate the history of the continent. Seen in this light, there is perhaps more to García Márquez's work than the echoes of Faulkner, Borges and other such literary influences and parallels so widely debated by some critics. In other words, readers have generally failed to recognize that although history is sometimes devoured by myth, every myth has its history. This novel is not about some undifferentiated fusing of 'history-and-myth', but about the myths of history and their demystification. García Márquez is undoubtedly attempting to reproduce a labyrinth in order to begin liberating it. One might call it a materialist deconstruction of Borges and all the other idealisms which precede him in Latin American thought.

If this conception of *One Hundred Years of Solitude* is accepted, all the hallowed references to Vico, Hegel and Croce, all talk of circularities and eternal returns become redundant (at least as 'influences': they are actually part of the work's subject matter). This is why the most convincing interpretations of the novel's apparent dualism have come from critics with a sociological approach, like the Ecuadorean Agustín Cueva, who argues that García Márquez 'is not seeking to put forward an irrationalist philosophy but merely to recreate a representation of a world that he knows is over and done with.'[27] Cueva shows that the work is a synthesis of elements belonging to two different genres, the epic and the novel, a line later followed by Tzvetan Todorov, who likewise brings out the clash between an individualist and a collective view of the world.[28] Similarly, Sergio Benvenuto, in a brilliant short study, affirms that 'living contradiction is the only appropriate language for this incredible intersection of universal culture and local unculture.'[29]

To those who already know Latin America, the culture traits in the text are unmistakable, though each is almost impossible to extricate from its anecdotic materiality: to those who do not know the continent, the novel is more abstract, and the incidents are recognizable as vehicles of universal experiences or truths distorted by Latin American eccentricity. Thus almost everything is at once familiar but unidentifiable inside this literary 'aleph': we see the world from genesis to apocalypse, from Renaissance to baroque, from Independence to neocolonialism; or from use values to exchange values, transparence to opacity, childhood innocence to adult guilt, lines and circles to labyrinths. The result has been called 'Magical Realism', but since Carpentier and Asturias, as we have seen, the same term is often used, consciously or unconsciously, as an ideological stratagem to collapse many different kinds of writing, and many different political perspectives, into one, usually escapist, concept. Like the Surrealist movement from which it ultimately derives, Magical Realism can in part be seen as an unconscious – irony of ironies! – conspiracy between critics eager to get away, in their imagination, to the colourful world of Latin America, and certain Latin American writers desperate to take refuge, in their writing, from the injustice and brutality of their continent's unacceptable reality.

Nevertheless, most critics and general readers have admired the novel precisely because it appears to conjure up a magical reality. In order to demonstrate such a view – and herein lies the contradiction, and the key to the influence of the deconstructionists, who appear to wish to weave a labyrinth that no socialism can fight its way out of – one has to know what reality is. So, here restated, an elementary hypothesis: whatever contemporary reality is, it is determined and defined by the metropolitan centres of culture in Europe and, above all now, the United States ('The ruling ideas of each age have ever been the ideas of its ruling class'). Latin America can therefore be viewed, by definition, as a home of irreality, where people are larger or smaller than life: there for my entertainment, specimens in the national–geographic catalogue of planetary showbiz safaris (in short, less than human). Critics accordingly praise the novel for its further confirmation that life is a dream, whereas it is at least plausible that what the novel is saying is that *Latin American life* is a dream – not just the 'unreality' and 'inauthenticity' spontaneously imposed by alienation under capitalism, but also shaped by five hundred years of colonialism – and that when a dream becomes a permanent living nightmare (example: we have plundered you for centuries and now you owe us billions of dollars) it is probably time to wake up. [30] The official history which the 'Triumph of the West' has ordained for itself is that of rationalism, progressive development and linear chronology. However contradictory and repressive this history may seem to any non-conformist European, it is, for the typical Latin American, organic and coherent by definition; whereas his own history is fragmented, discontinuous, absurd ('time itself underwent jolts and accidents, and thus could splinter and leave an eternalized instant in a room').[31] It is his fate actually to be one of the despised inhabitants of a 'banana republic', victim of a 'comic-opera regime' or a 'tinpot junta'. He is a 'mimic man'. Or so 'we' would have him think.

Thus far, then, on the whole, this book has been attempting to examine Latin American fiction through Latin America's own self-generated myths and stereotypes. *One Hundred Years of Solitude*, the first Latin American novel ever to achieve international bestseller status apparently on its own terms, raises the question of what those foreign – especially Anglo-American – readers saw in the book, and whether there is not some need for a book on 'South Americanism' to match Edward Said's book on Orientalism. America has acted as Utopia or as Exotic Other ever since it was discovered, and as a combination of natural paradise and political fantasy since the nineteenth century, when Byron, who named his yacht 'Bolívar', lamented: 'Europe's decrepitude is increasing; everybody here is the same, everything repeats itself. There the people are as fresh as their New World, and as violent as their earthquakes.'[32] Conrad's *Nostromo* explored this new world reality from a similar perspective early in the present century.

It is instructive in this, as in so many other ways, to compare García Márquez more closely with Borges. However 'Argentine' Borges may or may not be, he went into production, to put it crudely, with a top-quality luxury product aimed implicitly at the European consumer. It proved a highly marketable finished commodity, albeit a minority one. García Márquez's work shows every sign of having been manufactured for the home market, Latin America, and yet it has been just as acceptable to European and North American – which is to say, 'universal' – taste. He became the first international bestseller in Latin American history.[33] If, as I believe, part of the novel's achievement is a socialist – though not either a Social Realist nor a socialist realist – reading of Latin American history, the most likely explanation for its sensational success in, say, Britain and the United States is that its subtle ambiguities make it almost as possible for readers to despise or sympathize with its Latin American characters as it would be in life outside the novel. None of this is so surprising. Almost four hundred years after Cervantes wrote *Don Quixote*, critics continue to assure us that it is about some eternal or frozen distinction between reality and illusion, rather than – as seems evident to me – about a nostalgia (deeply felt by its author but all the more strongly satirized for that in its characters) for a mythologized aristocratic world view in an age of mercantilist relations. *One Hundred Years of Solitude*, it is arguable, was born of a nostalgic longing for certain precapitalist rural relations in an age of rapid urbanization and the implantation of industrial capitalism. Sometimes the most 'limpid' and transparent works are really the most opaque.

García Márquez is such a master of magic and mystery, his writing is so consistently enjoyable, that one is tempted to forget that to believe, even temporarily, in illusions is to settle for a world that is undecipherable and unknowable. But this is surely not the job of criticism. My view is that the essential point of departure for any analysis of *One Hundred Years of Solitude* must be an examination of its perception of the relation between ideology and consciousness and between lived reality, historiography and literature.

Indeed, the topic now under consideration – how magical and how realist is García Márquez? – is relevant to all his fictional production (not excluding some of his journalism),[34] but *One Hundred Years of Solitude* is unquestionably the pivotal work and by far the most complex. In *Leafstorm* (1955), *In Evil Hour* (1962), or, quintessentially, *No One Writes to the Colonel* (1958), the basic narrative conventions are those of critical realism, with implicit but perfectly straightforward economic, social and political – that is, historical – explanations for the psychological motivations of each of the characters (Angel Rama speaks of 'a pronounced social determinism').[35] Any picturesqueness in them is no more than eccentricity born of ex-centricity. In the much later *Autumn of the Patriarch* (1975), as we shall see, the weakness for hyperbole – what J. Mejía Duque has called 'the crisis of disproportion'[36] – and the temptation of the *tour de force* between them sweep almost all grasp on historical reality away, and it is worth recalling that the novel was written in Spain, where García Márquez was living during the last seven years of the Franco regime. In this novel he appeared – as the price of playing to the gallery – to become lost in the same ideological and linguistic labyrinths into which he had unintenionally lured so many other unsuspecting writers with the glittering success of *One Hundred Years of Solitude*. That work remains the only text of his in which the mix of real and fantasy elements is both perfectly fused and, analytically, perfectly separable.

In an early article on García Márquez, Angel Rama noted an 'oscillation in the author himself with regard to the plane on which any given explanation should rest: whether on the social or the metaphysical level.'[37] By the time of *One Hundred Years of Solitude*, however, the technical sleight of hand had become almost invisible, and most critics began to emphasize the blend of myth and history, fiction and reality, and to view with approval the apparent impossibility of distinguishing between them. Julio Ortega insisted that 'the play of reality and fantasy is never dual in this novel'.[38] José Miguel Oviedo declared that the novelist had 'mixed the real and the fantastic in so perfect and inextricable a fashion that no one can tell where the frontier between them may lie';[39] and Ernst Völkening commented admiringly that García Márquez was blessed with 'the uncommon gift of seeing both sides of the moon at one and the same time'.[40]

At first sight, indeed, García Márquez allows us both the pleasures of exoticism and difference or otherness and the satisfaction of feeling superior. In it, as in most of García Márquez's work, nothing ever turns out as people expect; everything surprises them; all of them fail; all are frustrated; few achieve communion with others for more than a fleeting moment, and most not at all. Most of their actions, like the structure of the novel as a whole and of course its first chapter, are circular. Ploughers of the sea, they are unable to make their lives purposive, achieve productiveness, break out of the vicious circle of fate. In short, like the characters of Rulfo's *Pedro Páramo*, they fail to become agents of history for themselves;[41] rather, they are the echoes of someone else's history, the last link in the centre–periphery chain, like the Indians in *Huasipungo* or Asturias's *Banana Trilogy*. The only explanation possible is that they are living out their lives in the name of someone else's values. Hence the solitude and distance, those recurrent themes of Latin American history: it is their abandonment in an empty continent, a vast cultural vacuum, marooned thousands of miles away from their true home. Conceived by Spain in the sixteenth century (the stranded galleon, the buried suit of armour), the characters awaken in the late eighteenth-century Enlightenment (magnet and telescope as symbols of the two pillars of Newtonian physics), but are entirely unable to bring themselves into focus in a world they have not made. Influences from outside are sporadic (the gypsies), piecemeal, throughout the notional hundred years of the novel, which is the span from the Independence era to the early 1960s, when it was being written.

Of course the characters are supposed – by themselves at least – to be living in 'our' world. Times of the day, days of the week, statistics of every kind are to be found everywhere in the novel, but are no more helpful or meaningful than the more obviously illusory temporal references such as 'many years later' which appear with equal frequency, from its very first sentence. The characters all believe that their actions are purposive, but whenever they follow their logical chain to its conclusion they find that they have come in a circle. Yet, despite the historical immobility which lies at its heart, the narrative literally teems with actions (part of what one critic has called its revival of the 'forgotten art of storytelling').[42]

Thus *One Hundred Years of Solitude* is the domain of the verb. The actions of which the verbs tell are individualistic, usually to the point of an extraordinary egotism – at least on the part of the male characters – and such individualism, given its relation to liberal ideology, might seem to suggest that they were genuinely historical, occurring only once in time and contributing more or less consciously to the movement of human history. But, once the reader is immersed in the narrative, each action begins to remind him or her of many other actions, since their inner meanings, like the names of the characters, constantly recur and refer, giving such apparently Borgesian concepts as the labyrinth and the mirror an inescapably material reading. Thus the very individualism and self-centredness of the characters is an obsessively repeated ritual. The fountainhead of this form of unreality is the first José Arcadio Buendía. It is he, progenitor of the novel who, soon after the start, initiates the pattern of bemused contemplation, self-absorption and withdrawal. The Aurelianos, by contrast, are actively selfish and individualistic, seekers of power rather than knowledge.[43] Ursula, who has been much studied, is the paradigm of the commonsensical mother figure, symbol of an entire epoch of family relations, but herself comes to believe that everything is circular (that the present is subordinate to the past), a conviction which brings her death and prompts the death of many others. Curiously enough, she makes her discovery, as we shall see, at precisely the moment when history, and the consciousness of modernity, has finally broken through to Macondo.

At this point, then, the Buendía line is doomed. I take this to mean that the end of neocolonialism is on the horizon, remembering that the novel was written during the early years of the Cuban Revolution, which García Márquez has continued to support through thick and thin. There seems little doubt that the family's morbid fear of a child cursed with a pig's tail is a condensed metaphor for the combined ideologies of original sin and biological determinism – so that, again, esoteric or essentialist arguments about the nature and meaning of the incest theme seem to me to be entirely beside the point: it is a historical era that is over, not a biological line. The religious concept of original sin circumscribed the whole of life in the colonial period, and was overlain by biological determinism after Independence, as an explanation of Latin America's continuing backwardness and a positivist justification of the rule of Europeanized minorities. The impact of Darwin and Spencer encouraged the ideologies of thinkers like Bunge and Arguedas in the early twentieth century, at a time when the European powers and the United States were still extending their colonial possessions. The reflection of these overlapping religious, philosophical and scientific theories in the self-image of the characters brings about an immensely subtle tragicomic fusion of fatalism and individualism. Most of the characters are aware that others have weaknesses and are doomed to failure, but none of them know this about themselves. The secret last analysis of every situation reverts to racial or metaphysical explanations. If you call a child Aureliano, he will turn out like 'an Aureliano'. There is no escape; and no second chance. Problems of underdevelopment, dependency or imperialism never occur to these characters (they have occurred to the author, but, like Borges's Pierre Menard, his genius lies in having apparently managed to 'forget' them). They are blissfully unaware of historical reality and know nothing of the world which has determined their destiny. Their only thoughts or memories are about things which relate to the structure of the novel, which is therefore the very fabric of their social history. This explains the exoticism for them of phenomena which to us are quite normal – it is to our discredit if we find this surprising or amusing – as it also explains the often cited dreamlike quality of the Banana Company massacre narrated in the later part of the text. Seen in this light, then, the novel seems less concerned with any 'magical' reality than with the general effect of a colonial history upon individual relationships: hence the themes of circularity, irrationality, fatalism, isolation, superstition, fanaticism, corruption and violence. The judgment as to whether these traits are inherent or produced by history is as much a political as a philosophical or scientific determination.

Even among critics who would follow me this far in the argument, there is little agreement about the meaning of the conclusion. Whilst not wishing to oversimplify it, I believe that it too is more straightforward than most readers have imagined. An old-fashioned biographical approach, as followed by Vargas Llosa in his pathbreaking critical study, can give us the first clue.[44] A number of critics have recognized the strike against the Banana Company and the ensuing massacre as the central shaping episode of the entire novel, but few have realized just how profoundly this is the case. It is the theme of proletarian struggle, however, which is the secret thread that can guide us out into the light at the end of the labyrinth. García Márquez was born in 1928, the very year in which the historic massacre took place. It is at about the same time that Meme Buendía's son, the illegitimate Aureliano, is born in the novel. His mother had been forbidden to see Mauricio, his father, because, as an apprentice mechanic in the company workshop and one-time employee of Aureliano Triste, he was from an inferior class. Mauricio's surname is Babilonia, conceivably because the proletariat, which he represents, will bring about the historical destruction of 'Macondo', which is less a place than the name García Márquez gives to an era. Interestingly, Mauricio looks like a gypsy,[45] which suggests that as a migrant manual worker, a member of the *hojarasca* ('trash') so despised by García Márquez's own family when he was a child, he is a vehicle of the same kind of internationalist consciousness and impact (what the Mexican government now calls 'exotic influences') as the real gypsies led by Melquíades in the earlier sections of the novel. Mauricio is permanently crippled in an accident at the end of chapter 14, shortly after Meme becomes pregnant, and appears no more. But, at the beginning of chapter 15, the arrival of his illegitimate son is made to coincide explicitly with the author's own prophecy of doom for Macondo: 'The events which were to deal Macondo its mortal blow were already on the horizon when they brought Meme Buendía's son home'.[46]

These apocalyptic 'events', then, are patently *historical* ones. It is of course Aureliano Babilonia himself who will eventually decipher Melquíades's parchments on the final page. All the disasters to come had in fact already been presaged by a previous textual moment, at the end of chapter 11, through a familiar image of progress: 'the innocent yellow train that was to bring so many insecurities and uncertainties, so many joys and misfortunes, so many changes, calamities and nostalgias to Macondo.'[47] We are a long way from Rómulo Gallegos and Santos Luzardo in *Doña Bárbara* (being written as García Márquez was born). The decision to bring the yellow train, inaugurating the final stage in the penetration of Macondo's introversion and self-centredness, was taken by Aureliano Triste, the man who turned the magical ice into a commodity, which we can construe as representative of the impact of the embryonic local bourgeoisie: 'they remembered him well because in a matter of hours he had managed to destroy every breakable object that passed through his hands.'[48] The little yellow train in its turn brings the multinational Banana Company, United States imperialism, and eventual disaster, a perfectly logical sequence of events carefully explained by the author himself, all of which has little to do with pigs' tails.

The Banana Company brings temporary prosperity around the time of the First World War, but as profits are threatened in the late 1920s the workers begin strike action. José Arcadio Segundo, great-uncle of the baby Aureliano Babilonia, and at first a foreman in the company, becomes a trade-union leader and plays a leading role in the conflict. He is one of the few survivors of the massacre, and insists on repeating his eye-witness account of the death of more than three thousand demonstrators until the day he dies. Indeed, his last words — to none other than Aureliano Babilonia, in Melquíades' old but ageless room — are: 'Always remember that there were more than three thousand and that they threw them in the sea.'[49] At which the narrator comments: 'Then he collapsed over the parchments and died with his eyes open.' The massacre had been denied by the authorities: 'In Macondo nothing has happened, nor is anything happening now, nor will it ever.'[50] Then all history and all memory were comprehensively blotted out by the rain which lasted 4 years, 11 months and 2 days, and which recalls the previous 'plague of insomnia' in chapter 3, significantly provoked on that occasion by the suppression of Colombian Indian history. Now proletarian history was to be erased. In this instance, however, despite assiduous efforts by Colombia's official historians to make even the memory of the murdered strikers 'disappear', it was not to be so easy. The massacre was perpetrated by troops under General Carlos Cortés Vargas at the Ciénaga (Magdalena) railway station on 5 December 1928, in direct connivance with the United Fruit Company. The conservative government of Miguel Abadía Méndez (1926–30) reported that a mere nine strikers were killed and, like all succeeding regimes, set about suppressing the true story. After some tempestuous parliamentary debates in September 1929, almost nothing of importance concerning these events appeared in Colombia in the forty years up to the publication of *One Hundred Years of Solitude*.[51] The rest was silence.

After the interminable rain, Ursula's own 'one hundred torrential years' come to an end, and with it her morality and her view of the world, the cement that has held the family together until these final chapters. When she dies, Macondo's decline accelerates, and the doom of the entire Buendía family rapidly approaches. Nevertheless, as García Márquez shows, all is not forgotten. First José Arcadio Segundo, then Aureliano Babilonia, keep the memory of the workers' struggles and their suppression alive, at the same time as they themselves strive to decipher the broader historical panorama encoded in the parchments in Melquíades's room. José Arcadio's first memory was of seeing a man executed by firing squad as a child, and as we decode his own life we perceive clearly that he is one of the few characters who has struggled in any way sincerely against injustice. He it is, then, who leads the strike; who begins to decipher the parchments, or 'true history', of the Buendía family; and who, as his legacy, educates young Aureliano Babilonia:

> In reality, although everyone took him for a madman, José Arcadio Segundo was at this time the most lucid member of the household. He taught little Aureliano to read and write, initiated him in the study of the parchments, and instilled in him so personal an interpretation of the meaning of the Banana Company for Macondo, that many years later, when Aureliano finally went out into the world, people would think that he was telling some hallucinatory story, because it was so radically opposed to the false version accepted by the historians and confirmed in the school textbooks.[52]

Nothing, surely, could be clearer. After José Arcadio Segundo's death, Aureliano Babilonia remains in Melquíades's room, continuing his own education and the deciphering of the parchments, sometimes aided by the ghost of Melquíades himself. The room, needless to say, is that timeless space of memory, domain of history and literature (García Márquez in his writer's solitude),[53] marked by the 'diaphanous purity of its air, its immunity against dust and destruction',[54] until, that is, Melquíades himself dies and time pursues its work in his room also. Aureliano, meanwhile, obsessed by the parchments, takes no interest in what is going on around him and makes only occasional excursions to buy reference works at the old Catalan's bookshop (the political aftermath of the Spanish Civil War and its impact in Latin America). At length, having deduced that the manuscripts are written in Sanskrit, he manages to translate the first page, only to discover that they are poems and still in code. Finally, 'firmly fortified within written reality', he emerges into the real world and makes four new friends at the bookshop, thereafter dividing his time between books and brothels: 'Only then did it occur to him that literature was the best game ever devised for pulling the wool over people's eyes.'[55]

One of his new friends, Gabriel, is none other than the author, and his fiancée, Mercedes, is none other than the author's wife. Gabriel leaves for Europe to become a writer after winning a competition. This would be in 1954, in the midst of *la Violencia*, when Colombia as a whole was indeed, like Macondo, in an advanced stage of social decomposition. It is to Gabriel that Aureliano, now left behind, had felt closest, for a very important reason. Both knew the story of the strike: 'Aureliano and Gabriel were linked by a sort of complicity, founded on real events in which no one else believed and which had so affected their lives that both were adrift in the wake of a world that was gone, and of which only their own nostalgic longings remained.'[56] Once again, could anything be clearer? García Márquez leaves the novel for Paris, but he also remains through the medium of Aureliano, who is so closely linked to him and to José Arcadio Segundo through their shared inter- pretation of the history of Macondo and of the Buendía family. Moreover, Aureliano is the character who eventually deciphers the parchments (the novel, his own life, Latin American history) on the very last page.

Before that hypnotic final section we have the famous metaphor of dialec- tical decline, which is the Buendía family's downward spiral as understood by Pilar Ternera: 'the history of the family was a system of irreparable repeti- tions, a turning wheel which would have gone on spinning until eternity were it not for the progressive and irremediable wearing of the axle.'[57] Needless to say, the family members themselves had perceived no spiral, only cycles of futility: '"I know this off by heart", shrieked Ursula. "It's as though time were going round in circles and we'd come back to the beginning again!"'[58] 'Once more she shivered at the realization that time did not pass, as she had just acknowledged, but merely went round and round in circles.'[59] Then, on the penultimate page, García Márquez explains not so much the nature of the family history as the inner theory of his novel: 'Melquíades had not arranged events in the order of man's conventional time, but had concentrated a whole century of daily episodes in such a way that they coexisted in a single instant.'[60] Again, the statement is not so much a philosophical speculation on the nature of time or the problems of literature, but a historical interpretation of reality in terms of what Cueva calls the 'great structural heterogeneity of Latin American social formations.'[61] This sudden focusing of the literary– structural problems involved in conveying uneven development through the classic bourgeois vehicle of the novel brings us at last to the central question of authorship and readership with which the novel ends.

It is the younger generation, that of García Márquez himself (Aureliano Babilonia and Gabriel), which finally comes to read and write the real history of the continent. They do so precisely by deciphering the magical reality and labyrinthine fantasies of the previous one hundred years of solitude, this very novel, which is their world, and in which so many other characters have been bewitched and bewildered. Hence the mirror/mirage (*espejos/espejismos*) ambiguity on the last page. There we find Aureliano Babilonia – and the author reminds us of his surname – 'deciphering the instant he was living, deciphering it as he lived it', or, as Leopoldo Zea would no doubt argue, negating the past dialectically in order to become, in Octavio Paz's phrase, 'contemporary with all men'. Thus he breaks out of false circularities, mean-ingless repetitions, the prehistory before the dawn of proletarian consciousness. Aureliano's reading literally puts an end to one hundred years of solitude, to *One Hundred Years of Solitude*, and turns the reader who is reading about him back out into the history outside the text.[62] The only remaining question is whether this is a logical outcome to the structural con-ception of the novel as a whole, or whether García Márquez has merely imposed it in a moment of inspiration, in order to escape, Houdini-like (Borges-like?), from the implications of his own 'Leopardian' pessimism (to echo Timpanaro).[63] I think not, precisely because, as has been said, this is not so much a literary narration of Latin American history as a deconstruc-tionist reading of that history. Once some of the characters become able to interpret their own past, the author is able to end on an optimistic note. The apocalypse of the Buendías is not – how could it be? – the end of Latin America but the end of primitive neocolonialism, its conscious or uncon-scious collaborators, and an epoch of illusions.

To those who may complain that the novel does not actually say this, one can only ask: What other significance is there in the chain of memory from the Banana massacre through José Arcadio Segundo, Aureliano Babilonia, the fictional and the real Gabriel García Márquez and the reader himself? Yet, if this reading is already Cervantine enough ('from Cide Hamete Benengeli to Melquíades the gypsy'), there is a further dimension to unfold. For the New Novelists of the 1960s, the two key signs of the impending transformation of Latin America were, as we have seen, the Cuban Revolution and the 'boom' of the Latin American novel itself.[64] Cuba was perceived by socialists – and even, for a time, by liberals – as the material conversion of the workers' struggle into historical reality. Looking back from this vantage point, many years later, it is quite obvious, as I have tried to show, that the 'boom' was heralded by *Where the Air is Clear* in 1958, announced by *Hopscotch* in 1963 and reached its apotheosis with *One Hundred Years of Solitude* in 1967; and that the latter, as text, is perfectly aware of its own literary–historical significance, one whose implicit claim is that the 'boom' itself was a proof of the end of neocolonialism and the begin-ning of true liberation. The intertextual references to Alejo Carpentier's *Explosion in a Cathedral*, *The Death of Artemio Cruz*, *Hopscotch* and *The Green House* are clear signs of this, in contrast with, say, the work of Borges, whose textual references are either to Argentina itself, or, overwhelmingly, to literatures outside Latin America. The sense of euphoria in the novel, and particularly in its final pages – one can almost hear García Márquez shout Eureka! – is palpable. It communicates to us the excitement of a writer who has at long last solved his artistic problems by deciphering his own life history, who is aware that in the process he has written a classic, and, not only that, is also conscious that his work will appear at the perfect culminating moment in the political and literary history of the continent, encapsulating that history and his own biography at one and the same time.[65] He had even, momentarily, found a means of reconciling his rather evident philosophical pessimisim about the human condition with his determinedly optimistic conception of the march of history.

To this extent one should perhaps revise the impression of a novel whose two levels, magical and realist, mythical and historical, are entirely inseparable, since after the massacre and the death of Ursula they slowly but surely begin to come apart. The opening of the novel – 'transparent', 'recent', bathed in light – is an evocation not only of Latin America's mythical innocence after Independence but of the magical childhood world which García Márquez inhabited in Aracataca with his grandfather the colonel.[66] The endless civil wars in the novel between liberals and conservatives bring no enlightenment, only disillusionment and despair. Nevertheless, as the novel wears on and García Márquez himself as narrator gradually metamorphoses from child into adult, finally becoming himself only on the last page of the book, the characters slowly, reluctantly come to understand, among other things, what it is that Latin American colonels are generally paid to do, and innocence comes to an end. Whereas at the start of the novel the characters are mainly optimistic and forward-looking, by the time the narrative is halfway through they begin to hear the music not of hope and destiny, but of nostalgia for the past and for innocence itself. Once Ursula loses her residual faith in the purpose and coherence of the present, she dies, and once she has died the solid unity – or mystification – of myth and history is broken. The rest of the novel condenses the decipherment of Colombian history which García Márquez and his generation – especialiy the Grupo de Barranquilla – carried out in the wake of the 1948 *Bogotazo* (he was twenty years old at the time), when the workers' movement was again denied its place in national life, and on through the dark years of *la Violencia*.[67] It seems clear that he was able to do this precisely by having distanced himself from these realities, escaping at last from Colombia, Aracataca and his family 'demons' (to quote Vargas Llosa). This is one more illustration of the truth that Latin American authors can best achieve greatness not through a national, still less a cosmopolitan perspective but from a continental standpoint: by conceiving of themselves as Latin Americans.

Seen in this multiple light, *One Hundred Years of Solitude* is clearly a demystification, though apparently one so scrupulously labyrinthine in itself that most readers have managed to get themselves as lost in its winding corridors and spiralling stairways as most Latin Americans, including the Buendías, in the phantasmagorical history which it reconstructs.[68] I say again that the major works of the 'boom' were largely misread by critics, and that the writers themselves were misled by critical reaction to their texts into mis-interpreting them, and thereafter – from about 1968 – into giving the public what they – perhaps mistakenly – thought it wanted. No misreading has been more serious for Latin American literary history than the 'mythreading' of its most celebrated work, *One Hundred Years of Solitude*. It is the culmination of that entire family of 'Ulyssean' novels which show their readers the way out of the historical labyrinth and at the same time flatter them, to quote Borges on 'Herbert Quain', that they are 'more perspicacious than the detective'.

8

Era's End:
Big Books and Great Dictators

The production of novels leads you, among other things, to a kind of omnipotence, but also, by the same token, to the impotence of its... inherent solitude.

David Viñas[1]

After a golden age comes a decline. After a boom comes a slump. There can be little doubt that the publication of *One Hundred Years of Solitude* marked the high point of the 'boom', and indeed the culmination of the New Latin American Novel as a whole. After that moment the hardening of the Cuban Revolution, the worldwide recession, the Chilean coup and other such revolutionary reverses coincided with a sense of voluntarism and surfeit on the part of authors who were now wanting to write big novels rather than proving able to write great ones. Needless to say, Latin American fiction has continued to produce large numbers of outstanding works, and remains perhaps the most fertile body of narrative in the world today, whilst publicity and sales have continued on an ever upward trend. Nevertheless, most readers seem to agree that the new works do not quite match the old ones in scale and perspective, and the genre has not developed very far beyond its position in the mid-1970s. Indeed, I would like to suggest 1975 as the year when the 'boom' finally ended, with the publication of a titanic failure, Fuentes's *Terra Nostra*, which effectively completed fifty years of Latin American fiction, and a promethean success, Roa Bastos's *I the Supreme*, which in some respects marked the end of an entire era in Latin American literary history, the one which had stretched from Sarmiento's *Facundo* in 1845.

The 'Boom' in Retrospect

As we have seen, the twentieth century began late in Latin America. The 1920s were felt to be the decade of the 'new' and of 'modernization', redefining Latin America once again as a continent which is always new yet always has to catch up with the so-called 'old' world. In the next period of accelerated political, economic and cultural change, between 1958 and 1969, Latin America became, through Cuba (not forgetting the Guatemalan affair of 1954), a direct protagonist of the Cold War; and, once again, in a second age of pluralist politics and easy money, newness, modernization and development became key concepts, but now with one crucial difference. Whereas in the 1920s the world's first Communist revolution had only just occurred, leaving intellectuals, including artists, free to choose, without definitive commitment, either the still untried Communist path (as many in Latin America did) or some other (usually populist) road (PRI in Mexico, APRA in Peru, Vargas and Perón in Brazil and Argentina), in the 1960s such pluralist illusions, although generated anew, were quicker to dissolve; and whereas in the 1920s the principal revolutionary model for Latin Americans, inevitably, was not the distant Soviet one but the equally complex and more ambiguous Mexican experience (Recabarren, Mella, Mariátegui, Prestes, Farabundo Martí and other Marxist intellectuals notwithstanding), in the 1960s it was Cuba's 'Third World' Communist revolution which provided the intellectual motor, whilst the populist, multiclass alliances which had united so many artists and intellectuals since the 1920s and allowed unbroken dialogue among them, rapidly disintegrated as both sides were forced explicitly to commit themselves – all the more so because the United States, looming ever larger with each passing decade, had now become the principal economic, political and ideological antagonist of that same Soviet Union on which Cuba, in the face of the imperialist blockade, had been forced to depend.

The young Arielist students of the 1918 Córdoba movement had quickly put most of Rodó's philosophical idealism and Darío's literary posturing behind them, identifying themselves, in the wake of the First World War, Mexico and the October Revolution, with the material world of the Latin American peasantry and its incipient workers' movements, on the lines envisaged by the great Peruvian intellectual González Prada. Sometimes missionaries (on the Vasconcelos model), sometimes revolutionaries, invariably educators and propagandists among the people (the muralists, the popular universities organized by Haya, Mella and others), that generation, born with the twentieth century, originated a link between students and workers and a practice of political activism which would henceforth characterize Latin American social life and would reach one of its great crescendoes in the

1960s, another great age of student revolt worldwide, when in Mexico of all places, exactly half a century after the Córdoba movement, the aspirations of another generation of student rebels came to a bitter end at Tlatelolco, as authoritarianism again became generalized in Latin America, a year after the death of Guevara and a few months after the frustration of the Parisian May.

This, in effect, was the half-century in which Latin America finally became integrated into the world's economic, political and cultural system. The inevitable result was that the Latin American historical labyrinth widened, deepened, ramified and expanded, but because it was also the moment when the analytical tools – for that very reason – at last became available, it was also the half-century in which literature, finally, was able to perceive and focus that labyrinth – 1967 was the high point – before Post-structuralist trends plunged us into our current Derridian chaos, in which history and myth, criticism and literature, all fuse inextricably together, beyond the moment of the novels of 'cultural knowledge'.[2] Because that same period, the 1960s, saw a remarkable intensification and flowering of Latin American fiction, it is not surprising, in retrospect, that the achievements of earlier generations should for a time have been eclipsed or, when recognized, radically differentiated from the 'boom' which, if some promoters of megaphone criticism had been believed, must either have been the product of a virgin birth or of some newly discovered island, like Columbus's America.[3]

The 'boom' was not only very largely the product of the fiction which had gone before, just as all literature is produced by varying combinations of real history and literary history, but it was also the climax and consummation of Latin American Modernism in the Anglo-American and Brazilian sense. Carlos Fuentes recognized this in his interview with Luis Harss in the mid-1960s when he acknowledged his debt to Dos Passos in the elaboration of *Where the Air is Clear*: 'As Latin America suffers a cultural lapse of at least forty or fifty years, new forms always tend to arrive late. So the substance is retarded also, it always lags behind; the moment came when the substance of our life found adequate form in the sort of novel Dos Passos was writing forty years ago.'[4] Of course, what was remarkable about the 'boom' was the way in which novelists evolved, within the decade, from mimetic beginnings to assume honoured places within the international literary avant-garde. Thus the development of Modernist fiction, which in Europe had really begun in Flaubert's day and reached its climax with Joyce (followed, as I see it, by a long decline which still continues), took slightly longer to complete in Latin America, where it began in the 1920s (although even here one must never forget the historical exception of Machado, Brazil's Sterne). This is partly because it took that long for conditions in Latin America to reach an equivalence, however inexact in the neocolonial context, to what they had been in

Europe in the 1920s, and partly because it takes time for influences in fiction to work their way through – particularly in this case, because, as we have seen, the new Latin American novel of the 1960s was a very specific kind of fiction, unequalled since Joyce himself in its structurally implicit claims and ambitions. At the same time, and in the light of these claims and ambitions, it is essential to underline once more that although a part of the explanation is based on concepts of cultural lag, dependency and one-way influences, it is by no means as simple as this, since, as has been shown, on the one hand there were many Latin American writers and artists, above all those resident in Europe – the 'Ulyssean' artists, forced into consciousness like wandering Jews – who in the 1920s were already producing avant-garde, 'Modernist' works; and on the other hand, there are many conventionally bourgeois or provincial artists in Europe (above all in Britain) and North America, as well as in Latin America itself, who have still not assimilated the impact and implications of 1920s Modernism and thus continue to produce what in style and even in ideology we could almost call nineteenth-century works. Moreover, there have been few Kafkas, Picassos, Joyces, Stravinskys or Einsteins anywhere since the 1920s, and even the cinema can hardly be said to have made 'progress' as an art form since the days of Griffith or Eisenstein. In other words, if we are to look for progress in recent art, it is not to 'high' art that we should look.

As we have seen, the Ulyssean model typologized in chapter 5, whose labyrinthine passage through everyday life – as well as the whole of history – was emulated by Woolf and Faulkner, was in fact peculiarly apposite for Latin America, where the challenge of uneven development was even more complex than in Joyce's Ireland. But in the 1920s, unsurprisingly, most Latin American writers were not fully ready for these innovations (nor, come to that, were most Europeans; nor are they yet), sensing, no doubt, that such a climax of bourgeois consciousness was the ultimate moment of balance and focus before a great many other things finally became clear, the result being an unhappy choice between a totally consumerist art or its total politicization. In any case, and ironically, Latin American writers had first to travel through the avant-garde and the consciousness of modernity before they could then turn again and conduct their own quest for identity, had first to understand the world before they could understand themselves. But this quest, for the Third World intellectual, involves more mirages and illusory reflections than even Alice had to negotiate, as soon as he or she tries to move beyond the culture and the aesthetics of hunger (witness Roa Bastos's road from *Son of Man* to *I the Supreme*). At any rate, it was the Parisian generation of Latin Americans of the 1920s who began this quest, which they completed shortly after the Second World War (when Asturias completed *Men of Maize* and Marechal completed '*Adam Buenosaires*') – significantly enough, at the time when Paz's *The Labyrinth of Solitude* was concluding that Latin Americans were now 'the contemporaries of all men', a historic statement which contained both a striking truth (some really were) and a great falsehood (the vast majority were not); and it was the next Parisian generation (some of whom also resided in London and Barcelona) – Cortázar, García Márquez, Fuentes and Vargas Llosa, *et al.* – who brought this literary–historical phenomenon to a close and a climax, back to Ithaca and Penelope, in the 1960s.

Each of their key novels was about a quest or quests; each was about the nature of Latin American identity; each also provided a metaphor or metaphors for the course of Latin American history – since the creation, the conquest, Independence, the birth of the author, etc.; each was linguistically exploratory and structurally mythological – labyrinthine, preoccupied with consciousness, obsessed with the woman both as muse and materiality: in short, they were Joycean, Ulyssean works, products of patriarchal idealism inspired by and dedicated (though only rarely addressed) to Penelope, the Other, the world of matter, the female, the people, the nation, Mother America. (It does not require a very extended analysis to see why, if only a few men were able to achieve the necessarily privileged experience required for writing this kind of work, it was almost out of the question for women between the 1920s and the 1960s; nor to note that the two most successful women writers of the last decade, Isabel Allende and Luisa Valenzuela, have both lived out the experience of exile and return as part of the process of literary production). The writers of those works had come to see, explicitly or implicitly, and largely thanks to the Cuban Revolution, that no writer could produce the Great Latin American Novel without a consciousness of colonialism as the determining structural fact of Latin American history, and without integrating this consciousness into the very structure of his or her fiction. This was not entirely new, however: it was just that a new generation had to learn again what had been known in the 1920s, and writers like Andrade, Asturias, Carpentier and Rulfo had already shown the way to a fiction which would make the Latin American Oedipal quest for historical self-knowledge and identity its central structuring motif. The real story of the New Novel, then, is of a moment in Latin American history when the Joycean novel became both generally writable and unavoidable. That process was demonstrably complete when, in 1976, Jorge Adoum's novel, '*Between Marx and a Naked Woman*', anticipating in a way Piglia's '*Artificial Respiration*' (see chapter 10), lamented not only the impossibility of writing 'after Joyce' but also, much more definitively, 'after Cortázar' (see below). However, a sense of intellectual inferiority and intimidation could hardly explain why this kind of novel could not go on being written after the 1960s. The answer might seem at first sight to be internal to literary development, but the real motivation was political. It was in fact the Cuban Revolution, which had focused the New Novel, which also brought it to an end, in its trajectory between Castro's *Words to the Intellectuals* (1961) and the Padilla Affair a decade later (see chapter 3).

As we have seen, Latin American society was not in the 1920s in such an infrastructural or superstructural condition as to give rise to the kinds of European and North American fiction written in the 1920s and 1930s, although the relation of European to Latin American poetry was much closer. Nevertheless, the model for such a literature existed and every so often individual writers, especially and indeed almost exclusively those with experience of life in Europe, were able sporadically to emulate it, without these emulations being fully recognizable as a pattern until the early 1960s. It was not until then that the typical Latin American novelist was socially and culturally in a position to produce texts equivalent to those which had been written, and which he knew had been written, in Europe in the period 1910 to 1930. At the same time it is important to note that these works were usually far more socially oriented than the works of European Modernism, and that this tradition has continued through the 'boom' to the present.

There are certain other very broad parallels that can be added in to the comparative analysis. For example, one key contradiction in Europe in the 1920s was that which existed between the bourgeois liberal democratic systems of the advanced capitalist world and the Communist ideology made feasible as a historical threat or promise by the October Revolution. These movements seemed to many writers at first to be going in roughly the same direction but at different speeds and with different priorities, and between them they allowed for the extraordinary explosion of the avant-garde in the period after the First World War, as has been shown above. At the same time the spectre of the dictatorship of the proletariat produced a rapid tactical extension of the franchise, especially to women, in the more advanced and stable capitalist states, such as Britain, the United States and France, and the rise and triumph of fascism in Italy, Germany and Spain. Once this latter development was fully asserted, at the same time as the great recession began to bite and Soviet attitudes began to harden, choices came to seem less free and literature was forced to divide into two camps, to the artistic detriment of both.

Latin America in the 1960s temporarily allowed a similar degree of choice to be perceived, as noted above. The economic expansion of the 1950s and 1960s, combined with the threat and lure of the Cuban Revolution – at first hastily matched, just as in Europe in the 1920s, with a promised extension of bourgeois democracy, the Alliance for Progress, Frei and Belaúnde, etc. – created for bourgeois liberal writers, in a new cosmopolitan era of consumer capitalism, a perspective of change, progress and apparently infinite choice – a benevolent labyrinth – which dazzled them and produced the fertile contradictions so characteristic of Latin American novels of the 1960s. Asturias, the precursor of the 1960s, had been through all this before in the 1920s and 1930s, and Borges, precursor of the post-'boom' 1970s, had anticipated what was to happen next. Then, as the true intentions of Cuban socialism took shape out of the mists of ideology and propaganda (Castro's declaration that he was a Communist, the USSR connection, the guerrilla struggles on the mainland, the Cabrera Infante and Padilla affairs), conflicts began to emerge and the stream of protest letters from Latin American writers on the subject of intellectual conscience were merely the outward sign of the fact that writers were no longer 'free' to imagine and to create whatever they liked, because reality was closing in on them once again. And once again they were forced, as writers had been in the 1930s, to choose, like Fuentes's Artemio Cruz. Most of them moved in practice (that is, in their writing) to the right (they at any rate became rapidly 'decentred'), whilst deeply deploring, naturally, the emergence of neofascist regimes all over the continent after the Brazilian coup of 1964, as the military, backed by the United States, responded to the threat of guerrillas who themselves were responding to the existing repression and ever present threat of United States intervention, from Guatemala to Santo Domingo. Most novelists wrote increasingly 'deconstructed' texts whose real message was that they were not prepared to confront the powers and authorities they saw only too clearly around them, on behalf of the peasants and workers of the continent, since, in an age when populism could no longer even appear to provide solutions, their own interests as bourgeois intellectuals were on the other side. And this can be seen very clearly indeed if we examine the sales and distribution of their books, including translations, after 1960. The paradox was that it was the Cuban Revolution itself which had given Latin America 'sex appeal' in the capitalist West, even if the realities of Cuban socialism and its intentions rapidly clarified the real position of Latin American bourgeois intellectuals in a way that had never happened before, and certainly not in the wake of the Mexican Revolution of 1910–17. What had come to an end was not a 'myth of authority', as Roberto González Echevárría has claimed,[5] but a myth of multiclass writing.

Not long after the announcement of Asturias's Nobel Prize came the news of Guevara's death in Bolivia. Cuba responded quickly by battening down the hatches, and elsewhere ferocious repression swept a continent in which film was able to record much more immediately than literature the horror of all that was going on, particularly in Argentina, Chile and Bolivia. In the face of this situation, some writers spoke left and wrote right, sustaining the contradictions of their situation ever more acutely, well into the new era. That era itself, however, belongs to yet another 'New Novel' (á la française), none other than the post-'boom' novel, which I would prefer to call post- or late Modernist, with the works of Severo Sarduy, Guillermo Cabrera Infante, Néstor Sánchez, some of Cortázar and the Mexican new wave. In the transition between the representative works of the 'boom', studied in the last chapter, and the developments of the 1970s, lies the moment where Latin America (meaning of course its novel-writing bourgeoisie) 'caught up' with Europe and finally produced equivalent, if still specifically Latin American, narrative forms to those produced in Europe and the United States. The next section examines this process in more detail.

Re-Joyce: Universality Beckons

The publication of Cortázar's *Hopscotch* in 1963 was the precise moment at which 'Joycism' came to dominate Latin American fiction, confirming retrospectively a development which had been almost half a century in the making. Paradoxically enough, it was in Cuba, always open to the lure of the baroque – it was in Havana that the 1920s Góngora revival was most enthusiastically celebrated – and at the same time especially vulnerable to North American popular culture, that Joyce's specifically linguistic lessons seem to have been easiest to learn. The *Orígenes* group, organized around the large figure of José Lezama Lima and younger men like Cabrera Infante, had been experimenting long before the 1960s with language, parody, satire and other forms of humour. Thus Lezama Lima's *Paradiso* (1966) and Cabrera Infante's *Three Trapped Tigers* (*Tres tristes tigres*, 1967) were by no means surprising products of the Caribbean island, and both were specifically applauded by Cortázar himself.[6] Other important Cuban proponents of the new vogue were Severo Sarduy, later a member of the *Tel Quel* circle, and Reinaldo Arenas.

It must be said at this point, however, as the Cuban cultural commissars were soon to say from their own standpoint, that while the technical and philosophical focus of the new fiction appeared immeasurably widened, the social relevance of the New Latin American Novel was, with some notable exceptions, becoming inexorably narrower. The Joyce of *Dubliners* and *Ulysses* was, when all is said and done, a social novelist applying new techniques to traditional everyday materials and by that means revolutionizing the realist novel. Many of the younger Spanish American writers of the 1960s and 1970s were interested only in certain aspects of the Joycean 'package', or in the somewhat whimsical works published by Cortázar after 1963, such as *Around the Day in Eighty Worlds* (*Vuelta al día en ochenta mundos*, 1967), *62/A Model Kit* (*62/Modelo para armar*, 1968) and *Last Round* (*Ultimo round*, 1969). *A Manual for Manuel* (*Libro de Manuel*, 1973), which decisively marks Cortázar's turn to commitment, was far less influential. Typical of the new mood were the young Mexicans of the *Onda*, or 'new wave', for whom Joyce was the great experimentalist of the twentieth century, rather than its exemplary craftsman, some of whom tended to use him and Cortázar less as an influence or an inspiration than as a pretext for engaging in 'semi-automatic' experiments that in reality had more to do with Surrealism or psychedelia. A reluctant precursor of such young writers is Salvador Elizondo (1932–), author of the pathbreaking French-style '*Farabeuf*' (1965), similar in conception to Cortázar's 'Blow-up'. Elizondo has written a number of articles on and around both Joyce and Borges, in addition to his pioneering translation and commentary of the first page of *Finnegans Wake*.[7] *The Princess of the Iron Palace* (*La princesa del Palacio de Hierro*, 1974) by Gustavo Sainz (1940–) may be construed as one long homage to the Molly Bloom soliloquy, whilst in '*Obsessive Circular Days*' (*Obsesivos días círculares*, 1969 and 1978) the narrator is trying to read *Ulysses* itself throughout his narrative, failing ever actually to achieve this objective because life – in its most incoherent and absurd contemporary forms – keeps getting in the way. What such works implicitly question, in the age of pop and television advertising, is whether 'Literature' can have any meaning or function for us now: Joyce brought the novel to an end, perhaps, but this was only the sign of a wider cultural and social malaise – we would like to be his equals, but civilization itself appears to be saying that the gesture would be futile, although one Mexican, Del Paso, as we shall see, not only pursues Joyce's example but literally swallows him whole in the gargantuan '*Palinurus of Mexico*' (1977).

At this point one should mention again '*Between Marx and a Naked Woman*' (*Entre Marx y una mujer desnuda*), that extraordinary novel by the Ecuadorean Jorge Adoum (1923–), first published in Mexico in 1976, and without doubt one of the most interesting and self-aware of all the works to have appeared 'after Cortázar'. Not only does the title itself effectively caricature the concerns of the New Left of the 1960s and early 1970s, but the novel's perspective can be considered paradigmatic from another point of view. Its very first page considers the problem of what on earth to write about and how on earth to write it in a post-Joycean and, still more embarrassing, a post-Cortázarian world:

Un ladrimugidolugúbre que venía de la cala just to amuse yourself, while there's still time, imagining the delight of your well-read compatriots who, after that phrase, could save themselves the bother of reading the rest of the book and say, when called upon, if called upon: Yes, but it's influenced by Joyce, just as they avoided reading the rest of Joyce himself, though when faced with a narrative that respects order – chronological, logical or grammatical – in other words, order as such, it never occurs to them to say: Influenced by Zola or Gorky – which they weren't in their day – and you screw it into a ball that ends up in a corner, in the basket, in the fireplace and, as if the suffering really were now about to start, you put in another sheet and believing that that is the beginning, you begin.

Irá a venir Juanmanuel?

Smiling, thinking of the smartasses leaping on the book like buzzards on carrion: Just like *Hopscotch* it begins with a question, as if *Hopscotch* began anywhere, forgetting that the first piece of nonsense we ever read in school began precisely with: 'Tell me, my son, is there a God?'! So, 'Yes, father, there is', you make another ball, you take another sheet and again you are up against that blank page.[8]

A similarly amusing token of Joyce's influence appeared in Buenos Aires in 1980, with Isidoro Blaisten's short story, 'Dublin in the South' ('Dublín al Sur'), from the collection of that name, in which Joyce is said to be guilty of the same disorientating effect on his readers as Cervantes and Flaubert had shown novels of chivalry and romantic novels to be in *Don Quixote* and *Madame Bovary* respectively. The protagonist, Esteban ('Stephen'), wins a 'mastermind' competition by answering correctly a series of questions about the life and works of James Joyce. The prize is a large sum of money with which he travels to Ireland, abandoning his former life and family in order to buy a tower and devote his days and nights to revering Joyce's works. Sadly but predictably, there is no happy ending for this latterday Ulysses: once in Ireland he begins to feel the same nostalgia for the Buenos Aires he has lost as he used to feel for the Dublin he had never known. 'Sensuality', he concludes, 'is a product of absence.'

Not all works of the past fifteen years have been as self-aware as Adoum's novel and Blaisten's story (one that is, Ricardo Piglia's '*Artificial Respiration*', 1980, will be examined in chapter 10), but Joyce and Cortázar can hardly be held responsible for all that has been done in their names. Joyce's intimate and profound love–hate relationship with Ireland, his knowledge of its many traditions, and his scholarly acquaintance with the English and continental heritages, are not always duplicated with regard to their own cultures by all his followers and imitators. Some young writers construct instant novels from transient snippets of pop culture, ad language, facile playboy eroticism and a laid-back, in-crowd style which is not always as lovable as they appear to imagine. Such works are frequently advertised as 'Joycean', although it is doubtful whether the master would have recognized his disciples, and their most striking feature is often an almost absolute lack of historical awareness. Again, a notable exception to the rule, as we shall see, is Manuel Puig, who has consistently attempted to set fantasy and linguistic experimentation within their material social coordinates, beginning with *Betrayed by Rita Hayworth* in 1968. (The 'ninth instalment' of *Heartbreak Tango*, 1969, is clearly based on the 'Ithaca' section of *Ulysses*.) This, indeed, was the view taken by a number of traditionalist writers and critics – whether of the nationalist–Americanist or Cuban–Communist variety – about the 'new' Latin American novel as a whole. While such views tend to oversimplification, they are important and must be taken into account. The history of Cuban objections to 'Modernist excesses' does not diverge very far from prior developments in the Soviet Union in the 1920s and 1930s, although censorship and repression have never been so severe under Castro's regime.[9] To illustrate their wider reverberations, one might examine the remarks of a veteran critic, Manuel Pedro González, typical of nationalist or regionalist objectors from all over Latin America, and those of José María Arguedas, a great novelist in the traditional indigenist mould. Such voices expressed a reluctance to accept the demise of the rather elemental realist–Naturalist fiction of the 1920s and 1930s in Spanish American and Brazilian literature, arguing that the logical next step was a classical realist moment on the lines of Balzac, Dickens, Zola, Galdós or Tolstoy. In the event, only Mario Vargas Llosa among the major postwar novelists even approximated to such developments, and turned away from them to some extent in the 1970s.

Manuel Pedro González had already waged a long campaign against the New Latin American Novel of the post-1945 era, asserting that nothing published after the war could match the social novels of the period 1885–1945 in terms of Americanist originality. While few would agree with this statement, more would sympathize with some of his other allegations. At any rate, the massive consolidation of Modernist trends after 1960 was clearly too much for González, who launched a series of brutal attacks on the New Novel and, both overtly and by implication, on its arch-inspirer, James Joyce.[10] Between 1962 and 1969 a torrent of abuse – one of the few expressions at the international level of a reaction deeply felt in every provincial town and mind in Latin America – streamed from González's poisoned pen in a vain attempt to hold back the tide of glamorous Hollywood-style publicity and adulation surrounding the new jetsetting novelists. Much of what he said merely re-echoed arguments of the 1920s, though again it is as well to remind ourselves that Joyce really does 'live' in the sense that he can still come as a shock to those who read him for the first time. (One might argue that the Salman Rushdie affair of 1989 was the result of a 'Ulyssean' novelist coming into conflict with a deeply traditional culture.) González himself was a grudging admirer of Joyce's encyclopaedic knowledge and literary skill, although he insisted, rather like Lukács before him, that Joyce's work was profoundly – and, more important, inherently – pessimistic and in the last analysis decadent: not at all the kind of reading suitable for young writers from a young continent.

Cortázar, in consequence, is presented as a mere poseur, who simply imitates the externals of Joyce's work; Vargas Llosa is accused of 'Cantinflism', Carlos Fuentes of 'Babelism'.[11] They are leaders of a narcissistic Sinatra-style literary mafia involved in a secret conspiracy whose external signs are mutual flattery and self-congratulation, and whose deeper meaning is the degeneration of Latin American society. Joyce produces mental sickness ('Ulyssomania'): 'Today, forty years after the appearance of *Ulysses*, the infection is as virulent as it was in the 1920s.'[12] Joyce is 'dangerous', 'damaging'; his influence on the young and impressionable, through the carriers of the epidemic known as the 'boom', has produced a body of literature which is merely a grotesque reflection of the moral decay of contemporary capitalism, rather than, as is sometimes claimed, a critique of it. As for the material results: 'Among others one might mention its byzantine forms and themes, baroque ornamentation, technical snobbery, desperate search for originality, cultivation of the extravagant or bizarre, preference for novelty, no matter how grotesque or uncouth, and above all, its perverse abuse of pornography and of the vocabulary of the tavern or the mortuary. These are all symptoms of decadence and sterility, and they are everywhere to be seen in our current fiction.'[13] The unrepentant 'young gentlemen' are further accused of 'puerility', 'tantrums', 'shameless pastiches', 'barefaced technical mimeticism', 'the most cynical plagiarism and theft' and, last but not least, 'intellectual lackeyism'. It is much the same language that was soon to be used in Cuba (as well as by Miguel Angel Asturias about García Márquez, who almost never acknowledged any Latin American precursors), which would reach its climax in Castro's famous attack on anti-Cuban writers and intellectuals resident in Europe at the height of the Padilla storm in 1971 (see chapter 3). It was a battle lost in advance.

The reaction is understandable in the Latin American context, where the oscillation between some original America and some monolithic Europe has swung throughout its independent history. The conflict is a real one, and such responses are not merely atavistic. Those who call all that preceded them 'preliterature' must expect some response, and of course, to add to the confusion, the single most important novel of the 'boom', *One Hundred Years of Solitude*, was – in appearance at least – an exception to the general trend, a traditional work of almost Cervantine limpidity. González's onslaught from the pages of the Venezuelan review *Zona Franca* was taken up in *Mundo Nuevo*, the Paris-based, CIA-financed magazine edited by Emir Rodríguez Monegal, the most important of all the vehicles for the 'boom' during its brief but influential run (1966–71). The first in a series of articles in 1968 and 1969, by Ignacio Iglesias, a member of the *Mundo Nuevo* staff, rather surprisingly supported González (Iglesias, a Spaniard, perhaps sharing peninsular ambiguity towards those who are supposed to be objects, not agents, of 'discovery'), identifying the Molly Bloom soliloquy as the original sin which had corrupted young Latin American novelists. *Ulysses*, he remarked, 'appears to be the basic textbook for not a few young Latin American novelists.'[14] Cortázar was inevitably seen as the main perverter of these adolescent writers, and Iglesias gave examples from his work and sometimes hilarious imitations of him by debutant novelists of the moment. Turning then to Carlos Fuentes and berating him, like González, for his 'linguistic Babelism' in *A Change of Skin* (*Cambio de piel*, 1967), Iglesias concluded: 'While not everyone is able to read this kind of novel, almost anyone is capable of writing them.'[15] In a subsequent number, Guillermo de Torre, the veteran Spanish critic, with all the authority of his massive lifelong study of avant-garde literatures, supported this deprecating view and alleged that few of these young men could have read *Ulysses* in the original and no doubt con-fined themselves 'to the French version or the very approximate Spanish one'. As for *Finnegans Wake*, it was certainly beyond them – far too diffi-cult! He concluded: 'To repeat inarticulate phrases, pseudo-infantile babblings, supposed expressions of the unconscious and other such devices, adds nothing of substance, at this moment in time, to the form or content of the novel.'[16]

The counterattack was taken up in the same issue by the Mexican Moisés Ladrón de Guevara, who quoted Adorno to the effect that old forms cannot express new contents;[17] and by the Argentinian Antonio Pagés Larraya, who gave a classic defence of the New Novel, quoting Borges – who else? – to the effect that there is nothing shameful or 'dependent' about influences. Pagés Larraya viewed the baroque as an integral part of Latin American aesthetic culture down to and including Lezama Lima and Cabrera Infante; mentioned the effect of Surrealism, first on Asturias, Borges and Carpentier, and then down to the present; and willingly acknowledged the Joycean roots of the New Novel and the role of Cortázar in making it accessible to Hispanic culture and language:

> Since its first discovery, the influence of *Ulysses* – a fertile and creative one, in my opinion – has continued to grow. The use of Joyce's methods... is sometimes total (Marechal's '*Adam Buenosaires*'), sometimes diffuse (*Hopscotch*), and sometimes partial, as in the case of Mallea and Onetti.... Latin American novelists are in no way diminished by the fact that Joyce has given them, as he has given so many novelists the world over, a means of resolving their own dilemmas.[18]

It was indeed the means, the form – that of the literary labyrinth – which allowed them to visualize and dramatize at last Latin America's historic quest for cultural identity.

In retrospect, perhaps the most surprising feature of the polemic is that the extent of Joyce's influence was taken for granted by both sides: they disa-greed only as to its benevolent or malevolent qualities. There is no reconciling such different positions. Just how complex and bitter the conflict can be, in the Latin American situation, was demonstrated by the debate that same year, 1969, between two emblematic figures, Julio Cortázar himself and José María Arguedas, perhaps the greatest nativist novelist this century, and the last, apparently, of the great regionalist writers of Spanish America. Cortázar was in self-imposed exile from Latin America, working in Paris as a translator for international organizations, whereas Arguedas, as we have seen, was a Quechua-speaking novelist, brought up among and for a time by the Indians of the Peruvian sierras. He never resolved his own traumas and inner conflicts, which were those of Peru as a whole, but in 1964 had produced his own supreme achievement, '*Everyone's Blood*', at the very moment when such writing appeared to have been definitively superseded by the new novel. Cortázar's reply to Arguedas's comments published in the Lima magazine *Amaru*, appeared in a deservedly famous interview with Rita Guibert in *Life en Español*.[19]

Arguedas reprinted his views in the 'First Diary', corresponding to May 1968, of his posthumously published novel, '*The Fox Above and the Fox Below*' (1971) – generally considered, ironically enough, Arguedas's first effort at self-referential fiction. Arguedas, genuinely shocked by Cortázar's self-conscious sophistication and pretensions to professionalism, exclaims: 'Writing novels and poems is not a profession.'[20] Arguedas presents himself as indigenist, provincial, Peruvian and American, deriding Cortázar's 'brilliance, his solemn conviction that one can understand the essence of one's own nation from the exalted spheres of some supranational perspective.'[21] As his episodic diatribe developed, Arguedas linked Joyce, Cortázar and Lezama Lima together as purveyors of an exclusivist literature born of the corrupt cities (Cortázar is 'consumed, exhausted by the stench and pollution of city streets'; Lezama Lima is 'densely and unscrupulously urban'), and declared himself proud to be among those excluded, 'marginalized' by the new literature:

> That is what we are like, we provincial writers, people who, once bitten by the literary bug, manage to understand Shakespeare, Rimbaud, Poe, Quevedo, but not *Ulysses....* Yet we are all provincials, Don Julio, provincials within our own nations and provincials within the supranational world, which is itself only another closed circuit.... All I have read of Cortázar's are his stories. I was frightened off by the instructions he gave at the front for reading *Hopscotch*; so I was deservedly excluded, for the time being, from entering that palace.[22]

Cortázar's reply to Arguedas's comments when they first appeared, was typically dazzling, and he makes some telling points; but to accuse a writer from Arguedas's background of a bad case of inferiority complex is not one of his better ones. It has to be said also that Cortázar, like other defenders of the New Novel, offered no strategy for reconciling the demands of the regional and the national, still less of the regional and the supranational;

while the concept of class is not mentioned once in twenty pages of discourse. Arguedas for his part committed suicide in November of the same year, whilst Cortázar, ironically, maintained his support for the Cuban Revolution (sorely tested but decisively reasserted in May 1971), wrote *A Manual for Manuel* in the early 1970s and became one of the most active and effective campaigners for the Allende regime in Chile after 1970 and the Nicaraguan Revolution after 1979.

Once again, then, the bifurcation which existed in the 1920s, when Joyce made his first impact, between the social novels of Rivera, Gallegos and Icaza, and the avant-garde currents of the time, centred on poetry, appeared to have come to an end, this time with the devouring of the regional by the cosmopolitan. In view of Latin American realities since the Second World War, this would not perhaps have been inappropriate, but it was not the end of the story. For once again history and politics were to take an unexpectedly direct hand in developments. As we have seen, Arguedas, who had previously declared, in a famous statement, that he was not 'acculturated', finally accepted that, like the Indians themselves, he was, in effect 'marginalized'. After his death, the other great representative of the regionalist current still alive at the time was Roa Bastos, with whom he had so much else in common. Whilst Arguedas had stayed in Peru on the margins, Roa, an exile, similarly branded himself a traitor and a fugitive, and resolved to assume the consequences of his Paraguayan condition. At the same time, however, he saw the inevitability of taking up the challenge of the new whilst resisting its temptations, and the result was *I the Supreme* (1974), as fearsomely complex, self-referential and metatextual as anyone could require, but reaffirming the previous collective tradition in new ways in the face of a much more complex world. In transforming his fictional method, he was able to become one of the most remarkable innovators in Latin American literary history, pointing the way to a literature which is not merely 'decentred' or 'deconstructionist', but truly self-critical and perhaps 'dialectical'. This really is another story; but one suspects that even that story would have been inconceivable without the lessons learned, both inside and outside Latin America, from James Joyce.

Big Books and Grand Failures

Carlos Fuentes's *Terra Nostra*, published in 1975, is the biggest Latin American novel of all, as we shall see. It had been preceded by a number of others which were similar to it. One might say they were Ulyssean novels but only at the level of space and myth, not time and history. Perhaps it would be more appropriate to call them Dantean novels, in the sense that their architecture and reference systems are essentially those of Western civilization itself.

Thus despite the fact that most of them respond to Carpentier's call for works which describe the face of Latin America's cities, most of them are, like the works of Borges, implicit declarations of universality, works which might have been written anywhere, without the loving realist detail or carefully framed historical information which would have given them some more lasting concrete materiality. These Dantean works essentially celebrate being alive in the midst of modernity, in cities which merely happen to be Latin American ones: if they seem to us to be inevitably imprinted with Latin Americanness – as in the case of Borges – this is something that is outside the will of the author. They are not works of national construction.

The Ulyssean novels, by contrast, are written at the intersection of the city (if only as refracted in the consciousness of the author) and the country, individual and mass, modern and traditional, history and myth. They are bicultural: their point of departure is dialectical, Indian and Spaniard (myth and history), female and male (Freud), country and city (Marx), nature and culture (Rousseau, Lévi-Strauss), barbarism and civilization (Engels, Sarmiento), a pattern of light, reason and history emerging from darkness, matter and myth which is the process of Western culture and which culminates in Modernism until the moment of Joyce, who begins the process of reversing the signs, preparing the way for post-Modernism. The New Latin American Novel of the 1920s to the 1960s was a Modernist creation, though some of its best known creators were 'always already' post-Modernist (Cortázar) and most of the others – Fuentes is the paradigm – turned in that direction. (García Márquez, the greatest of all, like the equally lucid Cervantes, had no need to veer off into the post-Modernist darkness of the baroque.)

The Ulyssean novels of Latin American Modernism used myth juxtaposed with, but invariably framed by, history. This meant that the personal psychic biography superimposed over national myth is also constrained by social and economic history and not only by psychic myth. It also meant that those great works incorporated both the rural-based focus of the 1920s and 1930s and the urban-based focus of the 1940s and 1950s together in one construct, as if one were to say Dos Passos/Faulkner plus Joyce, something which, incidentally, European literature itself never managed to achieve. What made this possible was a completion of the trajectory undertaken between the nineteenth century, the 1920s and the 1960s, namely a national, subnational (regional) and continental focus at one and the same time, with the latter predominating and fixing the whole.

Male members of a large family

The first, and in some ways the most impressive, of these wayward block-busters, was '*Adam Buenosaires*' (*Adán Buenosayres*, 1948) by the Argentine Leopoldo Marechal (1900–70), which appeared in the Argentine capital not long before Asturias's *Men of Maize*. This monstrous construction of almost eight hundred pages is set, significantly enough, in the 1920s, and is specifically addressed to readers in the Argentine capital itself. It is undoubtedly one of the great neglected works of Latin American Modernism, partly due to its Catholic framework and partly due to Marechal's enthusiastic support for Peronism at a time when most other artists and intellectuals – such as his close associate of the 1920s, Borges – were in opposition. This is the most obviously Dantesque of all these novels, since the Inferno itself appears to be situated not far below the streets of Buenos Aires. It was the first Latin American novel to attempt a close approximation to what Joyce had done for Dublin – not to mention fiction and the world – in *Ulysses*. Such a project, however, did not emerge naturally from Latin America's historical experience – not even that of Buenos Aires – and one should not forget that *Ulysses* is actually the tale of many cities, not just Dublin.

Nevertheless, Marechal's extraordinary and exasperating novel contains many of the formal and structural devices with which we have been concerned. Buenos Aires and human life are both conceived as intricate labyrinths, with paths branching in all directions, decisive crossroads, and excavations necessary at every turn. There are doubles, mirrors and masks, life and death hang on words, and parody rules. (The enigmatic last line reads: 'Solemn as an Englishman's fart.') There is little in the post-'boom' that is not here lying dormant – which brings us to the novel's first mention of its hero, Adam:

Adam Buenosaires awoke as if returning: Irma's song, fishing him out of the depths of sleep, hoisted him for an instant through torn scenes and vanishing phantoms; but the musical thread snapped, and Adam descended once more into the depths, given over to the dissolution of delicious death.... Adam, with his back turned on the new day, deserting the violent city, fleeing the light, forgot himself as he slept and forgetting himself cured his woes; because our personage is fatally wounded, and his agony is the fine thread which will weave the episodes of my novel. Unfortunately Mount Egmont Street was oblivious to all; and Irma, whose singing would have awoken Ulysses himself, piped up with the second verse. [23]

Any reader interested in *On Heroes and Tombs* or *Hopscotch* would find Marechal's novel an illuminating antecedent.

The Brazilian Erico Veríssimo (1905–75) also set out to produce grand novels on the scale, and with some of the characteristics, of Tolstoy, Joyce and Proust, though legibility was always a primordial objective of his work. Nevertheless he was also concerned with self-referentiality, the role of the writer and the function of fiction. His best known works are *The Rest is Silence* (*O resto é silencio*, 1942) and his largest project, the three-volume *Time and the Wind* (*O tempo e o vento*, 1949, 1951, 1962), a historical epic about the people of his home state of Rio Grande do Sul. Even here however the city predominates, both in subject matter and in structural presentation, and Veríssimo has little interest in the world which lies outside. Nevertheless his experiments with simultaneity and multiplicity on the lines of Dos Passos, Huxley and Woolf – so well suited to Latin America's pluralist realities – predate those of Fuentes and Vargas Llosa by many years and make him an important innovator.

At the height of the 'boom', in 1966, the Cuban José Lezama Lima (1910– 76), an important member of the *Orígenes* generation, which had been so influenced by the Góngora revivals of the 1920s, produced a stunning novel with the Dantean title of *Paradiso*, mixing both classical and Catholican imagery, lovingly but also scandalously, achieving the remarkable double coup of offending both the Catholic Church and the Cuban Revolution through its approach to eroticism in general and homosexuality in particular. Lezama had been writing the work since 1949, just as Marechal had been composing his novel since the 1920s (indeed, both are set mainly in that decisive decade). Where Dante's patriarchal vision implies that the woman can never be found on earth, and will always cause torment, Lezama's very title opts for fulfilment, and it may be that sexual inversion and its consequent democratization of gender relations is here proposed as one key to future social transformation, as it was in a way for Goyo Yic in Asturias's *Men of Maize*, and for many of the characters of *Mulata*, not to mention the conclusion of Fuentes's *Terra Nostra*. For a Cuba undergoing the seemingly unavoidable puritanical backlash consequent on revolutionary consolidation, with its historically masculine gestures, Lezama's book appeared a somewhat provocative way of celebrating the city of Havana, whose traditions of sinfulness the authorities were keen to put behind them. It has now been thoroughly rehabilitated, however.[24]

Although the novel does give some space to events in the outside world, notably the student movement of the 1920s (in which Carpentier had been involved, as well as such legendary heroes as Julio Antonio Mella), Lezama's vision is closely focused on the concepts of language and literature themselves, with the protagonist, José Cemí, conceived as *puersenex* ('a man's old age begins the day his mother dies'), endlessly attempting to come to terms with the world through a poetic apprehension of reality. This does not make for easy reading:

It was thus in the intersection of that spatial ordering of the two points of analogy with the unknown temporal motive, that Licario situated what he called his Poetic Syllogistics. He based it upon one of Dante's syllogisms, which appears in his *De monarchia*, where the minor premise, 'All grammaticals run', succeeded in working back through the poetic logos on the rain of non-locatable motives, wandering points and dust-storms, disposed only to enmesh themselves on the two parallel points of an irreality gravitating around a conclusion. At other times, that third wandering point, embedded in its own identity, succeded in creating a reappeared evidence, usually distanced from the first nature of its reality.... Licario nourished himself, in his cogitated extensiveness, with those two currents: an ascension of the seed to the point of participation, which is knowledge for death, and then the poetic awakening of a cosmos which reverted from the act to the seed through the mysterious labyrinth of the cognizant image.[25]

Not all of *Paradiso* is this impenetrable, and the work appears somewhat less Latinized in Spanish, but its hermeticism, allusiveness and complexity have ensured that it will never be read by more than a few highly educated readers and scholars. Undoubtedly, however, this is a major work of the Latin American baroque imagination by a writer at once idiosyncratic yet representative. The initials of the unmistakably autobiographical protagonist José Cemí give the clue to the novel's conception of the child as holy infant constituted through sensuality and language within the trinity completed by his mother and father. Lezama's arrested development – his family history was surprisingly similar to that of Borges, though he almost never left his native island – explains a work which is the product of great intensity and introspectiveness but little extension in comparison with the novels studied in this book. A work of genius, but one which, like its author, does not travel far.

In some ways there is a similar story to tell of Guillermo Cabrera Infante (1929–), by general consent, with his *Three Trapped Tigers* (*Tres tristes tigres*; first version 1964, definitive version 1967), author of the first Latin American comic classic. The novel was set in the prerevolutionary era, with a similar theme to that of Desnoes's *Memories of Underdevelopment*, but when it transpired that Cabrera, like his characters, preferred unrepentantly to go on being a 'sad tiger' even after the Revolution, the authorities rapidly lost patience with this born iconoclast and in due course he went into exile. This was a pity, though perhaps an inevitable one, since Cabrera was one of the most talented writers of the new wave. His linguistic exuberance makes comparison with Lezama (as well as Carpentier and Sarduy) inevitable, but there is one major difference: where Lezama's work relies heavily on a Greek and Roman Catholic philosophical background, Cabrera Infante turns to popular – indeed, pop – culture, and was the first to introduce the mass media into his fiction as a solid proposition and without parody or apology. On the contrary, it was educated or official culture which seemed to him to be risible. In view

of the subsequent development of consumer capitalism and its associated pop
subcultures, this now seems more than questionable, and it is difficult not to
feel that the road taken subsequently by Manuel Puig was the more productive. Cabrera began with an unmistakable left-wing critical edge, but his
subsequent works lost this completely, and sometimes seemed to celebrate
banality and alienation. His difficulties with the Castro government separated
him for a time from the literary mainstream, distorted his literary development and left him arrested, so to speak, as a sometimes hysterical – despite
the insouciance and iconoclasm – harker back to the good old days of a notoriously corrupt past.

Nevertheless *Three Trapped Tigers*, with its hilarious vision of three
hangers on and hangers around in prerevolutionary Havana is undoubtedly a
tragicomic classic. (The presentation of male friendship is a recurrent theme
in Cuban fiction: Villaverde's *Cecilia Valdés*, 1882, is based on a three-man
friendship as is Lezama's *Paradiso*). Moreover, his most ambitious work, *La
Habana para un infante difunto* (1979), appropriately translated as *Infante's
Inferno*, is also a major work by any standards, not least in length, and an
important biographical document, though not of course one to be 'trusted'. It
is in effect an almost interminable sexual odyssey, with Cabrera, writing
from London, recalling his early erotic experiences as an adolescent and as a
young man in the tropical fleshpots of old Havana. Eventually, and unsurprisingly, the labyrinth turns out to be not Havana nor even his own feverish
mind, but that object of desire, site of fantasy itself, the female interior,
entered in the cinematic darkness:

> Was it a hallucination? No one answered my question and I discovered that I was
> alone in a woman's world. Or almost alone: I had my flashlight for company.
> When one is alone even a flashlight is a soulmate. Unless, perish the thought, I was
> in some solitary confinement. Search, search! *Felix qui potuit.*
>
> I turned thus the corner – to find another fork. *Rerum cognoscere.* I was in a
> labyrinth. For the snark was a *bollo*, you see. There was no doubt about that.
> *Causas.* Following a rule of thumb I established at that very moment, I rejected,
> also without doubt, the wide peasant path for the straight and narrow footpath.
> After walking a few steps along this way I found myself in a cul-de-sac. (Also
> called blind alley or dead end in pictures.) Was I lost? Impossible! He who has
> found himself is never lost. The exit, and ensuing success, was right there on the
> right. On the right? Was the exit to the real of the movie on the right or on the left?
> I was going to pull out a coin to use it as a compass and decide my reckoning on
> heads or tails, a Raft toss-up, when the earth and the walls trembled again and the
> whole cavern, measureless to man, shook in spasms.[26]

Unfortunately for Cabrera, who has translated Joyce's *Portrait of the Artist*
and possibly sees himself as the Irishman's only true heir in Latin America,

there is no fun without pun and, as this section shows, his obsession with word play and sexual inuendo can become wearisome in the end, if not in the beginning. Here at any rate is the conclusion of the section quoted, and, indeed, the end of the novel:

> Silly as it might sound, after the boom I felt proud, my pride coming from the fact that never for a moment had I let go of my torch, which was the light. But precisely at this moment as I was falling I realized to my chagrin that I had lost the book. Me, myself, and I, flying limbs and all, began then to spin in a wild whirlpool with no center, a mauve maelstrom, the chaos as before. Stop! Then there was light, a streak lightning or street lightning, the freak bolt followed by something like a crash in a crack, a fall into the fault, a death rattle in the spelunca and when I was about to wake up screaming – I fell freely into a horizontal abbess, *abyss*!
> Here's where I came in.[27]

The emphasis on the cinema, as both subversive and colonizing, stimulator of eroticism and inducer to consumerism, dates from Asturias's *The President* and is prolonged today in Puig's brilliant critiques. In Cabrera, however, as in Vargas Llosa's *Aunt Julia and the Script-Writer* (1978), the cinema and pop culture generally are celebrated rather than criticized and it is for this reason that Cabrera's later work lacks historical relevance.

We follow two Cuban writers with two Mexicans. The first, Fernando del Paso (1935–),[28] is a writer who has tried harder than most to reconcile avant-garde literature with political writing, most notably in *José Trigo* (1966), which is partly organized around the crucial railwaymen's strike in the late 1950s. Like Cabrera Infante, Vargas Llosa and Fuentes, Del Paso has spent much time in London since the 1960s, including a long spell with the BBC World Service. In 1977 he produced a huge novel, inspired directly by James Joyce's *Ulysses* and Rabelais' *Gargantua and Pantagruel*, as well as chival-resque and picaresque fiction, entitled *Palinurus of Mexico* (*Palinuro de México*). The echo of '*Adam Buenosaires*' is obvious in the title, as well as the fact that Palinurus, like Adam, is dead before the work starts. (Indeed, the last chapter of *Paradiso* relates the death of Cemí's alter ego, Oppiano Licario, and Cabrera's Spanish title, 'Havana for a Dead Infante' – a pun, naturally – suggests a similar conception of the meaning of these colossal lit-erary self-projections.) Ironically enough, the weakness of Del Paso's work is the opposite of Lezama's, namely that the linguistic texture itself is perhaps insufficiently demanding to stretch the reader's consciousness to the dimen-sions required by Del Paso's Ulyssean perspective. Thus although Del Paso is an entertaining and knowledgeable writer, and although the novel's fiction-ality fuses with Mexico's recent reality when Palinurus dies at the Tlatelolco massacre ('*Acta est Fabula*: The Comedy is Over'), the narrative ultimately fails to achieve historical transcendence and is more of a Joycean improvization than a successful Ulyssean novel. Del Paso's latest work is another monster production, '*News of the Empire*' (*Noticias del imperio*, 1987), about the episode involving the imposition of Emperor Maximilian and Queen Carlota on Mexico in the nineteenth century.

Carlos Fuentes, *Terra Nostra*

The second Mexican writer is Carlos Fuentes, whose *The Death of Artemio Cruz* we examined in the last chapter. His *Terra Nostra* (1975) is the biggest of all Latin American novels thus far, in both length (almost nine hundred pages) and ambition. Its title makes plain an intention which, in retrospect, was that of Marechal, Lezama, Cabrera and Del Paso, namely to lay claim to a territory and its history through a literary reconstruction which identifies that temporal space with the life of its author. Fuentes's ambition is the greatest of all, since his work is not only not confined to a capital city, or even a capital and its country, but to the whole of Latin America and Spain, the whole Hispanic region over the whole of its history; indeed, it is more ambitious still because it also whimsically modifies that history and invents its own variants. This is Magical Realism with a vengeance: the vengeance of Latin American culture against its Spanish paternity, the culmination of almost a century of literary parricide.

Fuentes's energy, stamina and sheer enthusiasm over more than thirty years of writing, diplomacy, travelling, teaching and journalism are almost staggering, and would be inconceivable in the British environment of internally and externally imposed constraints. The same could be said of Mexico, and there is little doubt that his early upbringing as the son of a diplomat in the United States, in what he himself has called a culture of 'boundless optimism', was a most fortunate start in life. He has made himself a literary professional on the North American model, an Entertainer who does it His Way, an undoubted star. Always left of centre, but never too far – Mitterrand is the ticket – he writes frequently about pop culture but only rarely about the masses themselves. The coarseness and even vulgarity of some of his writing is crisscrossed with sudden insights of something close to genius, and there are paragraphs, pages and sometimes entire works (*Aura*, 1962) of a brilliance which few contemporary writers can surpass.

Yet there is also something rather sad about Carlos Fuentes. His writing is not universally admired (as the writings of, say, Vallejo, Borges, Rulfo and Paz are) in Latin America, and few critics believe that many of his works, taken alone, are of the very highest stature. Mexican culture has often reacted to him as an outsider, a man who does not really know the country or the way Mexicans think, speak and act, a man for whom Mexico is above all an idea (it was somehow characteristic of him that he experienced both the Prague and Paris springs of 1968 but not the Tlatelolco massacre in Mexico itself,

perhaps the most important single event in Mexican history since 1917).[29]
Mexicans consider Paz a greater essayist and Rulfo a greater novelist – even
though he wrote only one novel. Similarly, although Fuentes is always seen
as one of the four central writers of the Latin American 'boom', which has
now permanently integrated Latin American literature into the Western mainstream, not a single one of his works is accorded classic status. The
apparently inevitable conclusion, given his extraordinary talents, is that here
is a man who is ultimately a communicator rather than a great voice in his
own right, a diplomat rather than a politician, a man more concerned to speak
than to have something to say, and one who wants to be accepted and to have
no enemies. All of this was underlined in 1987 in a brutal polemic launched
by one of Mexico's younger intellectuals, Enrique Krauze, arguing that
Fuentes writes for the sake of it, narcissistically, with no rootedness in
Mexico and no apparent system of coherent and consistent beliefs.[30]

One is reminded of the Laurence Olivier phenomenon. Fuentes, perhaps
the most inherently talented writer of the past thirty years in Latin America,
is the 'karma chameleon' of its contemporary literature, to quote one of his
own pop references.[31] Profligate with his talents, he has no hesitation in imi-
tating and often surpassing his fellow writers, hijacking intellectual fashions,
shamelessly name-dropping or plunging into the world of popular culture
(*The Old Gringo*, 1986, was written with Jane Fonda in mind), in between
his periods as professor at the two Cambridges and his visits to Madrid,
Caracas and Paris to receive some of the most prestigious literary prizes his
cultural universe has to offer. *Where the Air is Clear* was an application of
Dos Passos to Mexico, expertly done. *The Death of Artemio Cruz* applied the
same approach to the Revolution itself, but now incorporated and buried the
literary modes of fellow Mexicans Azuela, Yáñez, Revueltas and Rulfo,
together with Paz's theories on the labyrinth of solitude. *A Change of Skin*
shows a clear influence from Cortázar, whilst *Holy Place* (*Zona sagrada*,
1967) betrays the impact of Structuralist thought on 'mythologies' so fashionable in the 1960s. *Terra Nostra* sets out to achieve for the whole Hispanic
world what Juan Goytisolo achieved for Spanish history and literature in his
'*Vindication of Count Don Julian*' (1970). '*Christopher Unborn*' (1987),
another novel for 1992, combines the vision of José Donoso's *Obscene Bird
of Night* with the pop humour typical of the Mexican younger generation,
especially Sainz and Agustín, since the 1960s. Anything they can do he can
do better.

Yet none of this can detract from Fuentes's extraordinary all-round
achievement. Krauze and others like him have failed to realize a simple fact
but one of extraordinary significance: that Fuentes is first and foremost a
Latin American writer, and only secondarily Mexico's most important novelist of modern times. One can see why this realization could be difficult to

swallow. For over thirty years he has been Mexico's leading novelist and one of the top four in Latin America, as well as playing a vital role as bridge between Mexican and North American culture. He has a wider range of contacts in the world of politics and letters than any other Latin American novelist, not excluding Mario Vargas Llosa. (Moreover, unlike Vargas Llosa, he has remained on the left of the liberal centre, has abstained from attacking a Cuban Revolution which he cannot wholeheartedly support, and has courageously defended the Nicaraguan Revolution against attack by the United States and Latin Americans such as Krauze himself.) More important even than this, however, it is arguable that he is the vertebral figure within the entire 'boom' of the Latin American novel, that he began it with *Where the Air is Clear* in 1958, the first truly professional urban-based novel, and ended it with *Terra Nostra* in 1975, a monumental attempt to review the whole psychological and political history of Spain and Spanish America. Its relative failure, as we shall see, marks the impossibility after the late 1960s, of continuing to write Ulyssean works based on coherent historical cycles, epiphanic insights and optimistic conclusions – now that Latin America, with the decline of the guerrillas, the rise of the dictators and the horizon of debt and drugs, has undergone an enforced reversion to historical type.

His pivotal status is outweighed, however, by something even less often acknowledged, namely his crucial integrative role in the propagation of the 'boom' over the past thirty years, although Fuentes himself is too shrewd and possibly even too generous to say so. His *Where the Air is Clear* was the first major novel as early as 1958; he it was who then set out to integrate Mexican literature into the mainstream, in a way that Paz could never have done (even had he deigned to); he, above all, who conspired and collaborated with Emir Rodríguez Monegal, the Uruguayan critic, to launch and sustain the extraordinary public relations and propaganda exercise which, twenty-five years later, shows no sign of abating before the great Spanish, Latin American and European jamboree of 1992. It was entirely appropriate that in the first number of the crucial magazine *Mundo Nuevo*, founded in Paris – partly as a counterweight to Cuba's even more important *Casa de las Américas* – the very first item was an interview of Fuentes by Rodríguez Monegal, in which Fuentes, with his customary generosity, praised other writers and above all pointed out, with remarkable acuity, that the two great precursors of the New Novel were Miguel Angel Asturias and Jorge Luis Borges. Moreover, he recognized the central importance of Alejo Carpentier in a general assessment of the development of Latin American fiction:

> I believe that our culture and our literature have passed through three more or less convulsive, more or less fluid phases in a way that has a universal projection.... These three chains – sometimes tangential circles – are utopia, epic and myth. America as a whole, the continent, was discovered and thought of as a utopia. It is

the world of Thomas More, but the world of Thomas More played out in practice. That proposed utopia is immediately negated, destroyed by the concrete necessities of history.... We have lived under the sign of the epic almost all our lives; our novels and our art have been epic, but at a moment where this epic capacity appears to be exhausted it seems that all that remains to us is a mythical possibility, the possibility of recuperating that past, of emerging from a past of history, an untamed past, and entering into the dialectic. To emerge from historiography, the writing of history, to enter the dialectic, which is the making of history with the myths provided by those Ariadne threads, that entire utopian and epic history, to turn it into something else. Through myth we reactivate the past, we reduce it to human proportions. That is the purpose of the dazzling novels by our great modern classic Alejo Carpentier.[32]

In 1969 it was Fuentes who wrote what many still consider the best short critical work on the new Spanish American novel;[33] he it was, more than anyone, who bridged the ideological and aesthetic distances between writers as different as Cortázar, García Márquez, Vargas Llosa and Borges, and who, with equal doses of generosity and self-interest, introduced the Spaniard Juan Goytisolo and the Chilean José Donoso into the magic circle;[34] and who in 1988 with his book of essays, *Myself with Others*, ceremonially completed the historic circle of Hispanic fiction from Cervantes to García Márquez, integrating the 'boom' writers – including himself – definitively into the orbital circuits of Western literature as a whole, whilst concentrating on his two favourite themes: the function of fiction and the problem of identity.

Nevertheless, if we look at *Terra Nostra* we can see the shortcomings in his approach to literary composition. Fuentes undoubtedly set out to write the Latin American novel to end all Latin American novels, a blockbusting total novel at the end of fiction, of the century, and, symbolically – given its apocalyptic overtones – of the world. (Again, the comparison with Marechal *et al.* is self-evident). The work rearranges half a millennium in the history of Spanish and Latin American history, beginning with the marriage of Philip II of Spain to Elizabeth Tudor of England, and speculates on what might have happened if... Although the objections to this falsification are obvious, they are also important. Roberto González Echevárría, who has condemned the Latin American New Novel as a whole for elaborating texts based on the quest for some illusory 'cultural knowledge' – obsessed with the power that they appear to be condemning and subverting – first excluded this novel from his critique and then decided that it was, after all, written from within that self-deluded tradition.[35] However, it seems obvious enough that the problem is not so much the search for cultural knowledge but the distortion of it, and it is the very elasticity of Fuentes's cultural perspective that gives rise to the problems. Spain's historical figures, from Philip and Cortés to Franco, intermingle with Spanish literary figures like Celestina, Don Quixote and Don

Juan, and Latin American ones (not to mention other literary and historical characters drafted in as required from the whole of Western culture).

If a critic like González Echevárría views the Ulyssean works already discussed as power-crazed, it is extraordinary to find him arguing that *Terra Nostra* is nonetheless on the way to the more 'radical' writing (as he sees it) exemplified by Sarduy. Could anything, at first sight, be more patriarchal than this novel, more of a *Cosa Nostra*, in which the whole of Latin American history and contemporary reality are seen as little more than a space with which Fuentes and his cronies are entitled to do as they literarily please. The novel is viewed not merely from 1992, like his more recent '*Christopher Unborn*', but from the last day of December 1999. However its point of departure, like that of '*Christopher Unborn*', is again 1492 and the Indian pre-existence is viewed as an impenetrable chaos which cannot even be turned into a labyrinth despite the attempt of the *conquistadores* to decipher it:

> I felt, Sire, as if I were going mad: the compass of my mind had lost its directional needle, my identities were spilling over and multiplying beyond all contact with minimal human reason, I was a prisoner of the most tenebrous magic, the magic represented in stone in this pantheon of all the gods and goddesses I could not conquer in this land, who with fearful grimaces mocked my oneness and imposed upon me their monstrous proliferation, destroying the arguments of unity I had meant to carry as an offering to this world, yes, and also the simple unity in which that unity was to be maintained: my own, the unity of my person. I looked upon the faces of the idols: they did not understand what I was saying.
>
> What proof did I have, except what I had carried from the coasts of Spain in the pocket of my doublet? Against the mirages of this land, against the fatal staff of the flayed god, against the limpid reflection in the head of the crane, against the very name of Smoking Mirror, against the incomprehensible images of the twenty days of my destiny, the destiny forgotten because it was still to be fulfilled, or perhaps the destiny fulfilled because it was already forgotten, I had opposed my own small mirror, the one Pedro and I used on the ship that brought us here when we performed the office of barber, the mirror I had shown to the distressed ancient of memories in the temple chamber: my mirror, and my scissors.[36]

Mirror and scissors involve imaging and cutting, imposing civilization upon barbarism, a key symbol in Fuentes's work, not unconnected to blindness. The subject matter and most of the concepts here are those already explored by Asturias (in '*Legends of Guatemala*', *Men of Maize*, *Mulata*, '*The Bad Thief*', 1969, and '*Three of Four Suns*'); whilst other concepts and the form of expression are unmistakably Borgesian. The vision as a whole is yet another version of our myth of Latin America.

So concerned is Fuentes to reproduce this myth entire and complete that in the last pages he actually lists the binary alternatives which he and every other New Novelist have been using since *Doña Bárbara* and '*Legends of Guatemala*' in 1929–30. Philip II is confronted retrospectively, like Artemio Cruz in 1962, with a series of alternatives which it is now too late to change, of which the following are a sample:[37]

Androgynous creator of a being invented in his image and likeness	Father creator of an incomplete man; where is woman?
The first being fecundates himself, multiplying himself like the earth, unstained	Man violates woman, and both offend Nature, which expels them from the sick garden
Harmony of the world of the sons prolongs the original harmony of the world of the fathers	Brother kills brother in order to possess a subjugated woman and an inhospitable earth
A diversity of peoples, tongues and beliefs is the result of a mixing of bloods that strengthens the unity of the human genre	The domination of vanquished woman and earth sets peoples against peoples: insufficiency is exalted as superiority, necessity as reason
The Spanish	I, the King
New world	Old world
Diversity	Unity
Life	Death

Apart from the surprising decision to incorporate Structuralist criticism into the body of his novel, Fuentes reveals here that his thinking is sometimes surprisingly coarse, that the need to conceptualize things in part from the Spanish perspective leads him astray and unbalances his schema, and, above all, that he lacks the third – dialectical – term, the one which originates from the New World, female and colonial standpoint. What he gives us instead is one patriarchal and one 'compromise' version. This is an instructive and revealing demonstration of the limitations of the liberal imagination, even when its exponent is a novelist of Fuentes's powers and the novel as vast and entertaining as *Terra Nostra*.

Exceptional post-script 1: *An Invincible Memory*

In Brazil the military coup of 1964 interrupted the normal development of narrative fiction before the 'boom' in Spanish America could really make its impact felt. Little overtly political writing has been possible until quite recently (the President at the time of writing, ironically enough, is himself a novelist), major exceptions being two valiant novels by Antônio Callado (1917–), linking country and city, *Quarup* (1967) and *Don Juan's Bar* (*Bar Don Juan*, 1971), and *The Emperor of the Amazon* (*Galvez, imperador do Acre*, 1976) by Márcio Souza (1946–), a satire which cost him his job in the civil service. Moreover since Mário de Andrade's formidable *Macunaíma*, no one has felt able to attempt a grand work uniting the whole of Brazilian history and culture in one vast novel. Now, however, João Ubaldo Ribeiro (1940–), whose *Sergeant Getulio* (*Sargento Getúlio*, 1971) was already widely admired, has written the most ambitious novel in the history of Brazilian narrative, with his *An Invincible Memory* (*Viva o povo brasileiro*, 1984), an English title which, although translated by the author, seems to me less satisfactory than a plain transcription, 'Long Live the Brazilian People'.

This novel of almost seven hundred pages covers the entire period from 1647 to the late 1970s, and although centred on the fertile Bahian coastal strip, it is clearly intended to embrace the whole vast surface of Brazil. The publishers announce the novel on its cover as 'the saga of a people in search of their self-affirmation', and indeed this is, more than any other Brazilian novel, the one which most determinedly confronts the theme of the quest for national identity through the exploration of a diverse but coherent collective unconscious. It begins with the Dutch occupation in the seventeenth century and returns us tongue in cheek to the 1920s anthropophagous theme with the opening lines of the narrative proper, in 1647: 'The Indian Capiroba enjoyed eating Dutchmen.' From this moment the narrative shows Brazil swallowing a series of different cultures and ideologies without ever arriving at any truly settled image of its own national identity. (Even so, some critics have argued that the work is essentially reductive, to the extent that it concentrates on the classic trinity of the 'three sad races' which make up Brazil's national bedrock and ignores more recent immigrants.) It is as if, unlike the Spanish American countries, Brazil's nineteenth-century empire delayed the beginning of this quest, which is only now reaching its culmination. Be that as it may, Ribeiro clearly feels that telling its story will reveal its central theme, as his epigraph suggests: 'The secret of the Truth is as follows: facts do not exist, only stories exist.'

Towards the end of the novel, in a flashback set in 1939, a retired general, one hundred years old, informs those gathered for his birthday that he has some stories to tell them. He would like to pass on the secret of life, but cannot, since it cannot be told: 'He wasn't happy, because he was a hundred years old and the Brazilian people still didn't know about themselves, knew nothing about themselves' (in Portuguese and Spanish, it should be noted, 'people' is in the singular).[38] And he goes on:

I can't die without guaranteeing... that the Brazilian people are not alone.... The Spirit of Man is universal and aspires to plenitude and grace, it has that aspiration as the common cause of its consciousness, which translates ultimately into the peace of existing without seeing existence, existing as essence, just existing, because the Spirit of Man longs for perfection, which is Goodness....

We have to be everything, but first we have to be ourselves, understand? What's your name? Everything, everything, everything. Psss. Long live the Brazilian people, long live us![39]

There is an inescapable reminder here of the conclusion of Carpentier's *Kingdom of this World*, in its theme of the quest and the struggle without end, the placing of existence before essence, life before theory. Moreover it also encapsulates other central themes such as solitude, the relation between the regional, the national and the universal, and the achievement of the future identity through the dialectical negation of current contradictions. Ironically enough, the listeners miss everything the old general says, and manage only to catch his dying words, 'Long live the Brazilian people'. The novel, not surprisingly, has been accused of flying very close to populism, but we should remember that in Portuguese and Spanish 'viva' literally means 'may it live' or 'let it live', so that the dominant sense of 'hurrah for!' is here juxtaposed with the primary significance: it is a prayer for survival. This becomes clearer as the novel ends with a storm blowing in from the ocean:

No one looked up and so no one saw, in the midst of the storm, the Spirit of Man, lost but full of hope, wandering above the unilluminated waters of the great bay.

The general laments the fact that he never managed to be a real Brazilian soldier, that is, a 'soldier of the people'. For all their apparent prepotency, Brazilian soldiers are slaves to the rich, because they are always subservient to them, and slaves to the poor, because they always fear their revenge. He predicts that the army will become even more estranged from the people than they are in 1939 and that there is much worse to come before things finally get better for Brazil. The novel attempts to emulate Brazil's own massive scale, and is written in an apocalyptic, sometimes overbearing tone, as if one were to imagine *One Hundred Years of Solitude* written by Jorge Amado. It is too soon to predict whether this work is a great Ulyssean achievement or a 'grand failure', but given the twenty-five-year military interruption one is inclined to think that it is a delayed version of the former. Certainly it is a torrid, passionate experience for the reader and a novel destined, one can be sure, to loom large in the history of Brazilian fiction.

Great Dictators and their Scribes

Carlos Fuentes's apparently manic gesture in writing *Terra Nostra*, which takes much of its force from Joyce, is not of course, as some have suggested, a lust for power but rather the artist's attempt to represent and perhaps even to shadow power and to grasp the whole of knowable reality, as Dante, Cervantes, Rabelais, Tolstoy, Proust and Joyce himself all did. The question that most concerns us here is why, between the 1940s and the 1970s, did this kind of novel, at once open, labyrinthine and total – Ulyssean – predominate in Latin America? And why did they come to an end?

Latin America is reputed the continent of dictators, but this is a travesty of its historical reality. Since the period of revolutions after 1810 it has been a region of liberal democratic constitutions on the European or North American models. It is precisely in the tension between aspiration and reality, viewed as both a national and continental problem, as well as an individual one, that much of the force of the theme is concentrated, from *Facundo* (1845) and *Amalia* (1851) through *The President* (1946) to the present.

There have been innumerable novels about individual dictators, or about the problems of dictatorship, *caudillismo*, *caciquismo*, militarism and the like. Few of them have managed successfully to unite the specific instance – Francia, Rosas, Estrada Cabrera, Gómez, Pinochet – with the more universal concerns of tyranny, power and evil. The first important works were inspired by Argentina's Rosas. *Facundo* examined the themes of civilization and barbarism, dictatorship and power, based on the case study of Facundo Quiroga and his relation to Rosas. Mármol's *Amalia* conceived the problem, as Asturias later did, partly as a problem of the State, manifested through the will of some Monstrous Personage violating the ordinary individual's privacy, both of home and of consciousness.

The 1920s saw a decisive transformation in Latin American historical awareness. In the period up to 1910, the Modernist–positivist generation, often writing from Europe, had developed a whole succession of historical theories about the continent's identity, through thinkers like Hostos, González Prada, Sierra, Rodó, Bunge, Arguedas, García Calderón and Ugarte, which had given some shape to Latin America's historical sense of itself, though largely without the benefit of up-to-date social-science thought. Similarly, literary critics like the Brazilian Sílvio Romero, the Argentinian Ricardo Rojas and the Dominican Pedro Henríquez Ureña, had begun to formalize the history of Latin American literature. But it was only in the 1920s, after Mexico, Moscow, Córdoba and – perhaps above all – the First World War, that sufficient autonomy of perspective appeared for writers and thinkers to see things clearly, within the perspective of modernity.

The nineteenth century had, in most places, been an era of disappointment, with dictatorial regimes predominating almost everywhere. In the twentieth century Central America and Cuba, Venezuela and Peru saw dramatic recurrences of the phenomenon – usually encouraged by the connivance of the United States – and thinkers began to see the continent in a comparativist light and to see dictatorship as a structural problem, rather than – as it had previously appeared – a biological or psychological one. In retrospect it is curious how pessimistic thinkers were, given the frequent European examples of tyrannies, thereby demonstrating of course the victory of ideology over science. In those days, when '*Maestros*' (indeed, 'Prosperos') were sought to offset the impact of corrupt '*doctores*' and brutal '*generales*', frequent references were also made to classical parallels (Rodó's *Ariel*, Asturias's use of Pericles in *The President*), as if to give some kind of solace through recalling the tyrants of ancient Athens and Rome. The most notable works of the era were Loveira's '*Generals and Doctors*', Guzmán's remarkable '*Shadow of the Caudillo*', and Gallegos's *Doña Bárbara*, inspired directly by Sarmiento's historic essay. On the whole, however, there was more enthusiasm for novels about the people, 'the underdogs', now apparently on the rise and on the march, than for lamenting the excesses of the tyrants, for this was an age of optimism, in which it was believed that the new democratic, liberal and socialist movements would soon consign authoritarianism to the past and that penetration by United States imperialism was by far the greater problem.

The major exception to this, once again, was Miguel Angel Asturias. Many of the other leading young writers were also from countries with dictatorships, and in Paris in the 1920s they all exchanged stories about them, just as in the late 1960s Fuentes and Vargas Llosa, from another generation far from home, suggested that a number of well-known novelists should try their hand at the theme.[40] Asturias had been perceptive enough to see the potential in the Maya ethnography he was studying and his original title for *The President* was 'Tohil', the name for the Maya–Quiche god of fire and war in the interpretations of the time. Asturias used the Maya myth in ways which would have been alien to him just a few years later, firstly by associating the Mayas to some extent with primitive savagery, and secondly by implying that in important respects the people 'asked for' the oppression to which they were subjected, not so much due to 'false consciousness' as to a deep desire for power and authority and a lack of courage at the individual level.

Asturias's novel should have appeared in the early 1930s and would thus have transformed our perception of the transition between the 1930s and the Magical Realist or 'new' novel. But the ironies – nay, the structures – of history saw him return in 1933 to a Guatemala in the hands of another great dictator (we use the term in the Chaplinesque sense), and the novel was not published until 1946, and not given continental circulation until 1948. It has therefore always appeared to be a postwar novel, and to form part of the new wave which in 1948–9 seemed to signal a completely new departure for Latin American literature. Even on that basis Angel Rama has acknowledged its importance as a literary precedent:

> In this line, as in so many others, one must concede the primacy of Miguel Angel Asturias. However controversial his perception of the Central American dictator may be for us today, there is no denying that the publication of *The President* (1946) is a point of departure that cannot be overlooked, for its attempt to deal with contemporary Latin American reality through a key figure who could enable us to understand the whole of society. In a conversation with Elena Poniatowska in *Exchange of Words*, Alejo Carpentier emphasized that the reason for the success of Asturias' novel was that he had dared to present a 'Latin American archetype'. In other words, he had produced a literature of recognition, not at the level of society's external manifestations but of its shaping forms, the unconscious energies which acquired form and expression through precise images, as in Jung's theory of archetypes.[41]

Asturias had also been the first to suggest, one might add, that in a theoretically liberal social order superimposed over an only incipiently liberal neocolonial economy, the dictator is the inevitable solution to many problems. He embodies within his own person the individualism which is announced by the official social philosophy but which must be denied to the overwhelming majority of citizens, uniting feudal paternalism and bourgeois individualism in one contradictory image. This was a perception which García Márquez would later develop still further in his narrative fiction.

Only a few years later, in 1952, a remarkable Colombian novelette, by Jorge Zalamea (1905–69), '*The Great Burundún-Burundá is Dead*' (*El gran Burundún-Burundá ha muerto*), was published in Buenos Aires. In it, indeed in its opening lines, the seeds of García Márquez's mature style, from *One Hundred Years of Solitude*, through – above all – *Big Mama's Funeral* (*Los funerales de la Mamá Grande*, 1962) to *The Autumn of the Patriarch* appear to be contained:

> No chronicle of the glory of his acts would be as convincing to future generations as the minute and factual description of the cortege which weighed his power in the hour of his death. For every step of that gloomy and grandiloquent procession was the fruit of his genius, symbol of his plans, echo of his celebrated flatulence.[42]

Asturias's novel had shown the inversion of values and corruption of language brought about by authoritarian regimes. In the '*Great Burundún-*

Burundá' we are informed that the dictator had effectively banned all com-
municable language. When his coffin lies in state a surprise awaits the
mourners:

> The Great Burundún-Burundá was not there – dead – inside the coffin! There,
> instead, irreverently, mysteriously, threateningly, lay a great big parrot, a
> voluminous parrot, an enormous parrot, all swollen, inflated and wrapped in
> documents, gazettes, mail from abroad, newspapers, reports, annals, broadsheets,
> almanacs, official bulletins.[43]

On the whole, however, neither the dictator novel, nor its more general
associate the novel of urban alienation, received much attention in the 1950s
and 1960s, because this again appeared to be a time of *'apertura'*, when the
people were on the move and the interior seemed to provide the answers to
the great themes of the continent and its future. Only Sarmiento, Gallegos
and Asturias have ever portrayed with clarity the relation between underdevelopment (internal colonialism) and capitalist development (external
imperialism) which makes of the dictator the 'necessary man'. At other times
writers have preferred to look elsewhere, if at all possible, or to treat dictatorship as an 'aberrant' and 'atavistic' phenomenon. In the 1950s and 1960s,
then, writers once again seemed to have the answers: the novels of the 1920s
had been about the land and the people of the future, whilst urban themes,
gathering pace in the 1930s, were about defeat and reverse; now in the 1950s
and 1960s, the future beckoned again, and again writers wished to settle
accounts with the past (as *The Vortex, Don Segundo Sombra* and *Doña
Bárbara* had sought to do), from the knowing standpoint of those who had
learned from the mistakes and the limitations of those previous writers. The
future in the 1960s was now in the cities, where the writers themselves were,
but they first had to tidy up the past, the country: this is what most of them
did between the mid-1940s and the mid-1960s, when the 'boom' writers
wrote their first and greatest works, which were either rural or urban–rural,
that is to say, bi- or transcultural in orientation. Naturally no Argentine writer
could easily contribute to this (their work had essentially gone urban ever
since Don Segundo Sombra's symbolic farewell, despite notable exceptions
like David Viñas's *'Men on Horseback'* and *'The Owners of the Land'*).
However, Cortázar's *Hopscotch* came up with one ingenious solution, in
which the whole of Argentina, focused on Buenos Aires, becomes 'the
country' and the whole of Europe, focused on Paris, becomes 'the city'.

The 'boom' itself was associated with the transition to liberal democracy
which had seemed to be evolving since the Second World War, with industrialization, import substitution and urbanization, and the growth of the middle
sectors. Then came revolution in a small Caribbean republic. It is no exagger-

ation to state that if the Southern continent was known for two things above all others in the 1960s, these were, first and foremost, the Cuban Revolution and its impact both on Latin America and the Third World generally, and second, the boom in Latin American fiction, whose rise and fall coincided with the rise and fall of liberal perceptions of Cuba between 1959 and the late 1960s, culminating abruptly in the events of 1971. But as we have seen, the 1960s, an age of optimism and energy in Latin America as elsewhere, can best be understood, both in politics and in literature, in comparison with the decade with which they are in any case most profitably compared, the 1920s. This is really the heart of this book's thesis, with its two timescales: 1810 to 1975 (from Sarmiento's *Facundo: Civilization and Barbarism* to Roa Bastos's *I the Supreme*), invoking the national question; and 1915 to 1975, with the rise of the Latin American novel (from *The Underdogs* to the end of the 'boom'), and the focusing of the inter-national question. The contemporary period since 1975 will be examined in chapter 10.

By the end of the 1960s, then, the literary party was over. Mario Vargas Llosa, whose *The Green House* had been more optimistic, 'despite everything', than might have been expected, produced in 1969, in *Conversation in the Cathedral*, a novel more pessimistic than anyone could have imagined, as if to signal the end of the celebratory cycle of the 'boom'. It was, as we have seen, an urban novel about 'Lima the horrible', a city the colour of excrement, and it was also about a dictatorship which had marked Vargas Llosa's own adolescence, that of Odría (1948–56). Vargas Llosa details its corrupting effect upon everything and everyone, including the smallest aspects of family and social life, as it sets about suppressing all hopes of popular political expression, especially the Apra party. Most remarkable, perhaps, was Vargas Llosa's grasp of the detailed mechanism of such mediocre but effective military regimes and the ruthless cynicism with which they pursue their objectives, including the degeneration of every natural urge and every tie of solidarity. The relation between the minister of information and security, Cayo Bermúdez, and the glamorous industrialist, Fermín Zavala, whom he both envies and loathes, is unforgettably portrayed.

The themes of Latin American society in the early 1970s, reflecting worldwide trends, were the growing gulf between left and right, with the gradual disappearance of the political centre, the struggle between guerrillas and military juntas (the Peruvian case being particularly contradictory), the contrast between the Cuban and Chilean roads to socialism, and the gradual reassertion of pessimism, disillusionment and despair, associated in the end with the defeat of socialism and popular governments almost everywhere in the continent until the – in a way anomalous – triumph of the Sandinista guerrillas in Nicaragua in 1979. Even this revolutionary process was contested and subverted every inch of the way by the United States, so that redemocratization of any meaningful kind was left until the mid 1980s and the socialist takeovers that had seemed inevitable were deferred, diverted or defeated. The everyday reality of repression and the worst forms of torture and disappearance, followed by the twin problems of debt and drugs, make this perhaps the most horrific period in all of Latin America's history.

Fiction rarely responds directly or immediately to such movements. Not even in Cuba have novelists been able to write successful histories of the postrevolutionary period, and this seems not primarily due to repression, whether overt or internalized, but rather to the problem of gaining distance. (The dictatorship beforehand has been extensively covered, of course, but it is well known that an adversary position is the easiest one for a novelist to take up, given the nature of the genre.) But respond Latin American fiction did. *Conversation in the Cathedral* is one symptom of the response, though possibly more of the lack of faith which brought the counterrevolution about in the first place. García Márquez made the ludicrous promise in 1975 that he would never write another novel whilst Pinochet remained in power in Chile, but was forced to renege on this oath. Pinochet remains in power at the time of writing.

In that year of 1974–5, however, three novels appeared which have remained inextricably linked together ever since in the history of Latin American fiction, each by an already distinguished author, and each on the theme of dictatorship: *I the Supreme* (*Yo el Supremo*, 1974) by Augusto Roa Bastos, *Reasons of State* (*El recurso del método*, 1975) by Alejo Carpentier, and *The Autumn of the Patriarch* (*El otoño del patriarca*, 1975) by García Márquez. The surprising thing about them is that none was situated in the present: two return to the early years of this century – implicitly they are about the period from 1810 to 1930 – whilst the other is set mainly in the early years of the last century. Certainly they are all major works of assimilation, like the novels of the 'boom' itself, but it is difficult to agree with those who say that the last two, *Reasons of State* and *The Autumn of the Patriarch*, inquire into 'the nature and ways of contemporary political power'.[44]

Although the three writers belonged to different literary generations, they were all supporters of the Cuban Revolution, and Carpentier indeed actually represented it as ambassador in Paris. This undoubtedly complicated the critical perception of the three anti-dictatorial novels. While the books by Carpentier and García Márquez appear to be revolutionary in orientation, judged by their subject matter, their extremely conservative approach to form – a relatively non-problematical presentation of both character and history – suggests contradictory underlying ideologies; whereas Roa Bastos, as we shall see, although apparently sceptical, pursues self-awareness and subjects the form of the novel to an interrogation in order to lay bare its normal ideological function within Western society in the last five hundred years (since *Don Quixote*), namely to teach people to distinguish between 'truth' and 'fiction'. Rather than self-referential, his posture is self-critical. Numerous readers who were also supporters of the Cuban Revolution, like Angel Rama or Mario Benedetti, seem to have been misled by their allegiance to that revolutionary process into interpreting the novels of Carpentier and García Márquez on the strength of their extra-literary postures, and to have neglected to consider whether those works are in fact 'revolutionary' in any convincing sense of the word.[45] It is an unfortunate fact, however, that novelists who support revolutionary movements can write novels which reveal that their unconscious ideology is profoundly contradictory and sometimes even reactionary. And this applies more to the novel than to any other literary form because the contradictions which give the novel its unique dynamism are, precisely, the contradictions of the bourgeois consciousness. The simple truth, which has been generally overlooked, is that both Carpentier and García Márquez aimed at easy targets – at the right from the left – whereas Roa Bastos made a critique of the left (for that is where Francia was) from within the left itself.

Reasons of State and *The Autumn of the Patriarch* are both highly entertaining works. They bring to mind Vargas Llosa's *Aunt Julia and the Scriptwriter*, published three years later (the work with which he 'joined the Latin American literary party', to quote the *New Republic*): that is, they are not entirely uncritical, by any means, but they are nowhere near as critical as they need to be and in that sense are ultimately self-indulgent and even complacent. Both also fell well below the standard of their writers' previous works, indicating a decline which appeared to be part of a generalized crisis among the New Novelists.[46] Perhaps the most immediately striking thing about them was that their dictators were not even historical figures, but composite and essentially imaginary ones (unlike Asturias's dictator, who was based on Estrada Cabrera but not named in order to generalize the message); that they belonged not to the present but to the distant past, which was in no way shown to be relevant to the present; and that they broke the tradition whereby the characterization of the dictator is oblique or in other ways problematical, without any obvious advantages accruing from such a risky venture. In short, they appeared to evade the challenges of the present (which continues to be one of the bleakest periods in Latin American history), shied away from the rigours of a genuinely historical interpretation, and eschewed attempting to resolve the essential structural problem confronting the Latin American novelist, which is that the novel is not so much a 'difficult' form in the tradition of Proust, Joyce and Faulkner, for whom the world was essentially incomprehensible and writing a form of compensation, as a 'problematical' form, precisely because the novel is a creation of the

European bourgeoisie and had developed in the light of its evolving consciousness. They accordingly ignore Lukács's recommendation that great men, even fictional ones, should be left offstage when historical interpretation is involved (as Vargas Llosa decided to do with Odría in *Conversation in the Cathedral*), and they enter the minds of their dictators at will. For most practical fictional purposes, total authorial omniscience has long been mistrusted, for obvious reasons; and in the particular case of a dictator, who is in any case – by definition – of all men the one whose consciousness is least available to others, that identification which characterizes the novel as a literary experience is surely entirely undesirable. Familiarity and certitude are in this case, to say the least, surprising and unwelcome.

Somewhat disconcertingly, then, given their subject matter, both writers appear to assume that they as authors will be taken as men of unfailing and undoubted 'good faith', in implicit contrast to their dictators (whereas Roa Bastos's doubt on this score – applied both to himself as author and to his narrators – was the very point of departure in *Son of Man*, as it is again in *I the Supreme*). It is almost as if there can be no doubt about the reaction of their readers to the very concept of dictatorship, as if dictators had no internal supporters. To be sure, both Carpentier and García Márquez, well aware that the whole history of Latin American culture may be conceived as a struggle between European forms and American contents, refer to the problem of doubt in their best-known narratives; but they choose – we are retrospectively brought to realize – to incorporate it as part of the content, not the form, of their works; the great exceptions being, as we have seen, *One Hundred Years of Solitude*, where, exactly like Carpentier in *The Lost Steps*, García Márquez uses his own certainty of tone (and apparent simplicity of form) ironically, as a form of subversion. But in these two later works neither writer seriously questions the problematic of writing as such, or of the novel as a genre, and they complacently lord it over their respective dictators, simple fellows in a simple world who appear to represent few interests other than their own and whose very ingenuousness leaves them at times looking almost lovable, and certainly pitiable. Angel Rama's assertion that García Márquez's Patriarch and Carpentier's First Magistrate demonstrate that Latin American fiction is at long last capable of producing genuine characters, is to say the least questionable: firstly, because the characters concerned are themselves non-problematical; and secondly, because there are no other major characters in either novel and there is no complexity of plot, everything springing as a matter of structural necessity from the actions and the point of view of the two despotic protagonists. They can in no sense be conceived as providing either explanations or implicit critiques of more recent repressive regimes in Latin America. Indeed, it is by no means easy to see that they have anything to do with the contemporary world of state terrorism, torture schools, mass disappearances on an almost Nazi scale and the technocratized juntas which have replaced those charismatic fathers of the people.

It is difficult, then, to resist the feeling that the authors' names themselves guaranteed the quality of the product, and that the admiration so widely felt for these two novels comes first from the ironic distance which, thanks to the temporal distance, they were able to establish, and, secondly, from the resulting ambiguity and maturity of vision – so unexpected in the black-and-white manichean world of the Latin American narrative – which they may be construed as exemplifying. But who cannot be mature about the past, especially if it is defined precisely as distant from and different from and to that extent irrelevant to the present? The liberal humanism of these works strikes me as having little to do with maturity (other than that false maturity, a form of collaborationism, which we noticed in Ciro Alegría), and much to do with an old-fashioned failure of commitment, not in the directly political sense, but in the sense of a failure to engage with the problem of Latin American reality and their own relation to it. Yet even Mario Benedetti, whose whole critical theme has been the need for literary commitment, suggested, in similar vein to Rama, that Carpentier's use of humour and satire to puncture the dignity of the dictator in *Reasons of State*, was a sign of the maturity of the present school of Latin American writing; and whilst conceding that *The Autumn of the Patriarch* is not a success, he attributes this to García Márquez's excessive use of hyperbole.[47]

However, it would be painful to accept that laughter is the most adequate response to the actions of Carpentier's murderous tyrant; and García Márquez's confusion seems more likely to have originated in a misconceived historical perspective. Indeed there are moments when the reader is tempted to think that the theme of the individualist dictator has attracted these two writers for reasons of nostalgia, a yearning for the days when, on the one hand, the enemy was a simple and straightforward *coronel* or *doctor* imbued with charisma and machismo, and not the anonymous, neo-fascist enemy of the 1970s; and when, on the other hand, novels were linear and chronological, and built around a central protagonist who was in some way or another a reflection or representation of his godlike author. In other words, while it is clearly not merely coincidental that these novels appeared when they did, corresponding obliquely to the phenomenon of military totalitarianism in Latin America since the late 1960s, it is probably significant that they both look back not, as in the case of *I the Supreme*, to the Independence period, but to the moment when the Latin American bourgeoisie became fully visible, that is to say, the moment when, but for the ironies of uneven development – the novelists were not yet ready – Latin American narrators would have been able to write the classic realist–psychological novel. This leaves the two writers reviewing the images of villains who are no longer enemies, characters who can be understood and perhaps forgiven, especially when compared – how could the reader resist it? – with the barbarians of today.[48]

This difficulty is particularly acute in the case of García Márquez's pathetic patriarch, whose lust for power causes him to miss all the fun in life, in contrast with a monolithic *pueblo* which knows reality when it sees it and knows how to live and love, as the end of the novel shows:

> He became convinced in the trail of yellow leaves of his autumn that he would never be master of all his power, that he was condemned to know life only from the other side, condemned to decipher the seams and straighten the threads of the woof and the warp of the tapestry of illusions of reality without ever suspecting even too late that the only livable life was the one on show, the one we saw over on this side which was not his, General sir, this poor people's side with its trail of yellow leaves of our countless years of misfortune and our ungraspable instants of happiness, where love was contaminated by the germs of death but was all love, General sir..., a comic tyrant who never knew which was the front and which the back of this life which we loved with an insatiable passion which you never dared even imagine for fear of knowing what we knew only too well, that it is arduous and ephemeral but there was no other, General sir, because we knew who we were whilst he was left never knowing it for ever... unaware of the cheers of the frenzied crowds who took to the streets singing hymns of joy at the joyful news of his death and unaware for ever more of the music of liberation and the rockets of jubilation and the chimes of glory which announced to the world the glad tidings that the endless time of eternity had finally come to an end.[49]

We know what García Márquez means of course, but the demagogy blinds him to the fact that the *pueblo*, too, is composed of individuals and that hundreds of thousands of them die at birth or are exploited throughout their average span of thirty-three years precisely because of this apparently meaningless craving for power. Power from where or power over what, the reader finds himself inquiring, only to be confronted with implicitly metaphysical or psychoanalytical answers. We know it will happen, of course, but it was hard in 1975 to bear the thought that Chile's Pinochet will some day have a sympathetic, if supercilious book written about him to demonstrate that he was the alienated one and not his tortured, exiled or murdered victims. Yet this is precisely what García Márquez appeared to be suggesting with his portrait of an elephantine dictator condemned to solitude and absurdity.

Similarly, the idea that Carpentier's more enlightened tyrant has his life's panorama spoiled at the very last (especially when the *Larousse Dictionary* excises his name after his downfall) is consoling only in some very lofty olympus but not in this Latin American twentieth century. García Márquez's ironic inversions of power and pleasure sometimes have truth in them – they are brilliantly juxtaposed in *Love in the Time of Cholera* (1985), for example

– but are counterproductive in this book about dictatorship. The brutal fact is that there is nothing absurd about Pinochet, any more than there was about Franco; or at least, that their absurdity is beside the point. Was Chaplin's laughter at Hitler effective? Probably not, but at least it was directed at Hitler himself, at the time, and not at the Kaiser. Satire is the last thing needed to deal with Latin American tyranny – unless written and published from within the frontiers of a nation so subjected and at the time in question – and fantasy seems inevitably trivial in the face of contemporary horrors.

It is difficult to understand how so great a writer could have been so mistaken. He declared repeatedly that he wanted to write a novel about dictatorship, but his great strength had always resided in the fact that themes suggested themselves or even imposed themselves upon him, springing directly out of life's experience and the moment he was undergoing at the time (like *One Hundred Years of Solitude* or *Love in the Time of Cholera*). Its 'phantasmagorical' texture amply explains why so many Europeans and North Americans welcomed the book so warmly. Naturally one cannot deny the familiar but ever wondrous power of evocation, and it must be conceded that the Patriarch is a great literary creation, a doleful, sometimes tragic – always pathetic – figure, wandering the solitary corridors of his government palace. In a way we wish it were so, and in a way it makes a satisfying commentary on some of the minor nineteenth-century tyrants, little men with dreams of power that were absurdly too big for them. But then one thinks again of all the great dictators who, like Carpentier's, effectively got away with it, not only financially but psychologically, and of the predicament of the Latin American people in the face of such tyrannies. The belief that power brings solitude and that powerlessness brings collective support and security may have meaning in some tribal communities, rural extended families and trade-union organizations, but not in the slums and on the highways of Mexico City, Lima and São Paulo, where the poor are atomized to the point of desperation and millions of children live orphaned and starving in the streets. The people, naturally, will console and defend themselves with humour and the carnival response whenever they are left enough economic, social or psychological room in which to manoeuvre, but life on the periphery has a nasty habit of taking even that away from them. Meanwhile, there has not been much great Latin American fiction about the contemporary dispossessed, no *Les Misérables*, no Dickens or Zola for them – at least, not since the 1930s, and at that time most writers wished to exalt the people rather than convey bad news about them. That is why in the 1970s and 1980s there has been an important move to documentary narrative, as fiction has failed in the face of the almost literally unbelievable horrors of reality itself.

Carpentier, as usual, in *Reasons of State*, uses Europe as an indispensable point of comparison, an inescapable double reality, whilst maintaining an attitude of ineffable irony towards it. This is in every sense of the phrase having the best of both worlds. Carpentier is only too well aware, needless to say (hence a title in Spanish which plays on Descartes), that even in Europe itself the rationalism claimed is usually – like the words 'freedom' and 'democracy' – a strategy rather than a sincerity or a reality, and shows how in Latin America the divorce between the two can leave the political stage representing a permanent farce. Nevertheless, given the characterization of the dictator in the novel, one is left wondering how this particular trick works and why the Latin American people put up with his transparent manoeuvres when the dictator is so obviously mediocre. To this Carpentier provides no answers: the explanatory vacuum is, perhaps, the other, empty side of utopianism. At the same time one has the sneaking suspicion that his rather comic – though sophisticated – dictator is really a bit of a rogue, almost a card. The first-person narrative, used to such ironic effect in *The Lost Steps*, may be used with similar intent here, but if so the self-criticism is benevolent and even self-indulgent. Of course there is no question of Carpentier justifying dictatorship, but the sense that the old-style dictators were not so bad as the present ones is only a step away from saying that the old-fashioned first-person monolinear narrative and individualist central character, apparently also used ironically, may after all have been better than all that experimentation and all that wordiness; or that the Belle Epoque and the *années folles* were a better time than the swinging sixties and gloomy seventies. If so, this is an example of the familiar phenomenon of laughter camouflaging despair. Uncertain as to whether it is ultimately a failure of engagement or of imagination, we turn to a novel which ensured that simplification and complacency would not be the path taken into the future by the Latin American political narrative.

Augusto Roa Bastos, *I the Supreme*

What books would there be here other than my own!

Augusto Roa Bastos, *I the Supreme*, 1974

Dictators have exactly this function: they replace writers, historians, artists, thinkers, etc.

Augusto Roa Bastos, Final note by the Compiler, *I the Supreme*, 1974

The most revolutionary artist would be one who was prepared to sacrifice even his own artistic vocation for the Revolution.

Fidel Castro, *Words to the Intellectuals*, 1961

The publication of *I the Supreme* in 1974 was an exceptional cultural phenomenon. It seemed to arrest the impending decline and fall of the new novel, and its author, who, it was said, had not previously shown signs of renewing either the forms or the contents of Latin American fiction, now appeared to have achieved both objectives in a novel which constituted a vast watershed, a literary labyrinth incorporating all the currents of the past, both aesthetic and political, and opening out a whole network of new channels into the future. It was more immediately and unanimously acclaimed than any novel since *One Hundred years of Solitude*, and critics seemed to suspect that its strictly historical importance might be even greater than that of García Márquez's fabulously successful creation, whose misreading of history through a grand opti(misti)cal illusion – the confusion of a bourgeois nationalist consciousness with a socialist consciousness, through the mistaken belief that anti-imperialism is the same thing as anti-capitalism – provides a fitting symbolic image of the New Novel of the 1960s in general. García Márquez's misreading of Latin American history – overestimating the likely impact of the Cuban Revolution in the rest of the continent – was no less dramatic than his misreading of the real political position and likely evolution of his fellow novelists; but the essential message of his novel remains: those who forget, or never learn to read their own history, will be destroyed by it.

All books are inexhaustible by definition, and it will be many years before this great work is even provisionally integrated into Latin American critical discourse. Yet it is possible to argue that its central problematic and basic intentions are remarkably clear and that if they continue to go largely unrecognized it is because the conclusions to which they lead are unacceptable to the majority of writers and readers concerned with the problems of contemporary Latin America. *I the Supreme* may be the most uncomfortable and unsettling novel written in Latin America in the past 150 years. Readers have perhaps been misled by Roa's supremely dialectical combination of minimum certainties, matters not open to discussion within his texts – above all that writing and politics are inseparable, and that the physical sufferings of the people are more important than the metaphysical anguish of artists and intellectuals – and more doubtful or speculative matters – what is life and how can it be made meaningful, what is language, how should one write. Thus, paradoxically, no novel opens up vaster speculative spaces for the nature of literary and linguistic practice, and yet those spaces are not absolutely free. So that in a curious and most illuminating way, the critical response to Roa's work has revealed a demand for absolute freedom of the imagination from Western writers and readers which may be intimately related to the Supremo's quest for absolute power. For his part Roa fully recognizes the 'ambiguity' of reality – his novel is almost Althusserian in its epistemological intentionality – but insists that the difficulty of interpreting the nature–society dialectic of human history in no way justifies ambiguities in the relation between the writer and the people or between the writer and the reader. These are quite separate problems.

In a sense, then, Roa Bastos, in surpassing the wildest expectations, finished off the 'boom' with a great implosion – taking the dictator motif back to Asturias's perspective of self-criticism (are we Latin Americans really that?), and writing a novel in which many of the central themes of Latin American culture are embedded and enciphered. Often, for example, we are reminded of Borges, only to find that his concerns have been radically historicized, politicized, materialized:

> You, half-breed with two souls, feel lost in this remote corner of nature. Intoxicated by the wild aroma of an idea. You are now riding toward the monastery of your trinitarian domain. You believe you are free. You are riding astride an idea: freeing your country. But you also see yourself shut up in a tiny cell writing by the light of a candle alongside the meteor you captured and hold prisoner with you.[50]

We are confronted, then, by one of the great Ulyssean, labyrinthine novels of Latin American history (by a writer who has lived in exile from Paraguay for forty years, mainly in Argentina and France), except that here the labyrinth is even more intricate, involving nothing less than the whole of language, culture and history as perceived in one's own consciousness and imagined in the consciousness of An Other:

> For the moment God does not occupy my mind. The question that preoccupies it is ruling over chance. Putting my daedal digit on the die, the die in the dicebox. Getting the country out of its labyrinth.
> (In the margin. Unknown hand.) You dug another one. The underground prisons for those poor cats of the patriciate. But on top of the labyrinth you built another one, deeper and more complicated still: the labyrinth of your solitude. Playing dice with words: Your sole-étude. Your lone-age. Your long age. You filled the labyrinth of your horror of nothing, old misanthrope, with the emptiness of the absolute. *Spongia solis....* Is this the spin you gave the die so as to get the Revolution moving? Did you believe Revolution to be the mark of one-alone-entirely-on-his-own? One alone is always wrong; truth begins with two and more.[51]

This is truly monstrous stuff – aspects of *Men of Maize*, *Hopscotch*, *The Death of Artemio Cruz* and *The Green House* all rolled into one – and its confrontation with Francia reminds one inescapably of Sarmiento's earlier man-to-man struggle with Facundo and Rosas in his 1845 prologue to *Facundo: Civilization and Barbarism*, that astonishing, exasperating document in which lay inscribed the story of *Doña Bárbara*, the sphynx of the plains, and the whirlpool of violence studied by Rivera in *The Vortex*. Both Sarmiento and Roa Bastos wrote as anguished exiles, and both used their central figures, Rosas and Francia, as points of departure for a discussion of the major themes of national and continental history. Sarmiento begins:

> Dread shadow of Facundo, I evoke you so that, in shaking off the bloodsoaked dust that covers your ashes, you may rise and explain to us the secret life and internal convulsions which tear at the entrails of a noble people! You hold the secret: reveal it to us! Ten years after your tragic death, the city man, the gaucho of the Argentine plains, as they take their different paths through the desert, still say: 'No, he hasn't died! He lives yet! He will return!' It is true! Facundo is not dead; he lives on in popular tradition, in Argentina's politics and revolutions; and in Rosas, his heir, his complement.[52]

No one could read the last pages of *I the Supreme* without recalling Sarmiento's imprecation. Of course in Roa Bastos's novel the man-to-man struggle is not only between the novelist, or 'compiler', as he insists on calling himself, and Francia; nor solely between Roa Bastos and the contemporary leaders Stroessner or Castro; nor even merely between Roa Bastos as writer and that other contemporary shadow on things called Barthes, Foucault and Derrida; but also between the novelist as artist and politician and his own conscience/consciousness (they are the same word, *conciencia*, in Spanish), as he tries to work out, once again, the nature of writing and history, the relation between the intellectuals and the people, and the bi-cultural character of Paraguay and Latin America as a whole.

I the Supreme is comparable only to *Facundo*, both in its historical significance and in its peculiar heterogeneity. It is the work which finally closes the era which *Facundo* itself opened, definitively reversing the signs of Sarmiento's work and completing that long trajectory of novels from *The Underdogs* through *The Vortex*, *Huasipungo*, *Men of Maize*, *Pedro Páramo* and *The Green House*, each of which, in different ways, and sometimes against the author's own apparent wishes, subjects the idealist values of European 'civilization' to a materialist critique. *Facundo* itself, conceived as a long political pamphlet, confronted a social and historical phenomenon through the techniques and perspectives of the creative imagination. Arrogant though he was, and despite his flights of fancy, Sarmiento was constrained by the essay genre to adopt an objectively humble and essentially historical approach to the life and significance of his protagonist (though there are the usual 'Magical Realist' elements in the story), and it is this stance which Roa Bastos emulates in his own creative biography of the great Paraguayan dictator; whereas, it need hardly be said by now, the most recent Latin American fiction has been characterized not so much by humility as by vanity and even narcissism in some cases (those that consider that 'linguistic experimentation for its own sake' is the true path of the modern novel). As the Supremo says of his own literary contemporaries, 'The more cultivated they seek to be, the less they wish to be Paraguayans.... What interests them is not recounting the facts, but recounting that they are recounting them.'[53] 'Literary diversions. I am not dictating one of those cheap novels in which the writer wallows in the sacred character of literature.'[54] Roa's novel is neither a 'documentary' nor a 'political' novel, but rather one that opens up a completely new way of confronting the problem of literary and political avant-gardes (hence numerous hidden connections with *The Lost Steps* and *Hopscotch*) through its use of a concept which the novel 'articulates' but does not 'utter': that of ideology.

Like *Facundo*, *I the Supreme* has an unavoidable Latin American specificity, and although it is informed by most of the important intellectual currents of its age – an advantage denied to Sarmiento, who was writing, moreover, within ten years of the death of his principal character, while the Other, Rosas, was still alive – and although its universal dimensions are wholly apparent, it cannot in most respects be separated from that specificity. Thus, while it is certainly a novel about dictatorship both as a universal and as a Latin American problem, it takes its concrete force from, and continually returns to, the life and works of José Gaspar de Francia, the Supreme and Perpetual Dictator of Paraguay from 1814 to 1840; and although it considers the function and meaning of writing in Western history as a whole, and the roles and duties of the Latin American writer since Independence, it cannot for a moment be separated from the predicament of one specific writer, Roa Bastos himself in the early 1970s, confronted with the dilemma of what to write, for whom to write, and whether in any case writing is anything other than an irrelevant or even cowardly thing to do in a continent where dictators are everywhere in power and where the great mass of the population is illiterate and condemned by uneven development to a consciousness anterior to that which has historically produced the novel as a literary form. The question, put very crudely, is this: does the practice of writing fiction have anything at all to contribute to the process of national and continental liberation? Or is the writer condemned, perhaps fatally, to be on the other side?[55]

The fact is that critics have not, in general, perceived the underlying problems to which this novel's structure offers provisional solutions and avenues into the future;[56] and have failed to recognize the thematic continuity between *I the Supreme* and the earlier *Son of Man*, whose central problematic – the gulf between the intellectual and the people, writing and reality, theory and practice – is precisely the same as that of the later and still more radical work, in which the link between the novel as a historical form and the development of bourgeois individualism is explored. Thus many readers came up with the extraordinary idea that the later novel was – simply – a condemnation of Francia, or that it was a mere open-ended exploration of Latin

American history and of fictional form. Whereas Roa Bastos makes it obvious that he shares the point of departure of Marx and Engels in *The German Ideology*, when they argue that with the division of labour, consciousness can 'flatter itself that it is something other than consciousness of existing practice' and can 'emancipate itself from the world' and proceed to the realm of 'pure' theory, producing a situation in which 'intellectual and material activity – enjoyment and labour, production and consumption – devolve on different individuals.'[57] The novel is thus based on the understanding that the development of class society involves the separation of mental and manual labour, a separation which, in its turn, at a particular moment in historical evolution, gives rise to the literary form we call the novel. The first irony is that in attempting to resolve this dilemma the Supremo only exacerbates it in the long term; the second is that writers themselves are in many regards as guilty as he is at the level of representation.

Roa Bastos rests his novel on a technique anticipated in *The Death of Artemio Cruz*, the distinction between 'I', the subjective experience of the individual, and 'HE', the objective historical self (a facet enormously magnified and hardened in this case given the Supremo's invulnerability): 'People all reassure themselves with the thought that they are a single individual. Difficult to be the same man constantly. What is the same is not always the same. I am not always I. The only one who doesn't change is HE.'[58] But Roa's enterprise is even more radical and complex than this. He moves on from the initial distinction to remind us that the structure of the classic bourgeois novel is the narration by a contemplative I of the actions of a less conscious, distanced HE, a relationship which we call irony and which is a manifestation of a certain relation of power.

Equally as important, however, is the indirect relation of the novelist, not only to his 'fiction', but to 'reality' itself, in the first place, and to his unknown audience, the readers, in the second place. The novelist does not speak, sing or chant, as the poet does in a literary genre wherein the I represents, not a distance from a HE, but the expression or the recuperation, even if only symbolic, of a WE. The novelist, despite the conversational tone which he adopted in the more confident days of the nineteenth century in order to naturalize his creations, is above all and by definition a man who writes.

Furthermore, he is not acquainted with his audience, but reaches them through commercial mediators, and they, the readers, obtain the book through the anonymous agency of the market and consume it in the solitude of their houses and in the solitude of their own silent individual consciousness. In other words, if the normal relationship of the intellectual with his society is established at the level of theory rather than practice, the relationship of writer to reader is that of any producer to his consumer within the capitalist mode of production. However, this is not how the writers themselves normally see things. As the Supremo puts it, 'Separated from their people and place by accident or vocation, they discover that they must live in a world made up of elements foreign to them with which they believe they are conjoined. They believe themselves to be providential figures of an imaginary populace.'[59]

In Latin America, however, the 'normal' distance between the novelist and his readers becomes an unbridgeable chasm. Whereas the poet who sings, chants and speaks, merely has to consider the universal problems of the level of formal and conceptual sophistication in order to determine the class character of his aesthetic construction, the novelist appears virtually condemned to represent only one class, the bourgeoisie. ('What meaning can writing have ... when by definition it does not have the same sense as the everyday speech of ordinary people'?[60]) Latin American poets have often felt sufficiently able to unite theory and practice as to join revolutionary struggles and take to the hills, in emulation of some of the great names of the romantic era; but it would be difficult to name many novelists who have done so. The poet can create as he goes, wherever he goes, and is not normally tied to a seat and a desk as the novelist is during long months and years, composing vast organic creations in compensation for, or even in order to mask, the fragmentation of society and the alienation from it of the writer himself. The abyss between the Latin American novelist and his indigenous, peasant and worker characters, is one of the aspects which gives rise to those central metaphors, 'solitude', 'absence' and 'distance'. For the intellectual the world is full of distances, gaps between himself and the world, between himself and the people, between writing and speech, language and reality, theory and practice. Such contradictions are the very fabric out of which *I the Supreme* is constructed, providing a classic example of the anguished self-consciousness of a writer who would claim to represent the 'Third World'.

Clearly acute problems of conscience and commitment are raised for a writer who sees things this way. Roa Bastos's conclusion is that the Latin American novelist, whether or not he or she follows a party line, is not 'free' to invent, because they are playing with the images of the lives of their people. Roa is in a line of writers – Azuela was the first, followed by Rivera, Asturias, Arguedas, Rulfo and the early Vargas Llosa – of whom he may be the most radical, who have built their existential dilemma into their novels, taking fragmentation as a structural principle instead of speaking with alien voices and donning the mask of organic form. Such writers accept logical discontinuity and the lack of an integrated psychological typology, not as proof of the innate absurdity of the world, but as the product of a colonized reality. After the high-point, in the mid 1960s, of the always dangerous and bewitching 'Ulyssean' journeys (the usual experience in a labyrinth is to get lost), the works of the most linguistically sophisticated 'new' novelists seemed to claim implicitly that in the age of mass communications and rapid transport the problems of uneven development were close to solution, which may have been true – for them. The cultural gap can now be made to appear invisible thanks to the new technology, and Europe and the United States are now 'in' Latin America. But it is arguable that such misconceptions and mystifications have only confused issues still more. Once again the Supremo's judgment (with which Roa may or may not agree) is merciless: 'They prophesied that they would turn this country into the new Athens. The Areopagus of the sciences, the letters, the arts of this Continent. What they were really out to do with their chimeras was to hand Paraguay over to the highest bidder.'[61]

It is to these problems that *I the Supreme* addresses itself, consciously and directly, continuing and updating the analysis offered by *Son of Man* as long ago as 1960. Roa Bastos, like Carpentier and García Márquez in their novels, enters the consciousness of his dictator, but it would be difficult to accuse him of implying that such an operation is an easy one to carry out: no novelist can have wrestled more exhaustingly yet more fairly with a fictional character than Roa Bastos. Besides, the Supremo himself is obsessively aware of the problems of knowing oneself and of writing history. His novel literally teems with epigrams, riddles, puns and other word games, but does so precisely to demonstrate the cantankerous dictator's conviction, shared by Roa Bastos, that language and literature have always been unreliable, treacherous tools, but particularly since that division of labour took place which gave some men verbal superiority over others as a reflection of the economic superiority of those same men and others over the same – now lower – classes:[62]

> Don't use improper words that are not my style, that are not steeped in my thought. I loathe relative talent that's begged and borrowed. What's more, your style is abominable. A labyrinthine alleyway paved with alliterations, anagrams, idiosyncratic idioms, barbarisms, paronomasias such as *pároli/párulis*, imbecilic anastrophes to dazzle imbecilic inverts who experience erections by virtue of the violent inversions of word order…. You have not yet destroyed oral tradition only because it is the one language that cannot be sacked, robbed, repeated, plagiarized, copied. What is spoken remains alive, sustained by the tone, the gestures, the facial expressions, the gaze, the accent, the breath of the speaker.[63]

Son of Man, as we have seen, dramatized the role of one leading protagonist who was a thinly veiled projection of the novelist himself, the difference being that Roa was fully aware of this where other novelists might remain oblivious. That narrative clearly underlined the gulf between social classes in Paraguay and seemed to imply that a novel, no matter what its subject matter or apparent point of view, was as sure a sign of the concentration of the means of production in a few hands as any of the more material manifestations. A few years earlier, Stalin had made the great discovery that language was not a superstructure, to the amusement of many literary critics; but few would deny that the use of language and its powers is class-based, or that literature itself is part of the superstructure, however that concept might now be defined. The result of this perception is that Roa Bastos is obsessively preoccupied with two of the central problems of Western literature and thought, truth and sincerity. This leaves him in what the Supremo might call 'grave danger' of a fatal case of bad faith, but not to face up to the possible implication of his real position would be worse:

> The one thing that is ours is what remains inside us. It is even farther inside us than what we ourselves are within ourselves. Those who feign modesty are the worst. Socrates hypocritically bows his head when he utters his famous sentence that is a lie: I only know that I know nothing. How could the peripatetic know that he knew nothing if he knew nothing? Hence he deserved the hemlock. He who says I lie and tells the truth lies, indubitably. But he who says I lie and really lies is telling the scriptest truth.[64]

Miguel Vera, the bourgeois intellectual who is the central character of *Son of Man*, lies to himself within his own subjectivity, and betrays the peasant revolutionaries on the objective plane of the narrative. Thus the first question Roa Bastos asks in *I the Supreme*, in terms of logical priority, is: can we know the truth? His long, fragmented answer to this question is cautious and sceptical, and already invokes the topic of language and its relation to reality and consciousness (he effectively pursues Marx's idea of language as 'practical consciousness'). The second question is: if we believe that we know the truth, will we tell it? Both Marx and Freud among others addressed themselves to these two questions, and each suggested, in his different way, that most of us cannot know the truth, and indeed, that even if we intuited it, the same or similar reasons to those which caused us to conceal it from ourselves would certainly ensure that we concealed it subsequently from others.[65] In this regard there is little doubt that Roa Bastos's novel must be counted a partial engagement with 'Post-structuralism', though without concessions to its implicit counsels of despair.

These are all inevitable dilemmas in a novel about politicians or intellectuals, and of course Francia, heir to the European Enlightenment and faced by the mythical *tabula rasa* or blank page of Latin American history, was both. They are questions which are considered in a host of Latin American novels, in which the author's uneasy conscience is almost the conventional, if implicit, point of departure (Onetti and Vargas Llosa are the best known exponents of this vein). However, there is a third question, which for Roa

Bastos is actually the most important of all, and which only he deals with in such complex yet unflinching detail, namely this: if the intellectual can cast off his alienation from the masses and know the truth (doubtful), and is prepared to tell it (still more doubtful), will he also act on it by putting it into practice? For practice, praxis, is part of the central problematic of both Roa Bastos's novels. The Supremo comments that the people are real, whereas intellectuals and politicians are merely 'probable beings' mounted on ideas which must be converted into reality. Hence his iron rule: 'To fulfil that which is spoken, written, agreed, signed.' With this the two great activist belief systems of the past two thousand years, Christianity and Marxism, come into parallel focus. Both were confronted in *Son of Man*, the first overtly – religion was given a materialist reading both by the peasant characters and by the author – and the second by implication, as we saw in chapter 3. Christianity, however, has been superseded as a problem by the time of *I the Supreme*, whereas Marxism is almost explicitly interrogated – though Roa is careful not to damage the novel's specific 1840 perspective on the one hand or universal applicability on the other – through nearly transparent references to revolutionary processes such as the Chinese and Cuban Revolutions.

Clearly, then, the question of Roa Bastos's point of view with regard to Francia as historical personage and fictional character must be clarified. Contrary to the conclusions of some readers, the presentation of Francia is, in relative terms, a positive one, in line with recent revisions of the nineteenth-century contradiction between so-called 'civilization' and 'barbarism'. In interviews Roa has described Francia unhesitatingly as 'the civil and political director of Paraguay's process of independence, creator of a state socialism with very specific characteristics.'[66] Instead of selling his country to nascent imperialism, as the leaders of the River Plate republics and Brazil were contemporaneously doing, thereafter to bemoan their distance from the metropolitan centres and their consequent 'solitude' – that of a marooned, parasitic bourgeoisie – Francia forced his countrymen to assimilate the realities of their historical heritage and predicament, consolidating through his policies the isolation which Spanish colonial rule had already imposed upon them. Thereupon, taking all political power – even fate itself – into his own hands, he set out to construct a true nation rather than a disguised dependency. His endeavour, he declares in the novel, is to 'restore the sovereignty of the Common People' thanks to his absolute possession of the 'Word of Independence'. In his Paraguay there were no landowners, no middle classes, no all-white marriages, no generals, no urbanization, no foreign trade to speak of, no church domination, no discrimination against the Indians, no corruption, no nepotism, no political parties, no elections, no beggars, no hunger, no poverty, no newspapers, no books: in short, no 'civilization'. In order to justify his right to such absolute power over the objective reality of the nation, the Left-Wing Dictator in a sense renounces his claim on humanity and converts himself into a totally abstract self-creation. He denies the effects of heredity ('confabulations of chance') or of the environment ('gestating myself through my own will') upon himself, and abstains from all pleasures of the senses in order to carry out his self-appointed task on behalf of the people who gave him *carte blanche*, in the most literal sense of that French expression, when they elected him as their Perpetual Dictator.

We are thus presented with the curious paradox of the ultimate individualist who proclaims his nonexistence as a person through his self-abnegation on behalf of his only nobility, 'the labouring–procreating mob'. He makes them truly isolated in order to make them self-reliant and independent, instead of allowing the establishment of a relation of dependency which paradoxically has made the rest of Latin America feel isolated. ('Precisely because the weight of events tends constantly to destroy equality, the weight of the Revolution must tend always to maintain it.') And through his advanced and lucid theoretical comprehension of what is now called neocolonialism, through his unchallengeable moral example and revolutionary integrity, and – above all – through his ruthless and remorseless conversion of theory into practice, the Supreme Dictator of the novel is able to persuade or force the people to accept the forms of his ideas without, however, changing the essential content to the same radical degree.

This is the bitter irony at the heart of *I the Supreme*. It is inevitable that once Francia dies – for no reality is absolute, no human life is perpetual – his successors will be the product of a conflict or contradiction that his authority was able to suppress but not eliminate. Roa Bastos appears to believe that, with all due respect to the dialectic and to the revolutionary vanguard, the normal movement of historical change is not that of form or theory 'pulling' content or practice along (a phenomenon symbolized in the novel by the capture of the 'meteor-chance' and the idealist conception of the empty skull as the philosophizing dictator's 'matrix-home'), but rather that of content bursting through form. As we have seen repeatedly in other novels, long before the current era of scepticism about Marxist claims to scientific truth, this was a characteristic position for Latin America's 'Third-Worldist' intellectuals suspicious of all imported doctrines which reduce the specificity of non-European or non-modern experience.[67] Roa also appears to believe that the normal progress of literature in the Western world has similarly been that of form running ahead of content in ways which do not necessarily or even normally point the way to the true future of the genre in question. Hence the central symbol of the egg (like Asturias's seed-stars), in contradistinction to the meteor and the empty skull, as an image of the way history gestates in the womb of time and cannot be rushed or speeded up without risk of deformation or without some later compensatory slowing-down. The Supremo's failure is perhaps as close to an image of authentic tragedy as the modern political novel is likely to offer us. He is not, contrary to what some critics have managed to deduce, simply held up to shame, ridicule or other forms of condemnation, as an easy target for writers and readers who are actually structurally inserted, without being aware of it, into the same kind of system as he was. He is, rather, presented as a model of the most that could be done in his time and place, a man who went as far as it was possible to go in carrying out objectives which may have been possible elsewhere at the same time or in the same place at some later date. Unfortunately, intellectuals themselves, like books, are a material proof of the contradictions of uneven development, and Francia's epic attempt was bound, 'in the last analysis', to fail. (There is some evidence in the text that the craving for absolute power is an unconscious projection of the desire to live for ever.) His failure is materialized, in the novel, in the flock of blind swallows which crash to their doom ('The Flood crossed their path'), and in the strange sexless Siamese twins who begin trekking in to the capital city at the end of the book, images of a people divorced on the one hand from the full totality of natural human–sensuous experience, and on the other from the possibility of developing their own conscious 'vision' in order to guide the direction of the Revolution collectively.

Francia is the most enlightened character in the book, but no one is enlightened enough to negate the objective realities and distortions of uneven development or to solve the insoluble. Thus, for example, the Supreme Dictator has more respect than others for such exploited groups as women in general or Paraguay's Indians in particular, but he still suppresses – rules out – the possible contribution they might make to his new social order:

> From age-old books, including Genesis, we know that in the beginning primitive man was male/female. No race is perfectly pure... The elders of the tribe here also know, without having read Plato's Symposium, that each one was originally two... Till thought tore them loose from nature. Separated them. Divided them in two. They continued to believe they were a single one, not knowing that one half was seeking the other half. Irreconcilable enemies in the impulse which the Man-of-Today calls love... They canceled out the difference between the sexes, so dear and so indispensable to Western thought, which can only operate by pairs... Though the man is the only reasonable sex. Only he is capable of reflection.[68]

Once more we see a re-examination of themes explored by Asturias in *Men of Maize* (the writers were close friends when exiled in Argentina together in the 1950s, and their work has much in common). Later Francia, who has acknowledged that for the Indians the body is primary because the soul is its dependent, insists that he has no evidence that he himself was ever actually

born: 'I don't want to be engendered in a woman's womb. I want to be
engendered in a man's thought.'[69] In short, for reasons which are apparently
progressive, Francia sets out to suppress or repress everything that he cannot
actually predict and control, not least his own response to the realm of the
senses, including all the world's 'indigenous' ancestral wisdom and all the
'feminine' cosmic cycles (despite his inner longing for the female-comet, the
'Star of the North').

So Francia fails, and the last pages see him burn all his writings before his
final restoration to the unspoken objectivity of the history of his people: 'I
am not flinging myself headfirst into your flames. I am throwing myself into
the Ethna of my Race. Some day its crater in eruption will eject only my
name. It will scatter the burning lava of my memory far and wide.'[70] Once
again language, history and literature are shown to be less important than acts
and their continuing and indeed endless echoes in folk memory. It is still too
early to say definitively what this structure and conclusion may mean, but it
is clear that Roa Bastos's novel has important implications for the relation of
literature to history in Latin America and of intellectuals to the political
process. Indeed, its influence on fiction since its publication is obvious, as we
shall see.

It is difficult to escape the conclusion that the novel was addressed above
all to Roa's friends in Cuba, who were similarly trying to force the hand of
history in the face of an imperialist blockade, while the relation of an austere
individualist leader to a revolutionary collectivity was similarly being
worked out.[71] (One might claim that just as with *Son of Man* he anticipated
liberation theology, so *I the Supreme* prophesied glasnost and perestroika.)
As a matter of fact, it is impossible to understand the full dialectical significance of *I the Supreme* without first recognizing that it contains an implied
critique of the New Latin American Novel, and secondly, and still more
important, that it is structured around two great presences and two great
absences. The presences are Francia, the all-powerful supreme dictator, the
man who is everything, whose every thought and action is translated at once
into objective reality, and whose audience is absolutely certain; and Roa
Bastos himself, the 'compiler' of the book, alluded to within it as a fugitive
and a traitor, a writer of fictions and fables, a man whose impact on his
country is negligible after thirty years of exile, and whose audience, like that
of all novelists, is wholly indeterminate. The two great absences are
Stroessner, then (and until this year) dictator of Paraguay and an example of
one of the worst kinds of Latin American tyrant; and Fidel Castro, who may
well be the current version of Francia in Roa Bastos's conception, in which
case the book would communicate his earnest hope that Cuba and Castro are
different from Paraguay and Francia in their respective relations to the
Russian Revolution and the French Revolution. Charles III of Spain's slogan,

'Everything for the people, nothing by the people', although not of course truly sincere in the case of the Spanish monarch, could easily have been adopted by Francia. Perhaps some might see connections between it and Castro's dictum: 'Within the Revolution, everything; outside the Revolution, nothing.' The following, at any rate, is the nub of Roa Bastos's last judgment on his dictator:

> You turned yourself into a great Obscurity for the people-mob; into the great Don-Amo, the Lord-and-Master who demands docility in return for a full belly and an empty head. Ignorance of a time at the crossroads. Better than anyone else, you knew that so long as the city and its privileges hold dominion over the totality of the people, Revolution is merely a caricature of itself. Every truly revolutionary movement, in the present era of our Republics, begins, solely and self-evidently, with sovereignty as a real whole in act.... No, little mummy; true Revolution does not devour its children. Only its bastards; those who are not capable of carrying it to its ultimate consequences. Beyond its limits if necessary. [72]

Roa's fears that Cuba's Revolution is heading for the same end as Francia's lead him neither to renounce socialism nor to counsel despair, but to renew old questions and resuscitate earlier debates in preparation for the new historical period to come. Much of his interrogation oscillates between the poles symbolized by two of the Supremo's personal inventions, his 'Portable Memory-Pen', which records historical reality with complete accuracy (and has passed into the hands of the compiler), and his 'Ray of Rectitude', which reduces all the complexities of experience to black and white. Needless to say, his implicit condemnation of government interference in intellectual activity is not an argument for creative licence (although Roa would be unlikely to condone legal sanctions). On the contrary, the essential project of the work is to explore the concept of the responsibility and commitment of the artist in a complex and rapidly changing world. Perhaps the key concept which he shares with the Supremo is this: 'Writing does not mean converting reality into words but making words real. Unreality exists only in the misuse of words, the misuse of writing.' [73] Typical of his dialectical thinking is his specific objection to the unbridled use of fantasy: 'As mercury is the element that separates gold from copper it is also the one that tinctures metals, the mediator of this union. Does it not resemble the imagination, mistress of error and falsehood. All the more deceiving in that it is not always so.' [74]

I the Supreme is also, then, a meditation on the meaning of writing: its relation to slavery at the very roots of civilization; its one-dimensional inefficiency and its tendency to freeze thought and language themselves. Hence references to 'lost senses', to 'our clumsy writing which has set us back millions of years'. The Supremo laments: 'I can only write; that is, deny life. Kill even more that which is dead already.' And: 'Forms disappear, but words remain, to signify the impossible. No story can be told... for true language is not yet born.' Writing, we see, is always the product of a distance, whether in time (it is always posterior, always after the event, always petrified) or in space (it mediates between those who are separated physically or socially). To sit down and write always takes one out of direct social action, and to write novels does so for a very long time, whereas speaking produces exactly the opposite effect. At the same time, writing is a form of power – or, at least, it is the shadow of power[75] – the possession of a rare and specific skill (rhetoric: persuasion and manipulation) which others do not possess and which carries with it a responsibility. That responsibility, Roa Bastos believes, is to the great mass of people who cannot read and write, the people of the Third World. His position is complicated by the fact that he finds himself condemned to write in a prerevolutionary situation, unsure of the ground – both political and literary – on which he is standing, and unconvinced of his worthiness to 'serve the people'. His unease is compounded by the intuition that being an exile in the non-socialist world leaves his fantasies and hopes for a better future intact, fertile, the raw materials of a vision not yet produced, or – still worse – reduced by the ruthless demystifying machine of dogmatic Marxism. Nevertheless, everything suggests that he follows his own version of the Maoist line of the 'struggle on two fronts', that is to say, the constant interpenetration of the literary with the political, in a tradition that is actually that of Latin America in its first Independence period.

Not least among the novel's virtues is its ability to engage with the most influential debates of the modern era, without referring directly to Marx, Freud, the *nouvelle critique* or, indeed, the *nueva novela*, in a narrative which for all its modernity manages also to stir echoes of the literature of Spain before the Independence of Latin America. Combined with this, but equally implicit, is a superbly challenging reading of the other key works of contemporary Latin American literature. The greatest triumph of all, however, is to have found a means of fusing 'literary revolution' with 'revolutionary literature' in a way that has allowed the novel to be hailed by both the radicals and the aesthetes among literary critics, thereby perhaps putting an end to a long century of debate – that of the 'national' or 'neocolonial' period – and opening up another. Now that we have this astonishing achievement to echo that of Sarmiento in 1845, it seems possible to propose that the 'true history' of Latin American literature may begin to be written. *I the Supreme* is an immense work, as closed as a labyrinth, as open as the stars. It is with this map that the slow process of liberating the labyrinth becomes truly conscious and thus truly begins.

Exceptional post-script 2: '*The General in His Labyrinth*'

'García Márquez directs Bolívar', the hallucinatory film ad would say. A novel written about Latin America's most famous and most glamorous historical figure of all time by perhaps its greatest ever novelist is undoubtedly a remarkable event, and one calculated to make any writer rush into print with an instant judgment even in the final stages of such a long volume as this – especially when the work is entitled '*The General in His Labyrinth*' (*El general en su laberinto*, 1989) and is about the great man's last journey towards his early death. The present personal response was composed at the moment of publication and before any of the – inevitably polemical – critical reactions were available.

The first thing to be said is that this is the opposite endeavour from that of Roa Bastos's confrontation with Bolívar's contemporary, Doctor Francia. García Márquez is questioning neither the nature of writing nor the status of his own text: on the contrary, he asserts its claims. If there is anyone who does not know Bolívar in this narrative it is Bolívar himself, not García Márquez: this is indeed the 'Autumn of Another Patriarch' with much the same relation between author and character. Neither is García Márquez questioning the basis of historical methodology. Although his acknowledgments following the body of the text confess his own 'absolute lack of experience and method in historical research', it is implicit in his comments and indeed in his approach to his task that this represents an effort to give us 'the real Bolívar' and that he has more than a suspicion that he has succeeded. Ironically enough, the acknowledgments thank a number of distinguished gentlemen, including an ex-president of Colombia, a Panamanian foreign secretary and sundry academics, who supplied the writer with the 'tyrannical documentation' which allowed him to base his novel as far as possible on such facts as are known. There is also a Succinct Chronology and a map of Bolívar's last journey – 'the least well documented time of his entire life' – from Bogotá down the Magdalena River to Santa Marta, where he died, between 8 May and 17 December 1830. It is this last journey which is the subject of the novel – seven months of solitude? – with a series of flashbacks to earlier periods in the Great Liberator's life. The result is a stunning piece of literary creation. It may prove to be García Márquez's definitive work.

The territory and its peculiar atmosphere are immediately familiar, as immediately recognizable as the tropical 'Greeneland' of heat, vultures and hopelessness in which García Márquez's English friend and colleague has so frequently immersed us. The novel begins with a presumption of death which is reminiscent of the real death with which *Love in the Time of Cholera* began. That novel had ended with an unmistakable reference to the conclusion of *No One Writes to the Colonel*; and this one ends with an actual death, that of Bolívar, which fuses the conclusion of *One Hundred Years of Solitude* with that of *The Autumn of the Patriarch*. As the General reaches 'the final objective' he murmurs 'How can I escape from this labyrinth!'. Then he gazes one last time at the mirror, hears the slaves singing outside his window and sees 'the diamond of Venus in the sky as it went away for ever, the eternal snows, the creeper whose yellow flowers he would not see bloom the following Saturday in a house closed down by mourning, the last splendour of that life that till the end of time itself would never ever be repeated.' Needless to say, the author is sailing very close here to the dangers of self-parody in a novel about the most venerated figure in Latin American history – a Venezuelan, moreover, when García Márquez is a Colombian. It would be foolish to deny that Bolívar is here a character from García Márquez's stock repertoire. Like the earlier colonel, endlessly waiting for his pension, Bolivar is waiting for a passport (though possibly hoping that it will never come). Like the patriarchal dictator wandering through the labyrinthine corridors of his palace (and through García Márquez's purple prose), Bolívar wanders through the wintry labyrinth of his stunning decline and fall.[76] And like all García Márquez's novels, the work is about defeat, not victory, about disillusionment, not the apotheosis of an idea. If we were not so accustomed to the García Márquez perspective, we might be surprised that a novel about the man who achieved the most glorious triumphs in Latin American history should focus upon his darkest hours. This is much more the 'Diary of Che in Bolivia' than 'We Shall Overcome' by Castro.

The question is whether Bolívar is also something other than a García Márquez character, and whether, given the new depths of psychological investigation revealed in the novelist's previous work, he has an independent status which can allow us to see him through the familiar rhetorical flourishes, hyperbolic *tours de force* and philosophical obsessions. The answer seems to be yes. We are able to see Bolívar for ourselves, as a man who has succeeded in his great task as liberator of a continent but failed in the even greater endeavour of uniting it; and as a man who, mightily fallen, somehow retains his courage and greatness of spirit in even the most desperate and humiliating circumstances, at the end of his 'mad chase between his woes and his dreams'. Clearly García Márquez believes that this is an even greater side to the Liberator, whose ultimate greatness – perhaps – lay in his becoming an ordinary Latin American in his last months, the predecessor of all those other magnificent failures who struggle through the pages of Latin American fiction in the arduous kingdom of this world. If this were so, then far from Bolívar becoming a García Márquez adaptation, we could see that it was Bolívar who had created all García Márquez's earlier characters – who had, in short, created the character of the Latin American, with his magnificent dreams, seemingly endless struggles, transient victories and shattering disappointments.

9

Writers and their Works:
The Labyrinth of Mirrors

Don Quixote was born for me alone, and I for him: his was to act, mine to write; we two together make but one.

> Miguel de Cervantes, *Don Quixote*, 1615

It's the other one, it's Borges, that things happen to... I live, I allow myself to live, so that Borges may contrive his literature and that literature justifies my existence... I do not know which of us two is writing this page.

> Jorge Luis Borges, 'Borges and I'

History, Stephen said, is a nightmare from which I am trying to awake.

> James Joyce, *Ulysses*, 1922

If one is going to insist on speaking about someone it's not enough to put oneself in his place: you have to be that someone. Only like can write about like.

> Augusto Roa Bastos, *I the Supreme*, 1974

As the reader may by now agree, there seems to be something in the labyrinthine relation of Latin American writers to culture and society, and therefore to their own works, which creates a curious and almost obsessive doubling over and interweaving of history and myth, fiction and reality. This gives a new meaning to the concept of 'intertextuality', though it might not have surprised Dante, Chaucer, Rabelais, Cervantes and Sterne. Each of those writers inserted themselves into their works in such a way as to puncture the concept of the sacred scriptural text, supplant the original creator and establish that separation of the Word from God which has been so decisive in opening the space of human endeavour and the human imagination.[1] The continuing significance of this act and the dangers involved even in the late twentieth century have recently been reemphasized by the affair of Salman

Rushdie's *Satanic Verses* and the Ayatollah in Iran. This chapter will be a diversion, a small labyrinthine odyssey through contemporary history and literature which may seem to take us off the track, away from the point, only the better to come home again, like any personage wilting back into obscurity at the end of another Bloomsday; or any reader returning – magically transformed – to the real, now defamiliarized world, after a journey through a book;[2] or anyone at all returning to his or her self after a quest through the corridors of memory, having met a fiction.

Borges's famous epilogue to *Dreamtigers* (1960) tells us that 'a man sets himself the task of portraying the world', only to find, shortly before his death, that 'that patient labyrinth of lines traces the image of his face'. In *Other Inquisitions* (1952) he had noted, whilst reflecting on *Don Quixote*, that 'if the characters in a story can be readers or spectators, then we, their readers or spectators, can be fictitious.'[3] In 1833, Borges goes on, 'Carlyle observed that universal history is an infinite sacred book that all men write and read and try to understand, and in which they too are written.' Joyce was the faust to try out the theseus this century, setting off through the labyrinth by writing a *Portrait of the Artist as a Young Man* and then, with *Ulysses*, composing a portrait of the artist as Everyman. In one of Borges's best-known stories, 'The Circular Ruins', a man wants to 'dream a man... down to the very last detail and insert him into reality.' The conclusion is expected: 'With relief, with humiliation, with terror, he realized that he too was a mere apparition, dreamed by another.'

In 1900 a Guatemalan Indian chief called Gaspar Ilóm led an uprising against the incursions of Mestizo farmers into Indian communal territories in the Northwestern highlands of the country following the Liberal government land reforms of the 1870s. After a bitter struggle Ilóm was trapped and treacherously poisoned by government forces. Many years later, as he faced a library magazine, a young Guatemalan writer, who had journeyed to Paris, read the story of Gaspar Ilóm in between translating Mayan works like the *Popol Vuh* into Spanish. Miguel Angel Asturias, for it was he, identified himself with the myth of the Indian god Quetzalcóatl, and dreamed of becoming a great Latin American novelist. He had been born a few weeks after his Argentine counterpart, Jorge Luis Borges, and a few weeks before Ilóm's unsuccessful struggle. The dead chief's tale took him back on a symbolic journey through the labyrinths of history and literature to the first Indian massacres by the early Spanish conquerors. He at once wrote a short story, 'Juan Garrafita', in which Ilóm appeared as a semi-mythological character. The writer returned from Paris to Guatemala, and little by little, over the next two decades, the story turned into a unique indigenist work called 'Gaspar Ilóm', published shortly after the Guatemalan Revolution of 1944. And in 1949 that same story appeared as the introductory section of one of

Latin America's great novels, *Men of Maize*, which foretold the eventual regeneration of the Latin American Indian and his culture. For stories are 'like rivers, they pick up what they can as they flow past, and if they can't pick up something and carry it along, they carry its reflection.' The critics, however, considered the novel a fiction, evidence of an overwrought tropical imagination. In the early 1940s the novelist's first wife presented him with a son, and he decided to give him the warlike name of Rodrigo. As a political precaution – this was the time of the dictator Ubico – he invited a soldier, Miguel Ydígoras Fuentes, to act as one of the boy's godfathers. In 1954 the writer, ambassador in El Salvador for the Arbenz government, was forced to go into exile after the United States-backed coup. Many years later Rodrigo, who called his own son Sandino, was captured among a band of revolutionary guerrillas in the Guatemalan countryside. The President, or dictator – *The President* was the title of the writer's most famous novel, an attack on dictators – was one Miguel Ydígoras Fuentes, who, as Borges might put it, rather than executing the rebel, decided to allow his godson to go into exile. In 1966, the year before he won the Nobel Prize, the writer returned once more to Paris as ambassador for his country's first civilian government for many years. During a brief visit to Guatemala – the first for twelve years and the last of his life – he was greeted by representatives of Guatemala's Indian communities, who named him 'Great Tongue' or spokesman for their cause. He also travelled secretly into the mountains to persuade Turcios Lima, leader of the FAR guerrillas, to lay down his arms. Turcios wisely refused, though a few months later he died in a car crash as the green berets took over his country, and it seemed that the revolutionary resistance might die with him. A few years later members of the FAR broke away to form a new Indian-oriented movement, the ORPA. Their leading spokesman, now a legendary Latin American freedom fighter, was the guerrilla commandant Gaspar Ilóm.

In 1928, many years earlier, whilst the Guatemalan was reading about Gaspar Ilóm in Paris, a notorious massacre was perpetrated in Colombia by government troops to suppress a strike by railways workers against the United Fruit Company (the same company against which, many years later, Miguel Angel would write his famous *Banana Trilogy*). The massacre took place at the railway station in Cíenaga, Magdalena. More than thirty thousand workers were on strike in the zone and more than four thousand were at the Cíenaga demonstration when the troops opened fire. The conservative government reported that a mere nine strikers were killed and, like all succeeding regimes, set about suppressing the true story. After some tempestuous parliamentary debates in September 1929, nothing of importance concerning these events was published in Colombia in the next forty years, until they were narrated in a celebrated historical novel and became perhaps the best known historical incident in Latin American literature. The writer, Gabriel García Márquez, had been born precisely in 1928, the year of the massacre, in the small town of Aracataca (which he would later rename Macondo), close to Ciénaga, just as Miguel Angel Asturias had been born at the time that Gaspar Ilóm was leading his rebellion against the forces of another ruthless government in another Latin American republic. One of the principal eyewitness accounts on which historians now depend was given by the parish priest of Aracataca. His testimony was used by deputy Jorge Eliécer Gaitán to back up his protest in the abortive parliamentary debates of 1929. Many years later, Gaitán's assassination, now as presidential candidate for the Liberal Party, led directly to the 1948 Bogotazo uprising and to twenty years of generalized and horrific violence in Colombia whose effects are felt to this day. In 1954 the writer left a country by now in an advanced stage of social decomposition and travelled to live in Paris. There he wrote and rewrote a work which refused doggedly to crystallize itself, doing so only at the appropriate moment, in 1967, the year in which Comandante Che Guevara died and Miguel Angel Asturias won the Nobel Prize (as the Colombian himself would do in 1982), when it became the symbol and con-summation of what wise heads and myth-makers called the New Latin American Novel. Its writer knew this only too well, but his characters were almost all of them lost in a dizzying labyrinth of history, ideology, fantasy and myth, though all set out to decipher this impenetrable world of words. They fail, like most of Gabriel's readers. The culminating episode prior to the conclusion concerned a massacre of striking banana workers. Most critics agreed that it was perhaps the most dreamlike passage in the novel, a stun-ning example of Magical Realism. One of the characters who appeared briefly at the end of the book, rather à la Hitchcock, among Colonel Buendía, Fuentes's Artemio Cruz, Carpentier's Victor Hugues and Cortázar's Rocamadour, was called Gabriel, together with his fiancée Mercedes, to whom García Márquez, many years later, would dedicate a famous love story set in the time of cholera. Gabriel left for Europe to become a writer after winning a literary prize. Wandering in a winding-sheet of words, he began to turn everyone he encountered into characters who seemed to have emerged from his own fictions. (Of his friend Salvador Allende, for example, he said that 'fate could only grant him that rare and tragic greatness of dying in armed defence of the anachronistic booby of bourgeois law'.) In the 1970s Gabriel, who had been living in Barcelona under the regime of the tyrant Franco, published a book designed to 'teach Miguel Angel Asturias how to write a dictator novel'. But Asturias had already written a dictator novel forty years before and died in 1974, a year before his teacher's work appeared. Though nothing would ever enable him to persuade the critics that his fiction in any way directly reflected historical

reality, Gabriel finally, fighting his way heroically out of such entangle-
ments, set out to write a novel about Latin America's greatest historical hero,
the liberator Símon Bolívar. He decided on the title 'The General in his
Labyrinth'.

In 1936 a boy was born in Peru. When, not so many years later – he was
almost a child prodigy – Mario Vargas Llosa's first novels appeared, critics
declared that here at last was a historic phenomenon, Latin America's first
master realist on the European model. This was curious, since the external
world of reality had scarcely penetrated the boy's consciousness in his early
years because he was obsessed with the disastrous comings and goings of the
relationship between his mother (who was always in) and his father (who was
always out): indeed they were separated at the moment of his birth.[4] Brought
up almost entirely by women, in the absence of external stimulants the young
man began to write about himself and his most intimate relationships.
Gradually he began to have intimate relationships in order to write about
them. No one was safe: all his experiences, all his relationships, dead or
alive, were devoured, digested and eventually excreted – condensed and dis-
placed – in a reproductive process even more obsessive than those that
afflicted Flaubert, Proust, Joyce and Faulkner before him, but one which
seemed exempt from the generative metaphors associated with myth-making
writers like the Nobel Miguel Angel and the Nobel Gabriel. This was fortunate, since incest and cannibalism were the obvious next steps and who could
tell whether Mario would have found himself able to resist.

Curiously, however, this perverse yet elegant realist, as the New Novel
began to be defined, began declaiming extraordinary things about the creative process: 'Writing novels is an act of rebellion against reality, against
God…. Each novel is a secret deicide, a symbolic assassination of reality….
The process of narrative creation is the transformation of our "demons" into
themes.' Many years later, readers would reflect that it was as well that
Mario had not at that time heard of an Islamic writer called Salman, for he
might have written a preemptive strike against his own religious creed
(perhaps entitled *Vatican's Seers*?). Instead Mario decided to become a 'New
Novelist' like Gabriel (at that time a good friend), whose literary biography
he later wrote, and took on another persona as he talked himself into it: 'The
new novelists, rather than inventors of stories, are inventors of languages, of
techniques…. Language has come to be the theme, the subject matter
itself…. The boundaries between the objective and the subjective world have
disappeared.' But who could really blame him? After all, once Latin
American writers became Magical Realists they gained consistently high
points on the international exchanges, whereas before import substitution,
when they were only producers of Social Realism (sorry, sugar), they
received consistently low marx. But we diversify: the most curious thing now

happened to Mario. As each of his books interwove things that had really happened to him, giving full names and addresses – ordinary things like marrying his Aunt Julia and then leaving her and marrying his cousin Patricia – with things that had happened to others or things he had only dreamed, the writer conjured himself into a fictional personage, eventually becoming the 'Varguitas' of *Aunt Julia and the Scriptwriter* and the famous novelist who appears in *The Real Life of Alejandro Mayta* or *'The Talker'* and lives in Vargas Llosa's house in Barranco, Lima. Emulating Borges, Mario could now say of his works, 'I do not know which one of us is writing this page.' Exhibitionist and voyeur at one and the same time, Mario might well claim that he is more honest than other writers about the true role of the novelist (a vulture which feeds on carry-on), although it is equally arguable that he really is, as he has often said, a striptease artist in reverse, one whose writings progressively cover up his real motives and eventually conceal his true identity altogether. Even from himself.[5] But even fantasy can become inadequate ultimately, and the writer can decide, like Aguirre, the 'Wrath of God', to 'make history as other men write plays'; so Mario, looking for real events to transpose, wrote a novel about a notorious massacre in Brazil, many years before, a war at the end of the world, and then joined a national commission to investigate a massacre of journalists in his own country of Peru; then, still seeking the unthinkable, wrote the first pornographic novel by a great Latin American novelist – another family romance entitled *'In Praise of the Stepmother'* – and finally decided that the only script which could still provide a frisson was the one in which he became President of Peru and thus journeyed – night errant along the Shining Path – through history as if through one of his favourite novels of chivalry.

Mario should have been born in Lima, but fate, and the separation of his parents, led him to the highlands and the city of Arequipa. Isabel Allende (anachronism: she will not appear until the next chapter) should have been born in the capital of Chile, but instead emerged, by chance, though prophetically, in unexpected exile in the capital of Peru, where Mario had failed to be born (his first and last failure in life). She was the niece of a Socialist Party politician who spent a lifetime failing to be elected, until 1970, when he finally became president of his country, only to be murdered in 1973 by barbarians whom no one had ever elected. Shortly after his death, his friend Pablo, the continent's greatest poet, also died, surrounded by soldiers, and Isabel marched behind the cortege to the graveyard. Unlike her masculine colleagues, Isabel had not planned to become a novelist (moreover she used to prefer Pablo's nature poetry to his political verse), but she found herself writing so-called fiction as a means of exorcizing the horrors of her uncle's assassination and the reign of terror which followed as Santiago tuned in to Chicago through international telephone and telegraph. Her book turned out to be the most successful novel in her continent since Gabriel's *One Hundred Years of Solitude*, which it somehow resembled, except that it had fallen to him to celebrate the opening of an era in Cuba in the early 1960s whilst it fell to her to lament its end in Chile in 1973; so his novel had ended with an incestuous reader deciphering a novel, his novel, in an empty room, whilst hers culminated with a writer composing a novel, Isabel's novel, in her prison cell, in preparation for letting the female genie, at last, out of the lamp and into the light. But enough. What is a nice girl like that doing in a His-Story like this? There must be some myth-take.

Eight years before Mario was born in Arequipa, six months after Gabriel was born in Aracataca, and fourteen years before Isabel was born in Lima, a Mexican baby emerged into the destiny of a magical reality, the world of North American culture: 'I was born on November 11, 1928, under the sign I would have chosen, Scorpio, and on a date shared with Dostoevsky, Cromelynck and Vonnegut. My mother was rushed from a steaming-hot movie-house in those days before Colonel Buendía took his son to discover ice in the tropics. She was seeing King Vidor's version of *La Bohème* with John Gilbert and Lilian Gish'.[6] It was, in short, the phantasmagorical story of a great baby (told in his book *Myself with Others*), now the Mexican novelist Carlos Fuentes, born into the best of all possible worlds and destined, come what may, to discourse his way, always triumphantly, through the labyrinths of the United States culture in which he was largely educated, the Mexican culture which he only fully discovered in his teens, and the European culture which is every Latin American's lost but always recoverable birthright through pilgrimage or conquest. Eventually Carlos became ambassador (of Mexico) in Paris, but resigned in protest when he heard that the author of a great massacre in 1968 was to become his close colleague in Madrid. In his *Terra Nostra* almost every other great writer and statesman in Hispanic history appears in the final pages, together with most of the great personages of Hispanic literature, whilst *Myself with Others*, possibly influenced by Mario's Cervantine reflections, includes Magical Realist essays entitled 'How I Started to Write' and 'How I Wrote One of my Books', and more conventional ones on – who else – Cervantes and Gabriel. The centrepiece was the only entirely fictional effort, 'Borges in Action', an intertextual tribute to the Great Deconstructor, starring Erasmus, Borges and Carlos himself, and centring on the function of fiction and the problem of identity, the mirror and the labyrinth. Carlos had always known how to keep the novel booming, and his strategy now was to use Borges's literary cosmopolitanism and transhistoricism to weave Latin American references, not least to himself, with remarkable sleight of hand, into his internationalist discourse, on equal terms. He had, as we have seen, two indisputable aces, Gabriel, the Latin American storyteller of the century, and Jorge Luis, the literary wizard.

Carlos played the hand as if his own future depended on it, for all he was worth, and got away with it. As Jorge Luis might have said, if all reality now is magical, then all writers are Latin Americans.

The list of them is long: Italo Calvino, Juan Goytisolo, Milan Kundera, Georges Perec, Umberto Eco, Salman Rushdie, Milorad Pavić and… Régis Debray. You do not have to be a Latin American in order to read – or even live – the great Latin American myth or write the great Latin American novel. Little Régis, born in France in the fateful year of 1940, claims in a self-fulfilling novel that he was really born (again?) as a political being in the United States in 1960, like the hero of Alejo Carpentier's *The Lost Steps*; rebounded from there in disgust to revolutionary Cuba, like the French eighteenth-century hero Victor Hugues in Carpentier's *Explosion in a Cathedral*; and was reborn again as a Latin American revolutionary in the tin mines of Bolivia in 1964.[7] His affair with Latin America really did begin, like Don Quixote's infatuation with knight errantry, through reading, in his case the works of Carpentier, himself yet another great reader. In Cuba Régis met Fidel, whom he thought to be an epic hero, king of the round table, and Che, a real-life knight errant pursuing the holy grail of revolution and bent upon a tragic death. The young Frenchman went underground in Venezuela and elsewhere with his first Latin American lover, wrote a series of influential but disastrously misguided (unfocused?) theoretical works, eventually followed Guevara to the Bolivian jungle, and after his death spent four years in a Bolivian prison, thereby missing May 1968 in Paris. For Régis Third World Revolution remained (as he puts it) a beautiful Dulcinea, and in his quest for her he pursued numerous real women who turned out, of course, to be mirages. But hold, Régis has written a biography, '*Masks*' (1987), out of Borges, Carpentier, García Márquez, Vargas Llosa and Fuentes, in which nothing is as it first appears. It seems the mirage of Revolution died in Santiago in 1973, when his friend Salvador Allende was murdered; there the French theoretician found a new lover, ex-companion of the martyred leader of the principal revolutionary party. He discovered that he was not, after all, a Latin American, as he had wished, and rediscovered his identity as revolution faded and he returned to his reason. Ironically, though, he really was entangled – the reader sees it more clearly than he – in a two-timing, double-crossing labyrinthine Latin American novel written, in life, by his new lover who betrayed him for ten years without him ever knowing it (one can but cry Fowles, *Mantissa*), and in book form by Régis himself once he found out. Having found out he attempted to rectify – rationalize – by writing a French novel, though he was actually – we see clearly – writing an archetypally Latin American novel. For the point of his story was, as he himself says, that he no longer knew what truth was or what fiction was, whether he was real or a character created by himself or someone else, but this still kept him one step ahead, which is important for a member of the avant-garde, because actually nobody knows these things and it is best to know this. Even when he became a minister in France's first government under the same Mitterrand who invited his friends Julio, Gabriel and Carlos to the grand inauguration, he had the sense that all he was doing was unreal. Though even then he failed to realize that the bewitching 'Silvia', his muse, his *fuego fatui*, his earth woman, his access to nature, had actually made him a character in her own life-text, a double of himself in spite of himself, a dupe and a dummy. Moreover, like Vargas Llosa's aunt and wife, Julia, who read about herself in his novel, found herself a character in a Colombian soap opera, and then took revenge by writing '*What Varguitas did not Say*', 'Silvia', alias Carmen, told her own life-story in a recent autobiography which is an even more exquisite retort, for there is not a mention of Régis between its covers. This story, surely, is a labyrinth to end all labyrinths.[8] Yet although, ironically (to us, not him), in escaping from the false realities of the Latin American Dream, he became entrapped in the Magical Reality of the Latin American Novel, the Frenchman tells us that the era of such adolescent longings is now over, and it is time to return to mature European realism once more – this is, after all, 1989. With one bound, realizing that the whole New World and its dream of the New Man had been naught but an illusion, he leapt free...

Meanwhile, across the Channel in London, that lit cit dominated not by Borges but by Burgess (and not just any old iron lady), another Ulyssean, Magical Realist writer sat meditating about his own journey through the cultural labyrinth. If Régis wanted out, Salman wanted in. He had been born in India (like Pamella, or Virtue Rewarded, or From Fleet Street to Wapping), in a Muslim family, at the very moment of its independence from the country in which he now lived. His first big novel, *Midnight's Children*, like Gabriel's big book, dealt with his country's experience since Independence, and ended on a similarly apocalyptic and enigmatic note, 'because it is the privilege and the curse of midnight's children to be both masters and victims of their times, to forsake privacy and be sucked into the annihilating whirlpool of the multitudes, and to be unable to live or die in peace.' Except if they are writers, one might have thought, but no, for it was written in the sacred book that if such a writer were to confuse reality and dreams by composing some satanic verses, forgetting that his fellows could not separate reality and dreams in the way that literary critics can, then, like one of Borges's characters, he would be dead from the moment of his crime, an arrow of vengeance would fly straight to his heart, already dead from the moment a Great Interpreter read those verses and proclaimed that it is the privilege and curse of midnight's child to be both master and victim of his times, to forsake privacy and be sucked into the annihilating whirlpool of the multitudes, and to be unable to live or die in peace.[9] Being thus confined to a vagabond, wandering, unsettled condition, Salman, archetypal twentieth-century exile, was without any certain abode; for though he had, in consequence of his angelic nature, a kind of empire in the liquid waste of air, yet this was certainly part of his punishment, that he was without any fixed place, or space, allowed him to rest the sole of his foot upon. All his fellow Magical Realists had been inspired to write by great massacres of the people, but only the ill-fated Salman's book provoked such massacres, demonstrating the dangers of writing Latin American novels aimed at other parts of the planet, lands of the past rather than the future, where truth and text were one and identity was not yet in doubt. Was it just a bad dream? Did it really happen? Impossible to say, because anything had become possible from the time that a Hollywood actor dreamed that he was a Great Communicator, president of the world's greatest country (commonly known at the time as the Great Satan), and woke up (briefly) to find that he was the president and anchorman of the world's greatest country, but what is certainly true and certain is that Salman became the most famous and the least celebrated writer the world has ever known.

In January 1989, at the same moment that Salman's satanic verses were proving, as Mario had once said, that literature is fire, a Supreme Pontiff attacked another bestselling work during a general audience, declaring that, contrary to the message of Umberto's two sacrilegious works, the path to God was not 'some labyrinth of the absurd' and that human life did not 'move inevitably towards death and nothingness'. John Paul, himself a poet ('Don't speak of unknowns,/ Man is not an unknown'), had perceived that both these works were distant Ecos of the Boom, as Latin American in lineage as the Liberation Theology for which he had publicly chastised one of his Cardinals in Managua. Umberto's earlier novel, *The Name of the Rose*, had paid homage to many world-renowned writers, including Cervantes and Conan Doyle, but above all to Latin America's Jorge Luis who becomes the blind librarian Jorge de Burgos, the ironic villain of the piece, lord of the library, land of the labyrinth into which Umberto's young narrator ventures: 'The image of Michael on the pyre became confused with that of Dolcino, and that of Dolcino with the beautiful Margaret. I felt again the uneasiness which had seized me in church. I put it out of mind and set off for the labyrinth. This was the first time I had entered it alone; the long shadows cast by the lamp on the floor terrified me quite as much as the visions of the previous night. At every moment I feared that I would find myself before another mirror, because such is the magic of mirrors that even when you know they are mirrors they still disturb you.'

No one knew better than Umberto that James the Irishman was really to blame, his works open to censure. James had written them, yes, in the period when Miguel, Luigi, Marcel, Thomas and André, yes, were elaborating

works about several or many counterfeiters searching through the mist, the
wasteland of lost time, for their illusive Author. James, for his part, started
one great novel about himself, wide awake, in the year the First World War
began and completed another, fast asleep, in the year the Second World War
began. Though dreaming all the while of Dublin and the past, he wrote some
of the first and all of the second in Paris, city of light and mirrors, which
taught the West to see, as Carlos, organizing an apocalyptic party for his literary friends, would later recall:

> Buendía, the Colombian, warned you when you arrived in France: Paris seems
> much larger than it really is because of the infinite number of mirrors that duplicate
> its true space: Paris is Paris, plus its mirrors.
>
> Late in life an aged Pierre Menard proposed that all beasts, men and nations be
> apportioned a supply of mirrors that would reproduce indefinitely their and other
> figures and their and other territories, for the purpose of appeasing for all time the
> imperative illusions of a destructive ambition for possession, although dominion
> only assures us the loss of what we have conquered as well as what is already ours.
> Only to a blind man could such a fantasy occur. And of course he was, in addition,
> a philologist.
>
> Oliveira, Buendía, Cuba Venegas, Humberto the mute, the cousins Esteban and
> Sofía, Santiago Zavalita, the man from Lima who lived every minute wondering at
> what precise moment Peru had fucked everything up, and who had come to Paris a
> refugee like all the others, wondering, like all the others – with the exception of the
> Cuban rumba-rhythm queen – at what moment Spanish America had fucked
> everything up.[10]

Why, from the very beginning, of course, García Márquez has said it time
and again, from time immemorial and forever more, but especially since, as
the Supremo said, they began writing 'great big novels in which the writer
parades the sacred nature of literature. False priests of the written word, their
works become lettered rituals, in which the characters fantasize with reality
or fantasize with language. They appear to officiate their ceremonies invested
with supreme authority, but become overwhelmed by the figures emerging
from their hands which they imagine they have created: this suffices to turn
their services into sir-vices. He who tries to relate his own life story becomes
lost in the immediate. One can only speak of an other.'

Gradually, these authors-in-search-of-a-character wrote less and less about
the ordinary people and more and more about themselves; yet, as if by magic,
their books, liberated, came to seem more imaginative the less imagination
was actually invested in them. Writing and writing and writing, like the
Graphographer whom Mario borrows from Salvador Elizondo to pen his epigraph at the start of *Aunt Julia and the Scriptwriter*, a novel about a boy
called Vargas Llosa who marries his aunt and will eventually write a novel

about a boy called Vargas Llosa who once married his aunt and would eventually, many years later, write a novel about a boy called Vargas Llosa who...: 'I write. I write that I am writing. Mentally I see myself write that I am writing and I can also see myself see that I am writing. I remember writing and also seeing myself writing. And I see myself remembering that I see myself writing and I remember seeing myself remember that I was writing and I write seeing myself write that I remember having seen myself write that I saw myself writing that I remembered having seen myself write that I was writing and that I was writing that I write that I was writing. I can also imagine myself writing that I had already written that I would imagine myself writing that I had written that I imagined myself writing that I had written that I imagined myself writing that I see myself writing that I write.' But then, as Augusto would have his Great Dictator say, somewhat self-righteously, writers, historically self-conscious, are sometimes naturally self-indulgent: 'They are not interested in recounting the facts but in recounting that they are recounting them'.[11]

If, say, on a winter's night a traveller, outside a town, leaning from the steep slope without fear of wind or vertigo, looks down in the gathering shadow in a network of lines that enlace, a network of lines that intersect on the carpet of leaves illuminated by the moon, what labyrinthine story there awaits its end? Why, of course, a Latin American story, *Around an Empty Grave*, by Calixto Bandera, one of the many pseudonyms of Italo Calvino, who was himself born on the Caribbean island of Cuba.[12] Efraín and María, Arturo Cova and Juan Preciado, Aureliano, Amaranta and Borges's Dahlmann – they are all there in those few pages, that Chinese box within a book. Earlier, however, Italo, thinking perhaps of Miguel Angel's Great Tribal Tongue, or Jorge Luis's Great Spirit of Literature, refers us to a legendary old Indian of a place called Cerro Negro, 'a man of immemorial age, blind and illiterate, who uninterruptedly tells stories that take place in countries and in times completely unknown to him. The phenomenon has brought expeditions of anthropologists and parapsychologists; it has been determined that many novels published by famous authors had been recited word for word by the wheezing voice of the Father of Stories several years before their appearance. The old Indian, according to some, is the universal source of narrative material, the primordial magma from which the individual manifestations of each writer develop; according to... others he is the reincarnation of Homer, of the storyteller of the Arabian Nights, of the author of the Popol Vuh, as well as of Alexandre Dumas and James Joyce; but there are those who reply that Homer has no need of metempsychosis, since he never died and has continued through the millennia living and composing, the author, besides the couple of poems usually attributed to him, also of many of the most famous narratives known to man'.[13]

Our revels now are ended. Latin America, for the time being and perhaps for many years yet, has become once more a great Home of the Story (but this time telling rather than being told), fount of labyrinths and mirrors (but now seeing as well as being seen), doubles and others (to be or to know, that is the subject), at the very time, 'tis said, when all the master narratives, and above all the supreme Author-ity of His-story, are at an end. Which we well may doubt, for, as Borges, reflecting on *Don Quixote*, once said, with definitive assurance, myth is at the beginning of literature and also (a way a lone a last a loved a long the) at its end.[14]

PART III

After the 'Boom'

10

Latin American Narrative Today

Latin America is always searching for its identity, I believe, because it is a 'Patria Grande', a great nationhood in formation, a job still to be done: it does not yet know its true face. Or, rather, it has not yet integrated its many faces, because when Latin America, now united by its contradictions, finally comes into being, it will be the result of the greatest mix of cultures, races, histories and geographies in the development of the human species.

The revelation of our identies, and of the common identity which will emerge from our astonishing diversity, depends on the recuperation of our history. Peoples who are unsure of where they come from, what roots, what mixtures, what acts of love, what violations, are unlikely to know where they are going. But this implies the discovery of our true history, lied about and betrayed by the winners, and it also means dragging history out of the museums: we are not the past. We have come from history, and history is the living memory of the times we have lived through and the tasks we have set ourselves.

Eduardo Galeano[1]

The 'boom' was really over by the time the three great dictator novels and *Terra Nostra* appeared in 1974–75, marking another moment of historical closure in Latin America. (*Terra Nostra*, like those dictator novels and *Conversation in the Cathedral* before them, was itself a meditation on patriarchy and authoritarianism.) In retrospect we can see that it was three different phenomena grouped under one name. Firstly, it was the culmination of fifty years of steady development in Latin American narrative, and to that extent was a climax (even though some wished to pretend that it was a break with the past or a self-generated upsurge of creativity). In this sense it corresponds to a particular phase within the process of modernity. But at the same time the reason why it was so visible from the start and, despite all the hype, so historically significant, is that it did mark the moment where Latin

311

American literature began to become generally internationalized and thus move fully 'into the mainstream' (Harss). That process of internationalization had begun in the 1920s, was complete by the 1960s, as far as the writers were concerned, and is now effectively complete as far as international publishing and readership is concerned – or will certainly be so by 1992. In this sense the 'boom' was not transient, but was the installation of a permanent state of affairs, in which Latin American culture is now fully integrated – however contradictorily – into Western culture, and is no longer considered under-developed or marginal. The third aspect, however, is that like most important historical moments, the 'boom' saw the completion of one development – Latin American Modernism – and the beginnings of another – Latin American post-Modernism. Here the great precursors once again were Asturias, in whose early linguistically experimental works much of Sarduy and the Mexican new wave can be found in embryo, but above all Borges, who has revolutionized our understanding of the relations between texts, especially the relation between 'literature' and 'criticism'. The great instiga-tor, however, was Julio Cortázar, whose *Hopscotch*, like the 'boom' itself, was trebly significant – in its own right, as a climax to Modernism, and as the point of departure for post-Modernism.

Looking back, we can see increasingly short timescales between the moments of effervescence, from Romanticism (1830s) through Modernismo and Naturalism (1890s), Avant-Gardeism and Social Realism (1920s), the New Novel (1940s), and the 'boom'(1960s). This suggests a sixth new wave to arrive some time in the 1990s. Given Latin America's own cultural momentum and the impetus of 1992, it will be surprising if the historical–generational rhythm does not produce something spectacular in the next decade – perhaps to do with Latin America's place among the plurality of nations and cultures. Clearly the present historical moment is a transitional one, and indeed we must believe it so, since the current four-sided frame of dictatorship and disappearance, debt and drugs, is not a scenario one would wish to imagine projected far into the future. At the same time it must be rec-ognized that the terms of trade remain historically against Latin America, as they have been for a century, and there are major political, social and ecolog-ical questions to be confronted. Only culturally do the prospects look positive: in this realm at least the world awaits Latin America's contribution with justifiable anticipation.

The last fifteen years have seen no settled pattern to Latin American fiction, though if one looks at individual national literatures there is a steadier and more familiar rhythm of evolution than the more varied continental scene: to make sense of that requires a long view, though many critics try to make continental judgments through virtual snapshots, which is easy if one merely wishes to be interesting, but difficult if one wishes to be reasonably accurate. Meanwhile European and North American readers and the press have warmly embraced the idea of a caricatured 'magical realist' style which is obviously supposed to reflect a stereotyped Latin America. This allows such readers both to enjoy the voluptuous delights of barbaric Otherness whilst satisfying the inherent sense of cultural superiority and ethnocentric attitudes that go with an ex-colonial mentality. And as we have seen, some Latin American novelists have responded to demand and played to the first-world gallery, sometimes losing sight of their own audience in the process. This is a historic error, without doubt, since the achievement of the great 'Ulyssean' novels lay precisely in their understanding of the relation between Latin America and the rest of the world, and in the construction of narratives which explored and mapped that history in a way accessible to both audiences. In this manner they attained that unity of the specific and the universal which has always been the key to artistic permanence.

There is no doubt that in a general way writers have been mesmerized – almost paralysed – by the horrors of the continent's contemporary history, a nightmare from which they are trying to wake up. This period has seen the death of old patriarchs (Neruda, Asturias, Carpentier, Borges; then Guimarães Rosa, Rulfo and even Cortázar), but also the unnatural deaths of numbers of younger writers due to political repression. Of the smaller countries by population, only Venezuela has remained reasonably stable and nonviolent over the period since 1960 but seems now to be entering a more turbulent era. Colombia, although formally democratic, has seen the continuation of appalling internal civil wars and violence as a national way of life. In Peru, the military experiment on the left was followed by a return to social democracy, the growth of Sendero Luminoso and the election of the first ever Aprista government at almost the worst possible moment. Ecuador's story is less dramatic but not dissimilar. Bolivia, convulsive as ever, has seen the end of its revolutionary MNR governments, populist military rule followed by right-wing repression growing to a crescendo in the 1980s with the despicable cocaine dictatorship of García Meza, now followed by a Chicago-type monetarist government under, of all people, the MNR's Paz Estenssoro. Chile, once the 'England of South America', has experienced the end of its Christian Democratic era, a brief but heroic socialist experiment and fifteen year's of Pinochet's barbaric military dictatorship. Uruguay, the 'Switzerland of South America', has seen the end of its much vaunted welfare state and democratic continuity, the Tupamaro struggle and savage military repression, with a huge proportion of the population imprisoned, exiled or murdered. Argentina has experienced its usual lurch between irreconcilable alternatives, from liberal democracy through military dictatorship, the return of Perón and the surreal reign of his widow, a decade of military repression unleashing unparalleled ferocity ended only by the absurd Falklands War, an Alfonsín

Radical government under constant pressure from all sides, and the return of the Peronists under Menem. Brazil, the first country in the continent to succumb to the new-style military governments, with blanket repression and censorship, death squads and other such innovations, and an economic miracle which turned out to be a mirage, is to be one of the last to return to the 'normality' guaranteed by all those essentially nineteenth-century constitutions. Most agonizing of all, Central America gropes ever more desperately for the necessary revolutions that will liberate the area from the twin scourge of ruthless oligarchical dictatorships at home and United States imperialism outside.

Only three countries, besides Venezuela, have seen virtually uninterrupted government stability in this period. In Paraguay General Stroessner remained in power until 1989 in the kind of comfortable, uninterrupted way that we associate with Porfirio Díaz, Salazar or Franco; and in Cuba, which opens this period of Latin American history, as it opened the century, Castro has maintained power and continued the revolution despite an international climate which has been essentially hostile ever since he took control. Stroessner and Castro are the only 'Supremos' who were in power throughout the period.

The third country is Mexico, where the survival of the one-party system controlled by PRI has looked increasingly problematical since 1968, but where the absence of military coups – indeed, of militarism *tout court* – the relative freedom of expression and absence from repression, make this large and contradictory country a political success, 'despite everything', as Fuentes's Artemio Cruz might say. Even there, however, the 1968 Tlatelolco massacre at the time of the Olympic Games marked the beginning of a period of crisis which shows no sign of abating, and the 1985 earthquake somehow confirmed this symbolically. Looking around at the alternatives, however, it may seem that even fragile continuity is better than none, and the benefits may be seen in the cultural ambit, where Mexico's stable national institutions, with few of the country's writers ever abroad for long,[2] gives the home scene a quite different feel to that of other countries.

It was in Mexico in one sense where the 'boom' was most strongly registered, because at least until 1968 Mexico's revolutionary past and stable present, together with a subtle 'Third Worldist' approach to Cuba–US (and later Chilean–US) relations, gave the country exceptional political and cultural prestige, and there was a concurrent boom in publishing in the 1960s, with the growth of influential new imprints such as the optimistically named Siglo XXI. Like the 'boom' itself in the cultural sphere, this only confirmed a tendency which had been evident since the 1920s. One of the defining features of Latin American intellectual life has been the absence of any settled centre other than Paris: no Latin American capital has been politically stable and open enough to maintain a continuity of cultural activity for more than a few years at a time, a fact which has had a decisive – and paradoxically beneficial – effect on the idea and the possibility of a 'Latin American Literature' and the particular Ulyssean shape it has taken during its voyage into the mainstream. Mexico City has undoubtedly been the nearest approximation to such a capital, but has operated more as a kind of safe harbour, given the continuing lure of Western Europe and the challenge of the pirate city of Havana.[3]

Given the difficulty of knowing which contemporary developments are likely to assert themselves and grow into significant historical movements of the kind identified by this study, the present chapter simply outlines current trends and identifies those writers and works which either display important continuities with the past or suggest promising avenues into the future

Popsters

> Where are the singers from?
>
> Severo Sarduy, (1967)[4]

Popular culture has been an increasingly influential source of material for Latin American writers since the transition from rural to urban fiction in the 1950s. Cortázar's interest in jazz was an early herald of the change. In view of the historical factors outlined above, Mexico proved a particularly fertile field for these new literary modes. Mexico City not only became, with Havana and Paris, a crucial axis of the ensuing period, but it also had its own mini-boom, with the emergence in the swinging sixties of that 'new wave' of hip young writers known as the 'Onda', centred on Mexico City's glitzy 'Pink Zone', and reminiscent of the 'Florida' group of avant-garde writers in Buenos Aires in the 1920s. The movement involved a curious mixing-in of United States beat, pop and psychedelic culture with Latin American literary ingredients like the works of Borges, Mexico's Arreola, Cuba's Lezama Lima, Cabrera Infante and Sarduy, and above all Cortázar's quintessentially 1960s mode. Its particular kind of linguistic frothiness was one more upsurge of the rather vacuous ornamentalism which has arisen every now and then in these baroque Indies from the age of Góngora through that of Darío and down to the present. In Mexico the new wave has taken most of its cues frrom the more volatile political and cultural avant-garde groups in Europe, the United States and Latin America itself, making for an extremely ambiguous relationship with the idea of consumer capitalism in general and the Mexican State in particular. The 'Onda' and its writers have continued to dominate Mexican cultural life in one form or another up to the present day, in an environment which still has a substantial number of little magazines and lively literary pages in both national and provincial newspapers. (A similar case in Argentina is Jorge Asís's *Flowers Stolen from the Quilmes Gardens'*, 1980). Without wishing to simplify excessively, it seems to me that the 'Onda', which has produced few historically transcendent works, should be counted less an example of European and North American influence and more as a Europeanizing and North Americanizing impulse, a desire for a cosmopolitan, non-Latin American, and in some cases anti-Latin American form of expression. It was, for the most part, in its juvenile and (essentially male-centred) playfulness, a false consciousness.[5] Needless to say, this is just as much a response to a neocolonial situation as the Americanist posture, except that the latter recognizes the realities of imperialism and seeks to produce counterrepresentations. Latin American artists will only be able to escape the conditions set by these interrelated force fields and the confusions to which they lead at the moment when imperialism itself comes to an end.

On the whole, then, this period has seen the divorce once more of Americanism and cosmopolitanism. Certainly the late 1970s and 1980s, despite growing world interest in the region, have not been a propitious time for literary Americanism, and in the late 1960s and especially after 1973 the pendulum swang away from this and its generally associated socialist criticism and culture, to be replaced by literature based essentially on the pleasure principle in the face of political despair. Given the predominance of labyrinthine structures in earlier fiction from the 1940s to the end of the 'boom', it is difficult to say whether the current situation is more or less confusing, but my own sense is that it is more so and that the misreading of a whole generation of fiction (1945–70), compounded by the failure to note the radical changes – essentially away from historical engagement – in the work of many leading writers since about 1970, would seem to confirm that critics are no more immune to the mirages created by their own situations than writers themselves. However, mythreading is something that none of us is ever exempt from, as the reader may even now be reflecting, close to the end of his or her long journey through this book.

It was probably developments in France once again (*nouveau roman* and *nouvelle vague*) which began to lead European and American literature back towards mystery, complexity and indecipherability, as writers turned away from such things as the Sartrean quest for meaning, self-invention and existential and political commitment. (Sartre's own loss of enthusiasm for Cuba at the end of the 1960s only served to deepen a development already evident in writers like Vargas Llosa, Fuentes and Goytisolo.) The French New Novel, powerfully influenced by Faulkner (though based on a highly selective reading of him), like Latin American fiction itself at this time, was picked up early by many writers (Carpentier's *'The Hunt'*, 1956, Cortázar, the Fuentes of *Holy Place*, Vargas Llosa), and exerted a somewhat sterile influence well into the 1970s. More pervasively influential, in fact, was its similarly anti-humanistic theoretical accompaniment, 'Structuralism', which ensured that Lévi-Strauss and Barthes were names that no fashionable Latin American writer could dare to overlook in interviews during the time of the 'boom' in magazines such as *Mundo Nuevo*.[6] Thus the 'post-boom' was under way at the very moment that the 'boom'itself became visible, and writers began to change direction at the very moment that their greatest literary achievements were being acclaimed. The 1980s have seen the hegemony of Derridian 'Post-structuralism', closely shadowed by the influence of Foucault and Lacan, whilst the left, in the midst of its acute disarray, has recuperated the dialogical Bakhtin – whose work is particularly helpful in the light of Latin America's 'bi-cultural' societies – and made out as best it could, in the face of a massive shift to French influence in the academies. This shift has been particularly noticeable in the United States (especially Yale). Its paradoxical features are many, not least the fact that the United States continues to cast an overwhelming spell over global 'popular culture' (which is nothing of the sort) in the widest sense, yet is currently, for the first time since the New World Independence movements in the half century after 1776, in the grip of the same French influence in 'high culture' as Latin America itself.[7]

The most successful of the writers who mix popular speech and popular culture into elusive avant-garde concoctions is not a Mexican, but Cuba's Severo Sarduy (1937–), a voluntary exile from the revolutionary island since 1960. Sarduy became an influential member of the *Tel Quel* group in Paris and produced a series of dazzling linguistic puzzles, such as *Gestures* (*Gestos*, 1963), *From Cuba with a Song* (*De donde son los cantantes*, 1967), *Cobra* (1975), *Maitreya* (1978) and *Hummingbird* (*Colibrí*, 1982). For some critics the neo-baroque Sarduy is one of the most important of all recent Latin American novelists, and it would be a mistake to think that his cruel, colourful miscegenations are merely escapist exercises which have no insights into Latin American cultural history. Nevertheless, when one considers what has been at stake in Cuba since he began to write, or, indeed, if one compares his narrative with the deadly serious explorations of Argentina's Manuel Puig (1932–), a writer with what at first sight would appear to be a similar project, Sarduy's work may be judged to be external – literally – to contemporary Latin American concerns.

Manuel Puig, in fact, seems by far the most important writer to have emerged out of the confused situation – which we must now call 'Post-modernist' – witnessed by and in Latin American fiction since the 'boom'. He is also one of the most successful both with the reading public and with critics. Puig in a sense combines Cortázar's pop Post-modernism with Roa

Bastos's dialectical self-awareness and steadiness of focus. He has made a certain way of reading contemporary society and a specific nexus of themes and problems virtually his own preserve. This problematic embraces mass and popular culture, Hollywood movies, TV soap operas and advertising, power relations and sexuality (especially machismo and homosexuality): in short, the tragic banality and distortion of life inside the capitalist cultural imperialist labyrinth. As the first writer to explore this world – dominated by mass-media developments in Mexico, Argentina and Brazil since the 1920s, and on the margins between lower-middle- and working-class culture – Puig has evolved a form of narrative composition and a flexible but always recognizable structural conception which contains and exposes the alienating effect of the mass media with almost Brechtian efficiency. In a sense he is the fictional equivalent of the Mexican cultural critic, Carlos Monsiváis, who likewise distances that which entraps and seduces him through irony and the techniques of the new journalism. One only has to compare Puig's approach with the undifferentiated world of Sarduy or with Vargas Llosa's standpoint in the hilarious but ultimately self-indulgent *Aunt Julia and the Scriptwriter*, to see the difference in ideological intention and critical edge.

Puig's major novels are *Betrayed by Rita Hayworth* (*La traición de Rita Hayworth*, 1968), *Heartbreak Tango* (*Boquitas pintadas*, 1969), *The Buenos Aires Affair* (1973), *The Kiss of the Spider Woman* (*El beso de la mujer araña*, 1976), *Pubis Angelical* (1979), *Eternal Curse on the Reader of These Pages* (*Maldición eterna a quien lea estas páginas*, 1980), and *Blood of Requited Love* (*Sangre de amor correspondido*, 1982).[8] Through his almost perfect parodies Puig gets close to the real world in which so many Latin Americans (not to mention Europeans and North Americans) are actually helplessly trapped, a labyrinth with no way out, because each time an exit is found through the raising of consciousness, some new stratagem is produced, a new corridor is opened, a new labyrinth of mirrors is constructed – as Julio Cortázar perceived with brilliant clarity in his Faustian interview for *Life* magazine.[9] Asturias's *The President*, through the love affair between his two central characters, showed his awareness that melodrama is the natural condition of much of Latin America's desperate – baroque? – emotional life. In his *The New Spanish American Novel*, published in 1969, Carlos Fuentes praised Vargas Llosa's *The Green House*, precisely for its 'acceptance of melodrama as one of the bases of Latin American social life.... When one lacks tragic consciousness, a sense of history or of oneself, melodrama supplies them: it is a substitute, an imitation, an illusion of being.'[10]

Puig's books were banned in his native Argentina for almost a decade. His most important novel is almost certainly *Kiss of the Spider Woman*, made into a famous film by Hector Babenco.[11] Its confrontation, in a prison cell, of a homosexual imprisoned for 'the corruption of minors' and a revolutionary

militant imprisoned for 'subversion', provides one of the most provoking
and illuminating episodes in contemporary fiction. Half the novel, presented
mainly through dialogue like a radio drama, is taken up with the stories told
by Molina, the lower middle class gay, to Valentín, the revolutionary activist
from an upper bourgeois background. These stories are not Molina's own,
but are his immensely detailed recollections of second-rate films he has seen
and loved. The other half of the novel is taken up with conversations
between the two men outside of these personalized film narratives, the occasional interior monologue, and such documentary materials as prison reports
and footnoted extracts from psychoanalytical and behaviourist theories of
homosexuality. The overall effect is stunning in lucidity and dialectical
impact.

As in other novels by Puig, the two characters are shown to be diametrical
opposites, but are brought closer together by their experiences, in one more
variation on Cervantes' partial rapprochement of Quixote and Sancho. As
Molina says:

> I don't know if you see what I mean... but we two are all alone, and our
> relationship – how can I put it? – can be moulded as we want it, it's not pressured
> by anyone else.... In a way we're completely free to act as we like towards one
> another, do you see? It's as if we were on a desert island. An island on which we
> may be alone together for years. Because our oppressors may be outside the cell,
> but not inside. Here no one is oppressing anyone else.[12]

The reader, who has already seen Valentín bullying and browbeating Molina
repeatedly in his efforts to 'liberate' him, nevertheless understands Molina's
utopian conception exactly, just as he or she also understands that it begs
every question there is about the internalization of repression and all its insid-
ious ideologies.

The point of departure is summarized effectively in the fact that Molina
calls Valentín by his first name, whereas Valentín, a socialist, distances his
cell-mate through the use of his surname. The authorities begin to poison
Valentín's food to weaken him for interrogation, and he is forced to rely
increasingly on Molina's ministrations, a physical dependence which
becomes increasingly psychological. Molina, meanwhile, is being bribed by
the authorities to betray Valentín by trapping him into releasing information
about his outside contacts: he responds by misleading them and playing for
time. Eventually the two men enter into a sexual relationship as Valentín's
emotional defences are lowered and he comes to need the stories which he
had originally scorned. Molina, whose entire life has been one of humiliation
and frustration, wishes his happiness to last for ever:

The great thing about being happy, you know, Valentín... is you feel it's for ever, you'll never feel bad again... Each time you've come to my bed... after... I've wanted to fall asleep and never wake up again. Of course I'd be sorry for Mama's sake, she'd be all on her own... but if it was just up to me, I'd want never to wake up again. But it's not just silly talk, really all I ask is to die.[13]

In a similar way, Molina feels that his brief happiness depends on not talking about it:

'Do you regret what happened?'
'No, I don't regret anything. I become more and more convinced that sex is innocence itself.'
'Can I ask you something... something really serious?'
'...'
'That we don't talk about anything, we don't discuss anything today. Just for today, I mean.'
'Whatever you say.'
'Don't you want to know why?'
'Why?'
'Because I feel... good... I feel... really good, and I don't want anything to take that away from me.'
'Whatever you say.'[14]

Undoubtedly it is Valentín whom the novel subjects to the most rigorous interrogation, given his own self-righteousness and his desire to transform society. He comes to understand that he has given in to desires – such as his attraction to the glamour of Europe and its women – which are in contradiction with his conscious values, and that he has failed to consider other groups of people – such as women in general, homosexuals, or those who have a lower level of political consciousness than himself – as full human beings with the right to lead their own lives, however 'deluded', in the way they choose and as best they can. He has in fact exploited them. The following dialogue, late in the novel, is typical of Puig's ability to marshal ironies and contradictions at every moment of his narrative. Valentín has finally come to accept Molina's sexuality and is trying to think seriously about his cell-mate's human rights:

'If you like being a woman... you shouldn't think less of yourself for it.'
'...'
'Do you see what I mean. What do you think?'
'...'
'I mean you don't have to pay with something, with favours, keep apologizing because you like it. You don't have to... lower yourself.'
'But if a man... is my husband, he has to give the orders, so he'll feel good.

That's only natural, because he... he's the man of the house.'

'No, the man of the house and the woman of the house have to be equal. If not, it's exploitation.'

'Then there's no fun in it.'

'Why?'

'Well, it's a bit embarrassing, but since you ask... Part of the fun is that when a man holds you... you feel a bit afraid.'

'No, that's wrong. Who put that idea in your head, that's all wrong.'

'But that's how I feel.'

'You don't really feel it, you were taken in by whoever fed you that garbage. To be a woman, you don't have to be... I don't know... a martyr.'[15]

Puig's book is clearly within the Hispanic tradition of prison literature discussed in chapter 4, in which the human mind itself is the site of the struggle for freedom which the cell would seem to negate. He uses the relation between its two characters to play off, often ironically, the various class, gender and political tensions implicit in their 'male–female' relationship (intellectuals and workers, law and fantasy, theory and practice, writing and speech, etc.). Most remarkable of all, perhaps, as in his other novels, is Puig's ability to maintain precisely the required distance from his materials and master the plurality of discourses available in his alienated neocolonial world. His chosen space is the realm of fantasy, but there is no question of the artist himself giving 'free' play to his own desires. On the contrary these are always mediated through a controlling vision which is sometimes cruel in its effects though never in its motivation. I know of no writer, moreover, who has shown more clearly the decisive influence of storytelling. Stories are not merely relevant to tribal cultures or to our own 'primitive' stage, when we are children, but to every moment of human existence. In everything we think or do, we tell ourselves stories about ourselves or others, in the present, the past or the future, and Puig's achievement is not only to give material form to this not always evident reality but to assist us in exploring what hidden impulses, fears or desires come together to shape the discourse of these stories at any given moment. We are reminded again of the historic shift in Latin American fiction from the open fields across which Gallegos gazed at the future horizon, to the labyrinths which later writers have been forced to enter.

The novel ends with Molina's death, killed soon after his release as he attempts to make contact with Valentín's comrades; and with Valentín's dream, after a savage torture session, about a tropical island on which there are only women – beautiful native girls, his mother, his girl friend and the sad Spider Woman of the title: 'I ask her why she is crying and in a closeup which fills the screen at the end of the film she says that is what no one knows, because it's an enigmatic ending...'[16] No recent work of fiction shows more clearly the contemporary Latin American novel's ability both to work within its own historical traditions and to explore the most difficult and controversial issues of modern society. Like *The President* in its day, Puig's novels make us look into the abyss, the ideological prison, in order to liberate ourselves from chains which are partly self-imposed. Who, in Britain or the United States, has written such radical, subversive and deconstructive texts as these? Looking back at the previous chapter, post-Puig, one can begin to see just how much Latin American fiction, produced in a continent fated always to be inventing, creating or developing itself, has contributed towards what one might call the narrativization of contemporary existence.

Political Writing

What we writers can do is insignificant in the face of the panorama of horror and oppression that the southern part of Latin America presents today; nevertheless we must do it and indefatigably seek new ways of intellectual struggle.

Julio Cortázar, 1978

Puig's clear-sighted fiction was one response to the challenge of what to write as the 'boom' reached its crescendo in the late 1960s and early 1970s. Meanwhile, of course, out in the real Latin America, if I may invoke such a concept, men, women and children were dying, disappearing and suffering torture on a historically unparalleled scale due to something even more horrendous than the usual slow death from poverty and enslavement over the centuries. Latin America became sucked into the Cold War and the diversion of global conflict into the world's underdeveloped regions after 1945, as world war has continued unabated in all parts of the planet. In that sense World War Three is already happening, and World War Four, nuclear holocaust, or Five, ecological catastrophe – are still waiting in the wings. These are all themes which must figure in any history of a continental culture today.

This is why the political posture of a line of great writers from González Prada and Martí through Neruda and Vallejo, Asturias and Carpentier, to Arguedas and Roa Bastos, is so important. It brings together a number of considerations which have been at or near the centre of our discussion, which are essential in any project to liberate the labyrinth, and may be summed up as consciousness and commitment. In that sense José María Arguedas marked out some of the outer limits of the era. *Deep Rivers* was an unfinished story, as Ernesto went off to join the Indians, perhaps as an ethnologist, perhaps as a missionary, perhaps even as a revolutionary. In '*Everyone's Blood*' Rendón Wilka sacrificed himself suicidally, as apparently the only historical gesture then available to him. Arguedas himself appears to have come to the conclusion, implied in 'The Fox Above and the Fox Below', that there was little else for an Indian-oriented novelist to do, and sacrificed himself too, possibly in a way that was historicaaly demoralizing, although it undoubtedly dramatized the intractable nature of the 'Indian problem' and the 'national question' in Peru. Manuel Scorza's five-part series, The Silent War (1978), continued this tradition, but Scorza too died before time in the air crash which also killed Angel Rama, Marta Traba and Jorge Ibargüengoitia in 1983.

The socialist realists – and others – had been commiting themselves to Latin America for half a century through the subject matter of their novels, and politically through the perspective a number of them adopted on revolution, emancipation and liberation. By the time of the 'boom' such writing was out of fashion. There have been rather few successful Communist novelists, except of course in Cuba, and the only well-known Marxist novelists to emerge after the 1930s movements in Ecuador and Brazil were Jorge Amado, who turned away to spicy bestsellers, and Miguel Angel Asturias, with his controversial Banana Trilogy, which effectively earned him the Lenin Peace Prize in 1966, the very year in which he fell out of favour by accepting an ambassadorship in Paris. What has happened since 1960, however, and more particularly since the Cuban Missile Crisis of 1962, is that as Latin America has entered the world's consciousness through television receivers and newspapers, the old social novels have been replaced by a more overtly political kind of writing which has, so to speak, entered via the space opened up by the 'boom'.[17]

Roa Bastos is particularly important in this regard, since the lessons he learned from the narrative experience of the half century before him led him to take up a distinctive standpoint. In Son of Man – Paraguay's belated equivalent of The Underdogs – the implicit posture is quite close to the Maoist position, in the sense that the people are encouraged to find their own leaders, mistrust petty-bourgeois elements, and apply the laws of practice and contradiction to politics and revolutionary action. Roa confronts head-on the challenge of the historical interpretation of reality. The history of Latin American fiction shows that, like Oedipus, many Latin American writers are blinded from the outset and have no intention of facing up to the questions Roa poses in a work published, appropriately enough, in 1960. Cuba then determined the historical parting of the ways, and the progression from self-doubt to historical blindness by a writer as intelligent as Vargas Llosa is exemplary in revealing the historical tensions involved for artists and intellectuals from that time. Paz had shown the way to this form of detachment and scepticism and has maintained the position ever since. Borges, apparently indifferent to history, never tried. For such writers reality is ultimately a labyrinth, history another, and all consciousness, including their own, in which the others are reflected, refracted aand distorted, the greatest labyrinth of all.

For Roa Bastos, however, this will not do. The structure of *Son of Man*, designed, like that of *Time of the Hero* and *Conversation in the Cathedral*, to discredit its intellectual protagonist, pursues the question of the relationship of consciousness to conscience with a tenacity which in practice must have brought him close to contemplating the position subsequently adopted by a movement like Sendero Luminoso. However, an acknowledgement of Latin American social realities gives his examination a Christian slant which makes it more reminiscent of Liberation Theology, at a time when the response of most intellectuals to the guerrilla struggles and military repression of the 1970s was to retreat into positions of agnosticism, apoliticism or simple despair, not to mention convenient conversions to right-thinking postures. Roa, too, ended with a declaration of despair, as his protagonist thinks about the peasant characters we have met in the novel:

> I don't think only of them. I think of all the other human beings like them, degraded to the very limits of their condition, as if suffering and humiliated man was always and at all times the only one fated to be immortal.
>
> There must be some way out of this monstrous contradiction of man crucified by man. Because otherwise one would have to think that the human race is accursed for ever, that this is hell and that we cannot hope for salvation. [18]

But of course this despairing reaction, though more than understandable in anyone who has studied or witnessed the condition of Latin America's Indian peasants over the course of time, is expressed by a character whom Roa has specifically discredited in advance – which does not of course mean that he excludes himself from the depiction.

Roa moved on from such an extremist position only because of its apparent non-functionality in practice – before the triumph of the Sandinistas in 1979 – but did not abandon the essential concept of moral and political commitment. *I the Supreme* was the result, perhaps the most challenging novel in contemporary Latin American history, a shift of ground from 'vulgar' reductionist, voluntarist or populist positions towards a self-analytical, self-critical but also profoundly dialectical form of fiction which has had few parallels in Western literature. The author appears in the novel not disguised as a character, but as himself, the 'compiler', as if to say: 'Look, the world is complex whatever we choose to do, but the voice behind this book is not just "the" voice, or "discourse", or "textuality", still less "your trustworthy nineteenth-century friend", but me, Augusto Roa Bastos, born in place X in year Y, history as follows, political posture as follows, point of view on the characters and events of this novel, also as follows; or if you do not believe me, work it out for yourself.' This is at the other extreme from , say, Güiraldes's *Don Segundo Sombra*, in which we do not know who is talking until the end, when it becomes someone decidedly other than the man, Güiraldes, who is really talking. That is also why Roa Bastos has always been reluctant to give interviews without a kind of 'health warning' appended to them, not to mention his belief that what the people say is more important than anything he will ever say, and that words are not the only way in which culture, history, experience are maintained: they are everywhere, in everything. In this, as in other questions, he moves in the same direction as *Men of Maize* ('I am not creator, but the vehicle, the medium through which these things have been said').

As mentioned above, the last such work in which a writer confronted his countrymen and a dictator in the same way was Sarmiento's *Facundo* 130 years before. There is a very real sense in which the arrogant and patriarchal Author, Sarmiento, and the self-effacing, self-doubting Compiler, Roa Bastos, open and close a whole chapter, a hundred years of solitude. Both works are documentaries, both are in a sense complied and selected, both are political acts that know their own status and their own – dialectically opposite – intentions.

Cuban Narrative Since the Revolution

Just like five years before, he remained trapped inside himself, incapable of escaping from his labyrinth; drowning in his lack of context. He probably never suspected the relation between his solitude and the country's confusion, nor the historical explanation for that confusion. He never suspected that his private notes formed part of the history of Cuba. Neither did I discover my modest historical self until after the triumph of the Revolution. Now I see my father like a lost child, with a pity perhaps similar to his the few times he saw me before he died; but I too am lost in another way in another labyrinth.

Cintio Vitier, '*From Peña Pobre*', 1975

In one sense Cuban fiction since the Revolution has been disappointing. There have been as many novels and short stories as one might expect from a country of Cuba's size, and many of them interesting and accomplished, but rather few of them have been about the postrevolutionary era as such, and none of those can be ranked unequivocally among the great Latin American classics. Nevertheless there have been many excellent novels: *Memories of Underdevelopment* (1965) by Edmundo Desnoes (1930–), '*The Children Say Goodbye*' (*Los niños se despiden*, 1968) by Pablo Armando Fernández (1930–), '*Rachel's Song*' (*Canción de Rachel*, 1969), an early testimonial novel by Miguel Barnet (1940–), '*The Last Woman and the Next Battle*' (*La última mujer y el próximo combate*, 1971), a socialist equivalent of *Doña Bárbara* by Manuel Cofiño (1936–), '*Bread and Sleep*' (*El pan dormido*, 1975), a historical novel set in Santiago de Cuba by José Soler Puig (1916–), and '*From Peña Pobre*' (*De Peña Pobre*, 1979) by Cintio Vitier (1921–), an ambitious panoramic work spanning the period from the 1890s to the 1970s and uniting the writer's Christian point of departure with his Marxist present. Vitier is one of the major members of the prerevolutionary *Orígenes* group, whose most influential figure was of course Lezama Lima, author of the monumental *Paradiso* (1966). Like Cabrera Infante's *Three Trapped Tigers*, Lezama's novel was essentially retrospective and in no important sense revolutionary. Perhaps Carpentier's '*Rite of Spring*' (*Consagración de la primavera*, 1978) is the closest to an approved revolutionary text, which integrates the past with the present, from 1920s Paris and Moscow to 1960s Havana and a window on the future, as testimony to a Revolution which, according to Carpentier, 'made me find myself in the context of a whole people'.[19] It is a kind of sequel to *Explosion in a Cathedral* (1962), an affectionate act of faith in the young revolutionary state, which ends at the moment of revolutionary triumph and the inauguration of a new socialist culture. As for the failure of works by younger writers to find success, political anxieties might be one of the explanations, but the more likely one is that writing fiction seems an unheroic and unassertive activity in comparison with film and television, poetry and song, art and dance. There is, moreover, the question of the usual time lapse required for perspective – particularly crucial here – and one might expect to see a great blockbuster, written probably by someone who was about twenty in 1959, some time in the 1990s.

Of course, if Vargas Llosa is correct, and great fiction feeds on misery as vultures feed on carrion, then Cuba will produce good fiction only through its exiled or imprisoned dissidents. The signs thus far are not encouraging. Either way, there seems little doubt that a novel with the dimensions of a *War and Peace* could be written about that country's turbulent but magnificent history, either since the 1830s, or since the 1890s, or the 1920s, or 1954, with the struggle in the mountains, the taking of power in 1959, the Bay of Pigs and Missile Crisis, and the military adventure in Africa. *Memories of Underdevelopment* remains the best-known novel about the revolutionary period, a work squarely in the tradition of feckless, disenchanted intellectuals incapable at first of believing in anything, least of all a revolution.

In *The Eyes of the Interred*, published in 1960, Asturias had ended his *Banana Trilogy* by imagining the eventual triumph of the Guatemalan workers' movement through a successful revolutionary upheaval, without actually dramatizing this counterfactual victory in his text. Roa Bastos's *Son of Man* was probably the last significant book about commitment completed before the triumph of the Cuban guerrillas. From 1959 it was known, at last, that socialist revolution was possible in the Americas, under some circumstances and against all the odds (though usually requiring some temporary loss of attention or softening of its stance on the part of the United States, as happened again with Nicaragua during the Carter presidency). Theorists began calculating the impact of Cuba and the prospects for revolution elsewhere in the continent throughout the 1960s, whilst the United States built its Alliance for Progress. Following Castro's *Words to the Intellectuals* in 1961 ('Inside the Revolution, everything; outside the Revolution, nothing'), Cuba underwent the same process of debate which had taken place in the USSR between 1917 and 1934, or in China after the Yenan discussions of 1937, culminating in the decisive events of 1971, and the parting of the ways and *prises de position* from that time onward. Article 38 of the 1976 Constitution specifies that 'Artistic creation is free so long as its content is not contrary to the revolution' and that 'Forms of expression in art are free'.

Discussions about art and society and art and politics were focused very much on Cuba's *Casa de las Américas* after 1960, challenged in due course by *Mundo Nuevo*, edited by Emir Rodríguez Monegal from Paris (both names tell their own story in terms of ideology and intention), and by *Libre*, in 1971, from that same home of emigrés, exiles, dissidents and mere apathetics or anti-Latin Americans (the best-known ones were on the right in the 1960s and 1970s, as they had been on the left in the 1920s and 1930s). The question that lay between them was: could the circle be squared, could a New Left revolutionary culture, committed to socialism, yet open to all currents, exist in the circumstances of the Cold War? There were innumerable discussions on this score up until 1973, most notably those published by Siglo XXI in Mexico on intellectuals and the Revolution, and the influential debates entitled *Revolution in Literature and Literature in the Revolution*, involving Oscar Collazos, Julio Cortázar and Mario Vargas Llosa.[20] Critics like Angel Rama and David Viñas appeared on the scene, and revolutionary fists were raised in meetings and newspapers everywhere on the continent and in 'Latin American' meetings elsewhere right up to and including 11 September 1973.

Reinaldo Arenas, *Farewell to the Sea*

Perhaps the most important of the dissident Cuban novelists is Reinaldo Arenas (1943–), whose early works were '*Celestino before Dawn*' (*Celestino antes del alba*, 1967) and the celebrated *Hallucinations* (*El mundo alucinante*, 1969), a magical history of the pre-Independence period in Latin America. Had he been born outside Cuba, Arenas would probably have become one of the most successful Latin American exponents of the Magical Realist mode, but fate decreed that he was to live in a country where the Social Realist – or, indeed, socialist realist – mode would dominate, and little by little he found this and other restrictions on his personal freedom not only unacceptable but quite literally intolerable. In 1980 he took refuge in the United States and in 1982 published his most substantial novel, *Farewell to the Sea* (*Otra vez el mar*, 1982). The novel bears the following postscript: 'First version disappeared, Havana, 1960. Second version confiscated, Havana, 1971. The present version smuggled out of Havana, 1974, and published in Barcelona, 1982.' It tells the story of a disillusioned revolutionary poet and his wife, whose marriage falls to pieces at the same pace as their revolutionary enthusiasm. Much of the book is written in the form of improvized poems. It is without doubt the most representative of the anti-Castro works, communicating with an edge perhaps too raw for full effect an experience of claustrophobia which Arenas could hardly bear:

> Go on?
> Not go on?
> That is the question.
> How are we to suffer the slings and arrows of the mere fact of being alive, the certainty that soon we will cease to be? How, then, are we to bear the standing in line for croquettes, the insult of aging, the prime minister's speeches, the unanswerable interrogations (the mockeries) that time always slings at us, the compulsory hunger praised in 'glorious' verbiage, the warmth of the tropics, the horror of the tropics, the irrevocable gestures of adolescents, the solitude without subterfuge or comfort, the tyrant's humiliation, the repeated betrayal by our friends, the weekly assembly, the food without salt, the dirty shirt, the full bus, the tap without water, the Bulgarian movies, the loss of almost all our hatreds and passions, the life reduced to one-dimensional stupor, the sexual persecution, the ostracism without appeal, the appropriation of our tiniest dreams.... Our unavoidable, clear condition of slavery, the fact of having been born into the muted crowing of an island, the terrifying helplessness of an island, the prison–prison–prison that is an island?... How, then, tolerate so much gibing and scorn, so much stupor, so much noise, so much implicit or explicit meaness, so much ass-wiggling, so much crowing, so many empty shrieking figures, so much sadness and impotence, fury and pain, when the light thrust of metal into my body, the sweet rope, or a bullet through the temple is enough?... Go on? Not go on? That is the question.[21]

For many readers this novel is a classic condemnation of life under Communism. Yet it has a hysterical tone which sits uneasily with the principled opposition which the case seems to require. Arenas escaped to the country which had been contributing to the claustrophobia by blockading Cuba for 20 years, and which had run it as an informal colony for the previous 60. He claims to have been disenchanted by the actual course of the Revolution, but seems so concerned by inessentials (I speak of deodorants, not freedom) that almost any Third World revolution might have repelled him. Above all, and this applies to Cabrera Infante and Padilla before him, his insistence on comparing Cuba not with, say, Nicaragua or Paraguay, but with France or the United States means that he is inevitably seeking to privilege the possibilities of the intellectual – who is always able to 'escape' if he wishes – as compared to the mass of the people. This may seem 'inevitable', but it needs to be taken into account. Cuban writers have undoubtedly been imprisoned and tortured. None has disappeared or been executed.

Jesús Díaz, 'The Initials of the Land'

Jesús Díaz (1941–) is a quite different case. He has participated fully in the Revolution since the beginning, and his story is one of astonishing ups and downs, that of a man who (like his fictional protagonist) has hung on to the twists and turns of the revolutionary dialectic with remarkable tenacity and suffered. He fought as a high-school student against Batista, became leader of those same students after 1959, took part in the Bay of Pigs campaign, founded the magazine El Caimán Barbudo in 1966 and won the Casa de las Américas prize that same year with his short stories 'The Hard Years' (Los años duros). In 1969 to 1970 he participated physically in the ill-fated campaign to harvest 10 million tons of sugar and then prepared a first version of 'The Initials of the Land' (Los iniciales de la tierra, 1987) at the height of the hard-line response to the Padilla affair in the early 1970s. The book was not well received and was not published. Díaz was by then working in the Cuban Film Institute (ICAIC) and became a successful director. He also produced a further short-story collection, 'Song of Love and War' (Canto de amor y de guerra, 1978), and an important documentary work, 'On the Fatherland and Exile' (De la patria y el exilio, 1979), based around a film he made on the same subject. However 'The Initials of the Land' is in a sense the distillation of his life thus far, and is probably the most important novel written from within the Revolution by a writer who has lived through 'the hard years' (to quote his short-story title). Its opening sequence also shows, unmistakably, that this is the first novel of the Revolution to adopt the conventions of the Great Latin American Novels of the 1960s:

He stopped reading, with the obscure certainty of being trapped in a labyrinth, and at that moment Gisela returned from ward duty dead with exhaustion, and leaned over the form, the straightforward tell-me-your-story in the face of which Carlos had spent the night trying to reconstruct his past and wondering why he had done this and not that, why he almost never achieved what he wanted but only what chance, or fate, or who knows what decided, as if his life was an irreversible blunder he always recognized too late and was now accusing him, from that still blank form, questioning and mute beneath Gisela's gaze, as she encouraged him with a conspiratorial kiss on her way to the bathroom, whilst he went back to his questions, his obsessions, his desperation, until he heard the hiss of urine like a call in the silence of the night with the curious certainty that he had already lived that moment. But no, it was Iraida then and things could have turned out differently: for example, if he hadn't slept with her he wouldn't have been expelled from the Youth Movement, nor caused Gisela such misery, nor suffered the torment of those blind days that surrounded him after; but then, where else did he find the strength to go and cut cane if not from that despair? No point going on, everything led to the labyrinth; even the hiss ceasing and the shower running, sending him on, for no reason, to José Antonio, perhaps the biggest mistake he'd ever made in his life, that ziz-zagging trajectory that was rattling around his memory and at times appeared indecipherable. What would they ask him at the assembly? What criticisms would they make? He, who had wished to be a hero and would still like to set an example, what was he in reality?[22]

This is an original approach to the problem of Latin American identity, as the 31-year-old protagonist wrestles with his life in order to justify to himself, and then to his comrades, that he deserves to be considered an 'exemplary worker' and thus a candidate for membership of the Communist Party. Like Artemio Cruz in Fuentes's novel, looking back over the aftermath of another revolution, Carlos examines his own past, his efforts to know and to be himself, the choices he took and the mistakes he made. A non-Cuban reader is inclined to respond with astonishment to the fact that a man who confronted as many challenges as Carlos, and made as few mistakes, should be subjected to such an arduous and discouraging odyssey away from revolutionary respectability and back again, and at that point reflects that this may be because the novel is substantially (though obviously not completely) autobiographical. The book interweaves the key episodes in Carlos's life with the key events of Cuban history since the late 1950s and gives unique insight into what it has been like to live through this passionate but also painful and contradictory experience. The interrelation of Carlos's failures with those of the Revolution, culminating in the disatrous failure to achieve the 1970 harvest, is less mechanical than in Fuentes's novel and more suggestive:

> If it was a case of telling the story of his life, he would have to start with his grandfather, because that was the first important memory he had, that and an illiterate girl called Toña he'd fallen in love with.... He stopped, panting. If he went on down that road, trying to escape from the stock formula he would end up in a labyrinth. What the hell did it matter that he'd fallen in love with Toña. What did that have to do with his trajectory? The comrades would have to forgive him, he was a bit nervous. [23]

The labyrinth referred to here and elsewhere is evidently the range of confusions involved in mixing the personal and the political. Carlos thus attempts to escape the 'temptation of the labyrinth' whilst his inquisitors attempt to find the 'line' that unites all his efforts and which for one of them is his persistent 'ideological weakness', though another – who speaks most directly to the reader – says that Carlos's story has been 'a desperate and sometimes pathetic struggle to live up to the standards of his times', times which involved commitment, taking risks and exposing oneself to life and its dangers and to history and its ironies. The book also makes strenuous efforts to integrate the Cuban popular culture and United States mass-media influence of his childhood. It then shows his adolescent days, recalling the same kind of *machista* camaraderie so exalted in Cabrera Infante's novels, and charting Carlos's slow movement away from this towards a more egalitarian relationship with the women in his life, culminating in his painful efforts to overcome his jealousy at his wife's unfaithfulness (provoked, in point of fact, by his own). Appropriately, and significantly, the novel culminates with a violent disagreement on this subject between the men and women present at the assembly, on the last page of the novel. The book then ends with the Chairperson (a man) inviting those present to vote for or against Carlos. The decision is of course the reader's.

Space precludes discussing the narrative fiction produced elsewhere in the Caribbean and Central America, a region where in general the tradition of revolutionary literature has been at its strongest over the past century. Such classics as 'Mamma United Fruit' (*Mamita Yunai*, 1941) by the Costa Rican Carlos Luis Fallas (1911–66) and Asturias's *Banana Trilogy* have been followed by *Ashes of Izalco* (*Cenizas de Izalco*, 1966) by the Salvadorean Claribel Alegría and her husband Darwin Flakoll from the United States, on the 1932 uprising in El Salvador in which 32,000 peasants were massacred; 'Poor Poet that I Was' (*Pobrecito poeta que era yo*, 1970), by Roque Dalton (1935–75), tragically murdered by his own guerrilla comrades; *To Bury our Fathers* (*Te dio miedo la sangre?*, 1977) by Sergio Ramírez (1942–), a leading Sandinista politician; the inspiring *Fire from the Mountain* (*La selva es algo más que una inmensa estepa verde*, 1981) by another revolutionary novelist, Omar Cabezas; the rumbustious *Macho Camacho's Beat* (*La guaracha del Macho Camacho*, 1980) by Luis Rafael Sánchez (1936–) of Puerto Rico; and an outstanding sequence of novels by Manlio Argueta (1935–) of El Salvador, including 'The Valley of the Hammocks' (*El valle de las hamacas*, 1970), 'Little Red Riding Hood in the Red Zone' (*Caperucita en la zona roja*, 1977), *One Day of Life* (*Un día en la vida*, 1980), and *Cuzcatlán* (*Cuzcatlán, donde bate la mar del sur*, 1986), which provide brilliantly focused solutions to the problems of writing about peasant characters at a time of repression and revolution.

Argentine Literature Since 1976

The first anniversary of the present military junta has been the occasion for many official documents and speeches evaluating the government's activities during the past year. However, what you call successes were, in fact, failures; the failures that you have recognized were crimes; and you leave out all mention of the calamities... These are the thoughts which I wished to share with the members of the junta on this first anniversary of your disreputable government, without hope of being listened to, in the certainty of persecution, but faithful to the commitment I made a long time ago to bear witness in difficult times.

Rodolfo Walsh, 'Open Letter', March 1977

Since 1973, when the Allende government was overthrown in Chile, and the peaceful socialist road was blocked, literature in Chile, Argentina and Uruguay has had to come to terms with a series of shattering experiences. In Chile José Donoso had published his *Obscene Bird of Night* in 1970, the year that Allende was elected, and became the fifth member of the 'boom' at a moment where such metaphysical explorations were soon to seem frivolous. After the overthrow Antonio Skármeta (1940–), with *I Dreamt the Snow was Burning* (*Soñé que la nieve ardía*, 1975) and *Burning Patience* (*Ardiente paciencia*, 1985), and Ariel Dorfman (1942–) with *Widows* (*Viudas*, 1981) and *The Last Song of Manuel Sendero* (*La última canción de Manuel Sendero*, 1982), among others, made the Chilean literary response to the coup. In Uruguay Carlos Martínez Moreno's *The Inferno* (*El color que el infierno me escondiera*, 1981) was a striking equivalent.

Peruvian literature has also provided interesting examples of the challenge of political engagement at a time of literary self-referentiality. In '*The Outrageous Life of Martín Romaña*' (*La vida exagerada de Martín Romaña*, 1981), Alfredo Bryce Echenique (1939–) tells the story of a young Peruvian in 1960s Paris delegated by an extreme left group to write a socialist realist novel about the Peruvian fishing unions. Instead, the protagonist, who frequently curses the well-known novelist Bryce Echenique, writes an experimental work on a non-transcendent subject in which its own author makes frequent appearances. Already in 1978 Manuel Scorza, the last of the great indigenist novelists, had included himself and some of his articles and documents in '*Tomb of the Lightning Flash*', the culmination of his five-part series, *The Silent War*, about the Indian struggle for survival in the high sierras and their unsuccessful battle against the Cerro de Pasco Mining Company. In '*The Motionless Dance*' (1983), published in the year of his tragic death, Scorza went even further by writing a novel on Bryce's theme, but one which moved in exactly the opposite direction (it is also eerily reminiscent of Debray's later '*Masks*', whose format it also inverts): a writer in Paris, member of a Peruvian guerrilla movement, falls in love with a beautiful Parisian bohemian as he tries to write a story about a guerrilla in which he ransacks the styles and motifs of Cortázar, García Márquez *et al.* Scorza effectively dramatizes the forking paths open to Latin American writers today and emphasizes hilariously the seductions and temptations to which they are subject, thereby making a most incisive comment on self-referentiality and intertextuality from the revolutionary Left. Finally in 1984, Peru's best-known writer, Mario Vargas Llosa himself, who had already played these games in *Aunt Julia and the Scriptwriter*, published *The Real Life of Alejandro Mayta*, about a Trotskyist guerrilla of the 1950s. In this a well-known novelist whose curriculum vitae appears to coincide precisely with that of Vargas Llosa, attempts, in an apocalyptic near future, to unravel the story of Mayta against a terrifying background of social dislocation. '*The Talker*' (1987) repeats the gesture.

However the most interesting case for a number of reasons is the Argentine one. (Argentine cinema since the early 1980s has also been a revelation.) It is in Argentina – always night to Chile's day – where one of the most shocking reversals of expectations took place, and where the national literary tradition was both worst and best placed to respond. Best placed, because hysteria and despair have long been a staple of Argentine fiction – that of a 'disappointed country' (Cambaceres, Arlt, Sábato) which has seen half a century of almost miraculous growth (1880–1930) followed by half a century of conflict and economic decline, climaxing in a decade (1973–82) which was enough to make the most optimistic despair; and worst, because the main tradition was also one of existential rather than political or historical focus, which made adaptation to the new situation particularly painful. It was in Argentina, more than anywhere else, where the crisis of realism had been evident, not merely since the 'boom', but since the 1920s, and therefore where Borges's lessons of intertextuality, deconstruction, the con-fusion of genres and the play of discourses and quotations was most advanced, indeed almost a national literary obsession. In the 1970s the sense of unreality which had characterized Argentine urban fiction since the beginning was projected eerily onto the screen of national history itself. Perón's farcical and disastrous return, opening with the violence at Ezeiza airport on the 20th June 1973, the bizarre interregnum of Isabelita and López Rega, the neo-Fascist regime of Videla with its almost unbelievable levels of repression, the symbolic triumph of the World Cup and the all too real defeat of the Falklands, mark a period as hallucinatory as anything Magical Realism might have wished to invent, and all this in a country for which the word 'sophisticated' is invariably the first to come to mind.

The fear most writers there had nurtured from the earliest times – with Rosas's Mazorca – was of anarchy and chaos, whether from the caudillos of the interior, the Indians, the proletariat, immigration or the terrorist state itself. Ironically enough, in 1976, when the military overthrew the regime of Perón's widow, chaos was what they said they were saving the country from and chaos was what they set out to sow through their own forms of terror, just as Rosas had done in the 1830s when an earlier generation of intellectuals was forced into silence, exile or disappearance. Mármol's *Amalia* (1851) had been one response, but the most graphic was *The Slaughterhouse* (*El matadero*, 1838) by Esteban Echeverría, the leader of that generation. In 1976 the slaughterhouse returned, with nightmarish proportions, to complete the process initiated by another writer of the nineteenth century, Sarmiento, who had been the one, ironically enough, to set up the national military academy. Thus an army which represented the sacred values of the fatherland and its history attempted once again to impose unity on its own terms, this time by eliminating all those who saw things differently – writers among them. In 1976 Haroldo Conti (1925–76), author of the excellent '*Mascaró, the American Hunter*' (*Mascaró, el cazador americano*, 1975), who was awakened to his Latin American identity by a visit to Cuba, disappeared; followed a year later by Rodolfo Walsh (1927–77), an excellent short-story writer whose best-known work was the documentary '*Operation Massacre*' (*Operación masacre*, 1957), an early exposé of military repression. Walsh too disappeared shortly after sending an 'open letter' to the military denouncing the policy of disappearances. After that writers knew what to expect if they told the truth and published it inside Argentina. Indeed, Walsh's heroic gesture represents the *ne plus ultra* of literary commitment. Most Argentine writers had not previously been much concerned with history as such. Now that it was banned, however, they began to look anew, as the crisis of realism was followed by a crisis of reality.

At this point a most interesting thing happened, as numbers of novelists, some from inside but most from outside the country, began to seek new ways of projecting what was going on within its borders. Among the most interesting works were Puig's early *Kiss of the Spider Woman* (1976); Daniel Moyano (1928–), *The Devil's Trill* (*El trino del diablo*, 1974), another novel anticipating what was to come; David Viñas (1929–), '*Body to Body*' (*Cuerpo a cuerpo*, 1979), on the military and their proletarian opponents over the past century, with the history of Argentina conceived as a war of conquest and extermination; Osvaldo Soriano (1943–), *A Funny, Dirty Little War* (*No habrá más penas ni olvido*, 1980), on the absurd contradictions of Peronism; Ricardo Piglia, '*Artificial Respiration*' (*Respiración artificial*, 1980; see p. 336); Mario Schizman (1945–), *At 8.25 Evita Became Immortal* (*A las 20.25 la señora entró en la inmortalidad*, 1981), on recent history viewed through the eyes of a bemused Jewish family; Juan Carlos Martini, '*Life Eternal*' (*La vida eterna*, 1981), on symbolic struggles for power among prostitutes and pimps; Marta Traba (1930–85), *Mothers and Shadows* (*Conversación al sur*, 1981), a widely diffused dialogue of resistance among ordinary women; Andrés Rivera (1928–), '*Nothing to Lose*' (*Nada que perder*, 1982), a reconstruction of the life of a union leader; Carlos Dámaso Martínez, '*Ashes in the Wind*' (*Hay cenizas en el viento*, 1982), on teachers turned undertaker burying murdered workers; Luisa Valenzuela (1938–), *The Lizard's Tail* (*Cola de lagartija*, 1983; see p. 356); Miguel Bonasso, '*Memory of Death*' (*Recuerdo de la muerte*, 1984; see p. 339); and Tomás Eloy Martínez, *The Perón Novel* (*La novela de Perón*, 1985: see p. 341).[24]

All these novels are covertly or overtly political, most interweave the chronicle and journalism with narrative fiction. Many are obsessed on the one hand with documents of every kind (especially those that are falsified to distort reality and those that inadvertently falsify it in the first place), not least with legal sentences and death certificates, and on the other with the almost ungraspable realm of memory or oral history. Above all, they are concerned with the nature of power, politics and reading, and their interaction in Argentine history. Is there any need to stress that this is the problematic carved out by Augusto Roa Bastos, who was still resident in Argentina when Perón made his fateful return in 1973? Like Roa Bastos's fiction, many of these recent works escape from the claustrophobia of Buenos Aires, where the 'dirty war' – in which the military used Montonero violence as a pretext to eliminate large sections of the left and to terrorize the entire population – was most intense, and back into the provinces. At the same time the Latin American dimension once more came to assume importance as a theme in Argentine literature for almost the first time since the 1830s. This 'end to solitude' in the Southern Cone, which a writer like David Viñas has been working towards for two decades, may turn out to be one of the most far-reaching phenomena of recent years.

Ricardo Piglia, '*Artificial Respiration*' (1980)

'Sometimes (no kidding) I think that we are the 1837 Generation. Lost in the diaspora. Which of us will write our *Facundo*?'

Like the Spaniard Juan Goytisolo in 1966 with *Marks of Identity* and Vargas Llosa in 1969 with *Conversation in the Cathedral*, Piglia wrote a book intended to work back through an authoritarian past to try to discover what had gone wrong in his country and indeed in his own family (Rulfo's *Pedro Páramo* was an early rural version of this endeavour). The novel opens in April 1976, the year of the military coup, and tells the story of the protagonist Renzi's search into his own family past. The first words are: 'Is there a history?' (story and history being the same word in Spanish). His search involves his family history, Argentina's national history, his own individual life and that of another, his uncle, Maggi, exiled from his family and from Buenos Aires (described by one of the characters as 'the Aleph of Argentina'). Maggi himself is a historian who is in turn searching for the story of a nineteenth-century political exile from the 1837 generation, which requires a Chinese box technique: 'You don't understand history, the Professor told me, Tardewski told me, Forgive me for saying so'.[25] The novel examines the lives of a number of marginal people, all exiled from something or other, and discusses other important exiles, such as Adolf Hitler, James Joyce, Franz Kafka and Ludwig Wittgenstein. One of the principal participants in the conversations which make up the entire book is Tardewski, an exiled Polish philosopher (one thinks of Gombrowicz), who claims to have discovered that Franz Kafka met Adolf Hitler in 1910 and based much of his own later work on Hitler's fantasies of power. (The reader wonders whether, in other circumstances, Piglia might have linked up Joyce and Lenin through Zurich.)

It is difficult to imagine where else a novel like this could have been so successful and have come to be considered a key literary and historical document (it is really a text for literary critics and historians). It continues the Cortázarian practice of having Argentinians argue away in colloquial speech about the world's most intellectual issues, with references that no one without a university education and a lifetime of thinking about the humanities could decipher. But in this case, given the political context, the game in which Piglia was engaged was a deadly one. There is a remarkable moment when Tardewski remembers something Maggi had read to him:

> The capacity to think through the fulfilment of one's own life in historical terms, said, Tardewski, reading Le Roy Ladurie's phrase from his book of quotations, was as natural for the men who took part in the French Revolution as it is for our contemporaries, when they get to forty, to meditate about their lives as a frustration of the ambitions of their youth. He saw condensed in that phrase, he said, as he took off his spectacles and returned the notebook to the drawer, what Marcelo called, not without irony, the historical gaze.[26]

The characters are agreed that the greatest literary figures of the century are Joyce, Kafka and Proust (with Faulkner close behind), but argue bitterly as to who is the greatest of all: for Renzi, it must be Joyce, the man who exhausted the possibilities of literary narrative, and for Tardewski, Kafka, the 'twentieth-century Dante', the man who foresaw Auschwitz and the state used as an instrument of terror, and thus went to the very suicide and silence of language. Needless to say, in view of the present book's juxtaposition of the Ulyssean novel and the city-as-prison novel, Piglia's discussion is a suggestive one at a moment where Latin American literature ended a long period of relative openness and plunged into closure. The same interrogation is made of Argentine literature, and of the relative importance of Sarmiento ('*Facundo* is the founding page of Argentine literature'), Lugones (whose role was to expunge all trace of 'Mestizo' influence from the Argentine language), Arlt, considered the most important writer of the century ('any primary school teacher, even my Aunt Margarita, could correct a page of his Spanish, but no one could write it'), and Borges, the point of reference for everything. Thus we get a very interesting four-sided relationship between Borges and Joyce, Arlt and Kafka, which space precludes us from exploring further.

Maggi, the internal exile, and Tardewski, exiled to Argentina from abroad, are constantly contrasted by Tardewski himself: 'We were opposites and yet united. Me, the sceptic, the man who lives outside of history; him, a man of principles, who could only think through history.'[27] And again: 'Me, the exile; him, a man who was born and died in his own country.'[28] Maggi is nowhere to be found, which is why Tardewski and Renzi spend so long in conversation, prompting one of many coded messages from Piglia: 'As you will have realized, says Tardewski, we've spoken this much, all night, in order not to speak, in other words, in order not to talk about him, the Professor. We have talked and talked because there is nothing we can say about him.'[29] It is at this point that it finally occurs to the reader that Maggi has 'disappeared' and that Piglia is risking his life on the assumption that the military is not capable of perceiving literary irony – for example, in the title itself. (For otherwise, apart from the initial mention of 1976, there is not a single direct indication that this might be a work about contemporary politics.) We then discover, close to the end of the novel, that Maggi has left Tardewski his writings on his nineteenth-century researches into a political exile to hand over to Renzi, the nephew who has never met him:

Now that he's free of all that stuff, which was all he really had, the Professor, wherever he is, no longer has anything to fear.

That's why, Tardewski said, he left me those papers to hand on to you. If he hasn't come himself, it's because it wasn't really necessary. It was more important, he said, to leave those papers, to decide to give them up and choose you to have them....

In a sense, he said, this book was the Professor's autobiography. This was his way of writing about himself. That's why in these papers I think you'll find all you need to know about him that I can't tell you. You will find there, I'm sure, the reason for his absence....

It's growing light, he said. It will soon be dawn.

I open one of the files.

'To whoever finds my body.

'I am Enrique Ossorio, born and died an Argentinian, who in life has wanted only one honour: that of being called a patriot, always ready to give his all for the Liberty of his country!'[30]

Piglia's work is curiously stimulating, a novel about Argentina written, as one might say, by Cortázar, Borges and Roa Bastos. In 1988 he published

'*Life Sentence*' (*Prisión perpetua*), a heterogeneous selection of texts, including a partial autobiography, a homage to a dead American writer he used to know, and other such pieces. In 'In Another Country' he remembers some of the things the American used to say:

> The glass skull. Prison is the psychic centre of a country.... Flaubert's light. The modern novel is a prison novel. It narrates the end of the experience. And when there are no experiences the narrative advances towards paranoid perfection. The void is covered over with the persecutory texture of perfect connections, a closed structure, *le mot juste*.... Prison is a story factory. Everyone tells the same stories, over and over again. What they did before, but above all what they are going to do.... He died without leaving anything behind, as if he were only an oral narrator.[31]

Such concepts, closely related to the space of literary creation, the human mind and the image of the city, show how much the themes outlined in chapter 4 continue to dominate the Latin American imagination.

Miguel Bonasso, '*Memory of Death*'

Piglia's tortuous coded message, written from within and profoundly intellectualized, contrasts with Miguel Bonasso's more straightforward realist encapsulation of the 'dirty war', and in particular the efforts of the guerrillas and the counterattack by the military. But it, too, mixes dramatized fictional re-enactments with documentary evidence, especially relating to repression and torture. Bonasso, himself an ex-Montonero, wrote the book from exile in Mexico, where he was a collaborator of the murdered journalist Manuel Buendía, and both Buendía and Bonasso appear as characters in the novel published in 1984. It focuses above all on the connections – and even the conspiracies – between the military and the guerrillas, and includes large numbers of historical figures, such as Galtieri, Astiz and the legendary Montonero leader Jaime Dri, the novel's central character. Curiously enough, like Piglia's 'In Another Country', its point of departure is the overthrow of Perón in 1955, which ruined the lives both of Dri's father and of Piglia's. The novel's frame of reference is very familiar: Dante and Quevedo ('I could find nothing to lay my eyes on which was not a memory of death') as symbols of the inferno, the prison and the nightmare; distance and solitude as marks of Argentine identity and isolation (the retrospective chapters are all entitled 'Distances'). Bonasso's novel is also notably Latin Americanist and Third Worldist (one of the characters ponders 'the defeated idea of that great Bolivarian America, trampled on by the people of Buenos Aires'), in the mode of Solanas's powerful but equally single-minded film *The Hour of the Furnaces*.

Towards the end of the novel, however, Bonasso finally gives in to the Cervantine impulse:

'DISTANCES'

Confession.

Forgive me for intervening. I can't help it. I know it's immodest. But I feel it's unavoidable. This chapter is one of those which has given me most trouble. And I want to tell the reader how it's being born. On a darkening July evening in Mexico City. Outside my window the two lanes of the Mariano Escobedo Avenue, soaked by the rain, reflecting the grey blue wash of an alien sky. A few metres beyond, the club, with its alien swimming pool which sometimes relaxes my eyes dulled by solitude and too long indoors. This isn't my air, nor my light, nor my landscape.

The passions of six, ten years ago, have turned into photographs on my desk. The whole of Argentina fitted into a pile of yellow files I consult with exasperation. Far away and long ago is no longer just Hudson's felicitous title, so well chosen it became a commonplace. It is an obsession which visits my thoughts day and night, moment by moment.[32]

Bonasso's intermingled nostalgia and despair are heightened, as so often in Latin American fiction, by the anguish of the blank sheet of paper, the impossibility of turning remembered reality into words: 'Through the window of my "Distances" I wanted to frame that ocean of occurrences we call an "epoch". And, as was to be expected, I could only display a few post-cards, with no apparent connections between them. Debris stirred around by memory.'[33] Parallels with Onetti's conclusion to 'The Pit' are obvious. Then Bonasso as narrator meditates on Argentina's tragic destiny:

I try to think about Perón's exile and end up thinking about our own. Because these days almost any smart politician, any run-of-the-mill sociologist has woken up to the fact that the great land of immigration has become the land of diaspora... Unitarians and federals, liberals and conservatives, nationalists and turncoats, Perónists and anti-Perónists, before and after the great wave of immigration, through persecution or nostalgia for the lights of the centre, through Indo-Americanism or Europeanizing tendencies, for cash, through impotence, audacity, fear, madness, almost all decisive Argentines ended up in exile. Alberdi, Sarmiento, San Martín, Rosas, to name just a few. Why this cruel law? What hidden forces work for dissolution, the decomposition of the social body? When will this sponsorship of distance, this brand mark of homesickness, end?[34]

He tries again to give shape to his 'real-novel or novelized reality' ('Everything in this book is strictly true and is based on a vast and conclusive documentary base'). Somehow, inspired by his literary masters Roberto Arlt and Rodolfo Walsh ('If I have said "I did", "I was", or "I discovered", it means "we did", "we were", "we discovered"'), he fills in the period which started with Perón's accession to power in 1945 and ended with his return in 1973, and manages to return to a somewhat desperate positive note:

> That 17th of November 1972 saw one of those moments of paralysis which Argentina produces quite often. It is not enough to call them social or political phenomena, because there is more to them than that: it would be truer to say they were atmospheric or cosmic. The rarification of reality engulfs all facets of life and from the pampa itself springs up the obscure certainty that everything is permitted. Everything can happen. The most patent sensation is this: there is no tomorrow, for the simple reason that it is impossible to imagine it. [35]

In its alternation between rationality and mysticism, individualism and collectivism, fact and assertion, the work gives a passionate and provoking insight into Argentina's recent past and some not altogether promising pointers to its likely future.

Tomás Eloy Martínez, *The Perón Novel*

Piglia's baleful and almost desperate rationality, Bonasso's almost messianic Montonero perspective and Valenzuela's quizzical, satirical gaze (see p. 356) were all different responses to the challenge of recent Argentinian history. In 1985 Tomás Eloy Martínez (1944–) applied a similar technique – the interweaving of fact, documents and fiction – to an exploration of the central protagonist of the last half century in Argentina, General Juan Domingo Perón, not exactly a dictator, but certainly the greatest caudillo in Argentine history since Rosas. Martínez was well qualified to undertake this task as perhaps the most inventive Argentine 'new' journalist of the 1960s on the staff of *Primera Plana*. Perón is still so controversial a figure on the one hand, and his story so incredible in itself on the other – the almost senile General ('I've retired now, even from exile'), his first wife Evita's embalmed corpse, the new wife, Isabelita, an ex-dancer, the private secretary José López Rega, a psychopathic astrologer, etc. – that it needed a cool eye and a sure hand to sift the material and mould it into a legible shape. This Martínez certainly achieves, and an explanation of how he did it appears on the cover:

> This is a novel where everything is true. For ten years I collected reams of documents, letters, testimonials, pages from diaries, photographs. Many were previously undiscovered. While in exile in Caracas, I reconstructed the Memoirs that Perón had dictated to me between 1966 and 1972 and the ones that López Rega read to me in 1970, explaining to me that they belonged to the General although he, López, had written them. Then, in Maryland, I decided that the truths of this book could not be expressed except in the language of the imagination. Thus appeared a Perón that no one had wanted to see: not the historical Perón, but the intimate one.[36]

The reader has no idea how far this statement may be 'trusted', but senses that it may not be very far.

Here, then, following all the years since Sarmiento's recreation of *Facundo*, and through him Rosas, is yet another scriptural recreation of a Latin American Man of Power. Nothing could dramatize more clearly the condition of Latin American woman as object than the treatment of Eva Perón: little more than a good-time girl turned actress, then the Virgin Mother of the People, then a mascot embalmed and carried around the world, for the deranged López Rega to prey on like a vampire:

> That night, no matter what, Evita's body was to remain emptied for all eternity. When the hour of Universal Resurrection strikes, she will be graced by another semblance, the Lord will know her by another name, the musical notes of her astrological sign will then have been changed. Her body will remain empty but her appearance will be unaltered. The same course of formaldehyde and potassium nitrate that keeps her body untainted will fill her veins, her heart will be awakened at the same point in her body each morning of history, nothing will becloud the divine serenity of her face. But her soul will have entered unfailingly this night into Isabel's soul.[37]

What we see is an old political leader, who still has power (the power that was his and the power that was Eva's), but not the ability to exercise it, being taken over by others, notably the bizarre astrologer–politician, here attempting to transfer Eva's spirit into Perón's new wife, Isabelita, who is already in his psychological clutches. Martínez carries out a cool examination of López Rega's psychology and methods:

> López Rega had learned some time before that the will to power was based not so much on what one does as on what one is ready to do. That all power resides in the knowledge of (he was going to say, sensitivity to) where the weaknesses of another lie: in his sexuality, his mind, his past.[38]

Like Bonasso (and, as we shall see, Luisa Valenzuela), Martínez decides that the only honest thing to do is to appear in his own work, as the character he is:

> First Person
> I've told this story many times, Zamora, but never before in the first person. I have no idea what obscure instinct of self-preservation prompts me to step back from myself now to talk about myself as though I were somebody else. The time has come for me to show my true colours, to bring my weaknesses out into the open. The profession of journalism is fiendish. It's a living-through, a feeling-with, a writing-for. Like actors. Today you're being a turn-of-the-century tough and tomorrow you're Perón. Period, new paragraph. For once, I'm going to be the main

character in my own life. I don't know just how. I want to tell the unwritten, purge myself of the untold, disarm myself of stories so that I can arm myself, finally, with the truth.[39]

Like so many major political figures in literature (and in life?), Perón himself is presented as a hollow man, an empty space on which others inscribe their own needs and desires. The Perón who reluctantly flies towards an Argentina that is no longer meaningful to him is charged with the contradictory meanings invested in him by his hundreds of thousands of delirious supporters. The question we inevitably ask is whether Perón ever really knew his own identity or imposed his own meaning on Argentina, or whether he – or all political leaders – merely channelled the desires of others. Was he a 'Non-Existent Gentleman'?[40] Martínez recalls his first meeting with Perón when the ex-president was exiled in Madrid:

> All at once, it was as though I were watching him on a movie screen and he had the same voice as Clark Gable or Gregory Peck.... For the first time in my life I could shake hands with a figure out of a drawing, could feel that a historical character wasn't just a written text.... He wasn't just a man. He was twenty years of Argentina, for better or worse...[41]

Martínez's book, by examining Perón's family background and hypothesizing about his emotional and political development, is able to construct a picture – it would be a mistake to call it a portrait – which carries much conviction and allows the reader to do his or her own imagining. Whilst giving a clearly demystificatory view of the Caudillo, the writer implies that he believed in his own myth more sincerely than some of his close associates, and also shows that real politics do not involve the easy moral choices which most bystanders like to imagine. Other imperatives always come to bear on action and take decision makers inexorably away from their initial point of departure:

> Political morality is always at the opposite pole from poetic morality. This is the abyss at which men part company; where the poet Trotsky is incomprehensible to the politician Stalin, Che to Fidel Castro, the Fascist Lugones to the Fascist Uriburu. Had Eva not died when she did, she and Perón would have come to a parting of the ways. They were birds of a different feather.[42]

Like Piglia, though only implicitly, Martínez plays on the associations of other major works of Argentine literature. When he says farewell to Perón after their first meeting, he echoes the end of *Don Segundo Sombra*:

> Night closed in on the garden. The General stretched out his arms and exclaimed:

Cooompañeero! His voice sounded youthful and husky, like it used to. I grasped his hands. And then I went away from there like one bleeding to death.[43]

And when talking about the relation of Perón to Eva, he reminds us of Borges's brief story 'The Sham', which includes the following: 'The mourner was not Perón and the blond doll was not the woman Eva Duarte, but neither was Perón Perón, nor was Eva Eva.'[44] Martínez's sequel goes like this:

> She was so anxious to black out her past that even before the General could say, 'I made her', she said, 'Perón made me.' It wasn't true. Everybody is at each moment another person. But how can they be another if, basically, they do not go on being basically the same one. Eva was already Eva when Perón met her.[45]

Perón, then, could not maintain his magical powers without Evita. López Rega could not exercise power himself without tapping into the charismatic current of Perón, and through him, into the mythical aura of Evita, Latin America's most potent and complex twentieth-century female archetype. And of course the novelist, distancing vampires through the sacred ritual of literary recreation, could not make them live again – as they were or different? – without inserting his own fangs into their veins and drawing sustenance from their lives. As we shall see, Luisa Valenzuela considers the serious implications of this writer–character situation in her own novel on late Perónism, *The Lizard's Tail*.

Women's Writing

> What *little* I have done in my life (and I don't call it little out of false modesty, but because my plans were more ambitious) I have done in spite of being denied the advantages of being a man. But I wouldn't have achieved this little bit without having the unshakable conviction that it is necessary to fight to win the place that belongs to half of humanity. In my case, the struggle consisted of following a vocation: that of letters. To be victorious in this sector – even if the victory were insignificant – would mean helping the great movement for emancipation that was under way. [46]
>
> Victoria Ocampo

It is appropriate to end with a brief survey of female writing and feminist writing, because its irruption is without doubt the single most important phenomenon of the post-'boom' era. The assumption by women of their own representation has inevitably put an end to the version of the great Latin American myth which reached its apotheosis with the 'boom' itself. If

Asturias's *Men of Maize* and Rulfo's *Pedro Páramo* symbolically initiated its inversion, it was only Latin American women themselves who could complete the process. At present the entire literary scene is still dominated by the leading 'boom' writers – García Márquez, Fuentes, Vargas Llosa – as it was twenty years ago. They, following the autumn and death of the patriarchs, have themselves moved into middle age and – in literary terms – relative decline, though they have continued to write as energetically as before. But even as they continue to make grand literary gestures – Fuentes's *Terra Nostra* (1975) and 'Christopher Unborn' (1988), Vargas Llosa's *War of the End of the World* (1981), García Márquez's *Love in the Time of Cholera* (1985) – all major novels, the results are somehow disappointing (a British equivalent would be Anthony Burgess's *Earthly Powers*). In a word, they strike the reader who has read their greatest books as essentially voluntarist works, there because the audience and the writers willed them, but not in any true sense from the heart. The best of these is *Love in the Time of Cholera*, but it is possibly fair to point out that if that novel succeeds it is precisely because it dramatizes our sense of a typically Latin American heroic failure. Its theme, after all, is one for the late 1980s: a brief, belated, totally private and largely symbolic triumph in the face of hopeless odds.

Outside of the big three, however, a number of women writers – Clarice Lispector, Elena Poniatowska, Luisa Valenzuela and Isabel Allende being the best known – have risen to a position where they are as successful as any of the other male contenders.[47] Allende, indeed, with her *House of the Spirits*, has produced one of the few works by a man or a woman that meets the three basic criteria implied by this study – eliciting a favourable response from both the reading public and the academic critics, and passing the test of historical relevance. Indeed, one might say that this was really a delayed novel of the 'boom', born late because Chile's post-1960s political experiment came to an end as late as 1973, giving a woman who was still young in the 1960s the opportunity both to learn from the 'boom' itself and to profit from the experience of history. As we have seen, there were no women members of the 'boom' at the time of its apotheosis: on the contrary, it was the cultural consummation and dissolution of five centuries of patriarchy.

The previous great works, at once nationalist, Americanist and internationalist Ulyssean novels, were grand literary gestures of a typically Latin American kind, Cortesian, Bolivarian, Guevaran, made – obviously enough – at a great historical conjuncture when they were confronted by 'the imaginative proximity of social revolution'.[48] Such gestures, until recently, are not easily made by women, who have not been conditioned to imagining the triumph of the Woman any more than protagonizing the triumph of the West. (In most of them, even if the characters do not liberate the labyrinth, the author certainly does.) Indeed, those 'boom' books, and the 'boom' itself, were perhaps structurally – though not all of them, nor any of them entirely – intrinsically male phenomena, masculine acts of the kind García Márquez (but not Borges, though both are relatives of colonels) criticizes implicitly in all his works, especially *One Hundred Years of Solitude*.

Perhaps when the next boom comes in the later 1990s, after masculine penetration has been finally definitively celebrated in 1992, and above all in the twenty-first century, when we penetrate space itself – or, rather, as we redefine all our activities, it sucks us in like Rivera's vaginal vortex – the women will also or primarily contribute the grand gestures. Or perhaps the time for grand gestures is past – perhaps novels themselves are irredeemable and anachronistic grand gestures, as Roa Bastos for one suspects. But this seems extremely doubtful given the historical situation of Latin America, the stimulus of 1992 and the global perspective and predicament of the human race as we reach the end of the twentieth century. In that sense, Isabel Allende – the first genuine female bestseller in Latin American history – may indeed be the sign of things to come, with her discreet corrective feminine rewriting of *One Hundred Years of Solitude*.

In the meantime it is, indeed, mainly the women who, during and after the 'boom' – post everything – have been doing the solid, collaborative, necessary jobs, such as labour history, documentary history and documentary fiction. Indeed, if we look back at the great women writers from the distant to the recent past (Sor Juana, Gertudis Gómez de Avellaneda, Clorinda Matto de Turner, Nellie Campobello, Raquel de Queirós, Rosario Castellanos), we can see that this current of enunciatory modesty, objectivism and high seriousness is a most important tradition in Latin American women's writing. Throughout the 1920s to the 1980s, Social Realism has been accompanied everywhere, in greater or lesser doses, by socialist realism, despite the jibes by cosmopolitan sophisticates at such phenomena as the 'Banana epic' or the 'Bolivian mining novel'. It is better understood today that the realist mode is less a representation than the token of an intention, and many women have adopted the technique, often in recognition of the fact that the pressing needs of a continent in struggle may for the time being remain as or more pressing than the needs of women in advanced bourgeois societies. (Nevertheless, the connection between Latin American women and the United States, especially universities and women's presses, is one that may have far-reaching implications for the future, reminiscent of the Latin America–Paris links of the male writers of the past and the assimilation of male literary critics into North American academe in the last two decades.)

Progress in the twentieth century has been arduous for women writers in Latin America, with few women in even the relatively privileged positions or vantage points from which, say, English women novelists were able to start their writing in the nineteenth century. Even in poetry women have had to take a back seat, with only the Uruguayan writer, the glamorous Juana de Ibarbourou, and the Chilean Gabriela Mistral, able to claim continental recognition. Mistral, indeed, was the first Latin American writer to win the Nobel Prize in 1945. Nevertheless, in many countries, above all Argentina (Victoria and Silvina Ocampo, Beatriz Guido, Silvina Bullrich, Marta Traba, Luisa Valenzuela, etc.), Uruguay (Cristina Peri Rossi), Chile (Marta Brunet, María Luisa Bombal, Isabel Allende), Brazil (Raquel de Queirós, Ligia Fagundes Telles, Clarice Lispector, Nélida Piñón) and Mexico (Nellie Campobello, Elena Garro, Rosario Castellanos, Elena Poniatowska, Luisa Josefa Hernández), much excellent writing has appeared and opportunities for women are gradually increasing. A few women have even become almost as well known as the best-known men, though none has yet become the best-known novelist or poet of their country. Similarly, in literary criticism women have begun to make their mark, but none are yet among the best-known critics of the continent, though there are rising stars such as Ana Pizarro, Beatriz Sarlo and Margo Glantz.

What is actually happening here, then, as so often in history, is that women in Latin America seem about to have their own emergence – if not boom – at a time when the same development is already well under way in Europe and the United States, and they will therefore be practising and coming to prominence in the very midst of advanced, future-oriented theorization about their practice – women's writing – and its social and historical significance. This is no easy situation in which to hold one's own picture steady, as the male writers discovered after about 1966.

Elena Poniatowska and documentary narrative: *Until We Meet Again*

Elena Poniatowska (1933–) is one of Latin America's most remarkable narrators. Outside of Paz and Fuentes, she is probably the most important writer in Mexico today. Her father was a French–Polish emigré aristocrat, her mother the daughter of a Mexican landowning family which fled the country during the Revolution. The family returned to Mexico when Elena was nine years old, and she was sent to an English school, largely learning Spanish from the family servants. In later life she strived desperately to integrate herself into Mexican national life, and today is the country's best known journalist and arguably Latin America's most important producer of documentary narrative. *Until We Meet Again* (*Hasta no verte Jesús mío*, 1969) is the moving story of a Mexican working-class woman's experience of the twentieth century, a work which makes most Social Realist novels seem artificial. *Massacre in Mexico* (*La noche de Tlatelolco*, 1971) is the single most influential record of any kind of the 1968 massacre, in which her brother Jan died, with a force reminiscent of the films of the Bolivian director Jorge Sanjinés. And her latest work, '*Nothing, No One*' (*Nada, nadie*, 1988), is a genuinely searing testimony to the experience of the 1986 earthquake. In short, Poniatowska has produced the most lasting memorials to the two most significant events of Mexican history in the last two decades, the Tlatelolco affair and the great earthquake, as well as a series of other works such as *Dear Diego* (*Querido Diego, te abraza Quiela*, 1978), *Lilus Kilus* (1976) and *'The Fleur de Lys'* (*La Flor de Lis*, 1988), something like a fictionalized autobiography. Another child of emigré parents, Margo Glantz, who has made a similarly wide-ranging contribution to fiction and literary criticism, is best known for her autobiographical *The Genealogies* (*Las genealogías*, 1981).

Until We Meet Again is perhaps the most substantial example of Latin American documentary narrative, a genre which in a sense has replaced the old journalistic 'chronicles' and the Social Realist novel (both of which still survive), though of course its roots go back to Sarmiento and Da Cunha – some would say to the first chronicles at the time of the discovery (though others might say that these were examples of Magical Realism and that the Spanish picaresque novel is the true ancestor of the documentary). Works by anthropologists and sociologists have been similar antecedents: Gilberto Freyre's *The Masters and the Slaves*, Ricardo Pozas's *Juan Pérez Jolote* (Mexico, 1956), the life of a Tzotzil Indian, and Oscar Lewis's enormously influential *Children of Sánchez* (1961) about the Mexico City slums and *La Vida* (1965) on prostitutes in Puerto Rico. From the late 1950s, however, as the Social Realist novel began to seem both patronizing and anachronistic, such documentary works began to take a more overtly political turn, with Walsh's *'Operation Massacre'* in 1957, the first of a series of committed, partly fictionalized – or merely narrativized – texts which have established an important and compelling tradition: Carolina Maria de Jesús, *Child of the Dark* (*Quarto de despejo*, 1960), on a woman's life in the São Paulo slums; Miguel Barnet, *The Autobiography of a Runaway Slave* (*Biografía de un cimarrón*, 1966); Domitila Chungara, *Let Me Speak* (*Si me permiten hablar*, 1977), *I, Rigoberta Menchú* (*Me llamo Rigoberta Menchú*, 1985); plus a whole series of harrowing prison memoirs by writers like Hernán Valdés, *Diary of a Chilean Concentration Camp* (*Tejas Verdes: diario de un campo de concentración en Chile*, 1974), or Jacobo Timerman, *Prisoner without a Name, Cell without a Number*, (1981), and Alicia Partnoy's *The Little School* (*La escuelita*, 1986). Recently Gabriel García Márquez returned to the documentary mode with *Miguel Littín's Clandestine Adventure in Chile* (*La aventura de Miguel Littín, clandestino en Chile*, 1986).

Whereas it was men, Audalio Dantas and Oscar Lewis respectively, who edited the statements of the women in *Child of the Dark* and *La Vida*, Poniatowska initiated a process in which middle-class women took over the task of assisting their peasant or working-class contacts in communicating through print. Although these relationships are inevitably problematical in class terms, and the status of the 'documents' is always ambiguous, the results are frequently compelling. Poniatowska's *Until We Meet Again* is the most elaborate and gives the fullest picture of its protagonist, Jesusa Palancares, a woman born in the interior, who took part in the Revolution and lived for more than forty years in Mexico City. Jesusa's view of the world excludes politics, and she has little sympathy for her fellow women (all 'soft touches'), but the political impact of the work is considerable. It is principally concerned with the endless work Jesusa has done throughout a long and lonely life, and her reflections on that and her other experiences. Although in a *machista* society independence has cost her dear, Jesusa is proud of her stance:

> I don't know what sadness is. I've never been sad. You might as well be talking Chinese, it means nothing to me. Ah, crying's one thing, sadness is another! It's bad, useless, no one cares about it other than yourself. I cry when I'm angry, but I've never been sad. I cry because I can't get my own back and then the tears start because I feel mad. I need to get even by biting, or kicking, whatever. But crying like some big soft baby so people'll say, 'Ah, poor thing!', I'd rather keep it to myself. Sad people are bad people who only think about their problems. I never told you that I was sad, I just said the life I'd led was sad, but not me.'[49]

Her story is in one sense representative of millions of Third World women who have had to endure the experience of moving from country to city during an explosive and disorientating period of history, with none of the stabilizing props that an education can give. Her mother died when Jesusa was a small child and she was often abandoned by her father. She was forcibly married to a revolutionary soldier at the age of fifteen (he was two years older), but both he and her father died before the conflict was over. She never had children of her own, though she fostered several. Interestingly enough, although Jesusa was treated badly by her husband until she resolved to threaten him with a gun, one of her fondest memories of life was the stories he used to read to her at night as they travelled the country, emphasizing once again the extent to which the power of the imagination is seen as a redemptive force in Latin American culture. Late in life Jesusa begins to long for the countryside she left so many years before:

> I truly fancy going out to die in the country, where I used to go roaming. With God's help I'd like to die under a tree far away! Once the buzzards had danced round me, that'd be it; you'd come looking for me and I'd be happy as anything flying round in the buzzards' bellies. Otherwise all your neighbours come round to watch you die and see you making a fool of yourself, because most folks come to laugh at people who are dying. That's life. You die to give other people a laugh....

That's why I don't want to die here in the city but out there on a hill-side, down a ravine, like my Dad who died in the open country under a tree. I ask God to get me ready and go where he wills, and end up as food for the animals, the coyotes, like my husband Pedro. It's not that I don't want to be buried, but who's going to bury me, can you tell me? They'll say:

'In God's charity, this old line died out.'

No, I don't believe people are good, to be perfectly honest. Only Jesus Christ, and I never knew him. And my father, though I never knew whether he loved me or not. But here on the earth, how can you expect to find anyone good?

Now stop bothering me. Bugger off. Let me sleep.[50]

Clarice Lispector, *The Hour of the Star*

Brazil's most celebrated woman writer was Clarice Lispector (1925–77), author of *Family Ties* (*Laços de familia*, 1960), *The Apple in the Dark* (*A maçá no escuro*, 1961), *The Foreign Legion* (*A Legião Estrangeira*, 1964), *The Passion According to G.H.* (*A paixão segundo G.H.*, 1964), and several other works of fiction and chronicles. Comparisons are often made with another Brazilian novelist with a penchant for intimate tales, Autran Dourado (1926–). Like Elena Poniatowska and Margo Glantz, Lispector was from a family of East European origin – she was two months old when her Ukrainian parents arrived in Brazil – and there seems little doubt that this identity question provides in the case of a number of women writers some equivalent to the impulse which the Ulyssean writers acquired through their usually voluntary experiences of mobility, exploration and discovery. On the whole Lispector was best known for her extraordinary explorations of feminine subjectivity, and the way in which women are entrapped and isolated in a private world of helpless rage and frustration which they often conceal even from themselves. In this she was similar to other women writers who have confined themselves, or been confined by circumstance, to relating the intimate sensibilities of the female consciousness, like Teresa de la Parra (Venezuela, 1895–1936), author of *Mama Blanca's Souvenirs* (*Las memorias de Mamá Blanca*, 1929), or María Luisa Bombal (Chile, 1910–80), author of *The House of Mist* (*La última niebla*, 1935) and *The Shrouded Woman* (*La amortajada*, 1938).

Lispector's best-known novel was her last, the very brief *The Hour of the Star* (*A hora da estrêla*, 1977), which later became a successful film. It significantly expanded her range by coming out of the kitchen and the bedroom, so to speak, and telling the story of the pathetic Macabéa, a half-literate typist from the country who comes to work in São Paulo, gets her intellectual sustenance from radio commercials and quiz shows, and ends up killed by a fast car just as she begins to dream of a Hollywood-style happy ending for herself. (Lispector's narrator notes that the story is written under 'the spon-

sorship of the most popular soft drink in the world'. People love it 'with ser-
vility and subservience' because it allows them 'to be modern and to move
with the times'.) The book has a dozen sub-titles, all conveying helplessness
and hopelessness, and is dedicated to many people, including 'all those musicians who have touched within me the most alarming and unsuspected
regions;... all those prophets of our age who have revealed me to myself and
made me explode into: me. This me that is you, for I cannot bear to be
simply me, I need others in order to stand up, giddy and awkward as I am.'[51]
Lispector gives self-referentiality a special meaning by having the story narrated by a highly introspective masculine voice:

> I, Rodrigo S.M. A traditional tale for I have no desire to be modish and invent
> colloquialisms under the guise of originality. So I shall attempt, contrary to my
> normal method, to write a story with a beginning, a middle, and a 'grand finale'
> followed by silence and rain....
>   It is true that I, too, feel no pity for my main character, the girl from the
> North-east: I want my story to be cold and impartial. Unlike the reader, I reserve
> the right to be devastatingly cold, for this is not simply a narrative, but above all
> primary life that breathes, breathes, breathes....
>   A simple shout that begs no charity. I know that there are girls who sell their
> bodies, their only real possession, in exchange for a good dinner rather than the
> usual mortadella sandwich. But the person whom I am about to describe scarcely
> has a body to sell; nobody desires her, she is a harmless virgin whom nobody
> needs. It strikes me that I don't need her either and that what I am writing could be
> written by another. Another writer, of course, but it would have to be a man for a
> woman would weep her heart out.[52]

Like Jesusa in *Until We Meet Again*, Macabéa clings to whatever belief
systems she can find to help her through her painful and humiliating life, and
proves astonishingly resilient. Lispector shows us only too starkly, however,
why no one should ever have to devote their existence to developing such
desperate and ultimately futile resourcefulness. The narrative device of
employing a masculine presence works brilliantly in a number of ways: not
only does it subvert possible hostility, conscious or unconscious, to feminine
special pleading; it so heightens the glare of knowledge and sophistication,
through the implied author's obsession with philosophy and the nature of
fiction, as to shine back upon the reader himself (or even herself), who is
almost certainly every bit as committed to consumer society and its messages
as the hapless protagonist whom he or she pities but probably disparages. In
short, the writer builds into the fiction a meditation about her relation to the
character which engages many of the issues which more directly documentary narrative also has to confront. Clarice Lispector's death from cancer in
the year in which this novel was published was particularly tragic, since *The*

Hour of the Star reveals a writer whose exploration of Latin American society and of the nature of fiction itself were both attaining new dimensions of subtlety and significance. Indeed, her presentation of Macabea, spoken by a voice reminiscent of the narrative persona of a Machado de Assis, not only insinuates Clarice's own metaphysical concerns but is also curiously prophetic of the central theme of Ribeiro's *An Invincible Memory*:

> First of all, I must make it clear that this girl does not know herself apart from the fact that she goes on living aimlessly. Were she foolish enough to ask herself 'Who am I?', she would fall flat on her face. For the question 'Who am I?' creates a need. And how does one satisfy that need? To probe oneself is to recognize that one is incomplete.[53]

The House of the Spirits: the rewriting of history

By far the most successful Latin American woman writer with the international reading public is Isabel Allende (1942–), author of *The House of the Spirits* (*La casa de los espíritus*, 1982), *Of Love and Shadows* (*De amor y de sombra*, 1984), and *Eva Luna* (1987). *The House of the Spirits*, indeed, is perhaps the only Latin American novel which has ever truly crossed the intellectual divide by appearing on bookstands at outlets like Woolworths whilst being taken seriously by academic readers. It has also met with controversy: many critics have accused the writer of plagiarizing García Márquez, some have suggested that her novel, which culminates with a plea for national reconciliation in Chile, is counterrevolutionary, and a few have even asserted that the book is little more than an amateurish sentimental romance.

Most of these objections seem to me to be misconceived. There is no question that the novel is something like a Chilean version of *One Hundred Years of Solitude*, but far more interesting are its differences from the prototype. Some of these differences are due to the point of writing – García Márquez wrote after the triumph of the Cuban Revolution and Allende wrote after the overthrow of her uncle Salvador Allende's regime in 1973 – but others are clearly gender-related. Thus where García Márquez leaves his reader wondering whether historical cycles are always vicious, Allende shows that progressive enlightenment is possible – and, indeed, essential if women are to emancipate themselves and play their part in bringing about a less violent world. (Her novel ends where it began, with the first entry made by Clara, her grandmother, in her 'notebooks that bore witness to life', but here the circle is clearly a dialectical spiral of experience and knowledge passed down from woman to woman.) His pivotal character, Ursula, was a woman, and so is Allende's – but again, Allende shows her as a personage resisting rather than underpinning the patriarchal society which both novels portray.

Moreover Allende traces her story down the female line, from great grand-mother Nívea, a suffragette, through Clara and Blanca to Alba, the principal narrator, and shows that Clara's notebooks are the intellectual link between them all, whereas García Márquez's lineages are notoriously masculine and the illuminating manuscripts are encoded not by a member of the family but by a magical outsider, the gypsy Melquíades. Similarly, where García Márquez repeats the names of his characters to show the confusion which dominates their lives, Allende has her characters given similar but different names, because 'repeated names sow confusion in notebooks that bear witness to life'.[54] Thus one of the major themes in the novel is that of who shall give names to newborn babies, and the women manage to wrest both the babies and the names from the men who have appropriated both through-out Western history. But perhaps the language itself is the most striking difference. García Márquez's novel seems non-rhetorical in comparison with most novels of the 'boom', but appears full of tricks, mirages and labyrinths as soon as one compares it with Allende's simple, self-effacing but effective narrative style. The child's-view 'magic' of the early sections gives way much more quickly than in García Márquez's book and by the end has been converted to the most painful – though always discreet – forms of realism. The matter-of-factness, indeed, is the novel's most singular achievement.

Allende's novel, like García Márquez's, is one that unites her own experi-ence of life with that of her country's contemporary history. Ambitious though this is, however, she does not attempt to add the further dimensions which would make her novel a metaphorical history of Latin America and mankind in the way that the Modernist, Ulyssean novelists so often set out to do. The novel traces four generations of middle-class women down through mother to daughter, from liberal Chile at the start of the century to socialist Chile at the time of Salvador Allende. Almost all the decisive events in the novel, apart from the military coup, are resolved by resourceful women. The novel climaxes as conservative Chile turns into fascist Chile to meet the socialist threat, leading to perhaps the world's most notorious military coup since the Second World War and to the regime of General Pinochet. The principal male character, Esteban Trueba, shares the narrative with Alba, his granddaughter. Trueba is a conservative landowner and senator of the tradi-tional patriarchal breed, who conspires in the coup, only to bring about the death of his son and the torture and violation of his beloved granddaughter, whose compañero is a militant left-wing revolutionary. The other main male character is Esteban García, one of his many illegitimate sons, whose justi-fied resentment leads him to abuse Alba on two different occasions before the climax to the novel, when he is a fascist officer and she, a left-wing mili-tant, falls into his clutches. When Alba is imprisoned her grandmother comes in spirit form to inspire her to resist and survive:

The doghouse was a small cell, like a tomb, airless, dark and frozen.... Alba gave up, decided to end her torment once and for all, stopped eating and only took a sip of water when her own weakness overcame her. She tried not to breathe, or move, and lay waiting for death with impatience. She stayed that way for a long time. When she had almost achieved her aim, her grandmother Clara appeared... to save her with the idea of writing with her thoughts, without pen or paper, to keep her mind occupied, escape from the doghouse and live. She suggested also that she write a testimony which one day would help to bring to light the terrible secret she was enduring, so the world would learn of the horror going on at the same time as the calm, well ordered life of those who didn't want to know.[55]

There is little doubt that Allende's book has achieved precisely this, and has brought the horrors of the Chilean coup to the attention of as many people as Costa-Gavras's film *Missing*, whose intentions were similar. Moreover, in a remarkably condensed manner, she has incorporated many of the most familiar emblematic personalities involved in recent Chilean history (Salvador Allende, whose farewell speech to the Chilean people she quotes, Pablo Neruda, Miguel Enríquez, Víctor Jara) in a surprisingly successful and coherent fashion. It is not this popularizing impulse but the closing reflections which Alba sets down almost at the end of the novel which seem most open to objection:

In the doghouse I wrote thinking that one day I would have Colonel García vanquished at my feet and be able to avenge all those who must be avenged. But now I doubt my hatred.... I suspect that nothing that has happened is fortuitous, but corresponds to a destiny sketched out before I was born and that Esteban García is part of that sketch. It is a clumsy, distorted outline, but each line is important. The day my grandfather dragged his grandmother Pancha García into the bushes down by the river added another link to the chain of events that was meant to be. Later the grandson of the violated woman repeated the act on the granddaughter of the violator and in another forty years, perhaps, my grandson will assault his by the river-side, and so on, for centuries to come, in an endless story of pain, blood and love.... At moments I have the feeling that I have really lived this and written these very same words, but I realize that it is not me, but another woman, who wrote them down in her notebooks so that I could use them. I write, she wrote, that memory is fragile and life is very short and passes so quickly that we can neither see the relations between events nor gauge the effects of our actions, believing in the fiction of time, in present, past and future, but it may be that everything happens simultaneously.... I want to believe that my task is life and that my mission is not to prolong hatred but just to fill these pages whilst I await the return of Miguel, bury the grandfather lying beside me in this room, and wait for better times, gestating the child I carry in my womb, child of so many violations, or perhaps Miguel's child, but above all my child.[56]

Isabel Allende herself was not arrested and tortured, but fled Chile a year after the coup. Few would question her right to communicate – which she does movingly – the kinds of experience other women had to endure at the hands of Pinochet's torturers, but there seems to be more doubt as to her right to assume the voice of one of them, albeit fictionalized, in order to appeal for reconciliation between all Chileans at a time when Pinochet was still in power after almost ten years. Obviously the line 'it is not me, but another', implicitly linking Alba with her grandmother, but also Allende with the female victims of the coup, shows her awareness of the problems and responsibilities involved, but it is notable that this conclusion determinedly eludes the concepts of class and gender conflict (other than stressing Alba's claim on her unborn child) which have characterized the novel up to this point. Nevertheless it is also clear that Allende has little doubt that time is on the side of justice, echoing her uncle's famous last words that 'Other men will put this moment behind them and sooner rather than later the great avenues will open up down which free men will walk to build a better society.' Needless to say, as long as violence rules it will be difficult for women to alter decisively their purchase on the direction of human development. Perhaps the epigraph, taken from her favourite poet, Pablo Neruda, who died shortly after the coup with his house surrounded by soldiers, may clarify her intentions: 'How long does man live, after all?/ A thousand years or just one?/ A week or several centuries?/ For how long does a man die?/ What does for ever mean?' This would seem to plant the novel squarely in that tradition of materialist readings of Latin American history in which positive values are passed on, both consciously and unconsciously, down the long chain of the generations. It may be that Isabel Allende, speaking as a woman, has managed to express an old message in a new tone of voice.

The Chilean's novel is undoubtedly a 'big book' of the kind which the 'Ulyssean' and 'boom' writers so frequently produced. Indeed, as mentioned above, it might well be considered as a belated novel of the 'boom' provoked by the Chilean coup which so brutally and decisively ended Latin America's brief utopian moment (1959–73). One should perhaps note here a similar recent endeavour from Brazil, 'The Republic of Dreams' (A República dos sonhos, 1984) by Clarice Lispector's best known successor, Nélida Piñón (1935–), yet another daughter of recent immigrants. Piñón, like Lispector, began by writing allusive, suggestive fiction, confirming the movement away from Social Realism after the 1940s; but she too, in the face of the military oppression of the 1960s and 1970s, has evolved towards a more historical mode. 'The Republic of Dreams', like Ribeiro's An Invincible Memory, returns with a will to the theme of Brazilian identity, in her case from the perspective of a woman whose grandparents migrated to Brazil from Galicia in Spain and made their fortune, despite the new land failing to turn out as the utopia of the deliberately ambiguous title. This very long book views Brazil alternately from within and without, and again combines a personal and family saga with the history of the country. As in Allende's book there is a surprising link-up between granddaughter and grandfather – symbol, obviously enough, of patriarchy. Piñón's novel ends in a scene involving the narrator, her grandfather Madruga, and his associate Venancio: 'Seeing me, grandfather smiles with undisguisable anxiety. Then, however, he manages to calm himself. Life no longer troubles him so much. Ever tactful, Venancio thanks me. I sit down with them. I don't know for how long. I only know that tomorrow I shall start to write the story of Madruga.' Which is of course, reminding us of the end of Allende's novel, what she has just completed with this statement.

The Lizard's Tail: a female avant-garde?

Not all women writers have felt compelled to follow the realist track in exploring Latin America's contemporary historical labyrinth. For Latin American women the short story, always liable to frame the fantastic, has generally proved a more accessible vehicle than the novel, which has always required some privileged access to, if not participation in, the world of work and politics. In Argentina and Uruguay women writers have proved as prone as the men to be seduced by the strange and the uncanny. Silvina Ocampo (1906–), sister of Victoria, wife of Adolfo Bioy Casares, and friend of Borges, was one of the pioneers of that characteristic River Plate genre, also worked by Onetti and Cortázar, in which the fantastic springs from everyday experience. More recently the Uruguayan writer Cristina Peri Rossi (1941–), in exile since 1971, has established a wide reputation for her ability to combine the fantastic and the political in both short stories and novels, including 'The Book of My Cousins' (El libro de mis primos, 1969) and the much admired La nave de los locos (1984), a novel about the experience of exile recently translated into English as The Ship of Fools and thus inevitably inviting comparison with Katherine Ann Porter's 1962 novel.

Another exile (since 1979), the Argentine Luisa Valenzuela (1938–), who lives in the United States, has written one of the most widely read novels about the period following Perón's return to Argentina in 1973, The Lizard's Tail (Cola de lagartija, 1983), whose name comes from one of the many instruments of torture recently invented in the Southern Cone. Her previous works include Other Weapons (Cambio de armas, 1977; published 1982), exploring the more disturbing aspects of male–female relations against the background of the prevailing military repression, and Strange Things Happen Here (Aquí pasan cosas raras, 1979). The same themes recur in the more free-wheeling, hypnotic Lizard's Tail, another work centred on the incredible José López Rega. The self-styled minister of social welfare is viewed as a deranged evil

genius engaged in some atavistic crusade to be achieved through hideous
blood rituals. Valenzuela's surrealistic language is reminiscent, inevitably, of
some of Cortázar's writing, but the closest parallel may be with the only prose
work of the Argentine poet Alejandra Pizarnik (1936–72), whose *The Bloody
Countess* (1968) has recently received wider circulation through translation.[57]
Valenzuela takes the most audacious risks in entering the mind of her historical personage, self-styled lord of the ants (*tacurús*):

> Wise *tacurús*, tubes through which the wind comes to bring music through my
> labyrinthine castle. A sound more like a moaning accordion of nostalgic childhood
> siestas. Underground castle, Aeolian, a miracle that I often celebrate by drinking a
> glass of the choicest formic acid. I've mentioned my floating island and I've
> mentioned my castle on land – underground. That's me, versatile. Master of all
> landscapes.[58]

At the same time she too uses her investigation of her bizarre personage to
question her own practice in writing about her country from exile:

> Sitting down to write when over there, almost beside you, only a step away,
> innocent people are being tortured, killed, and one writes as the only possible way
> to counterattack. Goddammit, what irony, what futility. What pain, above all. If I
> could stop other hands by stopping my hand.... I wonder how far this
> government's hunger for repression will go, what gluttony they're acting in
> response to, what gland it can be that secretes this indiscriminate hate, how we can
> ever put a halt to this chemical discharge.[59]

Valenzuela then comes up with an idea not altogether distant from that of
Allende, a renunciation of violence. In this case, however, the operation is
more complex, for unlike Allende's spectacularly unassertive prose
Valenzuela's writing carries all the contradictory force of its Surrealist ances-
try in an effort to communicate the strange evil banality of Isabel Perón's
Svengali. In this case, then, the strategy is perhaps a rather violent renunciation of violence, as the writer, rather like Roa Bastos, asks herself what she
thinks she is doing in handling such obscene materials and repackaging them
for a wider audience:

> Messianic, eh? I, too, am turning messianic, and there's the real contagion, the
> sorcerer's impregnation. He would like to dominate the world by putting his foot
> on it and crushing it whenever he chooses. He hopes – through action – to destroy
> at whim. And I, with such a passive form of action as writing, would like to stay
> his hand, put an end to his influence by lapsing into total passivity, perhaps even
> silence. Holding back the horror by not naming it, that might be it. Gag myself?
> No: a gag implies knowledge forcibly silenced, censorship. And now I realize that
> I don't know anything, I can't know anything, and I was deceiving myself all the

while I thought it necessary to keep memory alive as a weapon of defense and enlightenment. Now I fear it's just the opposite, I fear that to name is to give life.[60]

The problem of naming takes us back to the themes of the 1920s, with which this book began, and to the more recent debate as to whether writers from the 1920s to the 1960s were attempting to communicate democratically with their compatriots or to reconquer and reappropriate Latin America symbolically through some lust for power of their own. Luisa Valenzuela writes her novel on the rack of these inescapable contradictions:[61]

> Yes sir. I plant the flag, I plant the pen, I plant the written word, and maybe all that will serve me as seed for a time.... Who finds paper finds a pen, who finds his voice finds ears, who seeks breaks away. Finding without searching? It could be so, and therefore, Red Ant Sorcerer, lord of the Tacurú, master of drums, high priest of the Finger, owner of *The Voice*, hoarder of mirrors, probable impregnator of your own ball, taster of blood, here I leave you free to your fate, and I hope it will be the worst of fates, the one you have earned for yourself.
>
> In this simple ceremony I abandon the pen with which, in other simple ceremonies, I took note of you. So you see. We're alike: I, too, think I have influence over others. By being silent now, I think I can make you silent. By erasing myself from the map, I intend to erase you. Without my biography, it will be as if you had never had a life. So long, Sorcerer, *felice morte*.
>
> L. Valenzuela

It will be some time before the historical image of this calmly horrifying novel has been focused, but its filiation with *I the Supreme* is unmistakable, in particular the would-be dictator's obsession with his own self-generation and his desire for the entire world – to him a mere abstraction – to be ordered according to the pulsations of his own perverted will. Valenzuela's inclusion of herself among the guilty cannot disguise the fact that this novel links thematically Argentine solitude, writing and masculine will into a chain which needs to be deconstructed before that still unhappy country can clarify its own past and invent a new future for itself.

Despite numerous efforts to characterize the post-'boom' novel, it seems clear that we are not yet in a position to do so. The post-'boom' narrative is, quite simply, the novels which have appeared since the mid 1970s, and efforts to demonstrate radical new departures are usually just grist for the academic mill which rarely manage to propose entirely convincing formulations.[62] The major phenomenon, undoubtedly, is the accumulation of a body of determinedly self-referential fiction on a scale unseen in other parts of the world. This would seem to confirm the thesis that Latin America's historically dualist experience continues to magnify in intensity the intellectual's paradoxical self-awareness of his or her responsibility to the objects of their contemplation and representation. It has also facilitated the return of Social Realism under another guise, through an ideologically self-conscious mode of enunciation which mitigates some of the technical and philosophical inadequacies of earlier exponents of the genre. Nevertheless, for the time being, the historic fault line between the political and the aesthetic seems to have opened up once more in the process of Latin American narrative.

Conclusion:
Out of the Labyrinth?

Latin America's contemporary reality does not derive from some indecipherable curse. My intention has been to explore its history in order to explain it and to help to make it by opening up those spaces of liberty in which the victims and the defeated of the past might become the protagonists of the present.

Eduardo Galeano, 'Notes towards a Self-portrait', 1983

'How can I get out of this labyrinth?'

Simón Bolívar, quoted by García Márquez,
'*The General in his Labyrinth*', 1989

This journey through the labyrinths of Latin American history and literature is almost at an end. As I remarked in the introduction, I have been especially concerned not to filter all Latin American cultural phenomena through our own preconceptions, whether those of Anglo-Saxon commonsense on the one hand or its more recent Post-structuralist antidotes on the other. Thus I have sought to show that a metaphor like that of 'solitude' has a quite concrete origin in Latin American historical experience, which has been fused and confused with romantic, existentialist or other ontologies in narrative fiction and other quests for meaning from Independence to the present day. Equally, 'intertextuality' takes on a special significance in a region whose writers and intellectuals used to quote only authorities external to their own cultural milieu, until the 1960s, when the 'boom' crystallized a whole century of narrative development and revealed, retrospectively, that it is through culture generally and narrative fiction in particular that Latin Americans have been able to move beyond the futile limitations of national identity in the direction of some humanistic continental culture as part of the global community of tomorrow. And doubles, dualisms or binary oppositions – those of a culture operating through exclusions and segregations – take on an added and unavoidable dynamism in a continent whose inhabitants have always been denied freedom to act, to develop and to find or make themselves by the existence of hostile outside forces. In such a context, where most people are prevented by social origin, lack of education and sheer economic constraint from consuming or producing literature, the concept of writing takes on an even more problematical and dramatic character than in the developed capitalist world where it has been so fiercely questioned and debated – by writers, needless to say – over the past quarter of a century.

One must now come clean. The labyrinth is everywhere. At the very moment where biology, physics and astronomy have allowed mankind to see to the inner and outer limits of the universe, the relativization of everything has brought the old Greek metaphor of the tapestry, and its topographical equivalent, the labyrinth, back to the forefront of human signification. Extrapolating from Derrida, one might say that there is nothing outside the labyrinth; paraphrasing Foucault, one could add that there is no other reality but the reality we are in. Since the Greeks, weaving – Penelope – has been perhaps the most persistent symbol for the unfolding of human destiny – Ulysses – and for the texts which, textualizing, tell of it. The twentieth century has rediscovered this metaphor with a vengeance, and for contemporary Derrideans and Foucauldians textuality, with its decentring and its difference and its gaze into the abyss, has been repeatedly likened to a web, a forest or, above all, a labyrinth. This is a long way from the fields, paths and horizons of the 1920s Social Realist romances of the land: nevertheless, to coin a slogan for survival, even post-Modern relativity is only relative.

Thus this book has not wished to dissolve the traces of history, with its successively and endlessly superimposed events and perceptions ('the totality of all effective statements': Foucault), into the ultimately univocal perspective of contemporary, and no doubt transitory, deconstructionist analysis. Personal scepticism apart, to have done so would have confused the issue and concealed the fact that the labyrinth, like the metaphors mentioned above, has its own entirely concrete basis in a continent at once unitary and diverse, where identity is never given, and where history and culture themselves have always seemed to be a question of opting between different, already existing choices and alternative forking paths. For Latin Americans the problem was not a deluded assumption of metaphysical 'presence', but a situational inability to achieve such blissful illusions in the first place: there writers were always feeling themselves colonized, barbarized, feminized, parodied. In Latin America, therefore, the peculiarly emphatic dualism of its destiny raised the old Western oppositions into stark visibility long before this occurred in Europe itself, where, until the end of colonialism after the Second World War, they were built into the assumptions of reality as a triumphalist 'one-way street'. Moreover, the defeatism which lies just below the surface of most deconstructionist criticism would be doubly debilitating in a context where there have always already been more than enough reasons for discouragement or despair.

The process of inverting the direction of the old binary oppositions – it is only recently that people have talked, for the moment still utopically, of going beyond them and liquidating the problem – had been anticipated by progressive intellectuals from the highpoint of Modernism itself in the 1920s. If Romanticism had plunged artists, only recently released from patronage into individualism, back into communion with the folk, the feminine and nature, the 1920s saw the first serious encounters between what would now be called – however uneasily – First World intellectuals and Third World peoples, in the period after the first great proletarian revolution and the first world war. In Latin America, however, the 1920s demonstrated that any artist attempting to represent the region's realities under the sign of the future was now obliged to engage with this perspective of rebellion and redefinition, if he or she was to resolve within a textual structure the acutely contradictory, heterogeneous or plural elements and discourses generated within uneven development. The most thoroughgoing attempts to do this were Asturias's *Men of Maize* (1949) and Neruda's *'General Song'* (1950). Later versions, such as Fernández Retamar's *Caliban* (1971) or Galeano's *Open Veins of Latin America* (1971) and *Memory of Fire* (1982–86), though undoubted classics, were beginning to sail against the contrary winds of history, and the ideological timbers were thus beginning to creak. These works were simple negations, mere inversions of an ideology, whereas the 'Ulyssean' masterworks of the era, from *One Hundred Years of Solitude* to *I the Supreme*, tended to be more dialectical, to see synthesis as a question of raising rather than reducing. The questions remain the same, of course: who writes, on behalf of what power, in what context, using what signifying systems, and to what end.

The new awareness of history, that it is not just there, in 'the past', but also here, where we are, explains the ever-growing self-consciousness of narrative fiction in the region since the 1960s. Ironically enough, Latin American writers have shown far more awareness of the problematical nature of the reading and writing subjects than most recent critics, who subject absolutely everything to their ironic gaze except the process of constitution of their own textualized selves. It seems sufficiently clear that for most Latin American writers, despite the inevitable temptations of narcissism, self-referentiality of text and author has involved a continuing tradition of responsibility and commitment, a recognition that while there is indeed an 'internal other', there also continue to be external others whose existence and predicament pose particularly pressing questions of self-definition and conscience for the Latin American intellectual. They continue to find themselves in the 'Mestizo' position (not to mention, increasingly, in the 'Androgynous' position), trying on the one hand to represent (sincerely or duplicitously) the forms of Latin America's own popular culture and on the other to appropriate, on the best terms available, the forms of international culture, not least in the sphere of narrative modalities. As we have amply seen, this has created an extremely complex and ambivalent perspective, but also one which has provided an equally rich corpus of cultural and historical materials and an unusually privileged, 'Joycean' (and/or 'Faulknerian') perspective upon the Modern and, more recently, the post-Modern: a generalization of what I have called the 'Ulyssean' conjuncture.

This process of 'Ulyssean' exploration began in the 1920s, not the 1960s, and the 'boom' celebrated an arrival, not a departure. That era is now coming to its end, as the writers who were young and triumphant during the 'boom' (García Márquez, Fuentes, Vargas Llosa) approach old age, surrounded by many outstanding younger writers but no obvious successors. Borges's fictions, from the late 1930s, implied that Latin American writers were in a position at last to contemplate – from the perspective of modernity – the whole of Western culture, to assess it for themselves and to determine their own position within it. Thus by revising Western culture, they would universalize their own culture and become contemporaries of all men. Asturias, with the 'Legends of Guatemala' and Men of Maize, made the same thing possible from his more anthropological and historical perspective, whilst Carpentier, more than either of them, made the relation between European and Latin American culture his point of focus (as Paz would later also do – albeit more from the European side, so to speak).

Borges declared that there was no point in writing novels, for there is no history, only myth. Asturias's novels said there is only history, but myth is its subjective face. Carpentier, in The Lost Steps, took the same view: like the narrator of The Vortex before him, Carpentier's faceless storyteller found that, in searching for the past one found only the present and the future. Latin America's astonishing process of self-recognition through literature, carried out by artists and intellectuals after the First World War and the Mexican Revolution, took a mere half century to reach the novel which encapsulated it, One Hundred Years of Solitude. This completed a sequence of great symbolic histories of Latin America: Men of Maize, 1949; The Lost Steps, 1953; The Devil to Pay in the Backlands, 1956; The Death of Artemio Cruz, 1962; Hopscotch, 1963; The Green House, 1966; and One Hundred Years of Solitude, 1967. All have their point of departure in Doña Bárbara, and all take their logic from the effort to invert the sign system which that work had inherited from Sarmiento and incorporated into narrative. Nothing after that date has made any substantive change to the picture other than the rise of women's writing, symbolized above all by Allende's The House of the

Spirits, adding a transsexual future to a transcultural and transnational present.

Roa Bastos's *I the Supreme*, by contrast, published in the same year as Fuentes's *Terra Nostra*, that somewhat monstrous *summa* of all that had gone before, added a postscript to the 'boom' which not only completed the 50 years of self-discovery and self-recognition, but also the 150 years of the national – read, neocolonial – period which *One Hundred Years of Solitude* had identified, redefined and deconstructed. Only then was it possible to return to the Independence era and look anew at the creation of those young republics which could only find an identity when they had found one another. Most continue to believe that it is through culture that they will find themselves, in the first instance, and that it is the novel, as the most materially historical cultural form, which has hitherto constituted the most effective artistic vehicle for that intercommunication which music, dance and football have already provided in their respective spheres.

In this picture, then, something was completed during the period 1967–75 which had commenced half a century before with the Mexican Revolution. That something was a literary cycle which began with the novels of the Mexican Revolution – turning 'Naturalism' into 'realism', or perhaps 'epic realism' – and ended with the Cuban Revolution and its historical aftermath. It is obvious enough that these two progressive historical events mark Latin America's concrete historical emergence into the modern world, and the second of them made possible a further leap of the imagination and a real opening of consciousness, which did not produce the 'New Novels' but certainly helped to make and shape the 'boom' before as suddenly contributing to its curtailment. Thus Fuentes, Cortázar, García Márquez and Vargas Llosa were able to complete the exploration of the relationship between America and Europe, Indian and European, country and city, labour and capital which we have now traced through the labyrinth of several dozen novels, and thus to comprehend the meaning of America in world history and the direction of its trajectory over the past 50, 150 or 500 years. In the light of such a trajectory, it is entirely appropriate that García Márquez's latest project has been a novel about the man who succeeded in liberating the continent but failed to integrate it, Simón Bolívar. ('Citizens! I blush to say it: independence is the only good we have achieved, at the cost of all the rest.')

Beyond the coincidences of anniversaries, then, is the present moment in Latin American culture a special one? Does the 1992 anniversary coincide with some wider historical conjuncture, at least in literature? And is the moment framed by some wider global pattern of relationships into which Latin America may be inserted? Certainly anyone writing on such a theme at this time is drawn inevitably to reflect that many things are at an end, including 2,000 years of Western culture, 500 years of Latin American culture, and almost 100 years of modernity. Moreover, if we consider that it is now very late in the West, we are also brought to reflect that it seems more than possible that, unlike previously declining civilizations, we shall take the others with us when we go. As late multinational capitalism commodifies every remaining aspect of human relations in every last remaining refuge, establishing an international market of messages in which all the old power relations continue, albeit more invisibly than ever, it becomes ever more difficult for local identities, traditions and memories to be forged and preserved. Nevertheless, the consciousness of that endeavour and its importance has been central to the process of Latin American narrative in this century and this tradition at least looks certain to continue vigorously into the next, as the artists of the continent, like the characters of *One Hundred Years of Solitude*, try to decipher and appropriate messages from outside before they become obsolete.

The development of most of the 'boom' writers as individual creators should normally be divided in two: the moment up to and after the creation of the 'Ulyssean' novels, in which Latin American consciousness returned to itself once more, refreshed, enlightened and transformed, not by European culture as such, but by the journey through European culture, the clash and interpenetration of reconquest, the intellectual adventures and explorations, the dialectical opening up of a mental space, a culture and its characteristic artistic forms. Asturias, Carpentier, Cortázar, Guimarães Rosa, Fuentes, Vargas Llosa, García Márquez and Roa Bastos had all travelled widely abroad before writing these 'Ulyssean' works, but none of them were unAmerican, anti-American or cosmopolitan, as so many accused them of being, or as so many of the Modernistas had indeed been at the turn of the century. They all returned sooner or later, prodigals, men of the planet, who, if they lost their own countries – like Cortázar – could become Americans instead. They knew now how America differed from and was similar to other parts of the world. They were also the first two generations of novelists who had experienced what the Modernista poets had experienced, namely working and travelling together, influencing one another. Asturias, Borges and Carpentier lived and travelled in Europe, then went away and two decades later turned their experience into the 'Ulyssean' works of the 1940s, 1950s and 1960s. The 'boom' novelists were even more privileged. They had the example of that earlier generation, born with the century, but also, in an age of much greater mobility, got to know one another from the start and began to write intertextual works and to cross-refer to one another in a way that had never been conceived of before. The result, by the end of the 1960s, was a gradual shift to the metafiction, an obsession with writing itself, and an unmistakable privileging of the ontological over the epistemological; though at the same time the very politics which had been gradually repelling most writers away from social and historical analysis began to be more directly reflected in a new wave of documentary and semi-documentary narrative which remains vigorous today.

Roa Bastos was the first novelist to survey this entire panorama, the past and present united, and to attempt to encompass the entire labyrinth – including his own participation in it and journey through it – as political problem. Only by reconstructing the entire labyrinth – a task we are warned is impossible – will it be possible to make it dissolve, for the labyrinth implies the quest for modernity itself from within uneven development. Borges, ironically enough, had no idea what a labyrinth actually was: it was, for him, precisely a stratagem for detaching himself from reality with all its contradictions and making sure that he never actually had to look. Thus he created a labyrinth of mirages, instead of mirrors, though he undoubtedly enabled many others to see more clearly.

The modern world had dawned in about 1870 and the Latin American poets began to unite and to prepare for it. Modernity itself, like Latin American modernization, arrived after 1917, at which point novelists began to engage with it, as poetry met prose and literature met criticism all over the West. Latin America's full entry into the modern world was patently visible after 1945 – celebrated by Octavio Paz in 1950 – albeit on radically unequal terms. Latin American fiction reflected the immense historical importance of the moment, and also began to portray – not always modestly in the 1960s – writers' own participation in raising the continental consciousness, inevitably substantial in a region of political and economic weakness. Most of the novels registered a totally new awareness of the female dimension, and Asturias, Rulfo, Cortázar and even Vargas Llosa (in *The Green House*) signalled the beginnings of a reversal of trends and a transformation in consciousness.

It follows from all the above that the period 1917 to 1967 forms a neat half-century cycle, though one should be wary of falsifying history and generating new optical illusions of our own: Azuela's *The Underdogs*, written at the very beginning of the period, needed the forty years of preparation which Azuela's own prior experience represented in collision with the shock of the revolutionary conflict. Similarly, the average age of the 'boom' writers in the early 1960s was approaching the same forty years, and they too required the impulse of the Cuban Revolution to turn individualist works into Ulyssean ones. Inevitably, of course, our suggestion that the work of most of the 'boom' writers should be seen in two phases may well prove to be false when we discover what new wave the second half of their trajectory will bring about and fuse into, at which point our 50-year cycle will be incorporated within an even wider historical trajectory of further-reaching significance within which the 1917-to-1967 arc will be subsumed as one of the many flows through the territory of what we continue to call literature. Nevertheless, it is already clear that all the major writers have moved inexorably in the past decade towards the apocalyptic obsession which Asturias and Borges displayed before them. Vargas Llosa's *War of the End of the World* and *Real Life of Alejandro Mayta*, García Márquez's *One Hundred Years of Solitude*, *Love in the Time of Cholera* and '*The General in his Labyrinth*', and, above all, Fuentes's *Terra Nostra* and '*Christopher Unborn*', are each, in their way, unmistakable portents of the possibly cataclysmic end of an era (1984, 1992, 2000), both in narrative and in history itself.

This book has resisted a number of temptations, first among them that of looking back into the past and finding only what conforms to present patterns of thought – such as pluralism, heterogeneity or carnival. Latin Americans need to discover their identities before they decide to discard them. (Indeed, every time cultural critics declare that the problem of identity is liquidated in Europe, it seems to arise again with renewed vigour, as appears to be happening now.) On the whole, in Latin American history, we find cruelty, oppression and exploitation, countered by suffering, resistance and frequent heroism. And we also find writers who have attempted to engage with this history by confronting such problems as uneven development and the continuing implications of the division of labour (between developed and developing nations, city and country, men and women, brain and hand, conscious and unconscious), in a context where all metanarratives may be thought guilty of embodying the repressive mechanisms of metaphysical authority; and we find others who have tried to avoid such engagement, to 'defer' commitment to real people – the always already exploited – until such moment as the nature of being, the status of the signifier and the relation of author to character should again become transparently clear. Thus the second temptation resisted is that of discarding the concept of a literary canon for Latin America before one has even been established. I have tried to include all the texts which, in my opinion, are the key documents of Latin America's written narrative culture this century.

Nevertheless, it seems that the Post-modernists are right about at least one thing. We have been moving into a new era ever since the 1920s – relativity and all that – and at an accelerated rate since the inauguration of the space age in the late 1960s, which happened to coincide with the rise of contemporary feminism. These two phenomena will change the age-old ideological matter of the 'point of view' or 'vantage point', not least in literature, in ways which are unpredictable except in their inevitably revolutionary impact. Of course, with developments in Europe, including the full incorporation of Spain and Portugal for the first time since the seventeenth century, radical changes in the Soviet Union, the rise of the Hispanics in the United States, and the probability now that Cuban and Nicaraguan socialism will survive, even if in modified or diluted form, Latin America may have an easier passage into its rightful place in the modern world, as a part of what has hitherto been called Western culture, but a part which does not have to suppress the identity and the contribution of the great majority of its population in order to be so, and as a full participant in and member of world culture. Writers may go on having to liberate the labyrinth, or we may perhaps discover, not many years later, as we face the past, that the labyrinth has already been liberated, and that, although we did not yet know it, all spaces, for the foreseeable future, are open.

Notes

1 Myths of the Mestizo Continent

1.   One of the most important works to appear in the early years of the 'boom' was Luis Harss's *Los nuestros* ('*Our Writers*', Buenos Aires, Sudamericana, 1966). Its original English version was entitled *Into the Mainstream* (New York, Harper & Row, 1967), which seemed to confirm the then general perception that the New Novel had brought Latin American fiction into line with 'universal' currents only in the 1960s. A closer reading of Harss's brilliant critical interviews, especially those with Asturias, Borges and Carpentier, shows clearly, however, that the process originated in the 1920s and was merely completed in the 1960s.

2.   The first great critical synthesis of the history of Latin American literature was Pedro Henríquez Ureña, *Literary Currents in Hispanic America* (Harvard University Press, 1945). Since that time there have been numerous further attempts at definitive treatments, but none has succeeded in equalling, still less replacing this early outline sketch. For a more general treatment of high culture, see my 'The Literature, Music and Art of Latin America from Independence to c.1870', in L. Bethell (ed.), *Cambridge History of Latin America*, vol. III (Cambridge, 1985), pp. 797–839, and 'The Literature, Music and Art of Latin America 1870-1930', *Cambridge History*, vol. IV (1986), pp. 443–526. The best general histories of Latin American literature in English are by Jean Franco (see bibliography).

3.   J.L. Borges, 'The Gospel According to Mark', in *Doctor Brodie's Report*, trans. N.T. di Giovanni (London, Allen Lane, 1974), p. 19.

4.   Daniel J. Boorstin, *The Discoverers: A History of Man's Search to Know His World and Himself* (New York, Random House, 1983). Boorstin had been the Librarian of Congress since 1975. He was one of the many distinguished commentators quoted in the world press when the American space shuttle Challenger exploded in February 1986. In response to the disaster President Ronald Reagan likened the spirit of space exploration to the daring of Francis Drake off the coasts of Latin America almost 400 years before. (He also quoted a poem by a United States Spitfire pilot in asserting that the dead astronauts had 'slipped the surly bonds of earth to touch the face of God'.) For an interesting insight into relations between the United States and Latin America, see F.B. Pike, 'Latin America and the Inversion of United States Stereotypes in the 1920s and 1930s: the case of Culture and Nature', *The Americas*, 42 (October 1985), pp. 131–62: 'As long as capitalist prosperity continues, a majority of North Americans will probably maintain a certain disdain for all those in their midst and beyond their borders who have given cause to be perceived as creatures of nature because of their communal or herd instincts and their lack of obsession with dominating nature so as to maximize profit. Those not so obsessed will continue to be hailed as the equivalent of the noble savage by alienated United States intellectuals' (p. 162). The most remarkable recent interpretation of the meaning of the

369

United States in contemporary culture is Jean Baudrillard's *America* (London, Verso, 1989).

5.   John Roberts, *The Triumph of the West* (London, BBC, 1985). The book was based on an extended television series.

6.   Simón Bolívar, 'Letter to General Flores' (1830), in *Doctrina del Libertador* (Caracas, Ayacucho, 1976), p. 321 (my translation). For general information on Latin American history see *Cambridge History*, the first five volumes of which have appeared since 1984. See also S. Collier, H. Blakemore and T.E. Skidmore, *Cambridge Encyclopedia of Latin America* (Cambridge, 1985).

7.   My critical edition of *Men of Maize* gives one version of the myth in microscopic form (*Hombres de maíz*, edición crítica, Klincksieck, Paris, and Fondo de Cultura Económica, Mexico, 1981). The cinema, both foreign and Latin American, has recently begun to work on this material: see Herzog's *Aguirre, Wrath of God* (1972) and the Venezuelan Diego Rísquez's *Amerika, tierra incógnita* (1988).

8.   The Argentinian novelist Julio Cortázar noted that the female as 'Eve' (woman of flesh and blood rather than ideal projection) arrived late in Latin American literature. Significantly he claimed that her first appearance was in the 1920s, in Pablo Neruda's *Twenty Love Poems and a Song of Despair* (1924): see 'Neruda parmi nous', *Europe*, 537–38 (January–February 1974), pp. 34–41. Neruda was indeed the writer who developed the same vision in poetry as Miguel Angel Asturias and Alejo Carpentier were to do through narrative fiction (see chapter 5). It is often overlooked that Cortázar's own first book, '*The Kings*' (*Los reyes*, 1949), is on the theme of Theseus and the Minotaur.

9.   See in particular C. Lévi-Strauss, *The Savage Mind* (London, 1962) and *Totemism* (London, 1962); G. Balandier, *Sens et puissance* (Paris, 1971); E. Terray, *Marxism and 'Primitive' Societies* (New York, 1972); G. Balandier, *Anthropo-logiques* (Paris, 1974); and M. Godelier, *Perspectives in Marxist Anthropology* (Cambridge, 1977). Hélène Cixous, 'Sorties', in *La Jeune Née* (Paris, 1975), reprinted in D. Lodge, *Modern Criticism and Theory* (London, Longman, 1982), pp. 286–93, gives a brief but incisive insight into the use of these oppositions in contemporary culture, as does Fredric Jameson, 'Magical Narratives', in his *The Political Unconscious* (Cornell U.P., 1981).

10.   On the theme of national mythologies closer to home, see H.A. MacDougall, *Racial Myth in English History* (Montreal and Hanover, 1982), for a study of the uses of Anglo-Saxonism in Britain's rise to imperial power. MacDougall, whose work was published in the year of the Falklands/Malvinas War, predicted that such myths would never again be used in British politics…

11.   One important exception to this general picture of neglect is Gordon Brotherston, *Image of the New World: The American Continent Portrayed in Native Texts* (London, Thames and Hudson, 1979).

12.   Autran Dourado, *The Bells of Agony* (*Os sinos da agonia*, 1974), trans. John M. Parker. (London, Peter Owen, 1988), p. 234.

13.   Both works were given more colourful titles in English translation. *Facundo* was entitled *Life in the Argentine Republic in the Days of the Tyrants*, trans. Mrs H. Mann (New York, 1868), and *Os sertões* was entitled *Revolt in the Backlands*, trans. Samuel Putnam, (London, 1947).

14.   This episode has inspired numerous works of art, the best known recent ones being Ruy Guerra's film *Os fuzis* (1964) and Mario Vargas Llosa's novel, *The War of the End of the World* (*La guerra del fin del mundo*, 1981). For a comparativist study, see S. Castro Klaren, 'Santos and Cangaceiros: Inscription without Discourse in *Os sertões* and *La guerra del fin del mundo*', *Modern Language Notes*, no. 101 (1986), pp. 366–88.

15.   The most uncompromising gesture of reversing the signs came, not surprisingly, from postrevolutionary Cuba, in the era of Fanon, Memmi and Césaire: see *Calibán* by Roberto Fernández Retamar, Director of the Casa de las Américas, written in June 1971 in the wake of the 'Padilla affair' (chapter 3). See also, among many other such Third Worldist texts, Chinweizu, *Decolonising the African Mind* (Lagos, Pero, 1987).

16.   For a historical perspective see John King, '*Sur*': *A Study of the Argentine Literary Journal and its Role in the Development of a Culture, 1931–1970* (Cambridge, 1986).

17.   There have been numerous studies of the identification of national territories with symbolic female figures. For one recent example, see Joanna Hubbs, *Mother Russia: The Feminine Myth in Russian Culture* (Indiana University Press, 1989). My only justification for

the relative absence of female voices in this work is the same as that of Annette Kolodny in her influential *The Lay of the Land* (Chapel Hill, N. Carolina University Press 1975): 'The omission of women's materials, in light of the study's subject matter, may strike some readers as curious – but it was intentional: insofar as the masculine appears to have taken power in the New World, it seemed necessary to understand its relationship to the landscape first' (p. ix). Women themselves are currently embarked on the recuperation of those alternative voices. See, for example, Jean Franco's *Plotting Women: Gender and Representation in Mexico* (London, Verso, 1989).

18. *Il pendolo di Foucault* had not appeared in English translation at the time of writing. Eco's earlier novel, *The Name of the Rose* (London, Picador, 1984, trans. William Weaver; *Il nomme della rosa*, 1980), pays homage to many world-renowned writers, including Cervantes and Conan Doyle, but above all to Latin America's Borges (who, in the shape of the blind librarian Jorge de Burgos, is the ironic villain of the piece).

19. In the last decade there have been a number of works on Latin American fiction which invoke the labyrinth or its associated concept, most of them from the United States. Their elegance and speculative prowess – Borgesian in tenor – is as striking as their remoteness from any real engagement with Latin America's concrete historical experience. See Alfred J. MacAdam, *Modern Latin American Narratives: The Dreams of Reason* (Chicago U. P., 1977); Ludmila Kapschutschenko, *El laberinto en la narrativa hispanoamericana contemporánea* (London, Támesis, 1982); Djelal Kadir, *Questing Fictions: Latin America's Family Romance* (Minneapolis, 1986); Roberto González Echevarría, *The Voice of the Masters: Writing and Authority in Modern Latin American Literature* (Austin, Texas, 1986); and Wendy Faris, *Labyrinths of Language: Symbolic Landscape and Narrative Design in Modern Fiction* (Baltimore, 1988). The last named treats both Latin American and other writers; the rest lay heavy interpretive weight on a few carefully selected Latin American texts. For comparative purposes, see also David Seed, *The Fictional Labyrinths of Thomas Pynchon* (London, Macmillan, 1988). Similar acts of identification of book with world are Gabriel Josipovici, *The World and the Book* (London, 1971), and Marilyn French, *The Book as World* (London, 1982) on Joyce. Clearly the labyrinth is a concept whose time, irresistibly, has come: our adoption of the concept in this study is intended to suggest a rehistoricization.

20. The best known work on this theme is M.S. Stabb, *In Quest of Identity: Patterns in the Spanish American Essay of Ideas, 1890–1960* (Chapel Hill, N. Carolina U. P., 1967). Useful on the relation between literature and identity is R. Campra, *América Latina: la identidad y la máscara* (Mexico, Siglo XXI, 1987). See also N. Canny and A. Pagden, *Colonial Identity in the Atlantic World, 1500–1800* (Guildford, Princeton, 1988), which is mainly about the consciousness of the Creoles; and Ernest Gellner, *Culture, Identity and Politics* (Cambridge, 1987), which takes a wider view of national and regional identity in the modern world.

21. Benedict Anderson, *Imagined Communities* (London, Verso, 1983), is already a classic study of the origins of national consciousness, and uses numerous Latin American illustrations.

22. C. Fuentes, 'Words Apart', *Guardian Weekly* (12 March 1989), p. 11. The article was on the Salman Rushdie affair.

23. For a consideration of this which is especially meaningful in the Latin American context, see Walter Benjamin, 'Fate and Character', in his *One-Way Street and Other Writings* (London, New Left Books, 1979).

2 Openings: Rediscovering America

1. Pedro Henríquez Ureña, 'El desencanto y la promesa', *Seis ensayos en busca de nuestra expresión*, in *La utopía de América* (Caracas, Ayacucho, 1978), p.33. My translation. The desolate spirit of nineteenth-century Latin America is recreated in the Mexican Fernando del Paso's recent novel, '*News of the Empire*' (*Noticias del Imperio*, 1988), about Maximilian and Carlota's ill-fated reign. Shortly before her death the deranged ex-queen remarks: 'I am María Carlota…, Princess of Nothing and Nowhere, Sovereign over the Foam and over Dreams, Queen of Chimeras and Oblivion, Empress of Deception.' Del Paso notes that the disastrous enterprise arose from Juárez' refusal to pay Mexico's foreign debt.

2.   Ibid., p. 43.

3.   This essentially Romantic sequence continues in Latin America the long Spanish literary tradition born of the medieval epics and the romances or ballad genre, which in certain respects might be said to live on today in the Cuban, Chilean and Nicaraguan 'new troubadour' movements. In general these literary forms have had to be wrested from the clutches of reactionary traditionalists like the Argentine poet Leopoldo Lugones (1874–1938), at one time a dabbler in Fascism, whose historical study *'The Gaucho Minstrel'* (*El payador*, 1916) is one of the most important works of nationalist mythology and a considerable influence on Borges's subsequent studies of gauchesque poetry.

4.   One of the most serious efforts to modify Argentina's consciousness in an Indigenist direction was Ricardo Rojas's essay *Eurindia* (1924), whose ideas were not dissimilar to the Bolivian Franz Tamayo's *'Creation of a National Pedagogy'* (1910) and the Mexican José Vasconcelos's *'The Cosmic Race'* (1925). Rojas, the patriarch of Argentine literary history, was a self-proclaimed Mestizo.

5.   Azuela, *Los de abajo*, part II, chapter 9 (ed. J. Ruffinelli, Paris, ALLCA, 1988), pp. 100–101. Although there is a published English translation by E. Munguía Jr, *The Underdogs*, I have preferred to make my own versions, both in the case of this text and most others in the rest of this book. For a general appraisal in English of the Novel of the Mexican Revolution, see J. D. Rutherford, *Mexican Society During the Revolution: A Literary Approach* (Oxford, Clarendon Press, 1971).

6.   *Los de abajo*, I, 6, p. 20.

7.   Ibid., I, 18, pp. 61–2.

8.   Ibid.

9.   *Generales y doctores* (1920) is the title of a novel by the Cuban Carlos Loveira (1882–1928) indicating the Machiavellian and mutually beneficial relationship between soldiers and lawyers which historically has characterized Latin American politics and government.

10.   *Los de abajo*, I, 15, pp. 48–9.

11.   Ibid., III, 7, pp. 139–40.

12.   Martín Luis Guzmán, *El águila y la serpiente*, part VII, chapter 4 (*Obras Completas*, vol. I, Mexico, FCE, 1985), pp. 497–98. There is a good English translation by Harriet de Onís, *The Eagle and the Serpent* (1930), but again this version is mine.

13.   Guzmán began to write the *Memorias de Pancho Villa* as soon as he returned to his country in 1936. There is a condensed English version, *Memoirs of Pancho Villa*, translated by Virginia H. Taylor (1965).

14.   G. López y Fuentes, *'Tierra*, in A. Castro Leal (ed.), *La novela de la Revolución Mexicana*, vol. II (Mexico, Aguilar, 6th edn, 1966), pp. 302–04.

15.   R. Gallegos, *Canaima* (Buenos Aires, Austral, 9th edn, 1968), pp. 9–13. The novel was translated into English as *Canaima* by Jaime Tello (1984).

16.   J.E. Rivera, *La vorágine* (Buenos Aires, Losada, 7th edn, 1962), pp. 167–8. There is an English translation by Earle K. James, *The Vortex* (1935). See E. Neale-Silva, 'The Factual Bases of *La vorágine*', *PMLA*, 54 (1939), pp. 316–31, for useful historical background.

17.   Ibid., p. 12.

18.   Ibid., p. 47.

19.   Ibid., p. 30.

20.   Ibid., pp. 95–6.

21.   Ibid., p. 175.

22.   That there were no 'characters' in the 'regionalist' or 'telluric' or Social Realist narrative of the 1920s and 1930s was a commonplace of sophisticated literary criticism in the 1960s, not least among the 'boom' writers themselves. It was Mario Vargas Llosa who, in an article in the *Times Literary Supplement* (14 November 1968, pp. 1287–8), coined the title 'Primitives and Creators' to distinguish between the achievements of his own generation and the 'rudimentary' works of the writers of Social Realist 'preliterature'. He quoted Rivera's conclusion ironically, as does Carlos Fuentes the following year as the point of departure for his *La nueva novela latinoamericana* (Mexico, Joaquín Mortiz, 1969).

23.   See E.L. Tinker, *The Horsemen of the Americas and the Literature they Inspired* (New York, 1953). There is a long bibliography on the gaucho by British authors, from Darwin's brief

notes to the works of W.H. Hudson (especially *Far Away and Long Ago*) and R.S. Cunninghame Graham. On the political implications, not only in Latin America, see S. Finer, *The Man on Horseback* (London, 1962).

24.   *Don Segundo Sombra* (Buenos Aires, Losada, 23rd edn, 1966), p. 17. There is an English translation by Harriet de Onís, but all versions used are my own. A recent book on Güiraldes's novel by Françoise Pérus, *Historia y crítica literaria: el realismo social y la crisis de la dominación oligárquica* (Havana, Casa de las Américas, 1982), sets the novel in historical context.

25.   *Don Segundo Sombra*, p. 166.

26.   Ibid., p. 79.

27.   Ibid., p. 51.

28.   Ibid., p. 182.

29.   Ibid., p. 185.

30.   *Doña Bárbara* (Buenos Aires, Austral, 23rd edn, 1967), p. 32. There is an English translation by Robert Malloy, *Doña Bárbara* (1931), but the English versions quoted here are mine.

31.   Ibid., p. 58. Among the many works on the North American landscape, two by Annette Kolodny are particularly useful for comparative purposes. The first was *The Lay of the Land* (1975), motivated by 'my growing distress at what we have done to our continent' (p. ix), and which, as we have seen, effectively presented the masculine view of the New World. The second was *The Land Before Her: Fantasy and Experience of the American Frontiers, 1630–1860* (Chapel Hill, N. Carolina U.P., 1988), presenting the feminine experience. See also George Dekker, *The American Historical Romance* (Cambridge, 1987) and Robert Lawson-Peebles, *Landscape and Written Expression in Revolutionary America: The World Turned Upside Down* (Cambridge, 1988). There are as yet no Latin American equivalents, but for a helpful treatment of Latin American frontiers, see A. Hennessy, *The Frontier in Latin American History* (London, Edward Arnold, 1978).

32..   *Doña Bárbara*, p. 20.

33.   For a stimulating if inherently tautological treatment of Gallegos's pioneering inscription of the Latin American landscape, see R. González Echevarría's excellent '*Doña Bárbara* Writes the Plain', in his *The Voice of the Masters* (Texas, 1986). *Doña Bárbara* is one of the great 'foundational fictions' to be reviewed in Doris Sommer's important forthcoming study, *Irresistible Romance: The Foundational Fictions of Latin America*.

34.   V.S. Naipaul, 'The Reality and the Romance', *Sunday Times Magazine* (27 October 1974), pp. 56–66.

35.   Ibid., p. 61.

36.   Ibid.

37.   Ibid., p. 56.

38.   Gallegos, *Reinaldo Solar* (Buenos Aires, Austral, 1969), chapter 10. Naipaul, talking about his own father's quest for identity in Trinidad, remarks: 'My father was a self-taught man, picking his way through a cultural confusion of which he was perhaps hardly aware and which I have only recently begun to understand; and he wished himself to be a writer. He read less for pleasure than for clues, hints and encouragement; and he introduced me to those writers he had come upon in his own search' ('Reality and Romance', p. 56). Borges could have said the same about his father's influence during his own childhood.

39.   Edward W. Said, 'Through Gringo Eyes: With Conrad in Latin America', *Harper's Magazine (*April 1988), pp. 70–72.

40.   Carpentier used the image a number of times, most notably in *The Lost Steps*, trans. H. de Onís (London, Gollancz, 1956; *Los pasos perdidos*, 1953), p. 74, where he says that the only worthwhile mission for the Latin American artist is 'Adam's task of giving things their names'. Like Rivera's 'the jungle devoured them', this has become one of the unavoidable clichés of Latin American literary and cultural discourse.

41.   *Reinaldo Solar*, p. 10.

42.   The line from Walter Scott through Cooper to Alencar is traced in R.R. Mautner Wasserman, 'Re-inventing the New World: Cooper and Alencar', *Comparative Literature* (1986) pp. 130–45. There has been renewed interest in Cooper in recent years. See Robert Clark

(ed.), *James Fenimore Cooper: New Critical Essays* (London, Vision Press, 1987), and James D. Wallace, *Early Cooper and his Audience* (New York, Columbia, 1987). Cambridge University Press republished the *Leatherstocking Tales* in two volumes in 1986. For the first major collection of essays comparing North American and Latin American literature, see Bell Gale Chevigny and Gari Laguardia, *Reinventing the Americas: Comparative Studies of Literature of the United States and Spanish America* (Cambridge, 1986).

3 Closures: Conflicts and Commitments

1. Graciliano Ramos, *Vidas sêcas* (São Paulo, Martins, 13th ed., 1965), pp. 121–22. My version. Despite the attractions of 'Barren Lives', the English version (1961; reprinted 1973), should perhaps have precisely translated the original, 'Dry Lives'.

2. Ibid., pp. 158–9. For other works on Brazil in English, see W. Grossman, (ed.), *Modern Brazilian Short Stories* (Los Angeles, California University Press, 1967), E. Bishop and E. Brasil, eds., *An Anthology of Twentieth-Century Brazilian Literature* (Middletown, Wesleyan University Press, 1972), and C.L. Hulet, *Brazilian Literature*, 3 vols. (Washington DC, Georgetown University Press, 1974), an anthology with texts in Portuguese and commentaries in English. A recent critical work is D. Patai, *Myth and Ideology in Contemporary Brazilian Fiction* (Rutherford and London, Associated University Presses, 1983).

3. Jorge Icaza, *Huasipungo* (Buenos Aires, Losada, 3rd edn, 1965), p. 18. My version. There are two English translations, *Huasipungo* (trans. Mervyn Savill, 1962), and *The Villagers* (trans. Bernard M. Dulsey, 1964). The latter title is somewhat misleading, given the subject matter.

4. Ibid., pp. 26–7.

5. Ibid., pp. 17–18.

6. Ibid., p. 15.

7. Ibid., p. 139. Possibly the most interesting indigenist novel to have been written by an Ecuadorean since Icaza is '*Why Have the Herons Flown Away?*' (*¿Porqué se fueron las garzas?*, 1979) by Gustavo Alfredo Jácome (1912–).

8. Perhaps surprisingly, *El tungsteno* has recently been translated (*Tungsten*, trans. Robert Mezey, Syracuse, 1988).

9. R. Haya de la Torre, 'Anti-Imperialism and Apra' (1936), quoted in R. Alexander, *Aprismo: The Ideas and Doctrines of Víctor Raúl Haya de la Torre* (Kent State, 1973). Haya's first version had been published in 1928 and was dedicated to 'the workers, manual and intellectual, of Indo-America'.

10. Ciro Alegría, *Los perros hambrientos* (Buenos Aires, Losada, 2nd edn, 1971), p. 7.

11. Ibid., pp. 9–11.

12. Haya, 'We are not ashamed to call ourselves Indo-Americans' (1938), quoted by Alexander, *Aprismo* pp. 353–5.

13. Alegría, *Los perros hambrientos*, p. 145.

14. Ibid., p. 93.

15. Ibid., p. 12.

16. Ibid., pp. 12, 19.

17. Ibid., p. 37.

18. Haya, 'Anti-Imperialism and Apra' in *Aprismo*, pp. 163–70.

19. *Broad and Alien is the World*, translated by Harriet de Onís (New York, Farrar and Rinehart, 1941), p. 7. Merlin Press, London, reissued the novel in 1983, with four previously unpublished chapters translated by Mike Gonzalez. Alegría's *La serpiente de oro* has also been translated (*The Golden Serpent*, 1943).

20. See Clifford Geertz, *Works and Lives: The Anthropologist as Author* (Oxford, Polity, 1988); and Daniel C. Dennett, 'Why everyone is a Novelist', *Times Literary Supplement* (16–22 September 1988), pp. 1016, 1028.

21. See Benedict Anderson, *Imagined Communities*, pp. 32–40.

22. Arguedas's most important literary successor was his fellow Peruvian Manuel Scorza, who died in 1983 in the same plane crash which killed Angel Rama, Marta Traba and Jorge

Ibargüengoitia. Scorza, who remains virtually unstudied, due to his late arrival on the scene of a genre widely considered an anachronism, was particularly important because he himself took part in the peasant uprising of 1960, which is the point of departure of his five major indigenist novels. This was just one example of Latin America's unknown struggles, what Scorza himself has called the 'invisible' or 'silent' wars which never come to the attention of the international press.

23.   The concept of 'transculturation' was invented by the Cuban ethnologist Fernando Ortiz. Rama's principal work on the theme is *Transculturación narrativa en América Latina* (Mexico, Siglio XXI, 1982), and uses Arguedas's *Deep Rivers* as its paradigm in much the same way that Pérus, *Historia*, uses Güiraldes.

24.   Rama, *Transculturación* , p. 207.

25.   Arguedas, 'No soy un aculturado' (1968): see appendix to his posthumous novel, '*The Fox Above and the Fox Below*' (*El zorro de arriba y el zorro de abajo* (Buenos Aires, Losada, 1971).

26.   There are those who disagree as to the merits of '*Everyone's Blood*'. Mario Vargas Llosa, who has written frequently on Arguedas, says that the work is 'simplistic, a caricature', 'the classic failure of an artistic talent due to the self-imposition of social commitment'. See 'The Writer in Latin America', in G. Theiner (ed.), *They Shoot Writers, Don't They?* (London, Faber and Faber, 1984), p. 171.

27.   Arguedas, *Todas las sangres* (Buenos Aires, Losada, 1970), vol.I, pp. 35–6.

28.   Ibid., II, p. 79.

29.   Ibid., II, pp. 252–3.

30.   Ibid., II, p. 258.

31.   Ibid., II, p. 259.

32.   The national question has been debated with particular vigour by anthropologists, historians and literary critics, especially in Mexico and Peru since 1917, and with increasing urgency in both countries since 1968. On Peru, see F. Sánchez Albavera *et al.*, *Problema nacional: cultura y clases sociales* (Lima, Desco, 1981), and A. Cornejo Polar *et al.*, *Literatura y sociedad en el Perú* (Lima, Hueso Húmero, 1981). On Mexico, see SEP, *Culturas populares y política cultural* (Mexico, 1982), and *Cultura y sociedad en México y América Latina* (Mexico, 1987).

33.   Vargas Llosa is the staunchest literary defender of liberalism, both in Peru and Latin America as a whole. For an overview of his position, see my 'Mario Vargas Llosa: Errant Knight of the Liberal Imagination', in J. King (ed.), *Modern Latin American Fiction: A Survey* (London, Faber and Faber, 1987), pp. 205–33.

34.   Roa Bastos, *Hijo de hombre* (Buenos Aires, Losada, 4th edn, 1971), p. 13. My version. There is an English translation by Rachel Caffyn, *Son of Man* (London, Gollancz, 1965).

35.   Roa Bastos, quoted in *Marcha* (Montevideo, 8 July 1973), p. 9.

36.   Roa Bastos, 'Entretiens', *Caravelle*, no.17 (Toulouse, 1971), p. 208.

37.   Ibid., pp. 208, 214.

38.   Roa Bastos, *Hijo de hombre*, pp. 280–1.

39.   Fidel Castro, closing speech at National Congress on Education and Culture, Havana 1971. This and other documents relating to the 'Padilla Affair' can be found in *Libre*, I, a magazine founded in Paris in 1971 by opponents of the official Cuban line, including Vargas Llosa, Carlos Fuentes and the Spanish novelist Juan Goytisolo. See also *Index*, I, 2 (1972) for the subsequent debate involving Cabrera Infante, Padilla and others.

40.   Roa Bastos, 'Entretiens', pp. 215–16.

41.   Final Declaration of the National Congress on Education and Culture, Havana, 1971. See *Libre*, I.

42.   *Hijo de hombre*, p. 61.

43.   Ibid., p. 168.

44.   Ibid., p. 38.

45.   Ibid., p. 19.

46.   Ibid., p. 14.

47.   Ibid., p. 123. The preoccupation with the transience of words and the incommunicability of experience has haunted Roa Bastos, as it did Miguel Angel Asturias. Both writers

meditated extensively on oral tradition and popular culture. The Christian basis of much of this reflection about word and spirit is suggested in 'Easter Vigil', a poem by Pope John Paul II from *Easter Vigil and Other Poems* (trans. Jerzy Peterkiewicz, London, Hutchinson, 1979): 'This I say: much of man dies in things,/ more than remains... Never separate man from things, the body/ of his history – Never separate/ people from Man who became/ the body of their history.' Roa pursued the theme with almost obsessive zeal in *I the Supreme*.

48.　*Hijo de hombre*, p. 273.
49.　Ibid., p. 247.
50.　Roa Bastos, 'Entretiens', p. 217.
51.　*Hijo de hombre*, p. 132.
52.　Roa Bastos, 'Entretiens', p. 216.

4　Dead Ends: Cities and Prisons

1.　See N. Sánchez-Albornoz, 'The Population of Latin America, 1850–1930', in L. Bethell (ed.), *Cambridge History of Latin America*, vol. IV (1986), pp. 121–152.

2.　For an overview, see José Luis Romero, *Latinoamérica: las ciudades y las ideas* (Mexico, Siglo XXI, 1976); also Angel Rama, *La ciudad letrada* (Hanover, N.H., Ediciones del Norte, 1984).

3.　There is of course a vast bibliography on these matters. Particularly useful for comparisons with the Latin American case are Raymond Williams, *The Country and the City* (London, Paladin, 1975), and Walter Benjamin, *Charles Baudelaire: A Lyric Poet in the Era of High Capitalism* (London, Verso, 1973).

4.　Alejo Carpentier, 'Problemática de la actual novela latinoamericana', in *Tientos y diferencias* (Havana, Casa de las Américas, 1966), p. 15. For case study treatments of Rio in the late nineteenth century and Buenos Aires in the 1920s, see Jeffrey D. Needell, *A Tropical 'Belle Epoque': Elite Culture and Society in Turn-of-the-Century Rio de Janeiro* (Cambridge, 1987), and Beatriz Sarlo, *Una modernidad periférica: Buenos Aires 1920 y 1930* (Buenos Aires, Nueva Visión, 1988).

5.　Pedro Calderón de la Barca, *La vida es sueño* II, 11 (Buenos Aires, Austral, 15th edn, 1967), p. 178. The play has been translated many times into English, once, improbably, as *Such Stuff as Dreams are Made of* (trans. E. Fitzgerald, London, 1853), and later, as *Life is a Dream* or *Life's a Dream*, by a succession of different writers. Present version mine.

6.　Inca Garcilaso de la Vega, *Comentarios reales (selección)*, II, 11 (Buenos Aires, Austral, 8th edn, 1967), pp. 139–42.

7.　Octavio Paz, *Sor Juana: Her Life and Her World*, trans. Margaret Sayers Peden (London, Faber, 1988).

8.　Sor Juana Inés de la Cruz, *Obras escogidas* (Buenos Aires, Austral, 10th edn, 1959), p. 45. There are many similar examples in Sor Juana's poetry. For example, one of her best known sonnets, 'Diuturna enfermedad de la esperanza' ('Unending Sickness of Hope'), uses the concept of prolonged torture as its shaping idea.

9.　J.M. Machado de Assis, *Epitaph of a Small Winner*, trans. William Grossman (London, Hogarth Press, 1985), p. 223.

10.　E. Cambaceres, *Sin rumbo* (Buenos Aires, Huemul, 1966), p. 28.

11.　G. Ramos, *Angústia* (São Paulo, Martins, 9th edn, 1936), pp. 7, 9. My version, though there is an English translation, *Anguish* (1946). Ramos's different approach to rural and urban fiction is typical of Latin American writers in most eras. When they write about the countryside they invariably centre around peasant characters, but when they move to the city they portray petty-bourgeois characters like themselves: which would seem to confirm the thesis outlined in this chapter. Indeed, it has to be said that the urban masses are, on the whole, only rarely the central focus of Latin American narrative in comparison with other groups. See I. Díaz Ruiz, 'El proletariado en la narrativa latinoamericana', *Latinoamérica*, no. 11 (National University of Mexico, 1978), pp. 43–57. One of the most important writers on the urban working classes is José Revueltas of Mexico, mentioned below. Prior to 1973 Chile was especially notable for its realist vein. See Nicomedes Guzmán (1914–64), widely recognized as the most 'proletarian' of all Latin American novelists, author of '*Obscure Men*' (*Los hombres oscuros*, 1939), '*Blood and Hope*' (*La sangre y la esperanza*, 1942), and '*The Light comes from the Sea*' (*La luz viene del mar*, 1951). Other important Chileans are Manuel Rojas (1896–1973), Láutaro Yankas (1902–) and Volodia Teitelboim (1916–).

12.   In *The Land Before Her* Annette Kolodny notes that whilst the men on the frontier were busy felling trees, the women were usually to be found planting gardens.

13.   J.C. Onetti, *El pozo* (Montevideo, Arca, 5th edn, 1969), pp. 45–6. Onetti has been considered an unappreciated novelist by those in the know for almost forty years, which may be a record. His only works available in English are *A Brief Life* (*La vida breve*, 1950) and *The Shipyard* (*El astillero*, 1961).

14.   The novel was translated by its author, first as *Inconsolable Memories* (London, Deutsch, 1968), and then as *Memories of Underdevelopment* (Harmondsworth, Penguin, 1971).

15.   M.A. Asturias, *El señor Presidente*, I, 6 (R. Navas Ruiz, ed., Klincksieck, Paris, and FCE, Mexico, 1978), p. 35. There is an English translation, *The President* (1972), but present versions are mine.

16.   *El señor Presidente*, I, 3, p. 18.

17.   E. Sábato, *Sobre héroes y tumbas* (Buenos Aires, Sudamericana, 12th edn, 1970), p. 347. There is a translation, *On Heroes and Tombs* (1981). This novel was especially successful in France and Italy.

18.   Sábato was educated as a physicist, but found he preferred metaphysics. His relation to national politics has been a tormented one, as he has often found himself under attack from both the left and the right. In 1983 he presided over the commission set up by President Alfonsín to investigate the 'Dirty War' carried out by the Argentine military during the 1976–82 period. The report was entitled *Nunca más* (Buenos Aires, 1984), but is also known as the 'Sábato Report'.

19.   C. Fuentes, *La región más transparente* (Mexico, FCE, 6th edn, 1968), pp. 459–60. There is a translation by Sam Hileman, *Where the Air is Clear* (1960).

20.   M. Vargas Llosa, *Conversación en la Catedral* (Barcelona, Barral, 6th edn, 1973), p. 13. An English version appeared in 1975.

21.   Ibid., pp. 26–7.

22.   '*Lima the Horrible*' was an essay on the Peruvian capital by Sebastián Salazar Bondy, published in 1964. Unfortunately, perhaps, it turned out to be one of those titles that stick.

23.   One of the most moving works about a Latin American city is Elena Poniatowska's '*Nothing, No One*' (*Nada, nadie*, Mexico, Era, 1988), a documentary evocation of the Mexico City earthquake of 1985. Poniatowska manages to discover hope where her male colleagues normally find only defeat and despair.

5   Into the Labyrinth: Ulysses in America

1.   For critical consideration of these questions, see César Fernández Moreno (ed.), *América Latina en su literatura* (Mexico, Siglo XXI, 1972), Angel Rama, *La novela latinoamericana: panoramas 1920–1980* (Bogotá, Instituto Colombiano de Cultura, 1982), Alejandro Losada, *La literatura en la sociedad de América Latina* (Frankfurt, Vervuert, 1983), and Ana Pizarro (ed.), *La literatura latinoamericana como proceso* (Buenos Aires, CEAL, 1985), and *Hacia una historia de la literatura latinoamericana* (Mexico, El Colegio de México, 1987).

2.   A rare attempt to acclimatize us to this new world is Marshall Berman's powerful essay *All that is Solid Melts into Air: the Experience of Modernity* (London, Verso, 1983).

3.   Attempts to define Magical Realism, whether inside or outside Latin America, have produced more heat than light. See A. Flores, 'Magical Realism in Spanish American Fiction', in *Hispania*, 38 (May 1955), E. Anderson Imbert, '*El realismo mágico*' *y otros ensayos* (Caracas, Monte Avila, 1976). We have no space to explore the concept fully here. J. Weisgerber, 'Le réalisme magique: la locution et le concept', *Rivista di Letterature Moderne e Comparate*, 35; 1 (1982), effects a useful archaeology of the term, whilst Fredric Jameson, 'On

Magic Realism in Film', *Critical Enquiry*, 12 (Winter 1986), pp. 301–25, gives an insightful if unsystematized reading of cinema applications.

4.   From his inaugural address to the James Joyce Centenary Symposium in Dublin in June 1982. Material in this and succeeding chapters draws on my own paper on 'James Joyce and Spanish American Fiction', subsequently published in *Estudos Anglo-Americanos*, 7–8 (São Paulo, 1983–4), pp. 106–130.

5.   In addition to the unique irradiating power of Joyce's influence, he also has 'normal' effects on writers in Latin America, as when his *Dubliners* inspired the Uruguayan Mario Benedetti to write *Montevideanos* (1959).

6.   The most notable exception – a 'rural' author profoundly motivated by readings of Joyce – is Brazil's João Guimarães Rosa, with *The Devil to Pay in the Backlands* (1956); see below, chapter 6.

7.   Asturias is quoted from a conversation with this writer in London, May 1967; Carpentier from the Cuban magazine *Social*, 16, 8 (Havana, 1931); and Borges from his now famous review of *Ulysses*, 'El *Ulises* de Joyce', accompanied by his translation of the last page in *Proa*, 6 (Buenos Aires, January 1925, pp. 3–6). Borges's much later poem, 'Invocation to Joyce', quoted from at the head of this section, ends: 'What does our cowardice matter/ if there is one brave man on earth,/ what does sadness matter if someone/ some time said he was happy,/ what does my lost generation matter,/ that hazy mirror,/ if it is justified by your books.' (*Obra poética*, Madrid, Alianza, 1972, pp. 350–1). Borges' most concrete homage to Joyce, however, came when he attended the 1982 centenary symposium in Dublin, at the age of 83.

8.   Even Borges, always allergic to long narratives, translated a novel of Faulkner – *The Wild Palms* – only a year after its publication in the United States (*Las palmeras salvajes*, Buenos, Aires, 1940). See below, this chapter.

9.   'El sánscredo latinizado: el *Wake* en Hispanoamérica', *Zona Franca*, 3rd series, 5 (Caracas, 1978), pp. 31–4. The article was previously published in *Triquarterly*, 38 (Winter 1977), pp. 54–62. Haroldo de Campos and his brother Augusto were founders of the 'Concrete Poetry' movement in Brazil and are the principal exponents and translators there of Joyce's work, especially *Finnegans Wake*. See *Panaroma do Finnegans Wake* (São Paulo, 1962). As an expert on Joyce's work, it is no coincidence that H. de Campos coined the term 'Open Work', later to be adopted by Umberto Eco in his influential theoretical opus.

10.   This, according to MacAdam, *The Dreams of Reason*, is the central current of the new Latin American fiction: he examines particularly the impact of Joyce on Cortázar and Cabrera Infante. Octavio Paz, similarly, interviewed in R. Guibert, *Seven Voices* (New York, Vintage, 1973), affirms that Joyce's essential achievement is to have permanently annulled the distinction between poetry and fiction: 'In his work the central element is language. His characters are, quite literally, puns' (p. 203).

11.   For a Spanish American view of this, see J. Loveluck, 'Crisis y renovación de la novela hispanoamericana', in Loveluck (ed.), *La novela hispanoamericana* (Santiago de Chile, 1969, pp. 11–29), p. 28. Loveluck was attempting at the time to convert '*joycismo*' into a neutral technical term instead of a criminal charge.

12.   G. Cabrera Infante, interviewed in Guibert, *Seven Voices*, pp. 341–436, argued that books like Joyce's really burst the confines of the 'novel' as genre and ought to be given some other name.

13.   Severo Sarduy, another virtuoso Cuban novelist, in an essay on the 'baroque' tendency in Latin American fiction ('El barroco y el neobarroco', in C. Fernández Moreno, *América Latina*), has given the following account of the relation between Joyce and Leopoldo Marechal: 'In *Adam Buenosaires*, Marechal underlines... his adherence to the category "writing/odyssey". The primary structure of this sequence is, of course, the one postulated by Joyce, whose authority, as model, derives from the entire Homeric tradition, that of a narrative whose orthogonal axes would be "book as journey/journey as book" '(pp. 180–1).

14.   Jean Franco, 'El viaje frustrado en la literatura hispanoamericana contemporánea', in *Actas del Tercer Congreso Internacional de Hispanistas* (Mexico, 1970, pp. 365–70), examines this theme in García Márquez, Cortázar and Vargas Llosa. For a view of the same general topic from a different perspective, see T. Todorov, *La Conquête de l'Amérique: la question de l'Autre* (Paris, Seuil, 1982).

15. One Spanish American equivalent of this literary–linguistic underground adventure would be Asturias's *Mulata* (*Mulata de tal*, 1963); published in London as *The Mulata and Mister Fly* (1967).

16. See H. de Campos, 'Superación de los lenguajes exclusivos', in Fernández Moreno, *América Latina* pp. 279–300.

17. On the problem of perfectionism, see the novel by J. E. Adoum, '*Between Marx and a Naked Woman*' (*Entre Marx y una mujer desnuda*, 1976): 'after long hours of effort, one cannot manage even half a page, like Joyce, or even to take out a comma, like Wilde' (Mexico, Siglo XXI, 3rd edn, 1980, p. 88); and on the question of actuality, see Borges, 'El *Ulises* de Joyce', p. 5: 'in no other book do we witness the actual presence of things with such firm conviction.'

18. See Borges's celebrated brief essay, 'Valéry as a Symbol', in his *Other Inquisitions 1937–1952* (London, 1973), pp. 73–4.

19. Cabrera Infante, quoted in Guibert, *Seven Voices*, p. 418, among other interesting comments claims that *Finnegans Wake* is 'writing that is deliberately hieroglyphic'.

20. 'Joyce y los neologismos', *Sur*, 62 (Buenos Aires, November 1939), pp. 59–61.

21. H. de Campos, 'El sánscredo latinizado', p. 32.

22. The two Latin American versions of fragments of *Finnegans Wake* appeared, significantly enough, at the beginning of the 'boom'. The Mexican writer Salvador Elizondo published an excellent version of the first page, together with an extended commentary, in a review he edited, *Snob*, 1 (Mexico, 20 June 1962). His tour de force persuades us that if only there were life enough and time ('A way a lone a last...', etc.), a Spanish equivalent could, after all, be achieved. The Campos brothers translated several sections into Portuguese, including the same first page, in their *Panaroma* in the same year. They also quote the references to Brazil ('from Blasil the Brast to our povotogesus portocall'; 'A disincarnated spirit, called Sebastion, from the Rivera in Januero'; and 'on the island of Breasil the width of me perished and I took my plowshure sadly, feeling pity for me sored').

23. Borges's brief translation ends: 'y Gibraltar de jovencita cuando yo era una Flor de la Montaña sí cuando me até la rosa en el pelo como las chicas andaluzas o me pondré una colorada sí y cómo me besó junto al paredón morisco y pensé lo mismo me da el que otro cualquiera y entonces le pedí con los ojos que me pidiera otra vez y entonces me pidió sí quería sí para decirle sí mi flor serrana y primero lo abracé sí y encima mío lo agaché para que sintiera mis pechos toda fragancia sí y su corazón enloquecido y sí yo dije sí quiero Sí'. It will not be necessary to remind the reader that Molly, principle of spontaneity and instinct, is recalling the days of the past when she was a mountain flower and Hispanic culture gave a wild and exotic romantic background to the naturalistic impulses of sexual love.

24. Borges was consistently interesting over the years on the subject of translation, and in particular on the – for him – self-evident superiority of English over other rival languages. He was thinking of things Joycean in his 1941 'fiction', 'Tlön, Uqbar, Orbis Tertius', when he translated a phrase from the idealist language of Tlön as 'Upward, behind the onstreaming, it mooned'.

25. A persistent prejudice among Latin American writers is that Joyce is a late product of 'Western civilization', a truly scholarly author, whereas Faulkner is a 'new barbarian'.

26. As we shall have more than one occasion to mention, Salman Rushdie, a novelist both 'Joycean' and 'magical realist', became an example of this syndrome in February 1989 with the uproar in the Islamic world over his *Satanic Verses*.

27. 'Períodos literarios en el México del siglo XX', in Aurora M. Ocampo, ed., *La crítica de la novela mexicana contemporánea* (Mexico, 1981), pp. 165–6.

28. 'El sánscredo latinizado', p. 34.

29. See L.A. Sánchez, *Historia comparada de las literaturas americanas* (Buenos Aires, Losada, 1974), vol. IV, p. 16.

30. 'El *Ulises* de Joyce', p. 3.

31. See R. Burgin, *Conversations with Jorge Luis Borges* (London, Souvenir Press, 1973), pp. 73, 78.

32. 'The Flower of Coleridge', in *Other Inquisitions*, p. 12. Borges, many of whose 'fictions' are actually about 'influences', 'antecedents', etc., paid Joyce the unequalled compliment that 'he has no literary precursors' ('El *Ulises*', p. 5). Another elegant tribute

closing the same review article was to quote the transparent Lope de Vega's respectful but partly ironic words on Góngora's opaque poetry: 'I shall love and esteem the divine wit of this gentleman, taking from him with humility what I understand and fervently admiring that which I shall never understand' (p. 6).

33. 'La exposición del año', *Social*, 17, 9 (Havana, 1932). Forty-five years later the title of the last chapter of Robert Adams's *Afterjoyce: Studies in Fiction after 'Ulysses'* (New York, Oxford U. P., 1977), 'The Joyce Era?', would still be asking – unnecessarily, in my opinion – whether such predictions had turned out to be true. The book includes chapters on Borges and Lezama Lima.

34. 'Formas en la novela contemporánea', in Loveluck, *La novela*. This is an influential article which focuses on Joyce's general influence on fictional form in Latin America; see especially pp. 224–5.

35. See also M.P. González, 'Leopoldo Marechal y la novela fantástica', in his *Notas críticas* (Havana, Casa de las Américas, 1969), pp. 74–88, in which the Joycean parallels are well brought out; also Harss's influential introduction to his collection of interviews, which identifies '*Adam Buenosaires*' as 'the first real attempt at a total novel in our literature. It is at the same time a Buenos Aires odyssey – with echoes of Joyce's *Ulysses* – and a Dantean allegory' (*Into the Mainstream*, p. 28).

36. 'The New Latin American Novelists', *Partisan Review*, 44, 1 (1977), p. 41. For a retrospective, see his 'The New Novelists', *Encounter*, 25, 3 (1965), pp. 97–109.

37. See R. Fiddian, 'James Joyce y Fernando del Paso', *Insula*, 455 (Madrid, October 1984), p. 10. Fiddian is a leading interpreter both of Del Paso and of Joyce's impact on Spanish America.

38. For a discussion of this, see A. Uslar Pietri's prologue to Miguel Angel Asturias, *El señor Presidente*, critical edition by R. Navas Ruiz (Klincksieck, Paris, and FCE, Mexico, 1978). A recent example of the phenomenon is Régis Debray's novelized autobiography, *Les Masques* (Paris, Gallimard, 1987). See chapter 9 below.

39. See H. de Campos, '*Macunaíma*: la fantasía estructural', in M. de Andrade, *Macunaíma* (Barcelona, Seix Barral, 1977), p. 11. For a general study of related matters, see Paulo de Carvalho-Neto, *Folklore y psicoanálisis* (Mexico, Joaquín Mortiz, 1968).

40. Mário de Andrade, *Macunaíma*, trans. E.A. Goodland (London, Quartet, 1984), p. 168.

41. Mário de Andrade, *Macunaíma*, critical edition by Telê Porto Ancona Lopez (Paris, ALLCA, 1988), p. 148.

42. Alejo Carpentier, *Ecue–Yamba–O* (Barcelona, Bruguera, 1979), pp. 192–3. A *ñáñigo* was a member of a secret religious society formerly set up by slaves for mutual protection and to worship the god Eribó. Asturias wrote a similar narrative involving native dance with his *Torotumbo* (1955).

43. *Ecue–Yamba–O*, p. 8.

44. For a recent review of Black writing in Latin America, see R. Jackson, 'The Black Novel in Latin America Today', *Chasqui* 16, 2–3 (November 1987).

45. M.A. Asturias, *Leyendas de Guatemala* (Buenos Aires, Losada, 1957), p. 74.

46. Ibid., pp. 22–6.

47. This only became clear with the publication of the critical edition coordinated by R. Navas Ruiz. See my '*El señor Presidente*: una lectura contextual' in that work, pp. lxxxii–cxxxix, and 'M.A.Asturias: '*El señor Presidente*', in P. Swanson (ed.), *Landmarks in Modern Latin American Fiction* (London, Routledge, 1989).

48. M.A. Asturias, *El señor Presidente*, p. 7. See William H. Gass, 'The First Seven Pages of the Boom', *Latin American Literary Review*, 29 (January–June 1987), pp. 33–56.

49. *El señor Presidente*, pp. 73–4.

50. See M.A. Asturias, 'A la sombra de la torre Eiffel: *Las lanzas coloradas*' (30 June 1931), in his *París 1924–1933: Periodismo y creación literaria*, coordinated by Amos Segala, edited by Gerald Martin (Paris, ALLCA, 1988), pp. 435–436. The same vision remained with him when, at the end of his life, he wrote '*Three of Four Suns*' (*Tres de cuatro soles*, ed. D. Nouhaud, Paris, Klincksieck, and Mexico, FCE, 1977): 'Creation. One's own. And oneself feeding off it. Free. Lit up. Cut into lighted pieces... Her. My surprised self. Eden's blush. Violent hope. Earthquake. Contact with woman, direct, immediate, cosmic' (pp. 60–1).

51.   A. Carpentier, *The Kingdom of this World*, trans. Harriet de Onís (London, Gollancz, 1967), pp. 148–9. Carpentier's idea here is similar to Borges's well known story, 'The Immortal', from *El Aleph*, though Borges as ever gives the theme of immortality a more abstract treatment. Carpentier's novel is similar in standpoint to Pablo Neruda's great poem 'The Heights of Macchu Picchu' ('Las alturas de Macchu Picchu', in his *Canto general*, 1950).

52.   G. Venaissin, 'M. A. Asturias: *M le Président*', *Esprit*, 21, 7 (July 1953), pp. 153–8.

53.   One of the first critics to see this was the Peruvian Julio Ortega in his excellent *La contemplación y la fiesta* (Caracas, Monte Avila, 1969). See his essay 'Borges, fundador'.

54.   See E. Rodríguez Monegal's excellent *Jorge Luis Borges: A Literary Biography* (New York, Dutton, 1978).

55.   See Ariel Dorfman, 'Borges y la violencia americana' in *Imaginación y violencia en América Latina* (Barcelona, Anagrama, 2nd edn, 1972); John Sturrock, *Paper Tigers: The Ideal Fictions of Jorge Luis Borges* (Oxford, 1977); Paul de Man, 'A Modern Master', in H. Bloom (ed.), *Jorge Luis Borges* (New York, Chelsea House, 1986), pp. 21–8; Julio Rodríguez-Luis, 'La intención política en la obra de Borges: hacia una visión de conjunto', *Cuadernos Hispanoamericanos*, 361–2 (Madrid, July–August 1980), pp. 1–29; John King, 'Jorge Luis Borges: A View from the Periphery', in his *Modern Latin American Fiction*, pp. 101–16; and Jean Franco, 'The Utopia of a Tired Man: Jorge Luis Borges', *Social Text*, no. 4 (Fall 1981), pp. 52–78. Franco makes one of the most devastating critiques of Borges's political ploys. However, whilst providing a brilliant explanation of Borges's attraction for conservatives, she declines to recuperate him for progressive thought.

56.   J.L. Borges, *Dreamtigers* (London, Souvenir Press, 1973), p. 79. There are now so many translations of Borges' work that it is impossible to list them all. The most useful compilation remains *Labyrinths: Selected Stories and Other Writings* (ed. Donald Yates and James E. Irby, New York, New Directions, 1962; Harmondsworth, Penguin, 1970), which includes most of the stories of *Fictions* and *El Aleph*, a number of key essays and extracts from *Dreamtigers*.

57.   Borges, 'The Argentine Writer and Tradition', in *Labyrinths*, pp. 217–18.

58.   Borges, 'The Far-flung Tongue', in *Encounter*, 25, 3 (September 1965), p. 86.

59.   Borges, in the prologue to Burgin, *Conversations*, p. 7.

60.   Borges, 'The Other Tiger', *Dreamtigers*, p. 70.

61.   Borges, 'Pascal's Sphere', in *Other Inquisitions*, p. 6.

62.   'Partial Enchantments of the *Quixote*', in ibid., p. 46.

63.   'Kafka and his Precursors', in ibid., p. 108.

64.   'On Chesterton', in ibid., p. 84., 'About William Beckford's *Vathek*', in ibid., p. 140.

65.   Ibid., p. 10.

66.   J.L. Borges and A. Bioy Casares, *Extraordinary Tales*, trans. Anthony Kerrigan, (London, Souvenir Press, 1973).

67.   *Other Inquisitions*, p. 167.

68.   *Extraordinary Tales*, p. 17.

69.   Introduction to *Labyrinths*, p. 18.

70.   *Extraordinary Tales*, p. 11.

71.   'Valéry as a Symbol', *Other Inquisitions*, p. 74.

72.   'El Aleph', in *El Aleph* (Madrid, Alianza, 1972), p. 155.

73.   'The Scripture of the God' ('La escritura del Dios'), in ibid., p. 122.

74.   Ibid., pp. 158–9.

75.   *Doctor Brodie's Report*, p. 9.

76.   'Poema conjetural', *Obra poética*, pp. 129–30. Carlos Fuentes has seemed to be attempting a similar return to Mexico in his recent works, *The Old Gringo* (1986), *Christopher Unborn* (1988) and *Myself With Others* (1988). And José Donoso, of Chile, has written an interesting article which sums up the tension in the Ulyssean writer between adventure and absence: 'Ithaca: the Impossible Return', in Doris Meyer (ed.), *Lives on the Line* (Berkeley, California U.P., 1988), pp. 181–95

77.   Harry Levin, *The Gates of Horn* (London, Oxford U.P., 1968), p. 422.

78.   However, English and Spanish culture produced no such conciliatory, diplomatic and integrative modes: in both countries great traditions were hurriedly revived, invented or consolidated.

6 The Rise of the New Novel

1. *El señor Presidente*, pp. 21–22. My version.

2. Eduardo Galeano, 'Oxford, Mississipi: Faulkner', in his *Memoria del fuego III, El siglo del viento* (Madrid, Siglo XXI, 1986), p. 148. There is an English translation, *Memory of Fire: Century of Wind*, by Cedric Belfrage (New York, Pantheon, 1988). In the second volume of his collected political articles, *'Against All Odds' (Contra viento y marea*, II, Barcelona, Seix Barral, 1986), Vargas Llosa includes a fascinating article from 1981 chronicling his visit to a Peruvian jungle town called, of all things, Labyrinth (Laberinto). Whilst there the novelist reflects, in a style reminiscent of Carpentier, on the community's unmistakably 'Faulknerian' character, 'life as an adventure which confuses, as inextricably as the jungle does the foliage of its trees, the grotesque, the sublime and the tragic' ('Faulkner en Laberinto', in ibid., p. 299). This must be counted one of Vargas Llosa's most revealing articles.

3. Ariel Dorfman, '*Hombres de maíz*: el mito como tiempo y palabra', in his *Imaginación y violencia en América*, p. 71.

4. Miguel Angel Asturias, *Men of Maize* (London, Verso, 1988), pp. 5–6. Some of the material used in this section is taken from my introduction to the translation. *The Popol Vuh*, an important source of Asturias's inspiration, is available in English: *Popol Vuh: The Sacred Book of the Ancient Quiche Maya* (ed. and trans. D. Goetz and S.G. Morley, Oklahoma U.P., 1961).

5. *Men of Maize*, pp. 6–7.

6. Ibid., p. 123.

7. Ibid., p. 222.

8. Ibid., pp. 217–18.

9. Borges, in 'The Flower of Coleridge', in *Other Inquisitions*, wrote: 'in the sphere of literature as in others, every act is the culmination of an infinite series of causes and the cause of an infinite series of effects' (p. 11). There are innumerable similar examples in the works of both writers.

10. Juan Rulfo, *Pedro Páramo* (Mexico, FCE, 8th edn, 1966), p. 7. My version.

11. *Pedro Páramo*, p. 45.

12. Ibid., pp. 64, 69–70.

13. Ernst Fischer, *The Necessity of Art* (Harmondsworth, Penguin, 1963), pp. 98–9.

14. *Pedro Páramo*, p. 16.

15. Ibid., p. 17.

16. Ibid., pp. 99–100.

17. Ibid., p. 129.

18. J. Guimarães Rosa, *The Devil to Pay in the Backlands*, trans. J.L. Taylor and H. de Onís (New York, Knopf, 1971), p. 482. This translation has almost inevitably simplified the most challenging novel in Brazilian fiction, but has produced an excellent English version. Two recent critical works on the novel in English are recommended: see Stephanie Merriam, '*Grande sertão: veredas*, a Mighty Maze but not without a Plan', *Chasqui*, 13, 2 (1983), pp. 32–68, and Charles A. Perrone, 'João Guimarães Rosa: an Endless Passage', in J. King, *Modern Latin American Fiction: A Survey*, pp. 117–35.

19. *The Devil to Pay in the Backlands*, pp. 48–9.

20. Ibid., p. 259.

21. Ibid., p. 439.

22. José María Arguedas, *Los ríos profundos* (Losada, Buenos Aires, 4th edn, 1972), p. 19. My version. The novel was translated as *Deep Rivers* (1978).

23. Ibid., pp. 45–6. An *ayllu* is a small Indian community.

24. Ibid., p. 11.

25. Ibid., pp. 11, 28.

26. Ibid., p. 28. A *huayno* is an Andean song and dance of Inca origin; a *charango* is a type of small guitar.

27. Edwin Williamson, 'Coming to Terms with Modernity: Magical Realism and the Historical Process in the Novels of Alejo Carpentier', in King, *Fiction*, p. 87. See also R. González Echevarría, *Alejo Carpentier: The Pilgrim at Home* (Ithaca, Cornell U.P., 1977), D.L.

Shaw, *Alejo Carpentier* (Boston, Twayne, 1985), and I.R. MacDonald, 'Magical Eclecticism: *Los pasos perdidos* and Jean-Paul Sartre', in S. Bacarisse (ed.), *Contemporary Latin American Fiction* (Edinburgh, Scottish Academic Press, 1980), pp. 1–17.

28.   Northrop Frye, *The Secular Scripture* (Harvard, 1976), p. 54.

29.   See for example García Márquez's Nobel speech, Vargas Llosa's 'Latin America: Fiction and Reality', reprinted in King, *Fictions*, pp. 1–17, and Fuentes's 'Gabriel García Márquez and the invention of America', in *Myself with Others* (London, Deutsch, 1988), pp. 180–95. All were originally speeches to foreign audiences.

30.   Alejo Carpentier, *The Lost Steps* , trans. Harriet de Onís (London, Gollancz, 1956), p. 14.

31.   Ibid., pp. 73–4.

32.   Ibid., p. 53.

33.   Ibid., p. 274.

7 The 'Boom' of the 1960s

1.   Scorza quoted from interview with Rosalba Campra, *América Latina: la identidad y la máscara*, p. 178.

2.   J. Cortázar, *Los premios* (Buenos Aires, Sudamericana, 11th edn, 1971), pp. 381–2. This version mine.

3.   A. MacAdam, *The Dreams of Reason*, p. 60.

4.   J. Cortázar, *Rayuela* (Buenos Aires, Sudamericana, 13th edn, 1972), p. 115. This version mine. For studies in English, see Steven Boldy, *The Novels of Julio Cortázar* (Cambridge, 1980) and Jason Wilson, 'Julio Cortázar and the Drama of Reading', in J. King, *Fiction*, pp. 173–90.

5.   Ibid., p. 116.

6.   Ibid., p. 189.

7.   Ibid., pp. 192–3.

8.   See my '*Yo el Supremo*: the Dictator and his Script', *Forum for Modern Language Studies*, 15, 2 (1979), pp. 169–183; 'On Dictatorship and Rhetoric in Latin American Writing: a counter-proposal', *Latin American Research Review*, 17 (1982), pp. 207–27; 'James Joyce and Spanish American Fiction', *Estudos Anglo-Americanos*, 7–8 (1983–4), pp. 106–30; and 'Boom, Yes; New Novel, No; Further Reflections on the Optical Illusions of the 1960s in Latin America', *Bulletin of Latin American Research*, 3, 2 (1984), pp. 53–63.

9.   Perry Anderson, 'Modernity and Revolution', *New Left Review*, 144 (March–April 1984), pp. 96–113 (p. 109).

10.   Ibid.

11.   Ibid., p. 105.

12.   C. Fuentes, *La región mas transparente*, pp. 58–9.

13.   *La muerte de Artemio Cruz* (Mexico, FCE, 3rd edn, 1967), p. 209. This version mine. For studies of Fuentes in English, see C. Brody and C. Rossman, eds., *Carlos Fuentes: A Critical View* (Texas U.P., 1983), Wendy Faris, *Carlos Fuentes* (New York, Ungar, 1983), and S. Boldy, 'Carlos Fuentes', in King, *Fiction*, pp. 155–72.

14.   *La muerte de Artemio Cruz*, p. 116.

15.   Ibid., pp. 308–13.

16.   Ibid., p. 279.

17.   Ibid., p. 314.

18.   Ibid., pp. 275–8.

19.   Mario Vargas Llosa, *La Casa Verde* (Barcelona, Seix Barral, 12th edn, 1972), p. 51. For critical works in English, see D. Gerdes *Mario Vargas Llosa* (Boston, Twayne, 1985) and R.J. Williams, *Mario Vargas Llosa* (New York, Ungar, 1986).

20.   *La Casa Verde*, p. 31.

21.   Ibid., p. 370.

22.   G. García Márquez, *Cien años de soledad* (Buenos Aires, Sudamericana, 2nd ed., 1968), p. 9. Present versions are mine. Studies in English include G. R. McMurray, *Gabriel*

García Márquez (New York, Ungar, 1977), R.J. Williams, *Gabriel García Márquez* (Boston, Twayne, 1984), S. Minta, *Gabriel García Márquez: Novelist of Colombia* (London, Cape, 1987), McGuirk and Cardwell, *Gabriel García Márquez: New Readings* (Cambridge, 1987), and W. Rowe, 'Gabriel García Márquez', in King, *Fictions*, pp. 191–204.

23.   Ibid., pp. 350–51.

24.   Borges, *Dreamtigers*, 'Epilogue', p. 93. García Márquez, in his interviews with Plinio Apuleyo Mendoza, *The Fragrance of Guava* (London, Verso, 1982), specifies not only Faulkner in general, but also two crucial pages as formative influences upon him: the first was the opening of Kafka's *Metamorphosis* and the second was the moment in Virginia Woolf's *Mrs Dalloway* when a limousine, presumed to be the King's, sweeps mysteriously and awesomely down a London street.

25.   See R. González-Echevarría, *The Voice of the Masters*, for an exposition of this theory which is at once stimulating and a classic example of the critic chasing his own tail.

26.   A. Rama, 'Un novelista de la violencia américana', in P.S. Martínez (ed.), *Recopilación de textos sobre Gabriel García Márquez* (Havana, Casa de las Américas, 1969), pp. 58–71 (p .64).

27.   A. Cueva, 'Para una interpretación sociológica de *Cien años de soledad*', *Revista Mexicana de Sociología*, 36 (1974), pp. 59–76 (p. 67).

28.   T. Todorov, 'Macondo à Paris', in J. Leenhardt (ed.), *Littérature latino-américaine d'aujourd'hui* (Paris, Union Générale, 1980), pp. 316–34.

29.   S. Benvenuto, 'Estética como historia', in Martínez, *Recopilación*, pp.167–75 (p. 169).

30.   This is effectively the view taken by Rama, Benvenuto and Cueva in the works already referred to, and by Jean Franco in various studies; significantly for literary history, it is also the view taken in the 1960s by Carlos Fuentes in his 'Macondo, sede del tiempo' (in *Recopilación*, pp. 119–22), and by Mario Vargas Llosa in his 'El Amadís en America' (*Recopilación*, pp. 113–18).

31.   *Cien años de soledad*, p. 296.

32.   Said's book was just the latest in a series of Third World deconstructions deriving from Fanon, Césaire and Memmi. L. Zea, *El pensamiento latinoamericano* (Mexico, Pormaca, 1965), uses Hegel's conception of the New World as his point of departure: 'America is the land of the future... It is a country longed for by those who are weary of Europe's historical museum.'

33.   García Márquez's stamp is visible in many other 'Third World' novels such as Ṣalman Rushdie's *Midnight's Children* (1982) – see especially its ending.

34.   Part of the problem with García Márquez is that he really does seem to have more difficulty than most men in distinguishing literature from reality, fiction from truth. Thus when he talks, for example, about Salvador Allende, or Simón Bolívar, they are immediately turned into people who might be characters from one of his novels.

35.   Rama, 'Un novelista', p. 62.

36.   J. Mejía Duque, '*El otoño del patriarca* o la crisis de la desmesura' (Bogotá, Oveja Negra, 1975).

37.   Rama, 'Un novelista', p. 63.

38.   J. Ortega, *La contemplación y la fiesta* (Caracas, Monte Avila, 1969), p. 125.

39.   J.M. Oviedo, 'Macondo: un territorio mágico y americano', in *Nueve asedios a García Márquez* (Santiago de Chile, Editorial Universitaria, 3rd edn, 1972), pp. 89–105 (p. 97).

40.   E. Völkening, 'Anotado al margen de "*Cien anos de soledad*"', in J. Lafforgue, ed., *Nueva novela latinoamericana* (Buenos Aires, Paidós, 1969), p. 168.

41.   See C. Blanco Aguinaga, 'Realidad y estilo de Juan Rulfo', in Lafforgue, *Nueva novela*, pp. 85–113.

42.   R. Gullón, *García Márquez o el olvidado arte de contar* (Madrid, Taurus, 1970).

43.   Borges's story 'The Theologians' (From '*El Aleph*') gives numerous insights into the possibility of characters based alternately on the thirst for knowledge and the hunger for power. There seems little doubt that some of the inspiration for *One Hundred Years of Solitude* springs from here (one of the characters is even called Aureliano).

44.   M. Vargas Llosa, *García Márquez: historia de un deicidio* (Barcelona, Barral, 1971). This remains the fundamental source work on García Márquez.

45.   *Cien años de soledad*, p. 232.

46.   Ibid., p. 249.

47. Ibid., p. 193.
48. Ibid., p. 191.
49. Ibid., p. 300.
50. Ibid., p. 263.
51. A recent documentary anthology, *1928: la masacre en las Bananeras* (Bogotá, n.d., c.1980), reprints the parliamentary debates of 1929, and in particular the protests of two politicians, Jorge Eliécer Gaitán and Gabriel Turbay, together with a number of eyewitness accounts, including the vital contribution of none other than the parish priest of Aracataca, Father Francisco Angarita (in a letter dated 16 July 1929). In the introduction the editors note, like García Márquez in his novel, that 'the official version of Colombian history has tried by every means to omit or distort this bloody episode' (p. 5). Turbay himself had underlined the policy of censorship in a speech on 3 September 1929 when he referred to the 'tragic and horrifying secret of the endless chain of ignominious acts committed during the apocalyptic march of the military through the banana zone.' Fifty years later H. Rodríguez Acosta, in his *Elementos críticos para una nueva interpretación de la historia colombiana* (Bogotá, Tupac Amaru, 1979), would still be making the same point, whose importance for the relation of fiction to history in Latin America is obvious: 'This episode of Colombian history has been repeatedly ignored by our historians because to reveal it would damage the reputation of the ruling class' (p. 203).
52. *Cien años de soledad*, p. 296.
53. Borges, 'The Garden of Forking Paths': 'he shut himself away for thirteen years in the Pavilion of Limpid Solitude. On his death his heirs found nothing but chaotic manuscripts' (*Ficciones*, p.109).
54. *Cien años de soledad*, p. 264.
55. Ibid., p. 327.
56. Ibid., p. 329.
57. Ibid., p. 334.
58. Ibid., p. 169.
59. Ibid., p. 284.
60. Ibid., p. 350.
61. Cueva, 'Una interpretación sociológica', p. 59. Cueva's exceptional analysis fails to recognize that García Márquez's critique of imperialism is always far more radical than his critique of capitalism itself. This is of course a feature of the entire New Novel as a historical phenomenon.
62. Gordon Brotherston indicates this effect in *The Emergence of the Latin American Novel* (Cambridge, 1977), noting that it '"opens" the novel to include and involve the reader, as Umberto Eco has defined that process' (p. 135).
63. See Sebastiano Timpanaro, *On Materialism* (London, Verso, 1975).
64. Thus Mario Vargas Llosa: 'This seems to me a symptom, the sign of great historical changes to come in Latin America.... All the great eras of the novel have taken place just before some social apocalypse', quoted in H. Cattolica, 'Vargas Llosa: Europa y el escritor latinoamericano', *El Escarabajo de Oro*, 33 (March 1967), pp. 20–32.
65. The parallels with Asturias's relation to *Men of Maize* are striking. See chapter 9.
66. M. Vargas Llosa, 'García Márquez: de Aracataca a Macondo', in *Nueve asedios*, pp. 126–46: 'Aracataca was living on its memories when he was born: his fictions, in turn, would live off his memories of Aracataca' (p. 128).
67. This historical thread in fact coincides with that of the life and death of Jorge Eliécer Gaitán, who in 1929 was the principal critic of the government's role in the Banana massacres ('We know to our sorrow that in this country the government points its murderous machine guns at the fatherland's own sons and its trembling knees to the ground in the face of yankee gold'), and whose assassination, as presidential candidate for the Liberal Party, led to the 1948 street riots known as the 'Bogotazo' and the horrific period of generalized violence that followed over the next two decades, of which García Márquez's *No One Writes to the Colonel* and *In Evil Hour* show only the blood-chilling icy tip.
68. See John Berger, 'Márquez's Tolerance', *New Society*, 28 April 1977, p. 180: '[*One Hundred Years of Solitude*] is a book which speaks to those who are aware of the scale and

turbulence of the struggles and tragedy of history. To those whose view of history is domestic and gradualist, it is bound to seem at the best "baroque" and at the worst phantasmagorical – which is actually the adjective the inept Penguin blurb writer uses.' Berger's argument contests in advance the deprecating put-downs of Magical Realism and shows that each case should be judged on its merits.

8 Era's End: Big Books and Great Dictators

1.   Quoted in Rosalba Campra, *América Latina: la identidad y la máscara*, pp. 193–4.

2.   R. González Echevarría, *The Voice of the Masters*, early chapters.

3.   The principal propagandist of the 'boom' was the eminent Uruguayan critic, Emir Rodríguez Monegal, and its principal vehicle was the magazine he edited from Paris between 1966 and 1971, *Mundo Nuevo*. His influential 'The New Novelists' appeared in the celebrated Latin American number of *Encounter* in September 1965. (Both *Encounter* and *Mundo Nuevo* turned out to have been partially funded by the CIA). He later became Professor of Latin American Literature at Yale, where he launched a generation of graduates schooled in French Post-structuralist ideology. Rodríguez Monegal later produced his own history of the movement, *El boom de la novela latinoamericana* (Caracas, Tiempo Nuevo, 1972). See the similar work by a Chilean member of the 'boom', José Donoso, *The Boom in Spanish-American Literature: A Personal History* (*Historia personal del boom*, 1972; New York, Columbia, 1977).

4.   Fuentes, cited by Luis Harss in *Los nuestros* pp. 361–2.

5.   See his 'The Dictatorship of Rhetoric/ The Rhetoric of Dictatorship: Carpentier, García Márquez and Roa Bastos', *Latin American Research Review*, 15, 3 (1980), pp. 205–28.

6.   Not everyone was as enthusiastic about *Three Trapped Tigers*. John Updike published a review in *The New Yorker* (29 January 1972), pp. 91–4, under the title 'Infante Terrible', which effectively accuses Cabrera Infante of producing a tired Joycean imitation, especially of the 'Oxen of the Sun' and 'Nighttown' sections of *Ulysses*. MacAdam, *The Dreams of Reason*, p. 61, makes a stout defence of the Cuban. See also D. Kadir, 'Stalking the Oxen of the Sun and Felling the Sacred Cows: Joyce's *Ulysses* and Cabrera Infante's *Three Trapped Tigers*', *Latin American Literary Review*, 4 (1976), pp. 15–22.

7.   Elizondo wrote an illuminating article, 'En torno al *Ulises* de Joyce', in *Estaciónes*, 4; 13 (Mexico, 1959), pp. 98–111. His *Cuaderno de escritura* (Guanajuato, Mexico, 1969) includes a number of essays which bear on Joyce.

8.   Adoum, *Entre Marx*, p. 9. The frustrated narrator later (p. 159) finds things still more embarrassing when he 'discovers', in the 1970s, how to write like Sterne did in 1759. This problem of culture-lag is of course one of the central themes of *One Hundred Years of Solitude*, exemplified in the early pages when José Arcadio Buendía discovers that the earth is round.

9.   See S. Menton, *Prose Fiction of the Cuban Revolution* (Austin, Texas U.P., 1975) and R. Souza, *Major Cuban Novelists: Tradition and Innovation* (Columbia, Missouri 1976); the evidence of the magazine *Libre*, no. 1 (Paris, 1971), mentioned previously; *Index*, I, 2 (1972); and the various diatribes published by Cabrera Infante, the most Joycean of the exiles, from his London refuge.

10.   See especially 'El *Ulysses* cuarenta años despues', in his *Ensayos críticos* (Caracas, 1963), pp. 5–21; 'Consideraciones sobre la novela' (1966) in his *Notas críticas*, pp. 189–94; and 'Apostillas a la novela latinoamericana', *Zona Franca*, no. 48 (Caracas, August 1967), pp. 4–9.

11.   'El *Ulysses* cuarenta años despues', p. 17. '*Cantinflismo*' has been invented, Joyce-like, by González in reference to the well-known Mexican comedian Cantinflas, known for spouting long incomprehensible sentences at great speed in a silly voice.

12.   Ibid.

13.   'Apostillas a la novela latinoamericana', p. 6.

14.   'Novelas y novelistas de hoy', *Mundo Nuevo*, 28 (October 1968), pp. 84–8 (p. 87).

15.   Ibid., p. 88.

16.   'Para una polémica sobre la nueva novela', *Mundo Nuevo*, 34 (April 1969), pp. 83–5 (p. 83).

17.   'En torno a la nueva novela latinoamericana', *Mundo Nuevo*, 34, pp. 86–7.

18.   'Tradición y renovación en la novela hispanoamericana', *Mundo Nuevo*, 34, pp. 76–82.

19.   'Un gran escritor y su soledad: Julio Cortázar', *Life en Español*, 33, 7 (Mexico 1969), pp. 43–55. The interview was conducted by Rita Guibert and translated into English in her *Seven Voices*, pp. 279–302.

20.   *El zorro de arriba y el zorro de abajo* (Buenos Aires, Losada, 5th edn, 1975), p. 23.

21.   Ibid., p. 18.

22.   Ibid., pp. 27–8 and p. 17.

23.   L. Marechal, *Adán Buenosayres* (Havana, Casa de las Américas, 1969), pp. 4–5.

24.   Cintio Vitier, like Lezama a Catholic member of the *Orígenes* poetic group, has recently produced the first major critical edition of the novel (Paris, ALLCA, 1988), with the full cooperation of the Cuban cultural institutions. This was particularly important since earlier editions of the text were notoriously erratic. Lezama's provocative insinuations, even in his critical essays, were always likely to prove a difficulty with the Cuban revolutionary authorities. Take, for example, the opening of the first essay in his *'America's Self-Expression'* (*La expresión americana*, Madrid, Alianza, 1969): 'Only that which is difficult is stimulating; only resistance which challenges us can raise, incite and maintain our capacity for knowledge' ('Myths and Classical Weariness', p. 9).

25.   Lezama Lima, *Paradiso*, pp. 428–9. Present version is mine. Of Lezama Lima's other novel, *Oppiano Licario* (1977), Julio Ortega has written: *'Oppiano Licario* is like a baroque gate whose hermetic emblems are reproduced in the interior of its fabled labyrinth among the double mirrors of its aggregated identity' (in *Paradiso*, ed. Vitier, p. 695).

26.   G. Cabrera Infante, *Infante's Inferno*, trans. S.J. Levine and author (London, Faber and Faber, 1984), p. 404. Cabrera's novel is full of references to Homer's *Odyssey* and to Joyce's own *Ulysses* and *Finnegans Wake*.

27.   Ibid., p. 410.

28.   On Del Paso see R. Fiddian, 'Beyond the Unquiet Grave: Resurrection in *Palinuro de Mexico*', *Iberoamerikanisches Archiv*, 8, 3 (1982), pp. 243–55, and *'Palinuro and Ulysses'*, *Comparative Literature Studies*, 18 (1982), pp. 220–35.

29.   Fuentes wrote a brief and notably enthusiastic book on the Parisian events, *París: la Revolución de Mayo* (Mexico, Era, 1969). This is one of the most representative and revealing documents of the era.

30.   Krauze's article was published in *Plural*, edited by Octavio Paz, in May 1988, and received wide international publicity. Krauze was in fact only saying out loud what many Mexican intellectuals had been whispering for years. Nevertheless the article was both mean-spirited and incoherent, and Fuentes never deigned to reply. However some months later the Peruvian critic Julio Ortega took up his defence in an article also given wide diffusion in Mexico.

31.   His 1988 book of essays, *Myself with Others* (London, Deutsch), typically brilliant, runs perilously close to self-parody.

32.   'Situación del escritor en América Latina', in *Mundo Nuevo*, 1 (July 1966), pp. 5–21 (pp. 14–15).

33.   *La nueva novela hispanoamericana* (Mexico, Joaquín Mortiz, 1969). This work was violently attacked for its ahistorical bias and 'cosmopolitanism' by Cuba's leading cultural critic, Roberto Fernández Retamar in his essay *Calibán* in June 1971, as part of the sequel to the Padilla Affair, at exactly the moment that Fuentes and others were founding *Libre* in Paris.

34.   Donoso would have received individual attention in this history if space had allowed. Among his most important works are *The Obscene Bird of Night* (*El obsceno pájaro de la noche*, 1970) and *A House in the Country* (*Casa de campo*, 1978). See Philip Swanson, *José Donoso: The 'Boom' and Beyond* (Liverpool, Francis Cairns, 1988).

35.   See R. González Echevarría in *Latin American Research Review* and *The Voice of the Masters*.

36.   C. Fuentes, *Terra Nostra*, (Harmondsworth, Penguin, 1978), pp. 544–5.

37.   Ibid., pp. 866–8.

38.   João Ubaldo Ribeiro, *The Invincible Memory* (*Viva o povo brasileiro*, Rio de Janeiro, Nova Fronteira, 5th edn, 1985), p. 661. The English translation is by the author (1989). Present

versions are mine.

39. Ibid., pp. 662–3.

40. Fuentes tells the story in his review of *I the Supreme*, 'A Show of Heads', *London Review of Books* (19 March 1987), p. 23. In his 'Testimonio' to the critical edition of Asturias's *The President*, Arturo Uslar Pietri recalls how a previous generation of writers had discussed the literary recreation of dictators in Paris in the 1920s just as Fuentes and Vargas Llosa set out to do in a London pub in 1967.

41. Angel Rama, *Los dictadores latinoamericanos* (Mexico, FCE, 1976), p. 6. For more on Carpentier's views, see his interview, 'The Latin American Novel', in *New Left Review*, 154 (November–December 1985), pp. 99–111.

42. J. Zalamea, *El Gran Burundún–Burundá ha muerto* (Bogotá, Carlos Valencia, 1979), pp. 9–10.

43. Ibid., p. 87.

44. R. González Echevarría 'The Dictatorship of Rhetoric...', p. 206.

45. See M. Benedetti, 'El recurso del supremo patriarca', *Casa de las Américas*, no. 98 (1976), pp. 12–23; A. Rama, *Los dictadores latinoamericanos*; and Michael Wood, 'Unhappy Dictators', *New York Review of Books*, 23, 20 (9 December 1976), pp. 57–8.

46. See my 'Yo el Supremo: the Dictator and his Script', *Forum for Modern Language Studies*, 15, 2 (1979) and an important article by Jean Franco, 'From Modernization to Resistance: Latin American Literature 1959–1976', *Latin American Perspectives*, 16 (Winter 1978), pp. 77–97.

47. 'El recurso', p. 15.

48. On the last page of her novel *The Lizard's Tail* (1987: see chapter 10), Luisa Valenzuela has two characters comment: 'Tyrannies are not what they used to be. Now they have replacement parts. One president falls and another is ready to take over. There's no shortage of generals.'

49. *El otoño del patriarca* (Barcelona, Plaza y Janés, 1975), pp. 270–1. This version mine.

50. A. Roa Bastos, *I the Supreme*, trans. Helen Lane (London, Faber and Faber, 1987), p. 97. For a study that takes up a suitably quirky and ironic perspective attuned to that of Roa Bastos himself, see D. Balderston, 'Worms in *Yo el Supremo*', *Modern Language Notes*, 101 (1986), pp. 418–23.

51. *I the Supreme*, pp. 97–8.

52. D.F. Sarmiento, *Facundo: civilización y barbarie* (Buenos Aires, Austral, 6th edn, 1962), pp. 231–2.

53. *I the Supreme*, p. 32.

54. Ibid., p. 57. My version.

55. As has been seen, these problems were dramatized by the character of Vera in *Son of Man*, but were also those of Roa himself (see chapter 3).

56. For one early exception, see A. Sicard's contributions to the *Seminario sobre 'Yo el Supremo' de Augusto Roa Bastos* (Poitiers, 1976), esp. p. 115. See also Salvador Bacarisse 'Mitificación de la historia y desmitificación de la escritura: *Yo el Supremo*', *Bulletin of Hispanic Studies*, 65, 2 (1988), pp. 153–68.

57. *The German Ideology*, Part I, ed. C.J. Arthur (London, Lawrence and Wishart, 1974), p. 52.

58. *I the Supreme*, p. 32.

59. Ibid., p. 18.

60. Ibid., p. 202.

61. Ibid., p. 6.

62. 'The production of ideas, of conceptions, of consciousness, is at first directly interwoven with the material activity and the material intercourse of men, the language of real life. Conceiving, thinking, the mental intercourse of men, appear at this stage as the direct efflux of their material behaviour' (Marx and Engels, *The German Ideology*, p. 47).

63. *I the Supreme*, p. 56.

64. Ibid., p. 415.

65. Thus Roa insists that his work is an ideological construct, even beyond the limits of his own awareness: 'What cannot be overlooked, however, is its ideological meaning: the nucleus from which irradiates or upon which converges the network of possible meanings. We know that

if a work is not itself ideological, ideology is still present not as a reflection but an irradiation of the writing even in the most carefully distilled fantasies' (*Les Langues Modernes*, 71, 1977, pp. 58–9).

66. Ibid.

67. This position is justified by the attitudes of those Marxist thinkers who, unlike Marx himself, rarely take 'human–sensuous activity' into consideration (see *Theses on Feuerbach*, I). The world of sexuality and emotion is, so to speak, a closed book to the Supremo (see especially the episode with Deyanira-Andaluza and the criticisms of him by his dog Sultan and his Negro valet, Pilar, both closer to Nature than he is). One might say, paraphrasing Senghor's dangerous dictum, that 'emotion is indigenous'.

68. *I the Supreme*, p. 132.

69. Ibid., p. 152.

70. Ibid., p. 414.

71. On p. 404 we learn, for example, that one Francisco Solano López (a future dictator of Paraguay) is in a school called 'School Number 1, Fatherland or Death', and on p. 325 that Paraguay is the 'First Free and Sovereign Country in South America', both clear references to Cuba; similarly the title given to Francia in the novel, 'Pilot-of-the-Storms', recalls that of Mao-Tse Tung, 'The Great Helmsman' of the People's Republic of China. This apart, the later sections of the novel are full of theorizing about revolutionary strategy in the Third World context.

72. *I the Supreme*, p. 423.

73. Ibid., p. 65. My translation.

74. Ibid., p. 19.

75. 'I believe that having power over the word is having an illusory power; or at least it is a power only over the word itself as speech or writing' (Roa Bastos, *Les Langues Modernes*, p. 60).

76. When, accordingly, we look back at Bolívar's own writings, we can see that he, too, in his famous 'Jamaica Letter' (1815), finds that his native Venezuela has been reduced to a state of 'fearful solitude', and 'its tyrants rule over a desert', so that its people are left 'abstracted, absent from the world' (Bolívar, *Doctrina*, p. 58).

9 Writers and their Works: The Labyrinth of Mirrors

1. 'This is a work of fiction. The reason why some of its characters may seem like people in real life is the same reason why some people in real life seem like characters in a novel. No one, therefore, has the right to feel included in this novel. No one, either, to feel excluded.' (Fernando del Paso, *Palinurus of Mexico*).

2. 'Reader, it is time for your tempest-tossed vessel to come to port. What harbour can receive you more securely than a great library?' (Italo Calvino, *If On a Winter's Night a Traveller*, 1979; trans. William Weaver, London, Picador, 1982, p. 200).

3. '*Producer*: I'd have you know that it is our boast that we have given life, here on these very boards, to immortal works!

Father: There you are! Oh, that's it exactly! To living beings... to beings who are more alive than those who breathe and wear clothes! Less real, perhaps, but truer! We're in complete agreement!' (Luigi Pirandello, *Six Characters in Search of an Author*, 1921; trans. Frederick May, London, Heinemann, 1954, p. 9).

4. 'I wish either my father or my mother, or indeed both of them, as they were in duty both equally bound to it, had minded what they were about when they begot me.' (Laurence Sterne, *Tristram Shandy*, 1759). Quotation from Fuentes, *Myself with Others*, p. 3.

5. 'It is my image that I want to multiply, but not out of narcissism or megalomania, as could all too easily be believed: on the contrary, I want to conceal, in the midst of so many illusory ghosts of myself, the true me, who makes them move. For this reason, if I were not afraid of being misunderstood, I would have nothing against reconstructing, in my house, the room completely lined with mirrors according to Kircher's design.' (Calvino, *If On a Winter's Night*, p. 129).

6.   'It would be senseless for the author to try to convince the reader that his characters once lived. They were not born of a mother's womb; they were born of a stimulating phrase or two from a basic situation.' (Milan Kundera, *The Unbearable Lightness of Being*, 1984; trans. Michael Henry Heim, London, Faber and Faber, 1985, p. 39). Blurb from *Cosmopolitan*: 'This is a brilliant novel from someone who, amongst Rushdie and Márquez, is one of our masters of magic realism.'

7.   '*Father*: My drama lies entirely in this one thing... In my being conscious that each one of us believes himself to be a single person. But it's not true... Each one of us is many persons... Many persons... according to all the possibilities of being that there are within us.' (Pirandello, *Six Characters*, p. 25).

8.   'I know there are readers in the world, as well as many other good people in it, who are no readers at all, – who find themselves ill at ease, unless they are let into the whole secret from first to last, of everything which concerns you.' (Sterne, *Tristram Shandy*, I: 4).

9.   'The Koran is the holy book about whose compositional process we know most. There were at least two mediations between the whole and the book: Mohammed listened to the word of Allah and dictated, in his turn, to his scribes. Once – the biographers of the Prophet tell us – while dictating to the scribe Abdullah, Mohammed left a sentence half finished. The scribe, instinctively, suggested the conclusion. Absently, the Prophet accepted as the divine word what Abdullah had said. This scandalized the scribe, who abandoned the Prophet, and lost his faith.

'He was wrong.' (Calvino, *If On a Winter's Night*, p. 144).

10.   '*Producer*: Pretence! Reality! Go to hell the lot of you! Lights! Lights! Lights!' (Pirandello, *Six Characters*, p. 69). Quotation from *Terra Nostra*, p. 871.

11.   'The absolute absence of a burden causes man to be lighter than air, to soar into the heights, take leave of the earth and his earthly being, and become only half real, his movements as free as they are insignificant.' (*The Unbearable Lightness of Being*, p. 5).

12.   'In that invisible city, world literature, Calvino is a grandee.' (Susan Sontag).

13.   'I can think of no finer writer to have beside me while Italy explodes, while Britain burns, while the world ends.' (Salman Rushdie, review of *If On a Winter's Night a Traveller*. Our quotation from pp. 94–5).

14.   'The history contained in these Notes is reduced to the fact that the story that should have been told in them has not been told. As a consequence, the characters and facts that figure in them have earned, through the fatality of the written language, the right to a fictitious and autonomous existence in the service of the no less fictitious and autonomous reader.' (Augusto Roa Bastos, *I the Supreme*).

'Friendship, history and literature have supplied me with some of the characters of this book. All other resemblances to living persons or to other people having lived in reality or fiction can only be coincidental.' (Georges Perec, *Life: A User's Manual*, 1970; trans. David Bellos, London, Collins Harvill, 1988). 'Preamble. The eye follows the paths that have been laid down for it in the work. Paul Klee' (ibid.).

'Here lies the reader who will never open this book. He is here forever dead.' (Milorad Pavić, *Dictionary of the Khazars: A Lexicon Novel: female edition*; trans. Christina Pribićević-Zorić, London, Hamish Hamilton, 1989).

'Chapter 136. "UNNECESSARY": And, if I am not greatly mistaken, I have just written an utterly unnecessary chapter.' (Machado de Assis, *Epitaph of a Small Winner* p. 202).

10   Latin American Narrative Today

1.   Cited in Rosalba Campra, *América Latina: la identidad y la máscara*, p. 156.

2.   Curiously, the Brazilian case is similar. Exile has not been a major theme of Brazilian literature, and writers have not felt that by living abroad they would gain access to some second dimension. The literature of exile is one of the major themes of recent Latin American studies. See, for example, a recent edition of *Third World Quarterly*, 9, 1 (1987) entitled 'The Politics of

Exile', which includes sections on Latin America and in particular articles on literature, dictatorship and exile by W. Rowe and T. Whitfield, and F. McQuade.

3.   Unfortunately for Spanish America in general, elements within the Franco regime were also subtle enough by the mid-1960s to recognise that Spain might soon return to cultural and even limited political influence in Latin America in the later years of the century. The Barcelona publishing house Seix Barral soon came to handle many of the writers of the 'boom', in conjunction with the Carmen Balcells literary agency. Latin America's contribution to the cultural modernization of Spain since 1960 has therefore included a notable boost to the economics of the Spanish publishing industry.

4.   The primary response to Sarduy's title, *De donde son los cantantes*, would be to assume a question mark: 'Where are the singers from?' Since there appear to be no question marks, the meaning would be an answer: '[Cuba,] where the singers are from', as in 'Brazil, where the nuts are from'. The English translation chose *From Cuba with a Song* (1973).

5.   On the 'Onda', see Margo Glantz (ed.), *Onda y escritura en México: jóvenes de 20 a 33* (Mexico, Siglo XXI, 1971), and R. Teichmann, *De la Onda en adelante* (Mexico, Posada, 1987). The great chronicler of the era, at once enthusiastic and satirical, is Carlos Monsiváis: his scintillating evocations include *Días de guardar* (1970) and *Escenas de pudor y liviandad* (1988). On what he calls the 'junior Boom', see D. L. Shaw's invaluable *Nueva narrativa hispanoamerica* (Madrid, Cátedra, 1981). On recent Mexican fiction, see J. Ann Duncan, *Voices, Visions and a New Reality: Mexican Fiction Since 1970* (Pittsburgh U.P., 1986), and S. Sefchovich, *México: país de novelas* (Mexico, Grijalbo, 1987).

6.   See William Rowe, 'Paz, Fuentes and Lévi-Strauss: the Creation of a Structuralist Orthodoxy', *Bulletin of Latin American Research*, 3, 2 (1984), pp. 77–82.

7.   The principal exponents have been mainly Yale and male: Paul de Man, J. Hillis Miller, Geoffrey Hartman and Harold Bloom on the English and general comparative literature side, plus Rodríguez Monegal and González Echevarría on the Latin American side.

8.   For criticism of Puig's work in English, see S. Merriam, 'Bridging the Gap: Freud and Film in G. Cabrera Infante's *Three Trapped Tigers* and M. Puig's *Kiss of the Spider Woman*', in J. King, *Fiction*, pp. 268–82 (there is also an article by Puig himself, pp. 283–90), and Pamela Bacarisse, *Necessary Dreams: A Study of the Novels of Manuel Puig* (Cardiff, University of Wales, 1988).

9.   Cortázar began his written response to the interview by explaining why he was reluctant to do it.

10.   Fuentes, *La nueva novela hispanoamerica*, p. 47.

11.   Babenco's previous film was the horrifying *Pixote* (1983), about a São Paulo street boy.

12.   M. Puig, *El beso de la mujer araña* (Barcelona, Seix Barral, 1976), p. 206.

13.   Ibid., pp. 238–9.

14.   Ibid., p. 224.

15.   Ibid., pp. 246–7.

16.   Ibid., p. 285.

17.   The story in Latin American poetry is quite different. Three of the greatest Latin American poets of the century – Vallejo, Guillén and Neruda – were Communists and even Paz flirted with Marxism in his youth. The greatest poet of the contemporary period, continuing the traditions of the Guillén of *West Indies Ltd*, the Vallejo of *Spain, Take this Cup From Me*, and the Neruda of '*General Song*', is Ernesto Cardenal. Sandinista, revolutionary priest, minister of culture and documentary poet (who uses, ironically enough, the collage-based techniques of the one-time fascist sympathizer Ezra Pound), Cardenal has inspired an entire generation of post-Nerudian troubadours of the everyday and the comonplace, with humble, deceptively simple, resonant yet non-triumphalist foot-soldier poetry which also owes much to the Vallejo of the *Human Poems*. Cardenal's relation with the anti-religious Cuban Revolution has been an interesting one, and of the many writers and thinkers who have written Cuban diaries since 1959, his may well be the most passionate and illuminating.

18.   A. Roa Bastos, *Hijo de hombre*, pp. 279–80.

19.   'Conciencia e identidad de América', in *La novela latinoamericana en víspera de un nuevo siglo* (Mexico, Siglo XXI, 1981), p. 87.

20.   See O. Collazos, J. Cortázar and M. Vargas Llosa, *Literatura en la revolución y*

revolución en la literatura (Mexico, Siglo XXI, 1971); also R. Dalton *et al.*, *El intelectual y la sociedad* (Mexico, Siglo XXI, 1969).

21.   R Arenas, *Farewell to the Sea* (*Otra vez el mar*, 1982; trans. Andrew Hurley, Harmondsworth, Penguin, 1987), pp. 375–6.

22.   J. Díaz, *Las iniciales de la tierra* (Havana, Letras Cubanas, 1987), p. 7.

23.   Ibid., p. 429.

24.   The list is incomplete, but reasonably representative. For general insight into the problems of this era, see Hernán Vidal (ed.), *Fascismo y experiencia literaturia: reflexiones para una recanonización* (Minneapolis, Institute for the Study of Ideologies and Literature, 1985).

25.   R. Piglia, '*Artificial Respiration*' (*Respiración artificial*, Buenos Aires, Pomaire, 1980), p. 237.

26.   Ibid., p. 263.

27.   Ibid., p. 237.

28.   Ibid., p. 275.

29.   Ibid., p. 272.

30.   Ibid., pp. 275–6.

31.   R. Piglia, '*Life Sentence*' (*Prisión perpetua*, Buenos Aires, Sudamericana, 1988), pp. 27–9.

32.   M. Bonasso, *Recuerdo de la muerte* (Mexico, Era, 1984), p. 348.

33.   Ibid., p. 349.

34.   Ibid., p. 350.

35.   Ibid., p. 350.

36.   Quoted from the back cover of Tomás Eloy Martínez, *The Perón Novel*, trans. Asa Zatz (New York, Pantheon, 1988).

37.   *The Perón Novel*, p. 242.

38.   Ibid., p. 136.

39.   Ibid., pp. 256–7.

40.   '*The Non-Existent Gentleman*' (*El no existente caballero*, Buenos Aires, Megápolis, 1975) is the title of an influential work of literary theory published by Noé Jitrik, one of Argentina's best known exiled literary critics.

41.   *The Perón Novel*, p. 258.

42.   Ibid., pp. 259–60.

43.   Ibid., p. 263.

44.   Borges, *Dreamtigers*, p. 31.

45.   *The Perón Novel*, p. 303.

46.   Victoria Ocampo, from her speech on being awarded the Vaccaro Prize in Argentina in 1966. Quoted by Doris Meyer, *Lives on the Line*, pp. 51–2.

47.   See Anne Pescatello (ed.), *Female and Male in Latin America* (Pittsburgh U.P., 1973); Asunción Lavrín (ed.), *Latin American Women: Historical Perspectives* (Westport, Conn., Greenwood Press, 1978); D. Meyer and M. Olmos (eds.), *Contemporary Women Authors of Latin America: Introductory Essays* (New York, Brooklyn College Press, 1983); Beth Miller, *Women in Hispanic Literature: Icons and Fallen Idols* (Berkeley, California U.P., 1983); Patricia Elena González and Eliana Ortega (eds.), *La sartén por el mango* (San Juan, Puerto Rico, Huracán, 1984); and S. Magnarelli, *The Lost Rib: Female Characters in the Spanish American Novel* (London and Toronto, Associated University Presses, 1985). B. G. Chevigny and G. Laguardia, *Reinventing the Americas*, has an important section on women's writing, and J. King, *Fiction*, includes Susan Bassnett, 'Coming Out of the Labyrinth: Women Writers in Contemporary Latin America' (pp. 247–67). See also A. Manguel (ed.), *Other Fires: Stories from the Women of Latin America* (London, Picador, 1986) and Jean Franco's *Plotting Women*.

48.   Perry Anderson 'Modernity and Revolution', p. 104.

49.   Elena Poniatowska, *Hasta no verte, Jesús mío* (Mexico, Era, 1969), p. 295. These versions mine. On the novel, see Lisa Davis, 'An Invitation to Understanding among Poor Women of the Americas: *The Color Purple* and *Hasta no verte, Jesús mío*', in Chevigny and Laguardia, *Reinventing the Americas*, pp. 224–41. For Poniatowska's own illuminating comments on her relationship with Jesusa, see 'And Here's to You, Jesusa', in Doris Meyer,

Lives on the Line, pp. 139–55. On women in Mexico, see A. Guadalupe Sánchez and A. E. Domínguez, 'Women in Mexico', in R. Rohrlich-Leavitt, *Women Cross-Culturally: Change and Challenge* (The Hague, Mouton, 1975), pp. 95–110.

50.   *Hasta no verte, Jesús mío*, p. 316.

51.   C. Lispector, *The Hour of the Star* trans. G. Pontiero (Manchester, Carcanet, 1987), p. 8.

52.   Ibid., pp. 13–14.

53.   Ibid., pp. 15–16.

54.   Isabel Allende, *La casa de los espíritus* (Barcelona, Plaza y Janés, 17th edn, 1985), pp. 107, 232.

55.   Ibid., p. 362. There is an English translation (1985), but present versions are mine. For Allende's autobiographical musings on her work, see 'The Spirits Were Willing', in Meyer, *Lives on the Line*, pp. 236–42.

56.   Ibid., pp. 379–380.

57.   Published in Manguel, *Other Fires*.

58.   Luisa Valenzuela, *The Lizard's Tail* trans. G. Rabassa (London, Serpent's Tail, 1987), p. 8. On Valenzuela, see Magnarelli, *The Lost Rib*, pp. 169–85. Valenzuela herself has contributed essays, 'The Other Face of the Phallus', to Chevigny and Laguardia, *Reinventing the Americas*, pp. 242–8, and 'A Legacy of Poets and Cannibals: Literature Revives in Argentina', to Meyer, *Lives on the Line*, pp. 292–7.

59.   *The Lizard's Tail* , p. 226.

60.   Ibid., pp. 226–7.

61.   Ibid., p. 227.

62.   Among the most useful works are *Nueva narrativa hispanoamericana* by Donald Shaw; *La novela latinoamericana 1920–1980* by Angel Rama, in which he says that all the younger Latin American writers of the post-'boom' are children of 1968 and proposes, rather less convincingly, that they might be labelled 'contesters of power'; and *Roa Bastos, precursor del post-boom* (1983) by Juan Manuel Marcos. As this went to press Shaw had just published an update article, 'Towards a Description of the Post-Boom', *Bulletin of Hispanic Studies*, 56 (1989), pp. 87–94, essentially tentative, which coincides with the present writer's impression that what we see currently are shifts of emphasis and minor trends rather than major changes of direction. As for the latter, history will resolve them.

Critical Bibliography

Aínsa, Fernando, *Los buscadores de la utopía*, Caracas, Monte Avila, 1977.

—— *Identidad cultural de Iberoamérica en su narrativa*, Madrid, Gredos, 1986.

Anderson, Benedict, *Imagined Communities*, London, Verso, 1983.

Anderson, Perry, 'Modernity and Revolution', *New Left Review*, 144, March–April 1984, pp. 96–113.

Anderson Imbert, Enrique, *Historia de la literatura hispanoamericana*, 2 vols. Mexico, FCE, 2nd edn, 1970.

Bacarisse, Salvador (ed.), *Contemporary Latin American Fiction*, Edinburgh, Scottish Academic Press, 1980.

Balderston, Daniel (ed.), *The Historical Novel in Latin America*, Gaithersburg, Md, Hispamérica, 1986.

Bell, Daniel, *The Cultural Contradictions of Capitalism*, London, Heinemann, 2nd edn, 1976.

Bellini, Giuseppe, *Historia de la literatura hispanoamericana*, Madrid, Castalia, 1985.

Berman, Marshall, *All that is Solid Melts into Air: the Experience of Modernity*, London, Verso, 1983.

Bloom, Harold (ed.), *Jorge Luis Borges*, New York, Chelsea House, 1986.

Boorstin, Daniel J., *The Discoverers: A History of Man's Search to Know his World and Himself*, New York, Random House, 1983.

Bosi, Alfredo, *História concisa da literatura brasileira*, São Paulo,Cultrix, 1979.

Brotherston, Gordon, *The Emergence of the Latin American Novel*, Cambridge University Press, 1977.

—— *Image of the New World: The American Continent Portrayed in Native Texts*, London, Thames and Hudson, 1979.

Brushwood, John, *The Spanish American Novel: A Twentieth Century Survey*, Austin, Texas University Press, 1975.

Calviño, Julio, *La novela del dictador en Hispanoamérica*, Madrid, Cultura Hispànica, 1985.

—— *Historia, ideología y mito en la narrativa hispanoamericana contemporánea*, Madrid, Ayuso, 1987.

Campra, Rosalba, *América Latina: la identidad y la máscara*, Mexico, Siglo XXI, 1987.

Candido, Antônio, *Literatura e sociedade*, São Paulo, Editora Nacional,1980.

—— *Formação da literatura brasileira*, 2 vols. Belo Horizonte, Itatiaia, 6th edn, 1981.

Chevigny, Bell Gale and Laguardia, Gari (eds), *Reinventing the Americas: Comparative Studies of Literature of the United States and Spanish America*, Cambridge University Press, 1986.

Collazos, O., Cortázar, J., and Vargas Llosa, M., *Literatura en la revolución y revolución en la literatura*, Mexico, Siglo XXI, 1971.

Coutinho, Afrânio, *An Introduction to Literature in Brazil*, New York, Columbia University Press, 1969.

Donoso, José, *Historia personal del boom*, Barcelona, Anagrama, 1972.

Dorfman, Ariel, *Imaginación y violencia en América*, Santiago de Chile, Editorial Universitaria, 1970.

Duncan, J. Ann, *Voices, Visions and a New Reality: Mexican Fiction Since 1970*, Pittsburgh University Press, 1986.

Faris, Wendy B., *Labyrinths of Language: Symbolic Landscape and Narrative Design in Modern Fiction*, Baltimore, Johns Hopkins University Press, 1988.

Fernández Moreno, César, *América Latina en su literatura*, Mexico, Siglo XXI, 1972.

Foster, David W., *The Twentieth-Century Spanish-American Novel: A Bibliographical Guide*, Metuchen, Scarecrow Press, 1975.

—— *Studies in the Contemporary Spanish American Short Story*, Columbia, Missouri University Press, 1979.

—— *Alternate Voices in the Contemporary Latin American Narrative*, Columbia, Missouri University Press, 1985.

Franco, Jean, *Society and the Artist: The Modern Culture of Latin America*, London, Pall Mall, 1967.

—— *An Introduction to Spanish American Literature*, Cambridge University Press, 1971.

—— *Spanish American Literature since Independence*, London, Benn, 1973.

—— 'From Modernization to Resistance: Latin American Literature 1959–1976', *Latin American Perspectives*, no.16, 1978, pp. 77–97.

French, Marilyn, *The Book as World: James Joyce's 'Ulysses'*, London, Abacus, 1982.

Fuentes, Carlos, *La nueva novela hispanoamericana*, Mexico, Joaquín Mortiz, 1969.

Gallagher, David, *Modern Latin American Literature*, Oxford University Press, 1973.

González Casanova, Pablo (ed.), *Cultura y creación intelectual en América Latina*, Mexico, Siglo XXI, 1984.

González Echevarría, Roberto, *The Voice of the Masters: Writing and Authority in Modern Latin American Literature*, Austin, University of Texas Press, 1986.

Guibert, Rita, *Seven Voices*, New York, Vintage, 1973.

Harlow, Barbara, *Resistance Literature*, London, Methuen, 1987.

Harss, Luis and Dohmann, B., *Into the Mainstream: Conversations with Latin*

American Writers, New York, Harper and Row, 1968.

Hulet, Claude L., *Brazilian Literature*, 3 vols, Washington DC, Georgetown University Press, 1974.

Jackson, Richard L., *The Black Image in Latin American Literature*, Albuquerque, New Mexico University Press, 1976.

Jameson, Fredric, 'Post Modernism, or the Cultural Logic of Late Capitalism', *New Left Review*, 146, July–August 1984, pp. 53–92.

Josipovici, Gabriel, *The World and the Book*, London, Macmillan, 1971.

Kadir, Djelal, *Questing Fictions: Latin America's Family Romance*, Minneapolis, University of Minnesota Press, 1986.

Kapschutschenko, Ludmila, *El laberinto en la narrativa hispanoamericana contemporánea*, London, Tamesis, 1982.

Katra, William H., *'Contorno'*: *Literary Engagement in Post-Peronist Argentina*, London, Associated University Presses, 1988.

King, John (ed.), *Modern Latin American Fiction: A Survey*, London, Faber and Faber, 1987.

Kolodny, Annette, *The Lay of the Land: Metaphor as Experience and History in American Life and Letters*, Chapel Hill, University of N. Carolina, 1975.

Lafforgue, Jorge (ed.), *Nueva novela latinoamericana*, Buenos Aires, Paidós, 1969.

Leenhardt, Jacques (ed.), *Idéologies, littérature et société en Amérique Latine*, Bruxelles University Press, 1975.

—— *Littérature latino-américaine d'aujourd'hui* (Colloque de Cérisy), Paris, Union Générale d'Editions, 1980.

Losada, Alejandro, *La literatura en la sociedad de América Latina*, Frankfurt, Vervuert, 1983.

Marcos, Juan Manuel, *Roa Bastos, precursor del post-boom*, Mexico, Katún, 1983.

Martin, Gerald, *Miguel Angel Asturias, Hombres de maíz. Edición crítica*, Paris, Klincksieck, and Mexico, FCE, 1981.

—— 'The Literature, Music and and Art of Latin America 1870–1930', in L. Bethell (ed.), *Cambridge History of Latin America*, IV Cambridge University Press, 1986, pp. 443–526.

McGuirk, B. and Cardwell, R. (eds), *Gabriel García Márquez: New Readings*, Cambridge University Press, 1987.

Mejía Duque, Jaime, *Narrativa y neocolonialismo en América Latina*, Bogotá, Oveja Negra, 1972.

Meyer, Doris, *Lives on the Line: The Testimony of Contemporary Latin American Authors*, Berkeley, University of California Press, 1988.

O'Gorman, Edmundo, *La invención de América*, Mexico, FCE, 1984.

Ortega, Julio, *La contemplación y la fiesta*, Caracas, Monte Avila, 1969.

—— *Crítica de la identidad: la pregunta por el Perú en su literatura*, Mexico, FCE, 1988.

Patai, D., *Myth and Ideology in Contemporary Brazilian Fiction*, Rutherford and London, Associated University Presses, 1983.

Pérus, Françoise, *Historia y crítica literaria: el realismo social y la crisis de la dominación oligárquica*, Havana, Casa de las Americas, 1982.

Picón Garfield, E. and Schulman, I., *'Las entrañas del vacío'*: *ensayos sobre la mod-*

ernidad hispanoamericana, Mexico, Cuadernos Americanos, 1984.

Putnam, Samuel, *Marvelous Journey: A Survey of Four Centuries of Brazilian Writing*, New York, Knopf, 1948.

Rama, Angel (ed.), *Más allá del boom: literatura y mercado*, Mexico, Marcha, 1981.

Rama, Angel, *Transculturación narrativa en América Latina*, Mexico, Siglo XXI, 1982.

—— *La novela latinoamericana: panoramas 1920–1980*, Bogotá, Instituto Colombiano de Cultura, 1982.

—— *La ciudad letrada*, Hanover, New Hampshire, Ediciones del Norte, 1984.

Rodríguez-Luis, Julio, *La literatura hispanoamericana entre compromiso y experimento*, Madrid, Espiral, 1984.

Rodríguez Monegal, Emir, *Narradores de esta América*, Montevideo, Alfa, 1969.

—— *El boom de la novela latinoamericana*, Caracas, Tiempo Nuevo, 1972.

—— 'The New Latin American Novelists', *Partisan Review*, 44: 1, 1977, pp. 40–51.

Ruffinelli, Jorge, *La escritura invisible*, Xalapa, Mexico, Universidad Veracruzana, 1986.

Schwartz, Kessel, *A New History of Spanish American Fiction*, 2 vols, Coral Gables, Florida, Miami University Press, 1972.

Shaw, Donald L., *Nueva narrativa hispanoamericana*, Madrid, Cátedra, 1981.

Sosnowski, Saúl (ed.), *Represión, exilio y democracia: la cultura uruguaya*, Montevideo, Banda Oriental, 1987.

Spivak, Gayatri Chakravorty, *In Other Worlds: Essays in Cultural Politics*, London, Methuen, 1987.

Stabb, Martin S., *In Quest of Identity: Patterns in the Spanish American Essay of Ideas, 1890–1960*, Chapel Hill, Univ. of N. Carolina Press, 1967.

Times Literary Supplement, 14 November 1968, 'Latin American Literature'.

Vidal, Hernán (ed.), *Fascismo y experiencia literaria: reflexiones para una recanonización*, Minneapolis, Institute for the Study of Ideologies and Literature, 1985.

Williams, Margaret Todaro, 'Psychoanalysis and Latin American History', in R. Graham and P. Smith (eds), *New Approaches to Latin American History*, Texas University Press, 1974, pp. 194–222.

Yurkiévich, Saúl, *Identidad cultural de Iberoamérica en su literatura*, Madrid, Alhambra, 1986.

Primary Texts

The following is a list of the major writers and works referred to in this book which are available in English translation. The list is comprehensive but not exhaustive. I have noted first date of publication in USA and UK. Most of these works were subsequently published in paperback editions, too numerous to detail, many of which are still in print.

ALEGRÍA, Ciro (Peru, 1909–67)
Broad and Alien is the World, (*El mundo es ancho y ajeno*, 1941), trans. Harriet de Onís, New York, Farrar and Rinehart, 1941; London, Merlin Press, 1983, with four previously unpublished chapters translated by Mike Gonzalez.
The Golden Serpent (*La serpiente de oro*, 1935), trans. Harriet de Onís, New York, Signet, 1943.

ALLENDE, Isabel (Chile, 1942–)
The House of the Spirits (*La casa de los espíritus*, 1982), trans. Magda Bogin, New York, Knopf, 1985; London, Cape, 1985.
Of Love and Shadows (*De amor y de sombra*, 1984), trans. Margaret Sayers Peden, New York, Knopf, 1987; London, Cape, 1987.
Eva Luna (1987), trans. Margaret Sayers Peden, New York, Knopf, 1988; London, Hamish Hamilton, 1989.

ALMEIDA, José Américo de (Brazil, 1887–1980)
Cane Trash (*A bagaceira* 1928), trans. Robert Scott-Buccleuch, London, Peter Owen, 1978.

AMADO, Jorge (Brazil, 1912–)
Jubiabá (1935), trans. Margaret A. Neves, New York, Avon, 1984.
Sea of Death (*Mar morto*, 1936), trans. Gregory Rabassa, New York, Avon, 1984.

Captains of the Sand (*Capitães de areia*, 1937), trans. Gregory Rabassa, New York, Avon, 1988.

The Violent Land (*Terras do sem-fim*, 1942), trans. Samuel Putnam, New York, Knopf, 1945.

Gabriela: Clove and Cinnamon (*Gabriela, cravo e canela*, 1958), trans. James L. Taylor and William Grossman, New York, Knopf, 1962; London, Chatto & Windus, 1963.

Dona Flor and her Two Husbands (*Dona flor e seus dois marido*s, 1966), trans. Harriet de Onís, New York, Knopf, 1969; London, Weidenfeld & Nicolson, 1969.

Tereza Batista: Home from the Wars (*Tereza Batista, cansada de guerra*, 1972), trans. Barbara Shelby, New York, Knopf, 1975; London, Souvenir, 1982.

Tieta (*Tiêta do agreste*, 1977), trans. Barbara Shelby, New York, Knopf, 1979; London, Souvenir, 1981.

Showdown (*Tocaia grande*, 1984), trans. Gregory Rabassa, New York, Bantam, 1988.

ANDRADE, Mário de (Brazil, 1893–1945)
Macunaíma (1928), trans. E.A. Goodland, New York, Random House, 1984; London, Quartet, 1984.

ARENAS, Reynaldo (Cuba, 1943–)
Hallucinations (*El mundo alucinante*, 1969), trans. Gordon Brotherston, New York, Harper & Row, 1971; London, Cape, 1972.

Farewell to the Sea (*Otra vez el mar*, 1982), trans. Andrew Hurley, New York, Viking, 1986; Harmondsworth, Penguin, 1988.

ARGUEDAS, José María (Peru, 1911–69)
The Singing Mountains: Songs and Tales of the Quechua People (*Canto Kechwa*, 1938), trans. Ruth Stephan, Texas University Press, 1971.

Yawar Fiesta (*Yawar fiesta*, 1941), trans. Frances H. Barraclough, Texas University Press, 1984; London, Quartet, 1985.

Deep Rivers (*Los ríos profundo*s, 1958), trans. Frances H. Barraclough, Austin, Texas University Press, 1978.

ARGUETA, Manlio (El Salvador, 1935–)
One Day of Life (*Un día en la vida*, 1980), trans. Bill Brow, London, Chatto & Windus, 1984.

Cuzcatlan (*Cuzcatlán, donde bate la mar del sur*, 1986), trans. Clark Hansen, London, Chatto & Windus, 1987.

ARLT, Roberto (Argentina, 1900–42)
The Seven Madmen (*Los siete locos*, 1929), trans. Naomi Lindstrom, Boston, Godine, 1984.

ASTURIAS, Miguel Angel (Guatemala, 1899–1974)
The President (*El señor Presidente*, 1946), trans. Frances Partridge, London, Gollancz, 1963; New York, Atheneum, 1969.

Men of Maize (*Hombres de maíz*, 1949), trans. Gerald Martin, New York, Delacorte Press, 1975; London, Verso, 1988.

The Cyclone (*Viento fuerte*, 1950), trans. F.D. Flakoll and C. Alegria, London, Peter Owen, 1967; also Gregory Rabassa, *Strong Wind*, New York, Delacorte Press, 1969.

The Green Pope (*El papa verde*, 1954), trans. Gregory Rabassa, New York, Delacorte Press, 1971.

The Eyes of the Interred (*Los ojos de los enterrados*, 1960), trans. Gregory Rabassa, New York, Delacorte Press, 1972; London, Cape, 1974.

The Bejeweled Boy (*El Alhajadito*, 1961), trans. Martin Shuttleworth, New York, Doubleday, 1971.

Mulata (*Mulata de tal*, 1963), trans. Gregory Rabassa, New York, Delacorte Press, 1967; London, Peter Owen, 1967.

AZUELA, Mariano (Mexico, 1873–1952)
Marcela, a Mexican Love Story (*Mala yerba*, 1909), trans. Anita Brenner, New York, Farrar & Rinehart, 1932.

The Underdogs (*Los de abajo*, 1915), trans. Enrique Munguía, New York, Brentano's, 1929; London, Cape, 1930.

Two Novels of Mexico: The Flies and The Bosses (*Los caciques*, 1917; *Las moscas*, 1918), trans. Lesley Byrd Simpson, Berkeley, California University Press, 1956; Cambridge University Press, 1956.

Three Novels: The Trials of a Respectable Family, The Underdogs and The Firefly (*Las tribulaciones de una familia decente*, 1919; *Los de abajo*, 1916; *La luciérnaga*, 1932), trans. Frances K. Hendricks and Beatrice Berler, San Antonio, Trinity University Press, 1963.

BENEDETTI, Mario (Uruguay, 1920–)
The Truce (*La tregua*, 1960), trans. Benjamin Graham, New York, Harper & Row, 1969.

BIOY CASARES, Adolfo (Argentina, 1914–)
The Invention of Morel and Other Stories (*La invención de Morel*, 1940; *La trama celeste*, 1948), trans. Ruth L.C. Simms, Austin, Texas University Press, 1961.

The Dream of the Hero (*El sueño de los héroes*, 1954), trans. Diana Thorold, London, Quartet, 1987.

BOMBAL, María Luisa (Chile, 1910–80)
The House of Mist (*La última niebla*,1935), trans. María Luisa Bombal, New York, Farrar, Straus, 1947.

The Shrouded Woman (*La amortajada*, 1938), trans. María Luisa Bombal, New York, Farrar, Straus, 1948.

BORGES, Jorge Luis (Argentina, 1899–1986)
Labyrinths: Selected Stories and Other Writings, ed. and trans. D. Yates, J.E. Irby *et al.*, New York, New Directions, 1962; Harmondsworth, Penguin, 1970.

A Universal History of Infamy (Historia universal de la infamia, 1935), trans. Norman Thomas di Giovanni, New York, Dutton, 1972; London, Allen Lane, 1973.

Fictions (Ficciones, 1944), trans. Anthony Kerrigan, Alastair Reid *et al.*, New York, Grove, 1962; London, Weidenfeld & Nicolson, 1962.

El Aleph and Other Stories 1933–1969 (El Aleph, 1948, etc.), trans. Norman Thomas di Giovanni, New York, Dutton, 1970; London, Cape, 1971.

Other Inquisitions (Otras inquisiciones, 1952, essays), trans. Ruth L.C. Simms, Austin, Texas University Press, 1964; London, Souvenir, 1973.

Dreamtigers (El hacedor, 1960), trans. Mildred Boyer and Harold Morland, Austin, Texas University Press, 1964; London, Souvenir, 1973.

Doctor Brodie's Report (El informe de Brodie, 1970), trans. Norman Thomas di Giovanni, New York, Dutton, 1972; Harmondsworth, Allen Lane, 1974.

The Book of Sand (El libro de arena, 1975), trans. Norman Thomas di Giovanni, New York, Dutton, 1977; Harmondsworth, Penguin, 1979.

CABRERA INFANTE, Guillermo (Cuba, 1929–)

Three Trapped Tigers (Tres tristes tigres, 1965), trans. Donald Gardner & Suzanne Jill Levine, New York, Harper & Row, 1971; London, Picador, 1980.

View of Dawn in the Tropics (Vista del amanecer en el trópico, 1974), trans. Suzanne Jill Levine, New York, Harper & Row, 1979; London, Faber & Faber, 1988.

Infante's Inferno (La Habana para un infante difunto, 1979), trans. Suzanne Jill Levine and author, New York, Harper & Row, 1984; London, Faber & Faber, 1984.

CALLADO, Antonio (Brazil, 1917–)

Quarup (1967), trans. Barbara Shelby, New York, Knopf, 1970.

Don Juan's Bar (Bar Don Juan, 1971), trans. Barbara Shelby, New York, Knopf, 1972.

CARPENTIER (Alejo, 1904–79)

The Kingdom of this World (El reino de este mundo, 1949), trans. Harriet de Onís, New York, Knopf, 1957; London, Gollancz, 1967.

The Lost Steps (Los pasos perdidos, 1953), trans. Harriet de Onís, New York, Knopf, 1957; London, Gollancz, 1956.

Explosion in a Cathedral (El siglo de las luces, 1962), trans. John Sturrock, London, Gollancz, 1963; Boston, Little, Brown, 1963.

War on Time (La guerra del tiempo, 1956, stories), trans. Frances Partridge, New York, Knopf, 1969; London, Gollancz, 1970.

Reasons of State (El recurso del método, 1974), trans. Frances Partridge, London, Gollancz, 1976; New York, Knopf, 1976.

CASTELLANOS, Rosario (Mexico, 1925–74)

The Nine Guardians (Balún-Canán, 1957), trans. Irene Nicholson, London, Faber & Faber, 1959; New York, Vanguard, 1960.

CORTÁZAR, Julio (Argentina, 1914–84)

End of the Game and Other Stories (Bestiario, 1951; *Final del juego*, 1956; *Las armas secretas*, 1959), trans. Paul Blackburn, New York, Pantheon, 1967; London, Collins, 1968.

The Winners (*Los premios*, 1960), trans. Elaine Kerrigan, New York, Pantheon, 1965; London, Allison & Busby, 1968.

Hopscotch (*Rayuela*, 1963), trans. Gregory Rabassa, New York, Pantheon, 1966; London, Collins, 1967.

Cronopios and Famas (*Historias de cronopios y famas*, 1962), trans. Paul Blackburn, New York, Pantheon, 1969; London, Marion Boyars, 1976.

62, A Model Kit (*62: modelo para armar*, 1968), trans. Gregory Rabassa, New York, Pantheon, 1972; London, Marion Boyars, 1977.

All Fires the Fire and Other Stories (*Todos los fuegos el fuego*, 1966), trans. Suzanne Jill Levine, London, Marion Boyars, 1971; New York, Pantheon, 1973.

Around the Day in Eighty Worlds (*La vuelta al día en ochenta mundos*, 1967), trans. Thomas Christensen, San Francisco, North Point, 1986.

A Manual for Manuel (*Libro de Manuel*, 1973), trans. Gregory Rabassa, New York, Pantheon, 1978; London, Harvill, 1984.

A Change of Light and Other Stories (*Alguien que anda por ahí* 1977), trans. Gregory Rabassa, New York, Knopf, 1980; London, Harvill, 1984.

A Certain Lucas (*Un tal Lucas*, 1979), trans. Gregory Rabassa, New York, Knopf, 1984.

We Love Glenda So Much and Other Tales (*Queremos tanto a Glenda*, 1981), trans. Gregory Rabassa, New York, Knopf, 1983; London, Harvill, 1984.

DESNOES, Edmundo (Cuba, 1930–)
Memories of Underdevelopment (*Memorias del subdesarrollo*, 1965), trans. E. Desnoes, Harmondsworth, Penguin, 1971.

DONOSO, José (Chile, 1924–)
Coronation (*Coronación*, 1957), trans. Jocasta Goodwin, New York, Knopf, 1965; London, Bodley Head, 1965.

This Sunday (*Este domingo*, 1965), trans. Lorraine O'Grady Freeman, New York, Knopf, 1967; London, Bodley Head, 1968.

The Obscene Bird of Night (*El obsceno pájaro de la noche*, 1970), trans. Hardie St. Martin and Leonard Mades, New York, Knopf, 1973; London, Cape, 1974.

A House in the Country (*Casa de campo*, 1978), trans. David Pritchard, New York, Knopf, 1983; London, Allen Lane, 1984.

DORFMAN, Ariel (Chile, 1942–)
Widows (*Viudas*, 1981), trans. Stephen Kessler, New York, Random House, 1983; London, Pluto, 1984.

The Last Song of Manuel Sendero (*La última canción de Manuel Sendero*, 1982), trans. George R. Shrivers, New York, Viking, 1987.

DOURADO, Autran (Brazil, 1926–)
A Hidden Life (*Uma vida em segrêdo*, 1964), trans. Edgar Miller, New York, Knopf, 1969.

The Voices of the Dead (Opera dos mortos, 1967), trans. John Parker, London, Peter Owen, 1980; New York, Tapingler, 1981.

Pattern for a Tapestry (O risco do bordado, 1970), trans. John Parker, London, Peter Owen, 1984.

The Bells of Agony (Os sinos da agonia, 1974), trans. John Parker, London, Peter Owen, 1988.

FERNÁNDEZ, Macedonio (Argentina, 1874–1952)

Macedonio: Selected Writings in Translation, trans. Jo Anne Englebert *et al.*, Fort Worth, Texas, Latitudes Press, 1984.

FUENTES, Carlos (Mexico, 1928–)

Where the Air is Clear (La región más transparente, 1958), trans. Sam Hileman, New York, Farrar, Straus & Giroux, 1960; London, Deutsch, 1986.

The Good Conscience (Las buenas conciencias, 1959), trans. Sam Hileman, New York, Farrar, 1971; London, Deutsch, 1986.

The Death of Artemio Cruz (La muerte de Artemio Cruz, 1962), trans. Sam Hileman, New York, Farrar, 1964; London, Collins, 1964.

Aura (1962), trans. Lysander Kemp, New York, Farrar, 1966.

A Change of Skin (Cambio de piel, 1967), trans. Sam Hileman, New York, Farrar, 1968; London, Cape, 1968.

Terra Nostra (1975), trans. Margaret Sayers Peden, New York, Farrar, 1976; London, Secker & Warburg, 1977.

The Hydra Head (La cabeza de la hidra, 1978), trans. Margaret Sayers Peden, New York, Farrar, 1978; London, Secker, 1979.

Burnt Water (Agua quemada, 1980), trans. Margaret Sayers Peden, New York, Farrar, 1980; London, Secker, 1981.

Distant Relations (Una familia lejana, 1980), trans. Margaret Sayers Peden, New York, Farrar, 1982; London, Secker, 1982.

The Old Gringo (El gringo viejo, 1986), trans. Margaret Sayers Peden, New York, Farrar, 1986; London, Deutsch, 1987.

GALEANO, Eduardo (Uruguay, 1940–)

Days and Nights of Love and War (Días y noches de amor y de guerra, 1978), trans. Judith Brisler, New York, Monthly Review Press, 1983; London, Pluto Press, 1983.

GALLEGOS, Rómulo (Venezuela, 1884–1969)

Doña Bárbara (1929), trans. Robert J. Malloy, Magnolia, Mass., Peter Smith, 1948.

Canaima (1935), trans. Jaime Tello, Caracas, North American Association of Venezuela, 1984.

GARCÍA MÁRQUEZ, Gabriel (Colombia, 1928–)

Leaf Storm and Other Stories (La hojarasca, 1955, trans. Gregory Rabassa, New York, Harper & Row, 1972; London, Cape, 1972.

No One Writes to the Colonel and Other Stories (El coronel no tiene quien le escriba,

1961, and *Los funerales de la Mamá Grande*, 1962), trans. J.S. Bernstein, New York, Harper & Row, 1968; Cape, London, 1971.
In Evil Hour (*La mala hora*, 1962), trans. Gregory Rabassa, New York, Avon, 1980; London, Cape, 1980.
One Hundred Years of Solitude (*Cien años de soledad*, 1967), trans. Gregory Rabassa, New York, Harper & Row, 1970; London, Cape, 1970.
Innocent Erendira and Other Stories (*La increíble y triste historia de la cándida Eréndira y de su abuela desalmada*, 1972), trans. Gregory Rabassa, New York, Harper & Row, 1978; London, Cape, 1979.
The Autumn of the Patriarch (*El otoño del patriarca*, 1975), trans. Gregory Rabassa, New York, Harper, 1976; London, Cape, 1977.
Chronicle of a Death Foretold (*Crónica de una muerte anunciada*, 1981), trans. Gregory Rabassa, New York, Knopf, 1982; London, Cape, 1982.
Love in the Time of Cholera (*El amor en los tiempos del cólera*, 1985), trans. Edith Grossman, New York, Knopf, 1988; London, Cape, 1988.

GARRO, Elena (Mexico, 1920–)
Recollections of Things to Come (*Los recuerdos del porvenir*, 1963), trans. Ruth L.C. Simms, Austin, Texas University Press, 1969; London, Sidgwick & Jackson, 1978.

GÜIRALDES, Ricardo (Argentina, 1886–1927)
Don Segundo Sombra (1926), trans. Harriet de Onís, New York, Farrar & Rinehart, 1935; London, Constable, 1935.

GUZMÁN, Martín Luis (Mexico, 1887–1976))
The Eagle and the Serpent (*El águila y la serpiente*, 1928), trans. Harriet de Onís, New York, Knopf, 1930.
Memoirs of Pancho Villa (*Memorias de Pancho Villa*, 1938–1940), trans. Virginia Taylor, Austin, Texas University Press, 1965.

IBARGÜENGOITIA, Jorge (Mexico, 1928–1983)
Lightning of August (*Los relámpagos de agost*, 1964), trans. Irene del Corral, New York, Avon, 1986; London, Chatto & Windus, 1986.
The Dead Girls (*Las muertas*, 1974), trans. Asa Zatz, New York, Avon Books, 1983; London, Chatto & Windus, 1983.
Two Crimes (*Dos crímenes*, 1979), trans. Asa Zatz, New York, Avon, 1984; London, Chatto & Windus, 1984.

ICAZA, Jorge (Ecuador, 1906–78)
Huasipungo (1934), trans. Mervyn Savill, London, Dennis Dobson, 1962; also *The Villagers*, trans. Bernard M. Dulsey, Carbondale, Southern Illinois University Press, 1964.

LEZAMA LIMA, José (Cuba, 1912–76)
Paradiso (1966), trans. Gregory Rabassa, New York, Farrar, Straus & Giroux, 1974; London, Secker & Warburg, 1974.

LIMA BARRETO, Afonso Henriques de (Brazil, 1881–1922)
The Patriot (*Triste fim de Policarpo Quaresma*, 1911), trans. Robert Scott Buccleuch, London, Rex Collings, 1978.

LINS DO REGO, José (Brazil, 1901–57)
Plantation Boy (*Menino de engenho*, 1932, *Doidinho*, 1933, and *Bangüê*, 1934), trans. Emmi Baum, New York, Knopf, 1966.
Pureza (1937), trans. Lucie Marion, London, Hutchinson, 1948.

LISPECTOR, Clarice (Brazil, 1925–77)
Family Ties (*Laços de familia*, 1960), trans. Giovanni Pontiero, Austin, Texas University Press, 1972; Manchester, Carcanet, 1985.
The Apple in the Dark (*A maçã no escuro*, 1961), trans. Gregory Rabassa, New York, Knopf, 1967; London, Virago, 1985.
The Foreign Legion (*A legião estrangeira*, 1964), trans. Giovanni Pontiero, Manchester, Carcanet, 1986.
The Passion According to G.H. (*A paixão segundo G.H.*, 1964), trans. Ronald W. Souza, Minneapolis, Minnesota University Press, 1988.
The Hour of the Star (*A hora da estrêla*, 1977), trans. Giovanni Pontiero, Manchester, Carcanet, 1986.

LÓPEZ Y FUENTES, Gregorio (Mexico)
El indio (1935), trans. Anita Brenner, Indianapolis, Bobbs-Merrill, 1937; and as *They that Reap*, London, Harrap, 1937.

MACHADO DE ASSIS, Joaquim Maria (Brazil, 1839–1908)
Helena (1876), trans. Helen Caldwell, Berkeley, California University Press, 1984.
Yayá Garcia (*Iaiá Garcia*, 1878), trans. Robert Scott Buccleuch, London, Peter Owen, 1976; trans. Albert Bagby, Lexington, Kentucky University Press, 1977.
Epitaph of a Small Winner (*Memórias póstumas de Brás Cubas*, 1881), trans. William Grossman, New York, Noonday, 1952; London, W.H. Allen, 1953.
Philosopher or Dog (*Quincas Borba*, 1891), trans. Clotilde Wilson, New York, Farrar, Straus & Giroux, 1954; and as *The Heritage of Quincas Borba*, London, W.H. Allen, 1954.
Dom Casmurro (1900), trans. Helen Caldwell, New York, Noonday, 1953; London, W.H. Allen, 1953.
Esau and Jacob (*Esaú e Jacó*, 1904), trans. Helen Caldwell, Berkeley, California University Press; London, Peter Owen, 1966.

MARTÍNEZ, Tomás Eloy (Argentina, 1934–)
The Perón Novel (*La novela de Perón*, 1985), trans. Asa Zatz, New York, Pantheon, 1988.

MARTINEZ MORENO, Carlos (Uruguay, 1917–86)
El Infierno (*El color que el infierno me escondiera*, 1981), trans. Ann Wright, London, Readers International, 1988.

MOYANO, Daniel (Argentina, 1930–)
The Devil's Trill (*El trino del diablo*, 1974), trans. Giovanni Pontiero, London, Serpent's Tail, 1988.

OCAMPO, Silvina (Argentina, 1903–)
Leopoldina's Dream (*Autobiografía de Irene*, 1948, and other story collections), trans. Daniel Balderston, Harmondsworth, Penguin, 1988.

ONETTI, Juan Carlos (Uruguay, 1909–)
A Brief Life (*La vida breve*, 1950), trans. Hortense Carpentier, New York, Grossman, 1976.
The Shipyard (*El astillero*, 1961), trans. Rachel Caffyn, New York, Scribner's, 1968.

PARRA, Teresa de la (Venezuela, 1895–1936)
Mama Blanca's Souvenirs (*Las memorias de Mamá Blanca*, 1929), trans. Harriet de Onís, Washington, Pan American Union, 1959.

PARTNOY, Alicia (Argentina, 1955–)
The Little School (*La escuelita*, 1981), trans. A. Partnoy *et al.*, London, Virago, 1988.

PERI ROSSI, Cristina (Uruguay, 1941–)
The Ship of Fools (*La nave de los locos*, 1984), trans. Psiche Hughes, London, Allison & Busby, 1989.

PONIATOWSKA, Elena (Mexico, 1932–)
Until We Meet Again (*Hasta no verte Jesús mío*, 1969), trans. Helen Lane, New York, Pantheon, 1987.
Massacre in Mexico (*La noche de Tlatelolco*, 1971), trans. Helen Lane, New York, Viking, 1975.
Dear Diego (*Querido Diego, te abraza Quiela*, 1978), trans. Katherine Silver, New York, Pantheon, 1986.

PRADA OROPEZA, Renato (Bolivia, 1937–)
The Breach (*Los fundadores del alba*, 1969), trans. Walter Redmond, Garden City N.J., Doubleday, 1971.

PUIG, Manuel (Argentina, 1934–)
Betrayed by Rita Hayworth (*La traición de Rita Hayworth*, 1968), trans. Suzanne Jill Levine, New York, Dutton, 1971; London, Arena, 1984.
Heartbreak Tango (*Boquitas pintadas*, 1969), trans. Suzanne Jill Levine, New York, Dutton, 1973; London, Arena, 1987.

The Buenos Aires Affair (1973), trans. Suzanne Jill Levine, New York, Dutton, 1976.
Kiss of the Spider Woman (*El beso de la mujer araña*, 1976), trans. Thomas Colchie, New York, Knopf, 1979; London, Arena, 1984.
Pubis Angelical (1979), trans. Elena Brunet, New York, Random House, 1986; London, Faber, 1987.
Eternal Curse on the Reader of These Pages (*Maldición eterna a quien lea estas páginas*, 1980), New York, Random House, 1982; London, Arena, 1985.
Blood of Requited Love (*Sangre de amor correspondido*, 1984), trans. Jan Grayson, New York, Vintage, 1984.

QUEIRÓS, Raquel de (Brazil, 1910–)
The Three Marias (*As três Marias*, 1939), trans. Fred P. Ellison, Austin, Texas University Press, 1963.
Dôra, Doralina (1975), trans. Dorothy Scott Loos, New York, Avon, 1984.

QUIROGA, Horacio (Uruguay, 1878–1937)
The Decapitated Chicken and Other Stories (*Cuentos de amor, de locura y de muerte*, 1917), trans. Margaret Sayers Peden, Austin, Texas University Press, 1976.
Stories of the Jungle (*Cuentos de la selva*, 1918), trans. Arthur Livingstone, London, Methuen, 1923.
The Exiles (*Los desterrados*, 1926), trans. J.D. Danielson, Austin, Texas University Press, 1987.

RAMIREZ, Sergio (Nicaragua, 1942–)
Stories (*Charles Atlas también muere*, 1976), trans. Nick Caistor, London, Readers International, 1976.
To Bury Our Fathers (*¿Te dio miedo la sangre?*, 1977), trans. Nick Caistor, London, Readers International, 1984.

RAMOS, Graciliano (Brazil, 1892–1953)
São Bernardo (1934), trans. Robert Scott Buccleuch, London, Peter Owen, 1975.
Anguish (*Angústia*, 1936), trans. L.C. Kaplan, New York, Knopf, 1946.
Barren Lives (*Vidas sêcas*, 1938), trans. Ralph E. Dimmick, Austin, Texas University Press, 1961.
Childhood (*Infância*, 1945), trans. Celso de Oliveira, London, Peter Owen, 1979.
Prison Memoirs (*Memórias do cárcere*, 1953), trans. Thomas Colchie, New York, Evans, 1974.

REVUELTAS, José (Mexico, 1914–76)
The Stone Knife (*El luto humano*, 1943), trans. H.R. Hays, New York, Reynal-Hitchcock, 1947.

RIBEIRO, Darcy (Brazil, 1922–)
Maíra (1978), trans. E.H. Goodland and Thomas Colchie, New York, Random House, 1984; London, Picador, 1984.

RIBEIRO, João Ubaldo (Brazil, 1940–)
Sergeant Getúlio (*Sargento Getúlio*, 1971), trans. J. U. Ribeiro, Boston, Houghton Mifflin, 1984), London, Faber & Faber, 1986.
An Invincible Memory (*Viva o povo brasileiro*, 1984; trans. J. U. Ribeiro, New York, Harper & Row, 1988; London, Faber & Faber, 1989.

RIVERA, José Eustasio (Colombia, 1888–1928)
The Vortex (*La vorágine*, 1924), trans. Earle K. James, New York, Putnam, 1935.

ROA BASTOS, Augusto (Paraguay, 1917–)
Son of Man (*Hijo de hombre*, 1961), trans. Rachel Caffyn, London, Gollancz, 1965.
I the Supreme (*Yo el Supremo*, 1974), trans. Helen Lane, New York, Knopf, 1986; London, Faber & Faber, 1987.

ROJAS, Manuel (Chile, 1896–1973)
Born Guilty (*Hijo de ladrón*, 1951), trans. Frank Gaynor, New York, Library Publishers, 1955; London, Gollancz, 1956.

ROSA, João Guimarães (Brazil, 1908–67)
Sagarana (1946), trans. Harriet de Onís, New York, Knopf, 1966.
The Devil to Pay in the Backlands (*Grande sertão: veredas*, 1956), trans. J.L. Taylor and Harriet de Onís, New York, Knopf, 1963.
The Third Bank of the River and Other Stories (*Primeiras estórias*, 1962), trans. Barbara Shelby, New York, Knopf, 1968.

RULFO, Juan (Mexico, 1918–86)
The Burning Plain (*El llano en llamas*, 1953), trans. George D. Schade, Austin, Texas University Press, 1967.
Pedro Páramo (1955), trans. Lysander Kemp, New York, Grove, 1959; London, John Calder, 1959.

SÁBATO, Ernesto (Argentina, 1911–)
The Outsider (*El túnel*, 1948), trans. Harriet de Onís, New York, Knopf, 1950; also, as *The Tunnel*, Margaret Sayers Peden, New York, Random House, 1988; London, Cape, 1988.
On Heroes and Tombs (*Sobre héroes y tumbas*, 1961), trans. Helen Lane, Boston, Godine, 1981; London, Cape, 1982.

SAINZ, Gustavo (Mexico, 1940–)
Gazapo (1965), trans. Hardie St. Martin, New York, Farrar, Straus & Giroux, 1968.
The Princess of the Iron Palace (*La princesa del Palacio de Hierro*, 1974), trans. Andrew Hurley, New York, Grove, 1987.

SÁNCHEZ, Luis Rafael (Puerto Rico, 1936–)
Macho Camacho's Beat (*La guaracha del macho Camacho*, 1976), trans. Gregory Rabassa, New York, Pantheon, 1981.

SARDUY, Severo (Cuba, 1937–)
From Cuba with a Song (*De donde son los cantates*, 1967), trans. S. J. Levine, New York, Dutton, 1973.
Cobra (1973), trans. S.J. Levine, New York, Dutton, 1975.
Maitreya (1978), trans. S. J. Levine, Hanover, New Hampshire, Ediciones del Norte, 1987.

SARNEY, José (Brazil, 1931–)
Tales of Rain and Sunlight, (*Noites das aguas*, 1969), trans. Wyvern-Sel, Worcester, Bringsty, 1986.

SCHIZMAN, Mario (Argentina, 1945–)
At 8.25 Evita Became Immortal (*A las 8.25 la señora entró en la inmortalidad*, 1981), trans. Roberto Piccioto, Hanover, N.H., Ediciones del Norte, 1983.

SCORZA, Manuel (Peru, 1928–83)
Drums for Rancas (*Redoble por Rancas*, 1970), trans. Edith Grossman, New York, Harper & Row, 1977; London, Secker & Warburg, 1977.

SKÁRMETA, Antonio (Chile, 1940–)
I Dreamt the Snow was Burning (*Soñé que la nieve ardía*, 1975), trans. Malcolm Coad, London, Readers International, 1985.
The Insurrection (*La insurrección*, 1983), trans. Paula Sharp, Hanover, New Hampshire, Ediciones del Norte, 1983.
Burning Patience (*Ardiente paciencia*, 1985), trans. Katherine Silver, New York, Pantheon, 1987; London, Methuen, 1988.

SOUZA, Márcio (Brazil, 1946–)
The Emperor of the Amazon (*Galvez, imperador do Acre*, 1976), trans. Thomas Colchie, New York, Avon, 1977; London, Sphere, 1982.
Mad Maria (*Mad Maria*, 1980), trans. Thomas Colchie, New York, Avon, 1985.

TORRES, Antônio (Brazil, 1940–)
The Land (*Essa terra*, 1976), trans. Margaret A. Neves, London, Readers International, 1987.

TRABA, Marta (Argentina, 1930–85)
Mothers and Shadows (*Conversación al sur*, 1981), trans. Jo Labanyi, London, Readers International, 1986.

USLAR PIETRI, Arturo (Venezuela, 1906–)
The Red Lances, (*Las lanzas coloradas*, 1931), trans. Harriet de Onís, New York, Knopf, 1963.

VALENZUELA, Luisa (Argentina, 1938–)
Clara; Thirteen Short Stories and a Novel (*Hay que sonreír*, 1966; and *Los heréticos*,

1967), trans. H. Carpentier and K. Castello, New York, Harcourt, Brace, Jovanovich, 1976.

Strange Things Happen Here (*Aquí pasa cosas raras*, 1975) trans. Helen Lane, New York, Harcourt, 1980.

Other Weapons (*Cambio de armas*, 1982), trans. Deborah Bonner, Hanover, New Hampshire, Ediciones del Norte, 1985.

The Lizard's Tail (*Cola delagartija*, 1983), trans. Gregory Rabassa, New York, Farrar, Straus & Giroux, 1983; London, Serpent's Tail, 1987.

VARGAS LLOSA, Mario (Peru, 1936–)

The Time of the Hero (*La ciudad y los perros*, 1962), trans. Lysander Kemp, New York, Grove, 1966; Harmondsworth, Penguin, 1966.

The Green House (*La casa verde*, 1966), trans. Gregory Rabassa, New York, Harper & Row, 1968; London, Cape, 1969.

The Cubs and Other Stories (*Los cachorros*, 1967), trans. Ronald Christ and Gregory Kolovakos, New York, Harper, 1980.

Conversation in the Cathedral (*Conversación en la Catedral*, 1969), trans. Gregory Rabassa, Harper & Row, New York, 1975.

Captain Pantoja and the Special Service (*Pantaleón y las visitadoras*, 1973), trans. Ronald Christ & Gregory Kolovakos, New York, Harper, 1978; London, Faber & Faber, 1987.

Aunt Julia and the Scriptwriter (*La tía Julia y el escribidor*, 1978), trans. Helen Lane, New York, Farrar, 1982; London, Faber, 1983.

The War of the End of the World (*La guerra del fin del mundo*, 1981), trans. Helen Lane, New York, Farrar, 1984; London, Faber, 1985.

The Real Life of Alejandro Mayta (*Historia de Mayta*, 1984), trans. Alfred J. MacAdam, New York, Farrar, 1986; London, Faber, 1986.

Who Killed Palomino Molero (*¿Quién mató a Palomino Molero?*, 1986), trans. Alfred J. MacAdam, New York, Farrar, 1987; London, Faber, 1988.

VERÍSSIMO, José (Brazil, 1905–75)

Crossroads (*Caminhos cruzados*, 1935), trans. L.C. Kaplan, New York, Macmillan, 1943); and as *Crossroads and Destinies*, London, Arco, 1956.

The Rest is Silence (*O resto é silencio*, 1943), trans. L.C. Kaplan, New York, Macmillan, 1945; London, Arco, 1956.

Time and the Wind (*O tempo e o vento*, 1949), trans. Linton Barrett, New York, Macmillan, 1951; London, Arco, 1954.

YÁÑEZ, Agustín (Mexico, 1904–80)

The Edge of the Storm (*Al filo del agua*, 1947), trans. Ethel Brinton, Austin, Texas University Press, 1963.

The Lean Lands (*Las tierras flacas*, 1962), trans. Ethel Brinton, Austin, Texas University Press, 1968.

Index

Extended references are in italics

413